3RD EDITION

The VISUAL HANDBOOK of Building and Remodeling

A Comprehensive Guide to Choosing the Right Materials and Systems for Every Part of Your Home

CHARLIE WING

The Taunton Press

The Taunton Press, Inc., 63 South Main Street, PO Box 5506, Newtown, CT 06470-5506

email: tp@taunton.com

Editor: Helen Albert
Copy editor: Seth Reichgott
Indexer: Jay Kreider
Cover design: Jean-Marc Troadec
Cover and interior illustrations: Charlie Wing
Interior design: Nick Anderson
Layout: Charlie Wing

Library of Congress Cataloging-in-Publication Data

Wing, Charles, 1939-

 The visual handbook of building and remodeling : a comprehensive guide to choosing the right materials and systems for every part of your home / Charlie Wing.

   p. cm.

 Includes bibliographical references and index.

 ISBN 978-1-60085-246-6

 1. House construction--Handbooks, manuals, etc. 2. Dwellings--Remodeling--Handbooks, manuals, etc. 3. Building materials--Handbooks, manuals, etc. I. Title.

 TH4813.W56 2009

 690'.8--dc22

                              2009033722

Printed in the United States of America

10 9 8 7 6 5 4 3

The following names/manufacturers appearing in the *Visual Handbook of Building and Remodeling* are trademarks: 3M Fastbond® 30NF, Bilco®, BoilerMate®,Com Ply®, Dulux® EL, Duxseal®, Faststeel® Epoxy Putty, GE® Silicone II, Grace Ice and Water Shield®, Hardiplank®, Heat Mirror®, Household Goop®, J-B Weld®, Krazy Glue®, LePage® Metal Epoxy, Loctite® 349, Octron®, Rhoplex™, Sobo®, Stur-I-Floor®, Super Glue™, Uhu® Glue, Gorilla Glue® Velux®, Weldbond®, Zap®

Homebuilding is inherently dangerous. Using hand or power tools improperly or ignoring safety practices can lead to permanent injury or even death. Don't try to perform operations you learn about here (or elsewhere) unless you're certain they are safe for you. If something about an operation doesn't feel right, don't do it. Look for another way. We want you to enjoy building, so please keep safety foremost in your mind whenever you're working.

For Ray Wolf, agent, sailor, and lifelong friend, without whom this book
would never have been born.

Acknowledgments

As the dedication indicates, without the experience, insight, and doggedness of my agent, Ray Wolf, this book would have remained but a personal dream.

As soon as I had committed to leading a Bowdoin College seminar titled "The Art of the House," I started gathering information, not only on how houses were constructed, but how they worked. The seminar, in reality, should have been called, "The Physics of the House."

In addition to nearly 100 books, I soon had filing cabinets full of useful scraps of information gleaned from every element of the building industry: architect and builder friends, lumberyards, hardware stores, contractors, manufacturers, and associations. When the usefulness of all of this seemingly disparate information became apparent, I began dreaming of gathering it all into a single book. Architects have their *Architectural Graphic Standards*; my book would be *Graphic Standards for Builders*.

For many years the dream remained just that. I could get no publisher to share my vision and enthusiasm. Simply put, they didn't get it. Then I met Ray Wolf. He had worked for many years at Rodale Press, publisher of *Organic Gardening* and *New Shelter Magazine*. He knew how publishers worked, how they thought. He knew how to present the project in terms they would understand. Better yet, he ran a set of numbers that promised profitability.

After signing the contract, the most trying task fell upon the shoulders of legendary editor, Maggie Balitas, who patiently tempered my vision with the realities of publishing. To her young associate, David Schiff, Maggie assigned the duty of assuring accuracy. I am sure that I am responsible for several years of his accelerated aging. These are the three individuals who helped me turn my dream into reality. I cannot thank them enough.

Of course there would never have been a dream were it not for the legions of manufacturers and building trades associations, listed on pp. 621–624, who first produced the information in my files. I thank them for their efforts and their generosity in sharing their information.

Not least, thank you, Wid, for understanding that sitting in front of a computer eight hours a day, seven days a week, for a whole year is how I make a living.

Contents

Introduction

Twenty years ago I proposed to Rodale Press a "visual handbook for small builders and do-it-yourselfers." In my opinion, I told them, such a book could sell 50,000 copies and might, with periodic revision and addition, enjoy an indefinitely long life.

"Let's just see how the first edition sells," was their dubious but predictable reply. (They later confided that they expected the book to sell only 5,000 to 10,000 copies.)

It turned out my gut instinct was right. In fact, I was so right I was almost wrong! The first edition sold not 50,000 but 200,000 copies and, at age seven, was showing little sign of slowing.

Eight years later Reader's Digest purchased the book and issued a second edition with an additional 100 pages containing:

- span tables for U.S. and Canadian lumber.
- checklists of building code requirements.
- a catalog of metal framing aids.
- design standards for access.
- three times as many framing details.

The Reader's Digest edition sold an additional 100,000 copies. In reading the Amazon reviews, I discovered that, in addition to small builders and do-it-yourselfers, people who were finding the book useful included home inspectors, energy auditors, codes officials, and vocational instructors.

Ten years later I am thrilled that Taunton Press—arguably the foremost publisher of building books—has agreed to publish a third edition, this time in large format and full color. In addition to bringing the previous content up to date, the 56-percent-larger third edition adds information on:

- sustainable ("green") building.
- storage options.
- the *International Residential Code*.

But let me go back and tell you why I felt compelled to create the handbook in the first place.

"Building a house requires thousands of decisions based on a million bits of information." This was the opening line of my lectures to thousands of potential owner/builders attending my three-week courses at Shelter Institute and, later, Cornerstones.

Teaching that course, and a precursor "physics of the house" seminar at Bowdoin College, taught me how to convey technical building information to people who are not professional builders. I put that training to work in five previous books, which covered every aspect of building, from retrofitting insulation to a drafty old house in *House Warming*, to siting, planning, and constructing a house from the ground up in *Breaking New Ground*.

But still, something was missing. I'd written all I had to say about designing and constructing a house, but I hadn't thoroughly covered the topic of what to construct a house of. What's more, it didn't seem to me that anyone else had, either. There was, and is, a plethora of technical literature for architects and structural engineers, but there was no thorough guide for people without formal technical training. The fact is, the majority of people who actually lay their hands on building materials—tradesmen, owner/builders, and do-it-yourselfers—are not trained architects or engineers. These people needed a book just as thorough as the ones the architects use but that also offered explanations, formulas, and charts that would make the information accessible. *The Visual Handbook of Building and Remodeling*, I believed, would be that book.

Naturally, in my previous books, I discussed materials in the context of how to install them, as have most other how-to writers. But the *Visual Handbook* focuses on the materials themselves. Its purpose is to enable one to decide how much of which material of what size should be used for any given house on any given site. Some how-to-install information is included because the way materials are used is often relevant in deciding which materials to use. However, the how-to is incidental to the what-to, instead of the other way around. For example, the chapter on siding discusses the pros and cons of each type of siding, from clapboards to vinyl, so you can make an informed decision about which is best for your particular site and climate. But it also illustrates construction details, to help you decide which will work best on your particular house.

I could see right away that this had to be a highly visual book. Nowhere is the saying, "A picture (or drawing, in this case) is worth a thousand words," more true. Further, there is no way words could describe, for example, every standard molding profile. It is possible, however, to show for each the full-scale cross-section.

Three things have made it possible for me to create this visual handbook. The first is software for illustrating (*Adobe Illustrator*) and desktop publishing (*Quark* and *InDesign*) that enabled me to create illustrations without training and camera-ready pages without being a printer. The second is that I am an information pack rat, a looter of lists, a burglar of booklets, a swiper of spec sheets. The third is the willingness of manufacturers and trade associations to let me adapt their diverse materials to a uniform format.

In the accretion of building information I am insatiable. No builder, no hardware clerk, no sawyer in the backwoods, not even architects are spared my quest. I raid their files, their bookshelves, and their minds. Over the years I have accumulated the best of what they found useful in the actual building of houses: tables, lists, government pamphlets, manufacturers' literature, building-trade association publications, even instructions from a package of asphalt shingles. And now there is the Internet and Google! Now I can sit at my computer and search for and download information that used to require road trips and photocopies.

The result is a book that should be useful to anyone who puts his or her hands on building materials or hires others who do so. If you hire a builder, you won't be limited to his preferences but will be able to take a more active role in deciding what materials to use. If you are an owner/builder, this book should complement the how-to books containing step-by-step instructions. And if you are a tradesman, I hope that you will keep a copy behind the seat of your truck for easy reference.

By the way, the opening line of my owner/builder course proved to be a bit off the mark. According to the computer, *The Visual Handbook of Building and Remodeling* now contains 59.7 million bytes of information.

Charlie Wing
Bath, Maine

Design

Houses are designed for the comfort and safety of human beings. House dimensions must, therefore, be related to *human dimensions*.

Tied to human dimensions—but too often overlooked in our excitement over cathedral-ceilinged great rooms, spectacular kitchens, and commodious baths—are critical *window, closet, and passage dimensions*.

Central to the home, and tops in our list of priorities, are kitchens and baths. We are fortunate in having permission to present most of the recommendations of the National Kitchen and Bath Association's *Kitchen Design Guidelines* and *Bath Design Guidelines*.

With more fatal in-the-home accidents occurring on stairs than in any other area, building codes are becoming ever more specific and stringent about *stair design*. We are again fortunate in having permission from the Stairway Manufacturers' Association to adapt the illustrations from their excellent *Visual Interpretation of the IRC 2006 Stair Building Code*.

Although the 1990 Americans with Disabilities Act (ADA) was written to guarantee physically handicapped citizens access to public buildings and the workplace, many of its design requirements are equally applicable to the home. Because homeowners generally prefer to remain in their homes as long as physically practical, we have illustrated the applicable ADA specifications in the section titled *Access*.

Finally, we provide you with a checklist of requirements so that your foundation will *meet the IRC Code*.

Human Dimensions

Why do we need typical human dimensions when designing buildings? Because buildings are for people. People need to reach shelves, move furniture from room to room, pass by each other, work side by side, and look outside through windows.

The typical human dimensions shown below are for an adult male of height 5 feet 9 inches. To determine typical dimensions for people who are taller or shorter than that, simply multiply the dimensions shown by the ratio of their heights.

Example: What is the standing eye level of a 5-foot (60-inch) person?

The standing height of the figure in the illustration is 69 inches and the height of the eye is 65 inches. The standing eye level of the 60-inch person is therefore $65 \times 60 \div 69 = 56\frac{1}{2}$ (inches).

Typical Dimensions of a Human Male

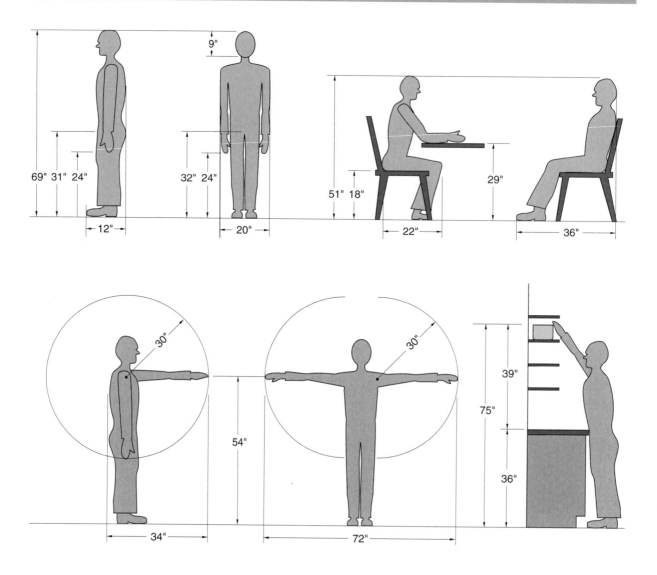

Window, Closet, and Passage Dimensions

Too often overlooked by inexperienced builders are the critical heights of windows and the widths of closets and passageways within the house.

Window heights are important on both the inside and the outside of buildings. For exterior symmetry the tops of all windows should align with the tops of exterior doors. Sill heights of windows adjacent to counters or furniture should be at least 42 inches; view window sills should not exceed 38 inches; no window sill except that of a patio door should be less than 10 inches high.

Closets are required for our ever-increasing wardrobes. Allow at least 36 inches of closet pole per occupant, with a hanger depth of 24 inches minimum. Provide at least one closet per bedroom, closets near front and rear entrances for coats, a linen closet, and at least one generous walk-in closet.

Passageway widths are dictated by the need to move large furnishings within the home and into or out of the home. The table below lists both minimum and recommended widths of passageways.

Widths of Passageways, inches

Passageway	Minimum	Recommended
Stairs	36	40
Landings	36	40
Main hall	36	40
Minor hall	36	40
Interior door	36	40
Exterior door	36	40
Basement door	36	48

Critical Window Dimensions

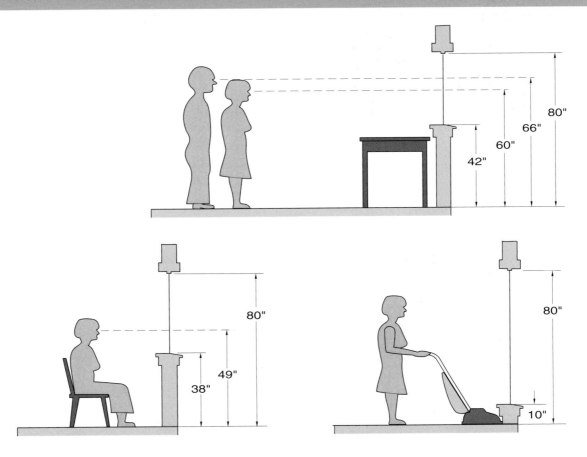

Kitchen Design Guidelines

More time is spent in the kitchen than in any other room of the home. The kitchen also accounts for the greatest cost per area. Thus its design merits careful consideration. As an aid, here are 21 of the 31 Kitchen Planning Guidelines of the National Kitchen & Bath Association. The complete set may be viewed at the NKBA website.

Distance between Work Centers

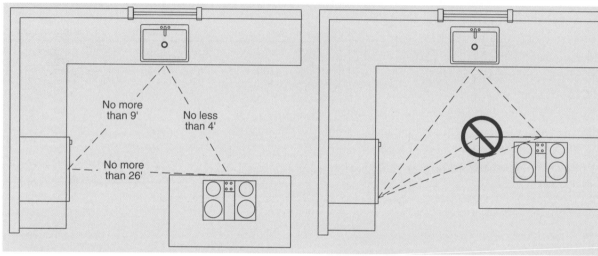

In a kitchen with three work centers, the sum of the three distances should total no more than 26', with no single leg of the triangle measuring less than 4' nor more than 9'.

No work triangle leg should intersect an island/peninsula or other obstacle by more than 12".

Separating Work Centers

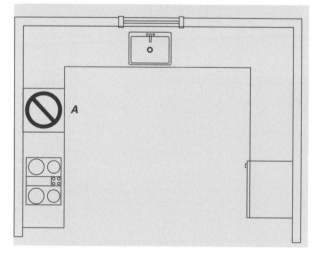

A full-height, full-depth, tall obstacle (A) should not separate two primary work centers. A properly recessed tall corner unit will not interrupt the workflow and is acceptable.

Work Triangle Traffic

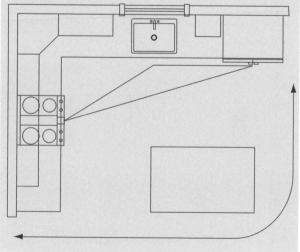

No major traffic patterns should cross through the basic work triangle.

Work Aisle

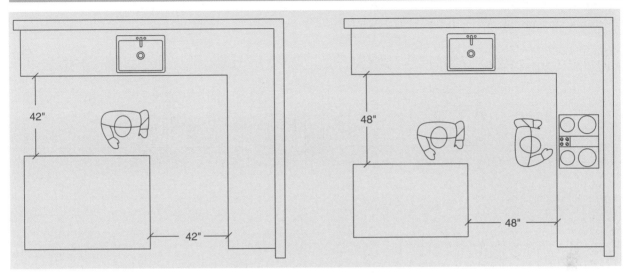

The width of a work aisle should be at least 42" for one cook and at least 48" for multiple cooks. Measure between the counter frontage, tall cabinets, and/or appliances.

Walkway

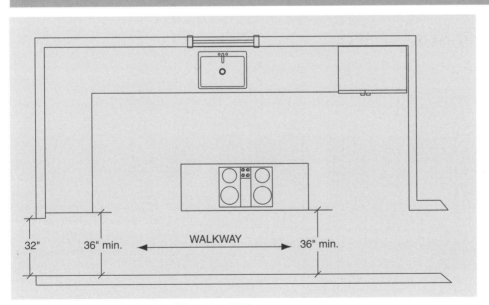

The width of a walkway should be at least 36".

Traffic Clearance at Seating

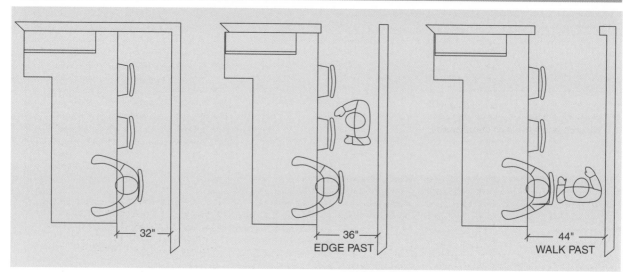

32"

36"
EDGE PAST

44"
WALK PAST

In a seating area where no traffic passes behind a seated diner, allow 32" of clearance from the counter/table edge to any wall or other obstruction behind the seating area.

If traffic passes behind the seated diner, allow at least 36" to edge past.

If traffic passes behind the seated diner, allow at least 44" to walk past.

Seating Clearance

Kitchen seating areas should incorporate at least the following clearances:

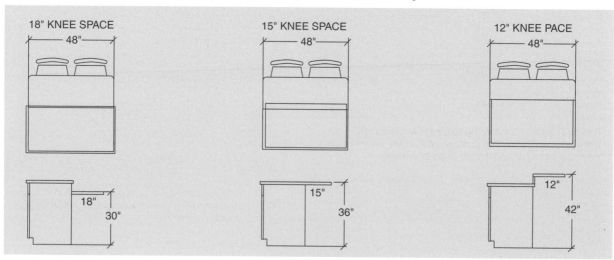

18" KNEE SPACE
48"
18"
30"

15" KNEE SPACE
48"
15"
36"

12" KNEE PACE
48"
12"
42"

30"-high tables/counters:
Allow a 24"-wide by 18"-deep counter/table space for each seated diner.

36"-high counters:
Allow a 24"-wide by 15"-deep counter space for each seated diner and at least 15" of clear knee space.

42"-high counters:
Allow a 24"-wide by 12"-deep counter space for each seated diner and 12" of clear knee space.

Cleanup/Prep Sink Placement

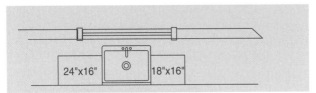

Include at least a 24"-wide **landing area***
to one side of the sink and at least an
18"-wide landing area on the other side.

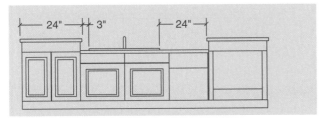

If all of the countertop at the sink is not at the same height, then
plan a 24" landing area on one side of the sink and 3" of countertop
frontage on the other side, both at the same height as the sink.

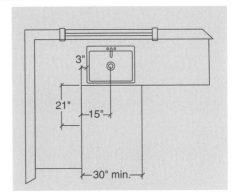

The 24" of recommended landing area can
be met by 3" of countertop frontage from the
edge of the sink to the inside corner of the
countertop if more than 21" of countertop
frontage is available on the return.

***Landing area** is measured as countertop
frontage adjacent to a sink and/or an appliance.
The countertop must be at least 16" deep and
must be 28" to 45" above the finished floor in
order to qualify.

Dishwasher Placement

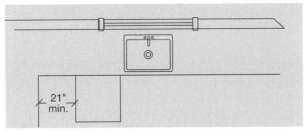

Provide at least 21" of standing space between the edge of the
dishwasher and countertop frontage, appliances, and/or cabinets
which are placed at a right angle to the dishwasher.

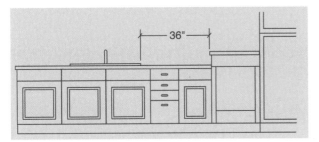

Locate nearest edge of the primary dishwasher within 36"
of the nearest edge of a cleanup/prep sink.

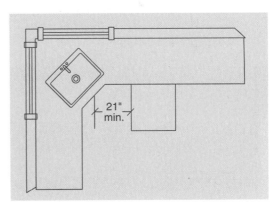

In a diagonal installation, the 21" is measured from
the center of the sink to the edge of the dishwasher
door in an open position.

Refrigerator Landing Area

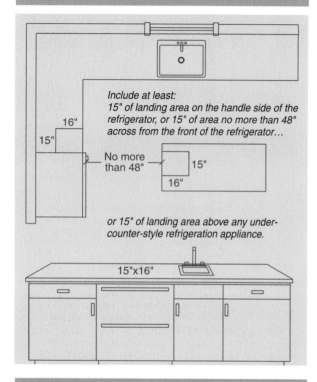

Include at least:
15" of landing area on the handle side of the refrigerator, or 15" of area no more than 48" across from the front of the refrigerator...

No more than 48"

or 15" of landing area above any under-counter-style refrigeration appliance.

15"x16"

Cooking Surface Landing Area

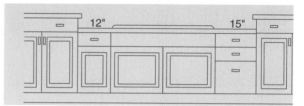

Include a minimum of 12" of landing area on one side of a cooking surface and 15" on the other side. If the cooking surface is at a different countertop height than the rest of the kitchen, then the 12" and 15" landing areas must be at the same height as the cooking surface.

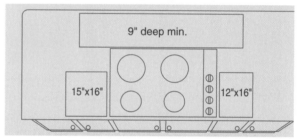

9" deep min.

15"x16"   12"x16"

For safety reasons, in an island or peninsula situation, the countertop should also extend a minimum of 9" behind the cooking surface if the counter height is the same as the surface-cooking appliance.

Cooking Surface Clearance

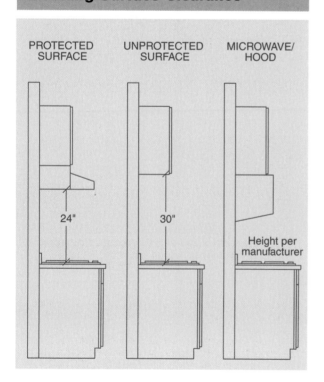

PROTECTED SURFACE | UNPROTECTED SURFACE | MICROWAVE/ HOOD

24" | 30" | Height per manufacturer

Cooking Surface Ventilation

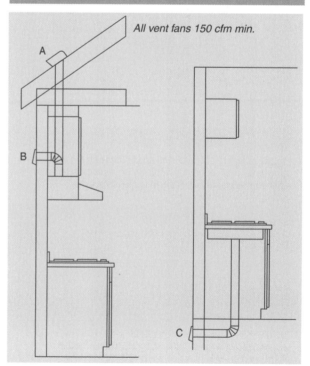

All vent fans 150 cfm min.

A

B

C

Oven Landing Area

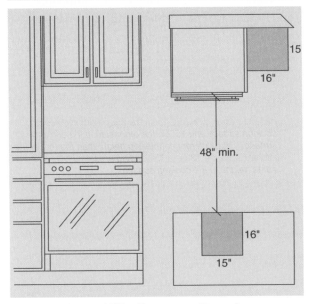

Include at least a 15" landing area next to or above an oven. At least a 15" landing area not more than 48" across from the oven is acceptable if the appliance does not open into a walkway.

Countertop Space

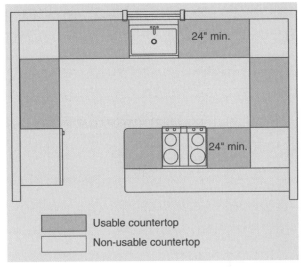

Usable countertop

Non-usable countertop

A total of 158" of countertop frontage, 24" deep, with at least 15" of clearance above, is needed to accommodate all uses, including landing area, preparation/work area, and storage.

Built-in appliance garages extending to the countertop can be counted toward the total countertop frontage recommendation, but they may interfere with the landing areas.

Electrical Receptacles

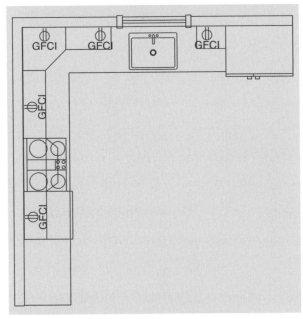

GFCI protection is required on all receptacles serving countertop surfaces in the kitchen (IRC E 3802.6). Refer to IRC E 3801.4.1 through E 3801.4.5 for placement.

Lighting

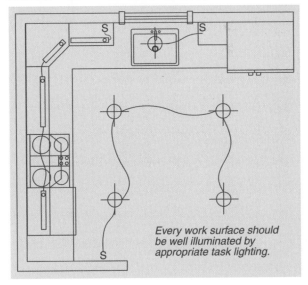

Every work surface should be well illuminated by appropriate task lighting.

At least one wall switch–controlled light must be provided. Switch must be placed at the entrance (IRC E 3803.2).

Window/skylight area equal to at least 8% of the total square footage of the kitchen, or a total living space which includes a kitchen, is required (IRC R 303.1, IRC R 303.2).

Bath Design Guidelines

Bathrooms, along with kitchens, assume greater importance and account for a greater portion of construction cost with every year. As an aid to bathroom design, here are 20 of the 27 *Bathroom* *Planning Guidelines* of the National Kitchen & Bath Association. The Guidelines assure compliance with the IRC, as well as comfort and convenience. The complete set may be viewed at the NKBA website.

Clear Space

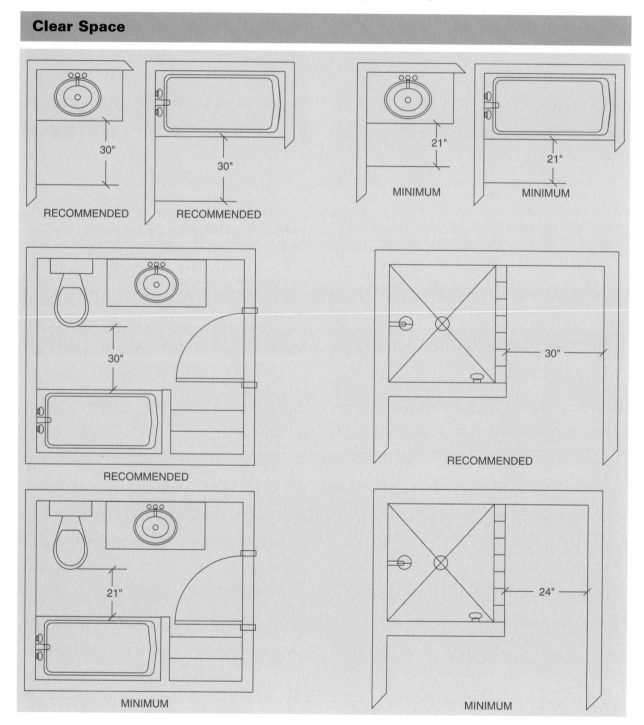

Single Lavatory Placement

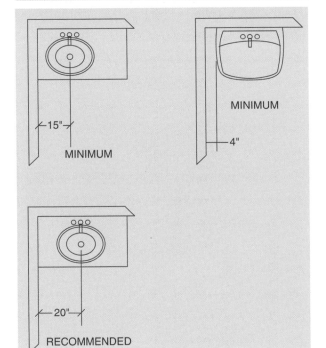

MINIMUM

15"

MINIMUM

4"

20"

RECOMMENDED

Double Lavatory Placement

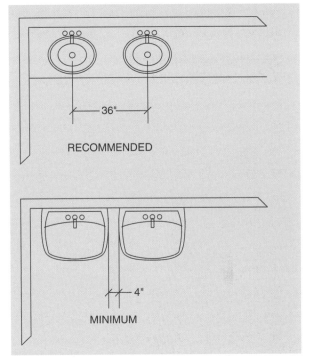

36"

RECOMMENDED

4"

MINIMUM

Lavatory/Vanity Height

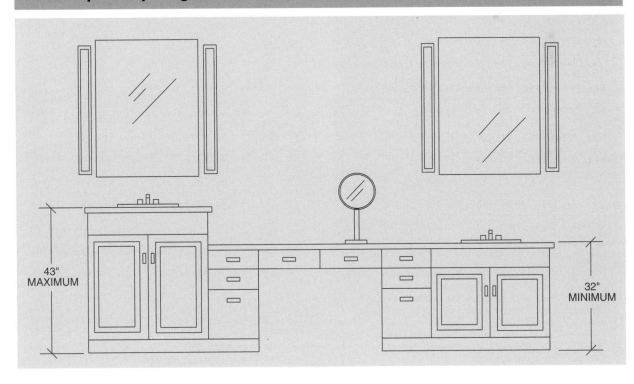

43"
MAXIMUM

32"
MINIMUM

Countertop Edges

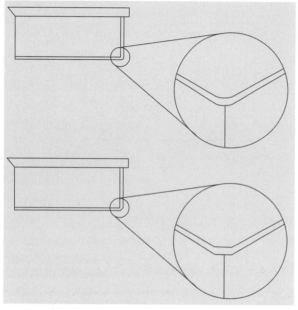

Specify clipped or round corners rather than sharp edges on all counters.

Shower Size

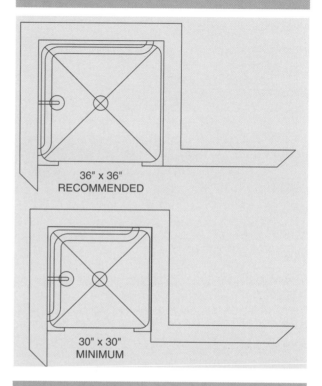

36" x 36"
RECOMMENDED

30" x 30"
MINIMUM

Tub/Shower Controls

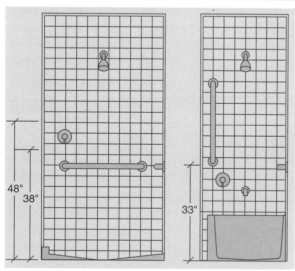

The shower controls should be accessible from both inside and outside the shower spray and be located between 38" and 48" above the floor, depending on user's height.

The tub controls should be accessible from both inside and outside the tub and be located between the rim of the bathtub and 33" above the floor.

Shower Seat

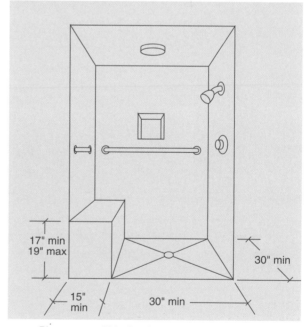

Plan a seat within the shower that is 17" to 19" above the shower floor and 15" deep.

Grab Bars

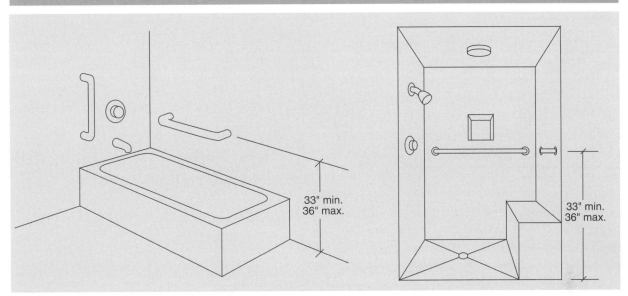

Plan grab bars to facilitate access to and maneuvering within the tub and shower areas. Tub and shower walls should be prepared (reinforced) at time of construction to allow for installation of grab bars to support a static load of 300 pounds.

Grab bars should be placed at least 33" to 36" above the floor. Grab bars must be 1¹/₄" to 1¹/₂" in diameter and extend 1¹/₂" from the wall.

Tub/Shower Surround

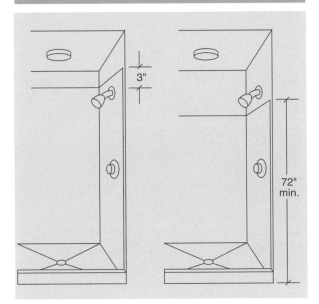

The wall area above a tub or shower pan should be covered in a waterproof material extending at least 3" above the showerhead rough-in.

Equipment Access

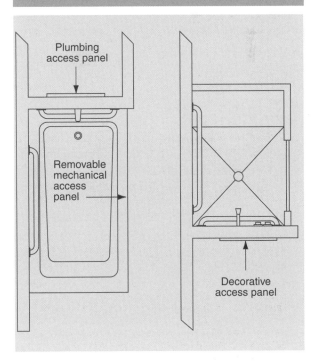

Toilet/Bidet Placement

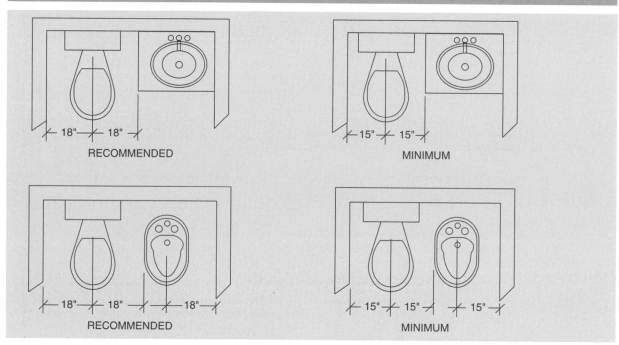

RECOMMENDED — 18" 18"

MINIMUM — 15" 15"

RECOMMENDED — 18" 18" 18"

MINIMUM — 15" 15" 15"

The distance from the centerline of toilet and/or bidet to any bath fixture, wall, or other obstacle must be at least 15".

Toilet Compartment

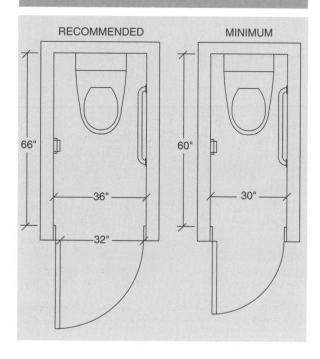

RECOMMENDED   MINIMUM

66"   60"

36"   30"

32"

Accessories

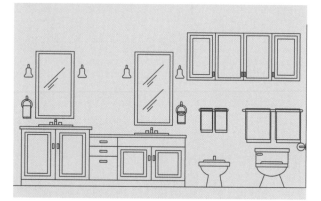

Place a mirror above or near the lavatory at a height that takes the user's eye height into consideration.

The toilet paper holder should be located 8" to 12" in front of the edge of the toilet bowl, centered at 26" above the floor.

Additional accessories, such as towel holders and soap dishes, should be conveniently located near all bath fixtures.

Ventilation

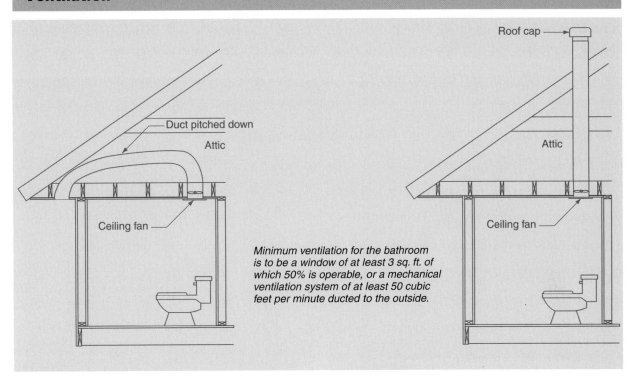

Minimum ventilation for the bathroom is to be a window of at least 3 sq. ft. of which 50% is operable, or a mechanical ventilation system of at least 50 cubic feet per minute ducted to the outside.

Electrical Receptacles

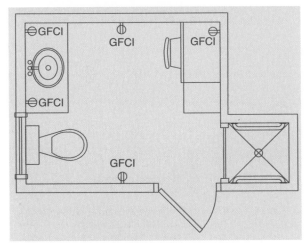

At least one GFCI-protected receptacle must be installed within 36" of the outside edge of the lavatory (IRC E 3801.6).

All receptacles must be protected by ground fault circuit interrupters (GFCI) (IRC 3802.1). A receptacle shall not be installed within a shower or bathtub space (IRC E 3902.10).

Switches shall not be installed within wet locations in tub or shower spaces unless installed as part of the listed tub or shower assembly.

Lighting

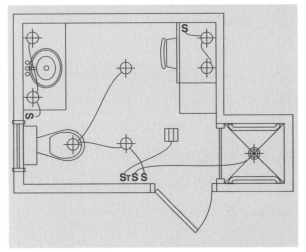

At least one wall switch–controlled light must be provided. Switch must be placed at the entrance (IRC E 3901.6, 3803.2).

All light fixtures installed within tub and shower spaces should be marked "suitable for damp/wet locations" (IRC E 3903.8).

Hanging fixtures cannot be located within a zone of 3' horizontally and 8' vertically from the top of the bathtub rim (IRC E 3903.10).

Stair Design

Stairs and stairways are all too often treated as afterthoughts. With stairway accidents accounting for a high percentage of all deaths and injuries in the home, the International Residential Code treats their proper design in great detail. A free 16-page *Visual Interpretation of the IRC 2006 Stair Building Code* is available in pdf format from the Stairway Manufacturers' Association (*www.stairways.org*).

Stairways

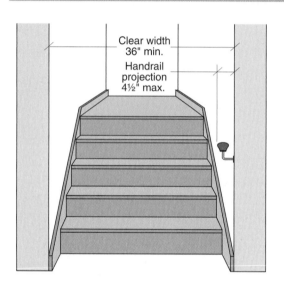

Clear width
36" min.

Handrail
projection
4½" max.

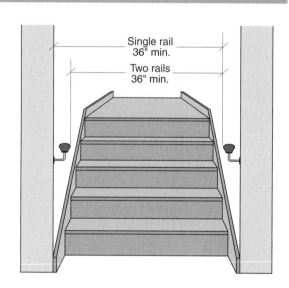

Single rail
36" min.

Two rails
36" min.

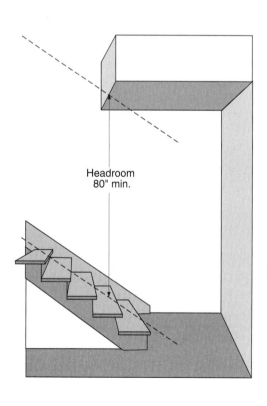

Headroom
80" min.

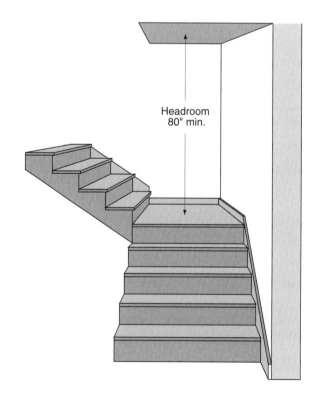

Headroom
80" min.

Handrails

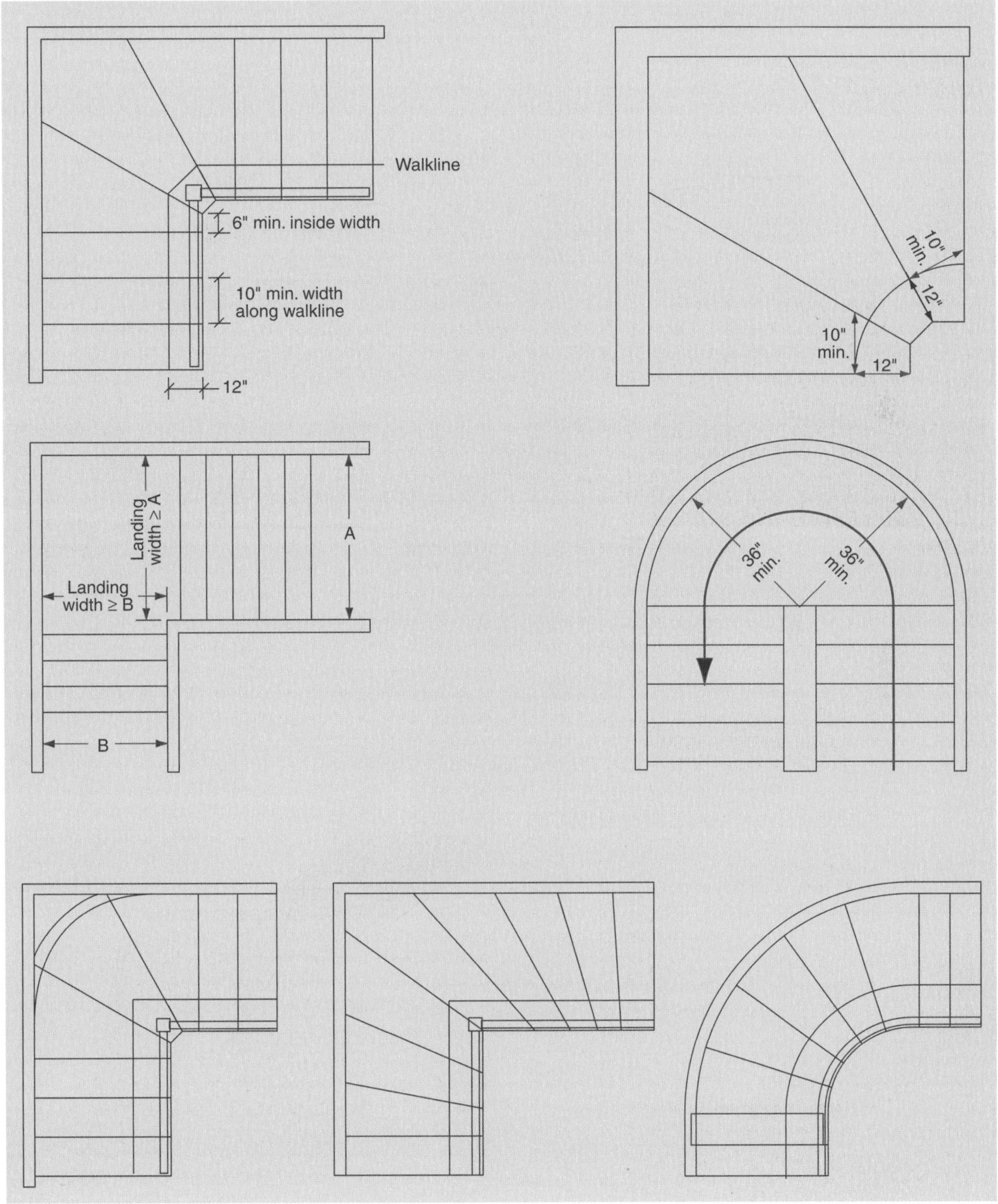
Walkline
6" min. inside width
10" min. width
along walkline
12"
10" min.
12"
10" min.
12"
Landing width ≥ A
A
Landing width ≥ B
B
36" min.
36" min.

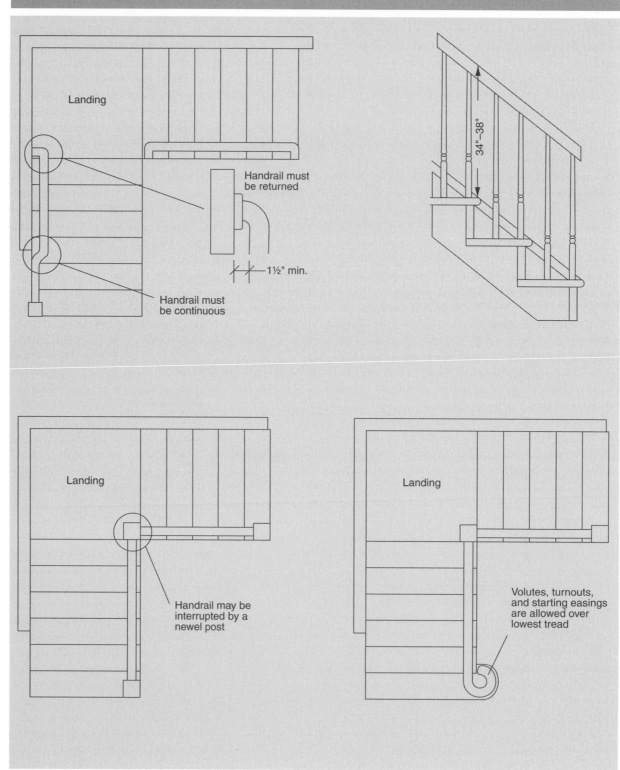

Landing

Handrail must
be returned

1½" min.

Handrail must
be continuous

34"–38"

Landing

Handrail may be
interrupted by a
newel post

Landing

Volutes, turnouts,
and starting easings
are allowed over
lowest tread

CIRCULAR CROSS SECTIONS

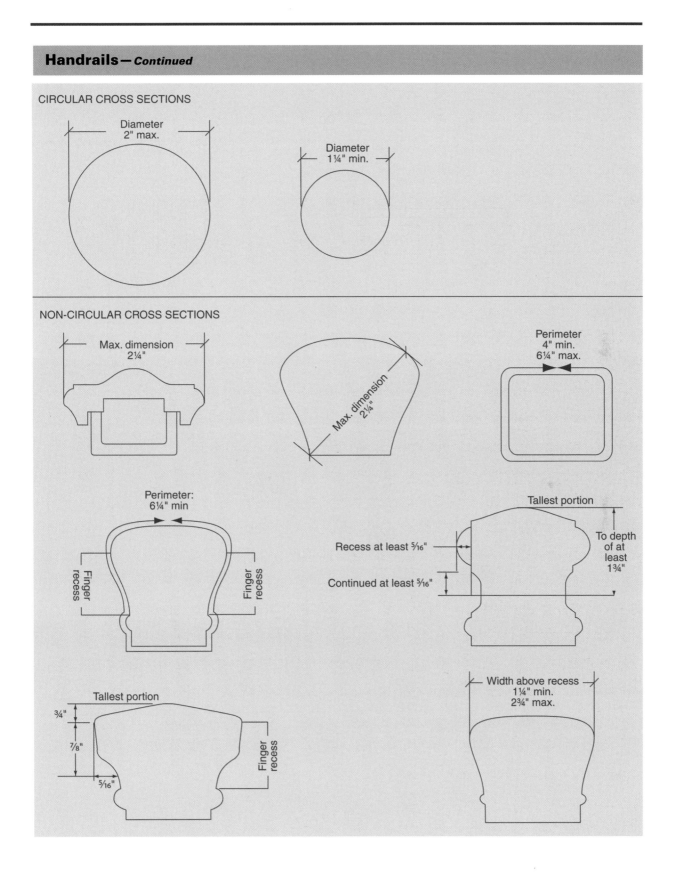

Diameter 2" max.

Diameter 1¼" min.

NON-CIRCULAR CROSS SECTIONS

Max. dimension 2¼"

Max. dimension 2¼"

Perimeter 4" min. 6¼" max.

Perimeter: 6¼" min

Finger recess

Finger recess

Recess at least ⁵⁄₁₆"

Continued at least ⁵⁄₁₆"

Tallest portion

To depth of at least 1¾"

Tallest portion

¾"

⁷⁄₈"

⁵⁄₁₆"

Finger recess

Width above recess 1¼" min. 2¾" max.

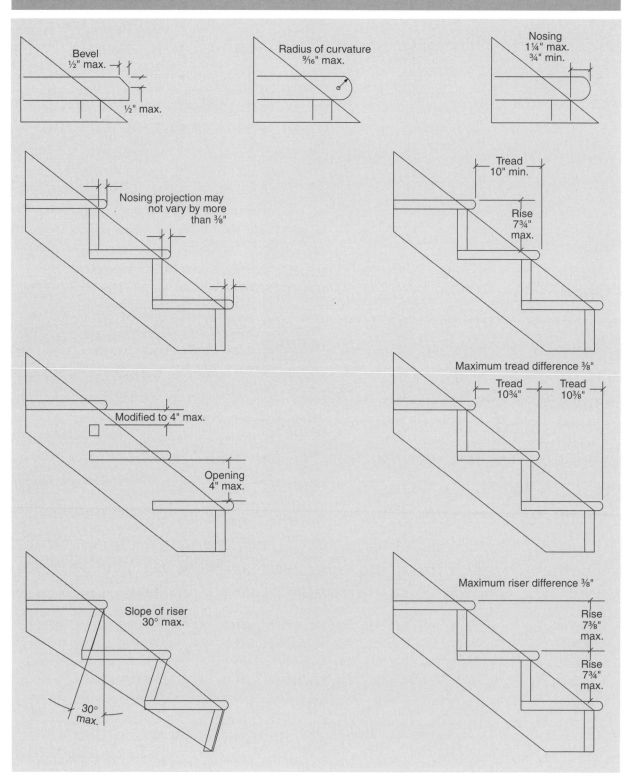

Bevel ½" max.
½" max.

Radius of curvature ⁹⁄₁₆" max.

Nosing 1¼" max. ¾" min.

Nosing projection may not vary by more than ⅜"

Tread 10" min.
Rise 7¾" max.

Modified to 4" max.
Opening 4" max.

Maximum tread difference ⅜"
Tread 10¾" Tread 10⅜"

Slope of riser 30° max.
30° max.

Maximum riser difference ⅜"
Rise 7⅜" max.
Rise 7¾" max.

Must not pass sphere
of 4" diameter

Must not pass sphere
of 6" diameter

then 36" min.

34" min.

If total rise over 30"

Access

The Americans with Disabilities Act of 1990 prohibits employers from discriminating against individuals having physical disabilities who are otherwise qualified for employment. The regulations are contained in 28 C.F.R. § 36.

The regulations regarding building design are useful in designing not only public buildings, but also homes that are "elder-friendly."

The illustrations on the following 10 pages are adaptations of those in Appendix A of Part 36. The complete *ADA Standards for Accessible Design* can be downloaded at *www.ada.gov/adastd94.pdf*.

Reach Limits

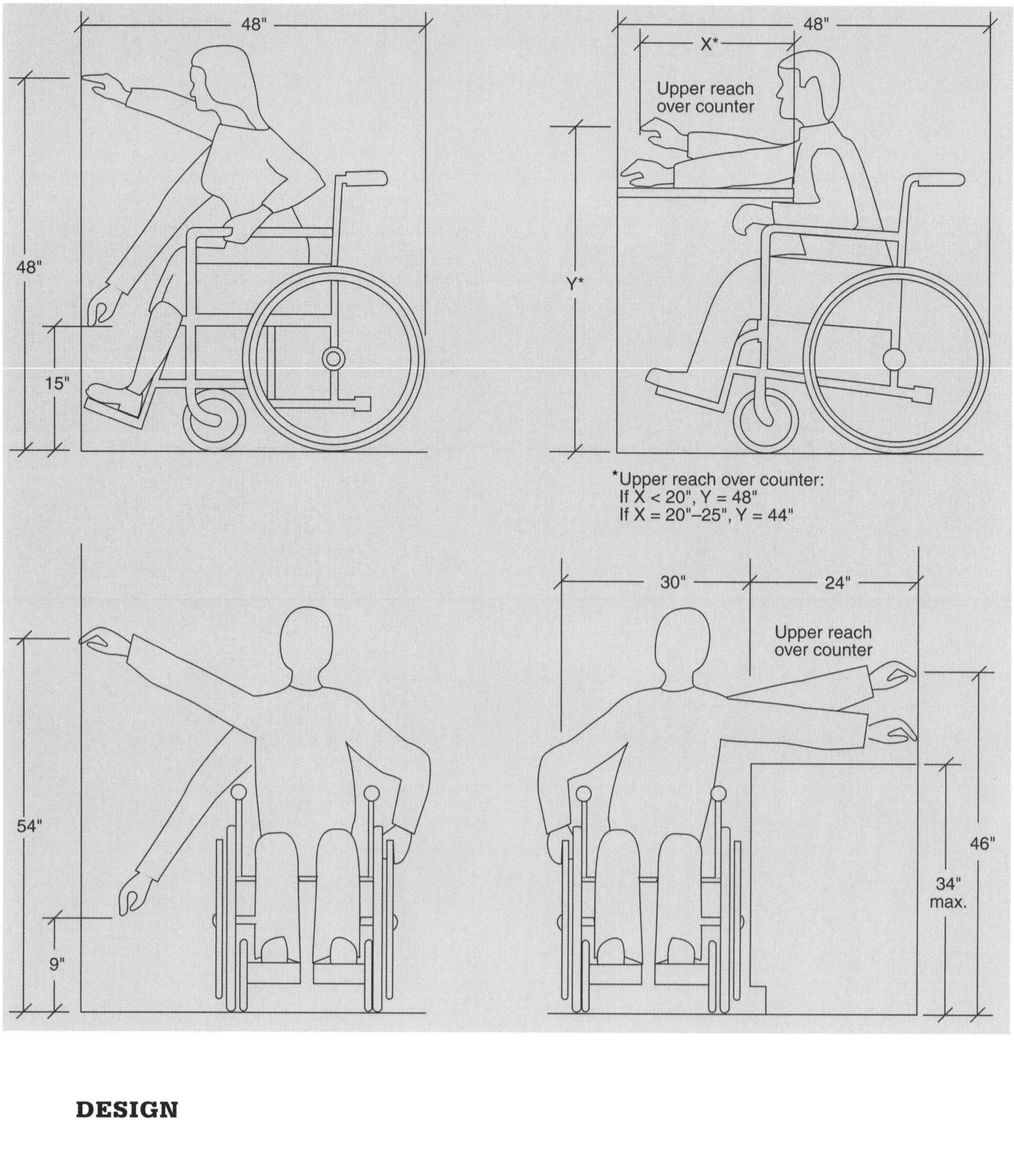

48"

48"

15"

48"

X*

Upper reach
over counter

Y*

*Upper reach over counter:
If X < 20", Y = 48"
If X = 20"–25", Y = 44"

54"

9"

30"

24"

Upper reach
over counter

46"

34"
max.

Clear Space and Turning

32" min.

24" max. depth for min. clearance

42" min.

48" min.

36" min.

42" min.

36" min.

36" min.

48" min.

36" min.

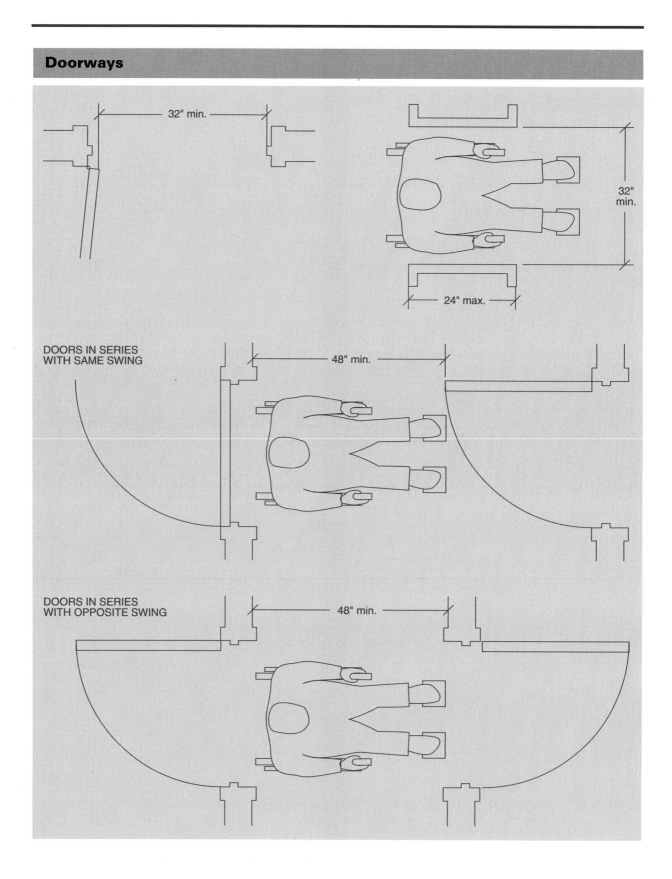

32" min.

32" min.

24" max.

DOORS IN SERIES WITH SAME SWING

48" min.

DOORS IN SERIES WITH OPPOSITE SWING

48" min.

Doorways—*Continued*

FRONT APPROACHES

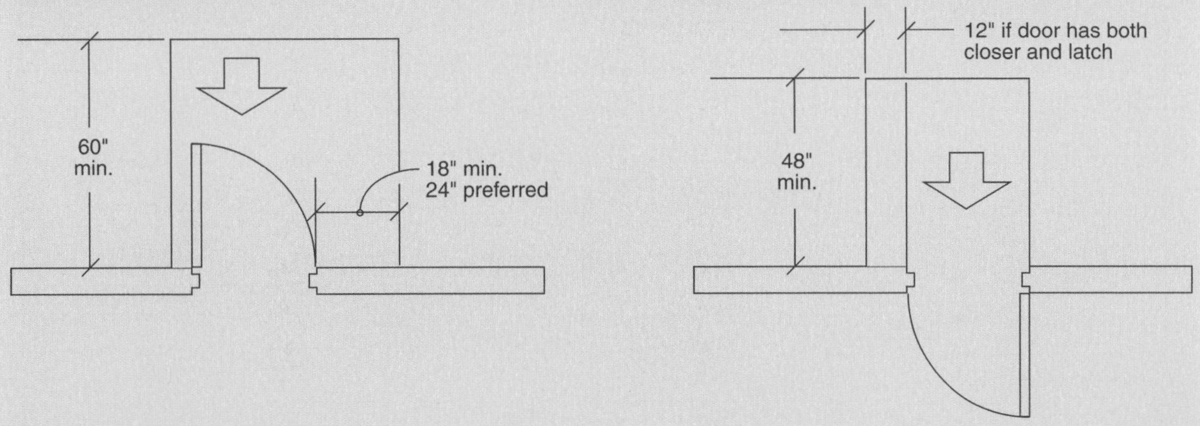
60" min.
18" min.
24" preferred
12" if door has both closer and latch
48" min.

HINGE-SIDE APPROACHES

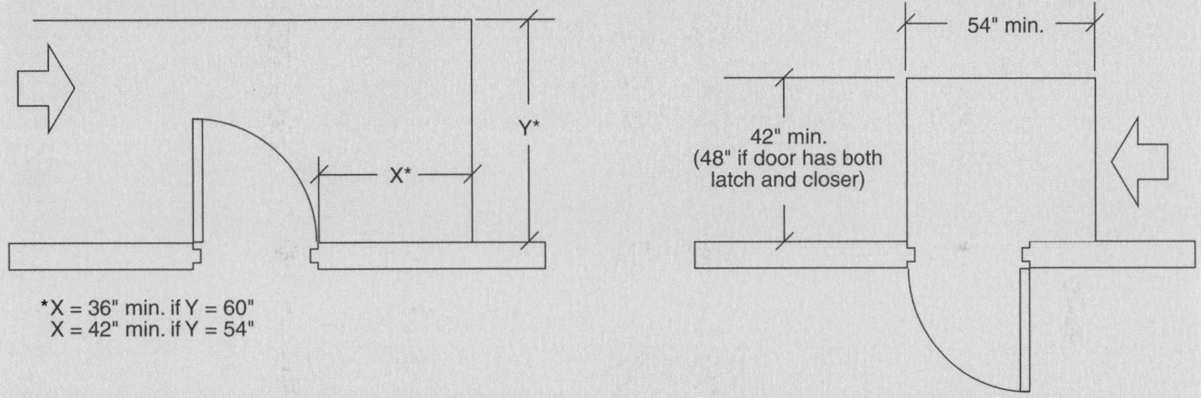
Y*
X*
54" min.
42" min.
(48" if door has both latch and closer)

*X = 36" min. if Y = 60"
X = 42" min. if Y = 54"

LATCH-SIDE APPROACHES

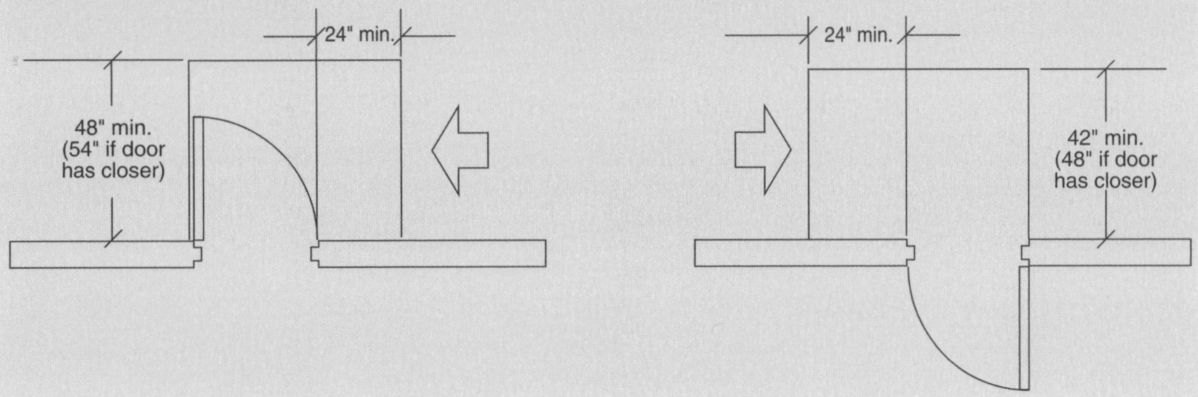
24" min.
48" min.
(54" if door has closer)
24" min.
42" min.
(48" if door has closer)

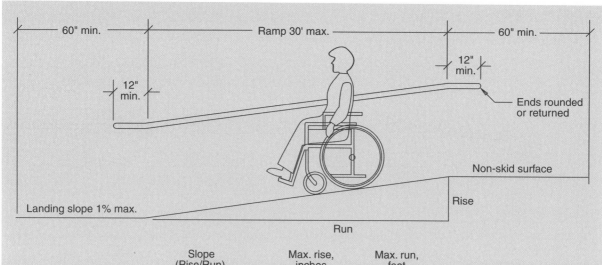

Slope (Rise/Run)	Max. rise, inches	Max. run, feet
1:12 to < 1:16	30	30
1:16 to < 1:20	30	40

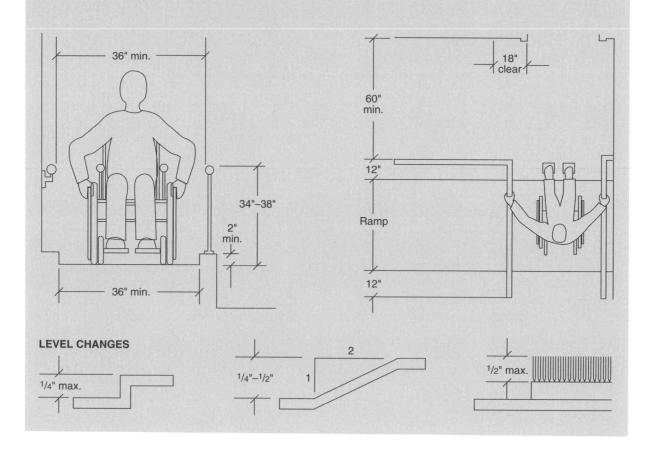

LEVEL CHANGES

Kitchens and Seating

COUNTERS AND RANGES

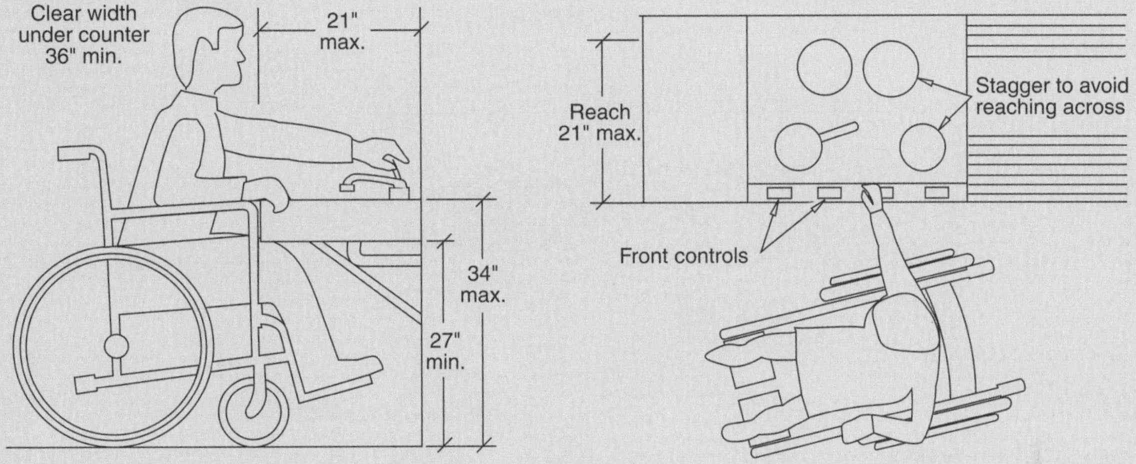

Clear width under counter 36" min.

21" max.

34" max.

27" min.

Reach 21" max.

Stagger to avoid reaching across

Front controls

ALONG TRAFFIC PATHS

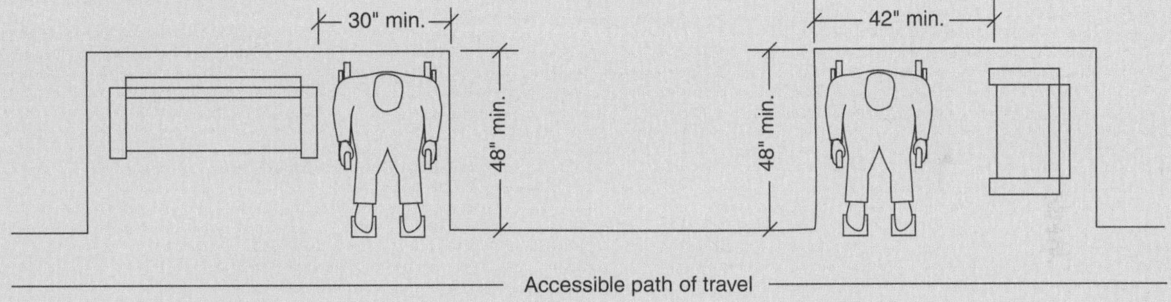

30" min.

48" min.

42" min.

48" min.

Accessible path of travel

SEATING AT TABLES

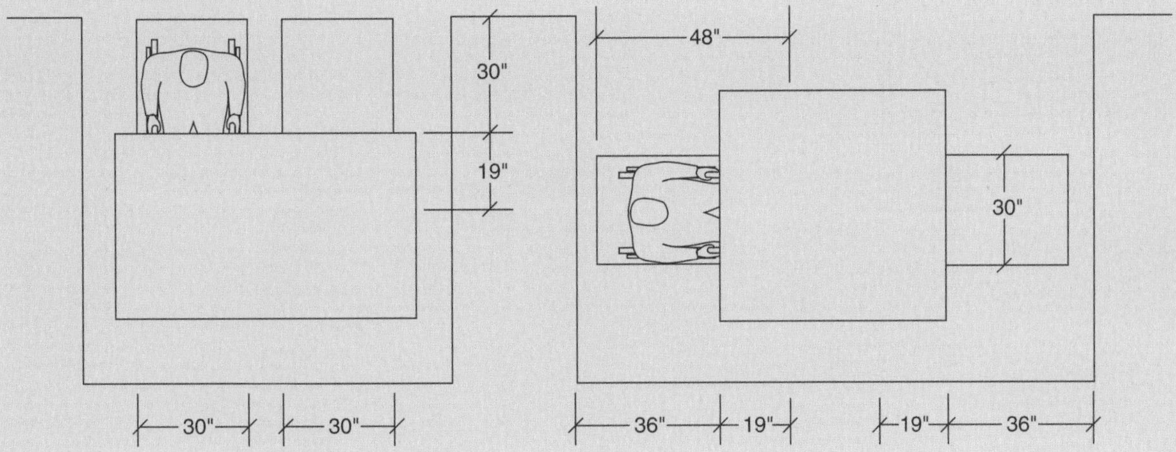

30"

19"

48"

30"

30"

30"

36"

19"

19"

36"

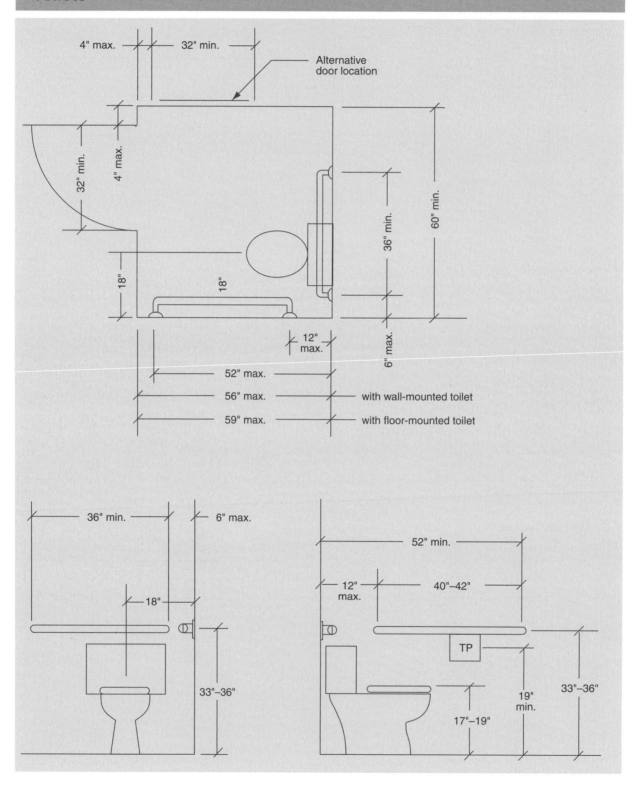

4" max. 32" min.

Alternative door location

32" min.

4" max.

18"

18"

36" min.

60" min.

12" max.

6" max.

52" max.

56" max. with wall-mounted toilet

59" max. with floor-mounted toilet

36" min. 6" max.

18"

33"–36"

52" min.

12" max. 40"–42"

TP

17"–19"

19" min.

33"–36"

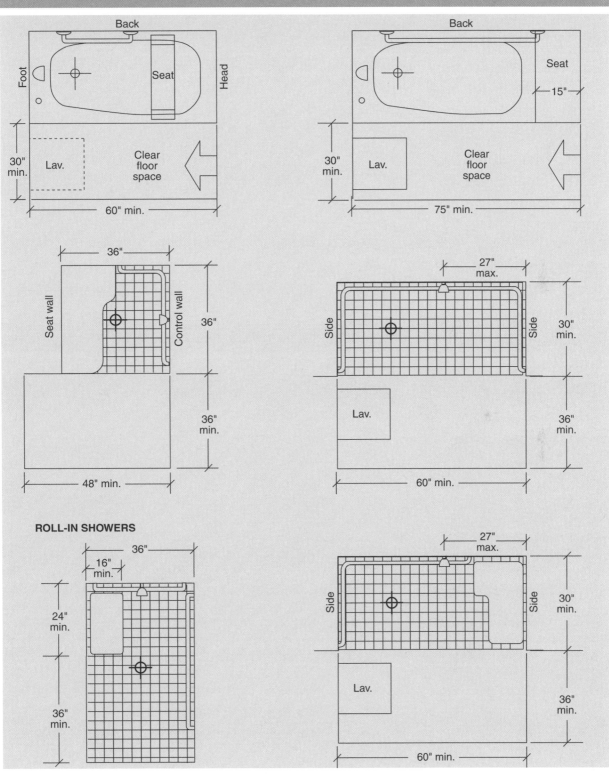

ROLL-IN SHOWERS

Tub Grab Bars

WITH SEAT IN TUB

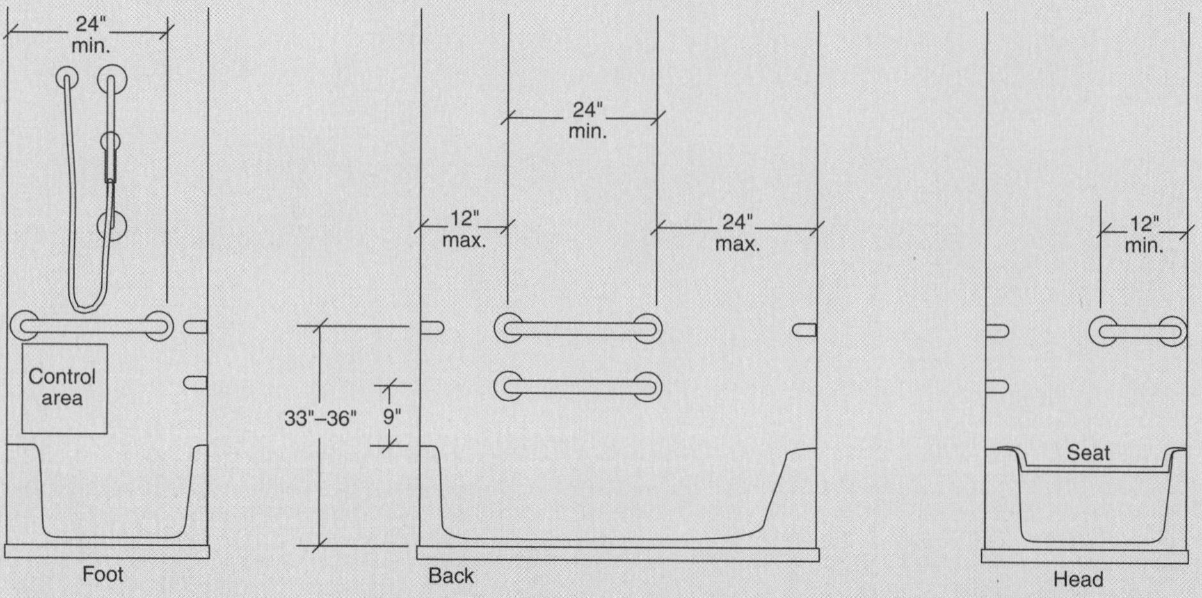

24" min.

Control area

Foot

24" min.

12" max.

24" max.

33"–36" 9"

Back

12" min.

Seat

Head

WITH SEAT AT HEAD OF TUB

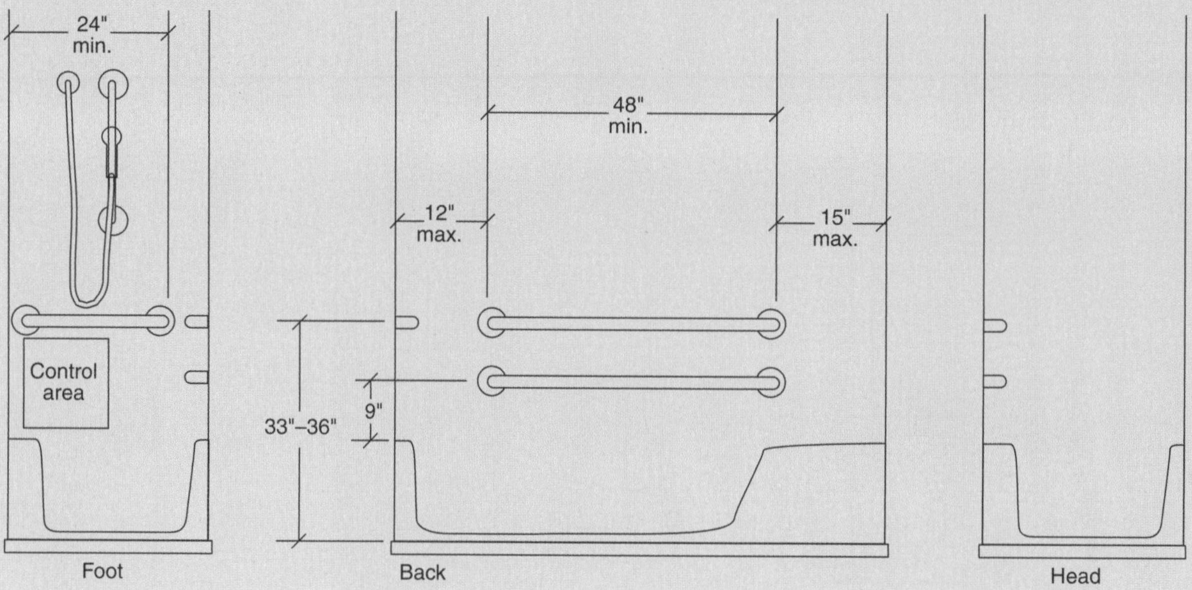

24" min.

Control area

Foot

48" min.

12" max.

15" max.

33"–36" 9"

Back

Head

Shower Grab Bars

36" by 36" STALL

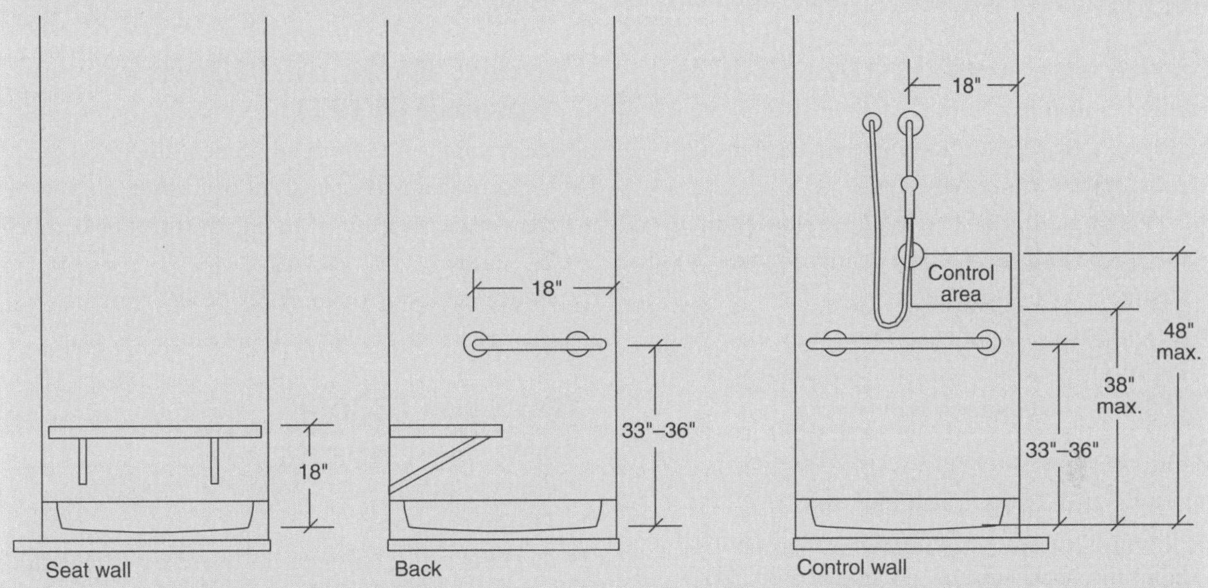

Seat wall

Back

18"

33"–36"

18"

Control wall

18"

Control area

48" max.

38" max.

33"–36"

30" by 60" STALL

Side

33"–36"

Back (long)

27" max.

Control area

48" max.

38" min.

33"–36"

Side

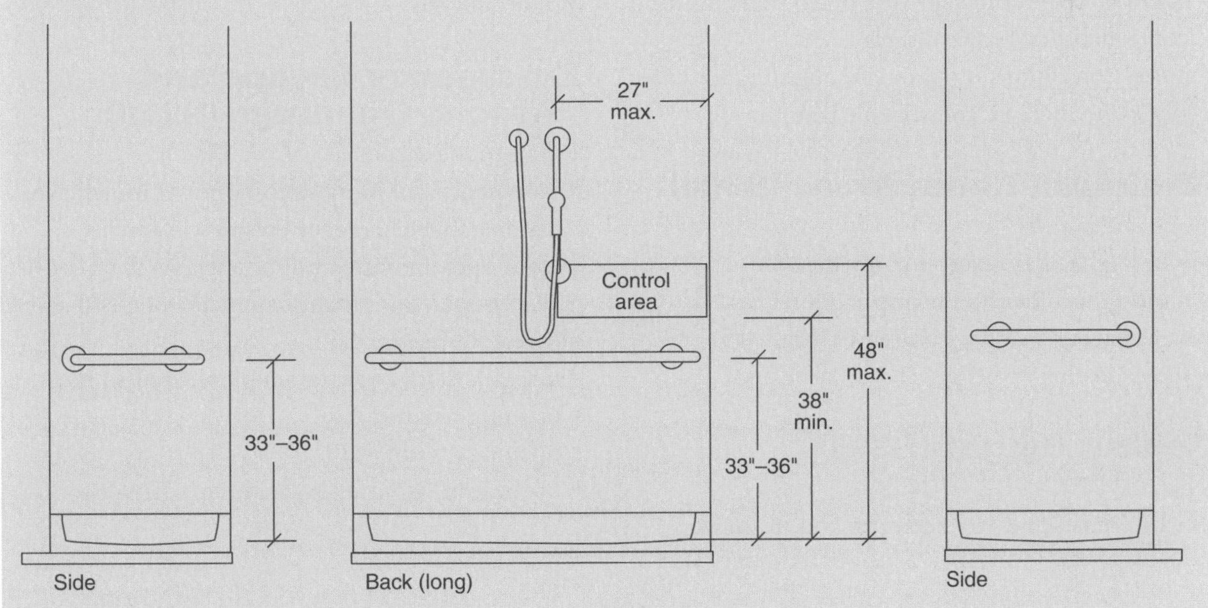

Meet the Code

The following is a partial list of requirements from the *2006 International Residential Code (IRC) for One- and Two-Family Dwellings*. Consult the publication for the full text and additional provisions.

Light and Ventilation (R303)

Habitable Rooms:

- glazing area ≥8% of floor area unless lighting provides ≥6 foot-candles
- ≥50% of glazing openable unless not required for egress, and mechanical ventilation of 0.35 air change per hour provided
- for purposes of light and ventilation, an adjoining room is considered part of a room when ≥50% of the common wall is open

Bathrooms:

- glazing area ≥3 sq ft, half openable
- glazing not required if provided with artificial light and ventilation to outside of ≥50 cfm

Stairway Illumination:

- interior stairs must be lighted to ≥1 foot-candle either at each landing or over each section of stairs
- exterior stairs must be lighted at top landing; basement bulkhead stairs at lower landing
- lighting for interior stairways of ≥6 stairs must be controllable from both levels
- unless continuous or automatic, lighting for exterior stairs must be controllable from inside

Minimum Room Areas (R304)

- one ≥120 sq ft
- others ≥70 sq ft (excepting kitchens)
- minimum dimension (excepting kitchens): 7'
- areas having a sloping ceiling of height <5' or furred ceiling of height <7' do not count

Ceiling Height (R305)

- general ≥7'0"
- bathrooms: ≥6'8" over fixtures and in showers

- basement (uninhabitable) ≥6'8"
- basement beams ≥6'4"
- beams spaced ≥4' oc may project 6" below required ceiling height

Toilet, Bath, and Shower Spaces (R307)

- toilet center line from adjacent wall: 15" min
- lavatory from adjacent wall or fixture: 4" min
- clear space in front of toilet, lavatory, or bathtub: 21" min
- shower stall dimensions: 30" × 30" min
- clear space at shower stall opening: 24" min

Garages (R309)

- doors to sleeping room prohibited
- doors to other rooms: solid 1⅜" wood or 20-min fire-rated
- dwelling walls: ½" gypsum board on garage side
- ceilings under habitable rooms: ⅝" Type X gypsum board on garage side
- dwelling walls within 3' of separate garage: ½" gypsum board on dwelling interior
- dwelling wall: ½" gypsum board on garage side
- floor: noncombustible and sloped toward exterior doorway

Emergency Escape and Rescue Openings (R310)

Emergency Escape:

- basements and every sleeping room must have an operable emergency escape window or door opening into a public way, yard, or court (exception: equipment basements of ≤200 sq ft)
- egress sill height: ≤44"
- net area: ≥5.7 sq ft (grade-floor ≥5.0 sq ft)
- opening height: ≥24"
- opening width: ≥20"
- operational from inside without a key or tools

Means of Egress (R311)

Doors:
- at least one egress door directly to outside from habitable area of house (not through garage)
- side-hinged
- width: 3'0" min
- height: 6'8" min
- operational from inside without a key or tools

Landings:
- landing each side of egress door: 3' × 3' min
- landing: ≤1½" lower than threshold, except ≤7¾" provided door doesn't swing over landing

Ramps:
- max. slope: 1/8 (12.5%)
- handrail required for slope >1/12 (8.3%)
- landing each end of ramp: 3' × 3' min

Stairways
- width above handrail: 36" min
- width at and below one handrail: 31½" min
- width at and below two handrails: 27" min
- headroom over nosing: 6'8" min

Landings for Stairways:
- landing top and bottom of each stairway, except interior stairway if door does not swing over stairs
- width of landing: ≥ width of stairs
- length of landing: 36" min
- stairway rise: ≤12' between floors or landings

Stair Treads and Risers:
- riser: 7¾" max
- riser variation: ⅜" max
- tread (nose to nose): 10" min
- tread variation: ⅜" max
- nosing: ¾" min to 1¼" max
- nosing not required if riser open
- riser sloped 0°–30° max from vertical

Winders:
- tread: ≥10" at 12" from narrower side
- tread: ≥6" at all points

- tread variation at 12" walk line: ⅜" max
- handrail required on narrow-tread side

Spiral Stairs:
- min. width: 26"
- tread: ≥7½" at 12" from narrower side
- all treads identical
- riser: ≤9½"
- headroom: 6'6" min

Handrails:
- 34" to 38" above tread nosing
- at least one side when ≥4 risers
- on outside of spiral stairways
- continuous except if interrupted by newel post at a turn
- ends return or terminate at newel posts
- spaced from wall: ≥1½"
- diameter if of circular section: 1¼" to 2"
- perimeter of non-circular section: 4" to 6¼" and max. diagonal dimension 2¼"

Guards (R312)
- required for floors and stair treads >30" above floor or grade below
- min. height of rail above floor: 36"
- min. height of rail above stair nosing: 34"
- not allow passage of 4" diameter sphere, except 6" for triangle formed by tread, riser, and bottom rail

Smoke Detectors (R313)
- all detectors to be interconnected
- in each sleeping room
- outside each sleeping area
- every floor, including basement, but not including crawl spaces or unfinished attics
- required as if new construction with renovation or addition requiring building permit
- must be powered by both unswitched house wiring and battery in new construction

Site and Climate

2

Architects often say, "You cannot build a good house on a bad site." They mean by this that the building site is, by far, the single most important element in a house design. Of course the qualities of a site involve a number of variables, some quantifiable, some not. In this limited space we describe the most important of those variables and how to deal with them.

We begin with the *plot plan*, the drawing which describes the dimensions of your site and your project, and which you must present to the building codes official in order to obtain your building permit.

Your site's soil properties can have a great effect on the cost of developing the site, particularly the costs of foundation and driveway, so we include the United Soil Classification System table of physical *soil properties*.

To take advantage of solar energy, whether photovoltaic or passive heating, you must know the geographic *orientation of your site*. We show how to determine true, or solar, south using a magnetic compass.

The topographic relief, or variations in elevation, of your site influence the costs of foundation, driveway, and grading, so we show a simple method of *determining relative elevations*.

Automobiles (and trucks of various sizes) play important roles in modern life. We show how to design *driveways* which safely access public highways and which provide adequate space in which to maneuver.

Throughout this book, whether predicting your heating bill or determining where to place windows for ventilation, you will have need for *climate data*, which we present in the form of simple maps.

In areas where too much winter wind results in high heating bills and drifting snow, *shelterbelts* consisting of strategically placed trees and bushes can provide significant relief.

Before purchasing trees and shrubs not native to your area, you will want to consult our map and table of *plant hardiness* to see if they have a chance of survival in your winters.

Important in selecting *trees* are the typical height and width at maturity. We have included a table of tree dimensions and a chart of tree silhouettes showing mature trees next to a typical house.

Last but not least, we have provided a table and map of grass seeds to consider in establishing *lawns*.

Plot Plans

Plot plans showing the building footprints, lot lines, setbacks, driveway, and locations of utilities and utility easements are usually required before a building permit can be secured. Plans showing elevation contours, both existing and planned, are additionally useful in setting foundation heights, laying out leach fields, and estimating excavation costs.

1. Using a 100-foot tape measure, stake out a base-line of elevation points along one of the property lines.

2. With a transit and tape, lay out a grid of secondary lines of points at right angles to the baseline.

3. Beginning at the lowest point, measure the relative elevation of each point in the grid (see p. 39).

4. Draw a plot plan to scale (check with your permitting official for an acceptable scale), interpolating lines of equal elevation (contour lines) between grid points. If grading is planned, draw the proposed final contours, as well.

Below is an example plot plan.

Sample Plot Plan

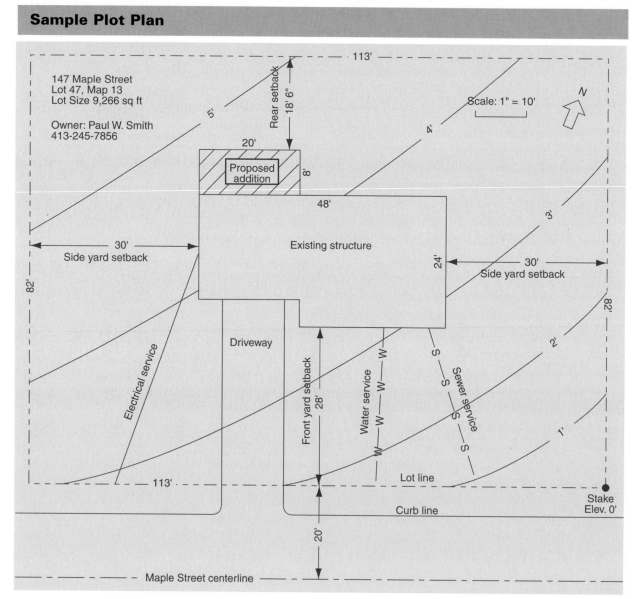

147 Maple Street
Lot 47, Map 13
Lot Size 9,266 sq ft

Owner: Paul W. Smith
413-245-7856

Scale: 1" = 10'

Rear setback
18' 6"

20'

Proposed addition

8'

48'

Existing structure

24'

30'
Side yard setback

30'
Side yard setback

82'

82'

Electrical service

Driveway

Front yard setback
28'

Water service
W — W — W — W

Sewer service
S — S — S — S — S

Lot line

Curb line

113'

113'

Stake
Elev. 0'

20'

Maple Street centerline

Soil Properties

Knowing the type(s) of soil on your property is useful, at least in preliminary planning. It is particularly important to know if your soil has diminished weight-bearing capacity or if it is likely to heave in winter.

If you are lucky your site has already been classified by the USDA Soil Conservation Service and described in one of the *Soil Surveys* available free through local soil and water conservation district offices in every state. Below are the characteristics of soils in the Unified Soil Classification System.

Unified Soil Classification System

Group	Soil Type	Description	Allowable Bearing[1] lb/sq ft	Drainage[2]	Frost Heave Potential	Expansion Potential[3]
NA	BR[4]	Bedrock	30,000	Poor	Low	Low
I	GW	Well-graded gravels or gravel-sand mixtures, little or no fines	8,000	Good	Low	Low
I	GP	Poorly graded gravels or gravel-sand mixtures, little or no fines	8,000	Good	Low	Low
I	SW	Well-graded sands, gravelly sands, little or no fines	6,000	Good	Low	Low
I	SP	Poorly graded sands or gravelly sands, little or no fines	5,000	Good	Low	Low
I	GM	Silty gravels, gravel-sand-silt mixtures	4,000	Good	Medium	Low
I	SM	Silty sand, sand-silt mixtures	4,000	Good	Medium	Low
II	GC	Clayey gravels, gravel-clay-sand mixtures	4,000	Medium	Medium	Low
II	SC	Clayey sands, sand-clay mixture	4,000	Medium	Medium	Low
II	ML	Inorganic silts and very fine sands, rock flour, silty or clayey fine sands with slight plasticity	2,000	Medium	High	Low
II	CL	Inorganic clays of low to medium plasticity, gravelly clays, sandy clays, silty clays, lean clays	2,000	Medium	Medium	Medium[5]
III	CH	Inorganic clays of high plasticity, fat clays	2,000	Poor	Medium	High[5]
III	MH	Inorganic silts, micaceous or diatomaceous fine sandy or silty soils, elastic silts	2,000	Poor	High	High
IV	OL	Organic silts and organic silty clays	400	Poor	Medium	Medium
IV	OH	Organic clays of medium to high plasticity	0	Unsat	Medium	High
IV	PT	Peat and other highly organic soils	0	Unsat	Medium	High

[1] Allowable bearing value may be increased 25% for very compact, coarse-grained, gravelly, or sandy soils or very stiff, fine-grained, clayey, or silty soils. Allowable bearing value shall be decreased 25% for loose, coarse-grained, gravelly, or sandy soils or soft, fine-grained, clayey, or silty soils.

[2] Percolation rate for good drainage is over 4"/hr, medium drainage is 2–4"/hr, and poor is less than 2"/hr.

[3] For expansive soils, contact a local soil engineer for verification of design assumptions.

[4] Classification and properties added by author for comparison.

[5] Dangerous expansion might occur if these soil types are dry but subject to future wetting.

Site Orientation

The earth has two sets of poles. The geographic poles are the ends of the axis upon which the earth turns. True north is the direction from your location toward the geographic north pole. The second set are the magnetic poles. The earth is a gigantic, but weak, magnet, and a freely rotating compass needle will point toward the north magnetic pole, roughly located at 76° N latitude and 101° W longitude in northern Canada.

Because of the difference in pole locations, a magnetic compass needle will point to either the east (east variation) or the west of true north. The direction of true north, important in solar design, can be found easily using a simple compass:

1. Select a reference point (a corner of the foundation, for example).

2. Find the local variation from the map below; 12° W for New York City, for example).

3. Hold a magnetic compass to your eye and turn your body until the needle points to the opposite of the local variation (12° E in our example). You are now sighting along the true north–south line. Mark a reference sighting point in the direction of the line.

Magnetic Compass Variation (2004)

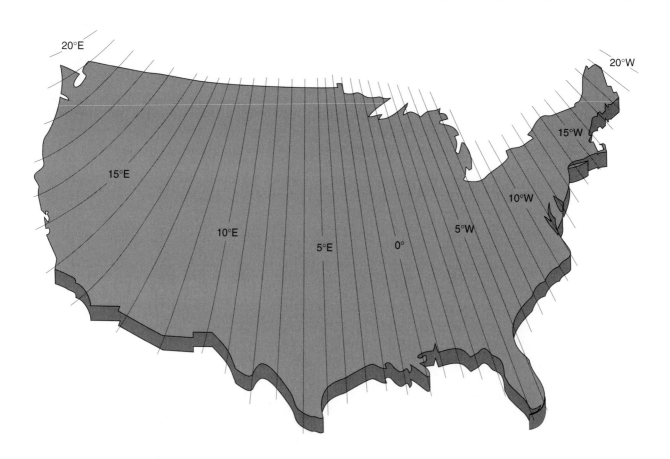

Determining Elevations

Relative elevations are important in laying out foundations, driveways and leach fields. Preliminary measurements can be made with a pocket sighting level, sometimes referred to as a "pop level." More precise measurements on the order of ¼ inch per 100 feet can be made with a builder's level or transit.

The method below requires two people: one to sight through the level; the other to hold and operate the grade pole. If the two are not too far apart, the person sighting may be able to read the feet and inches on the grade pole directly. At greater distances the grade pole operator slides a target up and down the scale and reads the level. More expensive automatic laser levels which project a rotating laser beam allow a single operator to hold the pole and read the level.

Measuring Relative Elevation

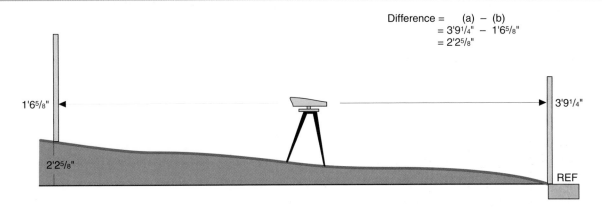

Difference =   (a) − (b)
= 3'9¹/₄" − 1'6⁵/₈"
= 2'2⁵/₈"

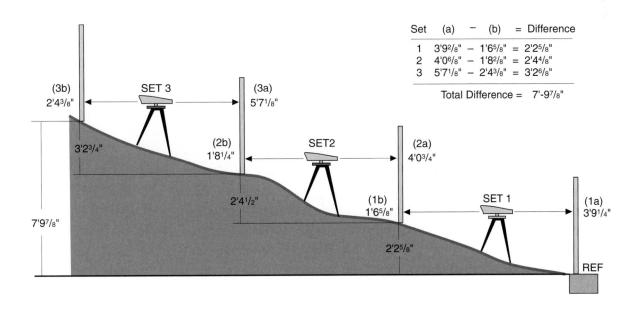

Set	(a)	−	(b)	= Difference
1	3'9²/₈"	−	1'6⁵/₈"	= 2'2⁵/₈"
2	4'0⁶/₈"	−	1'8²/₈"	= 2'4⁴/₈"
3	5'7¹/₈"	−	2'4³/₈"	= 3'2⁶/₈"

Total Difference =   7'-9⁷/₈"

Driveways

In addition to drainage and, in northern states, ease of snow removal, issues to consider in planning a driveway include the following:

- Permission to enter a public way
- Grade limits
- Vehicle turning radii

Entering a Public Way

Where and how a private drive enters a public road is a safety issue. You must obtain a permit from the town, city, or state that maintains the road or street. The key consideration is the safe sight distance at the highway's posted speed limit.

Safe Sight Distances for Passenger Cars Entering Two-Lane Highways

Speed, mph	Distance to Left	Distance to Right
30	350	260
40	530	440
50	740	700
60	950	1050

In the illustration below, the permit will depend on the visibility for traffic in the lane being entered. Entrances may be denied in the shaded areas.

Grade Limits

The *slope* of a surface is defined as the ratio of horizontal run to vertical rise. *Grade* is the percentage ratio of vertical rise to horizontal run. The table below shows recommended minimum and maximum grades for traffic surfaces.

Minimum grades are for the purpose of drainage; maximum grades are related to traction.

Slope versus Grade

Example

Driveway

Rise 4'

Run 64'

Slope = 64'/4' = 16:1
Grade = (4'/64') x 100 = 6%

Grades for Traffic Surfaces

Surface	Minimum	Maximum
Driveways in the North	1%	10%
Driveways in the South	1%	15%
Walks	1%	4%
Ramps	—	15%
Wheelchair ramps	—	8%

Danger Zones for Driveway Entrances

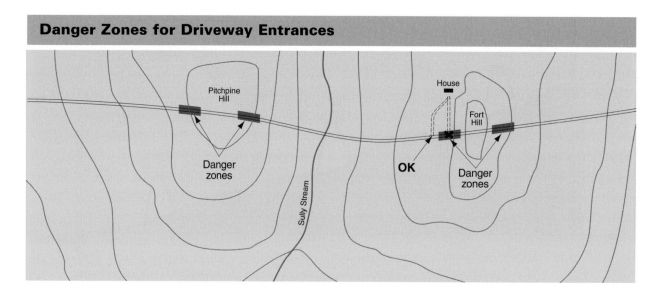

Turning Radii

The illustration at top shows the recommended minimum dimensions of driveways and parking turnarounds for one- and two-car garages.

At bottom are the minimum required inside and outside diameters of circular drives for small to large vehicles.

Minimum Turning Radii for Driveways and Turnarounds

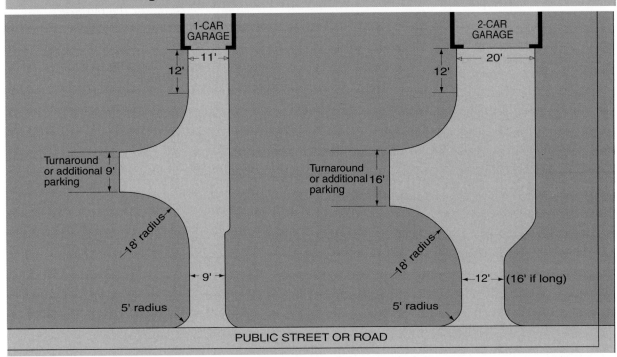

Circular Drive Radii

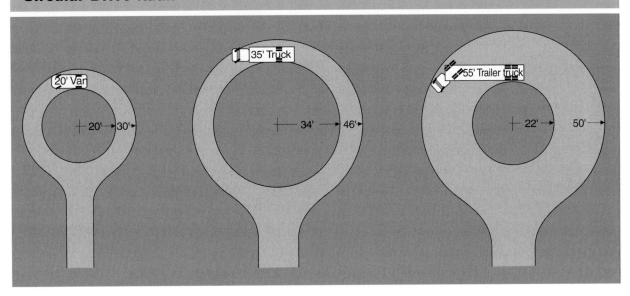

Climate Data

**Winter Design Temperature, °F
(colder 2.5% of hours)**

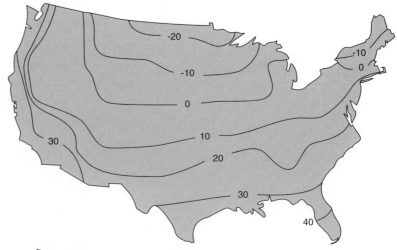

**Heating Degree-Days
(base 65°F)
The accumulated difference
between the average daily
temperature and 65°F for
the heating season**

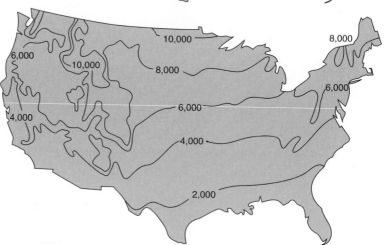

Average Frost Penetration (in)

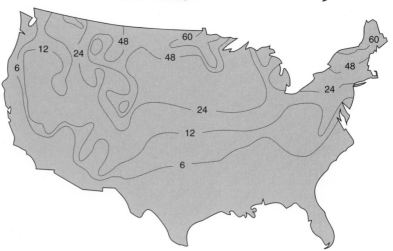

Summer Design Temperature, °F
(warmer 2.5% of hours)

Cooling Degree-Days
(base 75°F)
The accumulated difference
between the average daily
temperature and 75°F for
the cooling season

Mean Relative Humidity, July

Mean Wind Speed and Power in Spring

W/m^2	mph	knots
50	7.8	6.8
100	9.8	8.5
150	11.5	10.0
200	12.5	10.9
300	14.3	12.4
400	15.7	13.6

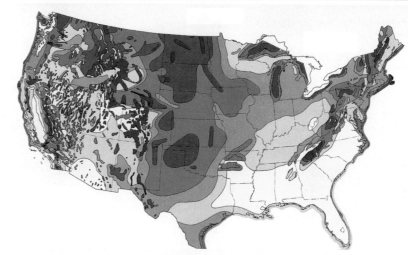

Mean Wind Speed and Power in Summer

W/m^2	mph	knots
50	7.8	6.8
100	9.8	8.5
150	11.5	10.0
200	12.5	10.9
300	14.3	12.4
400	15.7	13.6

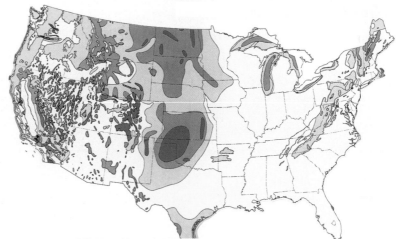

Mean Wind Speed and Power in Fall

W/m^2	mph	knots
50	7.8	6.8
100	9.8	8.5
150	11.5	10.0
200	12.5	10.9
300	14.3	12.4
400	15.7	13.6

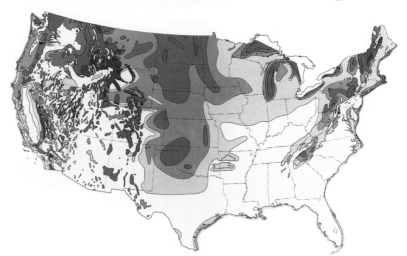

Mean Wind Speed and Power in Winter

W/m²	mph	knots
50	7.8	6.8
100	9.8	8.5
150	11.5	10.0
200	12.5	10.9
300	14.3	12.4
400	15.7	13.6

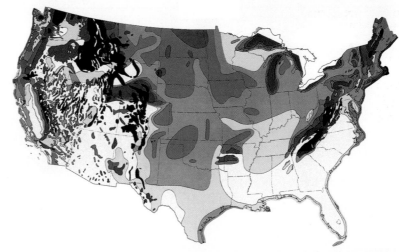

Mean Wind Direction in Summer

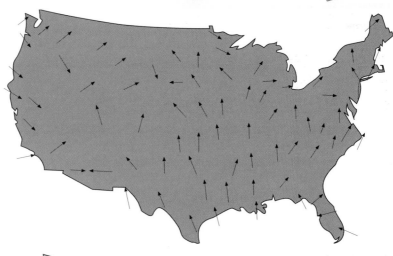

Mean Wind Direction in Winter

Shelterbelts

Effect of Shelterbelt on Wind Speed

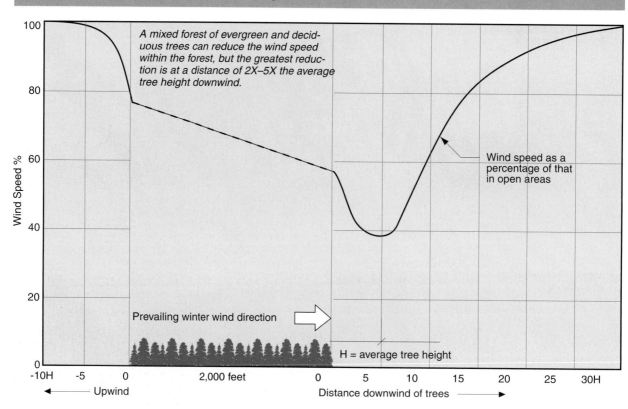

A mixed forest of evergreen and deciduous trees can reduce the wind speed within the forest, but the greatest reduction is at a distance of 2X–5X the average tree height downwind.

Wind Speed %

Wind speed as a percentage of that in open areas

Prevailing winter wind direction

H = average tree height

-10H   -5   0   2,000 feet   0   5   10   15   20   25   30H

◄── Upwind   Distance downwind of trees ──►

Effect of Shelterbelt on Snow Accumulation

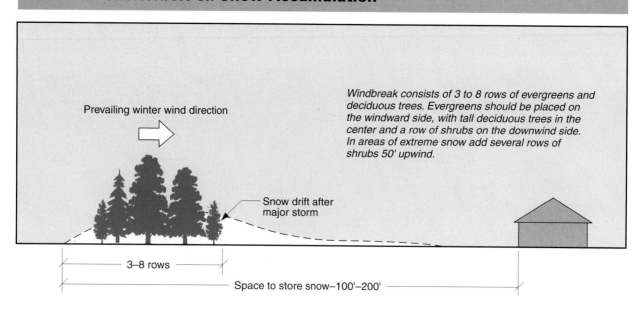

Prevailing winter wind direction

Windbreak consists of 3 to 8 rows of evergreens and deciduous trees. Evergreens should be placed on the windward side, with tall deciduous trees in the center and a row of shrubs on the downwind side. In areas of extreme snow add several rows of shrubs 50' upwind.

Snow drift after major storm

3–8 rows

Space to store snow—100'–200'

Landscaping Strategies for Winter and Summer

LANDSCAPING FOR WINTER WIND ONLY

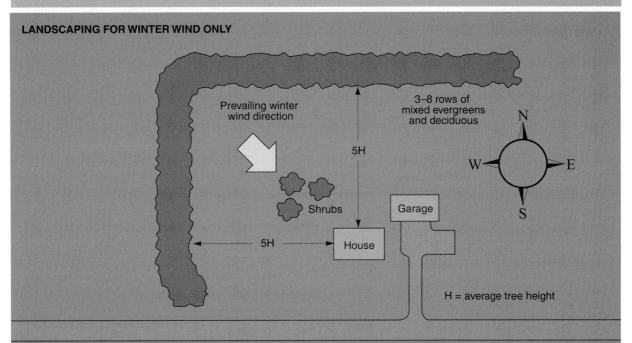

Prevailing winter wind direction

3–8 rows of mixed evergreens and deciduous

5H

Shrubs

Garage

5H

House

H = average tree height

LANDSCAPING FOR WINTER AND SUMMER WIND AND SUN

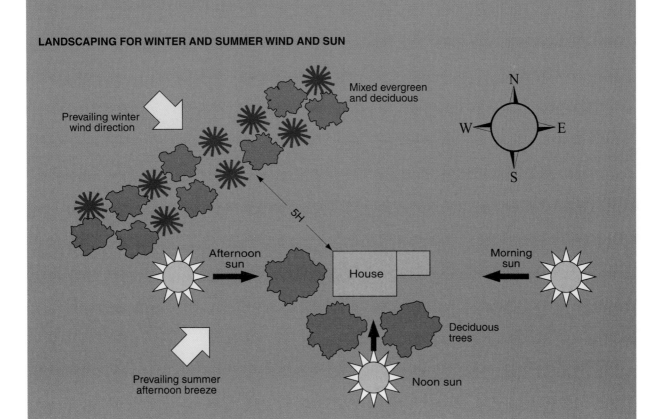

Prevailing winter wind direction

Mixed evergreen and deciduous

5H

Afternoon sun

House

Morning sun

Deciduous trees

Noon sun

Prevailing summer afternoon breeze

Plant Hardiness

The map below is a simplification of the highly detailed (to the county level) map published by the American Horticultural Society in cooperation with the U.S. Department of Agriculture. This 2003 version supercedes the earlier USDA Miscellaneous Publication 1475.

The map shows zones of average annual minimum temperature in 10°F increments. In order to make the map readable at this scale small, isolated pockets one zone higher or lower are not shown. Such aberrations are due to elevation (temperature decreasing with elevation by about 6°F per 1,000 feet), location in an urban area (higher temperature), and proximity to a large body of unfrozen water (higher temperature).

The average annual minimum temperatures are based on the lowest temperatures recorded for each of the years 1974 to 1986. The map shows 10 different zones, each of which represents an area of winter hardiness for agricultural plants and trees.

Use the map to find your hardiness zone, then consult the table on the facing page to find those plants which can survive your winters. The zone listed for the plant is the coldest zone it can be expected to survive.

To look up your zone by 5-digit zip code, go to *www.arborday.org/treeinfo/zonelookup.cfm.*

USDA Plant Hardiness Zone Map

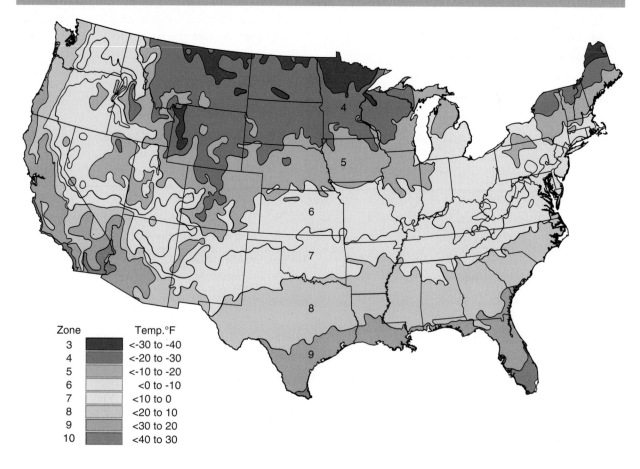

Zone	Temp.°F
3	<-30 to -40
4	<-20 to -30
5	<-10 to -20
6	<0 to -10
7	<10 to 0
8	<20 to 10
9	<30 to 20
10	<40 to 30

Plant Hardiness Zones

Botanical (and Common) Name	Zone
Abetiophyllum distichum (white forsythia)	5
Acer platanoides (Norway maple)	4
Aesculus x camea (red horsechestnut)	4
Araucaria araucana (monkey puzzle)	7
Arctostaphylos uva-ursi (bearberry)	2
Aristolochia durior (Dutchman's pipe)	4
Aucuba japonica (Japanese aucuba)	7
Bauhinia variegata (purple orchid tree)	9
Berberis danvinii (Darwin barberry)	8
Betula pendula (European white birch)	3
Bouvardia 'Coral' (Coral bouvardia)	9
Butia capitata (Pindo palm)	8
Camellia reticulate (reticulate camellia)	9
Camellia sasanqua (sasanqua camellia)	7
Carya illinoinensis 'Major' (pecan)	5
Casuarina equisetifolia (Australian pine)	9
Ceanothus impressus (Santa Barbara ceanothus)	8
Cedrus deodara (deodar cedar)	7
Cercis chinensis (Chinese redbud)	6
Chamaecyparis lawsoniana (Lawson cypress)	6
Chamaecyparis pisifera (Sawara cypress)	5
Cinnamomum camphora (camphor tree)	9
Cistus laurifolius (laurel rockrose)	7
Cistus x purpureus (purple rockrose)	8
Comus alba (Tatarian dogwood)	3
Comus kousa (Japanese dogwood)	5
Cunninghamia lanceolata (cunninghamia)	7
Cytisus x praecox (Warminster broom)	6
Elaeagnus multiflora (cherry elaeagnus)	5
Elaeagnus pungens (thorny elaeagnus)	7
Eriobotrya japonica (loquat)	8
Euonymus alatus (winged euonymus)	3
Euphorbia pulcherrima (poinsettia)	10
Fatshedera lizei (botanical-wonder)	8
Forsythia ovata (early forsythia)	4
Forsythia suspensa (weeping forsythia)	5
Fremontodendron mexicanum (flannel bush)	9
Ginkgo biloba (ginkgo, maidenhair-tree)	5
Hibiscus rosa-sinensis (Chinese hibiscus)	9
Hibiscus syriacus (shrub althea)	5

Botanical (and Common) Name	Zone
Hypericum 'Hidcote' (Hidcote St. Johnswort)	6
Iberis sempervirens (evergreen candytuft)	5
Ilex crenata 'Convexa' (convexleaf Jap. holly)	6
Jacaranda acutifolia (green ebony)	10
Juglans regia (English or Persian walnut)	6
Juniperus horizontalis (creeping juniper)	3
Koelreuteria paniculata (golden rain-tree)	6
Laburnum x watereri (Waterer laburnum)	7
Lagerstroemia indica (crapemyrtle)	5
Mahonia aquitolium (Oregon hollygrape)	5
Malus x amoldiana (Arnold crabapple)	4
Melia azedarach (chinaberry)	7
Metasequoia glyptostroboides (dawn redwood)	5
Myrtus communes (true myrtle)	8
Nandina domestics (heavenly bamboo)	7
Nerium oleander (oleander)	8
Olea europaea (common olive)	8
Osmanthus heterophyflus (holly osmanthus)	7
Picea abies (Norway spruce)	3
Pieris japonica (Japanese andromeda)	6
Pinus mugo var. *mughus* (Mugo pine)	3
Pinus radiata (Monterey pine)	7
Pinus strobus (eastern white pine)	3
Prunus yedoensis (Yoshino cherry)	6
Rhaphiolepis indica 'Rosea' (Indian hawthorn)	8
Rhododendron 'America' (hybrid rhododendron)	5
Rhododendron 'Loderi King George' (hybrid)	8
Rhododendron mollis hybrids (mollis azalea)	4
Rhododendron prinophyllum (roseshell azalea)	7
Rhododendron 'Purple Splendor' (hybrid)	8
Rosa rugosa (rugosa rose)	3
Schinus terebinthifolius (Brazilian pepper-tree)	9
Sequoia sempervirens (redwood)	8
Sequoiadendron giganteum (giant sequoia)	7
Stewartia pseudocamellia (Japanese stewartia)	6
Syringa vulgaris (common lilac)	3
Ulmus americana (American elm)	2
Vibumum burkwoodii (Burkwood viburnum)	5
Zelkova serrata (Japanese zelkova)	5

Trees

Trees for Shade and Shelter

Common Name	Hardiness Zones[1]	Type[2]	Height feet	Width feet	Spacing feet	Features
1. Quaking aspen	2–5	D	35	5	7	Excellent visual screen
2. Paper birch	2–5	D	45	20	15	White bark, very hardy
3. White spruce	2–5	E	45	20	10	Good for windbreak
4. Bur oak	2–5	D	45	20	15	Requires good soil for full size
5. Eastern red cedar	2–8	E	50	10	7	Good screen, tolerates dry soil
6. Norway maple	3–6	D	50	30	25	Grows in city, grows fast
7. Sugar maple	3–6	D	80	50	40	Beautiful foliage, sugar sap
8. Norway spruce	3–5	E	60	25	14	Grows fast, prefers sun
9. Red maple	3–6	D	40	30	25	Brilliant foliage, grows fast
10. Green ash	3–6	D	50	30	25	Grows fast in most soils
11. Eastern white pine	3–6	E	70	40	12	Grows very fast in most soils
12. Eastern hemlock	3–7	E	60	30	8	Good screen, grows in shade
13. White poplar	3–5	D	50	12	10	Grows very fast, short life
14. Pin oak	4–7	D	80	50	30	Keeps leaves in winter
15. Japanese cryptomeria	6–8	E	70	20	10	Good screen, grows fast
16. Oriental arborvitae	7–9	E	16	6	3	Grows fast in most soils
17. Rocky Mountain juniper	4–7	E	25	10	6	In West only, dry soils
18. Black haw	4–7	D	15	15	5	White flowers, red berries
19. American holly	6–9	E	20	8	8	Spined leaves, red berries
20. Lombardy poplar	6–8	D	40	6	4	Grows fast, all soils
21. Weeping willow	6–8	D	30	30	30	Drooping branches, wet soils
22. Sea grape	10	E	20	8	4	Very decorative
23. Northern white cedar	3–6	E	30	12	8	Good screen, loamy soil
24. Southern magnolia	8–9	E	30	10	5	Large white flowers
25. Douglas fir	4–6	E	60	25	12	Grows fast, up to 200'

Source: W. R. Nelson, Jr., *Landscaping Your Home* (Urbana-Champaign: University of Illinois, 1975).

[1] See Plant Hardiness Zones map, p. 48.

[2] D = deciduous, E = evergreen.

Lawns

Use the map below to select grass seed for your area. The table on the facing page lists the characteristics of each of the grasses listed.

Grass Seed Zones

1. Best adapted to this cool zone are fine fescues, Kentucky bluegrass, and creeping bentgrass. Winter kill can be the limiting factor for tall fescue and perennial ryegrass.

2. Warmer than zone 1. Perennial ryegrass and tall fescues do well here, either alone or mixed.

3. Zone characterized by high heat and humidity. Best grasses would be tall fescue, perennial ryegrass, Bermuda-grass, and zoysiagrass.

4. Even warmer and more humid than Zone 3. Best grasses in sunlight are Bermuda-grass, zoysiagrass, and Bahiagrass. Tall fescue does well here in shade.

5. This zone is characterized by cold winters and hot and dry summers. Bluegrass, perennial ryegrass, tall and fine fescues, bentgrass, Bermuda-grass, and zoysiagrass do well here. Irrigation is required. If irrigation is not possible, use either tall or fine fescue.

6. Zone is extremely hot and dry during summer. In areas of full sun use Bermuda-grass and zoysiagrass. In shady locations, especially where irrigation is possible, plant tall fescue. Overseeding with annual or perennial ryegrass during the dormant season is recommended for golf courses and other high-use areas.

7. Climate is extremely variable in this mountainous zone. Bluegrass is most popular in the northern areas. Tall fescue is more common in the southern areas of the zone.

Grass Seed Zones

Grasses for Lawns

Seed Name	Appearance	Texture	Common Applications	Relative Cost	Relative Maintenance	Planting Depth, in	Spread Rate lb/1,000 sq ft
Bahiagrass Argentine	Good	Coarse to medium	Lawns and traffic areas	Low	Low	¼"–½"	5–10
Bahiagrass Pensacola	Average	Medium	Lawns and roadways	Low	Low	¼"–½"	5–10
Bentgrass	Excellent	Fine	Putting greens	High	High	¼"–½"	½–1
Bermuda Common	Average	Fine	Lawns and sports fields	Low	Medium	¼"	2–3
Bermuda Improved	Excellent	Fine	Lawns and traffic areas	Medium	High	¼"	2–3
Bluegrass Kentucky	Good	Medium to fine	Lawns	Low	Low	¼"–½"	1–3
Bluegrass Rough	Good	Medium	Lawns and roadways	Low	Low	¼""–½"	1–3
Carpetgrass	Poor	Medium	Wet areas	Low	Low	¼"–½"	4–5
Centipede	Poor to medium	Medium	Lawns	Medium	Low	¼"	¼–1
Fescue Fine	Excellent	Fine	Lawns	Medium	Medium	¼"–½"	3–5
Fescue Tall	Good	Medium	Lawns and sports fields	Medium	Medium	¼"–½"	5–10
Ryegrass Annual	Poor	Fine	In conservation seed mixes	Low	Low	¼"–½"	5–10
Ryegrass Perennial	Poor	Medium	Lawns and sports fields	Medium	Low	¼"–½"	1–10
St. Augustine	Good	Coarse	Lawns	High	Medium	¼"–½"	½–1
Zoysiagrass	Excellent	Medium to fine	Lawns	High	High	¼"–½"	2–3

Masonry

Masonry constitutes man's oldest building material. Remnants of masonry structures more than 3,000 years old still exist, bearing witness to the material's resistance to the elements.

Chief among masonry materials are *concrete*, which can be poured into forms, and *mortar*, which is the glue used to fasten solid masonry units together.

Aside from floor slabs, most concrete in residential construction is used in concrete masonry units (CMU). We begin with the details of typical *CMU wall construction*. In addition to the ubiquitous 8×8×16 concrete block there is a wide variety of other *typical CMU sizes*. In addition to walls, driveways, walks, and patios are often constructed of *concrete pavers*.

A second whole class of masonry consists of brick. As with concrete, there is a wide range of standard *brick sizes*. More than with CMU, brick is used in a variety of *wall positions and patterns* to achieve architectural designs.

Walls consisting entirely of brick are rare today. Instead, cost and practical considerations have led to the development of three hybrid systems: *brick masonry cavity walls*, *brick veneer/steel stud walls*, and *brick veneer/wood stud walls*.

In both design and construction our tables for *brick wall heights* and for *estimating brick and mortar* will prove time savers. And as with concrete, bricks are often used in walks and patios as *brick pavement*.

The last type of masonry is stone. Stone is a very difficult and expensive material for residential construction. However, cultured stone—concrete cast and colored to resemble a variety of natural stones—makes possible *stone veneer construction*.

Finally, we provide another handy crib sheet to make sure your masonry design will *meet the IRC Code*.

Concrete

Concrete is reconstituted stone. Consisting of gravel aggregate, sand, and portland cement, it is as strong as most naturally occurring rock and will last as long. Made improperly, it cracks and crumbles and may have to be replaced within a few years.

Properly made concrete has four characteristics:

1. Correct ratio of clean and well-sized materials. The proper ratio of materials ensures that all sand grains are surrounded by cement and that all gravel pebbles are surrounded by sand.

2. Correct amount of water. Portland cement chemically combines with the water (the cement hydrates). Too little water results in unhydrated cement; too much water leaves voids when the water eventually escapes.

3. Long curing time. Complete hydration requires many days. To prevent evaporation of the water, the surface of the concrete should be kept damp for up to a week.

4. Air entrainment. When concrete is exposed to freezing, water within the cured concrete can freeze and expand and crack the concrete. Air-entraining admixtures form billions of microscopic air bubbles which act as pressure relief valves for freezing water.

Recommended Concrete Mixes

Application	Cement 94-lb Sacks	Sand cu ft	Gravel cu ft	Gal. Water if Sand Dry	Wet	Makes cu ft
Slabs > 3" thick, sidewalks, driveways, patios	1.0	2.2	3.0	6.0	5.0	4.1

Estimating Concrete for Slabs, Walks, and Drives (cubic yards)

Slab Area sq ft	Slab Thickness, in							
	2	3	4	5	6	8	10	12
10	0.1	0.1	0.1	0.2	0.2	0.3	0.3	0.4
50	0.3	0.5	0.6	0.7	0.9	1.2	1.4	1.9
100	0.6	0.9	1.2	1.5	1.9	2.5	3.0	3.7
300	1.9	2.8	3.7	4.7	5.6	7.4	9.4	11.1
500	3.1	4.7	6.2	7.2	9.3	12.4	14.4	18.6

Estimating Concrete for Footings and Walls (cubic yards per linear foot)

Depth/Height in	Width or Thickness, in				
	6	8	12	18	24
8	0.012	0.017	0.025	0.037	0.049
12	0.019	0.025	0.037	0.056	0.074
24	0.037	0.049	0.074	0.111	0.148
72	0.111	0.148	0.222	0.333	0.444
96	0.148	0.198	0.296	0.444	0.593

Mortar

Mortar is a mixture of cement, lime, and sand for bonding unit masonry (bricks, blocks, or stone) together. It differs from concrete in two ways: 1) Because it is used in thin layers, it contains no gravel aggregate, and 2) Because brick and block laying is a slow process, it contains hydrated lime to retain water and retard setup.

Availability

For small jobs requiring up to 1 cubic foot of mortar (about thirty 8×8×16-in blocks or seventy 2×4×8-in bricks), purchase a bag of mortar mix which requires only the addition of water. For larger jobs buy sacks of masonry cement. To each sack add 3 cubic feet of clean, sharp sand and enough water to make the mix plastic. Precolored mortar mixes are also available through masonry supply outlets.

Mixing

Unless you are a professional mason, or more than one bricklayer is at work, mix small batches of mortar by hand, because it must be used within approximately 1 hour. Do not lay masonry when there is any danger of freezing. Calcium chloride accelerator is sometimes used to speed setup and lessen the chances of freezing, but it can later cause efflorescence (a white, powdery deposit) on wall surfaces. Use the table below to estimate quantities of mortar for various masonry wall constructions.

Recommended Mortar Mixes

Mortar Type	Compressive Strength @ 28 days	Portland Cement	Masonry Cement	Sand
M	2,500 psi	1 Bag	1 Bag	6 cu ft
S	1,800 psi	½ Bag	1 Bag	4.5 cu ft
N, S, or M	750 psi	0	1 Bag	3 cu ft

Estimating Mortar (per 1,000 masonry units)

Masonry Unit Dimensions	Mortar Type	Portland Cement, lb	Masonry Cement, lb
3⅝"x2¼"x8" standard brick	M	329	245
3⅝"x2¼"x8" standard brick	S	219	327
3⅝"x2¼"x8" standard brick	N, S, or M	0	490
3⅝"x3⅝"x8" utility brick	M	423	315
3⅝"x3⅝"x8" utility brick	S	260	420
3⅝"x3⅝"x8" utility brick	N, S, or M	0	700
3⅝"x2¼ x8" Norman	M	329	245
3⅝"x2¼"x8" Norman	S	235	350
3⅝"x2"x8" Norman	N, S, or M	0	560
8"x8"x16" block	M	1,034	770
8"x8"x16" block	S	705	1,050
8"x8"x 16" block	N, S, or M	0	1,750

CMU Wall Construction

Exterior residential walls up to 35 feet in height may be constructed of 8-inch-thick concrete masonry units (blocks), Interior load-bearing walls may be the same, or they may be 6 inch thick up to 20 feet in height.

Unless protected by shallow-foundation insulation (see Chapter 4), footings must be poured beneath the local frost depth. Mortar should be applied only to the perimeter of the block, except on all faces of blocks to be filled.

The top course of the wall should be made solid, preferably by filling and reinforcing a continuous bond beam. Vertical rebar should be placed 16 or 24 inches on-center.

Typical CMU Wall Construction

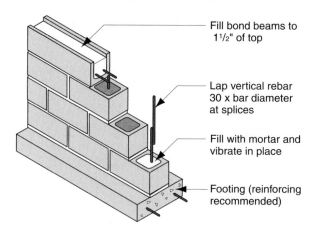

Fill bond beams to 1¹/₂" of top

Lap vertical rebar 30 x bar diameter at splices

Fill with mortar and vibrate in place

Footing (reinforcing recommended)

Corners and Intersections

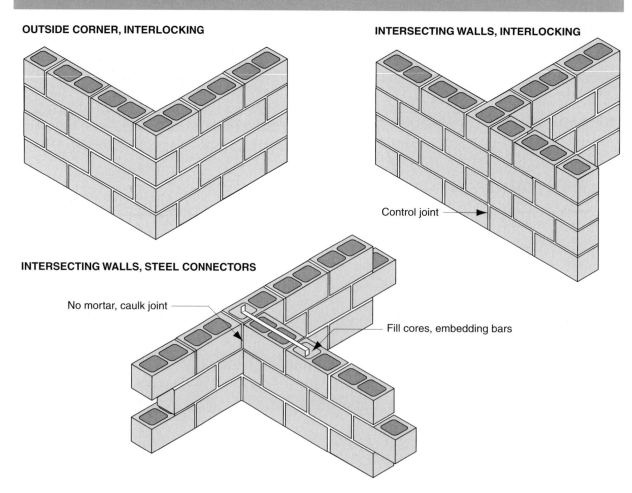

OUTSIDE CORNER, INTERLOCKING

INTERSECTING WALLS, INTERLOCKING

Control joint

INTERSECTING WALLS, STEEL CONNECTORS

No mortar, caulk joint

Fill cores, embedding bars

Typical Walls with Exterior Insulation

WITH STUCCO FINISH

Rafter tie

Vent

Rebar

Bond beam

Window unit

Cast sill

Solid backing

Drip edge

Wall finish

Drainage layer

Strapping

Rigid foam insulation

Rebar (per code)

Stucco coating

Isolation joint

Footing

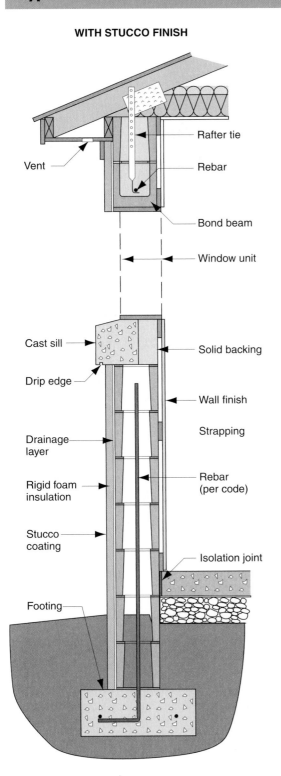

WITH HORIZONTAL LAP SIDING

Rafter tie

Vent

Rebar

Bond beam

Window unit

Cast sill

Solid backing

Drip edge

Wall finish

Insulation/ vertical strapping

Strapping

Lap siding

Rebar (per code)

Isolation joint

Footing

CMU Sizes

Dimensions actual WxLxH

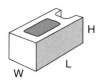

Partition
$3^5/_8$"x$7^5/_8$"x$3^5/_8$"

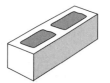

Half partition
$3^5/_8$"x$15^5/_8$"x$3^5/_8$"

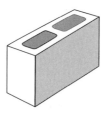

Partition
$3^5/_8$"x$15^5/_8$"x$7^5/_8$"

Double ends
$3^5/_8$"x$7^5/_8$"x$7^5/_8$"

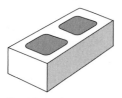

Double ends
$5^5/_8$"x$15^5/_8$"x$3^5/_8$"

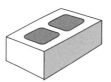

Double ends
$5^5/_8$"x$11^5/_8$"x$3^5/_8$"

Double ends
$5^5/_8$"x$7^5/_8$"x$7^5/_8$"

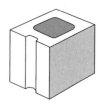

Half jamb
$5^5/_8$"x$7^5/_8$"x$7^5/_8$"

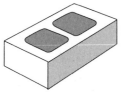

Half-high double end
$7^5/_8$"x$15^5/_8$"x$3^5/_8$"

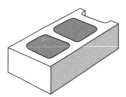

Half-high
$7^5/_8$"x$15^5/_8$"x$3^5/_8$"

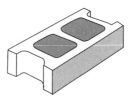

Half-high stretcher
$7^5/_8$"x$15^5/_8$"x$3^5/_8$"

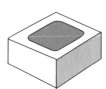

Half-high
$7^5/_8$"x$7^5/_8$"x$3^5/_8$"

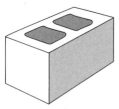

Double end
$7^5/_8$"x$15^5/_8$"x$7^5/_8$"

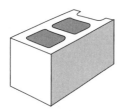

Regular
$7^5/_8$"x$15^5/_8$"x$7^5/_8$"

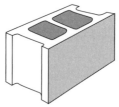

Stretcher
$7^5/_8$"x$15^5/_8$"x$7^5/_8$"

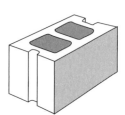

Steel sash jamb
$7^5/_8$"x$15^5/_8$"x$7^5/_8$"

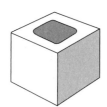

Plain ends
$7^5/_8$"x$7^5/_8$"x$7^5/_8$"

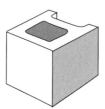

Half block
$7^5/_8$"x$7^5/_8$"x$7^5/_8$"

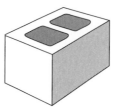

Double ends
$7^5/_8$"x$11^5/_8$"x$7^5/_8$"

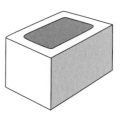

Plain ends
$7^5/_8$"x$11^5/_8$"x$7^5/_8$"

Dimensions actual WxLxH

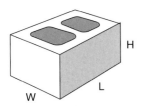

Double ends
$11^{5}/_{8}$"x$15^{5}/_{8}$"x$7^{5}/_{8}$"

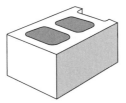

Regulars
$11^{5}/_{8}$"x$15^{5}/_{8}$"x$7^{5}/_{8}$"

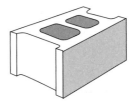

Stretcher
$11^{5}/_{8}$"x$15^{5}/_{8}$"x$7^{5}/_{8}$"

Single bullnose
$11^{5}/_{8}$"x$15^{5}/_{8}$"x$7^{5}/_{8}$"

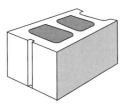

Steel sash jamb
$11^{5}/_{8}$"x$15^{5}/_{8}$"x$7^{5}/_{8}$"

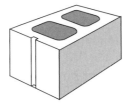

Jamb
$11^{5}/_{8}$"x$15^{5}/_{8}$"x$7^{5}/_{8}$"

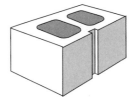

Twin
$11^{5}/_{8}$"x$15^{5}/_{8}$"x$7^{5}/_{8}$"

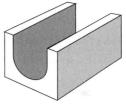

Solid bottom U block
$11^{5}/_{8}$"x$15^{5}/_{8}$"x$7^{5}/_{8}$"

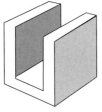

Beam
$7^{5}/_{8}$"x$7^{5}/_{8}$"x$11^{5}/_{8}$"

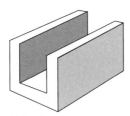

U lintel
$7^{5}/_{8}$"x$15^{5}/_{8}$"x$7^{5}/_{8}$"

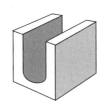

U lintel
$7^{5}/_{8}$"x$7^{5}/_{8}$"x$7^{5}/_{8}$"

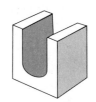

U lintel
$7^{5}/_{8}$"x$3^{5}/_{8}$"x$7^{5}/_{8}$"

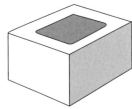

Pilaster & chimney block
$15^{5}/_{8}$"x$15^{5}/_{8}$"x$7^{5}/_{8}$"

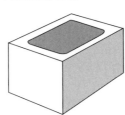

Pilaster
$11^{5}/_{8}$"x$15^{5}/_{8}$"x$7^{5}/_{8}$"

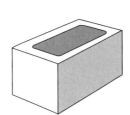

Pilaster
$7^{5}/_{8}$"x$15^{5}/_{8}$"x$7^{5}/_{8}$"

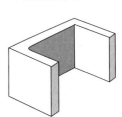

Pilaster
$7^{5}/_{8}$"x$15^{5}/_{8}$"x$7^{5}/_{8}$"

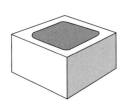

Chimney block
14"x14"x$7^{5}/_{8}$"

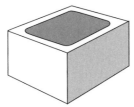

Column style no. 1
$15^{5}/_{8}$"x$15^{5}/_{8}$"x$7^{5}/_{8}$"

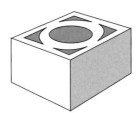

Flue block
$15^{5}/_{8}$"x$15^{5}/_{8}$"x$7^{5}/_{8}$"

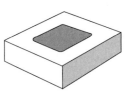

Flue block
$15^{5}/_{8}$"x$15^{5}/_{8}$"x$3^{5}/_{8}$"

Concrete Pavers

The details for paving patios, walks, and drives with CMU pavers are similar to those for brick pavers (see "Brick Pavement" on p. 72). There is an almost infinite variety of shapes and sizes of CMU pavers. Some of the most common are shown below. Many of the shapes are available in several earthtone colors. Check with local suppliers before designing your project.

Laying CMU Pavers

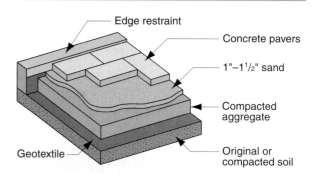

- Edge restraint
- Concrete pavers
- 1"–1½" sand
- Compacted aggregate
- Geotextile
- Original or compacted soil

Common CMU Paver Sizes

Dimensions actual WxLxH

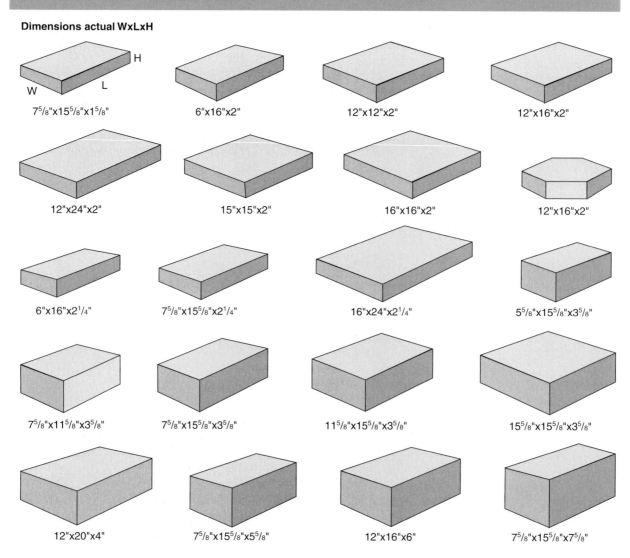

7⅝"x15⅝"x1⅝"

6"x16"x2"

12"x12"x2"

12"x16"x2"

12"x24"x2"

15"x15"x2"

16"x16"x2"

12"x16"x2"

6"x16"x2¼"

7⅝"x15⅝"x2¼"

16"x24"x2¼"

5⅝"x15⅝"x3⅝"

7⅝"x11⅝"x3⅝"

7⅝"x15⅝"x3⅝"

11⅝"x15⅝"x3⅝"

15⅝"x15⅝"x3⅝"

12"x20"x4"

7⅝"x15⅝"x5⅝"

12"x16"x6"

7⅝"x15⅝"x7⅝"

PLASTIC EDGE RESTRAINT

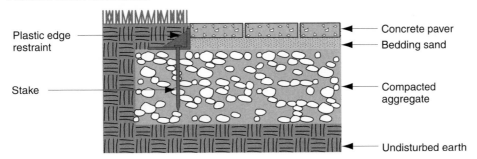

Plastic edge restraint

Stake

Concrete paver

Bedding sand

Compacted aggregate

Undisturbed earth

LANDSCAPE TIMBER RESTRAINT

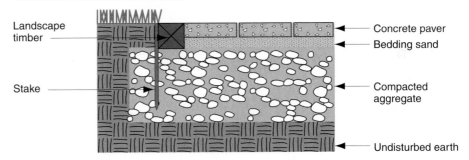

Landscape timber

Stake

Concrete paver

Bedding sand

Compacted aggregate

Undisturbed earth

STEEL ANGLE RESTRAINT

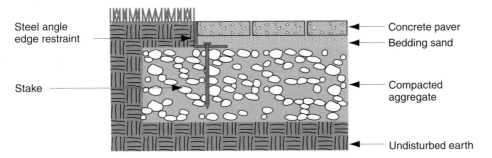

Steel angle edge restraint

Stake

Concrete paver

Bedding sand

Compacted aggregate

Undisturbed earth

PRECAST CONCRETE RESTRAINT

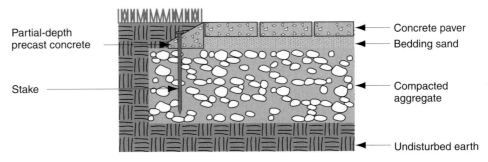

Partial-depth precast concrete

Stake

Concrete paver

Bedding sand

Compacted aggregate

Undisturbed earth

Brick Sizes

Dimensions of Common Bricks

NON-MODULAR BRICK
(dimensions actual WxLxH)

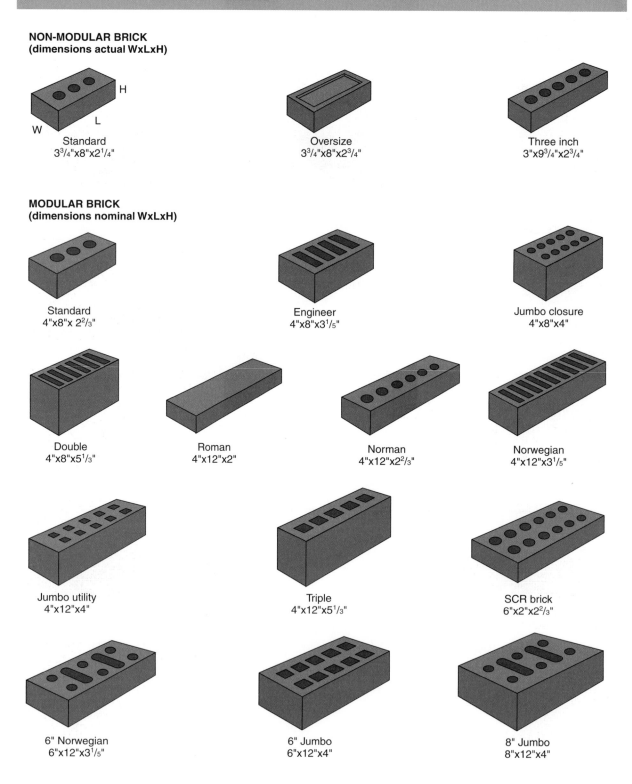

Standard
$3^3/_4$"x8"x$2^1/_4$"

Oversize
$3^3/_4$"x8"x$2^3/_4$"

Three inch
3"x$9^3/_4$"x$2^3/_4$"

MODULAR BRICK
(dimensions nominal WxLxH)

Standard
4"x8"x $2^2/_3$"

Engineer
4"x8"x$3^1/_5$"

Jumbo closure
4"x8"x4"

Double
4"x8"x$5^1/_3$"

Roman
4"x12"x2"

Norman
4"x12"x$2^2/_3$"

Norwegian
4"x12"x$3^1/_5$"

Jumbo utility
4"x12"x4"

Triple
4"x12"x$5^1/_3$"

SCR brick
6"x2"x$2^2/_3$"

6" Norwegian
6"x12"x$3^1/_5$"

6" Jumbo
6"x12"x4"

8" Jumbo
8"x12"x4"

Brick Wall Positions and Patterns

Brick Position and Pattern Terminology

BRICK POSITIONS

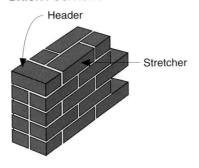

Header

Stretcher

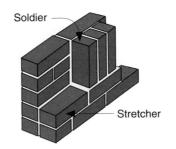

Soldier

Stretcher

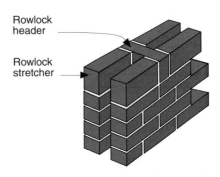

Rowlock header

Rowlock stretcher

BRICK PATTERNS

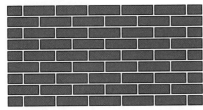

RUNNING

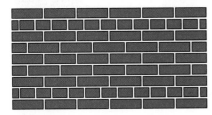

COMMON

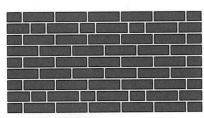

COMMON WITH
FLEMISH HEADERS

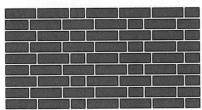

GARDEN WALL

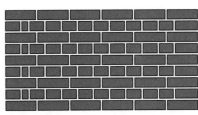

ENGLISH

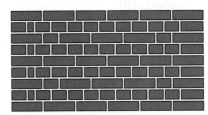

DUTCH

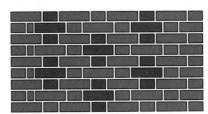

FLEMISH CROSS

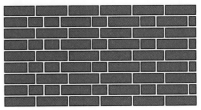

FLEMISH

Brick Masonry Cavity Walls

Brick and concrete masonry unit cavity wall construction is common in commercial and southern residential building. Best building practice requires the use of durable brick (grade SW in ground contact and freeze areas) and adherence to proper detailing.

Proper detailing requires the use of drips at sills, flashing at wall top and bottom, flashing at window and door heads and sills, provision for weep holes at all flashings, and caulking at the junctions of masonry and non-masonry materials.

Insulation is required in most locations, and a draining cavity is recommended in areas of wind-driven rain.

Brick/Masonry Cavity Construction

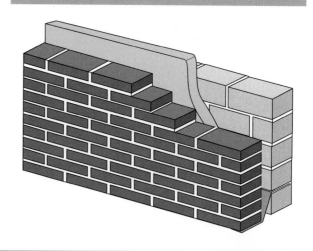

Wall Ties

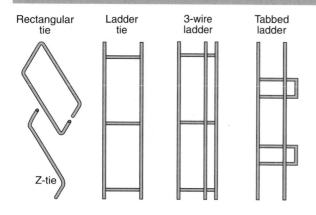

Rectangular tie   Ladder tie   3-wire ladder   Tabbed ladder

Z-tie

Wall Tie Spacing Requirements

Tie Wire Size in. (mm)	Wall Area per Tie No. per ft² (m²)	Max. Tie Spacing Horizontal · Vertical
W1.7 (MW11) 0.125 (3.06)	2⅔ (0.25)	36 · 24 (914 · 610)
W2.8 (MW18) 0.188 (4.76)	4½ (0.42)	36 · 24 (914 · 610)
Adjustable, with 2 W2.8 (MW18) 1.88 (4.76) legs	1.77 (0.16)	16 · 16 (406 · 406)

Floor Load Bearing

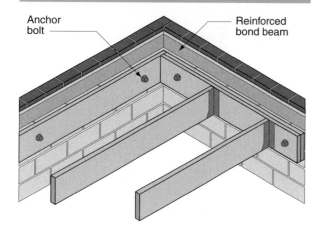

Anchor bolt

Reinforced bond beam

Roof Load Bearing

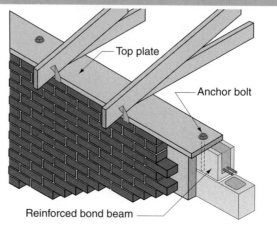

Top plate

Anchor bolt

Reinforced bond beam

Flashing at Bottom of Wall

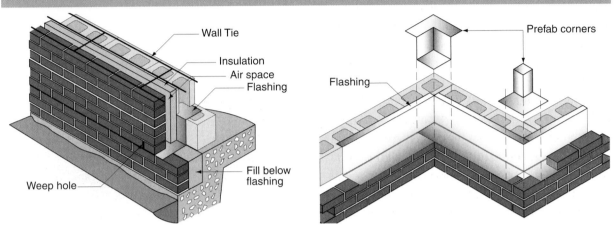

Wall Tie

Insulation

Air space

Flashing

Fill below flashing

Weep hole

Prefab corners

Flashing

Flashing at Heads

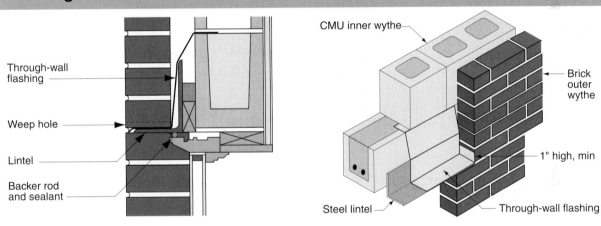

Through-wall flashing

Weep hole

Lintel

Backer rod and sealant

CMU inner wythe

Brick outer wythe

1" high, min

Steel lintel

Through-wall flashing

Flashing at Sills

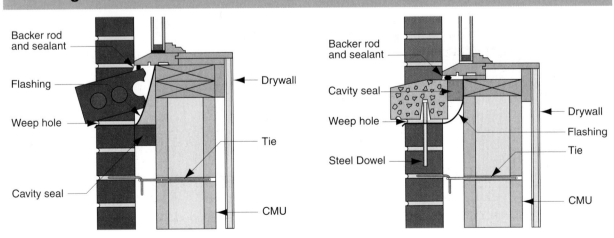

Backer rod and sealant

Flashing

Weep hole

Cavity seal

Drywall

Tie

CMU

Backer rod and sealant

Cavity seal

Weep hole

Steel Dowel

Drywall

Flashing

Tie

CMU

Brick Veneer/Steel Stud Walls

The brick veneer/steel stud wall system has grown, from its introduction in the 1960s, to one of the most widely used in commercial, industrial, and institutional building.

Because this style of building rarely has overhangs or gutters, the wall is not as well protected from rain, and the resulting incursion of water has required careful detailing of windscreen and flashings. The illustrations below detail flashings at wall bottoms, heads over doors and windows, and window sills.

As with all brick construction, best practice requires the use of durable brick (grade SW) in ground contact and freeze areas.

Brick Veneer and Steel Framing

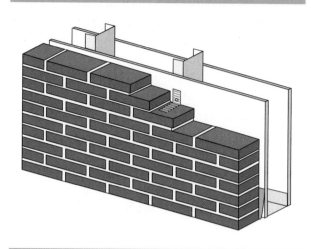

Wall Ties

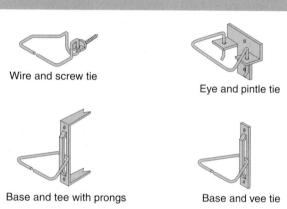

Wire and screw tie

Eye and pintle tie

Base and tee with prongs

Base and vee tie

Flashing at Bottom of Wall

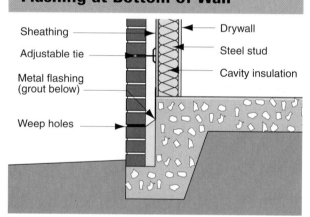

Sheathing

Adjustable tie

Metal flashing (grout below)

Weep holes

Drywall

Steel stud

Cavity insulation

Flashing at Heads

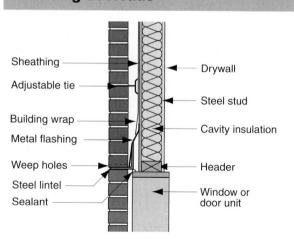

Sheathing

Adjustable tie

Building wrap

Metal flashing

Weep holes

Steel lintel

Sealant

Drywall

Steel stud

Cavity insulation

Header

Window or door unit

Flashing at Sills

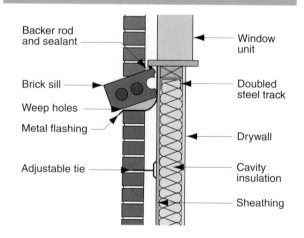

Backer rod and sealant

Brick sill

Weep holes

Metal flashing

Adjustable tie

Window unit

Doubled steel track

Drywall

Cavity insulation

Sheathing

Brick Veneer/Wood Stud Walls

Despite its obvious strength in compression, brick veneer over a wood frame wall functions as a low-maintenance exterior finish only and not as a structural element. This is because brick and wood expand and contract with moisture and temperature differently and so cannot be rigidly bonded in the vertical plane. Because a thin brick withe has little bending strength against wind and earthquake, however, it must be tied to the stronger wood stud wall horizontally.

The illustrations below show the most common connecting wall ties and detail the recommended flashing at wall bottoms, heads, and sills.

Brick Veneer and Wood Framing

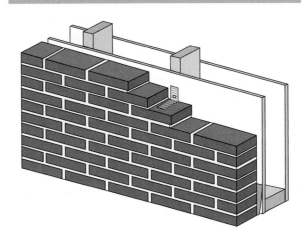

Wall Ties

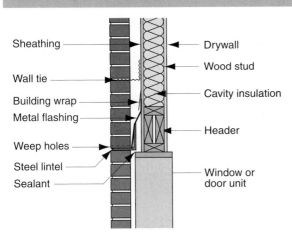

Eye and pintle tie

Wire and screw tie

Base and tee with prongs

Corrugated

Corrugated and wire

Flashing at Bottom of Wall

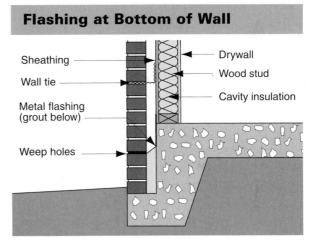

Sheathing

Wall tie

Metal flashing (grout below)

Weep holes

Drywall

Wood stud

Cavity insulation

Flashing at Heads

Sheathing — Drywall

Wall tie — Wood stud

Building wrap — Cavity insulation

Metal flashing — Header

Weep holes

Steel lintel

Sealant — Window or door unit

Flashing at Sills

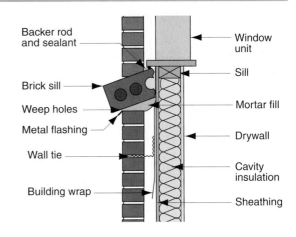

Backer rod and sealant — Window unit

Brick sill — Sill

Weep holes — Mortar fill

Metal flashing — Drywall

Wall tie — Cavity insulation

Building wrap — Sheathing

Brick Veneer/Wood Stud Walls **69**

Brick Wall Heights

Heights of Nonmodular Brick Walls

Number of Courses	2 1/4-in Thick Bricks		2 5/8-in Thick Bricks		2 3/4-in Thick Bricks	
	3/8-in Joint	1/2-in Joint	3/8-in Joint	1/2-in Joint	3/8-in Joint	1/2-in Joint
1	0'2 5/8"	0'2 3/4"	0'3"	0'3 1/8"	0'3 1/8"	0'3 1/4"
2	0'5 1/4"	0'5 1/2"	0'6"	0'6 1/4"	0'6 1/4"	0'6 1/2"
3	0'7 7/8"	0'8 1/4"	0'9"	0'9 3/8"	0'9 3/8"	0'9 3/4"
4	0'10 1/2"	0'11"	1 0"	1'1/2"	1'1/2"	1'1"
5	1'1 1/8"	1'1 3/4"	1'3"	1'3 5/8"	1'3 5/8"	1'4 1/4"
6	1'3 3/4"	1'4 1/2"	1'6"	1'6 3/4"	1'6 3/4"	1'7 1/2"
7	1'6 3/8"	1'7 1/4"	1'9"	1'9 7/8"	1'9 7/8"	1'10 3/4"
8	1'9"	1'10"	2'0"	2'1"	2'1"	2'2"
9	1' 11 5/8"	2' 3/4"	2' 3"	2' 4 1/8"	2' 4 1/8"	2' 5 1/4"
10	2'2 1/4"	2'3 1/2"	2'6"	2'7 1/4"	2'7 1/4"	2'8 1/2"
11	2'4 7/8"	2'6 1/4"	2'9"	2'10 3/8"	2'10 3/8"	2'11 3/4"
12	2'7 1/2"	2'9"	3'0"	3'1 1/2"	3'1 1/2"	3'3"
13	2'10 1/8"	2'11 3/4"	3'3"	3'4 5/8"	3'4 5/8"	3'6 1/4"
14	3'0 3/4"	3'2 1/2"	3'6"	3'7 3/4"	3'7 3/4"	3'9 1/2"
15	3'3 3/8"	3'5 1/4"	3'9"	3'10 7/8"	3'10 7/8"	4'3/4"

Heights of Modular Brick Walls

Number of Courses	Nominal Height (thickness) of Brick				
	2-in	2 2/3-in	3 1/5-in	4-in	5 1/3-in
1	0'2"	0'2 11/16"	0'3 3/16"	0'4"	0'5 5/16"
2	0'4"	0'5 5/16"	0'6 3/8"	0'8"	0'10 11/16"
3	0'6"	0'8"	0'9 5/8"	1'0"	1'4"
4	0'8"	0'10 11/16"	1'13/16"	1 4"	1 9 5/16"
5	0'10"	1'1 5/16"	1'4"	1 8"	2'2 11/16"
6	1'0"	1'4"	1'7 3/16"	2'0"	2'8"
7	1'2"	1'6 11/16"	1'10 3/8"	2'4"	3'1 5/16"
8	1'4"	1'9 5/16"	2'1 5/8"	2'8"	3'6 11/16"
9	1'6"	2'0"	2'4 13/16"	3'0"	4'0"
10	1'8"	2'2 11/16"	2'8"	3'4"	4'5 5/16"
11	1'10"	2'5 5/16"	2'11 3/16"	3'8"	4'10 11/16"
12	2'0"	2'8"	3'2 3/8"	4'0"	5'4"
13	2'2"	2'10 11/16"	3'5 5/8"	4'4"	5'9 5/16"
14	2'4"	3'1 5/16"	3'8 13/16"	4'8"	6'2 11/16"
15	2'6"	3'4"	4'0"	5'0"	6'8"

Estimating Brick and Mortar

Nonmodular Brick[1] and Mortar[2] Required for Single-Wythe Walls in Running Bond

Size of Brick, in TxHxL	With 3/8-in Joints			With 1/2-in Joints		
	Number of Brick/ 100 sq ft	Cubic Feet of Mortar/ 100 sq ft	Cubic Feet of Mortar/ 1,000 Brick	Number of Brick/ 100 sq ft	Cubic Feet of Mortar/ 100 sq ft	Cubic Feet of Mortar/ 1,000 Brick
2¾ x2¾ x9¾	455	3.2	7.1	432	4.5	10.4
2⅝ x2¾ x8¾	504	3.4	6.8	470	4.1	8.7
3¾ x2¼ x8	655	5.8	8.8	616	7.2	11.7
3¾ x2¾ x8	551	5.0	9.1	522	6.4	12.2

[1] Add at least 5% for breakage

[2] Add 10% to 25% for waste

Modular Brick[1] and Mortar[2] Required for Single-Wythe Walls in Running Bond

Nominal Size of Brick, in TxHxL	Number of Brick/ 100 sq ft	Cubic Feet of Mortar Per 100 sq ft		Per 1,000 Brick	
		3/8-in Joints	1/2-in Joints	3/8-in Joints	1/2-in Joints
4 x2⅔ x8	675	5.5	7.0	8.1	10.3
4 x3⅕ x8	563	4.8	6.1	8.6	10.9
4 x4 x8	450	4.2	5.3	9.2	11.7
4 x5⅓ x8	338	3.5	4.4	10.2	12.9
4 x2 x12	600	6.5	8.2	10.8	13.7
4 x2⅔ x12	450	5.1	6.5	11.3	14.4
4 x3⅕ x12	375	4.4	5.6	11.7	14.9
4 x 4 x12	300	3.7	4.8	12.3	15.7
4 x5⅓ x12	225	3.0	3.9	13.4	17.1
6 x2⅔ x12	450	7.9	10.2	17.5	22.6
6 x 3⅕ x12	375	6.8	8.8	18.1	23.4
6 x4 x12	300	5.6	7.4	19.1	24.7

[1] Add at least 5% for breakage

[2] Add 10% to 25% for waste

Brick Pavement

Compared with asphalt and concrete paving, brick paving is more attractive, will not crack (the cracks are part of the design), and is easy to repair.

Below are designs for a walkway, a driveway, and two patios. The use of SW grade brick is recommended in all cases. All should incorporate a slope for drainage. Walks and drives should slope at least ¼ inch per foot (2-percent grade), but no more than 1¾ inches per foot (15-percent grade).

Patios should slope from ⅛ to ¼ inch per foot (1-percent to 2-percent grade). The slopes can be from one edge to the other or from the center to the edges.

Bases for Brick Pavement

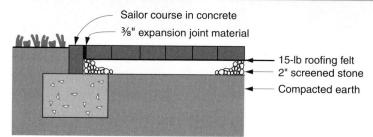

WALKWAY–GRAVEL BASE

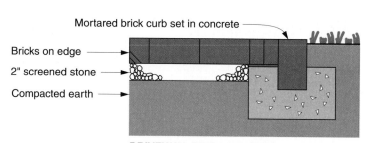

DRIVEWAY–BRICK ON EDGE

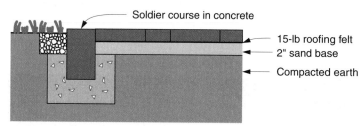

PATIO–SAND BASE

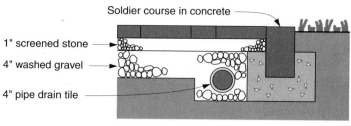

PATIO–GRAVEL BASE

Brick Pavement Patterns

STACK BOND
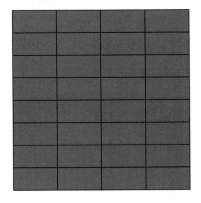

BASKET WEAVE

HERRINGBONE
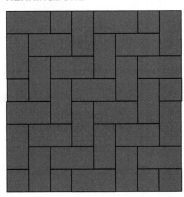

RUNNING BOND

HALF-BASKET
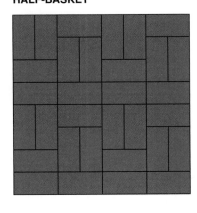

BASKET ON EDGE

OFFSET BOND

DOUBLE-BASKET
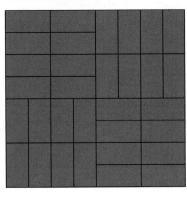

BASKET/WOOD GRID
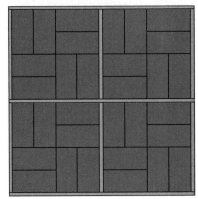

Stone Veneer Construction

Stone walls may be built entirely of stone or they may be cultured stone (cast concrete) over a base wall of solid concrete, concrete masonry units, or wood frame and sheathing. Cultured stone is preferred today, as it allows for thermal insulation.

Mortar joints should be ½ to 1 inch thick for rubble and ⅜ to ¾ inch thick for ashlar patterns.

To prevent staining, all fasteners should be stainless, flashing should be either stainless or hot-dipped galvanized steel, and mortar should be nonstaining.

Stone Veneer Construction Details

OVER CONCRETE BLOCK

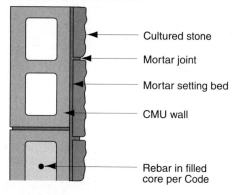

- Cultured stone
- Mortar joint
- Mortar setting bed
- CMU wall
- Rebar in filled core per Code

OVER POURED CONCRETE

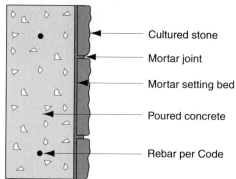

- Cultured stone
- Mortar joint
- Mortar setting bed
- Poured concrete
- Rebar per Code

OVER TILT-UP CONCRETE

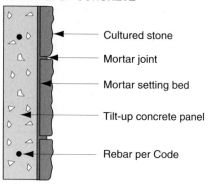

- Cultured stone
- Mortar joint
- Mortar setting bed
- Tilt-up concrete panel
- Rebar per Code

OVER OPEN STUD WALL

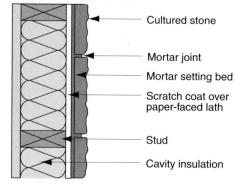

- Cultured stone
- Mortar joint
- Mortar setting bed
- Scratch coat over paper-faced lath
- Stud
- Cavity insulation

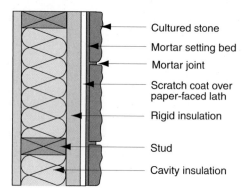

- Cultured stone
- Mortar setting bed
- Mortar joint
- Scratch coat over paper-faced lath
- Rigid insulation
- Stud
- Cavity insulation

OVER SHEATHING

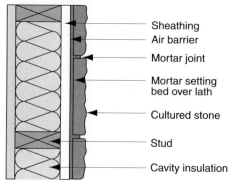

- Sheathing
- Air barrier
- Mortar joint
- Mortar setting bed over lath
- Cultured stone
- Stud
- Cavity insulation

Stone Patterns

COURSED ASHLAR

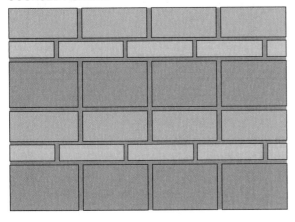

FIELDSTONE

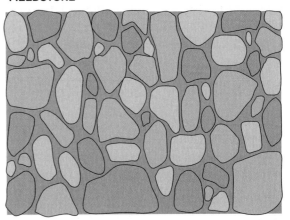

RANDOM ASHLAR

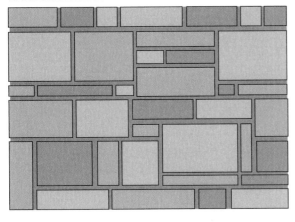

MOSAIC

THREE-HEIGHT RANDOM ASHLAR

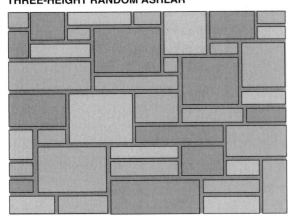

COURSED RUBBLE

Meet the Code

The following is a partial list of requirements from the *2006 International Residential Code (IRC) for One- and Two-Family Dwellings.* Consult the publication for the full text and additional provisions.

Concrete Floor on Ground (R506)
- slab thickness: ≥3.5"
- reinforcement supported at center to upper third of slab during pour

Compressive strength:
- exposed to negligible or no weathering, 2,500 psi
- exposed to moderate weathering, 3,000 psi
- exposed to severe weathering, 3,500 psi

Base preparation:
- vegetation, topsoil, and foreign material removed
- fill free of vegetation and foreign material
- fill compacted to assure uniform support
- fill depths ≤24" for clean sand and gravel and ≤8" for earth
- 4" base course of clean sand, gravel or crushed stone when the slab is below grade
- base course not required if slab on well-drained or sand-gravel mixture soils classified as Group I in Unified Soil Classification System (see page 37)
- 6 mil vapor barrier with joints lapped ≥6" between slab and base course or prepared subgrade

Exceptions—may be omitted from
1. garages and other unheated structures
2. driveways, walks, and patios

General Masonry (R606)
- minimum thickness of masonry bearing walls more than one story high 8"
- minimum thickness of solid masonry walls ≤9' high in 1-story dwellings and garages 6", except an additional 6 ' is permitted to a gable peak
- minimum thickness of rough, random or coursed rubble stone masonry walls 16"
- a course of solid masonry is required where hollow unit walls or masonry-bonded hollow walls decrease in thickness

- masonry walls to be laterally supported at intervals shown in Table R606.9

Table R606.9

Construction	Max. Wall Length/Thickness or Wall Height/Thickness
Bearing walls:	
Solid or solid grouted	20
All other	18
Nonbearing walls:	
Exterior	20
Interior	18

Unit Masonry (R607)
Mortar placement:
- unless otherwise required, head and bed joints ⅜" thick, except bed of starting course over foundations shall be ¼" to ¾"
- mortar joint thickness shall be within the following tolerances from the specified dimensions:
  1. Bed joint: + ⅛"
  2. Head joint: ¼" + ⅜"
  3. Collar joints: ¼" + ⅜"

Exception: non-load-bearing and masonry veneers
- mortar plasticity and pressure sufficient to extrude mortar from the joint and produce a tight joint
- no furrowing of bed joints producing voids
- if bond broken after initial placement, unit must be relaid in fresh mortar
- mortared surfaces clean and free of deleterious materials
- solid masonry units laid with full head, bed, and interior vertical joints filled
- hollow masonry unit head and bed mortar joints not less than the thickness of the face shell
- wall tie ends embedded in mortar joints
- wall tie ends to engage outer face shells of hollow units by at least ½"
- wire wall ties embedded at least 1½" into mortar bed of solid masonry units or solid grouted hollow units
- wall ties must not be bent after embedment

Grouted Masonry (R609)

Definitions:

Grouted multiple-wythe masonry is where the space between the wythes is solidly filled with grout. It is not necessary for the cores of masonry units to be filled with grout.

Grouted hollow unit masonry is where certain cells of hollow units are continuously filled with grout.

- grout to consist of cementitious material and aggregate in accordance with ASTM C 476
- type M or type S mortar with pouring consistency can be used as grout
- if grout pour stopped for 1 hour, horizontal joints shall be formed by stopping all tiers at same elevation with grout 1" below top
- mortar projecting >0.5" into grout space removed before inspection and grouting
- grout mixed thoroughly and suitable for pumping without segregation of the constituents
- grout to be placed before any initial set and <1½ hours after water added
- maximum pour heights and minimum spaces for grout placement to conform to Table R609.1.2
- grout poured continuously in lifts ≤5'
- grout to be consolidated by puddling or vibration during placement
- no grout pumping through aluminum pipes
- grout cleanouts may be required by official
- cleanouts to be sealed before pour
- cleanouts required at bottom course at each pour of grout, where pour exceeds 4' in height
- fine grout required if vertical space ≤2"
- vertical grout barriers of solid masonry entire height of wall to control horizontal flow of grout
- grout barriers to be >25' apart
- grouting between vertical barriers to be completed in one day with no interruptions >1 hour

Reinforcement of hollow unit masonry:

- horizontal grout or mortar between units and reinforcement ≥¼"
- reinforced hollow-unit masonry must preserve unobstructed vertical continuity of cells to be filled
- walls and cross webs forming filled cells to be full-bedded in mortar to prevent leakage of grout
- head and end joints to be filled with mortar not less than the thickness of the longitudinal face shells
- bond provided by lapping units in successive vertical courses
- align filled cells to maintain an unobstructed vertical cell of dimensions prescribed in Table R609.1.2.
- vertical rebar held in position at top and bottom and at intervals of ≤200 reinforcement diameter
- cells containing rebar filled solidly with grout
- grout to be poured in lifts of ≤8', except if pour >8', grout to be placed in lifts of ≤5' and inspection during pour required
- horizontal steel to be fully embedded in grout in an uninterrupted pour

Table R609.1.2

Grout Type	Max. Pour Height, ft	Min. Space[a,b] Width, in	Min. Space[b,c] Hollow Units, in
Fine	1	0.75	1.5x2
	5	2	2x3
	12	2.5	2.5x3
	24	3	3x3
Coarse	1	1.5	1.5x3
	5	2	2.5x3
	12	2.5	3x3
	24	3	3x4

[a] For grouting between masonry wythes

[b] Grout space dimension is the clear dimension between any masonry protrusion and shall be increased by the horizontal projection of the diameters of the horizontal bars within the cross-section of the grout space.

[c] Area of vertical reinforcement shall not exceed 6 percent of the area of the grout space.

Foundations

Many homeowners—even builders—think the words "foundation" and "basement" are synonymous. In northern states this is understandable, because about 90 percent of homes there have basements. But as the *foundation design* section shows, there are many other options for foundations. Your choice should be determined by the functions you want the foundation to perform.

After you choose the style (*full basement, crawl space,* or *slab on grade*), you must choose the material (poured concrete, masonry, or all-weather wood).

In this age of dwindling energy supplies, foundations must be insulated against heat loss. Tables for each style of foundation show how much insulation should be installed in each of 10 regions of the country.

Additional sections cover the details of *moisture control, termite control,* and *radon control.*

In all, eighteen different foundation designs are presented and detailed. You should have no problem following the large, clear illustrations of each.

Finally, we provide you with a checklist of requirements so that your foundation will *meet the IRC Code.*

Foundation Design

Vitruvius (80 B.C. to 25 B.C.), in his *De architecture,* had it right, "Durability will be assured when foundations are carried down to the solid ground and materials wisely and liberally selected."

Functions of Foundations

The longevity of many Roman public buildings are testimony to Vitruvius having identified that most important function of the foundation—transferring the weight of the building to stable ground. Since his day, however, we have added considerably to the foundation's list of duties. In selecting or designing an appropriate building foundation, one must now keep in mind all these possibilities:

- transfer building loads to the ground
- anchor the building against wind
- anchor the building against earthquakes
- isolate the building from frost heaving
- isolate the building from expansive soil
- support the building above ground moisture
- retard heat loss from the conditioned space
- provide dry storage space
- provide possible comfortable living space
- house the mechanical systems

Designing the Foundation

The design (decision-making) process should involve these eight steps:

1. Select the basic foundation style.

2. Select the material of which the foundation will be constructed (poured concrete, masonry units, or pressure-treated wood).

3. Decide if it is to be unconditioned or conditioned (heated to 65°F and cooled to 75°F).

4. Select the type and R-value of its insulation.

5. Detail its structure, insulation application, and possible finish.

6. Detail its control of moisture (including surface runoff, groundwater, and water vapor).

7. Detail its barriers against termites.

8. Detail its built-in radon mitigation.

The illustration below shows the three basic foundation types (full basement, crawl space, and slab on grade), each of which will be fully detailed in a number of variations in the following pages. Regardless of foundation type, however, all designs should conform, where applicable, to the list of best practices described on the facing page.

Three Basic Foundation Types

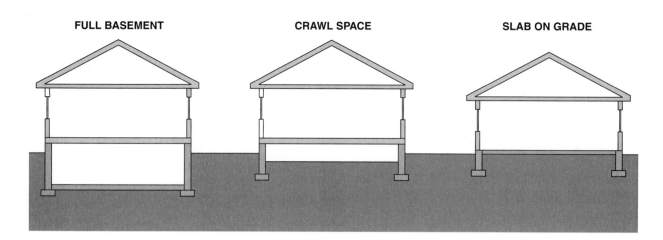

FULL BASEMENT   CRAWL SPACE   SLAB ON GRADE

Foundation Best Practices

Surface Drainage The surface next to the foundation should slope downward at least 6 inches in 10 feet to steer surface runoff away from the building. If practical, gutters should be used to collect roof runoff.

Backfill Foundation backfill should be topped with low-permeability soil to divert surface runoff. Porous sand or gravel should be placed against the walls to provide an easy path to the drain tile. In place of porous backfill, a drainage mat or insulating board with drainage channels may be placed against the foundation wall.

Dampproofing A dampproof coating covered by a 4-mil or 6-mil layer of polyethylene is recommended to reduce water vapor transmission from the soil to the basement. Parging is recommended over masonry unit (CMU) walls before dampproofing. Waterproofing applied directly to the foundation surface from grade level to drain tile is recommended for soils with poor drainage.

Filter Fabric A filter fabric over (and ideally around) the gravel bed and drainpipe is recommended to prevent clogging of the drain pipe.

Drainage System Where drainage problems are possible, a 4-inch-diameter perforated drainpipe should be installed in a gravel bed either outside or inside the footing. The pipe should be placed with holes facing downward and sloping 1 inch in 20 feet to an outfall or sump. The pipe should be below the level of the underside of the floor slab. Surface or roof drainage systems should not be connected to the foundation drainage system.

Exterior Insulation Acceptable materials include extruded polystyrene boards, molded polystyrene boards when porous backfill and adequate drainage are provided, and fiberglass drainage boards when drainage is provided at the footing. Insulation materials should be protected to at least 6 inches below grade by a material such as fiberglass panel, latex-modified cementitious coating, or other rigid weatherproof board—extending at least 6 inches below grade.

Footings All footings must be beneath the maximum frost depth or insulated to prevent frost penetration. They must be sized to distribute the load uniformly and have a minimum compressive strength of 2,500 psi.

Crack Control Two no. 4 bars running continuously 2 inches below the top of the wall and above/below window openings are recommended to minimize shrinkage cracking.

Anchor Bolts $\frac{1}{2}$-inch anchor bolts embedded at least 7 inches into concrete should be placed at a maximum spacing of 6 feet and no further than 1 foot from any corner.

Isolation Joint An isolation joint between slab and foundation wall reduces cracking by allowing relative movement. In radon areas, a liquid sealant should be poured into the joint over backing rod.

Concrete Slabs A slab of at least 4 inches thickness compressive strength of 2,500 psi is recommended. Chopped fiberglass additive or welded wire reinforcement held in place 2 inches below the top of the slab is recommended in areas with radon and termites. To avoid cracking due to soil settlement, slabs should not rest on foundation walls. To maximize strength and minimize cracking, slabs poured directly over insulation board or plastic vapor barrier should have a minimum water/cement ratio. Alternatively, the slab may be poured on a layer of sand over the foam insulation or vapor barrier.

Sill The foundation sill should be at least 8 inches above grade and should be pressure-treated to resist decay.

Caulking/Sealing Caulking against air leakage should include foundation wall/sill plate, sill plate/rim joist, rim joist/subfloor, and subfloor/above-grade wall plate.

Full Basements

Recommended configurations and R-values of basement insulation are given below and on the facing page for exterior and interior, as well as rigid foam and blanket insulations. *Recommended* means the configurations possessing the lowest estimated 30-year life-cycle cost (cost to install insulation plus cost of heat loss through the insulation over 30 years). Although the results listed are from the 1991 *Builder's Foundation Handbook*, optimum insulation R-value depends on only real dollar (adjusted for inflation) costs, so the results remain nearly constant over time. For those wishing to do their own calculations, Chapter 5 of the *Handbook* offers a handy worksheet and detailed instructions.

Basement Insulation Configurations

Concrete wall with 4' exterior insulation

Masonry wall with 8' exterior insulation

Concrete wall with 8' interior insulation

Masonry wall with 8' interior insulation

All-weather wood foundation with blanket insulation

Concrete wall with ceiling insulation

Recommended Insulation for Basements

Location	HDD$_{65}$[1]	CDD$_{75}$[2]	Conditioned[3]–Full		Conditioned–Half		Unconditioned		
			Masonry[4]	Wood	Masonry	Wood	Masonry	Wood	Ceiling
Minneapolis	8,007	98	8' R15	R19	R19/15	R19	4' R5	R19	R30
Chicago	6,177	181	8' R10	R19	R19/10	R19	4' R5	R11	R30
Denver	6,014	83	8' R10	R19	R19/15	R19	4' R5	R11	R30
Boston	5,593	74	8' R10	R19	R19/10	R19	4' R5	R11	R30
Washington	4,122	299	8' R10	R19	R19/10	R19	none	R11	R11
Atlanta	3,021	415	8' R5	R19	R19/10	R19	none	none	none
Fort Worth	2,407	1,139	8' R10	R19	R19/10	R19	none	none	none
Phoenix	1,442	1,856	8' R10	R19	R19/5	R19	none	none	none
Los Angeles	1,595	36	none	none	R19/0	R11	none	none	none
Miami	199	1,257	none	none	R19/0	R11	none	none	none

[1] *Heating degree-days,* base 65°F, the accumulated difference between the average daily temperature and 65°F for the heating season.

[2] *Cooling degree-days,* base 75°F, the accumulated difference between the average daily temperature and 75°F for the cooling season.

[3] *Conditioned* means heated to 65°F and cooled to 75°F.

[4] *Masonry* here means masonry block or poured concrete below grade (bg) and wood above grade (ag). Insulation values are presented as R(ag)/R(bg).

Concrete Basement Wall with 4-Foot Exterior Insulation

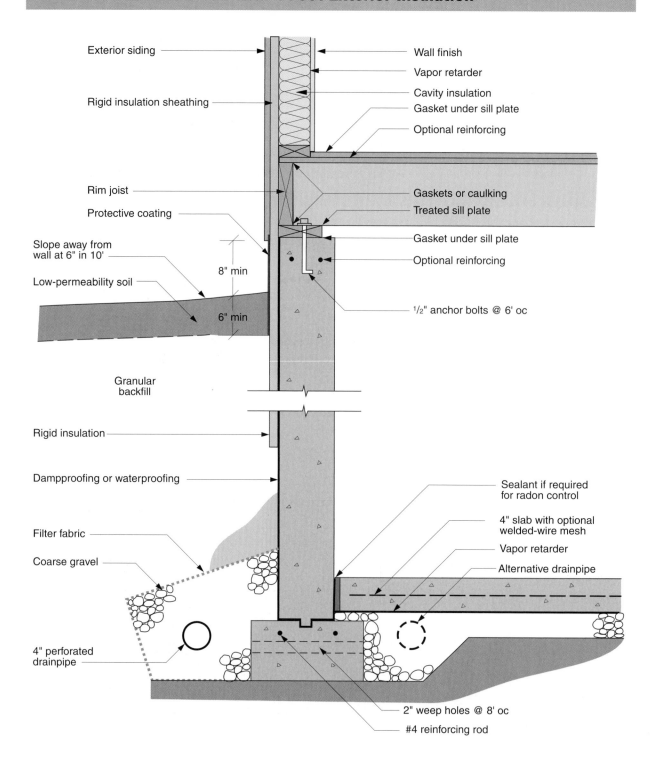

Exterior siding

Rigid insulation sheathing

Rim joist

Protective coating

Slope away from wall at 6" in 10'

Low-permeability soil

8" min

6" min

Granular backfill

Rigid insulation

Dampproofing or waterproofing

Filter fabric

Coarse gravel

4" perforated drainpipe

Wall finish

Vapor retarder

Cavity insulation

Gasket under sill plate

Optional reinforcing

Gaskets or caulking

Treated sill plate

Gasket under sill plate

Optional reinforcing

$1/2$" anchor bolts @ 6' oc

Sealant if required for radon control

4" slab with optional welded-wire mesh

Vapor retarder

Alternative drainpipe

2" weep holes @ 8' oc

#4 reinforcing rod

Masonry Basement Wall with 8-Foot Exterior Insulation

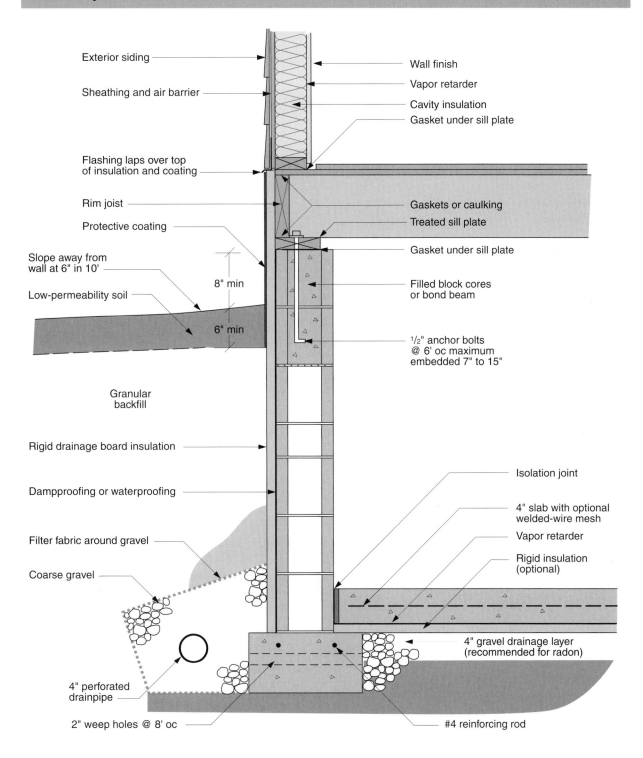

Exterior siding

Sheathing and air barrier

Flashing laps over top
of insulation and coating

Rim joist

Protective coating

Slope away from
wall at 6" in 10'

Low-permeability soil

8" min

6" min

Granular
backfill

Rigid drainage board insulation

Dampproofing or waterproofing

Filter fabric around gravel

Coarse gravel

4" perforated
drainpipe

2" weep holes @ 8' oc

Wall finish

Vapor retarder

Cavity insulation

Gasket under sill plate

Gaskets or caulking

Treated sill plate

Gasket under sill plate

Filled block cores
or bond beam

$1/2$" anchor bolts
@ 6' oc maximum
embedded 7" to 15"

Isolation joint

4" slab with optional
welded-wire mesh

Vapor retarder

Rigid insulation
(optional)

4" gravel drainage layer
(recommended for radon)

#4 reinforcing rod

Concrete Basement Wall with Interior Insulation

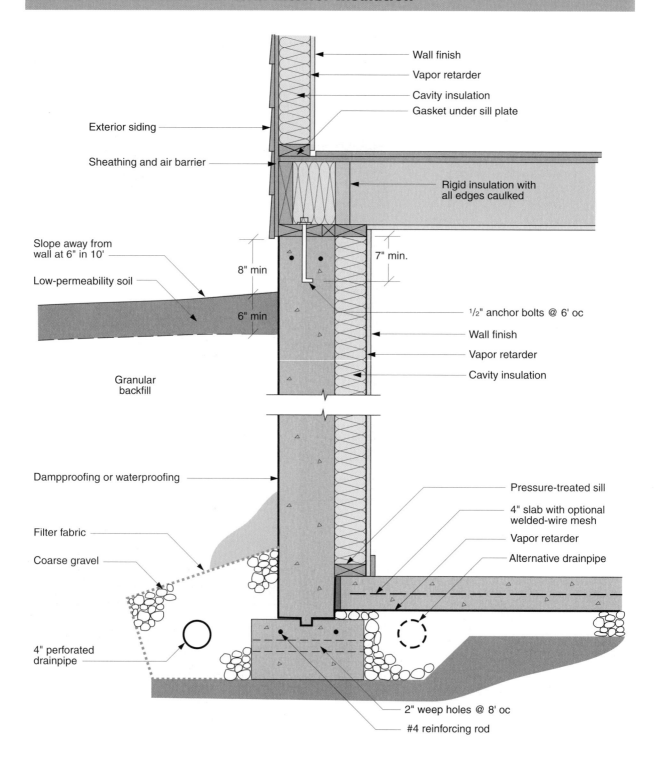

Wall finish

Vapor retarder

Cavity insulation

Gasket under sill plate

Exterior siding

Sheathing and air barrier

Rigid insulation with all edges caulked

Slope away from wall at 6" in 10'

Low-permeability soil

8" min

7" min.

6" min

½" anchor bolts @ 6' oc

Wall finish

Vapor retarder

Cavity insulation

Granular backfill

Dampproofing or waterproofing

Pressure-treated sill

4" slab with optional welded-wire mesh

Vapor retarder

Alternative drainpipe

Filter fabric

Coarse gravel

4" perforated drainpipe

2" weep holes @ 8' oc

#4 reinforcing rod

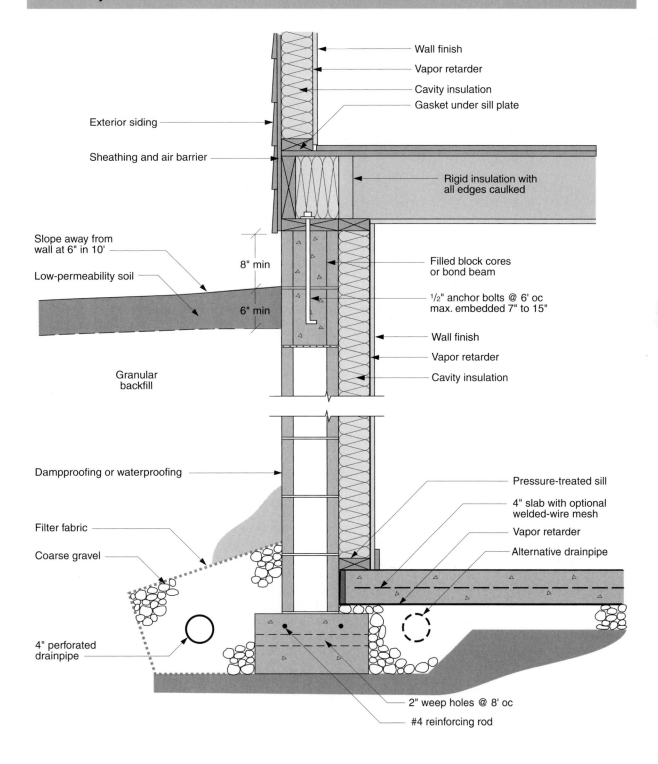

Wall finish

Vapor retarder

Cavity insulation

Gasket under sill plate

Exterior siding

Sheathing and air barrier

Rigid insulation with all edges caulked

Slope away from wall at 6" in 10'

Low-permeability soil

8" min

6" min

Filled block cores or bond beam

$1/2$" anchor bolts @ 6' oc max. embedded 7" to 15"

Wall finish

Vapor retarder

Cavity insulation

Granular backfill

Dampproofing or waterproofing

Pressure-treated sill

4" slab with optional welded-wire mesh

Vapor retarder

Filter fabric

Coarse gravel

Alternative drainpipe

4" perforated drainpipe

2" weep holes @ 8' oc

#4 reinforcing rod

All-Weather Wood Foundation

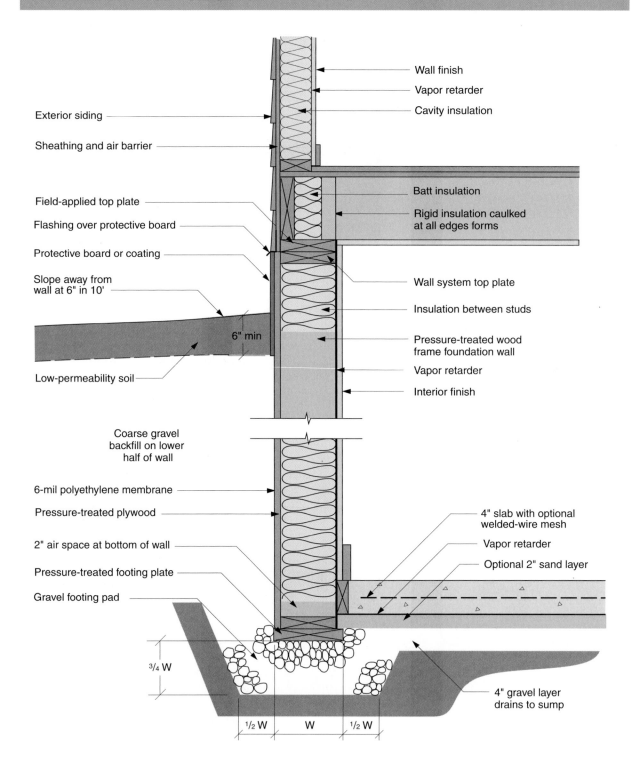

Wall finish

Vapor retarder

Cavity insulation

Exterior siding

Sheathing and air barrier

Batt insulation

Rigid insulation caulked at all edges forms

Field-applied top plate

Flashing over protective board

Protective board or coating

Slope away from wall at 6" in 10'

Wall system top plate

Insulation between studs

Pressure-treated wood frame foundation wall

6" min

Vapor retarder

Interior finish

Low-permeability soil

Coarse gravel backfill on lower half of wall

6-mil polyethylene membrane

Pressure-treated plywood

4" slab with optional welded-wire mesh

Vapor retarder

Optional 2" sand layer

2" air space at bottom of wall

Pressure-treated footing plate

Gravel footing pad

3/4 W

4" gravel layer drains to sump

1/2 W   W   1/2 W

Concrete Basement Wall with Ceiling Insulation

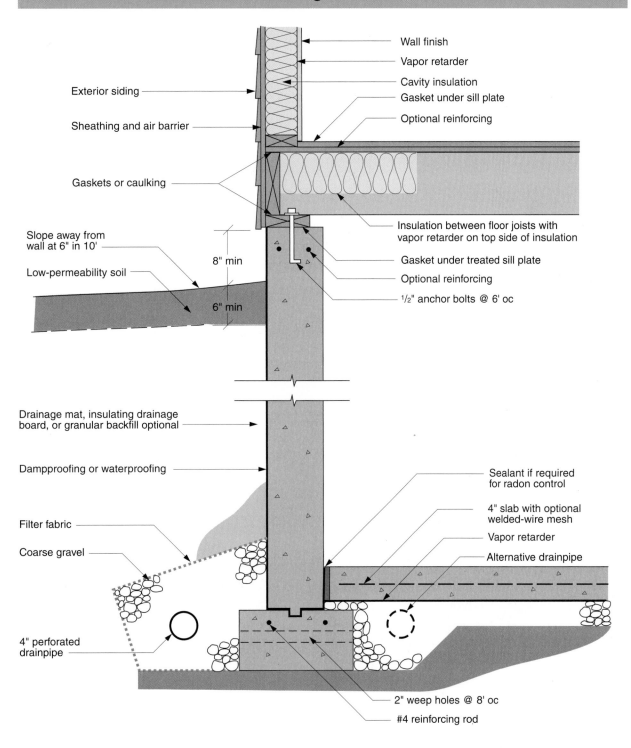

Wall finish

Vapor retarder

Cavity insulation

Gasket under sill plate

Optional reinforcing

Exterior siding

Sheathing and air barrier

Gaskets or caulking

Insulation between floor joists with vapor retarder on top side of insulation

Slope away from wall at 6" in 10'

8" min

Gasket under treated sill plate

Optional reinforcing

Low-permeability soil

6" min

$1/2$" anchor bolts @ 6' oc

Drainage mat, insulating drainage board, or granular backfill optional

Dampproofing or waterproofing

Sealant if required for radon control

4" slab with optional welded-wire mesh

Vapor retarder

Alternative drainpipe

Filter fabric

Coarse gravel

4" perforated drainpipe

2" weep holes @ 8' oc

#4 reinforcing rod

Crawl Spaces

Recommended configurations and R-values of crawl space insulation are given below for exterior and interior, as well as rigid foam and blanket insulations. *Recommended* means the configurations possessing the lowest estimated 30-year life-cycle cost (cost to install insulation plus cost of heat loss through the insulation over 30 years). Although the results listed are from the 1991 *Builder's Foundation Handbook*, optimum insulation R-value depends on only real dollar (adjusted for inflation) costs, so the results remain nearly constant over time. For those wishing to do their own calculations, Chapter 5 of the Handbook offers a handy worksheet and detailed instructions.

Crawl Space Insulation Configurations

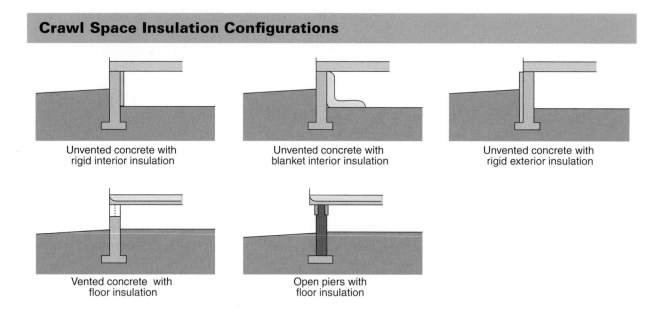

Unvented concrete with rigid interior insulation

Unvented concrete with blanket interior insulation

Unvented concrete with rigid exterior insulation

Vented concrete with floor insulation

Open piers with floor insulation

Recommended Insulation for Crawl Spaces

Location	HDD$_{65}$[1]	CDD$_{75}$[2]	Unvented 4ft Wall of Masonry	Wood	Unvented 2ft Wall of Masonry	Wood	Vented 2ft Wall of[3] Masonry	Wood
Minneapolis	8,007	98	4' R5	R19	2' R10	R19	R30	R30
Chicago	6,177	181	4' R5	R11	2' R10	R19	R19	R30
Denver	6,014	83	4' R5	R11	2' R10	R11	R19	R30
Boston	5,593	74	4' R5	R11	2' R10	R19	R19	R30
Washington	4,122	299	4' R5	none	2' R5	R11	R19	R30
Atlanta	3,021	415	4' R5	none	2' R5	none	R11	R11
Fort Worth	2,407	1,139	4' R5	none	2' R5	none	R11	R11
Phoenix	1,442	1,856	4' R5	none	2' R5	none	R11	R11
Los Angeles	1,595	36	none	none	none	none	R11	R11
Miami	199	1,257	none	none	none	none	none	none

[1] *Heating degree-days,* base 65°F, the accumulated difference between the average daily temperature and 65°F for heating season

[2] *Cooling degree-days,* base 75°F, the accumulated difference between the average daily temperature and 75°F for cooling season

[3] R-values for ceiling insulation

Unvented Concrete Crawl Space with Rigid Interior Insulation

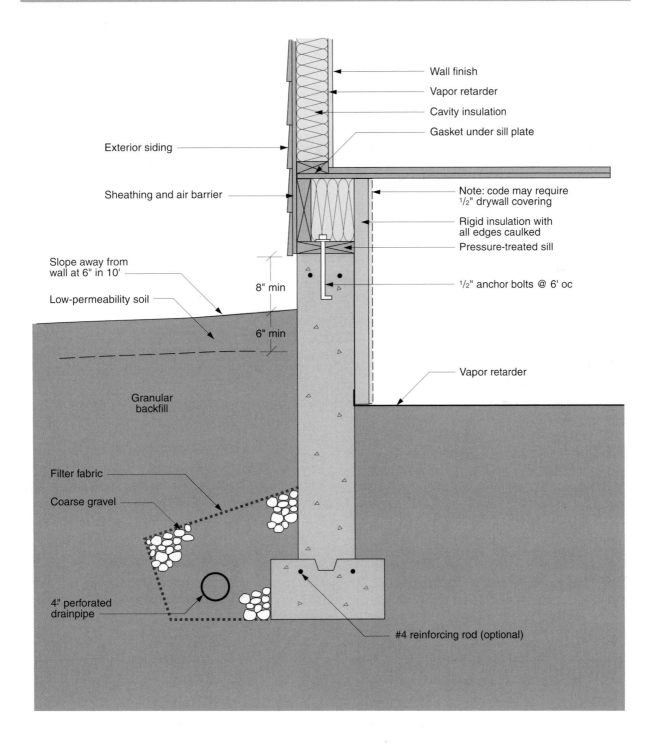

Wall finish

Vapor retarder

Cavity insulation

Gasket under sill plate

Exterior siding

Sheathing and air barrier

Note: code may require 1/2" drywall covering

Rigid insulation with all edges caulked

Pressure-treated sill

Slope away from wall at 6" in 10'

8" min

Low-permeability soil

6" min

1/2" anchor bolts @ 6' oc

Vapor retarder

Granular backfill

Filter fabric

Coarse gravel

4" perforated drainpipe

#4 reinforcing rod (optional)

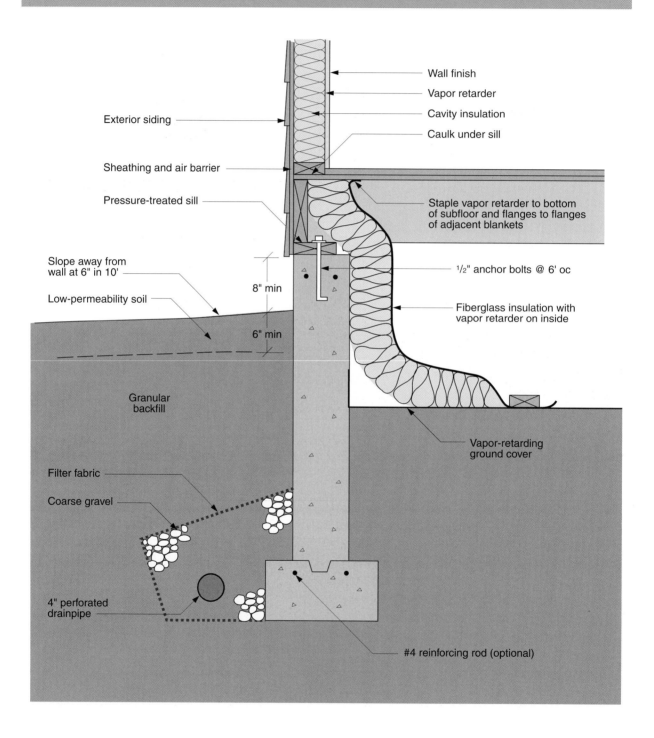

Wall finish

Vapor retarder

Cavity insulation

Caulk under sill

Exterior siding

Sheathing and air barrier

Pressure-treated sill

Staple vapor retarder to bottom of subfloor and flanges to flanges of adjacent blankets

Slope away from wall at 6" in 10'

Low-permeability soil

8" min

6" min

1/2" anchor bolts @ 6' oc

Fiberglass insulation with vapor retarder on inside

Granular backfill

Vapor-retarding ground cover

Filter fabric

Coarse gravel

4" perforated drainpipe

#4 reinforcing rod (optional)

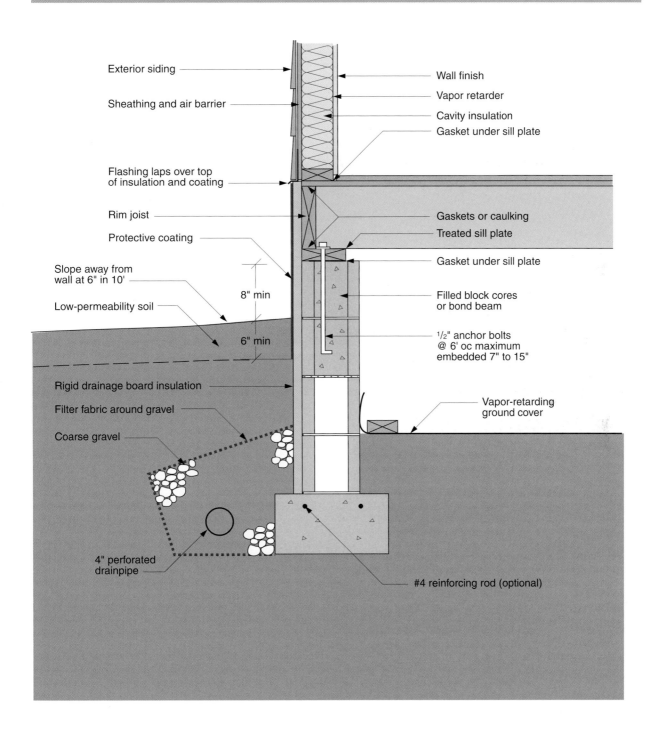

Exterior siding

Sheathing and air barrier

Flashing laps over top of insulation and coating

Rim joist

Protective coating

Slope away from wall at 6" in 10'

Low-permeability soil

Rigid drainage board insulation

Filter fabric around gravel

Coarse gravel

4" perforated drainpipe

Wall finish

Vapor retarder

Cavity insulation

Gasket under sill plate

Gaskets or caulking

Treated sill plate

Gasket under sill plate

Filled block cores or bond beam

$1/2$" anchor bolts @ 6' oc maximum embedded 7" to 15"

Vapor-retarding ground cover

#4 reinforcing rod (optional)

8" min

6" min

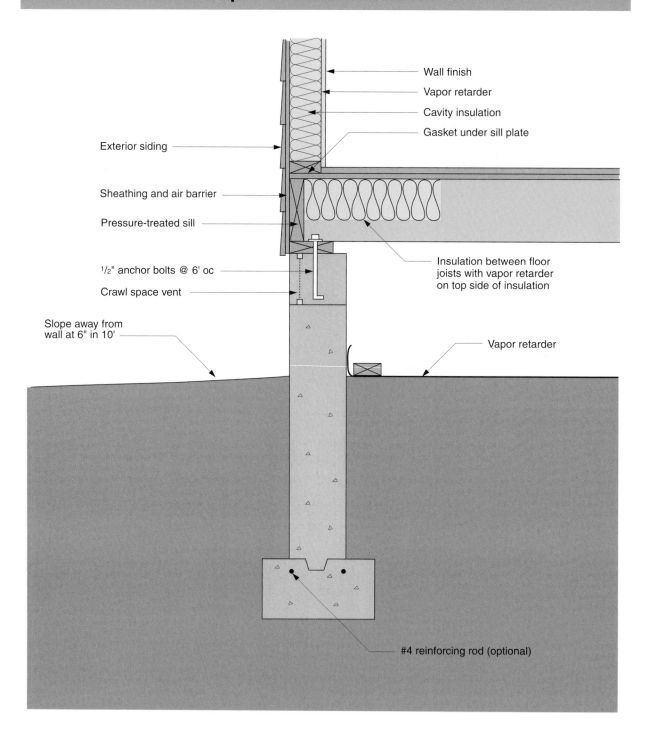

Wall finish

Vapor retarder

Cavity insulation

Gasket under sill plate

Exterior siding

Sheathing and air barrier

Pressure-treated sill

Insulation between floor joists with vapor retarder on top side of insulation

1/2" anchor bolts @ 6' oc

Crawl space vent

Slope away from wall at 6" in 10'

Vapor retarder

#4 reinforcing rod (optional)

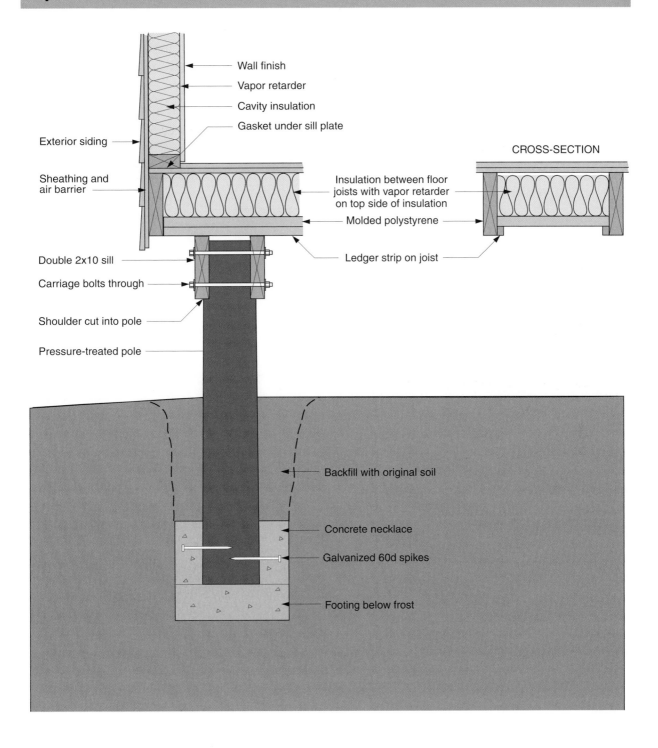

Wall finish

Vapor retarder

Cavity insulation

Gasket under sill plate

Exterior siding

Sheathing and air barrier

CROSS-SECTION

Insulation between floor joists with vapor retarder on top side of insulation

Molded polystyrene

Double 2x10 sill

Ledger strip on joist

Carriage bolts through

Shoulder cut into pole

Pressure-treated pole

Backfill with original soil

Concrete necklace

Galvanized 60d spikes

Footing below frost

Slabs on Grade

Recommended configurations and R-values of slab-on-grade foundation insulation are given below for both exterior and interior rigid foam insulation. *Recommended* means the configurations possessing the lowest estimated 30-year life-cycle cost (cost to install insulation plus cost of heat loss through the insulation over 30 years). Although the results listed are from the 1991 *Builder's Foundation Handbook*, optimum insulation R-value depends on only real dollar (adjusted for inflation) costs, so the results remain nearly constant over time. For those wishing to do their own calculations, Chapter 5 of the Handbook offers a handy worksheet and detailed instructions.

Slab-on-Grade Insulation Configurations

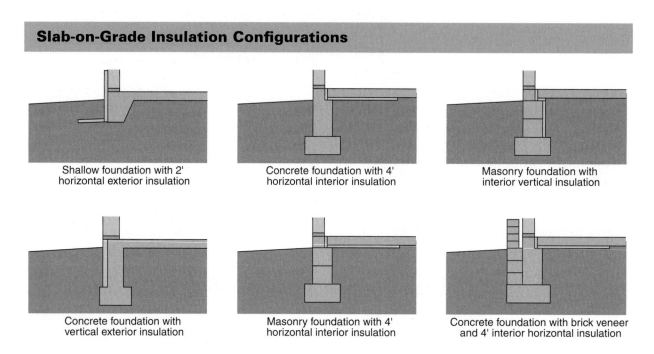

Shallow foundation with 2' horizontal exterior insulation

Concrete foundation with 4' horizontal interior insulation

Masonry foundation with interior vertical insulation

Concrete foundation with vertical exterior insulation

Masonry foundation with 4' horizontal interior insulation

Concrete foundation with brick veneer and 4' interior horizontal insulation

Recommended Insulation for Slabs on Grade

Location	HDD_{65}[1]	CDD_{75}[2]	Exterior Insulation	Interior Insulation
Minneapolis	8,007	98	2' R5 horizontal	4' R5 vertical
Chicago	6,177	181	2' R5 horizontal	4' R5 horizontal
Denver	6,014	83	2' R5 horizontal	4' R5 horizontal
Boston	5,593	74	2' R5 horizontal	4' R5 horizontal
Washington	4,122	299	2' R5 horizontal	4' R5 vertical
Atlanta	3,021	415	2' R5 horizontal	4' R5 vertical
Fort Worth	2,407	1,139	2' R5 horizontal	4' R5 vertical
Phoenix	1,442	1,856	2' R5 horizontal	4' R5 vertical
Los Angeles	1,595	36	none	none
Miami	199	1,257	none	none

[1] *Heating degree-days,* base 65°F, the accumulated difference between the average daily temperature and 65°F for heating season

[2] *Cooling degree-days,* base 75°F, the accumulated difference between the average daily temperature and 75°F for cooling season

Shallow Foundation with Exterior Insulation

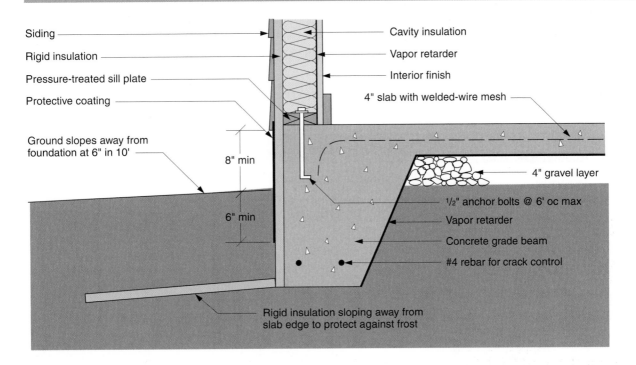

Siding

Rigid insulation

Pressure-treated sill plate

Protective coating

Ground slopes away from foundation at 6" in 10'

8" min

6" min

Cavity insulation

Vapor retarder

Interior finish

4" slab with welded-wire mesh

4" gravel layer

1/2" anchor bolts @ 6' oc max

Vapor retarder

Concrete grade beam

#4 rebar for crack control

Rigid insulation sloping away from slab edge to protect against frost

Slab on Grade and Concrete Foundation Wall with Exterior Edge Insulation

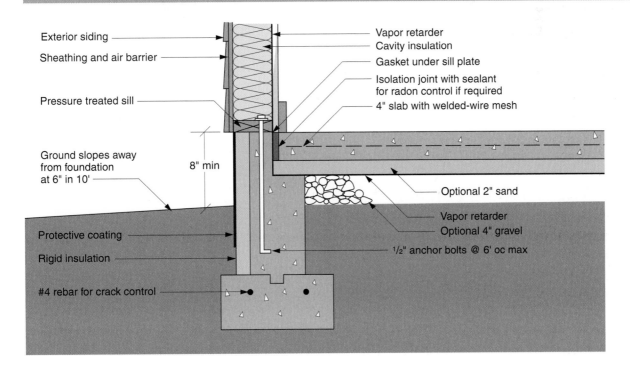

Exterior siding

Sheathing and air barrier

Pressure treated sill

Ground slopes away from foundation at 6" in 10'

8" min

Protective coating

Rigid insulation

#4 rebar for crack control

Vapor retarder

Cavity insulation

Gasket under sill plate

Isolation joint with sealant for radon control if required

4" slab with welded-wire mesh

Optional 2" sand

Vapor retarder

Optional 4" gravel

1/2" anchor bolts @ 6' oc max

Slabs on Grade   **97**

Slab on Grade and Concrete Foundation Wall with Interior Slab Insulation

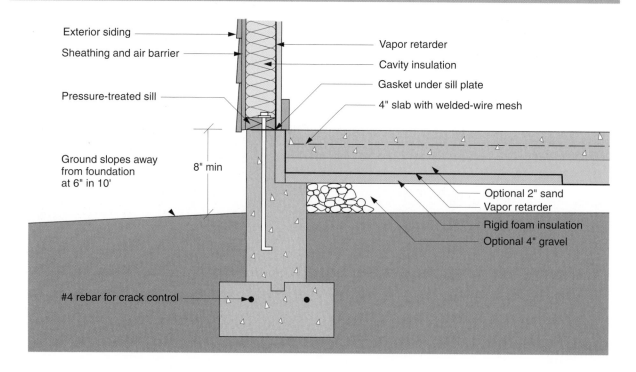

Exterior siding

Sheathing and air barrier

Pressure-treated sill

Ground slopes away from foundation at 6" in 10'

8" min

#4 rebar for crack control

Vapor retarder

Cavity insulation

Gasket under sill plate

4" slab with welded-wire mesh

Optional 2" sand

Vapor retarder

Rigid foam insulation

Optional 4" gravel

Slab on Grade and Masonry Foundation Wall with Interior Slab Insulation

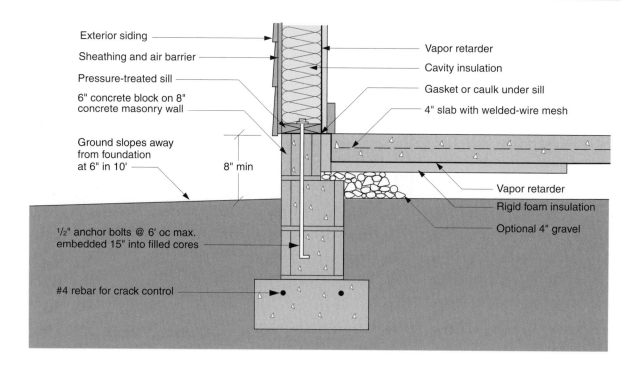

Exterior siding

Sheathing and air barrier

Pressure-treated sill

6" concrete block on 8" concrete masonry wall

Ground slopes away from foundation at 6" in 10'

8" min

1/2" anchor bolts @ 6' oc max. embedded 15" into filled cores

#4 rebar for crack control

Vapor retarder

Cavity insulation

Gasket or caulk under sill

4" slab with welded-wire mesh

Vapor retarder

Rigid foam insulation

Optional 4" gravel

Slab on Grade and Masonry Foundation Wall with Interior Edge Insulation

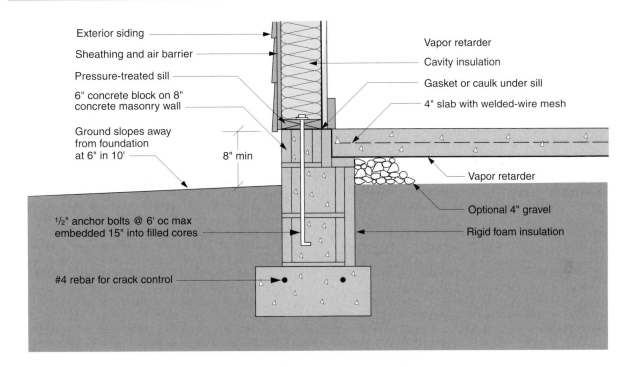

Exterior siding

Sheathing and air barrier

Pressure-treated sill

6" concrete block on 8" concrete masonry wall

Ground slopes away from foundation at 6" in 10'

8" min

1/2" anchor bolts @ 6' oc max embedded 15" into filled cores

#4 rebar for crack control

Vapor retarder

Cavity insulation

Gasket or caulk under sill

4" slab with welded-wire mesh

Vapor retarder

Optional 4" gravel

Rigid foam insulation

Slab on Grade and Concrete Foundation Wall with Interior Slab Insulation

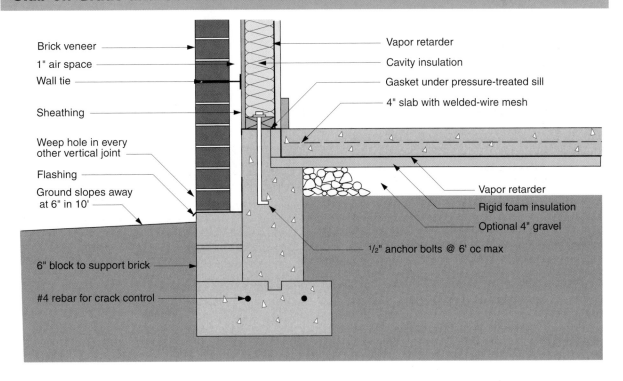

Brick veneer

1" air space

Wall tie

Sheathing

Weep hole in every other vertical joint

Flashing

Ground slopes away at 6" in 10'

6" block to support brick

#4 rebar for crack control

Vapor retarder

Cavity insulation

Gasket under pressure-treated sill

4" slab with welded-wire mesh

Vapor retarder

Rigid foam insulation

Optional 4" gravel

1/2" anchor bolts @ 6' oc max

Moisture Control

Excessive moisture in a basement or crawl space gives rise to two sorts of problems:

1. The wood structure—particularly the sills and floor joists—can be infected by a fungus and, over time, destroyed by "dry rot."

2. Basement surfaces and wall stud cavities can support the growth of various molds which can seriously affect the health of occupants.

Prevention of excess moisture generally involves at least several of the following tactics:

1. Choose a site with permeable soil and a water table reliably below the foundation floor level.

2. Direct roof and ground-surface water away from the building with gutters and downspouts and by grading the surrounding ground surface away from the foundation.

3. Install a system of perforated drainage pipes around the foundation footing to lower the local water table to below the foundation floor.

4. Diminish the amount of water vapor evaporating from the soil into the foundation space with vapor-retarding ground covers.

5. Ventilate unconditioned foundation enclosures to remove excess water vapor from the air.

Drainage Systems

Footing drains (illustration below) have two functions. They draw down the groundwater level to below the basement walls and floor, and they collect and drain away water that seeps down through the backfill from rain and melting snow. They may be aided by vertical wall and underfloor drainage blankets and, especially in the case of exterior footing drains, by weep holes through the footing.

The drain must be placed so that the top of the pipe is beneath the bottom of the floor slab and the bottom of the pipe above the bottom of the footing. Drains can be located outside the foundation or inside next to the footing beneath the floor slab. When the drain line is inside, a gravel fill should still be provided at the outside, and weep holes should be provided through the footing every 8 feet.

Exterior placement beside the footing is more effective at drawing down the water table. Interior drains are more effective for collecting soil gas in radon-control systems.

The pipe is placed with the two rows of holes facing down. A fabric filter keeps coarse sediment from washing into the drain line. The pipe should be sloped at least 1 inch in 20 feet, although 1 inch in 10 feet compensates for settling after construction.

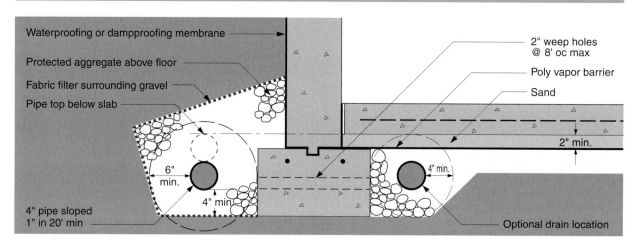

Perimeter Drain System

- Waterproofing or dampproofing membrane
- Protected aggregate above floor
- Fabric filter surrounding gravel
- Pipe top below slab
- 4" pipe sloped 1" in 20' min
- 6" min.
- 4" min.
- 2" weep holes @ 8' oc max
- Poly vapor barrier
- Sand
- 2" min.
- 4" min.
- Optional drain location

Ventilation Requirements

The IRC requires unconditioned crawl spaces to be ventilated to prevent moisture buildup. A rectangular crawl space requires a minimum of four vents, one on each wall, located no farther than 3 feet from each corner. The vents should be as high on the wall as possible to capture breezes, and landscaping should be planned to prevent obstruction. The free (open) area of all vents must total no less than $\frac{1}{150}$ of the floor area. The gross area of vents depends on the type of vent cover. The gross area can be found by multiplying the vent's free area by one of the factors in the table at right.

Two exceptions to the passive ventilation requirement are as follows: 1) the ground surface is covered by a qualified ground cover, and 2) forced ventilation is provided.

Ground Covers

A ground cover (vapor retarder) that restricts evaporation of soil moisture is the most effective way to prevent condensation and wood decay problems in a crawl space, as well as in an unheated full basement.

The vapor retarder should have a permeability rating of 1.0 perm maximum and should be rugged enough to withstand foot traffic. Recommended materials include 6-mil polyethylene and 45-mil ethylene polymer membrane (EPDM). Retarder sheet edges must overlap by 6 inches and be sealed or taped. The retarder must also extend at least 6 inches up the foundation walls and be fastened and sealed to the wall.

Forced Ventilation

It is not necessary to passively vent a crawl space if it is continuous with an adjacent basement or if its walls are insulated and a minimum of 1 cfm per 50 square feet ventilating air is delivered by mechanical ventilation. Venting is also incompatible with crawl spaces that are used as heat distribution plenums (in which the foundation walls are insulated and the space acts as a giant warm-air duct).

Crawl Space Vent Area Requirements

Vent Cover Material	Multiply Free Vent Area by
¼" mesh hardware cloth	1.0
⅛" mesh screen	1.25
16-mesh insect screen	2.0
Louvers + ¼" hardware cloth	2.0
Louvers + ⅛" mesh screen	2.25
Louvers + 16-mesh insect screen	3.0

Termite Control

Termites occur naturally in woodlands, where they help break down dead plant material and play an important role in the nutrient cycle. The problem lies in the fact that termites don't distinguish between the wood in dead trees and the dead wood in structures. Subterranean termites, which account for 95 percent of all termite damage, are found throughout the United States wherever the average annual air temperature is 50°F or above and the ground is sufficiently moist (see map below).

Termite Identification

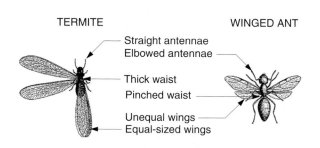

TERMITE   WINGED ANT

Straight antennae
Elbowed antennae
Thick waist
Pinched waist
Unequal wings
Equal-sized wings

Termite Hazard Distribution

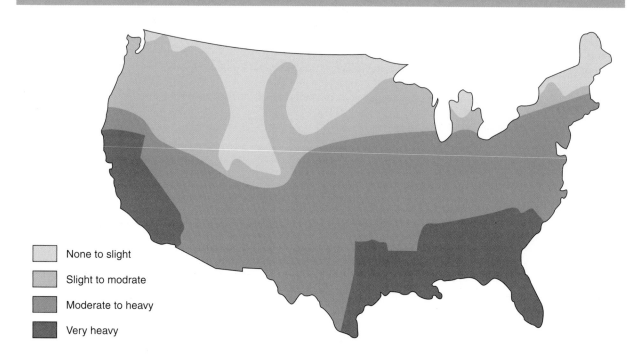

- None to slight
- Slight to modrate
- Moderate to heavy
- Very heavy

Points of Entry

Because termites occur naturally in forests and brush lands, clearing wooded sites robs them of their food supply. They adapt by feeding on the wood in structures. Termite control starts with blocking easy routes of entry from the soil to the wood in the structure. The most common points of entry are shown on the facing page.

Control Measures

Termite control is simple in concept, but difficult in practice, because termites can pass through cracks as narrow as $1/32$ inch. The major strategies of termite control include separating wood structures from the soil, minimizing cracks in slabs and walls, barriers to force termites into the open, soil treatment with chemicals, and keeping the soil and foundation dry.

Points of Termite Entry

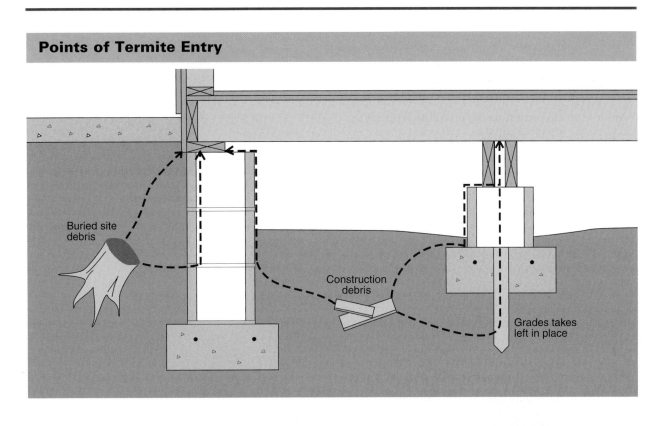

Buried site debris

Construction debris

Grades takes left in place

Preventive Steps

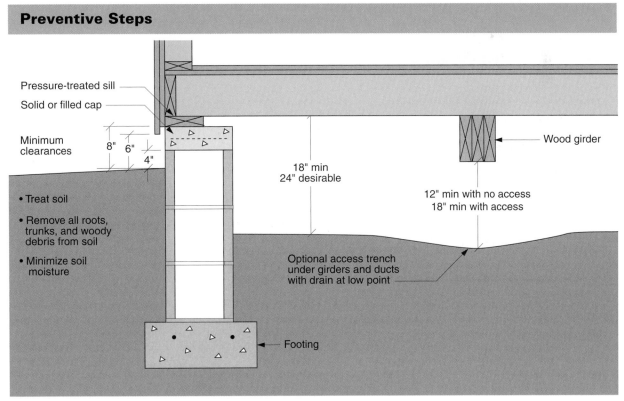

Pressure-treated sill

Solid or filled cap

Minimum clearances

8" 6" 4"

- Treat soil

- Remove all roots, trunks, and woody debris from soil

- Minimize soil moisture

18" min
24" desirable

Wood girder

12" min with no access
18" min with access

Optional access trench under girders and ducts with drain at low point

Footing

Radon Control

Radon is a colorless, odorless, radioactive gas. It is produced by the natural decay of radium and exists at varying concentrations throughout the United States (see map below). Radon is emitted from the ground and diluted to an insignificant level in the atmosphere. Being a gas, radon can travel through the soil and into a building through cracks and other openings in the foundation. Radon from well water can also contribute to radon levels in indoor air.

Radon is drawn from the soil through the foundation when indoor pressure is less than that in the soil. Radon levels are generally higher in winter due to the buoyancy of warm indoor air, furnace and fireplace drafts, and power exhaust fans. There are two effective approaches to radon management. Neither cost much, so they should be standard practice in new construction.

The Barrier Approach

Like a boat in water, the barrier approach keeps radon out by making it difficult for it to get in. What works to keep a basement dry also works to keep radon out. Because radon is a gas, the approach relies on infiltration-control measures such as minimizing cracks, joints, and other openings through the foundation. Waterproofing and dampproofing membranes outside the wall and under the slab are excellent barriers.

The Suction Approach

Suction systems collect radon from under the foundation and vent it to the outdoors. They do this by creating a stronger suction than that of the building itself. Suction systems are preferred where high potential for radon exists.

The systems have two parts: collection and discharge. A collection system adds little to construction cost, and the discharge system can be deferred until proven necessary. The collection system may utilize the existing moisture drainage system, or individual suction taps may be installed at the rate of one tap per 500 square feet of floor. A single tap, however, is adequate for a slab poured over a 4-inch layer of clean, coarse gravel.

Geologic Radon Potential

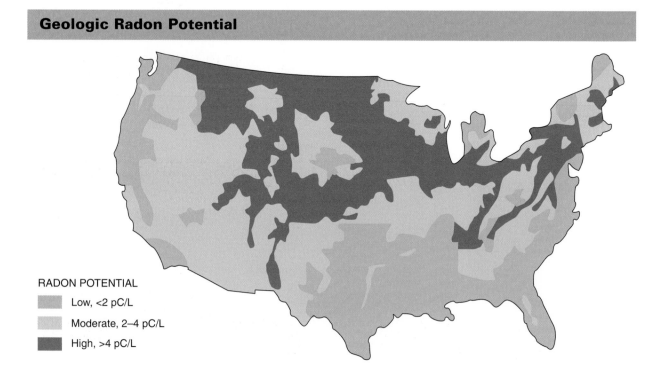

RADON POTENTIAL

- Low, <2 pC/L
- Moderate, 2–4 pC/L
- High, >4 pC/L

Passive Suction Under Slabs

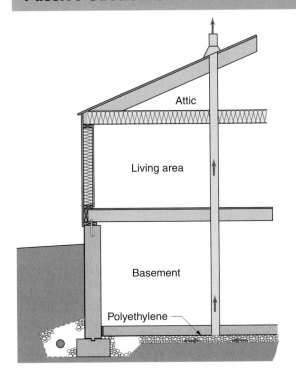

Attic

Living area

Basement

Polyethylene

Active Suction Under Slabs

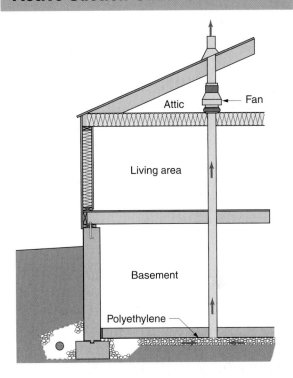

Attic

Fan

Living area

Basement

Polyethylene

Passive Suction in Crawlspace

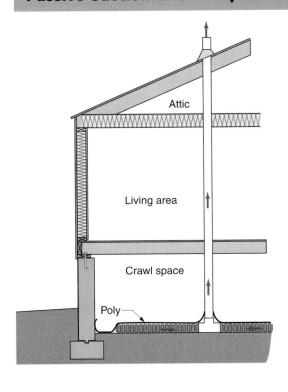

Attic

Living area

Crawl space

Poly

Crawlspace Groundcover Details

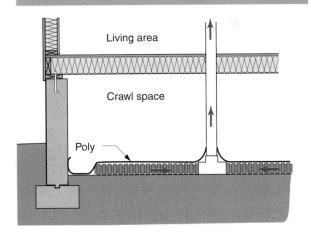

Living area

Crawl space

Poly

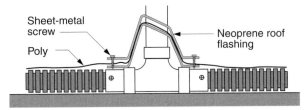

Sheet-metal screw

Poly

Neoprene roof flashing

Meet the Code

The following is a partial list of requirements from the *2006 International Residential Code (IRC) for One- and Two-Family Dwellings*. Consult the publication for the full text and additional provisions.

General (R401)

Drainage:
- diverted to a storm sewer or other collection point
- graded ≥6"/10' away from foundation
- swales sloped ≥2 percent within 10' of foundation
- impervious surfaces within 10' of foundation slope ≥2 percent away from building

Materials (R402)

Concrete:
- minimum compressive strength in Table R402.2
- subject to moderate or severe weathering to be air entrained

Table R402.2
Minimum Strength of Concrete, psi

Type or Location	Weathering Potential		
	Negligible	Moderate	Severe
Foundations & slabs (exc. garage)	2,500	2,500	2,500
Vertical walls exposed to weather	2,500	3,000	3,000
Porches, steps, garage, & carport slabs exposed to weather	2,500	3,000	3,500

Fasteners:
- for below-grade plywood or in knee walls, 304 or 316 stainless steel
- for above-grade plywood and lumber, 304 or 316 stainless steel, silicon bronze, copper, hot-dipped galvanized steel or hot-tumbled galvanized steel
- electrogalvanized steel, nails and galvanized steel staples not permitted

Wood:
- lumber and plywood treated to AWPA Std. U1
- lumber or plywood cut after treatment, to be field treated with copper naphthenate until rejection

Footings R403

General:
- exterior walls supported on continuous concrete footings, or approved systems to accommodate loads
- supported on undisturbed soil or engineered fill
- exterior footings ≥12" below undisturbed ground

Minimum size:
- minimum sizes per Table R403.1
- spread footings ≥6"thick
- footing projections ≥2" and less than thickness of footing
- pier and column footings based on tributary load and allowable soil pressure

Table R403.1
Minimum Width of Footings, inches

	Load Bearing Value of Soil, psf			
	1,500	2,000	3,000	4,000
Conventional light-frame construction				
1-story	12	12	12	12
2-story	15	12	12	12
4" brick veneer over light frame or 8" hollow masonry				
1-story	12	12	12	12
2-story	21	16	12	12
8" solid or fully grouted masonry				
1-story	16	12	12	12
2-story	29	21	14	12

Reinforcement:
- foundations with stem walls, one No. 4 bar within 12" of top of wall and one No. 4 bar 3"–4" from bottom of footing
- slabs on ground with turned-down footings, one No. 4 bar at top and bottom of footing, except if monolithic, 1 No. 5 bar or 2 No. 4 bars in middle third of footing depth

Frost protection:
- foundation walls, piers, and other supports to be protected by one or more of following methods:

1. extended below frost line
2. frost-protected shallow foundation (R403.3)
3. erected on solid rock

Exceptions:
1. freestanding light-framed structures of ≤600 sq. ft., with eave height ≤10'
2. other freestanding structures of ≤400 sq ft, with eave height ≤10'
3. decks not supported by dwelling

Foundation Walls (R404)

Lateral support:
- foundation walls that meet all of the following shall be considered laterally supported:
    1. full basement floor ≥3.5" concrete slab poured tight against bottom of foundation wall
    2. floor joists and blocking connected to sill plate
    3. sill plate bolt spacing per Table R404.1(2)
    4. floor full-blocked perpendicular to joists within two joist spaces of foundation wall
- no backfill until wall cured and anchored to floor above or braced to prevent damage, except bracing not required for <4' of unbalanced backfill

Table R404.1(2)
Maximum Anchor Bolt Spacing, inches

Wall Height ft	Backfill ft	USC Soil Classes		
		GW, GP SW, SP	GM, GC SM-SC, ML	SC, MH, ML-CL Inorganic CL
7	4	12	12	12
	5	12	12	12
	6	17	12	12
8	4	12	12	12
	5	16	12	12
	6	16	12	12
	7	16	12	12

Anchorage:
- ≥½" bolts @ ≤6' o.c. and embedded ≥7"
- two bolts per plate section min.
- one bolt ≤12" from each end of plate section

Foundation Drainage (R405)

Concrete or masonry foundations:
- drains around foundations enclosing usable space below grade
- drain tiles, gravel or crushed stone, or perforated pipe at or below area to be protected and discharged into approved drainage system
- gravel or crushed stone drains ≥1' outside and 6" above footing and covered with filter membrane
- drain tiles or perforated pipe on ≥2" and covered with ≥6" of washed gravel or crushed stone

Exception: drainage not required when foundation on well-drained ground (USC, Group I soils)

Wood foundations:
- ≥4" gravel, stone, or sand under basement floor
- automatic draining of subslab and wall footings
- 6-mil poly under basement floor
- unless USC Group I soil, a sump ≥24" in diameter or 20" square, extending ≥24" below bottom of basement floor, and discharging into approved sewer system or to daylight

Dampproofing (R406)

- basement walls dampproofed footing to grade
- masonry walls ≥⅜" parging plus dampproofing

Exception: parging not required for material approved for direct application to masonry
- waterproofing required in areas of high water table or other severe soil-water conditions
- membrane joints to be sealed with compatible adhesive

Crawlspace Ventilation (R408)

- net vent area ≥1 sq ft per 150 sq ft of floor
- 1 vent within 3' of each building corner
- ventilation not required where earth covered with continuous vapor retarder having lapped and sealed joints and edges, and there is continuous mechanical ventilation of ≥1 cfm/50 sq ft
- access to under-floor areas: ≥18"×24" through floor, or ≥16"×24" through perimeter wall

Wood

Wood is nature's must wonderful building material. Its combination of strength and beauty has never been surpassed in the laboratory. The first section of this chapter explores the *nature of wood*.

The beauty of wood, however, is partly due to its imperfections. So next the chapter looks at how *lumber defects* affect its grading and how *lumber grade stamps* are interpreted.

Wood is categorized as being either softwood (from evergreens) or hardwood (from deciduous trees). The *properties of North American species* table lists the qualities of 56 species. A second table compares *moisture and shrinkage* of 34 of the wood species.

And when is a 2×4 really a 2×4? Building projects often require that we know the exact dimensions of the lumber. The table of *standard lumber sizes* lists both nominal and actual dimensions of all standard categories and sizes of lumber.

Wood will last a long time if kept dry. The building codes recognize that many outdoor and underground applications lead to decay, however. This chapter lists and illustrates the applications for which the codes call for *pressure-treated wood*.

The Nature of Wood

The fibrous nature of wood largely determines how it is used. Wood is primarily composed of hollow, elongate, spindle-shaped cells arranged parallel to each other along the trunk of a tree. When lumber and other products are cut from the tree, the characteristics of these fibrous cells and their arrangement affect such properties as strength and shrinkage as well as the grain pattern of the wood.

Reading a Tree Trunk

Bark is a thick layer of dead cells, similar in function to the outer layers of human skin, that protects the living parts of the tree from insects and fire. A tree is very resistant to insects as long as its bark forms a complete barrier.

Phloem is the inner bark, consisting of live cells that transmit nutrients, as do the cells of the sapwood.

The *cambium* is a single layer of cells where, remarkably, all tree growth occurs. The cells of the cambium continually divide, first adding a cell to the phloem outside and then a cell to the sapwood

inside. As a result, a tree limb that first appears at a height of 5 feet above ground will remain 5 feet high, even though the tree grows taller.

Sapwood consists of the most recently formed layers of wood and, as its name implies, it carries sap up and down the tree. When the rate of growth varies throughout the year, or even ceases during cold winters, the sapwood shows annual growth rings. Wide rings are due to rapid growth in wet summers; narrow rings indicate dry summers.

Heartwood is formed of dead sapwood cells. Chemicals and minerals are deposited in and between the heartwood cells, making the wood more dense, strong, dark, and resistant to decay than the sapwood.

The *pith,* at the very center of the tree, is the overgrown remnant of the original shoot.

Rays are at right angles to the circular rings. Not defects or cracks, as they appear, rays are bundles of cells that transport and store food across the annual rings.

Reading a Tree Trunk

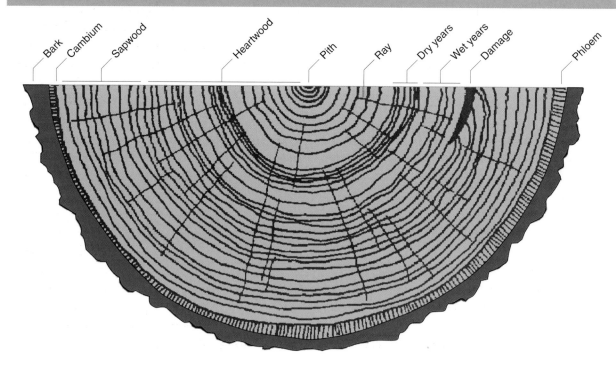

Bark | Cambium | Sapwood | Heartwood | Pith | Ray | Dry years | Wet years | Damage | Phloem

Growth Rings

In most species the difference between wood formed early in the growing season and that formed later produces well-marked annual growth rings. The age of a tree can be determined by counting these annual rings. However, if the growth is interrupted, by drought or defoliation by insects for example, more than one ring may be formed in the same season. In this case the inner rings do not have sharply defined boundaries and are called false rings.

The inner part of the growth ring formed early in the growing season is called earlywood, and the outer part formed later in the growing season, latewood. Earlywood is characterized by cells with relatively large cavities and thin walls. Latewood cells have smaller cavities and thicker walls.

Growth rings are most readily seen in species with sharp contrast between latewood formed in one year and earlywood formed in the following year, such as in the hardwoods ash and oak, and in softwoods like southern pine. In some species, such as water tupelo, aspen, and sweetgum, differentiation of earlywood and latewood is slight and the annual growth rings are difficult to recognize. In many tropical regions, growth is continuous throughout the year, and no well-defined growth rings are formed.

When growth rings are prominent, as in most softwoods and ring-porous hardwoods, earlywood differs markedly from latewood in physical properties. Earlywood is lighter in weight, softer, and weaker than latewood. Because of the greater density of latewood, the proportion of latewood is sometimes used to judge the strength of the wood. This method is useful with such species as the southern pines, Douglas fir, ash, hickory, and oak.

Wood Cells

Wood cells—the structural elements of wood tissue—are of various sizes and shapes and are firmly cemented together. Dry wood cells may be empty or partly filled with deposits, such as gums and resins. The majority of wood cells are considerably elongated and pointed at the ends; these cells are customarily called fibers. The length of wood fibers is highly variable within a tree and among species. Hardwood fibers average about ¹⁄₂₅ inch in length; softwood fibers range from ⅛ to ⅓ inch in length.

In addition to fibers, hardwoods have cells of relatively large diameter known as vessels or pores. These cells form the main conduits in the movement of sap.

Both hardwoods and softwoods also have cells that are oriented radially from pith toward bark. These groups of cells conduct sap across the grain and are called rays. The rays are most easily seen on edge-grained or quartersawn surfaces, and they vary greatly in size in different species. In oaks the rays are very conspicuous and add to the decorative features of the wood. Rays also represent planes of weakness along which seasoning (drying) checks develop.

Chemical Composition

Dry wood is primarily composed of cellulose, lignin, hemicelluloses, and minor amounts (5 percent to 10 percent) of extraneous materials. Cellulose, the major component, constitutes approximately 50 percent of wood by weight. It is a high-molecular-weight linear polymer. During growth the cellulose molecules are arranged into ordered strands called fibrils, which in turn are organized into the larger structural elements that make up the cell walls of wood fibers. Most of the cell wall cellulose is crystalline. Delignified wood fibers, which consist mostly of cellulose, are used in making paper. Delignified fibers may also be chemically altered to form textiles, films, lacquers, and explosives.

Lignin constitutes 23 percent to 33 percent of the wood substance in softwoods and 16 percent to 25 percent in hardwoods. Although lignin occurs in wood throughout the cell wall, it is concentrated toward the outside of the cells and between cells. Lignin is the cementing agent that binds the cells together. It is necessary to remove lignin from wood to make high-grade paper.

Defects and Grading

Defects in Lumber

Lumber is sawn from trees, and trees grow in an ever-changing environment. As a result, the material composition of trees and lumber varies. Some of the variations are valued for their beauty, whereas others reduce the strength or utility of the lumber. The most common "defects" are illustrated on the facing page and described below.

Bow is deviation from a flat plane of the wide face, end to end. It is caused by a change in moisture content after sawing and by fibers not being exactly parallel to the surfaces. It has no effect on strength. Therefore, feel free to use a piece wherever nailing will constrain it to a flat plane.

Cup is deviation from a flat plane of the narrow face, edge to edge. It is caused by a change in moisture content after surfacing. It tends to loosen fasteners.

Crook is deviation from a flat plane of the narrow face, end to end. It is caused by change of moisture content after sawing and by fibers not parallel to the surfaces. It makes wood unsuitable for framing.

Twist is deviation from a flat plane of all faces, end-to-end. It results from spiral wood grain and changes in moisture content. Twist also makes lumber unsuitable for framing.

Knots are very strong but not well connected to the surrounding wood. The rules for use in joists and rafters are 1) tight knots are allowed in the top third, 2) loose or missing knots are allowed in the middle third, and 3) no knots at all over 1 inch are allowed in the bottom third. Knots are the high-density roots of the limbs.

Check is the lumber version of a stretch mark, a rift in the surface caused when the surface of a timber dries more rapidly than the interior. End checks weaken a timber in shear; other checks are mostly cosmetic. The development of check can be very dramatic and unsightly in exposed beams that are dried rapidly in a warm house the first winter. Solutions include air drying for several years before use, or treatment of timber surfaces with oil to retard the drying process.

Split passes clear through the wood and is often the result of rough handling. It constitutes a serious structural weakness. Lumber with splits should not be used in bending (joists and rafters) or in compression as a post.

Shake is a separation of growth rings. Lumber with shake should not be used to support bending loads (beams, joists, and rafters), because it must be presumed that the zone of weakness extends the entire length of the piece.

Wane is the presence of bark or lack of wood at an edge. It results from a slight miscalculation on the part of the sawyer. It has very little effect on strength. The main drawback is the lack of a full-width nailing surface.

Cross grain occurs when a board is sawn from a crooked log. Because wood is ten times stronger in the direction of grain than across the grain, a cross-grain angle greater than one part in ten seriously weakens the wood in bending (beams, joists, and rafters).

Decay is destruction of the wood structure by fungi or insects. It prohibits structural use of the wood but may enhance its decorative value, provided the decay process has been halted.

Pitch pockets are accumulations of natural resins. They have little effect on strength but will bleed through paint and should not be allowed in lumber that will be painted.

Lumber Grade Stamps

A grade stamp assures the lumber customer that the piece of lumber carrying the stamp meets the minimum standard for the stated purpose. Some stamps certify strength for use in framing, whereas others certify appearance for use in millwork.

There is a bewildering array of grade stamps, but all stamps from certified agencies conform to the guidelines set by the American Lumber Standards Committee. Reading grade stamps is quite simple, as demonstrated by the example on the facing page.

Lumber Defects

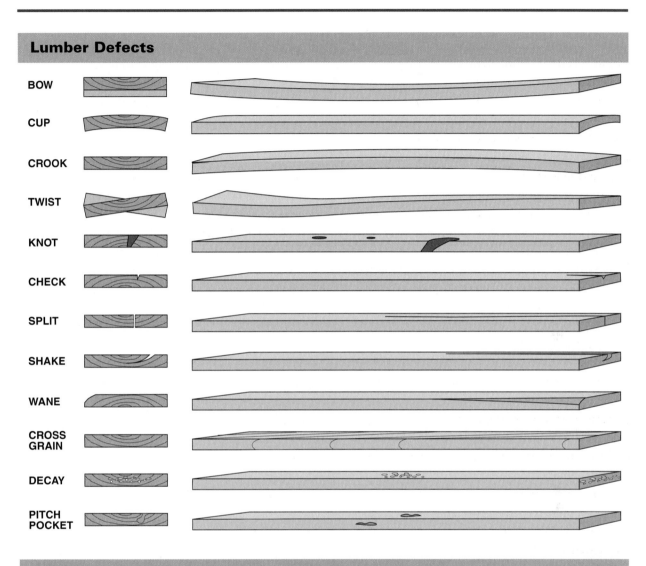

BOW	
CUP	
CROOK	
TWIST	
KNOT	
CHECK	
SPLIT	
SHAKE	
WANE	
CROSS GRAIN	
DECAY	
PITCH POCKET	

Typical Lumber Grade Stamp

Mill number where the lumber was manufactured → **MILL 10**

Certified agency under whose rules the lumber was graded → WCLB®

NO.2

Species may be a single species or a group of species having similar characteristics → **DOUG FIR**   **S·DRY**

Grade:
SEL.STR. = Select Structural
1 = N0. 1
2 = No. 2
3 = No. 3
CONST. = Construction
STAND. = Standard
UTIL. = Utility
STUD = Stud

Moisture content (MC) at the time of surfacing (planing):
S-GRN = MC 20% or more
S-DRY = MC 19% or less
MC 15 = MC 15% or less

Properties of North American Species

Below is a table of properties of North American wood species. For all of the numerical ratings, 1 is best and 5 is worst.

Density is an indirect measure of strength. Refer to Chapter 21 for tables of wood density versus the holding power of nails and screws.

Paintability refers to the relative ease of maintaining exterior painted surfaces such as clapboards, decking, and trim.

Cupping, or deviation of the wide face of a board from a flat plane, tends to loosen nails. Only species with cupping ratings of 1 or 2 should be considered for exterior siding and trim.

Checking is cracking of the exterior surface due to drying too quickly. It does not usually affect strength but is unsightly.

R/inch is the thermal resistance to heat flow, just as with insulation.

Physical Properties of Selected North American Hardwoods

Species	Density lb/cu ft	Paint- ability	Resistance to Cupping	Resistance to Checking	R/in Oven-Dry	R/in 12% MC	Color of Heartwood
Alder, red	25.6	3	–	–	–	–	Pale brown
Ash, white	37.4	–	–	–	1.0	0.84	Gray-brown
Aspen, quaking	24.3	3	2	1	1.5	1.2	Pale brown
Basswood, American	23.1	3	2	2	1.6	1.3	Cream
Beech. American	40.0	4	4	2	0.96	0.78	Pale brown
Birch, yellow	38.7	4	4	2	0.98	0.81	Light brown
Butternut	23.7	3–5	–	–	–	–	Light brown
Cherry, black	31.2	4	–	–	1.2	0.98	Brown
Chestnut	26.8	3–5	3	2	1.4	1.1	Light brown
Cottonwood, black	21.8	3	4	2	1.7	1.4	White
Cottonwood, eastern	26.8	3	4	2	1.4	1.2	White
Elm, American	31.2	4–5	4	2	1.2	0.96	Brown
Elm, rock	34.9	–	4	2	0.97	0.80	Brown
Elm, slippery	41.8	–	–	–	1.1	0.93	Brown
Hickory, pecan	41.2	4–5	4	2	0.95	0.77	Light brown
Locust, black	43.1	–	–	–	–	–	Golden brown
Magnolia, southern	31.2	3	2	–	1.2	1.0	Pale brown
Maple, sugar	39.3	4	4	2	0.98	0.81	Light brown
Oak, red	39.3	4	4	2	1.0	0.82	Light brown
Oak, white	42.4	4–5	4	2	0.91	0.75	Brown
Poplar, yellow	26.2	3	2	1	1.3	1.1	Pale brown
Sycamore, American	30.6	4	–	–	1.2	0.96	Pale brown
Walnut, black	34.3	3–5	3	2	–	–	Dark brown

Physical Properties of Selected North American Softwoods

Species	Density lb/cu ft	Paint-ability	Resistance to Cupping	Resistance to Checking	R/in Oven-Dry	R/in 12% MC	Color of Heartwood
Bald cypress	32.0	–	–	1	1.3	1.1	Brown
Cedar, Alaska	27.5	1	1	1	–	–	Golden brown
Cedar, Atlantic white	21.2	1	1	1	1.7	1.4	–
Cedar, eastern red	30.0	1	1	1	1.3	1.1	Pale red
Cedar, Incense	23.1	1	–	–	–	–	Brown
Cedar, Port Orford	26.8	1	–	1	1.4	1.2	Cream
Cedar, western red	20.0	1	1	1	1.7	1.5	Brown
Cedar, white	19.3	1	1	–	1.7	1.4	Light brown
Cypress	28.7	1	1	1	1.3	1.1	Light brown
Fir, balsam	23.0	–	–	–	1.6	1.3	–
Fir, Douglas	30.0	4	2	2	1.2	1.0	Pale red
Fir, white	24.3	3	2	2	1.5	1.2	White
Hemlock, eastern	25.0	3	2	2	1.4	1.2	Pale brown
Hemlock, western	28.1	3	2	2	1.3	1.1	Pale brown
Larch	32.4	4	2	2	1.1	0.93	Brown
Pine, eastern white	21.8	2	2	2	1.6	1.3	Cream
Pine, loblolly	33.7	–	–	–	1.2	0.96	–
Pine, lodgepole	33.7	–	–	–	1.4	1.2	–
Pine, longleaf	38.7	–	–	–	1.0	0.87	–
Pine, Norway	–	2	2	2	1.3	1.1	Light brown
Pine, pitch	33.1	–	–	–	1.2	0.98	–
Pine, ponderosa	25.0	3	2	2	1.4	1.2	Cream
Pine, red	28.7	–	–	–	1.3	1.1	–
Pine, shortleaf	33.7	–	–	–	1.2	0.96	–
Pine, southern	34.3	4	2	2	1.2	0.96	Light brown
Pine, sugar	22.5	2	2	2	1.6	1.3	Cream
Pine, western white	23.7	2	2	2	15	1.2	Cream
Redwood	22.5	1	1	1	1.5	1.2	Dark brown
Spruce, black	26.8	3	2	2	1.4	1.2	–
Spruce, Engelmann	23.1	3	2	2	1.4	1.2	–
Spruce, sitka	26.2	3	2	2	1.4	1.2	–
Spruce, white	21.8	3	2	2	1.6	1.3	White
Tamarack	33.1	4	2	2	–	–	Brown

Moisture and Shrinkage

The amount of water in wood is expressed as a percentage of its oven-dry (dry as possible) weight. For example, 1 cubic foot of oven-dry red oak weighs 39.3 pounds. In drying from the just-cut, or green, stage, the sapwood loses 69 percent of 39.3, or 27.1 pounds of water.

As wood dries, it first loses moisture from within its cells without shrinking; after reaching the fiber saturation point (cells empty), further drying results in shrinkage. Eventually wood comes to dynamic equilibrium with the relative humidity of the surrounding air—interior wood typically shrinking in winter and swelling in summer. Average summer indoor equilibrium moisture content (EMC) ranges from 6 percent in the southwest to 11 percent in the south and east coastal states. Indoor EMC can drop to 4 percent in northern states in winter.

In the table on the facing page, the terms *radial* and *tangential* refer to orientation relative to the growth rings. Because shrinkage tangential to growth rings averages twice that in the radial direction, lumber tends to distort in cross section in drying.

As shown in the illustration below, the pattern of distortion depends on the direction of the rings in the lumber. The greatest distortion occurs in plainsawn lumber; the least in radial-sawn, or edge-grained lumber.

Shrinkage Patterns of Lumber from Green to Oven Dry

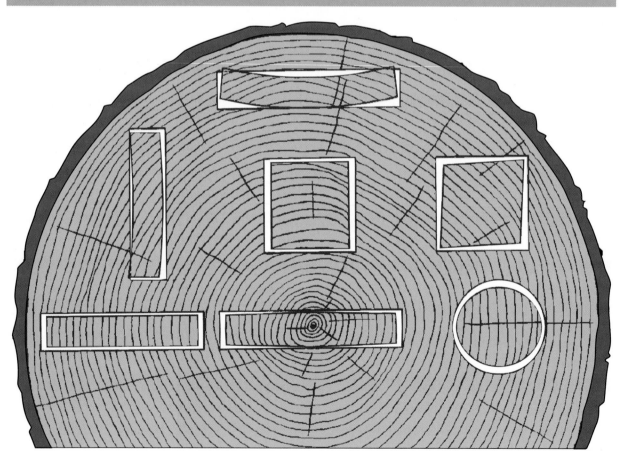

Moisture Content and Shrinkage of Hardwoods and Softwoods

Species	Moisture Content Green (%)[1]		Shrinkage, from Green to Oven-Dry (%)		
	Heartwood	Sapwood	Radial	Tangential	Volume
HARDWOODS					
Ash, white	46	44	4.9	7.8	13.3
Aspen, quaking	95	113	3.5	6.7	11.5
Basswood, American	81	133	6.6	9.3	15.8
Beech. American	55	72	5.5	11.9	17.2
Birch, yellow	74	72	7.3	9.5	16.8
Cherry, black	58	—	3.7	7.1	11.5
Chestnut, American	120	—	3.4	6.7	11.6
Elm, American	95	92	4.2	9.5	14.6
Hickory, pecan	80	54	4.9	8.9	13.6
Locust, black	—	—	4.6	7.2	10.2
Magnolia, southern	80	104	5.4	6.6	12.3
Maple, sugar	65	72	4.8	9.9	14.7
Oak, red	80	69	4.0	8.6	13.7
Oak, white	64	78	5.6	10.5	16.3
Poplar, yellow	83	106	4.6	8.2	12.7
Walnut, black	90	73	5.5	7.8	12.8
SOFTWOODS					
Cedar, Alaska	32	166	2.8	6.0	9.2
Cedar, Port Orford	50	98	4.6	6.9	10.1
Cedar, western red	58	249	2.4	5.0	6.8
Cedar, white	–	–	2.2	4.9	7.2
Cypress	121	171	3.8	6.2	10.5
Fir, Douglas	37	115	4.8	7.6	12.4
Fir, white	98	160	3.3	7.0	9.8
Hemlock, eastern	97	119	3.0	6.8	9.7
Hemlock, western	85	170	4.2	7.8	12.4
Larch, western	54	110	4.5	9.1	14.0
Pine, eastern white	—	—	2.1	6.1	8.2
Pine, lodgepole	41	120	4.3	6.7	11.1
Pine, longleaf	31	106	5.1	7.5	12.2
Pine, sugar	98	219	2.9	5.6	7.9
Pine, western white	62	148	4.1	7.4	11.8
Redwood	86	210	2.6	4.4	6.8
Spruce, sitka	41	142	4.3	7.5	11.5
Tamarack	49	–	3.7	7.4	13.6

[1] Moisture content is expressed as percentage of oven-dry weight. When the moisture in the wood weighs more than oven-dry wood, this percentage will be more than 100%.

Standard Lumber Sizes

Standard Lumber Sizes by Western Wood Products Association Rules

Product	Nominal Dimensions, in		Dressed Dimensions, in	
	Thickness	Width	Thickness	Width
Dimension	2	2	1½	1⁹⁄₁₆
	3	3	2½	2⁹⁄₁₆
	4	4	3½	3⁹⁄₁₆
		5	4½	4⅝
		6	5½	5⅝
		8	7½	7½
		10	9¼	9½
		12	11¼	11½
Scaffold plank	1¼ and thicker	8 and wider	Same as for "dimension"	
Timbers	5 and larger	5 and larger	nominal less ½	
Decking	2	5	1½	4
		6		5
		8		6¾
		10		8¾
		12		10¾
	3	6	2½	5¼
	4		3½	
Flooring	⅜	2	⁵⁄₁₆	1⅛
	½	3	⁷⁄₁₆	2⅛
	⅝	4	⁹⁄₁₆	3⅛
	1	5	¾	4⅛
	1¼	6	1	5⅛
	1½		1¼	
Ceiling and partition	⅜	3	⁵⁄₁₆	2⅛
	½	4	⁷⁄₁₆	3⅛
	⅝	5	⁹⁄₁₆	4⅛
	¾	6	¹¹⁄₁₆	5⅛
Factory and shop lumber	1 (4/4)	5 and wider	¾	random width
	1¼ (5/4)		1⁵⁄₃₂	
	1½ (6/4)		1¹³⁄₃₂	
	1¾ (7/4)		1¹⁹⁄₃₂	
	2 (8/4)		1¹³⁄₁₆	
	2½ (10/4)		2⅜	
	3 (12/4)		2¾	
	4 (16/4)		3¾	

Standard Lumber Sizes by Western Wood Products Association Rules — *Continued*

Product	Nominal Dimensions, in		Dressed Dimensions, in	
	Thickness	Width	Thickness	Width
Selects and commons	1 (4/4)	2	$3/4$	$1\frac{1}{2}$
	$1\frac{1}{4}$ (5/4)	3	$1^{5}/_{32}$	$2\frac{1}{2}$
	$1\frac{1}{2}$ (6/4)	4	$1^{13}/_{32}$	$3\frac{1}{2}$
	$1\frac{3}{4}$ (7/4)	5	$1^{19}/_{32}$	$4\frac{1}{2}$
	2 (8/4)	6	$1^{13}/_{16}$	$5\frac{1}{2}$
	$2\frac{1}{4}$ (9/4)	7	$2^{3}/_{32}$	$6\frac{1}{2}$
	$2\frac{1}{2}$ (10/4)	8 and wider	$2^{3}/_{8}$	nominal less $3/4$
	$2\frac{3}{4}$ (11/4)		$2^{9}/_{16}$	
	3 (12/4)		$2^{3}/_{4}$	
Finish and boards	$3/8$	2	$5/16$	$1\frac{1}{2}$
	$1/2$	3	$7/16$	$2\frac{1}{2}$
	$5/8$	4	$9/16$	$3\frac{1}{2}$
	$3/4$	5	$5/8$	$4\frac{1}{2}$
	1	6	$3/4$	$5\frac{1}{2}$
	$1\frac{1}{4}$	7	1	$6\frac{1}{2}$
	$1\frac{1}{2}$	8 and wider	$1\frac{1}{4}$	nominal less $3/4$
	$1\frac{3}{4}$		$1\frac{3}{8}$	
	2		$1\frac{1}{2}$	
	$2\frac{1}{2}$		2	
	3		$2\frac{1}{2}$	
	$3\frac{1}{2}$		3	
	4		$3\frac{1}{2}$	
Rustic and drop siding	1	6	$23/32$	$5^{3}/_{8}$
		8		$7^{1}/_{8}$
		10		$9^{1}/_{8}$
		12		$11^{1}/_{8}$
Paneling and siding	1	6	$23/32$	$5^{7}/_{16}$
		8		$7^{1}/_{8}$
		10		$9^{1}/_{8}$
		12		$11^{1}/_{8}$
Ceiling and partition	$5/8$	4	$9/16$	$3^{3}/_{8}$
	1	6	$23/32$	$5^{3}/_{8}$
Bevel siding	$1/2$	4	$15/32$ butt, $3/16$ tip	$3\frac{1}{2}$
		5		$4\frac{1}{2}$
		6		$5\frac{1}{2}$
	$3/4$	8	$3/4$ butt, $3/16$ tip	$7\frac{1}{4}$
		10		$9\frac{1}{4}$
		12		$11\frac{1}{4}$

Pressure-Treated Wood

Pressure-treated lumber is softwood which has been treated by forcing chemicals into the wood cells. The result is lumber that is nearly immune to decay.

Most pressure-treated wood used in residential applications is southern yellow pine framing lumber. Because it must meet the structural requirements of framing, and because it is also pressure-treated, each piece carries two separate quality stamps or tags, typical examples of which are illustrated below:

1. An inked grade mark conforming to the rules of the Southern Pine Inspection Bureau.

2. A stamp or tag conforming to the rules of the American Wood-Preservers' Association.

Building codes generally require the use of pressure-treated wood in the applications shown in the illustrations on the facing page.

Typical Southern Pine Lumber Grade Stamp

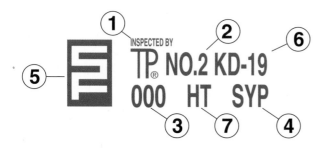

1 Inspection service: Timber Poducts Inspection, Inc. (TP)
2 Lumber grade
3 Mill identification number
4 Lumber species
5 Southern Forest Products Association logo (optional)
6 Moisture content: kiln dried (KD) to 19% maximum
7 Heat treated

Typical Quality Stamp for Treated Lumber

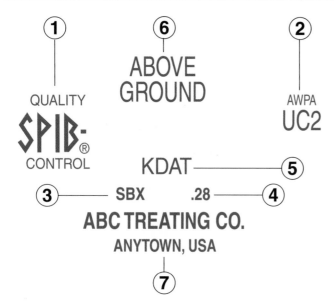

1 Trademark of inspection agency accredited by American Lumber Standard Committee (ALSC)
2 American Wood Preservers Association (AWPA) use category
3 Preservative used for treatment
4 Retention level
5 Dry or kild dried after treatment (KDAT)
6 Exposure category
7 Treating company and location

Applications Where Code Requires Pressure-Treated Wood

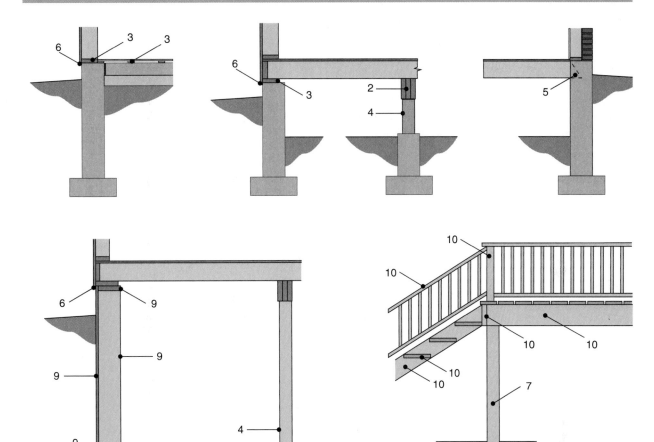

KEY:

1. wood embedded in, or in direct contact with, earth for support of permanent structures

2. floor joists less than 18 inches and girders less than 12 inches from the ground

3. foundation plates, sills, or sleepers on a masonry slab or foundation in earth contact

4. posts or columns placed direcly on masonry exposed to the weather, or in basements

5. ends of girders entering concrete or masonry walls without a ½-inch air space

6. wood in permanent structures and located less than 6 inches from earth

7. wood structural members supporting moisture-permeable floors or roofs exposed to the weather unless separated by an impervious moisture barrier

8. retaining walls (not illustrated)

9. all-weather wood foundations (see details in Chapter 4)

10. in hot and humid areas, structural supports of buildings, balconies, porches, etc., when exposed to the weather without protection from a roof, overhang, or other covering to prevent moisture accumulation

Framing

6

To make a human analogy, the frame of a building is its skeleton. To assure that this skeleton is strong enough, we need to specify how much weight it will support—the *building loads*. Knowing the loads and the design values (maximum allowable loads) for structural lumber, we can consult *span tables* to select the proper size joists and rafters.

Builders are increasingly turning to engineered-wood *I-joists* and *wood trusses*, so span tables for both are included here. Span tables are also given for *plank floors and roofs*, often used with the greater-than-usual joist and rafter spacing that results from timber framing. When loads become too large for ordinary lumber, you can turn to *glued laminated (glulam) beams, panel and lumber beams,* and even *steel beams*. This chapter includes simple span tables for all three.

The section on *timber framing* traces the origins of this revitalized art and illustrates the joinery that many find so beautiful. If you are remodeling an older home, you may be dealing with *balloon framing*. If your home is less than 50 years old, you will probably recognize its *platform framing*. If building a new home, you should consider the energy- and cost-efficiencies of *advanced (OVE) framing*.

Finally, we provide you with a checklist of *code requirements* relating to framing.

Building Loads

In this chapter we will consider the variety of forces acting on a building's frame. Understanding these forces (*loads* in building parlance), we can calculate the total load on an individual framing member. Being able to calculate loads is a powerful tool. It is the key that allows us to use span tables.

Building loads are the forces a building frame must support or resist. Building codes recognize five types of load:

- Dead—the weight of the building materials.
- Live—the weight due to occupancy; i.e., the weight of people, furnishings, and stored materials.
- Snow—the weight of snow on the roof.
- Wind—the force of the wind against exterior building surfaces, including the roof.
- Seismic—the force of the reaction of the building to the acceleration of the earth beneath.

Dead Loads

For a floor or roof, the dead load in pounds per square foot (psf) is found by adding the weights of the materials of which it is constructed using the table at right.

Example 1: A first floor framed with 2×8 joists, spaced 16 inches on-center, and covered with 5/8-inch plywood and wall-to-wall carpet weighs 2.2 psf + 1.8 psf + 0.6 psf = 4.6 psf.

Example 2: A second floor framed with 2×6 joists, spaced 16 inches on-center, with 1/2-inch drywall ceiling below and floored with 1/2-inch plywood and 3/4-inch hardwood above, weighs 1.7 psf + 2.2 psf + 1.5 psf + 3.0 psf = 8.4 psf.

Example 3: A roof with 2×8 joists 16 inches on-center, 6-inch fiberglass batts, 1/2-inch plywood sheathing, and asphalt shingles weighs 2.2 psf + 1.8 psf + 1.5 psf + 2.5 psf = 8.0 psf.

Weights of Building Materials

Component	Material	psf
Framing	2x4 @ 16" oc	1.1
	2x4 @ 24" oc.	0.7
	2x6 @ 16" oc	1.7
	2x6 @ 24" oc	1.1
	2x8 @ 16" oc	2.2
	2x8 @ 24" oc	1.5
	2x10 @ 16" oc	2.8
	2x10 @ 24" oc	1.9
Flooring	Softwood, per inch	3.0
	Hardwood, per inch	4.0
	1/2" Plywood	1.5
	5/8" Plywood	1.8
	3/4" Plywood	2.3
	1 1/8 " Plywood	3.4
	Sheet vinyl	1.5
	Carpet and pad	0.6
	3/4" Tile	10.0
	3/4" Gypcrete	6.5
	Concrete, per inch	12.0
	Stone, per inch	13.0
Ceiling	1/2" Drywall	2.2
	Plaster, per inch	8.0
	Acoustic tile	1.0
Roofing	Asphalt shingles	2.5
	Asphalt roll roofing	1.2
	Asphalt, built-up	6.0
	Wood shingles	3.0
	Wood shakes	6.0
	Roman tile	12.0
	Spanish tile	19.0
	Slate, 3/8"	12.0
	Steel	2.0
Insulation	Fiberglass wool, per inch	0.3
	Fiberglass board, per inch	1.5
	Foam, per inch	0.2

Live Loads

Minimum live load capacities are specified by building code. The table at right lists the IRC requirements for one- and two-family residential construction. The roof loads shown assume a maximum loaded area of 200 square feet per rafter.

Snow Loads

The snow load on a roof is taken over its horizontal projection; i.e., its span. It is thus the same as the ground snow load. The map below is simplified from the Ground Snow Load in the International Residential Code.

Important: if you live in one of the unshaded (mountainous) areas, consult your code official.

Live Loads (IRC)

Area	psf
Attics with storage	20
Attics without storage	10
Decks	40
Exterior balconies	60
Fire escapes	40
Passenger vehicle garages	50
Rooms other than sleeping rooms	40
Sleeping rooms	30
Stairs	40
Roof, rise < 4" per foot	20
rise 4"–12" per foot	16
rise >12" per foot	12

Ground Snow Loads, PSF

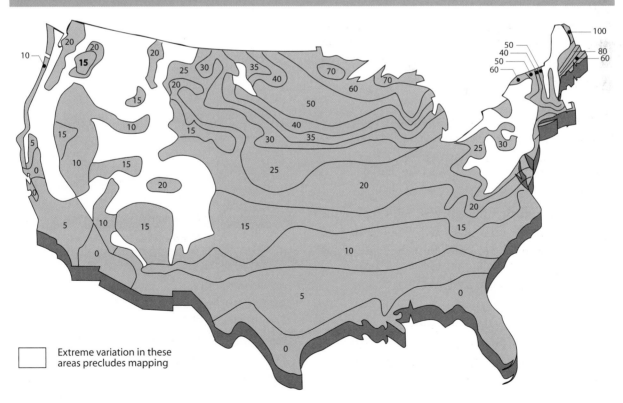

Extreme variation in these areas precludes mapping

Span Tables for U.S. Species

The span tables on pp. 127–147 are adapted from *The U.S. Span Book for Major Lumber Species.* The book, available from the Canadian Wood Council, was created in conformance with the procedures of U.S. grading and building authorities and with the design methods of the American Forest and Paper Association's *National Design Specification for Wood Construction.*

The book provides a convenient reference for the common species of U.S. and Canadian dimension lumber, fully in accord with U.S. building codes and Federal Housing Administration (FHA) requirements. It is important to note, however, that the tables apply only to construction in the United States.

Online Span Calculator

For those who prefer computers to books, the Canadian Wood Council offers a handy on-line span calculator. The free and user-friendly calculator allows even more dead-and-live load combinations than contained in this book. To access *SpanCalc*, go to: *www.twperry.com/spancalc/index.html.*

Allowable Span

The allowable span is the maximum clear horizontal distance between supports. For horizontal members such as joists, the clear span is the actual length between supports (see illustration at right). For sloping members such as roof rafters, a factor must be applied to the horizontal rafter span to determine the actual clear length or sloping distance. The table at right provides a method for converting horizontal span to sloping distance, and vice versa.

Spans are based on the use of lumber in dry conditions, as in most covered structures. They have been calculated using strength and stiffness values adjusted for size, repetitive member use, and appropriate duration of load.

Allowable spans in some cases (e.g., ceiling joists) may exceed available lengths. Availability should be confirmed before specification for a project.

Definition of Span

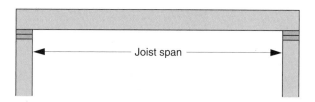

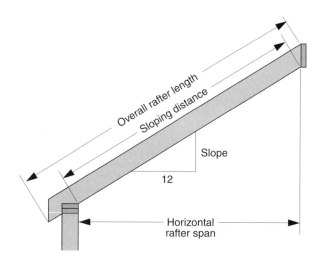

Conversion Factors for Rafters

Slope in 12	Slope Factor	Slope in 12	Slope Factor
1	1.003	13	1.474
2	1.014	14	1.537
3	1.031	15	1.601
4	1.054	16	1.667
5	1.083	17	1.734
6	1.118	18	1.803
7	1.158	19	1.873
8	1.202	20	1.944
9	1.250	21	2.016
10	1.302	22	2.088
11	1.357	23	2.162
12	1.414	24	2.236

Floor Joists

Sleeping Rooms and Attics: 30 PSF Live, 10 PSF Dead

Species Group	Spacing in oc	2 x 6 Sel Str	2 x 6 No.1	2 x 6 No.2	2 x 6 No.3	2 x 8 Sel Str	2 x 8 No.1	2 x 8 No.2	2 x 8 No.3	2 x 10 Sel Str	2 x 10 No.1	2 x 10 No.2	2 x 10 No.3	2 x 12 Sel Str	2 x 12 No.1	2 x 12 No.2	2 x 12 No.3
Douglas fir-larch	12	12-6	12-0	11-10	9-11	16-6	15-10	15-7	12-7	21-0	20-3	19-10	15-5	25-7	24-8	23-4	17-10
	16	11-4	10-11	10-9	8-7	15-0	14-5	14-2	10-11	19-1	18-5	17-5	13-4	23-3	21-4	20-3	15-5
	19.2	10-8	10-4	10-1	7-10	14-1	13-7	13-0	10-0	18-0	16-9	15-11	12-2	21-10	19-6	18-6	14-1
	24	9-11	9-7	9-3	7-0	13-1	12-4	11-8	8-11	16-8	15-0	14-3	10-11	20-3	17-5	16-6	12-7
Hem-fir	12	11-10	11-7	11-0	9-8	15-7	15-3	14-6	12-4	19-10	19-5	18-6	15-0	24-2	23-7	22-6	17-5
	16	10-9	10-6	10-0	8-5	14-2	13-10	13-2	10-8	18-0	17-8	16-10	13-0	21-11	21-1	19-8	15-1
	19.2	10-1	9-10	9-5	7-8	13-4	13-0	12-5	9-9	17-0	16-7	15-6	11-10	20-8	19-3	17-11	13-9
	24	9-4	9-2	8-9	6-10	12-4	12-1	11-4	8-8	15-9	14-10	13-10	10-7	19-2	17-2	16-1	12-4
Southern pine	12	12-3	12-0	11-10	10-5	16-2	15-10	15-7	13-3	20-8	20-3	19-10	15-8	25-1	24-8	24-2	18-8
	16	11-2	10-11	10-9	9-0	14-8	14-5	14-2	11-6	18-9	18-5	18-0	13-7	22-10	22-5	21-1	16-2
	19.2	10-6	10-4	10-1	8-3	13-10	13-7	13-4	10-6	17-8	17-4	16-5	12-5	21-6	21-1	19-3	14-9
	24	9-9	9-7	9-4	7-4	12-10	12-7	12-4	9-5	16-5	16-1	14-8	11-1	19-11	19-6	17-2	13-2

Maximum Allowable Span (feet-inches)

All Rooms Except Sleeping Rooms and Attics: 40 PSF Live, 10 PSF Dead

Species Group	Spacing in oc	2 x 6 Sel Str	2 x 6 No.1	2 x 6 No.2	2 x 6 No.3	2 x 8 Sel Str	2 x 8 No.1	2 x 8 No.2	2 x 8 No.3	2 x 10 Sel Str	2 x 10 No.1	2 x 10 No.2	2 x 10 No.3	2 x 12 Sel Str	2 x 12 No.1	2 x 12 No.2	2 x 12 No.3
Douglas fir-larch	12	11-4	10-11	10-9	8-11	15-0	14-5	14-2	11-3	19-1	18-5	18-0	13-9	23-3	22-0	20-11	16-0
	16	10-4	9-11	9-9	7-8	13-7	13-1	12-9	9-9	17-4	16-5	15-7	11-11	21-1	19-1	18-1	13-10
	19.2	9-8	9-4	9-2	7-0	12-10	12-4	11-8	8-11	16-4	15-0	14-3	10-11	19-10	17-5	16-6	12-7
	24	9-0	8-8	8-3	6-3	11-11	11-0	10-5	8-0	15-2	13-5	12-9	9-9	18-5	15-7	14-9	11-3
Hem-fir	12	10-9	10-6	10-0	8-8	14-2	13-10	13-2	11-0	18-0	17-8	16-10	13-5	21-11	21-6	20-4	15-7
	16	9-9	9-6	9-1	7-6	12-10	12-7	12-0	9-6	16-5	16-0	15-2	11-8	19-11	18-10	17-7	13-6
	19.2	9-2	9-0	8-7	6-10	12-1	11-10	11-3	8-8	15-5	14-10	13-10	10-7	18-9	17-2	16-1	12-4
	24	8-6	8-4	7-11	6-2	11-3	10-10	10-2	7-9	14-4	13-3	12-5	9-6	17-5	15-5	14-4	11-0
Southern pine	12	11-2	10-11	10-9	9-4	14-8	14-5	14-2	11-11	18-9	18-5	18-0	14-0	22-10	22-5	21-9	16-8
	16	10-2	9-11	9-9	8-1	13-4	13-1	12-10	10-3	17-0	16-9	16-1	12-2	20-9	20-4	18-10	14-6
	19.2	9-6	9-4	9-2	7-4	12-7	12-4	12-1	9-5	16-0	15-9	14-8	11-1	19-6	19-2	17-2	13-2
	24	8-10	8-8	8-6	6-7	11-8	11-5	11-0	8-5	14-11	14-7	13-1	9-11	18-1	17-5	15-5	11-10

Maximum Allowable Span (feet-inches)

Ceiling Joists

Drywall—No Future Rooms and No Attic Storage: 10 PSF Live, 5 PSF Dead

		Maximum Allowable Span (feet-inches)															
		2 x 4				2 x 6				2 x 8				2 x 10			
Species Group	Spacing in oc	Sel Str	No.1	GRADE No.2	No.3	Sel Str	No.1	GRADE No.2	No.3	Sel Str	No.1	GRADE No.2	No.3	Sel Str	No.1	GRADE No.2	No.3
Douglas fir-larch	12	13-2	12-8	12-5	11-1	20-8	19-11	19-6	16-3	27-2	26-2	25-8	20-7	34-8	33-5	32-9	25-2
	16	11-11	11-6	11-3	9-7	18-9	18-1	17-8	14-1	24-8	23-10	23-4	17-10	31-6	30-0	28-6	21-9
	19.2	11-3	10-10	10-7	8-9	17-8	17-0	16-8	12-10	23-3	22-5	21-4	16-3	29-8	27-5	26-0	19-10
	24	10-5	10-0	9-10	7-10	16-4	15-9	15-0	11-6	21-7	20-1	19-1	14-7	27-6	24-6	23-3	17-9
Hem-fir	12	12-5	12-2	11-7	10-10	19-6	19-1	18-2	15-10	25-8	25-2	24-0	20-1	32-9	32-1	30-7	24-6
	16	11-3	11-0	10-6	9-5	17-8	17-4	16-6	13-9	23-4	22-10	21-9	17-5	29-9	29-2	27-8	21-3
	19.2	10-7	10-4	9-11	8-7	16-8	16-4	15-7	12-6	21-11	21-6	20-6	15-10	28-0	27-1	25-3	19-5
	24	9-10	9-8	9-2	7-8	15-6	15-2	14-5	11-2	20-5	19-10	18-6	14-2	26-0	24-3	22-7	17-4
Southern pine	12	12-11	12-8	12-5	11-6	20-3	19-11	19-6	17-0	26-9	26-2	25-8	21-8	34-1	33-5	32-9	25-7
	16	11-9	11-6	11-3	10-0	18-5	18-1	17-8	14-9	24-3	23-10	23-4	18-9	31-0	30-5	29-4	22-2
	19.2	11-0	10-10	10-7	9-1	17-4	17-0	16-8	13-6	22-10	22-5	21-11	17-2	29-2	28-7	26-10	20-3
	24	10-3	10-0	9-10	8-2	16-1	15-9	15-6	12-0	21-2	20-10	20-1	15-4	27-1	26-6	23-11	18-1

Drywall—No Future Rooms and Limited Attic Storage: 20 PSF Live, 10 PSF Dead

		Maximum Allowable Span (feet-inches)															
		2 x 4				2 x 6				2 x 8				2 x 10			
Species Group	Spacing in oc	Sel Str	No.1	GRADE No.2	No.3	Sel Str	No.1	GRADE No.2	No.3	Sel Str	No.1	GRADE No.2	No.3	Sel Str	No.1	GRADE No.2	No.3
Douglas fir-larch	12	10-5	10-0	9-10	7-10	16-4	15-9	15-0	11-6	21-7	20-1	19-1	14-7	27-6	24-6	23-3	17-9
	16	9-6	9-1	8-11	6-10	14-11	13-9	13-0	9-11	19-7	17-5	16-6	12-7	25-0	21-3	20-2	15-5
	19.2	8-11	8-7	8-2	6-2	14-0	12-6	11-11	9-1	18-5	15-10	15-1	11-6	23-7	19-5	18-5	14-1
	24	8-3	7-8	7-3	5-7	13-0	11-2	10-8	8-1	17-2	14-2	13-6	10-3	21-3	17-4	16-5	12-7
Hem-fir	12	9-10	9-8	9-2	7-8	15-6	15-2	14-5	11-2	20-5	19-10	18-6	14-2	26-0	24-3	22-7	17-4
	16	8-11	8-9	8-4	6-8	14-1	13-7	12-8	9-8	18-6	17-2	16.0	12-4	23-8	21-0	19-7	15-0
	19.2	8-5	8-3	7-10	6-1	13-3	12-4	11-7	8-10	17-5	15-8	14-8	11-3	22-3	19-2	17-10	13-8
	24	7-10	7-7	7-1	5-5	12-3	11-1	10-4	7-11	16-2	14-0	13-1	10-0	20-6	17-1	16-0	12-3
Southern pine	12	10-3	10-0	9-10	8-2	16-1	15-9	15-6	12-0	21-2	20-10	20-1	15-4	27-1	26-6	23-11	18-1
	16	9-4	9-1	8-11	7-1	14-7	14-4	13-6	10-5	19-3	18-11	17-5	13-3	24-7	23-1	20-9	15-8
	19.2	8-9	8-7	8-5	6-5	13-9	13-6	12-3	9-6	18-2	17-9	15-10	12-1	23-2	21-1	18-11	14-4
	24	8-1	8-0	7-8	5-9	12-9	12-6	11-0	8-6	16-10	15-10	14-2	10-10	21-6	18-10	16-11	12-10

Rafters

Snow Region, Light Roof, Drywall, No Attic Space: 20 PSF Live, 10 PSF Dead

Species Group	Spacing in oc	2 x 6 Sel Str	2 x 6 GRADE No.1	No.2	No.3	2 x 8 Sel Str	2 x 8 GRADE No.1	No.2	No.3	2 x 10 Sel Str	2 x 10 GRADE No.1	No.2	No.3	2 x 12 Sel Str	2 x 12 GRADE No.1	No.2	No.3
								Maximum Allowable Span (feet-inches)									
Douglas fir-larch	12	16-4	15-9	15-6	12-4	21-7	20-10	20-5	15-7	27-6	26-4	24-11	19-1	33-6	30-6	28-11	22-1
	16	14-11	14-4	14-0	10-8	19-7	18-8	17-8	13-6	25-0	22-9	21-7	16-6	30-5	26-5	25-1	19-2
	19.2	14-0	13-5	12-9	9-9	18-5	17-0	16-2	12-4	23-7	20-9	19-9	15-1	28-8	24-1	22-10	17-6
	24	13-0	12-0	11-5	8-9	17-2	15-3	14-5	11-0	21-10	18-7	17-8	13-6	26-5	21-7	20-5	15-7
Hem-fir	12	15-6	15-2	14-5	12-0	20-5	19-11	19-0	15-3	26-0	25-5	24-3	18-7	31-8	30-1	28-1	21-7
	16	14-1	13-9	13-1	10-5	18-6	18-2	17-2	13-2	23-8	22-6	21-0	16-1	28-9	26-1	24-4	18-8
	19.2	13-3	12-11	12-4	9-6	17-5	16-10	15-8	12-0	22-3	20-6	19-2	14-8	27-1	23-10	22-3	17-1
	24	12-3	11-10	11-1	8-6	16-2	15-0	14-0	10-9	20-8	18-4	17-2	13-2	25-1	21-3	19-11	15-3
Southern pine	12	16-1	15-9	15-6	12-11	21-2	20-10	20-5	16-5	27-1	26-6	25-8	19-5	32-11	32-3	30-1	23-1
	16	14-7	14-4	14-1	11-2	19-3	18-11	18-6	14-3	24-7	24-1	22-3	19-10	29-11	29-4	26-1	20-0
	19.2	13-9	13-6	13-2	10-2	18-2	17-9	17-0	13-0	23-2	22-7	20-4	15-4	28-1	26-11	23-10	18-3
	24	12-9	12-6	11-9	9-2	16-10	16-6	15-3	11-8	21-6	20-3	18-2	13-9	26-1	24-1	21-3	16-4

Snow Region, Light Roof, Drywall, No Attic Space: 30 PSF Live, 10 PSF Dead

Species Group	Spacing in oc	2 x 6 Sel Str	2 x 6 GRADE No.1	No.2	No.3	2 x 8 Sel Str	2 x 8 GRADE No.1	No.2	No.3	2 x 10 Sel Str	2 x 10 GRADE No.1	No.2	No.3	2 x 12 Sel Str	2 x 12 GRADE No.1	No.2	No.3
								Maximum Allowable Span (feet-inches)									
Douglas fir-larch	12	14-4	13-9	13-6	10-8	18-10	18-2	17-8	13-6	24-1	22-9	21-7	16-6	29-3	26-5	25-1	19-2
	16	13-0	12-6	12-1	9-3	17-2	16-2	15-4	11-8	21-10	19-9	18-9	14-3	26-7	22-10	21-8	16-7
	19.2	12-3	11-8	11-0	8-5	16-1	14-9	14-0	10-8	20-7	18-0	17-1	13-1	25-0	20-11	19-10	15-2
	24	11-4	10-5	9-10	7-7	15-0	13-2	12-6	9-7	19-1	16-1	15-3	11-8	22-10	18-8	17-9	13-6
Hem-fir	12	13-6	13-3	12-7	10-5	17-10	17-5	16-7	13-2	22-9	22-3	21-0	16-1	27-8	26-1	24-4	18-8
	16	12-3	12-0	11-5	9-0	16-2	15-10	14-11	11-5	20-8	19-6	18-2	13-11	25-1	22-7	21-1	16-2
	19.2	11-7	11-4	10-9	8-3	15-3	14-7	13-7	10-5	19-5	17-9	16-7	12-9	23-7	20-7	19-3	14-9
	24	10-3	10-3	9-7	7-4	14-2	13-0	12-2	9-4	18-0	15-11	14-10	11-5	21-11	18-5	17-3	13-2
Southern pine	12	14-1	13-9	13-6	11-2	18-6	18-2	17-10	14-3	23-8	23-2	22-3	16-10	28-9	28-2	26-1	20-0
	16	12-9	12-6	12-3	9-8	16-10	16-6	16-2	12-4	21-6	21-1	19-3	14-7	26-1	25-7	22-7	17-4
	19.2	12-0	11-9	11-5	8-10	15-10	15-6	14-9	11-3	20-2	19-7	17-7	13-4	24-7	23-4	20-7	15-10
	24	11-2	10-11	10-2	7-11	14-8	14-5	13-2	10-1	18-9	17-6	15-9	11-11	22-10	20-11	18-5	14-2

Rafters

Snow Region, Light Roof, Drywall, No Attic Space: 40 PSF Live, 10 PSF Dead

| | | Maximum Allowable Span (feet-inches) | | | | | | | | | | | | | | | |
| | | 2 x 6 | | | | 2 x 8 | | | | 2 x 10 | | | | 2 x 12 | | | |
Species Group	Spacing in oc	Sel Str	No.1	No.2	No.3	Sel Str	No.1	No.2	No.3	Sel Str	No.1	No.2	No.3	Sel Str	No.1	No.2	No.3
Douglas fir-larch	12	13-2	12-6	12-3	9-6	17-2	16-6	15-10	12-1	21-10	20-4	19-4	14-9	26-7	23-7	22-5	17-1
	16	11-10	11-5	10-10	8-3	15-7	14-5	13-8	10-6	19-10	17-8	16-9	12-9	24-2	20-5	19-5	14-10
	19.2	11-1	10-5	9-10	7-7	14-8	13-2	12-6	9-7	18-8	16-1	15-3	11-8	22-9	18-8	17-9	13-6
	24	10-4	9-4	8-10	6-9	13-7	11-9	11-2	8-7	17-4	14-5	13-8	10-5	20-5	16-8	15-10	12-1
Hem-fir	12	12-3	12-0	11-5	9-4	16-2	15-10	15-1	11-9	20-8	20-1	18-9	14-5	25-1	23-4	21-9	16-8
	16	11-2	10-11	10-5	8-1	14-8	14-3	13-4	10-3	18-9	17-5	16-3	12-6	22-10	20-2	18-10	14-6
	19.2	10-6	10-3	9-7	7-4	13-10	13-0	12-2	9-4	17-8	15-11	14-10	11-5	21-6	18-5	17-3	13-2
	24	9-9	9-2	8-7	6-7	12-10	11-8	10-10	8-4	16-5	14-3	13-3	10-2	19-9	16-6	15-5	11-10
Southern pine	12	12-9	12-6	12-3	10-0	16-10	16-6	16-2	12-9	21-6	21-1	19-11	15-1	26-1	25-7	23-4	17-11
	16	11-7	11-5	11-2	8-8	15-3	15-0	14-5	11-0	19-6	19-2	17-3	13-0	23-9	22-10	20-2	15-6
	19.2	10-11	10-8	10-2	7-11	14-5	14-1	13-2	10-1	18-4	17-6	15-9	11-11	22-4	20-11	18-5	14-2
	24	10-2	9-11	9-2	7-1	13-4	13-1	11-9	9-0	17-0	15-8	14-1	10-8	20-9	18-8	16-6	12-8

Snow Region, Light Roof, Drywall, No Attic Space: 50 PSF Live, 10 PSF Dead

| | | Maximum Allowable Span (feet-inches) | | | | | | | | | | | | | | | |
| | | 2 x 6 | | | | 2 x 8 | | | | 2 x 10 | | | | 2 x 12 | | | |
Species Group	Spacing in oc	Sel Str	No.1	No.2	No.3	Sel Str	No.1	No.2	No.3	Sel Str	No.1	No.2	No.3	Sel Str	No.1	No.2	No.3
Douglas fir-larch	12	12-1	11-8	11-5	8-9	15-11	15-3	14-5	11-0	20-3	18-7	17-8	13-6	24-8	21-7	20-5	15-7
	16	11-0	10-5	9-10	7-7	14-5	13-2	12-6	9-7	18-5	16-1	15-3	11-8	22-5	18-8	17-9	13-6
	19.2	10-4	9-6	9-0	6-11	13-7	12-0	11-5	8-9	17-4	14-8	13-11	10-8	20-11	17-1	16-2	12-4
	24	9-7	8-6	8-1	6-2	12-7	10-9	10-3	7-10	16-1	13-2	12-6	9-6	18-8	15-3	14-6	11-1
Hem-fir	11-5	11-5	11-2	10-8	8-6	15-0	14-8	14-0	10-9	19-2	18-4	17-2	13-2	23-4	21-3	19-11	15-3
	16	10-4	10-2	9-7	7-4	13-8	13-0	12-2	9-4	17-5	15-11	14-10	11-5	21-2	18-5	17-3	13-2
	19.2	9-9	9-5	8-9	6-9	12-10	11-11	11-1	8-6	16-5	14-6	13-7	10-5	19-11	16-10	15-9	12-1
	24	9-1	8-5	7-10	6-0	11-11	10-8	9-11	7-7	15-2	13-0	12-1	9-4	18-0	15-1	14-1	10-9
Southern pine	12	11-10	11-8	11-5	9-2	15-7	15-4	15-0	11-8	19-11	19-7	18-2	13-9	24-3	23-9	21-3	16-4
	16	10-9	10-7	10-2	7-11	14-2	13-11	13-2	10-1	18-1	17-6	15-9	11-11	22-0	20-11	18-5	14-2
	19.2	10-2	9-11	9-4	7-3	13-4	13-1	12-0	9-2	17-0	16-0	14-4	10-10	20-9	19-1	16-10	12-11
	24	9-5	9-3	8-4	6-5	12-5	12-0	10-9	8-3	15-10	14-4	12-10	9-9	19-3	17-1	15-1	11-7

Rafters

Snow Region, Heavy Roof, Drywall, No Attic Space: 20 PSF Live, 20 PSF Dead

Species Group	Spacing in oc	2 x 6 Sel Str	No.1	No.2	No.3	2 x 8 Sel Str	No.1	No.2	No.3	2 x 10 Sel Str	No.1	No.2	No.3	2 x 12 Sel Str	No.1	No.2	No.3
Douglas fir-larch	12	16-4	14-9	14-0	10-8	21-7	18-8	17-8	13-6	27-6	22-9	21-7	16-6	32-4	26-5	25-1	19-2
	16	14-11	12-9	12-1	9-3	19-7	16-2	15-4	11-8	24-2	19-9	18-9	14-3	28-0	22-10	21-8	16-7
	19.2	14-0	11-8	11-0	8-5	18-1	14-9	14-0	10-8	22-1	18-0	17-1	13-1	25-7	20-11	19-10	15-2
	24	12-9	10-5	9-10	7-7	16-2	13-2	12-6	9-7	19-9	16-1	15-3	11-8	22-10	18-8	17-9	13-6
Hem-fir	12	15-6	14-6	13-7	10-5	20-5	18-5	17-2	13-2	26-0	22-6	21-0	16-1	31-3	26-1	24-4	18-8
	16	14-1	12-7	11-9	9-0	18-6	15-11	14-11	11-5	23-4	19-6	18-2	13-11	27-1	22-7	21-1	16-2
	19.2	13-3	11-6	10-9	8-3	17-5	14-7	13-7	10-5	21-4	17-9	16-7	12-9	24-8	20-7	19-3	14-9
	24	12-3	10-3	9-7	7-4	15-7	13-0	12-2	9-4	19-1	15-11	14-10	11-5	22-1	18-5	17-3	13-2
Southern pine	12	16-1	15-9	14-5	11-2	21-2	20-10	18-8	14-3	27-1	24-9	22-3	16-10	32-11	29-6	26-1	20-0
	16	14-7	14-4	12-6	9-8	19-3	18-1	16-2	12-4	24-7	21-5	19-3	14-7	29-11	25-7	22-7	17-4
	19.2	13-9	13-1	11-5	8-10	18-2	16-6	14-9	11-3	23-2	19-7	17-7	13-4	28-1	23-4	20-7	15-10
	24	12-9	11-9	10-2	7-11	16-10	14-9	13-2	10-1	21-6	17-6	15-9	11-11	25-9	20-11	18-5	14-2

Maximum Allowable Span (feet-inches)

Snow Region, Heavy Roof, Drywall, No Attic Space: 30 PSF Live, 20 PSF Dead

Species Group	Spacing in oc	2 x 6 Sel Str	No.1	No.2	No.3	2 x 8 Sel Str	No.1	No.2	No.3	2 x 10 Sel Str	No.1	No.2	No.3	2 x 12 Sel Str	No.1	No.2	No.3
Douglas fir-larch	12	14-4	13-2	12-6	9-6	18-10	16-8	15-10	12-1	24-1	20-4	19-4	14-9	28-11	23-7	22-5	17-1
	16	13-0	11-5	10-10	8-3	17-2	14-5	13-8	10-6	21-7	17-8	16-9	12-9	25-1	20-5	19-5	14-10
	19.2	12-3	10-5	9-10	7-7	16-1	13-2	12-6	9-7	19-9	16-1	15-3	11-8	22-10	18-8	17-9	13-6
	24	11-4	9-4	8-10	6-9	14-5	11-9	11-2	8-7	17-8	14-5	13-8	10-5	20-5	16-8	15-10	12-1
Hem-fir	12	13-6	13-0	12-2	9-4	17-10	16-6	15-4	11-9	22-9	20-1	18-9	14-5	27-8	23-4	21-9	16-8
	16	12-3	11-3	10-6	8-1	16-2	14-3	13-4	10-3	20-8	17-5	16-3	12-6	24-2	20-2	18-10	14-6
	19.2	11-7	10-3	9-7	7-4	15-3	13-0	12-2	9-4	19-1	15-11	14-10	11-5	22-1	18-5	17-3	13-2
	24	10-9	9-2	8-7	6-7	13-11	11-8	10-10	8-4	17-1	14-3	13-3	10-2	19-9	16-6	15-5	11-10
Southern pine	12	14-1	13-9	12-11	10-0	18-6	18-2	16-8	12-9	23-8	22-2	19-11	15-1	28-9	26-5	23-4	17-11
	16	12-9	12-6	11-2	8-8	16-10	16-2	14-5	11-0	21-6	19-2	17-3	13-0	26-1	22-10	20-2	15-6
	19.2	12-0	11-9	10-2	7-11	15-10	14-9	13-2	10-1	20-2	17-6	15-9	11-11	24-7	20-11	18-5	14-2
	24	11-2	10-6	9-2	7-1	14-8	13-2	11-9	9-0	18-9	15-8	14-1	10-8	22-10	18-8	16-6	12-8

Maximum Allowable Span (feet-inches)

Rafters

Snow Region, Light Roof, No Ceiling, 20 PSF Live, 10 PSF Dead

		Maximum Allowable Span (feet-inches)															
		2 x 4				2 x 6				2 x 8				2 x 10			
Species Group	Spacing in oc	Sel Str	No.1	GRADE No.2	No.3	Sel Str	No.1	GRADE No.2	No.3	Sel Str	No.1	GRADE No.2	No.3	Sel Str	No.1	GRADE No.2	No.3
Douglas fir-larch	12	11-6	11-1	10-10	8-5	18-0	17-0	16-2	12-4	23-9	21-6	20-5	15-7	30-4	26-4	24-11	19-1
	16	10-5	10-0	9-7	7-3	16-4	14-9	14-0	10-8	21-7	18-8	17-8	13-6	27-6	22-9	21-7	16-6
	19.2	9-10	9-2	8-9	6-8	15-5	13-5	12-9	9-9	20-4	17-0	16-2	12-4	25-6	20-9	19-9	15-1
	24	9-1	8-3	7-10	5-11	14-4	12-0	11-5	8-9	18-8	15-3	14-5	11-0	22-9	18-7	17-8	13-6
Hem-fir	12	10-10	10-7	10-1	8-3	17-0	16-8	15-8	12-0	22-5	21-3	19-10	15-3	28-7	26-0	24-3	18-7
	16	9-10	9-8	9-2	7-1	15-6	14-6	13-7	10-5	20-5	18-5	17-2	13-2	26-0	22-6	21-0	16-1
	19.2	9-3	9-1	8-6	6-6	14-7	13-3	12-5	9-6	19-2	16-10	15-8	12-0	24-6	20-6	19-2	14-8
	24	8-7	8-1	7-7	5-10	13-6	11-10	11-1	8-6	17-10	15-0	14-0	10-9	22-0	18-4	17-2	13-2
Southern pine	12	11-3	11-1	10-10	8-9	17-8	17-4	16-8	12-11	23-4	22-11	21-6	16-5	29-9	28-7	25-8	19-5
	16	10-3	10-0	9-10	7-7	16-1	15-9	14-5	11-2	21-2	20-10	18-8	14-3	27-1	24-9	22-3	16-10
	19.2	9-8	9-5	9-2	6-11	15-2	14-10	13-2	10-2	19-11	19-0	17-0	13-0	25-5	22-7	20-4	15-4
	24	8-11	8-9	8-2	6-2	14-1	13-6	11-9	9-2	18-6	17-0	15-3	11-8	23-8	20-3	18-2	13-9

Snow Region, Light Roof, No Ceiling: 30 PSF Live, 10 PSF Dead

		Maximum Allowable Span (feet-inches)															
		2 x 4				2 x 6				2 x 8				2 x 10			
Species Group	Spacing in oc	Sel Str	No.1	GRADE No.2	No.3	Sel Str	No.1	GRADE No.2	No.3	Sel Str	No.1	GRADE No.2	No.3	Sel Str	No.1	GRADE No.2	No.3
Douglas fir-larch	12	10-0	9-8	9-6	7-3	15-9	14-9	14-0	10-8	20-9	18-8	17-8	13-6	26-6	22-9	21-7	16-6
	16	9-1	8-9	8-3	6-4	14-4	12-9	12-1	9-3	18-10	16-2	15-4	11-8	24-1	19-9	18-9	14-3
	19.2	8-7	7-11	7-7	5-9	13-6	11-8	11-0	8-5	17-9	14-9	14-0	10-8	22-1	18-0	17-1	13-1
	24	7-11	7-1	6-9	5-2	12-6	10-5	9-10	7-7	16-2	13-2	12-6	9-7	19-9	16-1	15-3	11-8
Hem-fir	12	9-6	9-3	8-10	7-1	14-10	14-6	13-7	10-5	19-7	18-5	17-2	13-2	25-0	22-6	21-0	16-1
	16	8-7	8-5	8-0	6-2	13-6	12-7	11-9	9-0	17-10	15-11	14-11	11-5	22-9	19-6	18-2	13-11
	19.2	8-1	7-10	7-4	5-8	12-9	11-6	10-9	8-3	16-9	14-7	13-7	10-5	21-4	17-9	16-7	12-9
	24	7-6	7-0	6-7	5-0	11-10	10-3	9-7	7-4	15-7	13-0	12-2	9-4	19-1	15-11	14-10	11-5
Southern pine	12	9-10	9-8	9-6	7-7	15-6	15-2	14-5	11-2	20-5	20-0	18-8	14-3	26-0	24-9	22-3	16-10
	16	8-11	8-9	8-7	6-7	14-1	13-9	12-6	9-8	18-6	18-0	16-2	12-4	23-8	21-5	19-3	14-7
	19.2	8-5	8-3	7-11	6-0	13-3	13-0	11-5	8-10	17-5	16-6	14-9	11-3	22-3	19-7	17-7	13-4
	24	7-10	7-8	7-1	5-4	12-3	11-9	10-2	7-11	16-2	14-9	13-2	10-1	20-8	17-6	15-9	11-11

Rafters

Snow Region, Light Roof, No Ceiling: 40 PSF Live, 10 PSF Dead

| | | Maximum Allowable Span (feet-inches) | | | | | | | | | | | | | | | |
| | | 2 x 4 | | | | 2 x 6 | | | | 2 x 8 | | | | 2 x 10 | | | |
Species Group	Spacing in oc	Sel Str	No.1	No.2	No.3	Sel Str	No.1	No.2	No.3	Sel Str	No.1	No.2	No.3	Sel Str	No.1	No.2	No.3
Douglas fir-larch	12	9-1	8-9	8-6	6-6	14-4	13-2	12-6	9-6	18-10	16-8	15-10	12-1	24-1	20-4	19-4	14-9
	16	8-3	7-10	7-5	5-8	13-0	11-5	10-10	8-3	17-2	14-5	13-8	10-6	21-7	17-8	16-9	12-9
	19.2	7-9	7-1	6-9	5-2	12-3	10-5	9-10	7-7	16-1	13-2	12-6	9-7	19-9	16-1	15-3	11-8
	24	7-3	6-4	6-0	4-7	11-4	9-4	8-10	6-9	14-5	11-9	11-2	8-7	17-8	14-5	13-8	10-5
Hem-fir	12	8-7	8-5	8-0	6-4	13-6	13-0	12-2	9-4	17-10	16-6	15-4	11-9	22-9	20-1	18-9	14-5
	16	7-10	7-8	7-2	5-6	12-3	11-3	10-6	8-1	16-2	14-3	13-4	10-3	20-8	17-5	16-3	12-6
	19.2	7-4	7-0	6-7	5-0	11-7	10-3	9-7	7-4	15-3	13-0	12-2	9-4	19-1	15-11	14-10	11-5
	24	6-10	6-3	5-10	4-6	10-9	9-2	8-7	6-7	13-11	11-8	10-10	8-4	17-1	14-3	13-3	10-2
Southern pine	12	8-11	8-9	8-7	6-9	14-1	13-9	12-11	10-0	18-6	18-2	16-8	12-9	23-8	22-2	19-11	15-1
	16	8-1	8-0	7-10	5-10	12-9	12-6	11-2	8-8	16-10	16-2	14-5	11-0	21-6	19-2	17-3	13-0
	19.2	7-8	7-6	7-1	5-4	12-0	11-9	10-2	7-11	15-10	14-9	13-2	10-1	20-2	17-6	15-9	11-11
	24	7-1	7-0	6-4	4-9	11-2	10-6	9-2	7-1	14-8	13-2	11-9	9-0	18-9	15-8	14-1	10-8

Snow Region, Light Roof, No Ceiling: 30 PSF Live, 10 PSF Dead

| | | Maximum Allowable Span (feet-inches) | | | | | | | | | | | | | | | |
| | | 2 x 4 | | | | 2 x 6 | | | | 2 x 8 | | | | 2 x 10 | | | |
Species Group	Spacing in oc	Sel Str	No.1	No.2	No.3	Sel Str	No.1	No.2	No.3	Sel Str	No.1	No.2	No.3	Sel Str	No.1	No.2	No.3
Douglas fir-larch	12	10-0	9-8	9-6	7-3	15-9	14-9	14-0	10-8	20-9	18-8	17-8	13-6	26-6	22-9	21-7	16-6
	16	9-1	8-9	8-3	6-4	14-4	12-9	12-1	9-3	18-10	16-2	15-4	11-8	24-1	19-9	18-9	14-3
	19.2	8-7	7-11	7-7	5-9	13-6	11-8	11-0	8-5	17-9	14-9	14-0	10-8	22-1	18-0	17-1	13-1
	24	7-11	7-1	6-9	5-2	12-6	10-5	9-10	7-7	16-2	13-2	12-6	9-7	19-9	16-1	15-3	11-8
Hem-fir	12	9-6	9-3	8-10	7-1	14-10	14-6	13-7	10-5	19-7	18-5	17-2	13-2	25-0	22-6	21-0	16-1
	16	8-7	8-5	8-0	6-2	13-6	12-7	11-9	9-0	17-10	15-11	14-11	11-5	22-9	19-6	18-2	13-11
	19.2	8-1	7-10	7-4	5-8	12-9	11-6	10-9	8-3	16-9	14-7	13-7	10-5	21-4	17-9	16-7	12-9
	24	7-6	7-0	6-7	5-0	11-10	10-3	9-7	7-4	15-7	13-0	12-2	9-4	19-1	15-11	14-10	11-5
Southern pine	12	9-10	9-8	9-6	7-7	15-6	15-2	14-5	11-2	20-5	20-0	18-8	14-3	26-0	24-9	22-3	16-10
	16	8-11	8-9	8-7	6-7	14-1	13-9	12-6	9-8	18-6	18-0	16-2	12-4	23-8	21-5	19-3	14-7
	19.2	8-5	8-3	7-11	6-0	13-3	13-0	11-5	8-10	17-5	16-6	14-9	11-3	22-3	19-7	17-7	13-4
	24	7-10	7-8	7-1	5-4	12-3	11-9	10-2	7-11	16-2	14-9	13-2	10-1	20-8	17-6	15-9	11-11

Rafters

Snow Region, Heavy Roof, No Ceiling: 20 PSF Live, 20 PSF Dead

Species Group	Spacing in oc	2 x 4 Sel Str	GRADE No.1	No.2	No.3	2 x 6 Sel Str	GRADE No.1	No.2	No.3	2 x 8 Sel Str	GRADE No.1	No.2	No.3	2 x 10 Sel Str	GRADE No.1	No.2	No.3
								Maximum Allowable Span (feet-inches)									
Douglas fir-larch	12	11-6	10-1	9-7	7-3	18-0	14-9	14-0	10-8	22-10	18-8	17-8	13-6	27-11	22-9	21-7	16-6
	16	10-5	8-9	8-3	6-4	15-7	12-9	12-1	9-3	19-9	16-2	15-4	11-8	24-2	19-9	18-9	14-3
	19.2	9-9	7-11	7-7	5-9	14-3	11-8	11-0	8-5	18-1	14-9	14-0	10-8	22-1	18-0	17-1	13-1
	24	8-9	7-1	6-9	5-2	12-9	10-5	9-10	7-7	16-2	13-2	12-6	9-7	19-9	16-1	15-3	11-8
Hem-fir	12	10-10	9-11	9-3	7-1	17-0	14-6	13-7	10-5	22-1	18-5	17-2	13-2	26-11	22-6	21-0	16-1
	16	9-10	8-7	8-0	6-2	15-1	12-7	11-9	9-0	19-1	15-11	14-11	11-5	23-4	19-6	18-2	13-11
	19.2	9-3	7-10	7-4	5-8	13-9	11-6	10-9	8-3	17-5	14-7	13-7	10-5	21-4	17-9	16-7	12-9
	24	8-5	7-0	6-7	5-0	12-4	10-3	9-7	7-4	15-7	13-0	12-2	9-4	19-1	15-11	14-10	11-5
Southern pine	12	11-3	11-1	10-1	7-7	17-8	16-7	14-5	11-2	23-4	20-10	18-8	14-3	29-9	24-9	22-3	16-10
	16	10-3	9-8	8-9	6-7	16-1	14-4	12-6	9-8	21-2	18-1	16-2	12-4	26-11	21-5	19-3	14-7
	19.2	9-8	8-10	7-11	6-0	15-2	13-1	11-5	8-10	19-11	16-6	14-9	11-3	24-7	19-7	17-7	13-4
	24	8-11	7-11	7-1	5-4	14-1	11-9	10-2	7-11	18-3	14-9	13-2	10-1	22-0	17-6	15-9	11-11

Snow Region, Heavy Roof, No Ceiling: 30 PSF Live, 20 PSF Dead

Species Group	Spacing in oc	2 x 4 Sel Str	GRADE No.1	No.2	No.3	2 x 6 Sel Str	GRADE No.1	No.2	No.3	2 x 8 Sel Str	GRADE No.1	No.2	No.3	2 x 10 Sel Str	GRADE No.1	No.2	No.3
								Maximum Allowable Span (feet-inches)									
Douglas fir-larch	12	10-0	9-0	8-6	6-6	15-9	13-2	12-6	9-6	20-5	16-8	15-10	12-1	24-11	20-4	19-4	14-9
	16	9-1	7-10	7-5	5-8	14-0	11-5	10-10	8-3	17-8	14-5	13-8	10-6	21-7	17-8	16-9	12-9
	19.2	8-7	7-1	6-9	5-2	12-9	10-5	9-10	7-7	16-2	13-2	12-6	9-7	19-9	16-1	15-3	11-8
	24	7-10	6-4	6-0	4-7	11-5	9-4	8-10	6-9	14-5	11-9	11-2	8-7	17-8	14-5	13-8	10-5
Hem-fir	12	9-6	8-11	8-4	6-4	14-10	13-0	12-2	9-4	19-7	16-6	15-4	11-9	24-1	20-1	18-9	14-5
	16	8-7	7-8	7-2	5-6	13-6	11-3	10-6	8-1	17-1	14-3	13-4	10-3	20-10	17-5	16-3	12-6
	19.2	8-1	7-0	6-7	5-0	12-4	10-3	9-7	7-4	15-7	13-0	12-2	9-4	19-1	15-11	14-10	11-5
	24	7-6	6-3	5-10	4-6	11-0	9-2	8-7	6-7	13-11	11-8	10-10	8-4	17-1	14-3	13-3	10-2
Southern pine	12	9-10	9-8	9-0	6-9	15-6	14-10	12-11	10-0	20-5	18-8	16-8	12-9	26-0	22-2	19-11	15-1
	16	8-11	8-8	7-10	5-10	14-1	12-10	11-2	8-8	18-6	16-2	14-5	11-0	23-8	19-2	17-3	13-0
	19.2	8-5	7-11	7-1	5-4	13-3	11-9	10-2	7-11	17-5	14-9	13-2	10-1	22-0	17-6	15-9	11-11
	24	7-10	7-1	6-4	4-9	12-3	10-6	9-2	7-1	16-2	13-2	11-9	9-0	19-8	15-8	14-1	10-8

Headers in Exterior Bearing Walls

Maximum Allowable Span (feet-inches)

Roof Live Load, psf		20			30			40			50		
Header Supporting	Size	Building Width, ft			Building Width, ft			Building Width, ft			Building Width, ft		
		20	28	36	20	28	36	20	28	36	20	28	36
	2-2x4	3-6	3-2	2-10	3-3	2-10	2-7	3-0	2-7	2-4	2-10	2-6	2-2
	2-2x6	5-5	4-8	4-2	4-10	4-2	3-9	4-5	3-10	3-5	4-1	3-7	3-2
	2-2x8	6-10	5-11	5-4	6-2	5-4	4-9	5-7	4-10	4-4	5-2	4-6	4-0
	2-2x10	8-5	7-3	6-6	7-6	6-6	5-10	6-10	5-11	5-4	6-4	5-6	4-11
	2-2x12	9-9	8-5	7-6	8-8	7-6	6-9	7-11	6-10	6-2	7-4	6-4	5-8
	3-2x8	8-4	7-5	6-8	7-8	6-8	5-11	7-0	6-1	5-5	6-6	5-8	5-0
	3-2x10	10-6	9-1	8-2	9-5	8-2	7-3	8-7	7-5	6-8	7-11	6-10	6-2
	3-2x12	12-2	10-7	9-5	10-11	9-5	8-5	9-11	8-7	7-8	9-2	8-0	7-2
	4-2x8	9-2	8-4	7-8	8-6	7-8	6-11	8-0	7-0	6-3	7-6	6-6	5-10
	4-2x10	11-8	10-6	9-5	10-10	9-5	8-5	9-11	8-7	7-8	9-2	7-11	7-1
	4-2x12	14-1	12-2	10-11	12-7	10-11	9-9	11-6	9-11	8-11	10-8	9-2	8-3

Maximum Allowable Span (feet-inches)

Roof Live Load, psf		20			30			40			50		
Header Supporting	Size	Building Width, ft			Building Width, ft			Building Width, ft			Building Width, ft		
		20	28	36	20	28	36	20	28	36	20	28	36
	2-2x4	3-1	2-9	2-5	2-10	2-6	2-3	2-8	2-4	2-1	2-6	2-2	2-0
	2-2x6	4-6	4-0	3-7	4-2	3-8	3-3	3-11	3-5	3-1	3-8	3-2	2-11
	2-2x8	5-9	5-0	4-6	5-3	4-8	4-2	4-11	4-4	3-11	4-8	4-1	3-8
	2-2x10	7-0	6-2	5-6	6-5	5-8	5-1	6-0	5-3	4-9	5-8	4-11	4-5
	2-2x12	8-1	7-1	6-5	7-6	6-7	5-11	7-0	6-1	5-6	6-7	5-9	5-2
	3-2x8	7-2	6-3	5-8	6-7	5-10	5-3	6-2	5-5	4-10	5-10	5-1	4-7
	3-2x10	8-9	7-8	6-11	8-1	7-1	6-5	7-6	6-7	5-11	7-1	6-2	5-7
	3-2x12	10-2	8-11	8-0	9-4	8-2	7-5	8-9	7-8	6-11	8-3	7-2	6-6
	4-2x8	8-1	7-3	6-7	7-8	6-8	6-0	7-1	6-3	5-7	6-8	5-10	5-3
	4-2x10	10-1	8-10	8-0	9-4	8-2	7-4	8-8	7-7	6-10	8-2	7-2	6-5
	4-2x12	11-9	10-3	9-3	10-10	9-6	8-6	10-1	8-10	7-11	9-6	8-4	7-6

Headers in Exterior Bearing Walls

Maximum Allowable Span (feet-inches)

Roof Live Load, psf		20			30			40			50		
Header Supporting	Size	**Building Width, ft**			**Building Width, ft**			**Building Width, ft**			**Building Width, ft**		
		20	28	36	20	28	36	20	28	36	20	28	36
	2-2x4	2-8	2-4	2-1	2-8	2-3	2-0	2-6	2-2	2-0	2-5	2-1	1-10
	2-2x6	3-11	3-5	3-0	3-10	3-4	3-0	3-8	3-2	2-11	3-6	3-0	2-9
	2-2x8	5-0	4-4	3-10	4-10	4-3	3-9	4-8	4-1	3-8	4-5	3-10	3-5
	2-2x10	6-1	5-3	4-8	5-11	5-2	4-7	5-8	4-11	4-5	5-5	4-8	4-3
	2-2x12	7-1	6-1	5-5	6-11	6-0	5-4	6-7	5-9	5-2	6-3	5-5	4-11
	3-2x8	6-3	5-5	4-10	6-1	5-3	4-9	5-10	5-1	4-7	5-6	4-10	4-4
	3-2x10	7-7	6-7	5-11	7-5	6-5	5-9	7-1	6-2	5-7	6-9	5-10	5-3
	3-2x12	8-10	7-8	6-10	8-8	7-6	6-8	8-3	7-2	6-6	7-10	6-10	6-1
	4-2x8	7-2	6-3	5-7	7-1	6-1	5-6	6-9	5-10	5-3	6-4	5-7	5-0
	4-2x10	8-9	7-7	6-10	8-7	7-5	6-8	8-3	7-2	6-5	7-9	6-9	6-1
	4-2x12	10-2	8-10	7-11	10-0	8-8	7-9	9-6	8-4	7-6	9-0	7-10	7-1

Maximum Allowable Span (feet-inches)

Roof Live Load, psf		20			30			40			50		
Header Supporting	Size	**Building Width, ft**			**Building Width, ft**			**Building Width, ft**			**Building Width, ft**		
		20	28	36	20	28	36	20	28	36	20	28	36
	2-2x4	2-7	2-3	2-0	2-6	2-2	2-0	2-5	2-1	1-11	2-3	2-0	1-10
	2-2x6	3-9	3-3	2-11	3-8	3-3	2-11	3-6	3-1	2-10	3-4	2-11	2-8
	2-2x8	4-9	4-2	3-9	4-8	4-1	3-8	4-5	3-11	3-6	4-3	3-9	3-4
	2-2x10	5-9	5-1	4-7	5-8	5-0	4-6	5-5	4-9	4-4	5-2	4-7	4-1
	2-2x12	6-8	5-10	5-3	6-7	5-9	5-2	6-4	5-7	5-0	6-0	5-3	4-9
	3-2x8	5-11	5-2	4-8	5-10	5-1	4-7	5-7	4-11	4-5	5-4	4-8	4-2
	3-2x10	7-3	6-4	5-9	7-1	6-3	5-7	6-10	6-0	5-5	6-6	5-8	5-2
	3-2x12	8-5	7-4	6-7	8-3	7-3	6-6	7-11	6-11	6-3	7-6	6-7	6-0
	4-2x8	6-10	6-0	5-5	6-8	5-11	5-4	6-5	5-8	5-1	6-1	5-5	4-10
	4-2x10	8-4	7-4	6-7	8-2	7-2	6-6	7-10	6-11	6-3	7-6	6-7	5-11
	4-2x12	9-8	8-6	7-8	9-6	8-4	7-6	9-1	8-0	7-3	8-8	7-7	6-11

Headers in Exterior Bearing Walls

		Maximum Allowable Span (feet-inches)											
Roof Live Load, psf		20			30			40			50		
Header Supporting	Size	Building Width, ft			Building Width, ft			Building Width, ft			Building Width, ft		
		20	28	36	20	28	36	20	28	36	20	28	36
	2-2x4	2-1	1-10	1-7	2-1	1-9	1-7	2-0	1-9	1-7	2-0	1-9	1-7
	2-2x6	3-1	2-8	2-4	3-0	2-7	2-4	3-0	2-7	2-4	2-11	2-7	2-3
	2-2x8	3-10	3-4	3-0	3-10	3-4	2-11	3-9	3-3	2-11	3-9	3-3	2-11
	2-2x10	4-9	4-1	3-8	4-8	4-0	3-7	4-7	4-0	3-7	4-7	3-11	3-6
	2-2x12	5-6	4-9	4-3	5-5	4-8	4-2	5-4	4-8	4-2	5-3	4-7	4-1
	3-2x8	4-10	4-2	3-9	4-9	4-2	3-8	4-9	4-1	3-8	4-8	4-1	3-7
	3-2x10	5-11	5-1	4-7	5-10	5-1	4-6	5-9	5-0	4-6	5-8	4-11	4-5
	3-2x12	6-10	5-11	5-4	6-9	5-10	5-3	6-8	5-10	5-2	6-7	5-9	5-1
	4-2x8	5-7	4-10	4-4	5-6	4-9	4-3	5-5	4-9	4-3	5-5	4-8	4-2
	4-2x10	6-10	5-11	5-3	6-9	5-10	5-3	6-8	5-9	5-2	6-7	5-8	5-1
	4-2x12	7-11	6-10	6-2	7-10	6-9	6-1	7-9	6-8	6-0	7-8	6-7	5-11

Headers in Interior Bearing Walls

Header Supporting	Size	Building Width, ft		
		20	28	36
	2-2x4	3-5	2-10	2-6
	2-2x6	4-11	4-2	3-8
	2-2x8	6-3	5-4	4-8
	2-2x10	7-8	6-6	5-9
	2-2x12	8-11	7-6	6-7
	3-2x8	7-10	6-8	5-10
	3-2x10	9-7	8-1	7-2
	3-2x12	11-1	9-5	8-3
	4-2x8	9-0	7-8	6-9
	4-2x10	11-1	9-4	8-3
	4-2x12	12-10	10-10	6-7

Header Supporting	Size	Building Width, ft		
		20	28	36
	2-2x4	2-3	1-11	1-9
	2-2x6	3-4	2-10	2-6
	2-2x8	4-3	3-7	3-3
	2-2x10	5-2	4-5	3-11
	2-2x12	6-0	5-2	4-7
	3-2x8	5-4	4-6	4-0
	3-2x10	6-6	5-6	4-0
	3-2x12	7-6	6-5	5-8
	4-2x8	6-1	5-3	4-8
	4-2x10	7-6	6-5	5-8
	4-2x12	8-8	7-5	6-7

Span Tables for Canadian Species

Floor Joists

Sleeping Rooms and Attics: 30 PSF Live, 10 PSF Dead

Species Group	Spacing in oc	2 x 6 Sel Str	2 x 6 No.1/ No.2	2 x 6 GRADE No.3	2 x 8 Sel Str	2 x 8 No.1/ No.2	2 x 8 GRADE No.3	2 x 10 Sel Str	2 x 10 No.1/ No.2	2 x 10 GRADE No.3	2 x 12 Sel Str	2 x 12 No.1/ No.2	2 x 12 GRADE No.3
Spruce-pine-fir	12	11-7	11-3	9-8	15-3	14-11	12-4	19-5	19-0	15-0	23-7	23-0	17-5
	16	10-6	10-3	8-5	13-10	13-6	10-8	17-8	17-2	13-0	21-6	19-11	15-1
	19.2	9-10	9-8	7-8	13-0	12-9	9-9	16-7	15-8	11-10	20-2	18-3	13-9
	24	9-2	8-11	6-10	12-1	11-6	8-8	15-5	14-1	10-7	18-9	16-3	12-4
D.Fir-L(N)	12	12-6	11-10	9-6	16-6	15-7	12-0	21-0	19-7	14-8	25-7	22-8	17-0
	16	11-4	10-9	8-2	15-0	13-11	10-5	19-1	16-11	12-8	23-3	19-8	14-8
	19.2	10-8	10-0	7-6	14-1	12-8	9-6	18-0	15-6	11-7	21-10	17-11	13-5
	24	9-11	8-11	6-8	13-1	11-4	8-6	16-8	13-10	10-4	20-3	16-1	12-0
Hem-Fir(N)	12	12-0	11-10	10-5	15-10	15-7	13-2	20-3	19-10	16-1	24-8	24-2	18-8
	16	10-11	10-9	9-0	14-5	14-2	11-5	18-5	18-0	13-11	22-5	21-4	16-2
	19.2	10-4	10-1	8-3	13-7	13-4	10-5	17-4	16-9	12-9	21-1	19-6	14-9
	24	9-7	9-4	7-4	12-7	12-4	9-4	16-1	15-0	11-5	19-7	17-5	13-2
Northern Species	12	10-5	10-5	8-1	13-9	13-6	10-3	17-6	16-5	12-7	21-4	19-1	14-7
	16	9-6	9-3	7-0	12-6	11-8	8-11	15-11	14-3	10-11	19-4	16-6	12-7
	19.2	8-11	8-5	6-5	11-9	10-8	8-2	15-0	13-0	9-11	18-3	15-1	11-6
	24	8-3	7-6	5-9	10-11	9-6	7-3	13-11	11-8	8-11	16-11	13-6	10-4

All Rooms Except Sleeping Rooms and Attics: 40 PSF Live, 10 PSF Dead

Species Group	Spacing in oc	2 x 6 Sel Str	2 x 6 No.1/ No.2	2 x 6 GRADE No.3	2 x 8 Sel Str	2 x 8 No.1/ No.2	2 x 8 GRADE No.3	2 x 10 Sel Str	2 x 10 No.1/ No.2	2 x 10 GRADE No.3	2 x 12 Sel Str	2 x 12 No.1/ No.2	2 x 12 GRADE No.3
Spruce-pine-fir	12	10-6	10-3	8-8	13-10	13-6	11-0	17-8	17-3	13-5	21-6	20-7	15-7
	16	9-6	9-4	7-6	12-7	12-3	9-6	16-0	15-5	11-8	19-6	17-10	13-6
	19.2	9-0	8-9	6-10	11-10	11-6	8-8	15-1	14-1	10-7	18-4	16-3	12-4
	24	8-4	8-1	6-2	11-0	10-3	7-9	14-0	12-7	9-6	17-0	14-7	11-0
D.Fir-L(N)	12	11-4	10-9	8-6	15-0	14-2	10-9	19-1	17-6	13-1	23-3	20-4	15-2
	16	10-4	9-9	7-4	13-7	12-5	9-3	17-4	15-2	11-4	21-1	17-7	13-2
	19.2	9-8	8-11	6-8	12-10	11-4	8-6	16-4	13-10	10-4	19-10	16-1	12-0
	24	9-0	8-0	6-0	11-11	10-2	7-7	15-2	12-5	9-3	18-1	14-4	10-9
Hem-Fir(N)	12	10-11	10-9	9-4	14-5	14-2	11-9	18-5	18-0	14-5	22-5	21-11	16-8
	16	9-11	9-9	8-1	13-1	12-10	10-3	16-9	16-5	12-6	20-4	19-1	14-6
	19.2	9-4	9-2	7-4	12-4	12-1	9-4	15-9	15-0	11-5	19-2	17-5	13-2
	24	8-8	8-6	6-7	11-5	11-0	8-4	14-7	13-5	10-2	17-9	15-7	11-10
Northern Species	12	9-6	9-6	7-3	12-6	12-1	9-2	15-11	14-9	11-3	19-4	17-1	13-0
	16	8-7	8-3	6-3	11-4	10-5	8-0	14-6	12-9	9-9	17-7	14-9	11-3
	19.2	8-1	7-6	5-9	10-8	9-6	7-3	13-7	11-8	8-11	16-7	13-6	10-4
	24	7-6	6-9	5-2	9-11	8-6	6-6	12-8	10-5	7-11	15-4	12-1	9-3

Ceiling Joists

Drywall—No Future Rooms and No Attic Storage: 10 PSF Live, 5 PSF Dead

| | | Maximum Allowable Span (feet-inches) | | | | | | | | | | |
| | | 2 x 4 | | | 2 x 6 | | | 2 x 8 | | | 2 x 10 | | |
Species Group	Spacing in oc	Sel Str	No.1/ No.2	GRADE No.3	Sel Str	No.1/ No.2	GRADE No.3	Sel Str	No.1/ No.2	GRADE No.3	Sel Str	No.1/ No.2	GRADE No.3
Spruce-pine-fir	12	12-2	11-10	10-10	19-1	18-8	15-10	25-2	24-7	20-1	32-1	31-4	24-6
	16	11-0	10-9	9-5	17-4	16-11	13-9	22-10	22-4	17-5	29-2	28-1	21-3
	19.2	10-4	10-2	8-7	16-4	15-11	12-6	21-6	21-0	15-10	27-5	25-8	19-5
	24	9-8	9-5	7-8	15-2	14-9	11-2	19-11	18-9	14-2	25-5	22-11	17-4
D.Fir-L(N)	12	13-2	12-5	10-7	20-8	19-6	15-5	27-2	25-8	19-7	34-8	32-0	23-11
	16	11-11	11-3	9-2	18-9	17-8	13-5	24-8	22-8	16-11	31-6	27-8	20-8
	19.2	11-3	10-7	8-4	17-8	16-4	12-3	23-3	20-8	15-6	29-8	25-3	18-11
	24	10-5	9-10	7-6	16-4	14-7	10-11	21-7	18-6	13-10	27-6	22-7	16-11
Hem-Fir(N)	12	12-8	12-5	11-7	19-11	19-6	17-0	26-2	25-8	21-6	33-5	32-9	26-4
	16	11-6	11-3	10-1	18-1	17-8	14-9	23-10	23-4	18-8	30-5	29-9	22-9
	19.2	10-10	10-7	9-2	17-0	16-8	13-5	22-5	21-11	17-0	28-7	27-5	20-9
	24	10-0	9-10	8-3	15-9	15-6	12-0	20-10	20-1	15-3	26-6	24-6	18-7
Northern Species	12	10-11	10-11	9-1	17-2	17-2	13-3	22-8	22-0	16-10	28-11	26-10	20-6
	16	9-11	9-11	7-10	15-7	15-0	11-6	20-7	19-1	14-7	26-3	23-3	17-9
	19.2	9-4	9-4	7-2	14-8	13-9	10-6	19-5	17-5	13-3	24-9	21-3	16-3
	24	8-8	8-5	6-5	13-8	12-3	9-5	18-0	15-7	11-11	22-11	19-0	14-6

Drywall—No Future Rooms, Limited Attic Storage: 20 PSF Live, 10 PSF Dead

| | | Maximum Allowable Span (feet-inches) | | | | | | | | | | |
| | | 2 x 4 | | | 2 x 6 | | | 2 x 8 | | | 2 x 10 | | |
Species Group	Spacing in oc	Sel Str	No.1/ No.2	GRADE No.3	Sel Str	No.1/ No.2	GRADE No.3	Sel Str	No.1/ No.2	GRADE No.3	Sel Str	No.1/ No.2	GRADE No.3
Spruce-pine-fir	12	9-8	9-5	7-8	15-2	14-9	11-2	19-11	18-9	14-2	25-5	22-11	17-4
	16	8-9	8-7	6-8	13-9	12-10	9-8	18-2	16-3	12-4	23-2	19-10	15-0
	19.2	8-3	8-0	6-1	12-11	11-9	8-10	17-1	14-10	11-3	21-8	18-2	13-8
	24	7-8	7-2	5-5	12-0	10-6	7-11	15-10	13-3	10-0	19-5	16-3	12-3
D.Fir-L(N)	12	10-5	9-10	7-6	16-4	14-7	10-11	21-7	18-6	13-10	27-6	22-7	16-11
	16	9-6	8-8	6-6	14-11	12-8	9-6	19-7	16-0	12-0	24-8	19-7	14-8
	19.2	8-11	7-11	5-11	14-0	11-7	8-8	18-5	14-8	10-11	22-6	17-10	13-4
	24	8-3	7-1	5-3	13-0	10-4	7-9	16-6	13-1	9-9	20-2	16-0	11-11
Hem-Fir(N)	12	10-0	9-10	8-3	15-9	15-6	12-0	20-10	20-1	15-3	26-6	24-6	18-7
	16	9-1	8-11	7-1	14-4	13-9	10-5	18-11	17-5	13-2	24-1	21-3	16-1
	19.2	8-7	8-5	6-6	13-6	12-6	9-6	17-9	15-10	12-0	22-1	19-5	14-8
	24	8-0	7-8	5-10	12-6	11-2	8-6	16-2	14-2	10-9	19-9	17-4	13-2
Northern Species	12	8-8	8-5	6-5	13-8	12-3	9-5	18-0	15-7	11-11	22-11	19-0	14-6
	16	7-11	7-3	5-7	12-5	10-8	8-1	16-4	13-6	10-3	20-10	16-5	12-7
	19.2	7-5	6-8	5-1	11-8	9-8	7-5	15-5	12-4	9-5	19-5	15-0	11-6
	24	6-11	5-11	4-6	10-10	8-8	6-8	14-2	11-0	8-5	17-4	13-5	10-3

Rafters

Snow Region, Light Roof, Drywall, No Attic Space: 20 PSF Live, 10 PSF Dead

| | | Maximum Allowable Span (feet-inches) | | | | | | | | | | | |
| | | 2 x 6 | | | 2 x 8 | | | 2 x 10 | | | 2 x 12 | | |
Species Group	Spacing in o.c.	Sel Str	No.1/ No.2	GRADE No.3	Sel Str	No.1/ No.2	GRADE No.3	Sel Str	No.1/ No.2	GRADE No.3	Sel Str	No.1/ No.2	GRADE No.3
Spruce-pine-fir	12	15-2	14-9	12-0	19-11	19-6	15-3	25-5	24-7	18-7	30-11	28-6	21-7
	16	13-9	13-5	10-5	18-2	17-5	13-2	23-2	21-4	16-1	28-2	24-8	18-8
	19.2	12-11	12-7	9-6	17-1	15-11	12-0	21-9	19-5	14-8	26-6	22-7	17-1
	24	12-0	11-3	8-6	15-10	14-3	10-9	20-2	17-5	13-2	24-1	20-2	15-3
D.Fir-L(N)	12	16-4	15-6	11-9	21-7	19-10	14-10	27-6	24-3	18-1	33-6	28-1	21-0
	16	14-11	13-7	10-2	19-7	17-2	12-10	25-0	21-0	15-8	30-5	24-4	18-2
	19.2	14-0	12-5	9-3	18-5	15-8	11-9	23-7	19-2	14-4	28-0	22-3	16-7
	24	13-0	11-1	8-3	17-2	14-0	10-6	21-7	17-2	12-10	25-1	19-11	14-10
Hem-Fir(N)	12	15-9	15-6	12-11	20-11	20-5	16-4	26-6	26-0	19-11	32-3	30-6	23-1
	16	14-4	14-1	11-2	18-11	18-6	14-2	24-1	22-9	17-3	29-4	26-5	20-0
	19.2	13-6	13-3	10-2	17-9	17-0	12-11	22-8	20-9	15-9	27-6	24-1	18-3
	24	12-6	12-0	9-1	16-6	15-3	11-7	21-1	18-7	14-1	24-7	21-7	16-4
Northern Species	12	13-8	13-2	10-1	18-0	16-8	12-9	22-11	20-4	15-7	27-11	23-7	18-0
	16	12-5	11-5	8-9	16-4	14-5	11-0	20-10	17-8	13-6	25-4	20-5	15-7
	19.2	11-8	10-5	7-11	15-5	13-2	10-1	19-7	16-1	12-4	23-10	18-8	14-3
	24	10-10	9-4	7-1	14-3	11-9	9-0	18-1	14-5	11-0	21-7	16-8	12-9

Snow Region, Light Roof, Drywall, No Attic Space: 30 PSF Live, 10 PSF Dead

| | | Maximum Allowable Span (feet-inches) | | | | | | | | | | | |
| | | 2 x 6 | | | 2 x 8 | | | 2 x 10 | | | 2 x 12 | | |
Species Group	Spacing in oc	Sel Str	No.1/ No.2	GRADE No.3	Sel Str	No.1/ No.2	GRADE No.3	Sel Str	No.1/ No.2	GRADE No.3	Sel Str	No.1/ No.2	GRADE No.3
Spruce-pine-fir	12	13-3	12-11	10-5	17-5	17-0	13-2	22-3	21-4	16-1	27-1	24-8	18-8
	16	12-0	11-9	9-0	15-10	15-1	11-5	20-2	18-5	13-11	24-7	21-5	16-2
	19.2	11-4	10-11	8-3	14-11	13-9	10-5	19-0	16-10	12-9	23-1	19-6	14-9
	24	10-6	9-9	7-4	13-10	12-4	9-4	17-8	15-1	11-5	20-11	17-6	13-2
D.Fir-L(N)	12	14-4	13-6	10-2	18-10	17-2	12-10	24-1	21-0	15-8	29-3	24-4	18-2
	16	13-0	11-9	8-9	17-2	14-11	11-2	21-10	18-2	13-7	26-7	21-1	15-9
	19.2	12-3	10-9	8-0	16-1	13-7	10-2	20-7	16-7	12-5	24-3	19-3	14-5
	24	11-4	9-7	7-2	15-0	12-2	9-1	18-9	14-10	11-1	21-8	17-3	12-10
Hem-Fir(N)	12	13-9	13-6	11-2	18-2	17-10	14-2	23-2	22-9	17-3	28-2	26-5	20-0
	16	12-6	12-3	9-8	16-6	16-2	12-3	21-1	19-9	14-11	25-7	22-10	17-4
	19.2	11-9	11-7	8-10	15-6	14-9	11-2	19-10	18-0	13-8	23-10	30-11	15-10
	24	10-11	10-5	7-11	14-5	13-2	10-0	18-4	16-1	12-3	21-3	18-8	14-2
Northern Species	12	11-11	11-5	8-9	15-9	14-5	11-0	20-1	17-8	13-6	24-5	20-5	15-7
	16	10-10	9-10	7-7	14-3	12-6	9-7	18-3	15-3	11-8	22-2	17-9	13-6
	19.2	10-2	9-0	6-11	13-5	11-5	8-9	17-2	13-11	10-8	20-10	16-2	12-4
	24	9-6	8-1	6-2	12-6	10-3	7-10	15-11	12-6	9-6	18-8	14-6	11-1

Rafters

Snow Region, Light Roof, Drywall, No Attic Space: 40 PSF Live, 10 PSF Dead

		Maximum Allowable Span (feet-inches)											
		2 x 6			2 x 8			2 x 10			2 x 12		
Species Group	Spacing in oc	Sel Str	No.1/ No.2	GRADE No.3	Sel Str	No.1/ No.2	GRADE No.3	Sel Str	No.1/ No.2	GRADE No.3	Sel Str	No.1/ No.2	GRADE No.3
Spruce-pine-fir	12	12-0	11-9	9-4	15-10	15-6	11-9	20-2	19-1	14-5	24-7	22-1	16-8
	16	10-11	10-8	8-1	14-5	13-6	10-3	18-4	16-6	12-6	22-4	19-2	14-6
	19.2	10-3	9-9	7-4	13-6	12-4	9-4	17-3	15-1	11-5	20-11	17-6	13-2
	24	9-6	8-9	6-7	12-7	11-0	8-4	16-0	13-6	10-2	18-8	15-7	11-10
D.Fir-L(N)	12	13-0	12-2	9-1	17-2	15-4	11-6	21-10	18-9	14-0	26-7	21-9	16-3
	16	11-10	10-6	7-10	15-7	13-4	9-11	19-10	16-3	12-2	23-9	18-10	14-1
	19.2	11-1	9-7	7-2	14-8	12-2	9-1	18-8	14-10	11-1	21-8	17-3	12-10
	24	10-4	8-7	6-5	13-7	10-10	8-2	16-9	13-3	9-11	19-5	15-5	11-6
Hem-Fir(N)	12	12-6	12-3	10-0	16-6	16-2	12-8	21-1	20-4	15-5	25-7	23-7	17-11
	16	11-5	11-2	8-8	15-0	14-5	10-11	19-2	17-8	13-5	23-3	20-5	15-6
	19.2	10-8	10-5	7-11	14-1	13-2	10-0	18-0	16-1	12-3	21-3	18-8	14-2
	24	9-11	9-4	7-1	13-1	11-9	8-11	16-5	14-5	10-11	19-1	16-8	12-8
Northern Species	12	10-10	10-2	7-9	14-3	12-11	9-10	18-3	15-9	12-1	22-2	18-4	14-0
	16	9-10	8-10	6-9	13-0	11-2	8-7	16-7	13-8	10-5	20-2	15-10	12-1
	19.2	9-3	8-1	6-2	12-2	10-3	7-10	15-7	12-6	9-6	18-8	14-6	11-1
	24	8-7	7-3	5-6	11-4	9-2	7-0	14-5	11-2	8-6	16-8	12-11	9-11

Snow Region, Light Roof, Drywall, No Attic Space: 50 PSF Live, 10 PSF Dead

		Maximum Allowable Span (feet-inches)											
		2 x 6			2 x 8			2 x 10			2 x 12		
Species Group	Spacing in oc	Sel Str	No.1/ No.2	GRADE No.3	Sel Str	No.1/ No.2	GRADE No.3	Sel Str	No.1/ No.2	GRADE No.3	Sel Str	No.1/ No.2	GRADE No.3
Spruce-pine-fir	12	11-2	10-11	8-6	14-8	14-3	10-9	18-9	17-5	13-2	22-10	20-2	15-3
	16	10-2	9-9	7-4	13-4	12-4	9-4	17-0	15-1	11-5	20-9	17-6	13-2
	19.2	9-6	8-11	6-9	12-7	11-3	8-6	16-0	13-9	10-5	19-1	15-11	12-1
	24	8-10	7-11	6-0	11-8	10-1	7-7	14-8	12-4	9-4	17-1	14-3	10-9
D.Fir-L(N)	12	12-1	11-1	8-3	15-11	14-0	10-6	20-3	17-2	12-10	24-8	19-11	14-10
	16	11-0	9-7	7-2	14-5	12-2	9-1	18-5	14-10	11-1	21-8	17-3	12-10
	19.2	10-4	8-9	6-7	13-7	11-1	8-4	17-1	13-7	10-2	19-10	15-9	11-9
	24	9-7	7-10	5-10	12-6	9-11	7-5	15-3	12-1	9-1	17-9	14-1	10-6
Hem-Fir(N)	12	11-8	11-5	9-1	15-4	15-0	11-7	19-7	18-7	14-1	23-9	21-7	16-4
	16	10-7	10-4	7-11	13-11	13-2	10-0	17-9	16-1	12-3	21-3	18-8	14-2
	19.2	9-11	9-6	7-2	13-1	12-0	9-2	16-9	14-8	11-2	19-5	17-1	12-11
	24	9-3	8-6	6-5	12-2	10-9	8-2	15-0	13-2	10-0	17-5	15-3	11-7
Northern Species	12	10-1	9-4	7-1	13-3	11-9	9-0	16-11	14-5	11-0	20-7	16-8	12-9
	16	9-2	8-1	6-2	12-1	10-3	7-10	15-4	12-6	9-6	18-8	14-6	11-1
	19.2	8-7	7-4	5-7	11-4	9-4	7-1	14-6	11-5	8-8	17-1	13-2	10-1
	24	8-0	6-7	5-0	10-6	8-4	6-4	13-2	10-2	7-9	15-3	11-10	9-0

Rafters

Snow Region, Heavy Roof, Drywall, No Attic: 20 PSF Live, 20 PSF Dead

Species Group	Spacing in oc	2 x 6 Sel Str	2 x 6 No.1/ No.2	2 x 6 GRADE No.3	2 x 8 Sel Str	2 x 8 No.1/ No.2	2 x 8 GRADE No.3	2 x 10 Sel Str	2 x 10 No.1/ No.2	2 x 10 GRADE No.3	2 x 12 Sel Str	2 x 12 No.1/ No.2	2 x 12 GRADE No.3
Spruce-pine-fir	12	15-2	13-9	10-5	19-11	17-5	13-2	25-5	21-4	16-1	29-6	24-8	18-8
	16	13-9	11-11	9-0	18-1	15-1	11-5	22-1	18-5	13-11	25-7	21-5	16-2
	19.2	12-11	10-11	8-3	16-6	13-9	10-5	20-2	16-10	12-9	23-4	19-6	14-9
	24	11-8	9-9	7-4	14-9	12-4	9-4	18-0	15-1	11-5	20-11	17-6	13-2
D.Fir-L(N)	12	16-4	13-7	10-2	21-7	17-2	12-10	26-6	21-0	15-8	30-8	24-4	18-2
	16	14-10	11-9	8-9	18-9	14-11	11-2	22-11	18-2	13-7	26-7	21-1	15-9
	19.2	13-6	10-9	8-0	17-1	13-7	10-2	20-11	16-7	12-5	24-3	19-3	14-5
	24	12-1	9-7	7-2	15-4	12-2	9-1	18-9	14-10	11-1	21-8	17-3	12-10
Hem-Fir(N)	12	15-9	14-9	11-2	20-10	18-8	14-2	26-0	22-9	17-3	30-1	26-5	20-0
	16	14-4	12-9	9-8	18-5	16-2	12-3	22-6	19-9	14-11	26-1	22-10	17-4
	19.2	13-3	11-8	8-10	16-10	14-9	11-2	20-6	18-0	13-8	23-10	20-11	15-10
	24	11-10	10-5	7-11	15-0	13-2	10-0	18-4	16-1	12-3	21-3	18-8	14-2
Northern Species	12	13-8	11-5	8-9	18-0	14-5	11-0	22-9	17-8	13-6	26-5	20-5	15-7
	16	12-5	9-10	7-7	16-2	12-6	9-7	19-9	15-3	11-8	22-10	17-9	13-6
	19.2	11-8	9-0	6-11	14-9	11-5	8-9	18-0	13-11	10-8	20-11	16-2	12-4
	24	10-5	8-1	6-2	13-2	10-3	7-10	16-1	12-6	9-6	18-8	14-6	11-1

Maximum Allowable Span (feet-inches)

Snow Region, Heavy Roof, Drywall, No Attic: 30 PSF Live, 20 PSF Dead

Species Group	Spacing in oc	2 x 6 Sel Str	2 x 6 No.1/ No.2	2 x 6 GRADE No.3	2 x 8 Sel Str	2 x 8 No.1/ No.2	2 x 8 GRADE No.3	2 x 10 Sel Str	2 x 10 No.1/ No.2	2 x 10 GRADE No.3	2 x 12 Sel Str	2 x 12 No.1/ No.2	2 x 12 GRADE No.3
Spruce-pine-fir	12	13-3	12-4	9-4	17-5	15-7	11-9	22-3	19-1	14-5	26-5	22-1	16-8
	16	12-0	10-8	8-1	15-10	13-6	10-3	19-9	16-6	12-6	22-10	19-2	14-6
	19.2	11-4	9-9	7-4	14-9	12-4	9-4	18-0	15-1	11-5	20-11	17-6	13-2
	24	10-5	8-9	6-7	13-2	11-0	8-4	16-1	13-6	10-2	18-8	15-7	11-10
D.Fir-L(N)	12	14-4	12-2	9-1	18-10	15-4	11-6	23-8	18-9	14-0	27-5	21-9	16-3
	16	13-0	10-6	7-10	16-9	13-4	9-11	20-6	16-3	12-2	23-9	18-10	14-1
	19.2	12-1	9-7	7-2	15-4	12-2	9-1	18-9	14-10	11-1	21-8	17-3	12-10
	24	10-10	8-7	6-5	13-8	10-10	8-2	16-9	13-3	9-11	19-5	15-5	11-6
Hem-Fir(N)	12	13-9	13-2	10-0	18-2	16-8	12-8	23-2	20-4	15-5	26-11	23-7	17-11
	16	12-6	11-5	8-8	16-6	14-5	10-11	20-1	17-8	13-5	23-4	20-5	15-6
	19.2	11-9	10-5	7-11	15-0	13-2	10-0	18-4	16-1	12-3	21-3	18-8	14-2
	24	10-7	9-4	7-1	13-5	11-9	8-11	16-5	14-5	10-11	19-1	16-8	12-8
Northern Species	12	11-11	10-2	7-9	15-9	12-11	9-10	20-1	15-9	12-1	23-7	18-4	14-0
	16	10-10	8-10	6-9	14-3	11-2	8-7	17-8	13-8	10-5	20-5	15-10	12-1
	19.2	10-2	8-1	6-2	13-2	10-3	7-10	16-1	12-6	9-6	18-8	14-6	11-1
	24	9-4	7-3	5-6	11-9	9-2	7-0	14-5	11-2	8-6	16-8	12-11	9-11

Maximum Allowable Span (feet-inches)

Rafters

Snow Region, Light Roof, No Ceiling: 20 PSF Live, 10 PSF Dead

Species Group	Spacing in oc	2 x 4 Sel Str	2 x 4 No.1/ No.2	2 x 4 GRADE No.3	2 x 6 Sel Str	2 x 6 No.1/ No.2	2 x 6 GRADE No.3	2 x 8 Sel Str	2 x 8 No.1/ No.2	2 x 8 GRADE No.3	2 x 10 Sel Str	2 x 10 No.1/ No.2	2 x 10 GRADE No.3
Spruce-pine-fir	12	10-7	10-4	8-3	16-8	15-11	12-0	21-11	20-2	15-3	28-0	24-7	18-7
	16	9-8	9-5	7-1	15-2	13-9	10-5	19-11	17-5	13-2	25-5	21-4	16-1
	19.2	9-1	8-7	6-6	14-3	12-7	9-6	18-9	15-11	12-0	23-3	19-5	14-8
	24	8-5	7-8	5-10	13-3	11-3	8-6	17-0	14-3	10-9	20-9	17-5	13-2
D.Fir-L(N)	12	11-6	10-9	8-0	18-0	15-8	11-9	23-9	19-10	14-10	30-4	24-3	18-1
	16	10-5	9-3	6-11	16-4	13-7	10-2	21-7	17-2	12-10	26-6	21-0	15-8
	19.2	9-10	8-6	6-4	15-5	12-5	9-3	19-9	15-8	11-9	24-2	19-2	14-4
	24	9-1	7-7	5-8	14-0	11-1	8-3	17-8	14-0	10-6	21-7	17-2	12-10
Hem-Fir(N)	12	11-1	10-10	8-10	17-4	17-0	12-11	22-11	21-6	16-4	29-2	26-4	19-11
	16	10-0	9-10	7-8	15-9	14-9	11-2	20-10	18-8	14-2	26-0	22-9	17-3
	19.2	9-5	9-2	7-0	14-10	13-5	10-2	19-5	17-0	12-11	23-8	20-9	15-9
	24	8-9	8-3	6-3	13-8	12-0	9-1	17-4	15-3	11-7	21-2	18-7	14-1
Northern Species	12	9-7	9-0	6-10	15-0	13-2	10-1	19-10	16-8	12-9	25-3	20-4	15-7
	16	8-8	7-10	5-11	13-8	11-5	8-9	18-0	14-5	11-0	22-9	17-8	13-6
	19.2	8-2	7-1	5-5	12-10	10-5	7-11	16-11	13-2	10-1	20-9	16-1	12-4
	24	7-7	6-4	4-10	11-11	9-4	7-1	15-3	11-9	9-0	18-7	14-5	11-0

Snow Region, Light Roof, No Ceiling: 30 PSF Live, 10 PSF Dead

Species Group	Spacing in oc	2 x 4 Sel Str	2 x 4 No.1/ No.2	2 x 4 GRADE No.3	2 x 6 Sel Str	2 x 6 No.1/ No.2	2 x 6 GRADE No.3	2 x 8 Sel Str	2 x 8 No.1/ No.2	2 x 8 GRADE No.3	2 x 10 Sel Str	2 x 10 No.1/ No.2	2 x 10 GRADE No.3
Spruce-pine-fir	12	9-3	9-1	7-1	14-7	13-9	10-5	19-2	17-5	13-2	24-6	21-4	16-1
	16	8-5	8-2	6-2	13-3	11-11	9-0	17-5	15-1	11-5	22-1	18-5	13-11
	19.2	7-11	7-5	5-8	12-5	10-11	8-3	16-5	13-9	10-5	20-2	16-10	12-9
	24	7-4	6-8	5-0	11-7	9-9	7-4	14-9	12-4	9-4	18-0	15-1	11-5
D.Fir-L(N)	12	10-0	9-3	6-11	15-9	13-7	10-2	20-9	17-2	12-10	26-6	21-0	15-8
	16	9-1	8-0	6-0	14-4	11-9	8-9	18-9	14-11	11-2	22-11	18-2	13-7
	19.2	8-7	7-4	5-6	13-6	10-9	8-0	17-1	13-7	10-2	20-11	16-7	12-5
	24	7-11	6-7	4-11	12-1	9-7	7-2	15-4	12-2	9-1	18-9	14-10	11-1
Hem-Fir(N)	12	9-8	9-6	7-8	15-2	14-9	11-2	20-0	18-8	14-2	25-6	22-9	17-3
	16	8-9	8-7	6-7	13-9	12-9	9-8	18-2	16-2	12-3	22-6	19-9	14-11
	19.2	8-3	7-11	6-0	13-0	11-8	8-10	16-10	14-9	11-2	20-6	18-0	13-8
	24	7-8	7-1	5-5	11-10	10-5	7-11	15-0	13-2	10-0	18-4	16-1	12-3
Northern Species	12	8-4	7-10	5-11	13-1	11-5	8-9	17-4	14-5	11-0	22-1	17-8	13-6
	16	7-7	6-9	5-2	11-11	9-10	7-7	15-9	12-6	9-7	19-9	15-3	11-8
	19.2	7-2	6-2	4-8	11-3	9-0	6-11	14-9	11-5	8-9	18-0	13-11	10-8
	24	6-8	5-6	4-3	10-5	8-1	6-2	13-2	10-3	7-10	16-1	12-6	9-6

Rafters

Snow Region, Light Roof, No Ceiling: 40 PSF Live, 10 PSF Dead

		Maximum Allowable Span (feet-inches)											
		2 x 4			2 x 6			2 x 8			2 x 10		
Species Group	Spacing in oc	Sel Str	No.1/ No.2	GRADE No.3	Sel Str	No.1/ No.2	GRADE No.3	Sel Str	No.1/ No.2	GRADE No.3	Sel Str	No.1/ No.2	GRADE No.3
Spruce-pine-fir	12	8-5	8-3	6-4	13-3	12-4	9-4	17-5	15-7	11-9	22-3	19-1	14-5
	16	7-8	7-3	5-6	12-0	10-8	8-1	15-10	13-6	10-3	19-9	16-6	12-6
	19.2	7-2	6-8	5-0	11-4	9-9	7-4	14-9	12-4	9-4	18-0	15-1	11-5
	24	6-8	5-11	4-6	10-5	8-9	6-7	13-2	11-0	8-4	16-1	13-6	10-2
D.Fir-L(N)	12	9-1	8-4	6-2	14-4	12-2	9-1	18-10	15-4	11-6	23-8	18-9	14-0
	16	8-3	7-2	5-4	13-0	10-6	7-10	16-9	13-4	9-11	20-6	16-3	12-2
	19.2	7-9	6-7	4-11	12-1	9-7	7-2	15-4	12-2	9-1	18-9	14-10	11-1
	24	7-3	5-10	4-5	10-10	8-7	6-5	13-8	10-10	8-2	16-9	13-3	9-11
Hem-Fir(N)	12	8-9	8-7	6-10	13-9	13-2	10-0	18-2	16-8	12-8	23-2	20-4	15-5
	16	8-0	7-10	5-11	12-6	11-5	8-8	16-6	14-5	10-11	20-1	17-8	13-5
	19.2	7-6	7-1	5-5	11-9	10-5	7-11	15-0	13-2	10-0	18-4	16-1	12-3
	24	7-0	6-4	4-10	10-7	9-4	7-1	13-5	11-9	8-11	16-5	14-5	10-11
Northern Species	12	7-7	7-0	5-4	11-11	10-2	7-9	15-9	12-11	9-10	20-1	15-9	12-1
	16	6-11	6-0	4-7	10-10	8-10	6-9	14-3	11-2	8-7	17-8	13-8	10-5
	19.2	6-6	5-6	4-3	10-2	8-1	6-2	13-2	10-3	7-10	16-1	12-6	9-6
	24	6-0	4-11	3-9	9-4	7-3	5-6	11-9	9-2	7-0	14-5	11-2	8-6

Snow Region, Light Roof, No Ceiling: 50 PSF Live, 10 PSF Dead

		Maximum Allowable Span (feet-inches)											
		2 x 4			2 x 6			2 x 8			2 x 10		
Species Group	Spacing in oc	Sel Str	No.1/ No.2	GRADE No.3	Sel Str	No.1/ No.2	GRADE No.3	Sel Str	No.1/ No.2	GRADE No.3	Sel Str	No.1/ No.2	GRADE No.3
Spruce-pine-fir	12	7-10	7-8	5-10	12-3	11-3	8-6	16-2	14-3	10-9	20-8	17-5	13-2
	16	7-1	6-8	5-0	11-2	9-9	7-4	14-8	12-4	9-4	18-0	15-1	11-5
	19.2	6-8	6-1	4-7	10-6	8-11	6-9	13-5	11-3	8-6	16-5	13-9	10-5
	24	6-2	5-5	4-1	9-6	7-11	6-0	12-0	10-1	7-7	14-8	12-4	9-4
D.Fir-L(N)	12	8-5	7-7	5-8	13-3	11-1	8-3	17-6	14-0	10-6	21-7	17-2	12-10
	16	7-8	6-7	4-11	12-1	9-7	7-2	15-4	12-2	9-1	18-9	14-10	11-1
	19.2	7-3	6-0	4-6	11-0	8-9	6-7	14-0	11-1	8-4	17-1	13-7	10-2
	24	6-8	5-4	4-0	9-10	7-10	5-10	12-6	9-11	7-5	15-3	12-1	9-1
Hem-Fir(N)	12	8-2	8-0	6-3	12-10	12-0	9-1	16-10	15-3	11-7	21-2	18-7	14-1
	16	7-5	7-1	5-5	11-8	10-5	7-11	15-0	13-2	10-0	18-4	16-1	12-3
	19.2	7-0	6-6	4-11	10-10	9-6	7-2	13-9	12-0	9-2	16-9	14-8	11-2
	24	6-6	5-10	4-5	9-8	8-6	6-5	12-3	10-9	8-2	15-0	13-2	10-0
Northern Species	12	7-1	6-4	4-10	11-1	9-4	7-1	14-7	11-9	9-0	18-7	14-5	11-0
	16	6-5	5-6	4-3	10-1	8-1	6-2	13-2	10-3	7-10	16-1	12-6	9-6
	19.2	6-0	5-0	3-10	9-6	7-4	5-7	12-0	9-4	7-1	14-8	11-5	8-8
	24	5-7	4-6	3-5	8-6	6-7	5-0	10-9	8-4	6-4	13-2	10-2	7-9

Rafters

Snow Region, Heavy Roof, No Ceiling: 20 PSF Live, 20 PSF Dead

| | | Maximum Allowable Span (feet-inches) | | | | | | | | | | | | |
| | | 2 x 4 | | | 2 x 6 | | | 2 x 8 | | | 2 x 10 | | |
Species Group	Spacing in oc	Sel Str	No.1/ No.2	GRADE No.3	Sel Str	No.1/ No.2	GRADE No.3	Sel Str	No.1/ No.2	GRADE No.3	Sel Str	No.1/ No.2	GRADE No.3
Spruce-pine-fir	12	10-7	9-5	7-1	16-5	13-9	10-5	20-10	17-5	13-2	25-6	21-4	16-1
	16	9-8	8-2	6-2	14-3	11-11	9-0	18-1	15-1	11-5	22-1	18-5	13-11
	19.2	8-11	7-5	5-8	13-0	10-11	8-3	16-6	13-9	10-5	20-2	16-10	12-9
	24	7-11	6-8	5-0	11-8	9-9	7-4	14-9	12-4	9-4	18-0	15-1	11-5
D.Fir-L(N)	12	11-6	9-3	6-11	17-1	13-7	10-2	21-8	17-2	12-10	26-6	21-0	15-8
	16	10-2	8-0	6-0	14-10	11-9	8-9	18-9	14-11	11-2	22-11	18-2	13-7
	19.2	9-3	7-4	5-6	13-6	10-9	8-0	17-1	13-7	10-2	20-11	16-7	12-5
	24	8-3	6-7	4-11	12-1	9-7	7-2	15-4	12-2	9-1	18-9	14-10	11-1
Hem-Fir(N)	12	11-1	10-1	7-8	16-9	14-9	11-2	21-3	18-8	14-2	26-0	22-9	17-3
	16	10-0	8-9	6-7	14-6	12-9	9-8	18-5	16-2	12-3	22-6	19-9	14-11
	19.2	9-1	7-11	6-0	13-3	11-8	8-10	16-10	14-9	11-2	20-6	18-0	13-8
	24	8-1	7-1	5-5	11-10	10-5	7-11	15-0	13-2	10-0	18-4	16-1	12-3
Northern Species	12	9-7	7-10	5-11	14-9	11-5	8-9	18-8	14-5	11-0	22-9	17-8	13-6
	16	8-8	6-9	5-2	12-9	9-10	7-7	16-2	12-6	9-7	19-9	15-3	11-8
	19.2	7-11	6-2	4-8	11-8	9-0	6-11	14-9	11-5	8-9	18-0	13-11	10-8
	24	7-1	5-6	4-3	10-5	8-1	6-2	13-2	10-3	7-10	16-1	12-6	9-6

Snow Region, Heavy Roof, No Ceiling: 30 PSF Live, 20 PSF Dead

| | | Maximum Allowable Span (feet-inches) | | | | | | | | | | | | |
| | | 2 x 4 | | | 2 x 6 | | | 2 x 8 | | | 2 x 10 | | |
Species Group	Spacing in oc	Sel Str	No.1/ No.2	GRADE No.3	Sel Str	No.1/ No.2	GRADE No.3	Sel Str	No.1/ No.2	GRADE No.3	Sel Str	No.1/ No.2	GRADE No.3
Spruce-pine-fir	12	9-3	8-5	6-4	14-7	12-4	9-4	18-8	15-7	11-9	22-9	19-1	14-5
	16	8-5	7-3	5-6	12-9	10-8	8-1	16-2	13-6	10-3	19-9	16-6	12-6
	19.2	7-11	6-8	5-0	11-8	9-9	7-4	14-9	12-4	9-4	18-0	15-1	11-5
	24	7-1	5-11	4-6	10-5	8-9	6-7	13-2	11-0	8-4	16-1	13-6	10-2
D.Fir-L(N)	12	10-0	8-4	6-2	15-4	12-2	9-1	19-4	15-4	11-6	23-8	18-9	14-0
	16	9-1	7-2	5-4	13-3	10-6	7-10	16-9	13-4	9-11	20-6	16-3	12-2
	19.2	8-3	6-7	4-11	12-1	9-7	7-2	15-4	12-2	9-1	18-9	14-10	11-1
	24	7-5	5-10	4-5	10-10	8-7	6-5	13-8	10-10	8-2	16-9	13-3	9-11
Hem-Fir(N)	12	9-8	9-0	6-10	15-0	13-2	10-0	19-0	16-8	12-8	23-3	20-4	15-5
	16	8-9	7-10	5-11	13-0	11-5	8-8	16-6	14-5	10-11	20-1	17-8	13-5
	19.2	8-1	7-1	5-5	11-10	10-5	7-11	15-0	13-2	10-0	18-4	16-1	12-3
	24	7-3	6-4	4-10	10-7	9-4	7-1	13-5	11-9	8-11	16-5	14-5	10-11
Northern Species	12	8-4	7-0	5-4	13-1	10-2	7-9	16-8	12-11	9-10	20-4	15-9	12-1
	16	7-7	6-0	4-7	11-5	8-10	6-9	14-5	11-2	8-7	17-8	13-8	10-5
	19.2	7-1	5-6	4-3	10-5	8-1	6-2	13-2	10-3	7-10	16-1	12-6	9-6
	24	6-4	4-11	3-9	9-4	7-3	5-6	11-9	9-2	7-0	14-5	11-2	8-6

Headers in Exterior Bearing Walls

		Maximum Allowable Span (feet-inches)											
Roof Live Load, psf		20			30			40			50		
Header Supporting	Size	Building Width, ft			Building Width, ft			Building Width, ft			Building Width, ft		
		20	28	36	20	28	36	20	28	36	20	28	36
	2-2x4	3-7	3-2	2-10	3-4	2-10	2-7	3-0	2-7	2-4	2-10	2-5	2-2
	2-2x6	5-5	4-8	4-2	4-10	4-2	3-9	4-5	3-10	3-5	4-1	3-7	3-2
	2-2x8	6-10	5-11	5-4	6-2	5-4	4-9	5-7	4-10	4-4	5-2	4-6	4-0
	2-2x10	8-5	7-3	6-6	7-6	6-6	5-10	6-10	5-11	5-4	6-4	5-6	4-11
	2-2x12	9-9	8-5	7-6	8-8	7-6	6-9	7-11	6-10	6-2	7-4	6-4	5-8
	3-2x8	8-6	7-5	6-8	7-8	6-8	5-11	7-0	6-1	5-5	6-6	5-8	5-0
	3-2x10	10-6	9-1	8-2	9-5	8-2	7-3	8-7	7-5	6-8	7-11	6-10	6-2
	3-2x12	12-2	10-7	9-5	10-11	9-5	8-5	9-11	8-7	7-8	9-2	8-0	7-2
	4-2x8	9-4	8-6	7-8	8-8	7-8	6-11	8-1	7-0	6-3	7-6	6-6	5-10
	4-2x10	11-11	10-6	9-5	10-10	9-5	8-5	9-11	8-7	7-8	9-2	7-11	7-1
	4-2x12	14-1	12-2	10-11	12-7	10-11	9-9	11-6	9-11	8-11	10-8	9-2	8-3
	2-2x4	3-1	2-9	2-5	2-10	2-6	2-3	2-8	2-4	2-1	2-6	2-2	2-0
	2-2x6	4-6	4-0	3-7	4-2	3-8	3-3	3-11	3-5	3-1	3-8	3-2	2-11
	2-2x8	5-9	5-0	4-6	5-3	4-8	4-2	4-11	4-4	3-11	4-8	4-1	3-8
	2-2x10	7-0	6-2	5-6	6-5	5-8	5-1	6-0	5-3	4-9	5-8	4-11	4-5
	2-2x12	8-1	7-1	6-5	7-6	6-7	5-11	7-0	6-1	5-6	6-7	5-9	5-2
	3-2x8	7-2	6-3	5-8	6-7	5-10	5-3	6-2	5-5	4-10	5-10	5-1	4-7
	3-2x10	8-9	7-8	6-11	8-1	7-1	6-5	7-6	6-7	5-11	7-1	6-2	5-7
	3-2x12	10-2	8-11	8-0	9-4	8-2	7-5	8-9	7-8	6-11	8-3	7-2	6-6
	4-2x8	8-3	7-3	6-7	7-8	6-8	6-0	7-1	6-3	5-7	6-8	5-10	5-3
	4-2x10	10-1	8-10	8-0	9-4	8-2	7-4	8-8	7-7	6-10	8-2	7-2	6-5
	4-2x12	11-9	10-3	9-3	10-10	9-6	8-6	10-1	8-10	7-11	9-6	8-4	7-6
	2-2x4	2-8	2-4	2-1	2-8	2-3	2-0	2-6	2-2	2-0	2-5	2-1	1-10
	2-2x6	3-11	3-5	3-0	3-10	3-4	3-0	3-8	3-2	2-11	3-6	3-0	2-9
	2-2x8	5-0	4-4	3-10	4-10	4-3	3-9	4-8	4-1	3-8	4-5	3-10	3-5
	2-2x10	6-1	5-3	4-8	5-11	5-2	4-7	5-8	4-11	4-5	5-5	4-8	4-3
	2-2x12	7-1	6-1	5-5	6-11	6-0	5-4	6-7	5-9	5-2	6-3	5-5	4-11
	3-2x8	6-3	5-5	4-10	6-1	5-3	4-9	5-10	5-1	4-7	5-6	4-10	4-4
	3-2x10	7-7	6-7	5-11	7-5	6-5	5-9	7-1	6-2	5-7	6-9	5-10	5-3
	3-2x12	8-10	7-8	6-10	8-8	7-6	6-8	8-3	7-2	6-6	7-10	6-10	6-1
	4-2x8	7-2	6-3	5-7	7-1	6-1	5-6	6-9	5-10	5-3	6-4	5-7	5-0
	4-2x10	8-9	7-7	6-10	8-7	7-5	6-8	8-3	7-2	6-5	7-9	6-9	6-1
	4-2x12	10-2	8-10	7-11	10-0	8-8	7-9	9-6	8-4	7-6	9-0	7-10	7-1

Headers in Exterior Bearing Walls

		Maximum Allowable Span (feet-inches)											
Roof Live Load, psf		20			30			40			50		
Header Supporting	Size	Building Width, ft			Building Width, ft			Building Width, ft			Building Width, ft		
		20	28	36	20	28	36	20	28	36	20	28	36
	2-2x4	2-7	2-3	2-0	2-6	2-2	2-0	2-5	2-1	1-11	2-3	2-0	1-10
	2-2x6	3-9	3-3	2-11	3-8	3-3	2-11	3-6	3-1	2-10	3-4	2-11	2-8
	2-2x8	4-9	4-2	3-9	4-8	4-1	3-8	4-5	3-11	3-6	4-3	3-9	3-4
	2-2x10	5-9	5-1	4-7	5-8	5-0	4-6	5-5	4-9	4-4	5-2	4-7	4-1
	2-2x12	6-8	5-10	5-3	6-7	5-9	5-2	6-4	5-7	5-0	6-0	5-3	4-9
	3-2x8	5-11	5-2	4-8	5-10	5-1	4-7	5-7	4-11	4-5	5-4	4-8	4-2
	3-2x10	7-3	6-4	5-9	7-1	6-3	5-7	6-10	6-0	5-5	6-6	5-8	5-2
	3-2x12	8-5	7-4	6-7	8-3	7-3	6-6	7-11	6-11	6-3	7-6	6-7	6-0
	4-2x8	6-10	6-0	5-5	6-8	5-11	5-4	6-5	5-8	5-1	6-1	5-5	4-10
	4-2x10	8-4	7-4	6-7	8-2	7-2	6-6	7-10	6-11	6-3	7-6	6-7	5-11
	4-2x12	9-8	8-6	7-8	9-6	8-4	7-6	9-1	8-0	7-3	8-8	7-7	6-11

Headers in Interior Bearing Walls

		Maximum Allowable Span (feet-inches)							
Header Supporting	Size	Building Width, ft			Header Supporting	Size	Building Width, ft		
		20	28	36			20	28	36
	2-2x4	3-5	2-10	2-6		2-2x4	2-3	1-11	1-9
	2-2x6	4-11	4-2	3-8		2-2x6	3-4	2-10	2-6
	2-2x8	6-3	5-4	4-8		2-2x8	4-3	3-7	3-3
	2-2x10	7-8	6-6	5-9		2-2x10	5-2	4-5	3-11
	2-2x12	8-11	7-6	6-7		2-2x12	6-0	5-2	4-7
	3-2x8	7-10	6-8	5-10		3-2x8	5-4	4-6	4-0
	3-2x10	9-7	8-1	7-2		3-2x10	6-6	5-5	4-11
	3-2x12	11-1	9-5	8-3		3-2x12	7-6	6-5	5-8
	4-2x8	9-1	7-8	6-9		4-2x8	6-1	5-3	4-8
	4-2x10	11-1	9-4	8-3		4-2x10	7-6	6-5	5-8
	4-2x12	12-10	10-10	9-7		4-2x12	8-8	7-5	6-7

I-Joists

The APA Performance Rated I-Joist (PRI) is an engineered wood structural member, designed for residential floor framing, with the following characteristics:

• Flanges are either sawn lumber or structural composite lumber. Top and bottom flanges are of the same type and grade of material.

• Webs consist of wood structural panels, consisting of Exposure I or exterior plywood or OSB.

• The four depths are: 9½ inches, 11⅞ inches, 14 inches, and 16 inches. Flange widths vary with strength.

• PRIs are manufactured in lengths to 60 feet, then cut to standard lengths such as 16 to 36 feet.

Sample Trademark

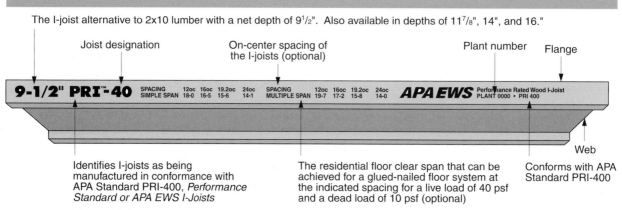

The I-joist alternative to 2x10 lumber with a net depth of 9½". Also available in depths of 11⅞", 14", and 16."

Joist designation

On-center spacing of the I-joists (optional)

Plant number

Flange

9-1/2" PRI™-40 SPACING SIMPLE SPAN 12oc 18-0 16oc 16-5 19.2oc 15-6 24oc 14-1 SPACING MULTIPLE SPAN 12oc 19-7 16oc 17-2 19.2oc 15-8 24oc 14-0 **APA EWS** Performance Rated Wood I-Joist PLANT 0000 • PRI 400

Identifies I-joists as being manufactured in conformance with APA Standard PRI-400, *Performance Standard or APA EWS I-Joists*

The residential floor clear span that can be achieved for a glued-nailed floor system at the indicated spacing for a live load of 40 psf and a dead load of 10 psf (optional)

Web

Conforms with APA Standard PRI-400

Typical Performance-Rated I-Joist Floor Framing (details on pp. 149–151)

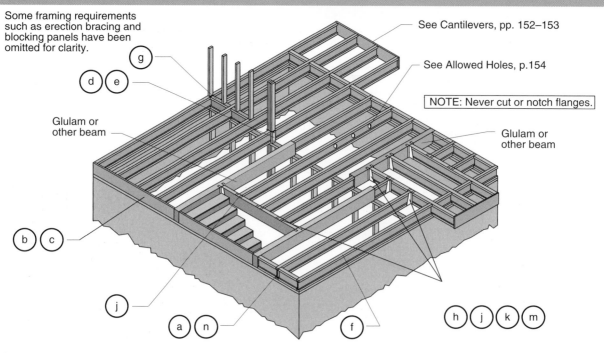

Some framing requirements such as erection bracing and blocking panels have been omitted for clarity.

See Cantilevers, pp. 152–153

See Allowed Holes, p.154

NOTE: Never cut or notch flanges.

Glulam or other beam

Glulam or other beam

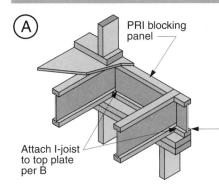

(A) PRI blocking panel

Attach I-joist to top plate per B

Blocking Panel or Rim Joist	Uniform Vertical Load Transfer Capacity* (plf)
PRI joists	2000

*The uniform vertical load capacity is limited to a joist depth of 16" or less and is based on the normal (10-yr) load duration. It shall not be used in the design of a bending member, such as joist, header, or rafter. For concentrated vertical load transfer capacity, see D.

8d nails @ 6" oc to top plate (when used for lateral shear transfer, nail to bearing plate with same nailing as required for decking)

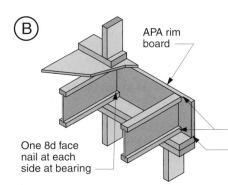

(B) APA rim board

One 8d face nail at each side at bearing

Blocking Panel or Rim Joist	Uniform Vertical Load Transfer Capacity* (plf)
1¹⁄₈" APA rim board plus	4850
1¹⁄₈" APA rim board	4400
1" APA rim board	3300

*The uniform vertical load capacity is limited to a rim board depth of 16" or less and is based on the normal (10-yr) load duration. It shall not be used in the design of a bending member, such as joist, header, or rafter. For concentrated vertical load transfer capacity, see D.

One 8d common or box nail at top and bottom flange

Attach APA rim board to top plate using 8d common or box toenails @ 6"oc

To avoid splitting flange, start nails at least 1¹⁄₂" from end of I-joist. Nails may be driven at an angle to avoid splitting of bearing plate.

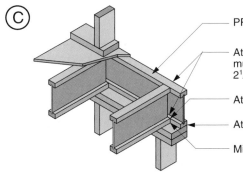

(C) PRI rim joist per A

Attach rim joist to floor joist with one nail at top and bottom. Nail must provide 1" minimum penetration into floor joist. For 2¹⁄₂" and 3¹⁄₂" flange widths, toe nails may be used.

Attach I-joist per B

Attach rim joist to top plate per 1A

Minimum 1³⁄₄" bearing required

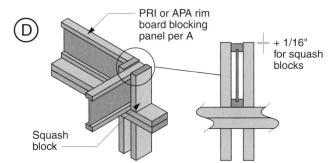

(D) PRI or APA rim board blocking panel per A

+ 1/16" for squash blocks

Squash block

Pair of Squash Blocks	Vertical load transfer capacity per pair of squash blocks (lb)	
	3¹⁄₂" wide	5¹⁄₂" wide
2x lumber	4,000	7,000
1¹⁄₈" APA rim board, rim board plus, or rated Sturd-I-Floor 48 oc	3,000	3,500
1" APA rim board or rated Sturd-I-Floor 32 oc	2,700	3,500

Provide lateral bracing per 1a, 1b, or 1c

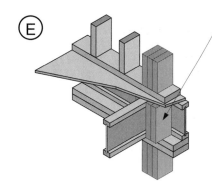

(E) Transfer load from above to bearing below. Install squash blocks per D. Match bearing area of blocks below to post above.

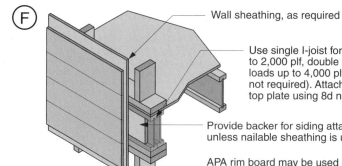

(F) Wall sheathing, as required

Use single I-joist for loads up to 2,000 plf, double I-joists for loads up to 4,000 plf (filler block not required). Attach I-joist to top plate using 8d nails at 6" oc.

Provide backer for siding attachment unless nailable sheathing is used.

APA rim board may be used in lieu of I-joists. Backer is not required when APA rim board is used.

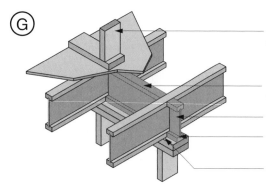

(G) Load bearing wall above shall align vertically with the wall below. Other conditions, such as offset walls, are not covered by this detail.

Blocking required over all interior supports under load-bearing walls or when floor joists are not continuous over support.

PRI blocking panel per A

8d nails at 6" oc to top plate

Joist attachment per detail B

(H)

Backer block (use if hanger load exceeds 250 lb) Before installing a backer block to a double I-joist, drive three additional 10d nails through the webs and filler block where the backer block will fit. Clinch. Install backer tight to top flange. Use twelve 10d nails, clinched when possible. Maximum capacity for hanger for this detail = 1,280 lb.

BACKER BLOCKS (Blocks must be long enough to permit required nailing without splitting)

Flange Width	Material Thickness Required*	Minimum Depth**
$1^1/2$"	$^{19}/_{32}$"	$5^1/2$"
$1^3/4$"	$^{23}/_{32}$"	$5^1/2$"
$2^5/_{16}$"	1"	$7^1/4$"
$2^1/2$"	1"	$5^1/2$"
$3^1/2$"	$1^1/2$"	$7^1/4$"

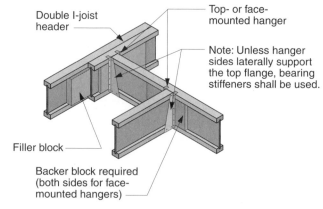

Double I-joist header

Top- or face-mounted hanger

Note: Unless hanger sides laterally support the top flange, bearing stiffeners shall be used.

Filler block

Backer block required (both sides for face-mounted hangers)

For hanger capacity, see hanger manufacturer's recommendations. Verify double I-joist capacity to support concentrated loads.

* Minimum grade for backer block material shall be utility grade SPF (south) or better for solid sawn lumber and rated sheathing grade for wood structural panels.
** For face-mount hangers use net joist depth minus $3^1/4$" for joists with $1^1/2$" thick flanges. For $1^5/_{16}$" thick flanges use net depth minus $2^7/8$".

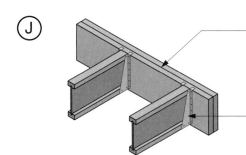

J

Glulam or multiple structural composite lumber beams

For nailing schedules for multiple SCL beams, see the manufacturer's recommendations.

Top- or face-mounted hanger installed per manufacturer's recommendations

Note: Unless hanger sides laterally support the top flange, bearing stiffeners shall be used.

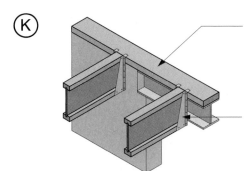

K

2x plate flush with inside face of wall or beam

Note: Unless hanger sides laterally support the top flange, bearing stiffeners shall be used.

Top-mounted hanger installed per manufacturer's recommendations

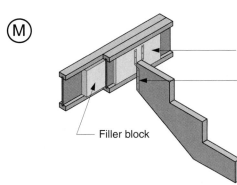

M

Multiple I-joist header with full-depth filler block shown. Glulam and multiple SCL headers may also be used. Verify double I-joist capacity to support concentrated loads.

Backer block attach per H. Nail with twelve 10d nails, clinch when possible.

Install hanger per manufacturer's recommendations.

Filler block

Maximum support capacity = 1,280 lb

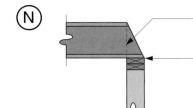

N

Do not bevel-cut joist beyond inside face of wall.

Attach I-joist per B.

Note: Blocking required at bearing for lateral support, not shown for clarity.

Cantilevers for Balconies

Balconies may be constructed using either continuous APA PRIs (first figure below) or by adding lumber extensions (second figure below) to the I-joists. Continuous I-joist cantilevers are limited to one-fourth the adjacent span when supporting uniform loads only. Applications supporting concentrated end loads, such as a wall, are shown on the facing page.

Unless otherwise engineered, cantilevers are limited to a maximum of 4 feet when supporting only uniform loads. Blocking is required at the cantilever support, as shown in both figures.

Uniform floor load shall not exceed 40 psf live load and 10 psf dead load. The balcony load shall not exceed 60 psf live load and 10 psf dead load.

Cantilever Details for Balconies

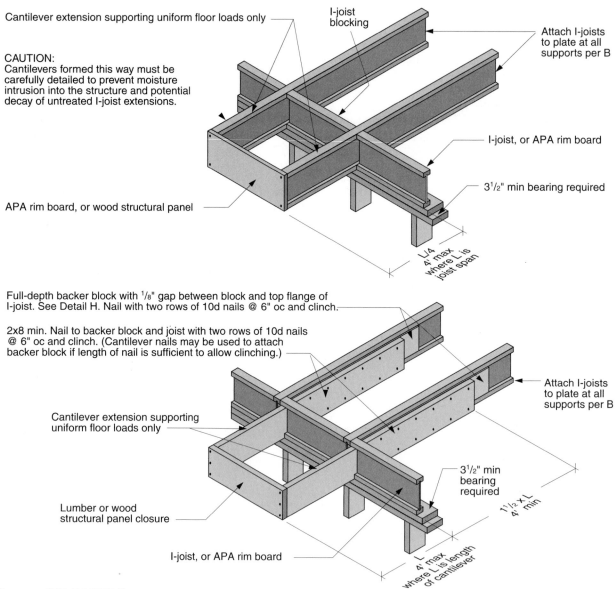

Cantilever extension supporting uniform floor loads only

I-joist blocking

Attach I-joists to plate at all supports per B

CAUTION:
Cantilevers formed this way must be carefully detailed to prevent moisture intrusion into the structure and potential decay of untreated I-joist extensions.

I-joist, or APA rim board

APA rim board, or wood structural panel

3¹/₂" min bearing required

L/4 4' max where L is joist span

Full-depth backer block with ¹/₈" gap between block and top flange of I-joist. See Detail H. Nail with two rows of 10d nails @ 6" oc and clinch.

2x8 min. Nail to backer block and joist with two rows of 10d nails @ 6" oc and clinch. (Cantilever nails may be used to attach backer block if length of nail is sufficient to allow clinching.)

Attach I-joists to plate at all supports per B

Cantilever extension supporting uniform floor loads only

Lumber or wood structural panel closure

3¹/₂" min bearing required

1¹/₂ x L/4 min

I-joist, or APA rim board

L 4' max where L is length of cantilever

Cantilevers for Building Offsets

I-joists may support a concentrated load applied to the end of the cantilever, such as with a vertical building offset. Whether an I-joist cantilever requires reinforcement should be determined by consulting Table 4 of the APA publication, *Performance Rated I-Joists*. For cantilever-end concentrated load applications that require reinforcing, the cantilever is limited to 2 feet maximum. In addition, blocking is required along the cantilever support and for 4 feet on each side of the cantilever area. Depending on roof loads and layout, three methods of reinforcing are allowed in load bearing cantilever applications: reinforcing sheathing applied to one side of the I-Joist (Method 1), reinforcing sheathing applied to both sides of the joist (Method 2), or double I-joists (Alternate Method 2).

Cantilever Details for Vertical Building Offsets

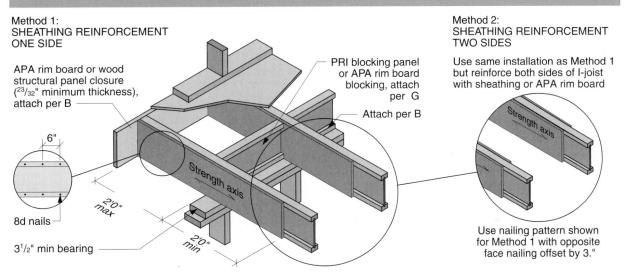

Method 1:
SHEATHING REINFORCEMENT
ONE SIDE

APA rim board or wood structural panel closure ($^{23}/_{32}$" minimum thickness), attach per B

6"

8d nails

3$^{1}/_{2}$" min bearing

2'0" max

2'0" min

Strength axis

PRI blocking panel or APA rim board blocking, attach per G

Attach per B

Method 2:
SHEATHING REINFORCEMENT
TWO SIDES

Use same installation as Method 1 but reinforce both sides of I-joist with sheathing or APA rim board

Strength axis

Use nailing pattern shown for Method 1 with opposite face nailing offset by 3."

APA RATED SHEATHING 48/24 (minimum thickness $^{23}/_{32}$") required on sides of joist. Depth shall match the full height of the joist. Nail with 8d nails at 6" oc, top and bottom flange. Install with face grain horizontal. Attach I-joist to plate at all supports per B.

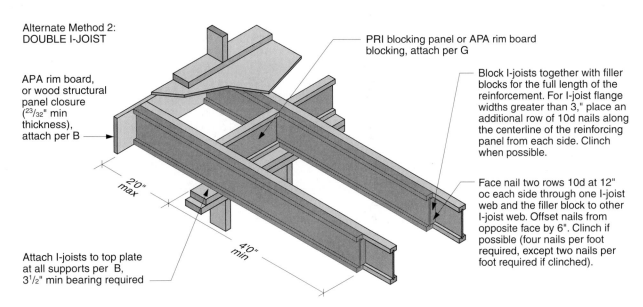

Alternate Method 2:
DOUBLE I-JOIST

APA rim board, or wood structural panel closure ($^{23}/_{32}$" min thickness), attach per B

2'0" max

4'0" min

Attach I-joists to top plate at all supports per B, 3$^{1}/_{2}$" min bearing required

PRI blocking panel or APA rim board blocking, attach per G

Block I-joists together with filler blocks for the full length of the reinforcement. For I-joist flange widths greater than 3," place an additional row of 10d nails along the centerline of the reinforcing panel from each side. Clinch when possible.

Face nail two rows 10d at 12" oc each side through one I-joist web and the filler block to other I-joist web. Offset nails from opposite face by 6". Clinch if possible (four nails per foot required, except two nails per foot required if clinched).

Allowed Holes in PRI Joists

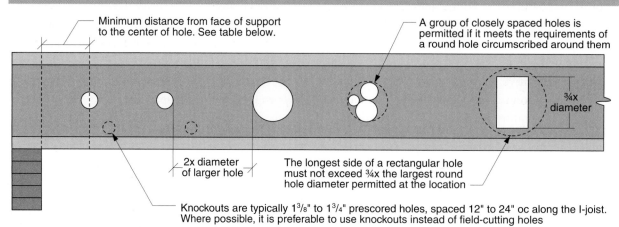

Minimum distance from face of support to the center of hole. See table below.

A group of closely spaced holes is permitted if it meets the requirements of a round hole circumscribed around them

¾x diameter

2x diameter of larger hole

The longest side of a rectangular hole must not exceed ¾x the largest round hole diameter permitted at the location

Knockouts are typically 1⅜" to 1¾" prescored holes, spaced 12" to 24" oc along the I-joist. Where possible, it is preferable to use knockouts instead of field-cutting holes

Minimum Distance from Joist Supports to Center of Hole

Depth, in	I-Joist Designation	Round Hole Diameter, in										
		2	3	4	5	6	7	8	9	10	11	12
9½	PRI-20	0-06	1-00	2-06	3-06	5-06	–	–	–	–	–	–
	PRI-30	1-00	2-00	3-06	5-00	6-06	–	–	–	–	–	–
	PRI-40	0-06	2-00	3-00	4-06	6-00	–	–	–	–	–	–
	PRI-50	1-06	2-06	4-00	5-00	6-06	–	–	–	–	–	–
	PRI-60	2-00	3-00	4-06	6-00	7-06	–	–	–	–	–	–
11⅞	PRI-20	0-06	0-06	0-06	0-06	2-00	4-00	6-00	–	–	–	–
	PRI-30	0-06	0-06	0-06	2-00	3-06	5-00	7-00	–	–	–	–
	PRI-40	0-06	0-06	1-06	2-06	4-00	5-06	7-00	–	–	–	–
	PRI-50	0-06	0-06	1-00	2-06	4-06	6-00	8-00	–	–	–	–
	PRI-60	1-00	2-00	3-06	4-06	6-00	7-06	9-00	–	–	–	–
	PRI-70	0-06	1-06	2-06	4-00	5-06	7-00	9-00	–	–	–	–
	PRI-80	2-00	3-06	4-06	6-00	7-06	9-00	10-06	–	–	–	–
	PRI-90	0-06	0-06	1-06	3-00	5-00	7-00	9-00	–	–	–	–
14	PRI-40	0-06	0-06	0-06	1-00	2-00	3-06	5-00	6-00	8-00	–	–
	PRI-50	0-06	0-06	0-06	0-06	1-00	2-06	4-06	7-00	9-00	–	–
	PRI-60	0-06	0-06	0-06	2-00	3-06	5-00	6-06	8-06	10-06	–	–
	PRI-70	0-06	0-06	0-06	1-00	2-06	4-06	6-00	8-00	10-06	–	–
	PRI-80	0-06	2-00	3-00	4-06	6-00	7-06	9-00	10-06	12-06	–	–
	PRI-90	0-06	0-06	1-00	2-06	4-00	6-00	7-06	9-06	11-06	–	–
16	PRI-40	0-06	0-06	0-06	0-06	0-06	1-06	3-00	4-06	5-06	7-00	9-00
	PRI-50	0-06	0-06	0-06	0-06	0-06	1-06	1-00	2-06	4-06	7-00	10-00
	PRI-60	0-06	0-06	0-06	0-06	0-06	2-00	3-06	5-06	7-06	9-06	12-00
	PRI-70	0-06	0-06	0-06	0-06	0-06	1-00	3-00	5-00	7-00	9-06	11-06
	PRI-80	0-06	0-06	0-06	2-00	3-06	5-00	6-06	8-06	10-06	12-06	14-06
	PRI-90	0-06	0-06	0-06	1-00	2-06	4-00	5-06	7-06	9-00	11-00	13-06

Notes: 1. Table for I-joist spacing of 24 in oc or less.

2. Hole location distance is measured from the inside edge of supports to the center of the hole.

3. Distances are based on uniformly loaded joists that meet the span requirements on the following page.

4. For continuous joists with more than one span, use the longest span to determine hole location in either span.

Residential Floor Spans

The table below indicates the allowable clear spans for various joist spacings under typical residential uniform floor loads (40 psf live load and 10 psf dead load) for glued-nailed systems. The spans shown are based on repetitive member usage which is typical for all wood products spaced 24 inches on center or less. In addition, floor sheathing must be field glued to the I-joist flanges to achieve the PRI allowable spans. APA PRIs can be used for other applications, such as roofs, to support line loads, or concentrated loads, etc., when properly engineered using the appropriate design properties.

Allowable Spans for APA EWS Performance Rated I-Joists

Depth, in	I-Joist Designation	Simple Spans				Multiple Spans			
		On Center Spacing, in				On Center Spacing, in			
		12	16	19.2	24	12	16	19.2	24
	PRI-20	16-07	15-02	14-04	13-05	18-01	16-06	15-07	13-05
	PRI-30	17-01	15-08	14-10	13-10	18-07	17-00	16-01	15-00
9½	PRI-40	18-00	16-05	15-06	14-06	19-07	17-11	16-04	14-07
	PRI-50	17-10	16-04	15-05	14-05	19-05	17-09	16-09	15-07
	PRI-60	18-11	17-04	16-04	15-03	20-08	18-10	17-09	16-06
	PRI-20	19-10	18-02	17-02	16-00	21-08	19-07	16-09	13-05
	PRI-30	20-06	18-09	17-08	16-06	22-04	20-05	18-10	15-00
	PRI-40	21-05	19-07	18-06	16-08	23-05	20-05	18-07	16-07
11⅞	PRI-50	21-04	19-06	18-05	17-02	23-03	21-02	20-00	16-01
	PRI-60	22-07	20-08	19-06	18-02	24-08	22-06	21-02	19-07
	PRI-70	23-00	21-00	19-10	18-06	25-01	22-10	21-07	18-06
	PRI-80	24-11	22-08	21-04	19-10	27-01	24-08	23-03	21-07
	PRI-90	25-08	23-04	22-00	20-05	27-11	25-05	23-11	22-02
	PRI-40	24-04	22-03	20-06	18-04	25-11	22-05	20-05	18-03
	PRI-50	24-04	22-02	21-0	19-07	26-06	24-02	20-02	16-01
14	PRI-60	25-09	23-06	22-02	20-08	28-00	25-07	24-01	19-09
	PRI-70	26-01	23-10	22-06	20-11	28-05	25-11	23-02	18-06
	PRI-80	28-03	25-09	24-03	22-07	30-10	28-00	26-05	23-11
	PRI-90	29-01	26-05	24-11	23-02	31-08	28-10	27-01	25-02
	PRI-40	26-11	24-03	22-01	19-09	27-11	24-02	22-00	19-08
	PRI-50	27-00	24-08	23-04	20-02	29-06	24-03	20-02	16-01
16	PRI-60	28-06	26-00	24-07	22-10	31-01	28-04	24-09	19-09
	PRI-70	29-00	26-05	24-11	23-01	31-07	27-10	23-02	18-06
	PRI-80	31-04	28-06	26-10	25-00	34-02	31-01	29-03	23-11
	PRI-90	32-02	29-03	27-07	25-07	35-01	31-10	30-00	26-07

Notes: 1. Allowable clear span applicable to residential floor construction with a design dead load of 10 psf and live load of 40 psf. The live load deflection is limited to span/480. The end spans shall be 40% or more of the adjacent span.

2. Spans are based on a composite floor with glued-nailed sheathing meeting the requirements for APA rated sheathing or APA rated STURD-I-FLOOR conforming to PRP-108, PS 1, or PS 2 with a minimum thickness of $^{19}/_{32}$ in (40/20 or 20 oc) for a joist spacing of 19.2 in or less, or $^{23}/_{32}$ in (48/24 or 24 oc) for a joist spacing of 24 in. Adhesive shall meet APA specification AFG-01 or ASTM D3498. Spans shall be reduced 1 ft when the floor sheathing is nailed only.

3. Minimum bearing length shall be 1-$^3/_4$ in for the end bearings, and 3$^1/_2$ in for the intermediate bearings.

4. Bearing stiffeners are not required when I-joists are used with the spans and spacings given in this table, except as required for hangers.

5. This span chart is based on uniform loads.

Wood Trusses

Anatomy of a Wood Truss

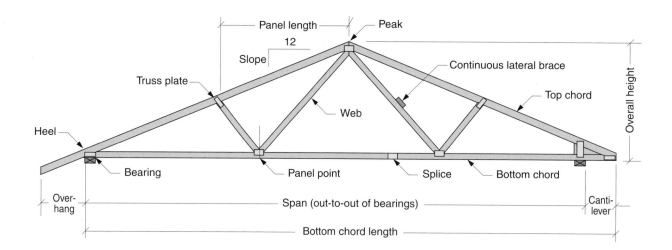

With the decreasing availability of large structural lumber, trusses offer cost savings in both roofs and floors. The reason they can do so—in spite of an added cost of fabrication—is that the lengths of lumber subjected to bending stress are broken into smaller sections.

The top left illustration on the facing page shows how a simple triangle formed by two rafters, a ceiling joist, and a vertical tie (a king post truss) divides a building's total clear span into two rafter clear spans, each half as long. The vertical load of the roof is transformed into forces of tension and compression in the directions of the members.

The next illustration shows how, by simple addition of two diagonal members, the queen post truss further divides the rafter clear span.

The facing page shows a small sample (30) of the variety of trusses available from truss manufacturers nationwide. Designed by computer and manufactured of stress-rated lumber in precision jigs, trusses offer precision, cost-effective solutions to any span problem.

P. 159–168 contain representative span tables showing clear spans as limited by the species/grades and sizes of the top and bottom chord members. All of the roof-truss tables assume wood moisture content of less than 19 percent in service, truss spacing of 24 inches on-center, and roof live and dead loads of 30 psf and 7 psf, respectively. The floor-truss tables assume moisture content of less than 19 percent and the spacings, dead loads, and live loads shown. Remember, these tables are for preliminary design guidance only and must be confirmed by the manufacturer.

Example: What is the maximum allowable clear span of queen post trusses (p. 159) of #2 southern pine with 24-inches on-center spacing, roof pitch of 4/12, top-chord (rafter) dead and live loads of 7 psf and 30 psf, and bottom-chord (ceiling joist) dead load of 10 psf, if the top chord is a 2×6 and the bottom chord a 2×4?

Turn to p. 159. Read horizontally across the row labeled Species Group Southern Pine and Grade #2 to the group of four spans under Pitch of Top Chord 4/12. For a 2×6 top chord the maximum span is 28-2. For a 2×4 bottom chord the maximum span is 18-9. The truss span is thus limited to 18-9 by the 2×4 bottom chord. If we increase the bottom chord to a 2×6 the span will be limited by the bottom chord to 26-3.

A Variety of Trusses (by No Means Complete)

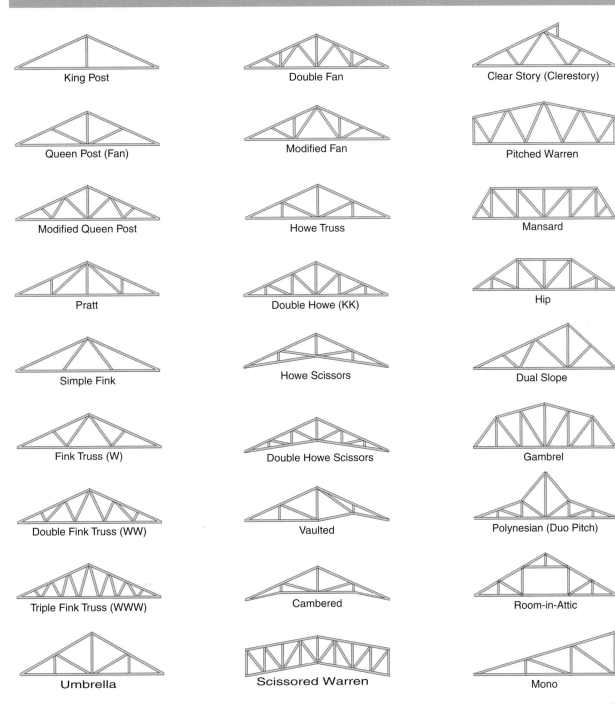

King Post

Queen Post (Fan)

Modified Queen Post

Pratt

Simple Fink

Fink Truss (W)

Double Fink Truss (WW)

Triple Fink Truss (WWW)

Umbrella

Gable End

Double Fan

Modified Fan

Howe Truss

Double Howe (KK)

Howe Scissors

Double Howe Scissors

Vaulted

Cambered

Scissored Warren

Double Inverted

Clear Story (Clerestory)

Pitched Warren

Mansard

Hip

Dual Slope

Gambrel

Polynesian (Duo Pitch)

Room-in-Attic

Mono

Scissors Mono

Roof Truss Bearing and Eave Details

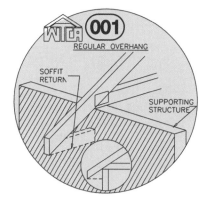

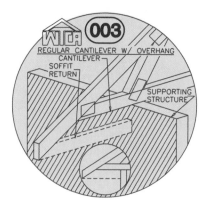

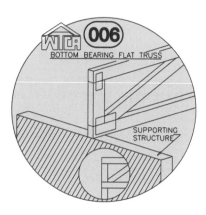

Queen Post Truss

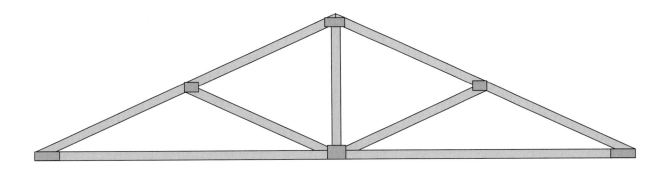

Maximum Allowable (smallest of four figures) Span, feet-inches

Species Group	Grade	Pitch of Top Chord											
		3/12				4/12				5/12			
		Top Chord		Bottom Chord		Top Chord		Bottom Chord		Top Chord		Bottom Chord	
		2×4	2×6	2×4	2×6	2×4	2×6	2×4	2×6	2×4	2×6	2×4	2×6
Southern Pine	#1 Dense	21-6	28-2	21-6	28-2	21-6	28-2	21-6	28-2	21-6	28-2	21-6	28-2
	#1	21-6	28-2	20-8	27-5	21-6	28-2	20-8	27-5	21-6	28-2	20-8	27-5
	#2 Dense	21-6	28-2	20-1	27-3	21-6	28-2	20-1	27-3	21-6	28-2	20-1	27-3
	#2	21-6	28-2	18-9	26-3	21-6	28-2	18-9	26-3	21-6	28-2	18-9	26-3
Douglas Fir-Larch	Sel. Str.	22-4	29-0	22-4	29-0	22-4	29-0	22-4	29-0	22-4	29-0	22-4	29-0
	#1 & Better	22-4	29-0	20-7	28-0	22-4	29-0	20-7	28-0	22-4	29-0	20-7	28-0
	#1	22-4	29-0	19-0	27-0	22-4	29-0	19-0	27-0	22-4	29-0	19-0	27-0
	#2	22-4	29-0	17-3	26-0	22-4	29-0	17-3	26-0	22-4	29-0	17-3	26-0
Southern Pine-Fir	Sel. Str.	19-9	25-10	19-9	25-10	19-9	25-10	19-9	25-10	19-9	25-10	19-9	25-10
	#1	19-9	25-10	16-10	24-6	19-9	25-10	16-10	24-6	19-9	25-10	16-10	24-6
	#2	19-9	25-10	16-10	24-6	19-9	25-10	16-10	24-6	19-9	25-10	16-10	24-6
Hem-Fir	Sel. Str.	20-8	26-8	20-8	26-8	20-8	26-8	20-8	26-8	20-8	26-8	20-8	26-8
	#1	20-8	26-8	18-1	25-5	20-8	26-8	18-1	25-5	20-8	26-8	18-1	25-5
	#2	20-8	26-8	16-6	23-8	20-8	26-8	16-6	23-8	20-8	26-8	16-6	23-8

Fink Truss

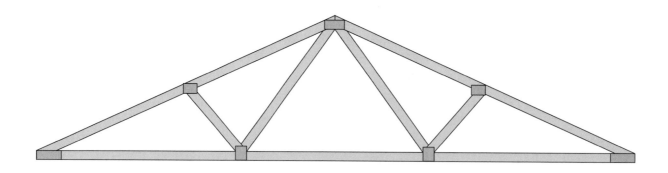

Maximum Allowable (smallest of four figures) Span, feet-inches

Species Group	Grade	Pitch of Top Chord											
		3/12				4/12				5/12			
		Top Chord		Bottom Chord		Top Chord		Bottom Chord		Top Chord		Bottom Chord	
		2×4	2×6	2×4	2×6	2×4	2×6	2×4	2×6	2×4	2×6	2×4	2×6
Southern Pine	#1 Dense	27-7	40-11	30-10	40-11	30-7	42-0	31-11	42-0	31-11	42-0	31-11	42-0
	#1	26-10	39-11	29-7	40-9	29-9	42-0	30-8	40-9	31-1	42-0	30-8	40-9
	#2 Dense	26-6	39-1	26-6	37-10	29-4	42-0	29-10	40-7	30-7	42-0	29-10	40-7
	#2	25-5	37-5	25-0	35-4	28-2	41-5	27-10	39-1	29-5	42-0	27-10	39-1
Douglas Fir-Larch	Sel. Str.	28-2	41-10	33-2	41-10	31-4	43-2	33-2	43-2	32-8	43-2	33-2	43-2
	#1 & Better	26-8	39-7	30-2	41-9	29-7	43-2	30-6	41-9	30-10	43-2	30-6	41-9
	#1	25-8	38-1	27-5	39-1	28-6	42-2	28-3	40-3	29-8	43-2	28-3	40-3
	#2	24-6	36-4	24-10	35-1	27-3	40-3	25-7	38-8	28-5	41-10	25-7	38-8
Southern Pine-Fir	Sel. Str.	26-0	38-5	29-0	38-5	29-0	38-5	29-4	38-5	29-4	38-5	29-4	38-5
	#1	23-8	34-11	21-4	29-8	26-5	38-5	24-7	34-5	27-7	38-5	25-0	36-5
	#2	23-8	34-11	21-4	29-8	26-5	38-5	24-7	34-5	27-7	38-5	25-0	36-5
Hem-Fir	Sel. Str.	26-11	39-9	30-9	39-9	30-0	39-9	30-9	39-9	30-0	39-9	30-9	39-9
	#1	24-9	36-7	25-10	36-5	27-6	39-9	26-10	37-11	28-9	39-9	26-10	37-11
	#2	23-8	34-10	23-0	32-5	26-3	38-7	24-5	35-2	27-5	39-9	24-5	35-2

Modified Queen Post Truss

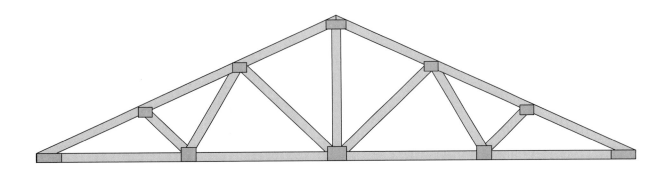

Maximum Allowable (smallest of four figures) Span, feet-inches

Species Group	Grade	Pitch of Top Chord											
		3/12				4/12				5/12			
		Top Chord		Bottom Chord		Top Chord		Bottom Chord		Top Chord		Bottom Chord	
		2×4	2×6	2×4	2×6	2×4	2×6	2×4	2×6	2×4	2×6	2×4	2×6
Southern Pine	#1Dense	33-2	46-5	33-2	46-5	38-4	54-6	38-8	54-6	41-10	55-10	42-5	55-10
	#1	32-5	46-5	31-9	44-6	37-4	54-6	37-0	52-4	40-9	55-10	40-9	54-2
	#2 Dense	32-1	46-5	27-11	39-7	36-10	54-6	33-0	46-11	40-2	55-10	36-11	52-7
	#2	30-9	45-7	26-4	37-0	35-5	52-5	31-1	43-10	38-8	55-10	34-9	49-1
Douglas Fir-Larch	Sel. Str.	34-0	50-10	40-0	50-10	39-2	57-5	44-0	57-5	42-9	57-5	44-0	57-5
	#1 & Better	32-2	48-1	33-0	46-6	37-1	55-4	37-11	53-10	40-6	57-5	40-6	55-5
	#1	31-1	46-4	29-7	41-10	35-10	53-4	34-4	48-9	39-1	57-5	37-5	53-6
	#2	29-8	44-1	26-8	37-2	34-2	50-9	31-1	43-7	37-5	55-5	33-10	48-5
Southern Pine-Fir	Sel. Str.	30-11	43-7	30-11	43-7	36-1	51-0	36-3	51-0	38-11	51-0	38-11	51-0
	#1	28-3	41-10	21-11	30-1	32-9	48-6	26-4	36-5	36-0	51-0	29-10	41-5
	#2	28-3	41-10	21-11	30-1	32-9	48-6	26-4	36-5	36-0	51-0	29-10	41-5
Hem-Fir	Sel. Str.	32-5	48-3	37-7	48-3	37-4	52-10	40-10	52-10	40-10	52-10	40-10	52-10
	#1	29-10	44-3	27-7	38-6	34-5	51-0	32-3	45-3	37-8	52-10	35-6	50-4
	#2	28-6	42-3	24-1	33-9	32-10	48-7	28-6	40-1	35-11	52-10	31-11	45-1

Double Fink Truss

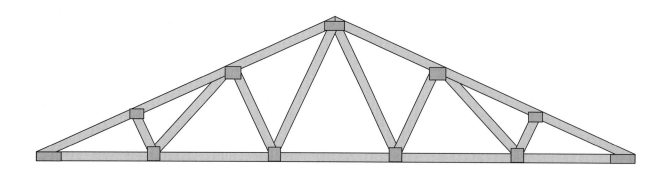

Maximum Allowable (smallest of four figures) Span, feet-inches

Species Group	Grade	3/12 Top Chord 2×4	3/12 Top Chord 2×6	3/12 Bottom Chord 2×4	3/12 Bottom Chord 2×6	4/12 Top Chord 2×4	4/12 Top Chord 2×6	4/12 Bottom Chord 2×4	4/12 Bottom Chord 2×6	5/12 Top Chord 2×4	5/12 Top Chord 2×6	5/12 Bottom Chord 2×4	5/12 Bottom Chord 2×6
Southern Pine	#1 Dense	33-3	49-3	35-5	49-3	38-3	57-0	42-4	57-0	41-8	60-0	47-9	60-0
	#1	32-4	48-4	33-11	47-1	37-2	55-7	40-7	56-10	40-7	60-0	45-9	60-0
	#2 Dense	31-11	47-6	29-5	41-7	36-9	54-6	35-9	50-7	40-1	59-4	40-9	57-10
	#2	30-7	45-5	27-9	38-11	35-3	52-3	33-8	47-3	38-6	56-11	38-5	54-0
Douglas Fir-Larch	Sel. Str.	33-11	50-8	43-9	50-8	39-0	58-2	50-11	58-2	42-7	60-0	54-11	60-0
	#1 & Better	32-1	47-11	35-7	49-11	36-11	55-1	42-0	58-2	40-4	60-0	46-11	60-0
	#1	31-0	46-2	31-9	44-7	35-8	53-1	37-9	53-4	39-0	57-11	42-5	60-0
	#2	29-6	43-11	28-4	39-3	34-1	50-7	34-0	47-4	37-3	55-3	38-4	53-8
Southern Pine-Fir	Sel. Str.	31-1	46-1	32-10	46-1	35-11	53-6	39-6	53-6	39-3	58-4	44-9	58-4
	#1	28-1	41-8	22-10	31-1	32-7	48-4	28-1	38-6	35-10	53-0	32-5	44-8
	#2	28-1	41-8	22-10	31-1	32-7	48-4	28-1	38-6	35-10	53-0	32-5	44-8
Hem-Fir	Sel. Str.	32-3	48-1	40-10	48-1	37-2	55-4	47-11	55-4	40-8	60-0	50-10	60-0
	#1	29-8	44-1	29-4	40-9	34-3	50-10	35-3	49-1	37-6	55-6	39-9	55-9
	#2	28-4	42-1	25-5	35-4	32-9	48-5	30-10	43-0	35-10	52-11	35-2	49-4

Mono Truss

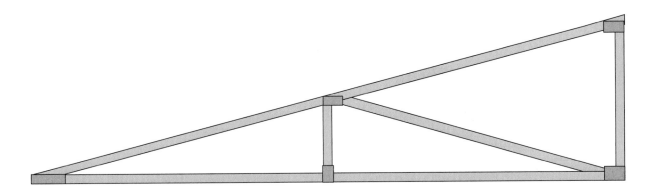

Maximum Allowable (smallest of four figures) Span, feet-inches

		Pitch of Top Chord											
		3/12				4/12				5/12			
		Top Chord		Bottom Chord		Top Chord		Bottom Chord		Top Chord		Bottom Chord	
Species Group	Grade	2×4	2×6	2×4	2×6	2×4	2×6	2×4	2×6	2×4	2×6	2×4	2×6
Southern Pine	#1Dense	16-0	23-5	21-6	23-5	16-6	24-1	21-6	24-1	16-10	24-6	21-6	24-6
	#1	15-6	22-11	20-8	23-5	16-0	23-7	20-8	24-1	16-3	23-11	20-8	24-6
	#2 Dense	15-2	22-1	20-1	23-5	15-7	22-8	20-1	24-1	15-10	23-0	20-1	24-6
	#2	14-6	21-0	18-9	23-5	14-11	21-6	18-9	24-1	15-1	21-9	18-9	24-6
Douglas Fir-Larch	Sel. Str.	16-5	24-1	22-4	24-1	17-0	24-9	22-4	24-9	17-4	25-3	22-4	25-3
	#1 & Better	15-3	22-5	20-7	24-1	15-9	23-0	20-7	24-9	16-0	23-4	20-7	25-3
	#1	14-7	21-4	19-0	24-1	15-0	21-10	19-0	24-9	15-2	22-2	19-0	25-3
	#2	13-10	20-3	17-3	24-1	14-2	20-8	17-3	24-9	14-5	20-11	17-3	25-3
Spruce-Pine-Fir	Sel. Str.	15-4	22-4	19-9	22-4	15-10	23-1	19-9	23-1	16-1	23-6	19-9	23-6
	#1	13-8	19-11	16-10	22-4	14-0	20-4	16-10	23-1	14-3	20-8	16-10	23-6
	#2	13-8	19-11	16-10	22-4	14-0	20-4	16-10	23-1	14-3	20-8	16-10	23-6
Hem-Fir	Sel. Str.	15-11	23-3	20-8	23-3	16-6	24-0	20-8	24-0	16-10	24-6	20-8	24-6
	#1	14-2	20-8	18-1	23-3	14-7	21-2	18-1	24-0	14-10	21-6	18-1	24-6
	#2	13-6	19-8	16-6	23-3	13-10	20-1	16-6	23-8	14-1	20-5	16-6	23-8

Mono Truss

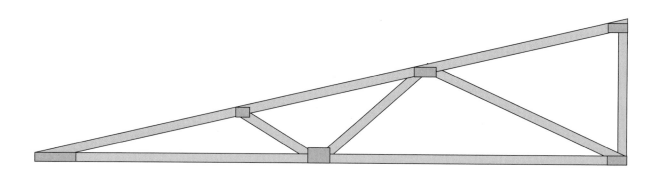

Maximum Allowable (smallest of four figures) Span, feet-inches

		Pitch of Top Chord											
		3/12				4/12				5/12			
		Top Chord		Bottom Chord		Top Chord		Bottom Chord		Top Chord		Bottom Chord	
Species Group	Grade	2×4	2×6	2×4	2×6	2×4	2×6	2×4	2×6	2×4	2×6	2×4	2×6
Southern Pine	#1Dense	21-6	28-2	21-6	28-2	21-6	28-2	21-6	28-2	21-6	28-2	21-6	28-2
	#1	21-6	28-2	20-8	27-5	21-6	28-2	20-8	27-5	21-6	28-2	20-8	27-5
	#2 Dense	21-6	28-2	20-1	27-3	21-6	28-2	20-1	27-3	21-6	28-2	20-1	27-3
	#2	21-3	28-2	18-9	26-3	21-6	28-2	18-9	26-3	21-6	28-2	18-9	26-3
Douglas Fir-Larch	Sel. Str.	22-4	29-0	22-4	29-0	22-4	29-0	22-4	29-0	22-4	29-0	22-4	29-0
	#1 & Better	22-4	29-0	20-7	28-0	22-4	29-0	20-7	28-0	22-4	29-0	20-7	28-0
	#1	21-5	29-0	19-0	27-0	22-4	29-0	19-0	27-0	22-4	29-0	19-0	27-0
	#2	20-6	29-0	17-3	26-0	22-4	29-0	17-3	26-0	22-4	29-0	17-3	26-0
Spruce-Pine-Fir	Sel. Str.	19-9	25-10	19-9	25-10	19-9	25-10	19-9	25-10	19-9	25-10	19-9	25-10
	#1	19-9	25-10	16-10	24-6	19-9	25-10	16-10	24-6	19-9	25-10	16-10	24-6
	#2	19-9	25-10	16-10	24-6	19-9	25-10	16-10	24-6	19-9	25-10	16-10	24-6
Hem-Fir	Sel. Str.	20-8	26-8	20-8	26-8	20-8	26-8	20-8	26-8	20-8	26-8	20-8	26-8
	#1	20-8	26-8	18-1	25-5	20-8	26-8	18-1	25-5	20-8	26-8	18-1	25-5
	#2	19-10	22-1	16-6	23-8	20-8	26-8	16-6	23-8	20-8	26-8	16-6	23-8

Howe Scissors Truss

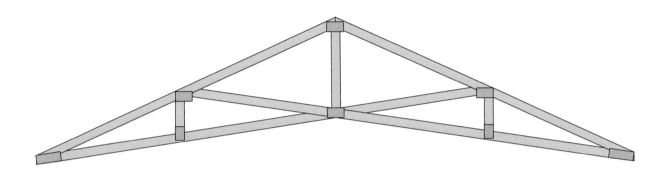

Maximum Allowable (smallest of four figures) Span, feet-inches

		Pitch of Top Chord											
		3/12				4/12				5/12			
		Top Chord		Bottom Chord		Top Chord		Bottom Chord		Top Chord		Bottom Chord	
Species Group	Grade	2x4	2x6	2x4	2x6	2x4	2x6	2x4	2x6	2x4	2x6	2x4	2x6
Southern Pine	#1Dense	20-2	30-0	21-8	30-0	22-5	33-5	26-7	33-5	24-1	35-11	30-8	35-11
	#1	19-7	29-4	20-8	28-7	21-10	32-7	25-5	33-5	23-6	35-0	29-4	35-11
	#2 Dense	19-4	28-10	17-9	25-1	21-6	32-0	22-0	31-2	23-2	34-4	25-7	35-11
	#2	18-6	27-7	16-9	23-6	20-8	30-8	20-9	29-2	22-3	32-11	24-2	34-0
Douglas Fir-Larch	Sel. Str.	20-6	30-8	27-8	30-8	22-10	34-1	33-2	34-1	24-7	36-8	36-6	36-8
	#1 & Better	19-5	29-0	22-1	30-8	21-8	32-4	26-10	34-1	23-4	34-9	30-8	36-8
	#1	18-9	28-0	19-6	27-4	20-11	31-2	23-11	33-8	22-7	33-6	27-5	36-8
	#2	17-10	26-8	17-4	23-11	20-0	29-9	21-4	29-6	21-7	32-0	24-7	34-3
Spruce-Pine-Fir	Sel. Str.	18-9	27-11	19-11	27-11	21-0	31-4	24-7	31-4	22-8	33-9	28-6	33-9
	#1	16-11	25-3	13-7	18-8	19-1	28-4	17-0	23-2	20-8	30-8	19-11	27-5
	#2	16-11	25-3	13-7	18-8	19-1	28-4	17-0	23-2	20-8	30-8	19-11	27-5
Hem-Fir	Sel. Str.	19-6	29-1	25-6	29-1	21-9	32-5	30-10	32-5	23-6	34-11	34-9	34-11
	#1	17-11	26-9	17-11	24-9	20-1	29-10	22-1	30-7	21-8	32-2	25-5	34-11
	#2	17-2	25-6	15-4	21-4	19-2	28-5	19-0	26-5	20-9	30-7	22-1	30-11

Queen Scissors Truss

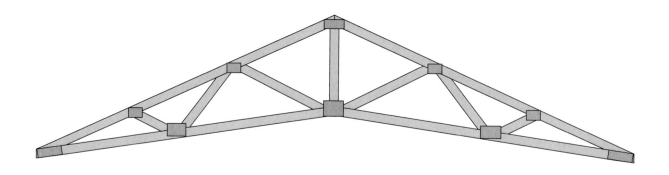

Maximum Allowable (smallest of four figures) Span, feet-inches

Species Group	Grade	Pitch of Top Chord 3/12				4/12				5/12			
		Top Chord		Bottom Chord		Top Chord		Bottom Chord		Top Chord		Bottom Chord	
		2×4	2×6	2×4	2×6	2×4	2×6	2×4	2×6	2×4	2×6	2×4	2×6
Southern Pine	#1Dense	20-5	28-5	20-5	28-5	25-2	35-1	25-2	35-1	28-6	40-8	29-1	40-8
	#1	20-5	28-5	19-7	27-1	25-1	35-1	24-1	33-6	27-8	40-8	27-10	38-11
	#2 Dense	20-5	28-5	16-9	23-10	24-10	35-1	20-9	29-5	27-5	40-8	24-3	34-5
	#2	20-5	28-5	15-10	22-4	23-9	35-1	19-7	27-6	26-3	39-1	22-10	32-2
Douglas Fir-Larch	Sel. Str.	22-11	34-5	26-2	34-5	26-4	39-6	31-7	39-6	29-0	43-5	35-10	43-5
	#1 & Better	21-7	32-5	20-10	29-2	24-10	37-3	25-5	35-9	27-5	41-1	29-2	41-1
	#1	20-10	31-4	18-5	25-11	24-1	36-0	22-8	31-10	26-7	39-9	26-1	36-10
	#2	19-9	29-7	16-5	22-9	22-10	34-2	20-2	27-11	25-4	37-9	23-4	32-6
Spruce-Pine-Fir	Sel. Str.	18-10	26-5	18-10	26-5	23-3	32-8	23-3	32-8	26-7	38-1	27-0	38-1
	#1	18-5	26-5	12-11	17-9	21-6	32-1	16-0	21-10	24-0	35-8	18-10	25-10
	#2	18-5	26-5	12-11	17-9	21-6	32-1	16-0	21-10	24-0	35-8	18-10	25-10
Hem-Fir	Sel. Str.	21-7	32-6	24-1	32-6	24-11	37-4	29-3	37-4	27-6	41-2	33-6	41-2
	#1	19-10	29-8	16-11	23-6	22-11	34-3	20-10	28-11	25-5	37-10	24-2	33-8
	#2	19-0	28-5	14-6	20-3	22-0	32-9	17-11	24-11	24-4	36-1	20-11	29-3

Double Howe Scissors Truss

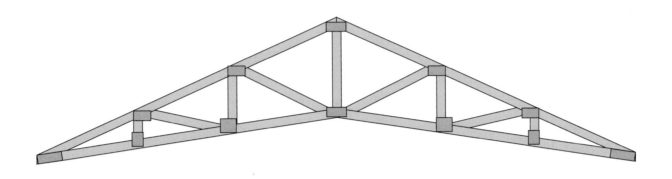

Maximum Allowable (smallest of four figures) Span, feet-inches

		Pitch of Top Chord											
		3/12				4/12				5/12			
		Top Chord		Bottom Chord		Top Chord		Bottom Chord		Top Chord		Bottom Chord	
Species Group	Grade	2×4	2×6	2×4	2×6	2×4	2×6	2×4	2×6	2×4	2×6	2×4	2×6
Southern Pine	#1Dense	20-11	29-0	20-11	29-0	25-9	36-6	26-6	36-6	28-4	42-4	31-6	42-4
	#1	20-11	29-0	20-0	27-7	24-11	36-6	25-4	34-9	27-6	41-2	30-1	41-6
	#2 Dense	20-11	29-0	17-0	24-2	24-8	36-6	21-6	30-4	27-2	40-7	25-9	36-3
	#2	20-5	29-0	16-1	22-8	23-7	35-3	20-3	28-5	26-1	38-10	24-3	33-11
Douglas Fir-Larch	Sel. Str.	22-9	34-2	27-5	34-2	26-2	39-3	34-4	39-3	28-10	43-2	40-4	43-2
	#1 & Better	21-5	32-2	21-6	30-0	24-8	37-0	27-2	37-8	27-3	40-10	32-1	43-2
	#1	20-9	31-1	18-11	26-7	23-11	35-9	23-11	33-4	26-5	39-5	28-4	39-9
	#2	19-7	29-5	16-9	23-2	22-8	33-11	21-2	29-0	25-2	37-6	25-2	34-7
Spruce-Pine-Fir	Sel. Str.	19-2	26-11	19-2	26-11	23-10	33-10	24-3	33-10	26-4	39-6	28-11	39-6
	#1	18-3	26-11	13-0	17-11	21-4	31-10	16-4	22-3	23-10	35-5	19-7	26-7
	#2	18-3	26-11	13-0	17-11	21-4	31-10	16-4	22-3	23-10	35-5	19-7	26-7
Hem-Fir	Sel. Str.	21-5	32-3	25-0	32-3	24-9	37-1	31-6	37-1	27-4	40-10	37-2	40-10
	#1	19-8	29-6	17-3	23-11	22-9	34-0	21-10	30-0	25-3	37-7	26-0	35-10
	#2	18-10	28-2	14-8	20-6	21-10	32-6	18-6	25-8	24-2	35-10	22-2	30-8

Floor Truss, 24 Inches On-Center

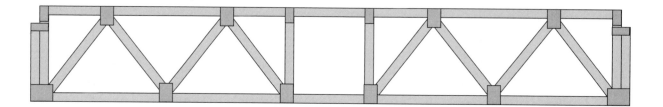

Maximum Allowable Span, feet-inches

Species Group	Grade	16 in Deep		20 in Deep		24 in Deep	
		Top Chord	Bottom Chord	Top Chord	Bottom Chord	Top Chord	Bottom Chord
Top chord: 40 psf live, 5 psf dead — Bottom chord: 0 psf live, 5 psf dead							
Southern Pine	#1Dense	20-5	22-4	29-2	25-3	34-0	28-0
	#1	24-9	22-0	28-9	24-6	33-0	27-0
	#2	24-0	19-1	28-3	21-3	31-2	24-0
Douglas Fir-Larch	Sel. Str.	26-8	26-6	31-6	30-0	36-0	33-0
	#1	25-6	21-4	28-8	24-3	31-8	26-6
	#2	23-6	19-6	26-8	22-2	29-6	24-3
Spruce-Pine-Fir	Sel. Str.	24-0	21-3	29-0	24-1	32-0	26-9
	#1	21-0	16-9	24-1	18-9	27-0	20-8
	#2	21-0	16-9	24-1	18-9	27-0	20-8
Hem-Fir	Sel. Str.	25-0	25-0	29-6	28-2	33-8	31-2
	#1	24-3	20-0	27-4	22-7	30-3	25-0
	#2	23-0	18-0	26-0	20-5	28-8	22-8
Top chord: 40 psf live, 10 psf dead — Bottom chord: 0 psf live, 10 psf dead							
Southern Pine	#1Dense	24-0	19-6	28-0	22-0	30-9	24-4
	#1	23-6	18-9	27-6	20-9	30-0	23-6
	#2	22-4	16-4	25-4	18-4	28-0	20-4
Douglas Fir-Larch	Sel. Str.	26-0	23-0	29-4	26-2	32-4	29-0
	#1	23-0	18-4	25-8	20-6	28-4	23-0
	#2	21-0	16-8	24-0	18-9	26-3	20-9
Spruce-Pine-Fir	Sel. Str.	23-0	18-8	26-0	21-0	29-0	23-4
	#1	19-2	14-3	22-0	16-1	24-1	17-9
	#2	19-2	14-3	22-0	16-1	24-1	17-9
Hem-Fir	Sel. Str.	24-3	22-0	27-4	24-9	30-3	27-4
	#1	21-9	17-0	24-6	19-4	27-0	21-4
	#2	20-7	15-3	23-2	17-3	25-8	19-2

Plank Floors and Roofs

Plank floors and roofs are used in plank-and-beam and post-and-beam constructions. The tables below are for tongue-and-groove planks applied in the alternating two-span style, as shown. Note that two spans are shown in each table:

- limited by fiber stress in tension, F_b
- limited by deflection (modulus of elasticity, E)

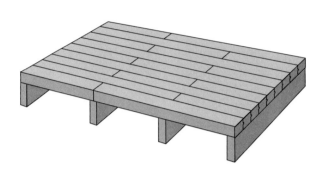

Roof: 40 PSF Live Load, Deflection Ratio 1/360, feet-inches

Thickness, in		Dead Load	Fb, psi				E, 10⁶ psi		
Nominal	(Actual)	psf	900	1,200	1,500	1,800	1.0	1.2	1.4
1	(³/₄)	5	3-10	4-6	5-0	5-6	2-9	2-11	3-1
2	(1¹/₂)	7	7-7	8-9	9-9	10-8	5-6	5-10	6-2
3	(2¹/₂)	12	12-0	13-10	15-6	16-11	9-2	9-9	10-3
4	(3¹/₂)	15	16-4	18-10	21-1	23-1	12-10	13-8	14-5
6	(5¹/₂)	20	24-7	28-5	31-9	34-9	20-4	21-8	22-9

Roof: 20 PSF Live Load, Deflection Ratio 1/180, feet-inches

Thickness, in		Dead Load	Fb, psi				E, 10⁶ psi		
Nominal	(Actual)	psf	900	1,200	1,500	1,800	1.0	1.2	1.4
1	(³/₄)	7	5-0	5-9	6-5	7-1	4-4	4-8	4-11
2	(1¹/₂)	10	9-6	10-11	12-3	13-5	8-9	9-4	9-9
3	(2¹/₂)	15	14-7	16-10	18-10	20-8	14-7	15-6	16-4
4	(3¹/₂)	20	19-2	22-2	24-9	27-1	20-5	21-8	22-10
6	(5¹/₂)	25	28-5	32-9	36-8	40-2	32-4	34-4	36-2

Roof: 40 PSF Live and Snow Load, Deflection Ratio 1/180, feet-inches

Thickness, in		Dead Load	Fb, psi				E, 10⁶ psi		
Nominal	(Actual)	psf	900	1,200	1,500	1,800	1.0	1.2	1.4
1	(³/₄)	7	3-9	4-4	4-10	5-4	3-5	3-8	3-10
2	(1¹/₂)	10	7-4	8-5	9-5	10-4	6-11	7-4	7-9
3	(2¹/₂)	15	11-8	13-5	15-1	16-6	11-7	12-4	12-11
4	(3¹/₂)	20	15-7	18-1	20-2	22-2	16-3	17-3	18-2
6	(5¹/₂)	25	23-7	27-3	30-6	33-5	25-8	27-3	28-8

Glulam Beams

Pound for pound, APA-EWS glulam beams are stronger than steel, and they are attractive enough to leave exposed.

The table below provides glulam floor-beam sizes in I-joist-compatible sizes for the 24F-1.8E stress classification.

The table on the facing page provides the more extensive range of sizes available when I-joist compatibility is not a factor.

Details for incorporating glulam beams into floor framing are shown on p. 172–173.

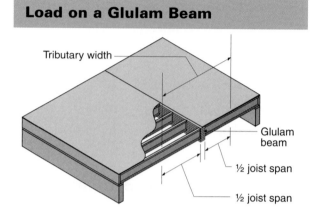

Load on a Glulam Beam

Tributary width — Glulam beam — ½ joist span — ½ joist span

24F–1.8E I-Joist Compatible (IJC) Floor Beams for Simple-Span or Multiple-Span Applications

Span, ft	Tributary Width, ft						
	8	10	12	14	16	18	20
8	3½ x 9½	3½ x 9½	3½ x 9½	3½ x 9½	3½ x 9½	3½ x 11⅞	3½ x 11⅞
	5½ x 9½	5½ x 9½	5½ x 9½	5½ x 9½	5½ x 9½	5½ x 9½	5½ x 9½
10	3½ x 9½	3½ x 9½	3½ x 11⅞	3½ x 11⅞	3½ x 11⅞	3½ x 14	3½ x 14₂
	5½ x 9½	5½ x 9½	5½ x 9½	5½ x 9½	5½ x 9½	5½ x 11⅞	5½ x 11⅞
12	3½ x 11⅞	3½ x 11⅞	3½ x 14	3½ x 14	3½ x 14	3½ x 16	3½ x 16
	5½ x 9½	5½ x 9½	5½ x 11⅞	5½ x 11⅞	5½ x 11⅞	5½ x 11⅞	5½ x 14
14	3½ x 11⅞	3½ x 14	3½ x 14	3½ x 16	3½ x 16	3½ x 18	3½ x 18
	5½ x 9½	5½ x 11⅞	5½ x 11⅞	5½ x 14	5½ x 14	5½ x 14	5½ x 16
16	3½ x 14	3½ x 16	3½ x 16	3½ x 18	5½ x 16	5½ x 16	5½ x 18
	5½ x 11⅞	5½ x 11⅞	5½ x 14	5½ x 14	7 x 14	7 x 14	7 x 16
18	3½ x 16	3½ x 18	3½ x 18	5½ x 16	5½ x 18	5½ x 18	7 x 18
	5½ x 11⅞	5½ x 14	5½ x 16	7 x 14	7 x 16	7 x 16	—
20	3½ x 18	5½ x 16	5½ x 16	5½ x 18	7 x 18	7 x 18	—
	5½ x 14	7 x 14	7 x 16	7 x 16	—	—	—
22	3½ x 18	5½ x 18	5½ x 18	7 x 18	—	—	—
	5½ x 16	7 x 16	7 x 16	—	—	—	—
24	5½ x 16	5½ x 18	7 x 18	—	—	—	—
	7 x 16	7 x 16	—	—	—	—	—

Notes: 1. Applicable to simple-span or multiple-span applications with a dead load of 10 psf and live load of 40 psf.

2. For multiple-span applications, the end spans shall be 40% or more of the adjacent span.

3. Service condition = dry.

4. Maximum deflection = span/360 under live load.

5. F_{bx} = 2,400 psi when tension zone is stressed in tension or 1,600 psi when compression zone is stressed in tension; F_{vx} = 195 psi; E_x = 1.8 x 10⁶ psi.

6. Beam weight = 36 pcf.

7. IJC refers to commonly available residential I-joist depths of 9½ in, 11⅞ in, 14 in and 16 in.

24F–1.8E Floor Beams for Simple-Span or Multiple-Span Applications

Span, ft	Tributary Width, ft						
	8	**10**	**12**	**14**	**16**	**18**	**20**
8	3⅛ x 7½	3⅛ x 9	3⅛ x 9	3⅛ x 10½	3⅛ x 10½	3⅛ x 10½	3⅛ x 12
	3½ x 7½	3½ x 7½	3½ x 9	3½ x 9	3½ x 10½	3½ x 10½	3½ x 10½
	5⅛ x 6	5⅛ x 7½	5⅛ x 7½	5⅛ x 7½	5⅛ x 9	5⅛ x 9	5⅛ x 9
	5½ x 6	5½ x 6	6¾ x 6	5½ x 7½	5½ x 7½	5½ x 9	5½ x 9
10	3⅛ x 9	3⅛ x 10½	3⅛ x 12	3⅛ x 12	3⅛ x 13½	3⅛ x 13½	3⅛ x 15
	3½ x 9	3½ x 10½	3½ x 10½	3½ x 12	3½ x 12	3½ x 13½	3½ x 13½
	5⅛ x 7½	5⅛ x 9	5⅛ x 9	5⅛ x 9	5⅛ x 10½	5⅛ x 10½	5⅛ x 12
	5½ x 7½	5½ x 7½	5½ x 9	5½ x 9	5½ x 10½	5½ x 10½	5½ x 10½
12	3⅛ x 10½	3⅛ x 12	3⅛ x 13½	3⅛ x 15	3⅛ x 15	3⅛ x 16½	3⅛ x 18
	3½ x 10½	3½ x 12	3½ x 12	3½ x 13½	3½ x 15	3½ x 15	3½ x 16½
	5⅛ x 9	5⅛ x 10½	5⅛ x 10½	5⅛ x 12	5⅛ x 12	5⅛ x 13½	5⅛ x 13½
	5½ x 9	5½ x 9	5½ x 10½	5½ x 10½	5½ x 12	5½ x 12	5½ x 13½
14	3⅛ x 13½	3⅛ x 15	3⅛ x 15	3⅛ x 16½	3⅛ x 18	3⅛ x 19½	3⅛ x 19½
	3½ x 12	3½ x 13½	3½ x 15	3½ x 15	3½ x 16½	3½ x 18	3½ x 18
	5⅛ x 10½	5⅛ x 12	5⅛ x 12	5⅛ x 13½	5⅛ x 13½	5⅛ x 15	5⅛ x 15
	5½ x 10½	5½ x 10½	5½ x 12	5½ x 12	5½ x 13½	5½ x 15	5½ x 15
16	3⅛ x 15	3⅛ x 16½	3⅛ x 18	3⅛ x 13½	3⅛ x 21	3⅛ x 21	3⅛ x 18
	3½ x 13½	3½ x 15	3½ x 16½	3½ x 18	3½ x 19½	3½ x 19½	3½ x 21
	5⅛ x 12	5⅛ x 13½	5⅛ x 13½	5⅛ x 15	5⅛ x 16½	5⅛ x 16½	5⅛ x 15
	5½ x 10½	5½ x 12	5½ x 13½	5½ x 15	5½ x 15	5½ x 16½	5½ x 16½
18	3⅛ x 16½	3⅛ x 18	3⅛ x 19½	3⅛ x 21	3⅛ x 18	3⅛ x 19½	3⅛ x 19½
	3½ x 15	3½ x 16½	3½ x 18	3½ x 19½	3½ x 21	3½ x 22½	3½ x 24
	5⅛ x 13½	5⅛ x 15	5⅛ x 16½	5⅛ x 16½	5⅛ x 15	5⅛ x 16½	5⅛ x 18
	5½ x 12	5½ x 13½	5½ x 15	5½ x 16½	5½ x 18	5½ x 18	5½ x 19½
20	3⅛ x 18	3⅛ x 21	3⅛ x 18	3⅛ x 19½	3⅛ x 19½	3⅛ x 21	3⅛ x 22½
	3½ x 16½	3½ x 19½	3½ x 21	3½ x 22½	3½ x 24	3½ x 19½	3½ x 21
	5⅛ x 15	5⅛ x 16½	5⅛ x 15	5⅛ x 16½	5⅛ x 18	5⅛ x 18	5⅛ x 19½
	5½ x 13½	5½ x 15	5½ x 16½	5½ x 18	5½ x 19½	5½ x 18	5½ x 19½
22	3⅛ x 19½	3⅛ x 18	3⅛ x 19½	3⅛ x 21	3⅛ x 22½	3⅛ x 22½	3⅛ x 24
	3½ x 18	3½ x 21	3½ x 22½	3½ x 24	3½ x 21	3½ x 22½	3½ x 24
	5⅛ x 16½	5⅛ x 15	5⅛ x 16½	5⅛ x 18	5⅛ x 19½	5⅛ x 21	5⅛ x 21
	5½ x 15	5½ x 16½	5½ x 18	5½ x 19½	5½ x 19½	5½ x 21	5½ x 21
24	5⅛ x 18	5⅛ x 19½	5⅛ x 21	5⅛ x 22½	5⅛ x 24	5⅛ x 25½	5⅛ x 27
	3½ x 21	3½ x 22½	3½ x 24	5½ x 21	5½ x 22½	5½ x 24	5½ x 25½
	6¾ x 15	6¾ x 16½	6¾ x 18	6¾ x 19½	6¾ x 21	6¾ x 22½	6¾ x 24
	5½ x 16½	5½ x 18	5½ x 19½	6¾ x 19½	6¾ x 21	6¾ x 22½	6¾ x 24

Notes: 1. Applicable to simple-span or multiple-span applications with a dead load of 10 psf and live load of 40 psf.

2. For multiple-span applications, the end spans shall be 40% or more of the adjacent span.

3. Service condition = dry.

4. Maximum deflection = span/360 under live load.

5. F_{bx} = 2,400 psi when tension zone is stressed in tension or 1,600 psi when compression zone is stressed in tension; F_{vx} = 215 psi; E_x = 1.8 x 10⁶ psi.

6. Beam weight = 36 pcf.

7. Beam widths of 3 in and 5 in may be substituted for 3⅛ in and 5⅛ in, respectively, at the same tabulated depth.

Glulam Connection Details

BEAM BEARING AT END WALL

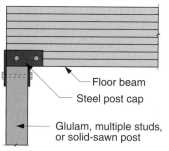

— Floor beam
— Steel post cap

Glulam, multiple studs,
or solid-sawn post

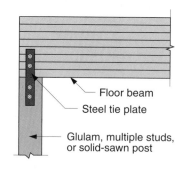

— Floor beam
— Steel tie plate

Glulam, multiple studs,
or solid-sawn post

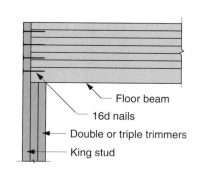

— Floor beam
— 16d nails
— Double or triple trimmers
— King stud

BEAM BEARING AT MASONRY WALL

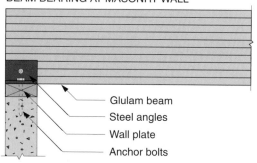

— Glulam beam
— Steel angles
— Wall plate
— Anchor bolts

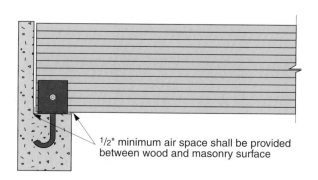

1/2" minimum air space shall be provided
between wood and masonry surface

CONTINUOUS BEAM OVER INTERMEDIATE STEEL COLUMN

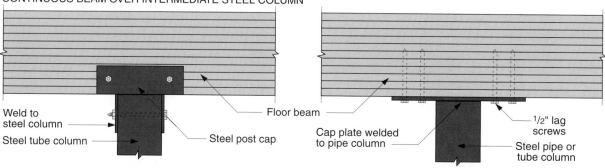

Weld to
steel column
Steel tube column

Floor beam

Steel post cap

Cap plate welded
to pipe column

1/2" lag
screws

Steel pipe or
tube column

CONTINUOUS FLOOR BEAM OVER INTERMEDIATE WOOD SUPPORTS

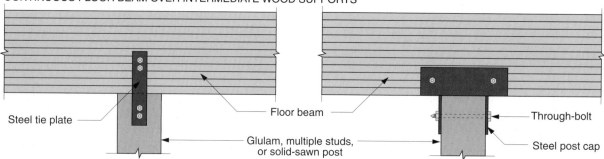

Steel tie plate

Floor beam

Glulam, multiple studs,
or solid-sawn post

Through-bolt

Steel post cap

172   **FRAMING**

BEAM SUPPORT AT END WALL WITH FLOOR JOIST OVER BEAM

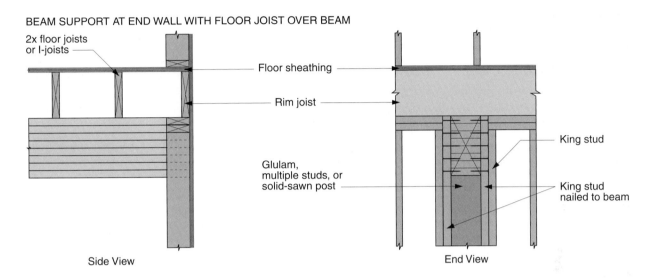

2x floor joists or I-joists

Floor sheathing

Rim joist

King stud

Glulam, multiple studs, or solid-sawn post

King stud nailed to beam

Side View

End View

BEAM SUPPORT AT END WALL WITH FLOOR JOISTS FLUSH WITH BEAM

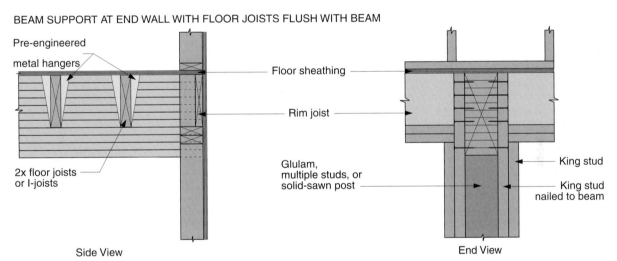

Pre-engineered metal hangers

Floor sheathing

Rim joist

2x floor joists or I-joists

Glulam, multiple studs, or solid-sawn post

King stud

King stud nailed to beam

Side View

End View

LUMBER JOISTS BEARING ON FLOOR BEAM

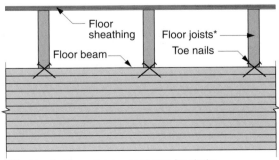

Floor sheathing

Floor joists*

Toe nails

Floor beam

*Blocking between joists not shown for clarity

JOISTS MOUNTED FLUSH WITH FLOOR BEAM

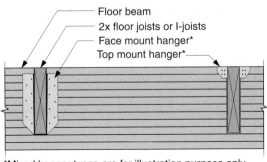

Floor beam

2x floor joists or I-joists

Face mount hanger*

Top mount hanger*

*Mixed hanger types are for illustration purpose only

Panel and Lumber Beams (Box Beams)

When roof load or span requirements are too great to allow use of commonly available dimension lumber or timbers, panel and lumber beams ("box beams") constructed of 2×4 and 2×6 lumber and APA trademarked structural-use panels can solve the problem. They offer inexpensive alternatives to steel or glued laminated wood beams.

The table below shows the allowable loads on beams, in pounds per linear foot, as functions of beam cross section and span.

The lumber is assumed to be No. 1 Douglas-fir or No. 1 southern pine, except No. 2 grades may be substituted if the table loads are reduced by 15 percent.

The structural panels are assumed to be APA rated sheathing Exposure I, oriented strand board (OSB), composite panels (COM-PLY®), or 4- or 5-ply plywood.

Panel and Lumber Beam Components

Labels: End stiffener, Upper flange, Panel web, Panel joint, Stiffener, Lower flange

Allowable Loads[1] for Panel and Lumber Beams

Panel	Section	Lb/linear ft 2×4	Lb/linear ft 2×6	Span, ft 10	12	14	16	18	20	22	24
12-IN DEEP ROOF BEAM OR HEADER											
15/32" 32/16	A	6	8	278[2]	232[2]	192	147	116	94	78	64
15/32" 32/16	B	9	12	339[2]	283[2]	242[2]	212	176	143	118	91
23/32" 48/24	B	11	14	408[2]	340	291	223	176	143	118	95
23/32" 48/24	C	13	17	–	–	–	234	198	160	133	105
16-IN DEEP ROOF BEAM OR HEADER											
15/32" 32/16	A	8	10	393[2]	328[2]	274	210	166	134	111	93
15/32" 32/16	B	10	13	475[2]	396[2]	340[2]	297	264	219	181	152
23/32" 48/24	B	13	16	569[2]	474[2]	406	342	270	219	181	152
23/32" 48/24	C	15	19	–	–	–	–	295	266	219	184
20-IN DEEP ROOF BEAM OR HEADER											
15/32" 32/16	A	9	11	515[2]	429[2]	357	273	216	175	144	121
15/32" 32/16	B	12	15	610[2]	509[2]	436[2]	381[2]	339[2]	297	246	207
23/32" 48/24	B	15	18	728[2]	607[2]	520[2]	455[2]	367	297	246	207
23/32" 48/24	C	17	22	–	–	–	–	385[2]	346	312	262
24-IN DEEP ROOF BEAM OR HEADER											
15/32" 32/16	A	11	13	643[2]	536[2]	439	336	266	215	178	149
15/32" 32/16	B	13	16	744[2]	620[2]	531[2]	465[2]	413	372	312	262
23/32" 48/24	B	16	20	885[2]	738[2]	632[2]	553	465	377	312	262
23/32" 48/24	C	18	24	–	–	–	–	474[2]	427	388	342

[1] Includes 15% snow loading increase.

[2] Lumber may be No. 2 Douglas-fir or No. 2 southern pine without reduction of tabulated capacity.

Cross Sections (see table column 1)

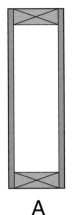 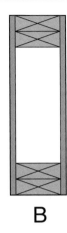 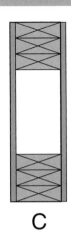

A   B   C

Nailing Pattern

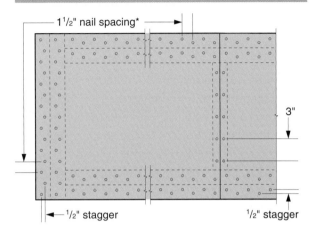

1½" nail spacing*

3"

½" stagger   ½" stagger

All beams in the load-span tables function with 8d common nails spaced 1½ inches on-center on each side of each flange lamination. The spacing may be doubled to 3 inches on-center in the middle half of the beam. Use corrosion-resistant nails if the beam is exposed to moisture. If staples or nails of other sizes or types are used, the spacing must be adjusted in proportion to the allowable lateral load for the fasteners selected.

Although the nailing shown is structurally adequate, additional stiffness can be developed by gluing the panels to the lumber. Any type of wood adhesive will work, but do not reduce the number of nails.

Web Joint Layouts

10' to 10½'

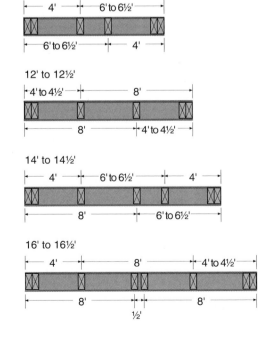

12' to 12½'

14' to 14½'

16' to 16½'

18' to 18½'

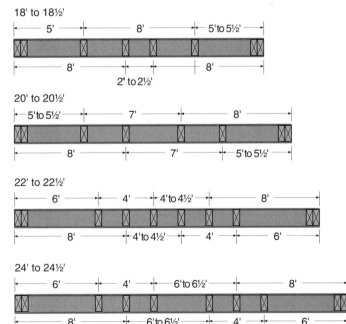

20' to 20½'

22' to 22½'

24' to 24½'

Steel Beams

Steel beams often provide the most cost-effective solution when the loads to be carried are large. The tables below and on the facing page show the maximum clear spans (distance between supports) for the most common steel beam; shape W, type A36.

The calculations are based on simple beams; i.e., beams supported only at their ends. The calculations are thus conservative for continuous beams with more than two supports. The beams are assumed to carry the uniformly distributed floor loads shown as the shaded areas in the figure at right, in addition to their own weight and the weights of any interior walls supporting upper level floors.

These tables are intended for planning purposes only. Consult a steel beam supplier or engineer for final specification.

Area Supported by a Simple Beam

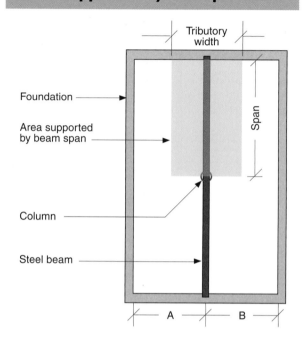

Center Beam Supporting a Single Floor: 40 PSF Live, 10 PSF Dead

	Maximum Allowable Span (feet-inches)									
	Tributary Width Supported by Beam, (A + B)/2									
Beam	6-0	8-0	10-0	12-0	14-0	16-0	18-0	20-0	22-0	24-0
W6x9	14-4	13-0	12-0	11-4	10-10	10-4	9-10	9-4	8-11	8-6
W6x12	15-10	14-4	13-4	12-6	11-11	11-5	10-11	10-7	10-2	9-10
W8x10	17-7	16-0	14-11	14-0	13-2	12-5	11-8	11-1	10-7	10-1
W6x16	17-11	16-2	15-1	14-2	13-6	12-11	12-5	12-0	11-7	11-4
W8x13	19-2	17-5	16-2	15-2	14-5	13-10	13-1	12-5	11-11	11-5
W8x15	20-5	18-7	17-2	16-2	15-5	14-8	14-2	13-7	12-11	12-5
W10x12	21-2	19-4	17-11	16-10	15-7	14-7	13-10	13-1	12-6	11-11
W8x18	22-2	20-2	18-8	17-7	16-10	16-0	15-5	14-11	14-5	14-0
W10x15	23-0	20-11	19-5	18-4	17-5	16-5	15-6	14-8	14-0	13-5
W8x21	23-8	21-7	20-0	18-10	17-11	17-1	16-6	15-11	15-5	15-0
W10x17	24-5	22-2	20-7	19-5	18-5	17-7	16-8	15-11	15-2	14-6
W8x24	24-6	22-2	20-8	19-5	18-6	17-8	17-0	16-5	15-11	15-5
W12x14	25-0	22-10	21-1	19-7	18-2	17-0	16-1	15-4	14-7	13-11
W10x19	25-8	23-5	21-8	20-5	19-5	18-7	17-11	17-1	16-4	15-7
W8x28	25-11	23-6	21-10	20-7	19-6	18-8	18-0	17-4	16-10	16-4
W12x16	26-4	23-11	22-2	20-11	19-5	18-2	17-2	16-4	15-7	14-11
W10x22	27-7	25-0	23-2	21-11	20-10	19-11	19-1	18-6	17-11	17-4
W12x19	28-6	25-11	24-0	22-7	21-6	20-4	19-2	18-2	17-5	16-7
W10x26	29-5	26-10	24-10	23-5	22-2	21-2	20-5	19-8	19-1	18-7

Center Beam Supporting Two Floors: 40+30 PSF Live, 10+10 PSF Dead

Maximum Allowable Span (feet-inches)

Beam	Tributary Width Supported by Beam, (A + B)/2									
	6-0	8-0	10-0	12-0	14-0	16-0	18-0	20-0	22-0	24-0
W6x9	11-11	10-7	9-7	8-10	8-2	7-8	7-2	6-11	6-7	6-4
W6x12	13-1	11-11	11-0	10-1	9-5	8-10	8-4	7-11	7-6	7-2
W8x10	14-5	12-7	11-5	10-5	9-8	9-1	8-7	8-2	7-10	7-6
W6x16	14-10	13-6	12-6	11-10	11-0	10-5	9-10	9-4	8-11	8-6
W8x13	15-11	14-2	12-10	11-8	10-11	10-2	9-8	9-2	8-10	8-5
W8x15	16-11	15-5	13-11	12-10	11-11	11-1	10-6	10-0	9-7	9-2
W10x12	16-11	14-11	13-5	12-4	11-5	10-8	10-1	9-7	9-2	8-10
W8x18	18-5	16-10	15-7	14-6	13-6	12-7	11-11	11-5	10-10	10-5
W10x15	19-0	16-8	15-1	13-10	12-10	12-1	11-5	10-10	10-4	9-11
W8x21	19-8	17-11	16-7	15-7	14-8	13-10	13-1	12-5	11-11	11-5
W10x17	20-2	18-1	16-4	15-0	13-11	13-0	12-4	11-8	11-2	10-8
W8x24	20-4	18-6	17-1	16-1	15-4	14-8	14-0	13-4	12-8	12-2
W12x14	19-10	17-5	15-7	14-5	13-5	12-6	11-10	11-4	10-8	10-4
W10x19	21-5	19-5	17-6	16-1	15-0	14-0	13-4	12-7	12-1	11-7
W8x28	21-6	19-6	18-1	17-1	16-2	15-6	14-11	14-4	13-8	13-1
W12x16	21-1	18-7	16-8	15-5	14-4	13-5	12-8	12-0	11-6	11-0
W10x22	22-11	20-10	19-4	17-11	16-7	15-7	14-8	14-0	13-5	12-10
W12x19	23-6	20-8	18-8	17-1	15-11	15-0	14-1	13-5	12-10	12-4
W10x26	24-5	22-2	20-7	19-5	18-2	17-1	16-1	15-4	14-8	14-1

Center Beam Supporting Three Floors: 40+30+30 PSF Live, 10+10+10 PSF Dead

Maximum Allowable Span (feet-inches)

Beam	Tributary Width Supported by Beam, (A + B)/2									
	6-0	8-0	10-0	12-0	14-0	16-0	18-0	20-0	22-0	24-0
W6x9	10-0	8-10	7-11	7-4	6-10	6-4	6-0	5-8	5-5	5-2
W6x12	11-5	10-0	9-1	8-4	7-8	7-4	6-11	6-6	6-2	6-0
W8x10	11-10	10-5	9-5	8-7	8-0	7-6	7-1	6-10	6-6	6-0
W6x16	13-2	11-10	10-8	9-10	9-1	8-7	8-1	7-8	7-5	7-1
W8x13	13-4	11-8	10-6	9-8	9-0	8-6	8-0	7-7	7-4	7-0
W8x15	14-6	12-8	11-6	10-7	9-10	9-2	8-8	8-4	7-11	7-7
W10x12	13-11	12-2	11-1	10-2	9-6	8-11	8-5	8-0	7-7	7-0
W8x18	16-5	14-5	13-0	12-0	11-1	10-6	9-11	9-5	9-0	8-7
W10x15	15-7	13-10	12-5	11-5	10-7	10-0	9-5	9-0	8-7	8-2
W8x21	17-6	15-10	14-2	13-1	12-2	11-5	10-10	10-4	9-10	9-5
W10x17	16-11	14-11	13-6	12-5	11-6	10-10	10-2	9-8	9-4	8-11
W8x24	18-0	16-5	15-2	14-0	13-0	12-4	11-7	11-0	10-6	10-1
W12x14	16-2	14-4	12-11	11-11	11-0	10-5	9-8	8-8	8-0	7-4
W10x19	18-2	16-0	14-6	13-4	12-5	11-7	11-0	10-6	10-0	9-7
W8x28	19-1	17-4	16-1	15-1	14-1	13-2	12-6	11-11	11-4	10-11
W12x16	17-5	15-4	13-10	12-8	11-10	11-1	10-6	10-0	9-6	8-10
W10x22	20-2	17-10	16-1	14-10	13-10	12-11	12-2	11-7	11-1	10-2
W12x19	19-5	17-1	15-5	14-2	13-2	12-5	11-8	11-1	10-7	9-11
W10x26	21-8	19-6	17-7	16-2	15-1	14-2	13-5	12-8	12-2	11-8

Timber Framing

History

Also known as post-and-beam, post-and-girt, and post-and-lintel, the timber framing system was already well developed in Europe before the discovery of America. The main method of fastening the heavy timbers, the mortise-and-tenon joint (see p. 181), was developed sometime between 200 B.C. and 500 B.C., and the self-supporting braced frame was developed around A.D. 900.

The system is characterized by the use of large, widely spaced load-carrying timbers. Vertical loads are carried by posts at corners and intersections of load-bearing walls. Plates and girts collect distributed roof and floor loads from rafters and joists and transfer them to the posts. Wall studs carry no vertical loads, being used only for attachment of wall sheathing.

Timber framing requires a higher degree of carpentry skill than the so-called stick systems. First, the integrity of the frame depends on the choice and meticulous execution of the wood-peg-fastened joints. Second, the entire frame is precut, each intersecting member being labeled. Finally—usually in a single day—the members are assembled into large wall sections called bents, and then raised with much human power and conviviality. Raising day is the moment of truth for the lead framer.

The timber-frame system evolved more from economic necessity than from aesthetic sensibility. Large timbers were more plentiful, circular-saw and band-saw mills were not available to slice timbers into sticks, and nails were still made by hand, which made them much too costly to use in the quantities needed for stick framing.

Today

The timber frame enjoys a new popularity today, but not for economic reasons. Even proponents acknowledge that a well-executed timber frame is more expensive than a frame employing wood-saving and labor-saving trusses, metal fasteners, and power nailing. The appeal of the timber frame lies in its material and craftsmanship, as well as in nostalgia.

The timber frame of today remains unchanged. In fact, most framers try to emulate the best of the past. What have changed, however, are the insulation and the sheathing systems. Few contractors still practice the classic in-fill system, whereby wall studs are placed between the load-carrying posts to support exterior sheathing and interior finish.

Foam-filled stressed-skin panels dominate the market now. Widely available from dozens of manufacturers, most consist of exterior panels of oriented strand board and interior sheets of gypsum drywall, separated by either urethane or expanded polystyrene foam.

Wiring and plumbing were developed after the timber frame. To this day, concealment of pipes and wires requires planning on the part of the designer and preboring of sheathing and roofing panels.

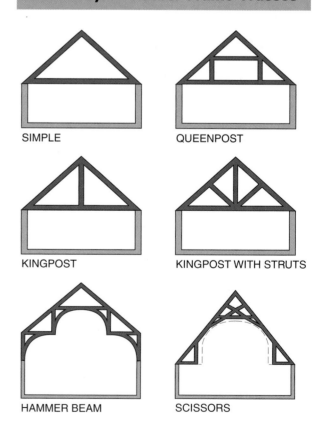

A Variety of Timber-Frame Trusses

SIMPLE

QUEENPOST

KINGPOST

KINGPOST WITH STRUTS

HAMMER BEAM

SCISSORS

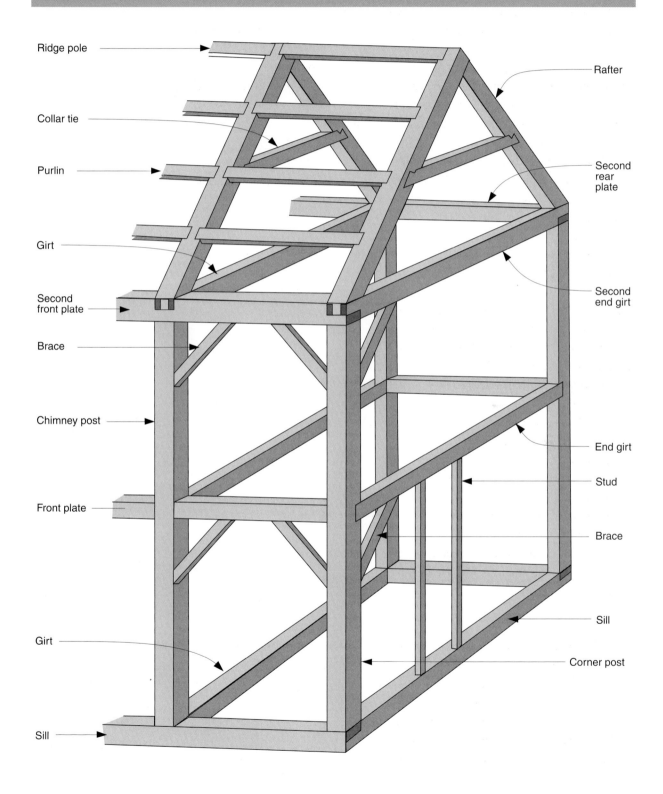

Ridge pole

Collar tie

Purlin

Girt

Second front plate

Brace

Chimney post

Front plate

Girt

Sill

Rafter

Second rear plate

Second end girt

End girt

Stud

Brace

Sill

Corner post

Timber Frame Joinery

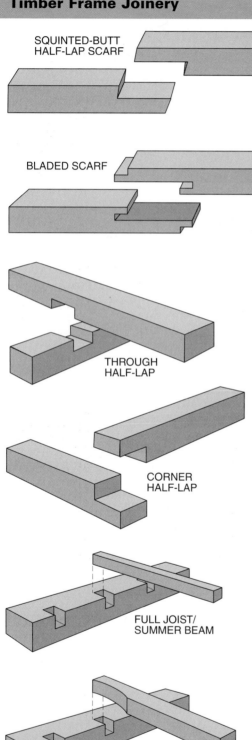

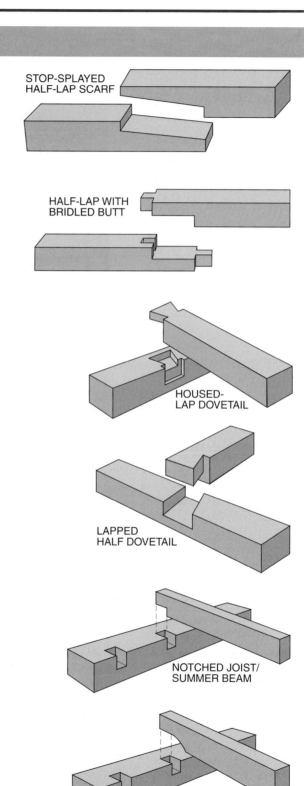

SQUINTED-BUTT HALF-LAP SCARF

STOP-SPLAYED HALF-LAP SCARF

BLADED SCARF

HALF-LAP WITH BRIDLED BUTT

THROUGH HALF-LAP

HOUSED-LAP DOVETAIL

CORNER HALF-LAP

LAPPED HALF DOVETAIL

FULL JOIST/ SUMMER BEAM

NOTCHED JOIST/ SUMMER BEAM

HALF DOVETAIL/ SUMMER BEAM

BEVELED JOIST/ SUMMER BEAM

Timber Frame Joinery—*Continued*

DOUBLE-TENON MORTISE AND TENON
THROUGH MORTISE AND TENON WITH SHOULDERS
THRU MORTISE WITH EXTENDED TENON AND WEDGES
OPEN MORTISE AND TENON
HOUSED MORTISE AND TENON
MORTISE AND TENON WITH DIMINISHED HAUNCH
SINGLE-SHOULDER MORTISE AND TENON
WEDGED-DOVETAIL MORTISE AND TENON
WEDGED-DOVETAIL MORTISE AND TENON
STUB MORTISE AND TENON
DIMINISHED-HAUNCH MORTISE AND TENON
HOUSED BIRD'S MOUTH
BEVELED-SHOULDER BIRD'S MOUTH
STEP-LAP SEAT

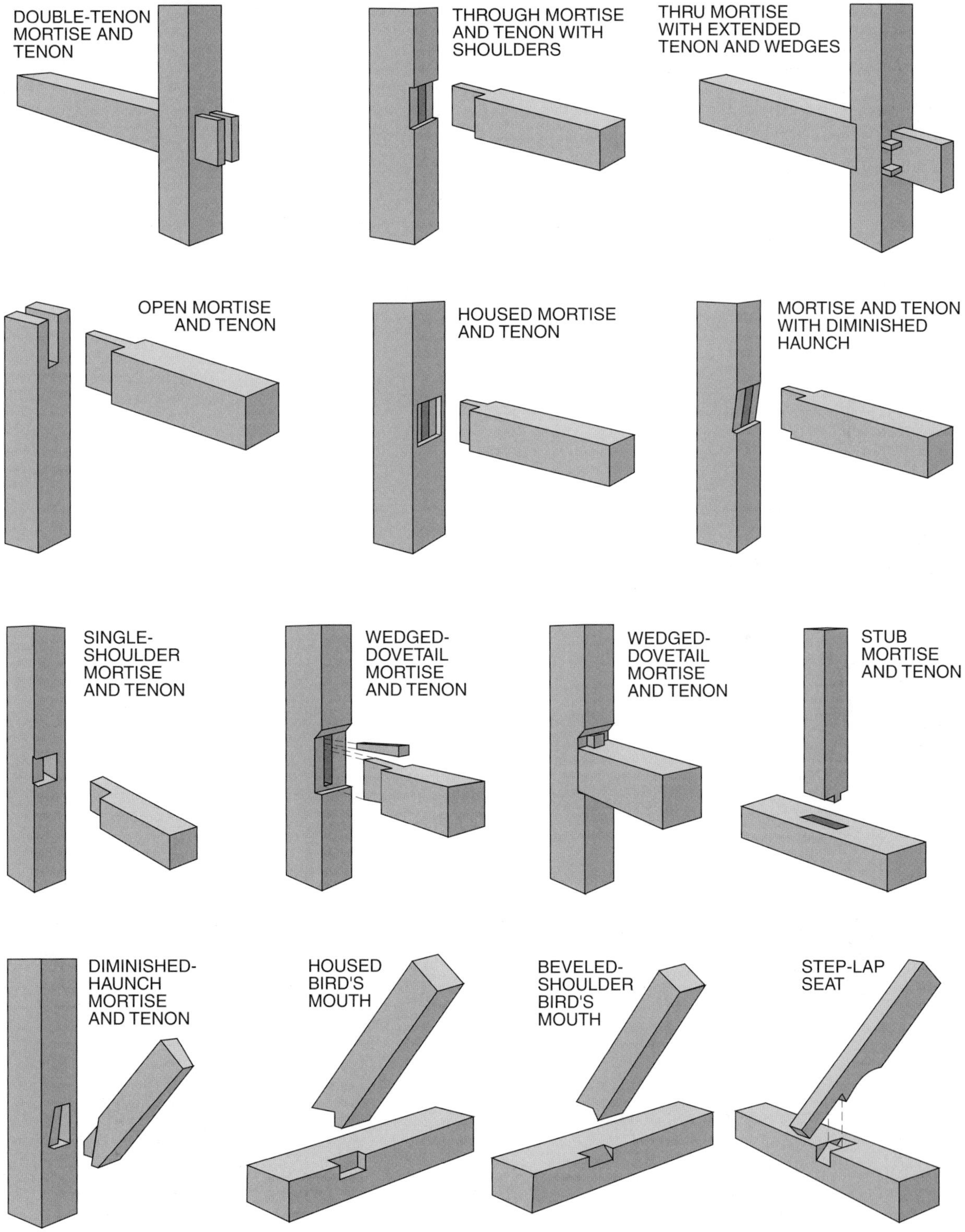

Balloon Framing

The balloon frame developed in response to at least three innovations in the construction industry:

• Invention of the machine-made nail, which made nailing less expensive than hand-pegging.

• More advanced circular-saw mills, which lowered the cost of standardized sawn lumber.

• Development of a housing industry, which promoted standardization of materials and methods.

In the balloon frame, there is no requirement for lumber more than 2 inches thick. Plates, sills, and posts are all built up from 2-inch stock. Front and rear girts are replaced by ribbons (or ribbands), 1×6 or 1×8 boards let into the studs as a support for the joists. Studs now carry most of the vertical load. Bracing is supplied by sheathing panels or by diagonally applied sheathing boards.

The balloon frame gets its name from the fact that the studs run unbroken from sill to top plate, regardless of the number of stories, making the frame like a membrane or balloon. Both the major advantage and disadvantage of the system derive from this fact. In drying, lumber may shrink up to 8 percent in width, but only 0.1 percent in length. Because the overall dimensions of a balloon frame are controlled by length, shrinkage cracks in stucco and plaster finishes are minimized.

The major disadvantage of the balloon frame is the necessity of fire-stopping the vertical wall cavities, which otherwise would act as flues in rapidly spreading fire from basement to attic. A related disadvantage is the difficulty of insulating the wall cavities, which typically open into the basement at the foundation sill.

Because of the fire danger, and because of the scarcity of long framing members, the balloon frame has been replaced almost entirely by the platform frame, discussed in the next section. Framing details for both systems are similar and are shown in later pages.

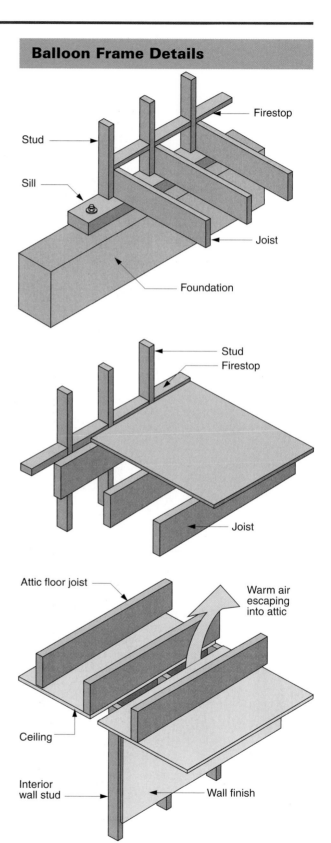

Balloon Frame Details

Stud

Sill

Firestop

Joist

Foundation

Stud
Firestop

Joist

Attic floor joist

Warm air escaping into attic

Ceiling

Interior wall stud

Wall finish

Typical Balloon Frame

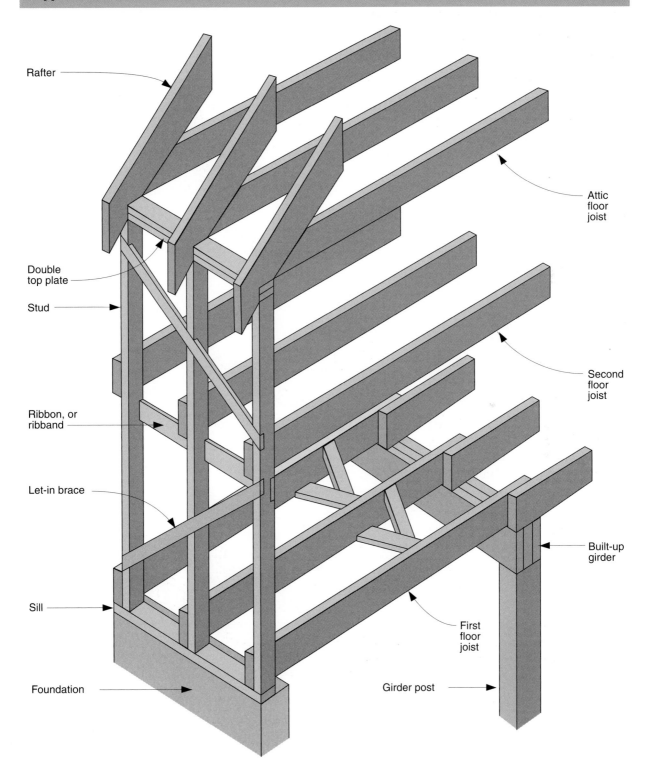

Rafter

Attic floor joist

Double top plate

Stud

Second floor joist

Ribbon, or ribband

Let-in brace

Built-up girder

Sill

First floor joist

Foundation

Girder post

Platform Framing

The platform frame solved the fire problem of the balloon frame. Each story of a platform frame is built upon a platform consisting of joists, band joists, and subfloor. After completion of the first-story walls, the second platform is built identical to the first as if the first-story walls were the foundation. Platform framing represented a great step forward in standardization, requiring the lowest levels of carpentry skill and the fewest standard sizes of lumber.

The platform frame also standardized the use of band joists and sole plates (aka bottom plates). The plates automatically provide fire-stopping and nailing surfaces for both exterior sheathing and interior drywall. The advent of gypsum drywall and other forms of paneling made frame shrinkage less important. Bracing is provided either by the structurally rated exterior sheathing panels, or by diagonally applied sheet metal braces.

Typical Platform Frame

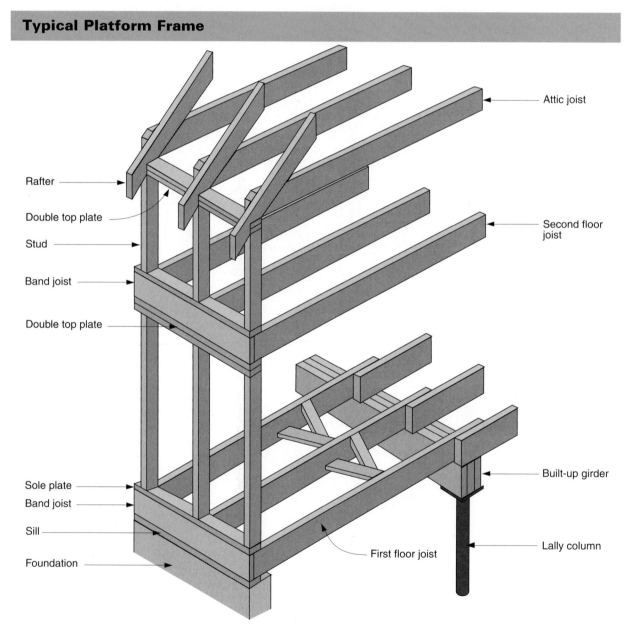

- Rafter
- Double top plate
- Stud
- Band joist
- Double top plate
- Sole plate
- Band joist
- Sill
- Foundation
- Attic joist
- Second floor joist
- Built-up girder
- Lally column
- First floor joist

OVERVIEW

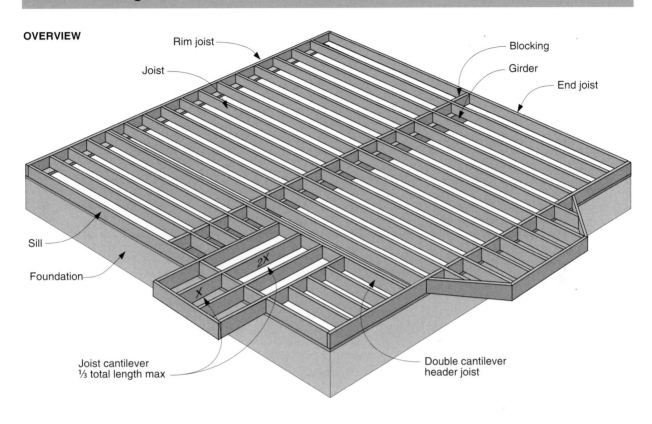

Rim joist

Joist

Blocking

Girder

End joist

Sill

Foundation

2X

X

Joist cantilever
⅓ total length max

Double cantilever
header joist

JOIST DETAILS

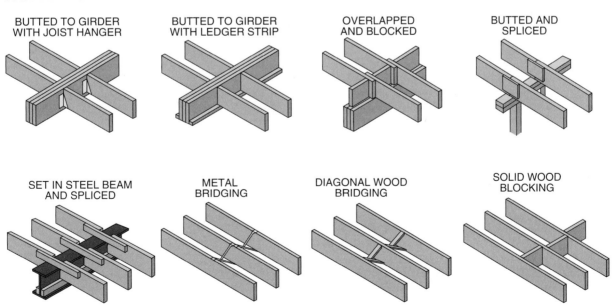

BUTTED TO GIRDER
WITH JOIST HANGER

BUTTED TO GIRDER
WITH LEDGER STRIP

OVERLAPPED
AND BLOCKED

BUTTED AND
SPLICED

SET IN STEEL BEAM
AND SPLICED

METAL
BRIDGING

DIAGONAL WOOD
BRIDGING

SOLID WOOD
BLOCKING

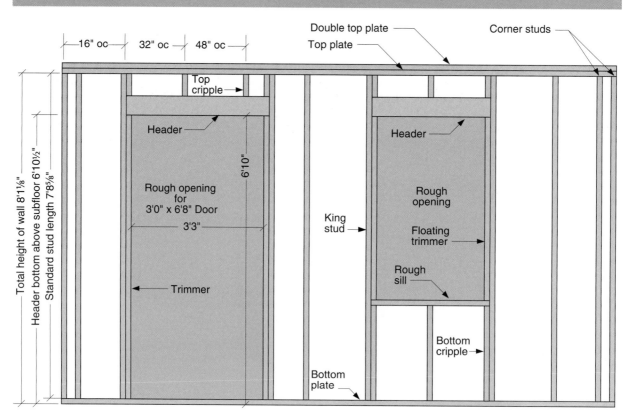

16" oc   32" oc   48" oc

Double top plate

Top plate

Corner studs

Top cripple

Header

6'10"

Header

Rough opening for 3'0" x 6'8" Door

3'3"

Rough opening

Total height of wall 8'1⅛"

Header bottom above subfloor 6'10½"

Standard stud length 7'8⅝"

King stud

Floating trimmer

Rough sill

Trimmer

Bottom cripple

Bottom plate

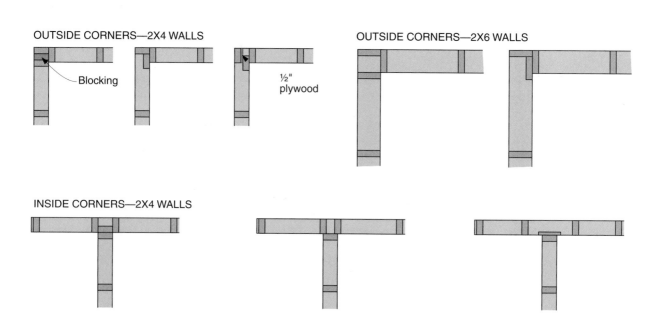

OUTSIDE CORNERS—2X4 WALLS

Blocking

½" plywood

OUTSIDE CORNERS—2X6 WALLS

INSIDE CORNERS—2X4 WALLS

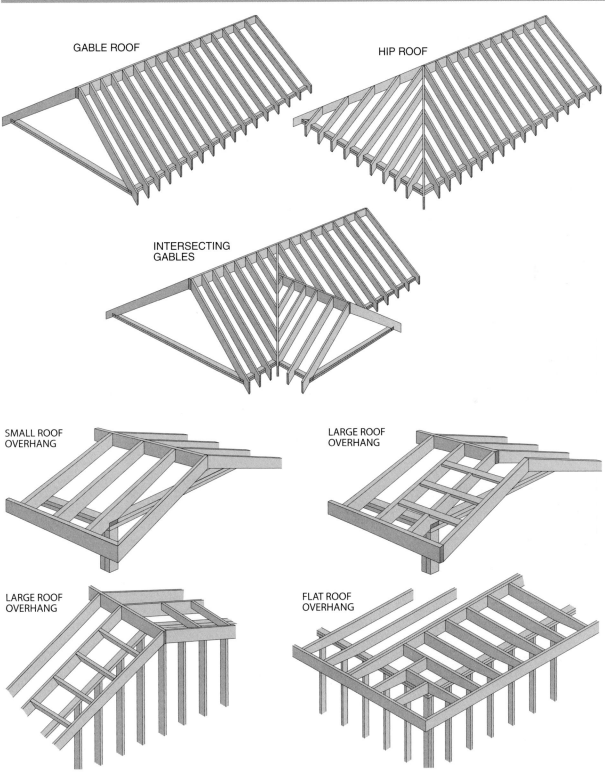

GABLE ROOF

HIP ROOF

INTERSECTING
GABLES

SMALL ROOF
OVERHANG

LARGE ROOF
OVERHANG

LARGE ROOF
OVERHANG

FLAT ROOF
OVERHANG

Dormer and Bay Framing

SHED
DORMER

GABLE
DORMER

CANTILEVERED
BAY

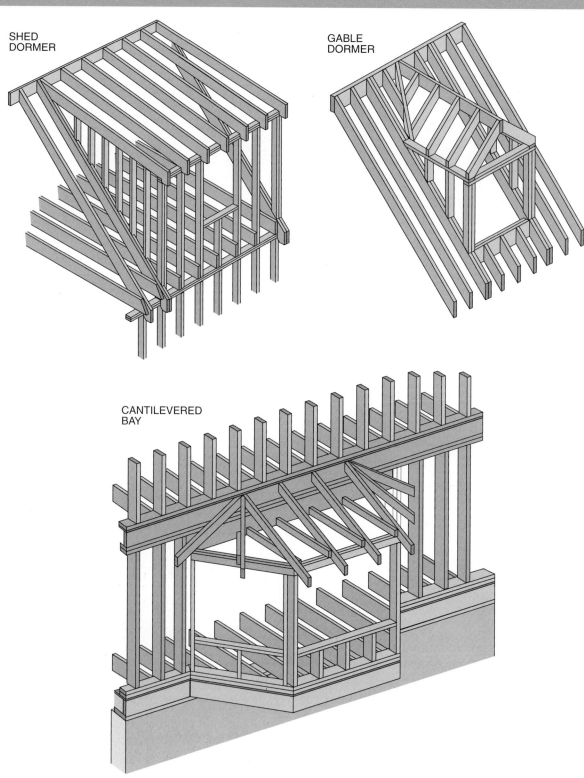

Stairway Framing

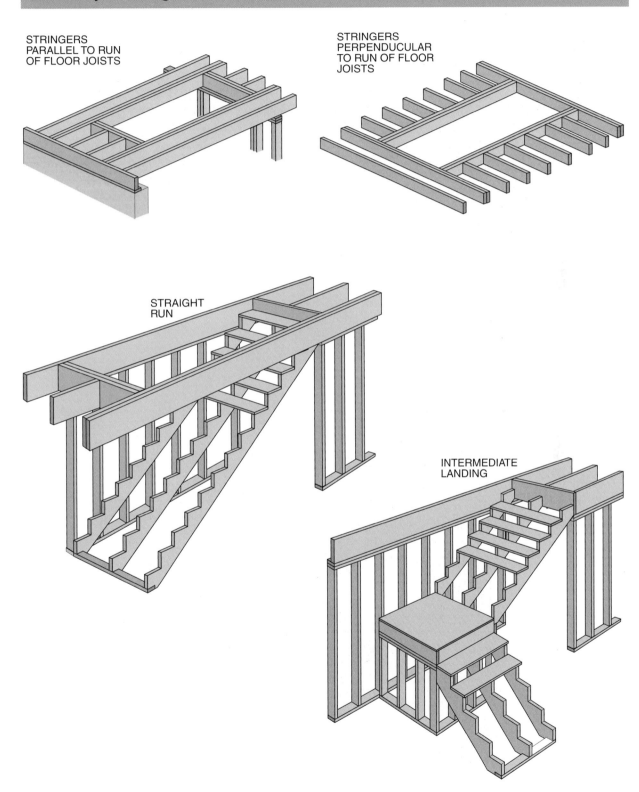

STRINGERS
PARALLEL TO RUN
OF FLOOR JOISTS

STRINGERS
PERPENDUCULAR
TO RUN OF FLOOR
JOISTS

STRAIGHT
RUN

INTERMEDIATE
LANDING

Advanced (OVE) Framing

In an effort to reduce waste in residential building, the National Association of Home Builders (NAHB) developed what they termed Optimum-Value Engineering (OVE), which reduces the amount of lumber in the frame without sacrificing performance. In fact, because the framing acts as a thermal short circuit (compared to insulation) in the building envelope, OVE saves energy, as well.

Unfortunately, both builders and buyers have been slow to adopt the cost-saving techniques. This is not surprising considering America's apparent faith that bigger is better (bigger portions, bigger vehicles, bigger homes). Attempting to make OVE more compelling, its proponents have begun calling it Advanced Framing. Advanced Framing or OVE, here are its features.

Advanced Framing Details

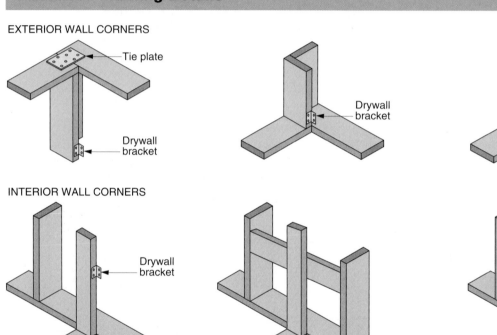

EXTERIOR WALL CORNERS

Tie plate

Drywall bracket

Drywall bracket

INTERIOR WALL CORNERS

Drywall bracket

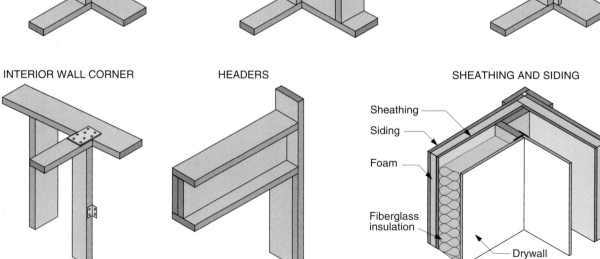

INTERIOR WALL CORNER

HEADERS

SHEATHING AND SIDING

Sheathing

Siding

Foam

Fiberglass insulation

Drywall

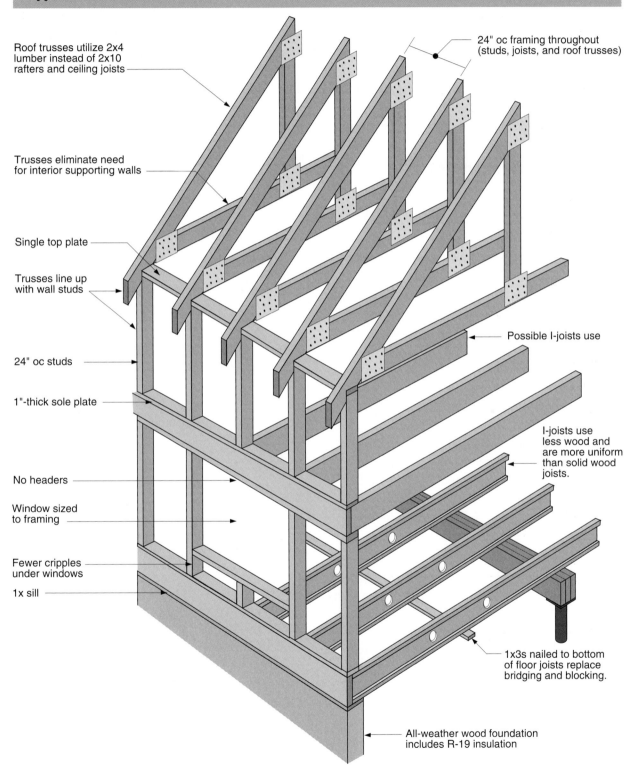

Roof trusses utilize 2x4 lumber instead of 2x10 rafters and ceiling joists

24" oc framing throughout (studs, joists, and roof trusses)

Trusses eliminate need for interior supporting walls

Single top plate

Trusses line up with wall studs

Possible I-joists use

24" oc studs

1"-thick sole plate

I-joists use less wood and are more uniform than solid wood joists.

No headers

Window sized to framing

Fewer cripples under windows

1x sill

1x3s nailed to bottom of floor joists replace bridging and blocking.

All-weather wood foundation includes R-19 insulation

Meet the Code

The following is a partial list of requirements from the *2006 International Residential Code (IRC) for One- and Two-Family Dwellings*. Consult the publication for the full text and additional provisions.

All Framing (R502, R602, R802)

Identification:

- all load-bearing dimension lumber to be identified by grade mark or have certificate of inspection
- preservative-treated lumber to bear the quality mark of an approved inspection agency

Wood Floor Framing (R502)

Design and construction:

- if supported by a wall, decks to be fastened without toenails or nails subject to withdrawal
- joist spans in American Forest & Paper Association (AF&PA) Span Tables for Joists and Rafters
- floor cantilever spans to not exceed the nominal depth of the wood floor joist
- joists under parallel bearing partitions to be of adequate size to support load. Double joists, separated for piping or vents, to be solid blocked @ ≤4' oc
- bearing partitions perpendicular to joists not offset from supporting girders, walls or partitions more than joist depth unless joists of sufficient size
- spans of girders fabricated of dimension lumber to be in accordance with AF&PA Span Tables
- ends of joists, beams, and girders to have ≥1.5" bearing on wood or metal and ≥3" on masonry or concrete except where supported on a 1x4 ribbon and nailed to the adjacent stud, or by joist hangers
- joists framed from opposite sides over a bearing support to lap ≥3" and be nailed together with ≥3 10d face nails or be spliced for equal strength
- joists butting a wood girder to be supported by framing anchors or ≥2×2 ledger strips
- joists supported at ends by solid blocking, or a header, band, or rim joist, or to an adjoining stud
- joists ≥2×12 nominal supported laterally by solid blocking, diagonal bridging, or a continuous 1× 3 strip nailed across bottoms at ≤8' oc

Notches in sawn joists, rafters, and beams:

- depth ≤⅙ of member depth, length ≤⅓ of member depth, and not located in middle ⅓ of span
- at the ends, ≤¼ depth of the member
- tension side of members of ≥4" nominal thickness not to be notched except at ends
- hole diameters ≤D/3 and ≥2" from edges or another hole.

Notches in engineered wood products:

- cuts, notches, and holes in trusses, structural composite lumber, structural glue-laminated members, or I-joists prohibited except where permitted by manufacturer recommendations or professional design

Floor openings:

- floor openings to be framed with header and trimmer joists. When header span ≤4', single header may be same size as floor joist. Single trimmer joists may carry a single header joist located ≤3' of trimmer bearing. When header span >4', trimmers and header to be doubled
- hangers to be used for header to trimmer connection when header span >6'
- tail joists >12' to be supported at header by framing anchors or on ≥2×2 ledger strips

Wood trusses.

- must comply with ANSI/TPI 1
- to be braced as shown on truss design drawings
- not to be cut, notched, or spliced
- additions of load (e.g., HVAC equipment, water heater, etc.), exceeding design load for the truss not permitted without verification
- truss design drawings to be submitted to building official and provided with delivered trusses

Draftstopping:

- where usable space exists above and below concealed space of a floor/ceiling assembly, draftstops to be installed so area of concealed space ≤1,000 sq ft and divided into equal areas

Wood Wall Framing (R602)

Exterior wall design and construction:

- exterior walls to be designed and constructed in accordance with AF&PA's NDS
- exterior walls with foam sheathing to be braced
- structural sheathing fastened directly to framing
- if double top plates are used, top plate joints are offset ≥24"
- single top plate allowed if plate tied at joints, corners and intersecting walls by a ≥3" by 6" galvanized steel plate nailed by six 8d nails on each side
- where joists, trusses, or rafters are spaced >16" oc and bearing studs spaced 24" oc, members to bear within 5" of studs. Exceptions: 2'2" by 6" top plates, 2'3" by 4" top plates, a third top plate, or solid blocking reinforcing the double top plate
- studs to bear fully on a ≥2" nominal plate

Interior wall design and construction:

- load-bearing walls to be constructed, framed and fireblocked as specified for exterior walls.
- 2×3 @ 24" oc nonbearing walls permitted

Drilling and notching:

- studs in exterior wall or bearing partition may be cut or notched to depth ≤25 percent of width
- studs in nonbearing partitions may be notched to a depth ≤40 percent of width
- stud holes ≤60 percent of width and ≥⅝" from edge
- studs in exterior and bearing walls drilled between 40 percent and 60 percent to be doubled
- if top plate cut >50 percent of width, a galvanized metal tie ≥0.054" by 1¼" to be fastened both sides with eight 16d nails or equivalent, except if wall covered by wood structural panel sheathing

Fireblocking required in:

- concealed spaces of stud walls and partitions, including furred spaces and parallel rows of studs or staggered studs: vertically at ceiling and floor, and horizontally at intervals not exceeding 10'

Roof Framing (R802)

Design and construction:

- for pitch ≥ 3/12, rafters fastened to ridge board or gusset plates. Ridge board full depth on cut rafter
- where ceiling joists and rafters not connected at top wall plate, rafter ties required
- where ceiling joists or rafter ties not provided, the ridge to be supported by a wall or girder
- collar ties or ridge straps, spaced ≤4' oc, to be connected in the upper third of attic space
- ceiling joists to be lapped ≥3" or butted and toenailed to a bearing member. Ceiling joists resisting rafter thrust to be fastened to resist such thrust
- ceiling joist and rafter spans as in AF&PA Span Tables for Joists and Rafters
- rafter and ceiling joist ends to have ≥1½" bearing on wood or metal and ≥3" on masonry or concrete

Drilling and notching:

- notches in solid lumber joists, rafters, and beams: depth ≤D/6, length ≤D/3, and not in the middle ⅓ of span
- notches at ends of the member ≤D/4
- tension edge if D≥4" not notched except at ends
- hole diameters ≤D/3 and ≥2" from edges or another hole

Exception: Notch on cantilever permitted if D of remaining portion ≥4" and the length ≤24"

- cuts, notches, and holes in trusses, structural composite lumber, structural glue-laminated members, or I-joists prohibited except where permitted by manufacturer recommendations or professional design
- rafters and ceiling joists >2×10 nominal braced against rotation
- rafters and ceiling joists ≥2×12 supported laterally by solid blocking, diagonal bridging, or a continuous 1×3 strip nailed across bottoms at ≤8' oc

Framing of roof openings same as floor openings
Wood roof trusses same as wood floor trusses

Sheathing

If the frame is the building's skeleton, then the sheathing is its skin. Sheathing functions to enclose the building in an airtight barrier, to strengthen its studs, joists, and rafters by tying them together, to brace the building against racking (twisting) under wind and seismic forces, and to provide a base for flooring, siding, and roofing. By far, most sheathing is done with panels manufactured according to standards established by the Engineered Wood Association (www.apawood.org). This trade organization (once known as the American Plywood Association, or APA) provides extensive technical support relating to all engineered wood products. Most of the material in this chapter is adapted from an APA booklet, *Engineered Wood Construction Guide*. The chapter begins by showing and explaining the grade stamps for all of the *APA sheathing panels*. Next, illustrations and tables show you all you'll ever need to know about *APA subflooring, underlayment, Sturd-I-Floor®, glued floor, wall sheathing, roof sheathing,* and *wall bracing.*

APA Sheathing Panels

Panels for construction can be manufactured in a variety of ways: as plywood (cross-laminated wood veneer), as oriented strand board (OSB), or as other wood-based panel products.

Some plywood is manufactured under the provisions of Voluntary Product Standard PS 1-95 for Construction and Industrial Plywood, a detailed manufacturing specification developed cooperatively by the plywood industry and the U.S. Department of Commerce. Other plywood panels, however, as well as composite and OSB panels, are manufactured under the provisions of APA Performance Standard PRP-108, or under Voluntary Product Standard PS 2-04.

These APA performance-rated panels are easy to use and specify because the recommended end use and maximum support spacings are indicated in the APA grade stamp (see illustration at right).

The list at right describes the face (outside) veneer grading system. The face veneers are often of different grades so that less expensive veneers can be used on the side of the panel that will not show.

The tables on the following pages constitute a lumberyard guide to APA sheathing, including veneered and nonveneered panels, and panels intended for exterior and interior conditions.

Bond Classification

The bond classification relates to moisture resistance of the glue bond, and thus to structural integrity of the panel.

Exterior panels are suitable for repeated wetting and redrying or long-term exposure.

Exposure 1 panels are intended to resist the effects of moisture during construction and for exterior use where not directly exposed to water. Exposure 1 panels are made with the same adhesives used in Exterior panels. However, due to other factors affecting bond performance, only Exterior panels should be used for long-term exposure to weather.

Interior panels are manufactured with interior glue and are intended for interior uses only.

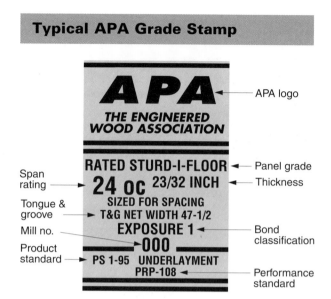

Typical APA Grade Stamp

Plywood Veneer Face Grades

A This smooth, paintable veneer allows not more than 18 neatly made repairs that run parallel to the grain. Wood or synthetic repairs permitted. It may be used as natural finish in less demanding applications.

B Solid-surface veneer permits shims, sled or router repairs, tight knots to 1 inch across the grain, and minor splits. Wood or synthetic repairs permitted.

C-Plugged Improved C veneer has splits limited to ⅛-inch width and knotholes and other open defects limited to ¼ by ½ inch. It admits some broken grain. Wood or synthetic repairs also permitted.

C This veneer has tight knots to 1½ inches. It has knotholes to 1 inch across the grain with some to 1½ inches if the total width of knots and knotholes is within specified limits. Repairs are synthetic or wood. Discoloration and sanding defects that do not impair strength permitted. Limited splits and stitching are allowed.

D Knots and knotholes to 2½-inch width across the grain, and ½ inch larger within specified limits, are allowed. Limited splits and stitching permitted. This face grade is limited to Exposure I or Interior panels.

APA Performance-Rated Panels

Typical APA Grade Stamp	Thicknesses	Grade Designation, Description, and Uses

$5/16$
$3/8$
$7/16$
$15/32$
$1/2$
$19/32$
$5/8$
$23/32$
$3/4$

APA RATED SHEATHING

Exposure Durability Classifications: Exterior, Exposure 1

Specially designed for subflooring and wall and roof sheathing.
Also good for a broad range of other construction and industrial applications.
Can be manufactured as OSB, plywood, or other wood-based panel.

APA
THE ENGINEERED
WOOD ASSOCIATION
RATED SHEATHING
40/20 19/32 INCH
SIZED FOR SPACING
EXPOSURE 1
000
PS 2-04 SHEATHING
PRP-108 HUD-UM-40

APA
THE ENGINEERED
WOOD ASSOCIATION
RATED SHEATHING
24/16 7/16 INCH
SIZED FOR SPACING
EXPOSURE 1
000
PRP-108 HUD-UM-40

$5/16$
$3/8$
$7/16$
$15/32$
$1/2$
$19/32$
$5/8$
$23/32$
$3/4$

APA STRUCTURAL I RATED SHEATHING

Exposure Durability Classifications: Exterior, Exposure 1

Unsanded grade for use where shear and cross-panel strength properties
are of maximum importance, such as panelized roofs and diaphragms.
Can be manufactured as OSB, plywood, or other wood-based panel.

APA
THE ENGINEERED
WOOD ASSOCIATION
RATED SHEATHING
STRUCTURAL I
32/16 15/32 INCH
SIZED FOR SPACING
EXPOSURE 1
000
PS 1-95 C-D PRP-108

APA
THE ENGINEERED
WOOD ASSOCIATION
RATED SHEATHING
32/16 15/32 INCH
SIZED FOR SPACING
EXPOSURE 1
000
STRUCTURAL I RATED
DIAPHRAGMS-SHEAR WALLS
PANELIZED ROOFS
PRP-108 HUD-UM-40

$19/32$
$5/8$
$23/32$
$3/4$
1
$1 1/8$

APA RATED STURD-I-FLOOR

Exposure Durability Classifications: Exterior, Exposure 1

Specially designed as combination subfloor-underlayment. Provides smooth
surface for application of carpet and pad and possesses high concentrated
and impact load resistance. Can be manufactured as OSB, plywood, or
other wood-based panel. Available square edge or tongue-and-groove.

APA
THE ENGINEERED
WOOD ASSOCIATION
RATED STURD-I-FLOOR
24 oc 23/32 INCH
SIZED FOR SPACING
T&G NET WIDTH 47-1/2
EXPOSURE 1
000
PS 2-04 SINGLE FLOOR
PRP-108 HUD-UM-40

APA
THE ENGINEERED
WOOD ASSOCIATION
RATED STURD-I-FLOOR
20 oc 19/32 INCH
SIZED FOR SPACING
T&G NET WIDTH 47-1/2
EXPOSURE 1
000
PRP-108 HUD-UM-40

$11/32$
$3/8$
$7/16$
$15/32$
$1/2$
$19/32$
$5/8$

APA RATED SIDING

Exposure Durability Classification: Exterior

For exterior siding, fencing, etc. Can be manufactured as plywood, as a
composite, or as an overlaid OSB. Both panel and lap siding available.
Special surface treatment such as V-groove, channel groove, deep groove
(such as APA Texture 1-11), brushed, roughsawn, and overlaid (MDO)
with smooth- or texture-embossed face. Span rating (stud spacing for
siding qualified for APA Sturd-I-Wall applications) and face grade
classification (for veneer-faced siding) indicated in trademark.

APA
THE ENGINEERED
WOOD ASSOCIATION
RATED SIDING
24 oc 19/32 INCH
SIZED FOR SPACING
EXTERIOR
000
PRP-108 HUD-UM-40

APA
THE ENGINEERED
WOOD ASSOCIATION
RATED SIDING
303-18-S/W
16 oc 11/32 INCH
GROUP 1
SIZED FOR SPACING
EXTERIOR
000
PS 1-95 PRP-108
HUD-UM-40

APA Sheathing Panels   **197**

APA Sanded and Touch-Sanded Plywood Panels

Typical APA Grade Stamp	Thicknesses	Grade Designation, Description, and Uses
A-A • G-1 • EXPOSURE 1-APA • 000 • PS1-95	$1/4$, $11/32$ $3/8$, $15/32$ $1/2$, $19/32$ $5/8$, $23/32$ $3/4$	**APA A-A** Exposure Durability Classifications: Interior, Exposure 1, Exterior Use where appearance of both sides is important for interior applications such as built-ins, cabinets, furniture, partitions; and exterior applications such as fences, signs, boats, shipping containers, tanks, ducts, etc. Smooth surfaces suitable for painting.
A-B • G-1 • EXPOSURE 1-APA • 000 • PS1-95	$1/4$, $11/32$ $3/8$, $15/32$ $1/2$, $19/32$ $5/8$, $23/32$ $3/4$	**APA A-B** Exposure Durability Classifications: Interior, Exposure 1, Exterior For use where appearance of one side is less important but where two solid surfaces are necessary.
APA THE ENGINEERED WOOD ASSOCIATION A-C GROUP 1 EXTERIOR 000 PS 1-95	$1/4$, $11/32$ $3/8$, $15/32$ $1/2$, $19/32$ $5/8$, $23/32$ $3/4$	**APA A-C** Exposure Durability Classifications: Exterior For use where appearance of only one side is important in exterior or interior applications, such as soffits, fences, farm buildings, etc.
APA THE ENGINEERED WOOD ASSOCIATION A-D GROUP 1 EXPOSURE 1 000 PS 1-95	$1/4$, $11/32$ $3/8$, $15/32$ $1/2$, $19/32$ $5/8$, $23/32$ $3/4$	**APA A-D** Exposure Durability Classifications: Interior, Exposure 1 For use where appearance of only one side is important in interior applications, such as paneling, built-ins, shelving, partitions, flow racks, etc.
B-B • G-2 • EXT-APA • 000 • PS1-95	$1/4$, $11/32$ $3/8$, $15/32$ $1/2$, $19/32$ $5/8$, $23/32$ $3/4$	**APA B-B** Exposure Durability Classifications: Interior, Exposure 1, Exterior Utility panels with two solid sides.
APA THE ENGINEERED WOOD ASSOCIATION B-C GROUP 1 EXTERIOR 000 PS 1-95	$1/4$, $11/32$ $3/8$, $15/32$ $1/2$, $19/32$ $5/8$, $23/32$ $3/4$	**APA B-C** Exposure Durability Classifications: Exterior Utility panel for farm service and work buildings, boxcar and truck linings, containers, tanks, agricultural equipment, as a base for exterior coatings, and other exterior uses or applications subject to high or continuous moisture.

Typical APA Grade Stamp	Thicknesses	Grade Designation, Description, and Uses
	$1/4$, $11/32$ $3/8$, $15/32$ $1/2$, $19/32$ $5/8$, $23/32$ $3/4$	**APA B-D** Exposure Durability Classifications: Interior, Exposure 1, Utility panel for backing, sides of built-ins, industry shelving, slip sheets, separator boards, bins, and other interior or protected applications.
	$1/4$, $11/32$ $3/8$, $15/32$ $1/2$, $19/32$ $5/8$, $23/32$ $3/4$	**APA UNDERLAYMENT** Exposure Durability Classifications: Interior, Exposure 1, For application over structural subfloor. Provides smooth surface for application of carpet and pad and possesses high concentrated and impact load resistance. For areas to be covered with resilient flooring, specify panels with "sanded face."
	$11/32$, $3/8$, $15/32$, $1/2$, $19/32$, $5/8$, $23/32$, $3/4$	**APA C-C PLUGGED** Exposure Durability Classifications: Exterior For use as an underlayment over structural subfloor, refrigerated or controlled atmosphere storage rooms, open soffits, and other similar applications where continuous or severe moisture may be present. Provides smooth surface for application of carpet and pad and possesses high concentrated and impact load resistance. For areas to be covered with resilient flooring, specify panels with "sanded face."
	$3/8$, $15/32$ $1/2$, $19/32$ $5/8$, $23/32$ $3/4$	**APA C-D PLUGGED** Exposure Durability Classifications: Interior, Exposure 1 For open soffits, built-ins, cable reels, separator boards, and other interior or protected applications. Not a substitute for underlayment or APA rated Sturd-I-Floor as it lacks their puncture resistance.

APA Subflooring

APA Panel Subflooring Details

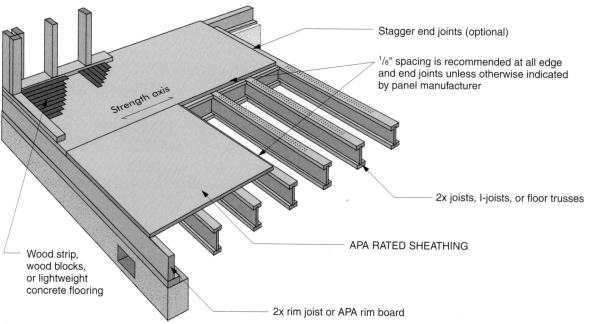

Stagger end joints (optional)

$^{1}/_{8}$" spacing is recommended at all edge and end joints unless otherwise indicated by panel manufacturer

Strength axis

2x joists, I-joists, or floor trusses

APA RATED SHEATHING

Wood strip, wood blocks, or lightweight concrete flooring

2x rim joist or APA rim board

Notes:
Provide adequate moisture control and use ground cover vapor retarder in crawl space. Subfloor must be dry before applying subsequent layers.

For buildings with wood or steel framed walls, provide $^{3}/_{4}$" expansion joints with separate floor framing members and discontinuous wall plates over the joints, at intervals that limit continuous floor areas to 80 ft maximum in length or width, to allow for accumulated expansion during construction in wet weather conditions.

APA Panel Subflooring (APA Rated Sheathing)[1]

Panel Span Rating	Thickness, in	Maximum Span, in	Nail Size and Type[4]	Maximum Nail Spacing, in	
				Supported Panel Edges[5]	Intermediate Supports
24/16	$^{7}/_{16}$	16	6d common	6	12
32/16	$^{15}/_{32}$, ½	16	8d common[2]	6	12
40/20	$^{19}/_{32}$, ⅝	20[3]	8d common	6	12
48/24	$^{23}/_{32}$, ¾	24	8d common	6	12
60/32	⅝	32	8d common	6	12

Source: *Engineered Wood Construction Guide* (Tacoma, WA: APA—The Engineered Wood Association, 2005)

[1] APA Rated Sturd-I-Floor may be substituted when span rating is ≥ tabulated maximum span.

[2] 6d common nail permitted if panel thickness ≤½".

[3] Span may be 24" if ≥1½" of lightweight concrete is applied over panels.

[4] Other code-approved fasteners may be used.

[5] Supported panel joints to lie along the centerline of framing with ≥1½" bearing. Fasteners to be ⅜" from panel edges.

APA Underlayment

APA Plywood Underlayment Details

APA plywood underlayment. See table below for underlayment recommendations for thin flooring products

Stagger end joints (optional for subfloor panels)

Stagger end joints in underlayment panels (optional under carpet and pad)

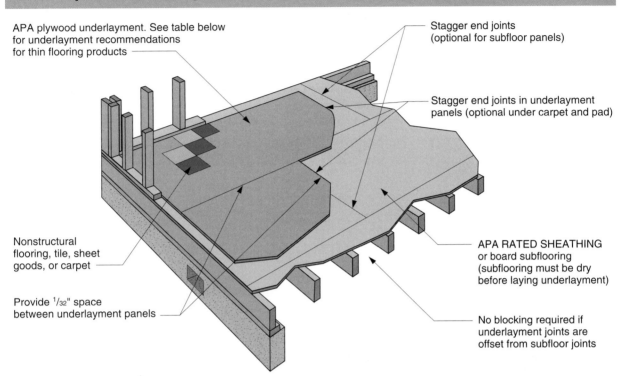

Nonstructural flooring, tile, sheet goods, or carpet

Provide ¹/₃₂" space between underlayment panels

APA RATED SHEATHING or board subflooring (subflooring must be dry before laying underlayment)

No blocking required if underlayment joints are offset from subfloor joints

APA Plywood Underlayment

Plywood Grades[1]	Application	Minimum Thickness	Fastener Size and Type	Max Fastener Spacing[4]	
				Panel Edges[3]	Intermediate Supports
APA Underlayment APA C-C Plugged Ext	Over smooth subfloor	¼"	3d × 1¼" ring-shank nails[2]	3"	6 each way
Rated Sturd-I-Floor (¹⁹/₃₂" or thicker)	Over lumber subfloor or uneven surfaces	¹¹/₃₂"	min 12½-ga (0.099") shank dia	6"	8 each way

Source: *Engineered Wood Construction Guide* (Tacoma, WA: APA—The Engineered Wood Association, 2005)

[1] In areas to be finished with resilient floor coverings such as tile or sheet vinyl, or with fully adhered carpet, specify Underlayment, C-C Plugged or veneer-faced Sturd-I-Floor with "sanded face." Underlayment A-C, Underlayment B-C, Marine Ext, or sanded plywood grades marked "Plugged Crossbands Under Face," "Plugged Crossbands (or Core)," "Plugged Inner Plies," or "Meets Underlayment Requirements" may also be used under resilient floor coverings.

[2] Use 4d × 1½" ring-shank nails, minimum 12½ gage (0.099") shank dia, for underlayment panels ¹⁹/₃₂" to ¾" thick.

[3] Fasten panels ⅜" from panel edges.

[4] Fasteners for 5-ply plywood underlayment panels and for panels greater than ½" thick may be spaced 6" oc at edges and 12" each way intermediate.

APA Sturd-I-Floor

The APA Rated Sturd-I-Floor is a span-rated APA proprietary product designed specifically for use in single-layer floor construction beneath carpet and pad. The product provides cost-saving and performance benefits of combined subfloor-underlayment construction. It is manufactured in conformance with APA PRP-108 Performance Standards and/or Voluntary Product Standard PS 1 or PS 2. It's easy to use because the maximum recommended spacing of floor joists (span rating) is stamped on each panel. Panels are manufactured with span ratings of 16, 20, 24, 32, and 48 inches. *These assume use of the panel is continuous over two or more spans with the long dimension or strength axis across supports.*

Glue-nailing is recommended for Sturd-I-Floor panels, though panels may be nailed only. Recommendations for both methods are given in

the top table on the facing page. (See "APA Glued Floor," p. 204, for more detailed gluing recommendations.) Recommended live loads are given in the bottom table on the facing page.

Although Sturd-I-Floor is suitable for direct application of carpet and pad, an additional thin layer of underlayment is recommended under tile, sheet flooring, or fully adhered carpet. The added layer restores a smooth surface over panels that may have been scuffed or roughened during construction, or over panels that may not have received a sufficiently sanded surface. When veneer-faced Sturd-I-Floor with "sanded face" is specified, the surface is also suitable for direct application of resilient floor covering. Glued tongue-and-groove edges are recommended under thin floor coverings to assure snug joints.

APA Rated Sturd-I-Floor Details

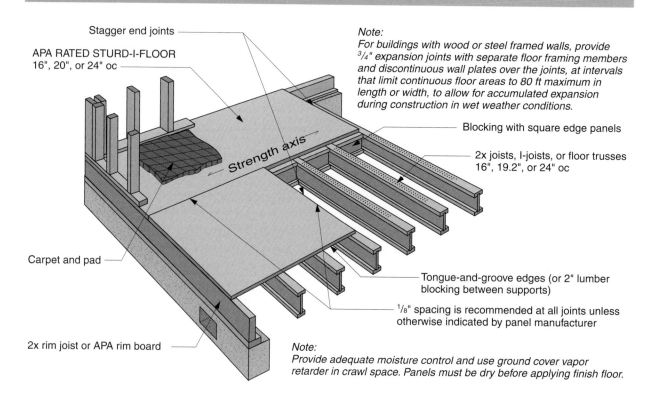

Stagger end joints

APA RATED STURD-I-FLOOR 16", 20", or 24" oc

Strength axis

Carpet and pad

2x rim joist or APA rim board

Note:
For buildings with wood or steel framed walls, provide ³/₄" expansion joints with separate floor framing members and discontinuous wall plates over the joints, at intervals that limit continuous floor areas to 80 ft maximum in length or width, to allow for accumulated expansion during construction in wet weather conditions.

Blocking with square edge panels

2x joists, I-joists, or floor trusses 16", 19.2", or 24" oc

Tongue-and-groove edges (or 2" lumber blocking between supports)

¹/₈" spacing is recommended at all joints unless otherwise indicated by panel manufacturer

Note:
Provide adequate moisture control and use ground cover vapor retarder in crawl space. Panels must be dry before applying finish floor.

APA Rated Sturd-I-Floor[1]

Joist Spacing[2] in	Panel Thickness[2] in	Fastening: Glue-Nailed[3]			Fastening: Nailed-Only		
		Nail Size and Type	Maximum Spacing, in[8]		Nail Size and Type	Maximum Spacing, in[8]	
			Supported Panel Edges[7]	Intermediate Supports		Supported Panel Edges[7]	Intermediate Supports
16	19/32	6d ring- or screw-shank[4]	12	12	6d ring- or screw-shank	6	12
20	19/32, 5/8	6d ring- or screw-shank[4]	12	12	6d ring- or screw-shank	6	12
24	23/32, 3/4	6d ring- or screw-shank[4]	12	12	6d ring- or screw-shank	6	12
	7/8	8d ring- or screw-shank[4]	6	12	8d ring- or screw-shank	6	12
32	7/8	8d ring- or screw-shank[4]	6	12	8d ring- or screw-shank	6	12
48	1 3/32, 1 1/8	8d ring- or screw-shank[5]	6	see ([6])	8d ring- or screw-shank[5]	6	see ([6])

[1] Special conditions may impose heavy traffic and concentrated loads that require construction in excess of the minimums shown.

[2] Panels in a given thickness may be manufactured in more than one span rating. Panels with a span rating greater than the actual joist spacing may be substituted for panels of the same thickness with a span rating matching the actual joist spacing. For example, 19/32" thick Sturd-I-Floor 20" oc may be substituted for 19/32" thick Sturd-I-Floor 16" oc over joists 16" oc.

[3] Use only adhesives conforming to APA Specification AFG-01 or ASTM D3498, applied in accordance with the adhesive manufacturer's recommendations. If OSB panels with sealed surfaces and edges are to be used, use only solvent-based glues; check with panel manufacturer.

[4] 8d common nails may be substituted if ring- or screw-shank nails are not available.

[5] 10d common nails may be substituted with 1 1/8" panels if supports are well seasoned.

[6] Space nails maximum 6" for 48" spans and 12" for 32" spans.

[7] Supported panel joints shall occur approximately along the centerline of framing with a minimum bearing of 1/2". Fasten panels 3/8" from panel edges.

[8] Increased nail schedules may be required where floor is engineered as a diaphragm.

Recommended Uniform Floor Live Loads for APA Rated Sturd-I-Floor and APA Rated Sheathing with Strength Axis Perpendicular to Supports

Sturd-I-Floor Span Rating	Sheathing Span Rating	Minimum Thickness, in	Maximum Span, in	Allowable Live Loads, psf[1]						
				Joist Spacing, in						
				12	16	20	24	32	40	48
16 oc	24/16, 32/16	7/16 [3]	16	185	100	–	–	–	–	–
20 oc	40/20	19/32, 5/8	20	270	150	100	–	–	–	–
24 oc	48/24	23/32, 3/4	24	430	240	160	100	–	–	–
32 oc	60/32 [2]	7/8	32	–	430	295	185	100	–	–
48 oc	–	1 3/32, 1 1/8	48	–	–	460	290	160	100	55

[1] 10 psf dead load assumed. Live load deflection limit is 1/360.

[2] Check with suppliers for availability.

[3] 19/32" is minimum thickness of rated Sturd-I-Floor.

APA Glued Floor

The APA glued floor system is based on field-applied construction adhesives that secure wood structural panels to wood joists. The glue bond is so strong that floor and joists behave like integral T-beam units. Floor stiffness is increased appreciably over conventional construction, particularly when tongue-and-groove joints are glued. Gluing also helps eliminate squeaks, floor vibration, bounce, and nail-popping.

Panels recommended for glued floor construction are T&G APA Rated Sturd-I-Floor for single-floor construction, and APA Rated Sheathing for the subfloor when used with a separate underlayment or with structural finish flooring.

Before each panel is placed, a line of glue is applied to the joists with a caulking gun. The panel T&G joint should also be glued. If square-edge panels are used, edges must be supported between joists with 2×4 blocking. Glue panels to blocking to minimize squeaks. Blocking is not required under structural finish flooring or separate underlayment.

Application

1. Snap a chalk line across joists 4 feet from wall for panel edge alignment and as a glue boundary.

2. Spread glue to lay 1 or 2 panels at a time.

3. Lay first panel tongue side to wall, tap into place with block and sledgehammer, and nail.

4. Apply a ¼-inch line of glue to framing members. Apply glue in a serpentine pattern on wide areas.

5. Apply two lines of glue on joists where panel ends butt to assure proper gluing of each end.

6. After first row is in place, spread glue in grooves of 1 or 2 panels at a time before laying next row.

7. Tap second-row panels into place, using a block to protect groove edges.

8. Stagger end joints. A ⅛ inch-space between end joints and edges, including T&G, is recommended.

9. Complete all nailing of each panel before the glue sets.

APA Glued Floor Details

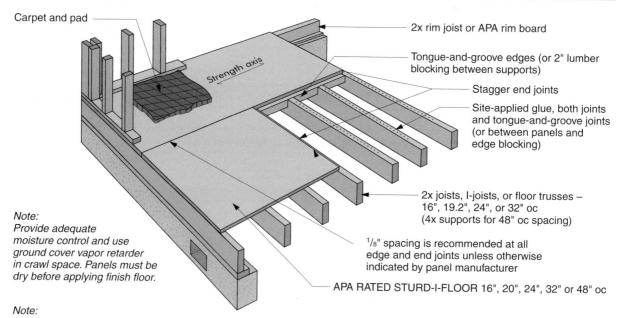

Carpet and pad

Strength axis

2x rim joist or APA rim board

Tongue-and-groove edges (or 2" lumber blocking between supports)

Stagger end joints

Site-applied glue, both joints and tongue-and-groove joints (or between panels and edge blocking)

2x joists, I-joists, or floor trusses – 16", 19.2", 24", or 32" oc (4x supports for 48" oc spacing)

⅛" spacing is recommended at all edge and end joints unless otherwise indicated by panel manufacturer

APA RATED STURD-I-FLOOR 16", 20", 24", 32" or 48" oc

Note:
Provide adequate moisture control and use ground cover vapor retarder in crawl space. Panels must be dry before applying finish floor.

Note:
For buildings with wood or steel framed walls, provide ¾" expansion joints with separate floor framing members and discontinuous wall plates over the joints, at intervals that limit continuous floor areas to 80 ft maximum in length or width, to allow for accumulated expansion during construction in wet weather conditions.

APA Wall Sheathing

APA Panel Wall Sheathing Details

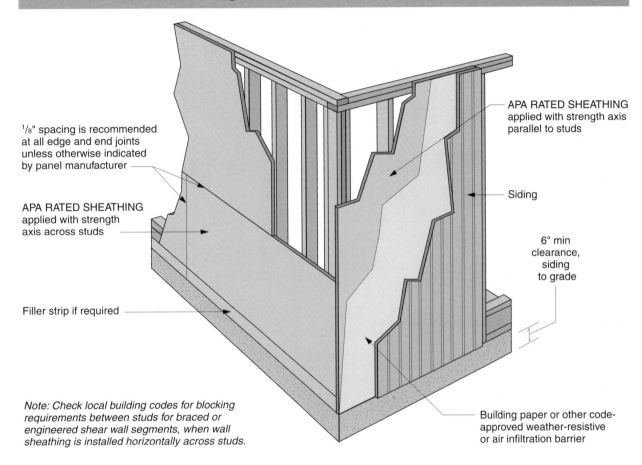

¹/₈" spacing is recommended at all edge and end joints unless otherwise indicated by panel manufacturer

APA RATED SHEATHING applied with strength axis across studs

Filler strip if required

APA RATED SHEATHING applied with strength axis parallel to studs

Siding

6" min clearance, siding to grade

Building paper or other code-approved weather-resistive or air infiltration barrier

Note: Check local building codes for blocking requirements between studs for braced or engineered shear wall segments, when wall sheathing is installed horizontally across studs.

APA Panel Wall Sheathing[1]
(APA Rated Sheathing panels continuous over two or more spans)

Panel Span Intermediate Rating	Maximum Stud Spacing, in	Nail Size[2,3]	Maximum Nail Spacing, in[5]	
			Supported Panel Edges[4]	Intermediate Supports
12/0, 16/0, 20/0 or Wall,16" oc	16	6d for panels ≤¹/₂" thick	6	12
24/0, 24/16, 32/16 or Wall, 24" oc	24	8d for panels >¹/₂"	6	12

[1] See requirements for nailable panel sheathing when exterior covering is to be nailed to sheathing.

[2] Common, smooth, annular, spiral-thread, or galvanized box.

[3] Other code-approved fasteners may be used.

[4] Fasteners shall be located ³/₈" from panel edges.

[5] Increased nail schedules may be required where wall is engineered as a shear wall.

APA Roof Sheathing

APA Panel Roof Sheathing Details

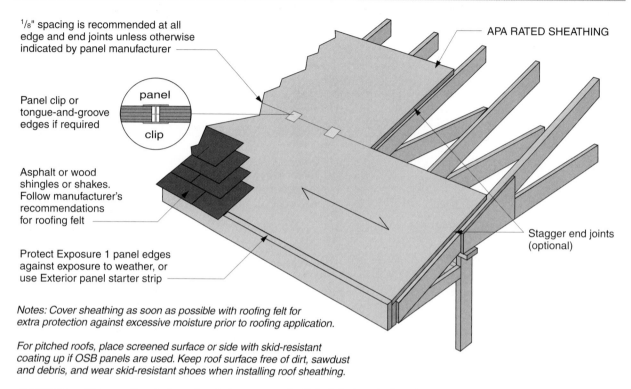

¹/₈" spacing is recommended at all edge and end joints unless otherwise indicated by panel manufacturer

Panel clip or tongue-and-groove edges if required

panel
clip

Asphalt or wood shingles or shakes. Follow manufacturer's recommendations for roofing felt

Protect Exposure 1 panel edges against exposure to weather, or use Exterior panel starter strip

APA RATED SHEATHING

Stagger end joints (optional)

Notes: Cover sheathing as soon as possible with roofing felt for extra protection against excessive moisture prior to roofing application.

For pitched roofs, place screened surface or side with skid-resistant coating up if OSB panels are used. Keep roof surface free of dirt, sawdust and debris, and wear skid-resistant shoes when installing roof sheathing.

For buildings with conventionally framed roofs (trusses or rafters), limit the length of continuous sections of roof area to 80' maximum during construction, to allow for accumulated expansion in wet weather conditions. Omit roof sheathing panels in each course of sheathing between sections, and install "fill in" panels later to complete roof deck installation prior to applying roofing.

Gluing of roof sheathing to framing is not recommended, except when recommended by the adhesive manufacturer for roof sheathing that already has been permanently protected by roofing.

Recommended Maximum Spans for APA Panel Roof Decks for Low-Slope Roofs[1]
(Panel perpendicular to supports and continuous over two or more spans)

Grade	Minimum Nominal Panel Thickness, in	Minimum Span Rating	Maximum Span, in	Panel Clips per Span[2]
APA Rated Sheathing	¹⁵/₃₂	32/16	24	1
	¹⁹/₃₂	40/20	32	1
	²³/₃₂	48/24	48	2
	⁷/₈	60/32	60	2
	¹⁹/₃₂	20 oc	24	1
	²³/₃₂	24 oc	32	1
	⁷/₈	32 oc	48	2

[1] Low-slope roofs are applicable to built-up, single-ply, and modified bitumen roofing systems. For guaranteed or warranted roofs contact membrane manufacturer for acceptable deck. Low-slope roofs have a slope that is less than 2/12 (2"/foot).

[2] Edge support may also be provided by tongue-and-groove edges or solid blocking.

Recommended Uniform Roof Live Loads for APA Rated Sheathing[3] and APA Rated Sturd-I-Floor with Strength Axis Perpendicular to Supports[5]

Panel Span Rating	Minimum Panel Thickness, in	Maximum Span, in		Allowable Live Loads, psf[4]							
		With Edge Support[1]	Without Edge Support	Joist Spacing, in							
				12	16	20	24	32	40	48	60
APA RATED SHEATHING[3]											
12/0	5/16	12 5/16	12	30	–	–	–	–	–	–	–
16/0	5/16	16	16	70	30	–	–	–	–	–	–
20/0	5/16	20	20	120	50	30	–	–	–	–	–
24/0	3/8	24	20[2]	190	100	60	30	–	–	–	–
24/16	7/16	24	24	190	100	65	40	–	–	–	–
32/16	15/32, 1/2	32	28	325	1180	120	70	30	–	–	–
40/20	19/32, 5/8	40	32	–	305	205	130	60	30	–	–
48/24	23/32, 3/4	48	36	–	–	280	175	95	45	35	–
60/32[7]	7/8	60	40	–	–	–	305	165	100	70	35
60/48[7]	1 1/8	60	48	–	–	–	305	165	100	70	35
APA RATED STURD-I-FLOOR[6]											
16 oc	5/16	24	24	185	100	65	40	–	–	–	–
20 oc	19/32, 5/8	32	32	270	150	100	60	30	–	–	–
24 oc	23/32, 3/4	48	36	–	240	160	100	50	30	25	–
32 oc	7/8	48	40	–	–	295	185	100	60	40	–
48 oc	1 3/32, 1 1/8	60	48	–	–	–	290	160	100	65	40

[1] Tongue-and-groove edges, panel edge clips (one midway between each support, except two equally spaced between supports 48" oc or greater), lumber blocking, or other.

[2] 20" for 3/8" and 7/16" panels. 24" for 15/32" and 1/2" panels.

[3] Includes APA-Rated sheathing/ceiling deck.

[4] 10 psf dead load assumed.

[5] Applies to panels 24" or wider applied over two or more spans.

[6] Also applies to C-C Plugged grade plywood.

[7] Check with supplier for availability.

Recommended Minimum Fastening Schedule for APA Panel Roof Sheathing (Increased nail schedules may be required in high wind zones and where roof is engineered as a diaphragm.)

Panel Thickness[2], in	Nail Size	Maximum Nail[3,4] Spacing, in	
		Supported Panel Edges[5]	Intermediate
5/16 to 1	8d	6	12[1]
1 7/8	8d or 10d	6	12[1]

[1] For spans 48" or greater, space nails 6" at all supports.

[2] For stapling asphalt shingles to 5/16" and thicker panels, use staples with a 5/16" min crown width and a 1" leg length. Space according to shingle manufacturer's recommendations.

[3] Use common smooth or deformed shank nails with panels to 1" thick. For 1 1/8" panels, use 8d ring- or screw-shank or 10d common smooth-shank nails.

[4] Other code-approved fasteners may be used.

[5] Supported panel joints shall occur approximately along the centerline of framing with a minimum bearing of 1/2". Fasteners shall be located 3/8" from panel edges.

Wall Bracing

The APA Narrow Wall Bracing Method was developed to permit narrow wall segments while satisfying the stringent wall bracing requirements of the IRC.

Sheath exterior walls with plywood or OSB and install headers extending beyond openings. The lapped-header/sheathing combination forms a semi-moment-resisting frame which provides greater resistance to wind and earthquake. Braced wall segments can be as narrow as 16 inches and hold-downs are not required. See p. 210–211 for details.

The IRC (Section R602.10.5) allows for wall segments as narrow as 24 inches, but the APA Narrow Wall Bracing Method (Section R602.10.6) adds enough structural support to safely reduce bracing width to 16 inches. As shown below, both methods can be used all around the house at garage, window, and door openings, creating a more pleasing appearance both inside and out. The table below summarizes minimum allowable bracing widths permitted by the IRC.

Narrow Bracing Options for a Fully Sheathed Home (details on facing page)

Allowable Bracing Segment Widths for Fully-Sheathed Homes

Bracing Construction	Minimum Width of Braced Wall Panel for Wall Height of:			Maximum Opening Height Next to the Braced Wall
	8 ft	9 ft	10 ft	
IRC R602.10.5 (see details 2, 5)	32"	36"	40"	85% of wall height
	24"	27"	30"	65% of wall height
APA Narrow Wall[1] Bracing (see details 1, 3, 5)	16"	18"	20"	to bottom of header

[1] The minimum width of braced wall segment for the APA Method is based on the height from the top of the header to the bottom of the sill plate. Framing, such as a cripple wall, may be built on top of the header, but it does not affect the height used to determine the minimum braced wall segment width.

Narrow Wall Bracing Details

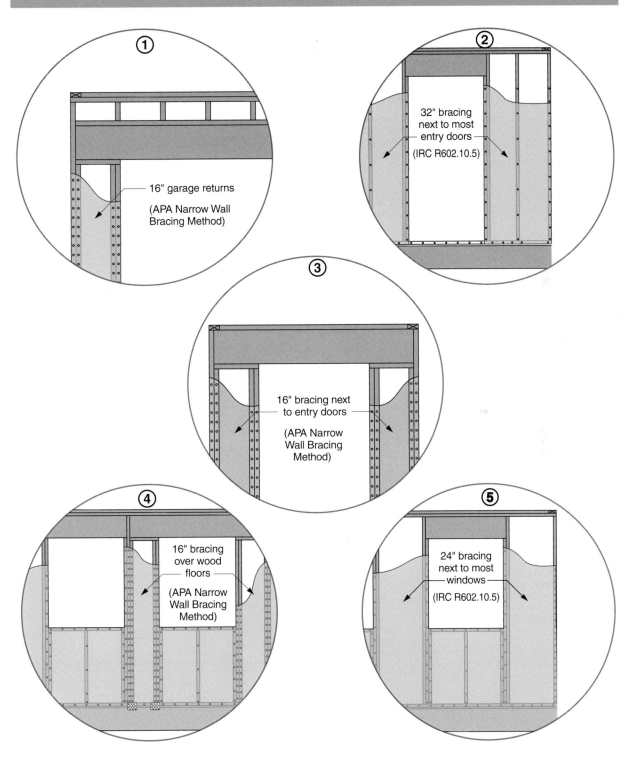

① 16" garage returns

(APA Narrow Wall Bracing Method)

② 32" bracing next to most entry doors

(IRC R602.10.5)

③ 16" bracing next to entry doors

(APA Narrow Wall Bracing Method)

④ 16" bracing over wood floors

(APA Narrow Wall Bracing Method)

⑤ 24" bracing next to most windows

(IRC R602.10.5)

Narrow Wall over Concrete or Masonry Block Foundation

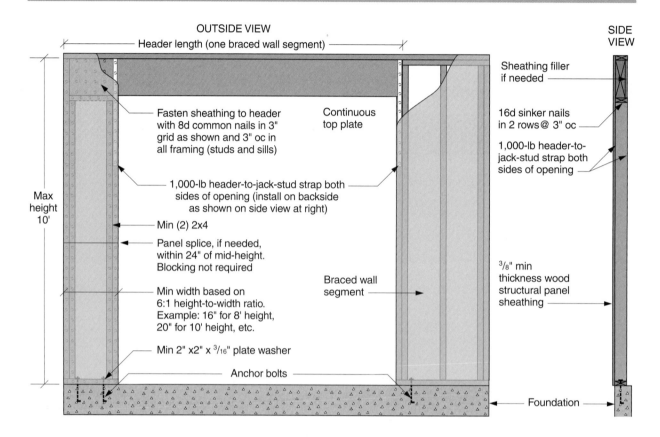

OUTSIDE VIEW

SIDE VIEW

Header length (one braced wall segment)

Fasten sheathing to header with 8d common nails in 3" grid as shown and 3" oc in all framing (studs and sills)

Continuous top plate

1,000-lb header-to-jack-stud strap both sides of opening (install on backside as shown on side view at right)

Max height 10'

Min (2) 2x4

Panel splice, if needed, within 24" of mid-height. Blocking not required

Braced wall segment

Min width based on 6:1 height-to-width ratio. Example: 16" for 8' height, 20" for 10' height, etc.

Min 2" x2" x $^3/_{16}$" plate washer

Anchor bolts

Sheathing filler if needed

16d sinker nails in 2 rows @ 3" oc

1,000-lb header-to-jack-stud strap both sides of opening

$^3/_8$" min thickness wood structural panel sheathing

Foundation

Example of Outside Corner Detail

Connect the two walls as shown to provide overturning restraint. The fully sheathed wall line perpendicular to the narrow bracing segment helps reduce the overturning force because the overturning moment acts over a longer distance.

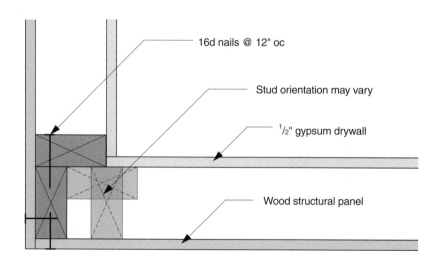

16d nails @ 12" oc

Stud orientation may vary

$^1/_2$" gypsum drywall

Wood structural panel

Narrow Wall over Raised Wood Floor or Second Floor—Framing Anchor Option

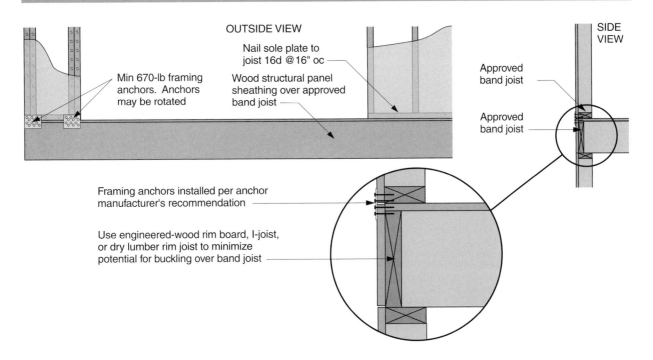

OUTSIDE VIEW

SIDE VIEW

Min 670-lb framing anchors. Anchors may be rotated

Nail sole plate to joist 16d @16" oc

Wood structural panel sheathing over approved band joist

Approved band joist

Approved band joist

Framing anchors installed per anchor manufacturer's recommendation

Use engineered-wood rim board, I-joist, or dry lumber rim joist to minimize potential for buckling over band joist

Narrow Wall over Raised Wood Floor or Second Floor—Panel Overlap Option

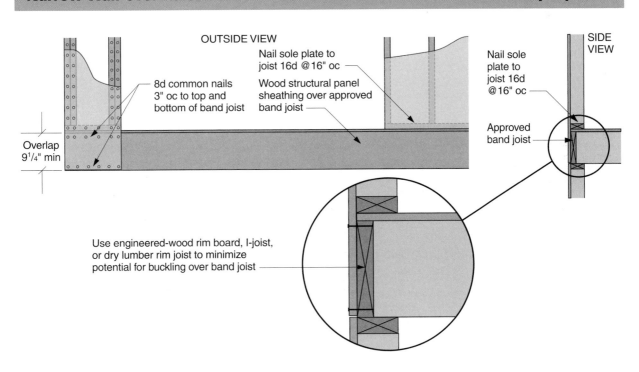

OUTSIDE VIEW

SIDE VIEW

8d common nails 3" oc to top and bottom of band joist

Nail sole plate to joist 16d @16" oc

Wood structural panel sheathing over approved band joist

Nail sole plate to joist 16d @16" oc

Approved band joist

Overlap 9¹/₄" min

Use engineered-wood rim board, I-joist, or dry lumber rim joist to minimize potential for buckling over band joist

Siding

8

The first section identifies the *function of siding* (protection of the walls from moisture) and illustrates three principles all sidings must follow.

Next, the advantages and disadvantages of all of the common *siding options* are compared.

The rest of this chapter is filled with illustrations and tables designed to help you successfully install *vinyl siding, hardboard lap siding, cedar shingles*, the various *horizontal wood sidings, vertical wood sidings*, combined *plywood sheathing/siding*, and *stucco*.

Finally, we provide you with a *checklist of code requirements* relating to siding.

Function

Aside from decoration and a sometimes dual role as structural sheathing, the function of siding is to keep the structure and interior of a building dry. If the siding is painted, it must be allowed to dry from both sides. Water penetrates siding in one or more of three ways:

- as bulk water flowing downward under the force of *gravity*
- as rain water driven horizontally by the pressure of *wind*
- as rain water drawn upward by *capillarity* (surface tension acting in small spaces).

The three problems are prevented in three very different ways:

- gravity—by flashing at horizontal junctures of building surfaces and materials
- wind—by venting the back side of siding to equalize air pressures
- capillarity—by eliminating capillary-sized gaps between siding courses, using round head nails or wedges.

The illustrations below show examples of each technique. Details specific to each type of siding are presented in the following pages.

Siding Moisture Control

GRAVITY
(FLASHING)

Air/water barrier

Z-flashing

Brickmold

Window sash

WIND SCREEN
(VERTICAL VIEW)

Air/water barrier

Wind screen
(vented
air space)

CAPILLARITY
(AIR GAPS)

Round-head nail

Capillary break

Options

Things to consider when selecting siding are your home's architectural style, the styles of other homes in the neighborhood, the material and its appropriateness in your climate, and the environmental/energy impact of the material and its manufacture. Other considerations, of course, are the type and amount of care required in its maintenance, its expected lifetime, and initial cost.

In the chart below, *care* includes maintenance of an attractive appearance as well as weathertightness. Vinyl and aluminum are not subject, except for occasional washing, to maintenance, but bright colors may fade over time from exposure to ultraviolet rays.

Life assumes proper maintenance and may vary widely under differing conditions.

Cost is for materials only and does not include the cost of professional installation. In general, labor costs are lowest for vinyl, aluminum, and plywood. Labor can also vary as much as 50 percent due to popularity of style (and, therefore, competitive pricing) and prevailing wages. For example, stucco would cost far less in the Southwest, where it predominates, than in the Northeast.

Sidings Compared

Material	Care	Life yrs	Relative Cost	Advantages	Disadvantages
Aluminum/Steel	None	30	Medium	Ease of installation Low maintenance Fire resistance	Susceptibility to denting Limited colors Difficult repairs
Fiber cement	Paint	30	Medium to High	Dimensionally stable Low maintenance Fire resistance	May rattle in high wind Cutting produces hazardous dust
Hardboard	Paint Stain	20	Low	Low cost Fast installation	Susceptibility to moisture Short life Limited availability
Horizontal wood	Paint Stain	50+	Medium to High	Classic appearance Simple repairs Environmentally friendly	High labor cost High maintenance Can rot
Plywood	Paint Stain	20	Low	Low material cost Low labor cost Doubles as sheathing	Appearance Short life
Shingles/Shakes	Stain None	50+	High	Classic appearance Low maintenance Environmentally friendly	Highest labor cost May rattle in high wind
Stucco	Paint None	50+	Low to Medium	Classic in Southwest Low cost where common Fast installation	Professional installation Easily damaged Difficult repairs
Vertical wood	Stain None	50+	Low to Medium	Low material cost Low labor cost Low maintenance	Farm building appearance Uneven weathering
Vinyl	None	30	Low	Fast installation Simple residing option Simple repairs	Fading of bright colors Low impact resistance Environmentally unfriendly

Vinyl

The most important rule for successful installation of vinyl siding is to allow for movement. The thermal expansion coefficient of vinyl (0.000035/°F) is 3× that of aluminum and 10× that of wood. To avoid buckling, all vinyl siding, soffit, and accessories used in exterior applications must be able to move freely as they expand and contract with temperature.

The rules for installation are, therefore, as follows:

- Nail in the center of slots.
- Do not nail too tightly.
- Leave at least ¼ inch clearance at stops.
- Do not pull horizontal sidings up tight.
- Strap and shim all uneven walls.

Vinyl Siding Components

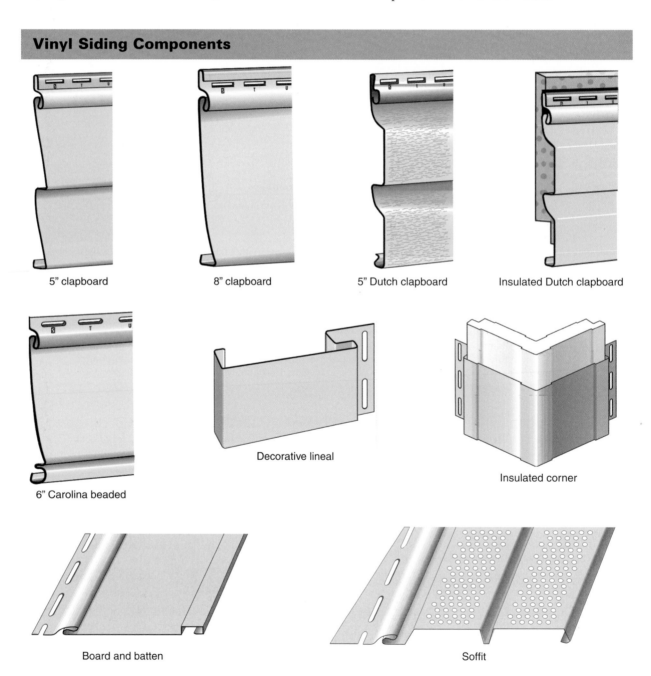

5" clapboard

8" clapboard

5" Dutch clapboard

Insulated Dutch clapboard

6" Carolina beaded

Decorative lineal

Insulated corner

Board and batten

Soffit

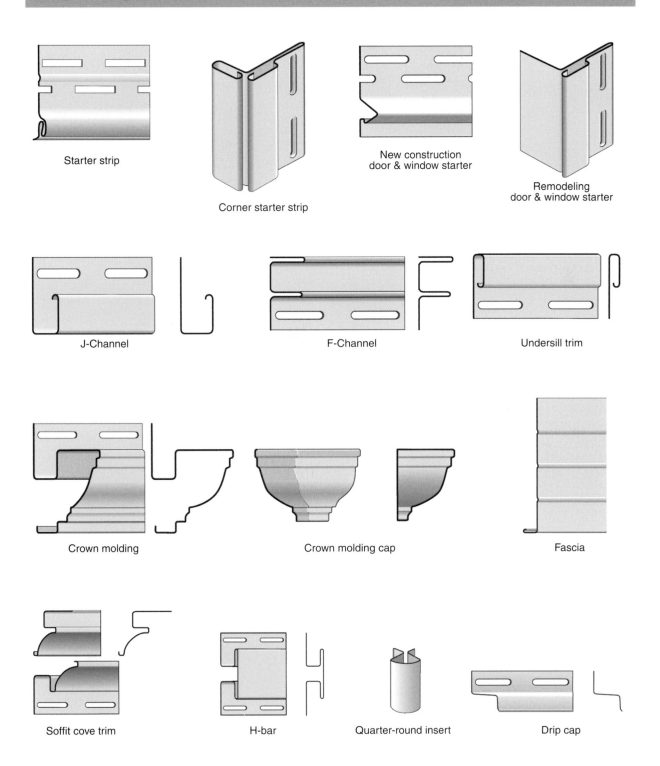

Starter strip

Corner starter strip

New construction
door & window starter

Remodeling
door & window starter

J-Channel

F-Channel

Undersill trim

Crown molding

Crown molding cap

Fascia

Soffit cove trim

H-bar

Quarter-round insert

Drip cap

RECTANGULAR WALL

$$\text{Area} = \text{Height} \times \text{Width} \ = \ \underline{\hspace{2cm}}$$

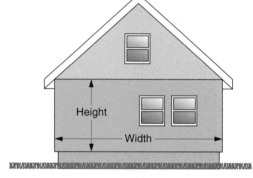

TRIANGULAR GABLE END WALL

$$\text{Area} = \frac{\text{Height} \times \text{Width}}{2} \ = \ \underline{\hspace{2cm}}$$

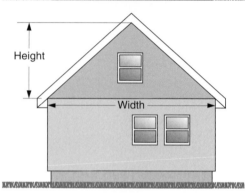

UPPER WALL OF GAMBREL

$$\text{Area} = \frac{(B + C) \times H}{2} \ = \ \underline{\hspace{2cm}}$$

$$+ \ \frac{C \times D}{2} \ = \ \underline{\hspace{2cm}}$$

$$\text{TOTAL} = \ \underline{\hspace{2cm}}$$

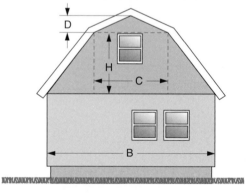

DORMER SIDES (BOTH)

$$\text{Area} = \text{Height} \times \text{Width} \ = \ \underline{\hspace{2cm}}$$

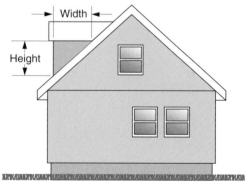

NAIL DRIVING

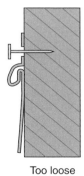
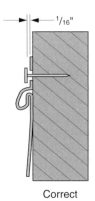

1/16"

Too tight

Too loose

Correct

HORIZONTAL LENGTHS

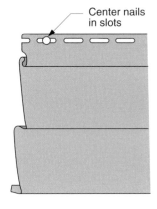

Center nails
in slots

Center staples
in slots

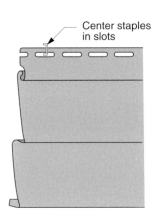

VERTICAL LENGTHS

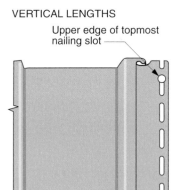

Upper edge of topmost
nailing slot

ENDS OF HORIZONTALS

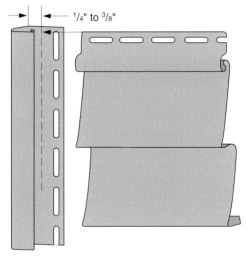

1/4" to 3/8"

ENDS OF VERTICALS

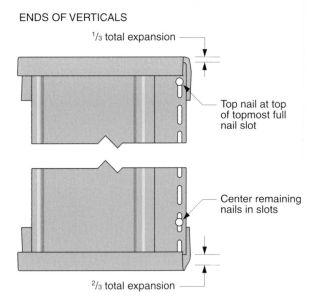

1/3 total expansion

Top nail at top
of topmost full
nail slot

Center remaining
nails in slots

2/3 total expansion

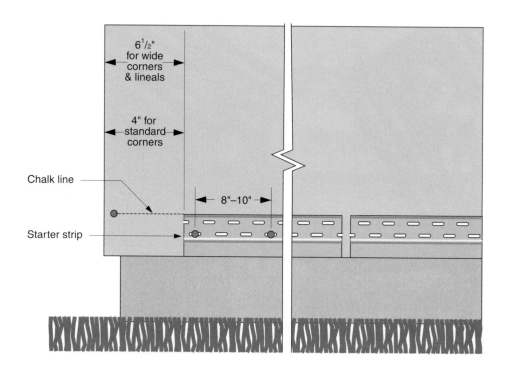

Chalk line

Starter strip

6¹/₂" for wide corners & lineals

4" for standard corners

8"–10"

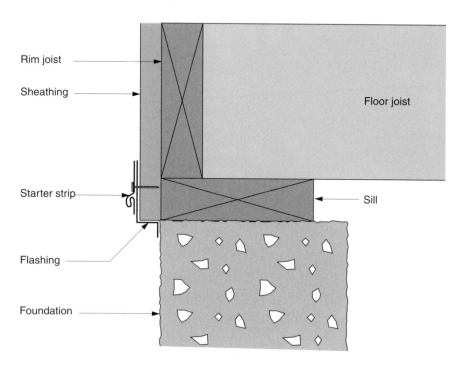

Rim joist

Sheathing

Floor joist

Starter strip

Sill

Flashing

Foundation

STARTING AT AN OUTSIDE CORNER

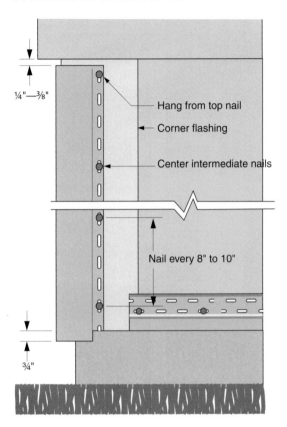

¼"—⅜"

Hang from top nail

Corner flashing

Center intermediate nails

Nail every 8" to 10"

¾"

OUTSIDE CORNER SPLICE

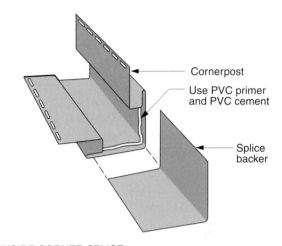

Cornerpost

Use PVC primer and PVC cement

Splice backer

INSIDE CORNER SPLICE

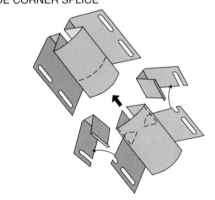

INSIDE CORNER OPTIONS

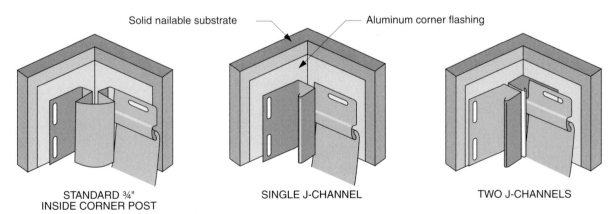

Solid nailable substrate

Aluminum corner flashing

STANDARD ¾"
INSIDE CORNER POST

SINGLE J-CHANNEL

TWO J-CHANNELS

The width of flashings depends on the width of the trim and where the final complete course of siding stops below the window. All flashings should extend past the window nailing flanges. The width of the flashing under the window is sized to allow for the iversion of water.

SEE NOTE
BELOW

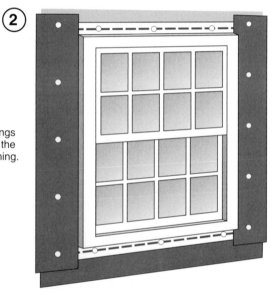

Apply the side flashings by overlapping the bottom flashing.

Apply the top flashing over the tops of the side flashings.

NOTE: Make sure the width of the bottom flashing is sufficient to overlap the nailing flange of the top course of complete siding panels.

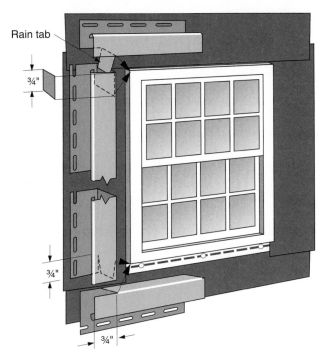

Rain tab

¾"

¾"

¾"

FOR SQUARE CORNERS

Using aviation snips, notch two side pieces of J-channel, as shown, butt against the window casings, and fasten in place.

Cut top and bottom J-channels so that the ends extend beyond the window casings to the outside edges of the side channels.

Place the top J-channel on the casing and fasten in place. Make two cuts in the bottom of the top channel and bend the tab down into the side channel. Repeat on the other side. This forms a water drain.

Make two cuts in the bottoms of the side channels to receive the notched bottom channel. Push the bottom channel up into the side channel slits and butt against the bottom window casing. When snug, fasten in place.

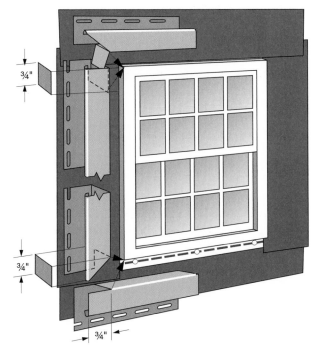

¾"

¾"

¾"

FOR MITERED CORNERS

Square cut the bottom J-channel so that its ends extend beyond the window casings to the outside of the J-channels on either side. Notch the ends for clearance, snug up under the bottom window casing, and fasten in place.

Measure the side J-channels, adding the widths of both top and bottom J-channels. Miter cut the lower ends of both side J-channels at 45 degrees. Notch the channels, position against the side casings and bottom channel, and fasten.

Mark the top J-channel so its ends extend beyond the casings to the outsides of the side J-channels. Miter cut both ends of the the front face, and cut and bend down the water tabs.

Position the top J-channel against the top of the window casing with the tabs inside the side channels, and fasten.

ROOF/WALL INTERSECTION

To prevent water infiltration along the intersection of roof and wall, install step flashing before installing J-channel. At points where vinyl siding and accessories will meet at a roof line—such as areas where a gable dormer or a second-story side wall intersect with the roof—it is best to position the J-channel so it is $^3/_4$" to 1" away from the roof line. Placing the J-channel directly on the roof line would subject it to a buildup of heat, which could result in excessive expansion.

NOTE: If you use more than one length of J-channel to span a wall surface, be sure to overlap J-channels $^3/_4$". Do not butt J-channel pieces end-to-end.

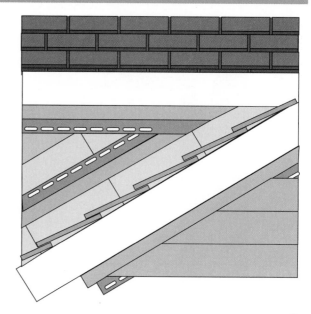

FITTING AT GABLE ENDS

Make a pattern duplicating the slope of the gable. Use this pattern as a cutting guide for panels to fit into the gable ends.

To make the pattern, lock a short piece of siding into the panel gable starter course, as shown in the illustration. Hold a second piece of siding against the J-channel at the slope. Run a pencil along the edge of this piece, transferring the slope angle to the first piece of siding. Cut along the pencil line using a power saw or tin snips. Use the resulting pattern to mark the siding panels before cutting.

NOTE: Double-check the angle of the pattern at every course. If necessary, cut new pattern.

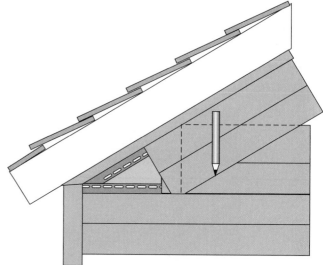

INSTALLING CUT PANELS

Slip the angled end of the panel into the J-channel along the gable edge, leaving space for expansion. Interlock with the siding panel below.

If necessary to securely fasten the last panel at the peak of the gable, face nail as shown in the illustration. This is the only place you will face nail. Use a 1$^1/_4$" to 1$^1/_2$" aluminum nail with painted head that matches the siding.

NOTE: Do not cover louvers in gables.

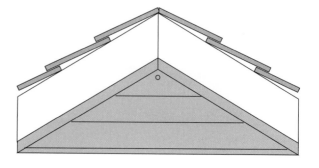

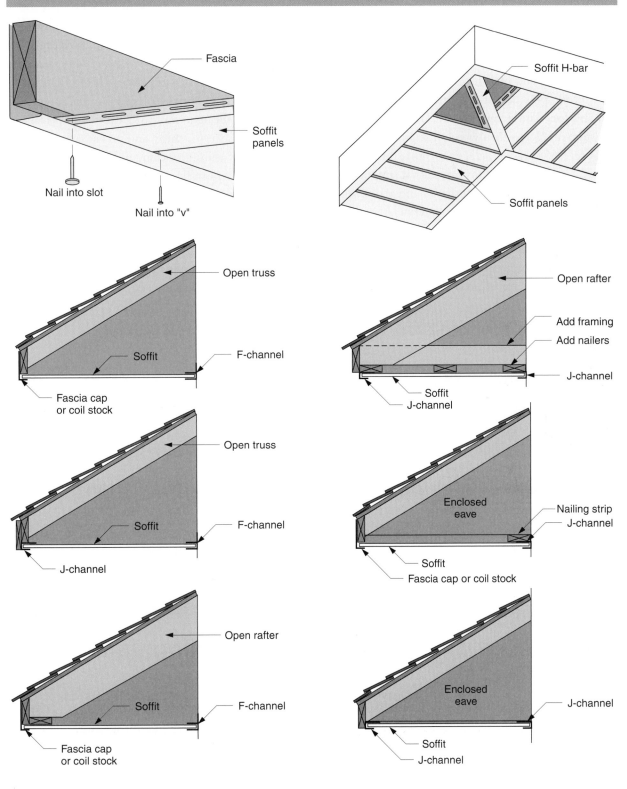

Fascia

Soffit panels

Nail into slot

Nail into "v"

Soffit H-bar

Soffit panels

Open truss

Soffit

F-channel

Fascia cap
or coil stock

Open rafter

Add framing

Add nailers

J-channel

Soffit
J-channel

Open truss

Soffit

F-channel

J-channel

Enclosed
eave

Nailing strip
J-channel

Soffit

Fascia cap or coil stock

Open rafter

Soffit

F-channel

Fascia cap
or coil stock

Enclosed
eave

J-channel

Soffit

J-channel

Fiber-Cement

Fiber-cement siding is exactly that—a mixture of wood fiber, sand, and Portland cement. The high percentage of sand and cement make it, essentially, a masonry siding. The wood fibers reduce the weight and reinforce the masonry. It shares characteristics of both wood and masonry.

On the plus side, it is immune to insect attack, rot, and fire. And because it swells and shrinks with moisture much less than wood, it retains paint well.

On the negative side, it is more brittle than wood. The 12-foot lengths can snap if supported at the midpoint in the flat position, and striking the edges or corners can chip the material. Also, direct contact between the cementitious siding and aluminum flashing will result in corrosion of the flashing unless the aluminum is anodized.

Lap sidings are typically available in lengths of 12 feet and widths from 5 to 12 inches. Fiber-cement trim is also available, but few builders use it because of its weight and because it's ⅝-inch thickness is insufficient to project beyond the siding.

Cutting fiber-cement with power saws produces copious cement dust that can be a health hazard, so dust masks are essential. For safety and accuracy, it's best to cut the material outdoors with specialized tools, such as shears, snips, and power saws designed to capture or minimize cement dust.

The siding can be installed over braced wood or steel studs spaced a maximum of 24" on-center or directly to minimum 7/16"-thick OSB sheathing. It can also be installed over foam insulation up to 1" thick. Fastening with a pneumatic nail gun is recommended. See the illustrations on the facing page for fastening and clearance details.

Estimated Number of 12-foot Hardiplanks® (assuming zero waste)

Net Area[1], sq ft	Siding Width/Exposure, in								
	5¼ 4	6¼ 5	7¼ 6	7½ 6¼	8 6¾	8¼ 7	9¼ 8	9½ 8¼	12 10¾
100	25	20	17	16	15	14	13	13	9
200	50	40	33	32	30	29	25	25	19
300	75	60	50	48	44	43	38	38	28
400	100	80	67	64	59	57	50	50	37
500	125	100	83	80	74	71	63	63	47
600	150	120	100	96	89	86	75	75	56
700	175	140	117	112	104	100	88	88	65
800	200	160	133	128	119	114	100	100	74
900	225	180	150	144	133	129	113	113	84
1000	250	200	167	160	148	143	125	125	93
1200	300	240	200	192	178	171	150	150	112
1500	375	300	250	240	222	214	188	188	140
2000	500	400	333	320	296	286	250	250	186
2500	625	500	417	400	370	357	313	313	233
3000	750	600	500	480	444	429	375	375	279
4000	1000	800	667	640	592	572	500	500	372
5000	1250	1000	834	800	740	714	626	626	467

[1] Net Area is wall area, less area of openings.

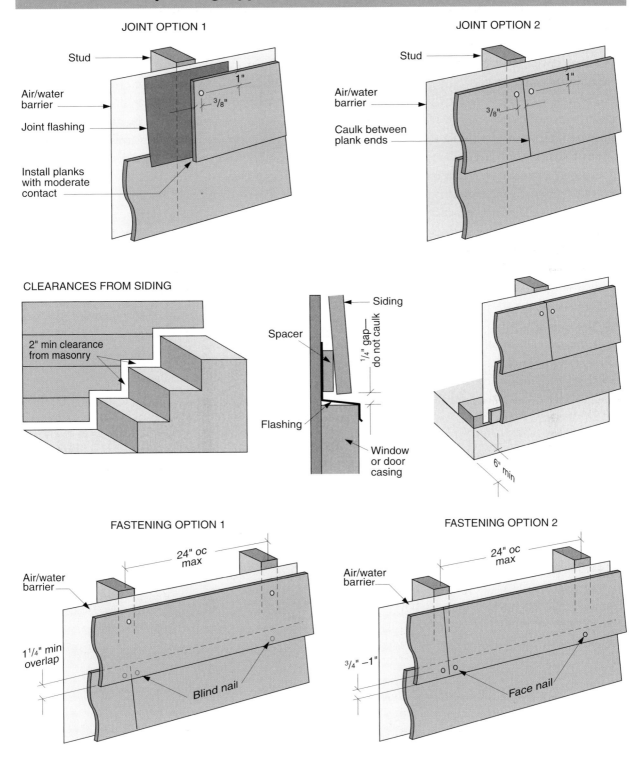

JOINT OPTION 1

Stud

Air/water barrier

Joint flashing

Install planks with moderate contact

1"

3/8"

JOINT OPTION 2

Stud

Air/water barrier

Caulk between plank ends

1"

3/8"

CLEARANCES FROM SIDING

2" min clearance from masonry

Siding

Spacer

1/4" gap – do not caulk

Flashing

Window or door casing

6" min

FASTENING OPTION 1

24" oc max

Air/water barrier

1 1/4" min overlap

Blind nail

FASTENING OPTION 2

24" oc max

Air/water barrier

3/4" –1"

Face nail

Hardboard Lap

Hardboard lap siding may be cut with either fine-tooth hand or power saws. The cutting action should be into the appearance face of the siding, i.e., face up with hand saws and tablesaws and face down with portable circular saws.

Lap siding may be applied directly to studs or over sheathing. Studs should be spaced 16 inches on-center in both cases. An air-barrier membrane should be used when the siding is applied directly to studs or over board sheathings.

Use only corrosion-resistant nails. Nails should penetrate framing members by 1½ inches minimum (8d nails for studs only; 10d nails over sheathing).

Allow at least 6 inches between the siding and the ground or any area where water may collect. A starter strip 1½ inches wide and the same thickness as the siding should be installed level with the bottom edge of the sill plate. Nail the starter strip with the recommended siding nails. Cut, fit, and install the first course of siding to extend at least ¼ inch, but no more than 1 inch, below the starter strip. Nail the bottom edge of the first course of siding 16 inches on-center and through the starter strip at each stud location. Maintain contact at the joints without forcing. Leave a space of ⅛ inch between the siding and window or door frames and corner boards. Caulk this space after the siding is installed.

All joints must fall over studs and be nailed on both top and bottom on each side of the joint. Stagger succeeding joints for best appearance.

The second and all succeeding courses of siding must overlap the previous course a minimum of 1 inch. Locate nails ½ inch from the bottom edge and not more than 16 inches on-center. Nail through both courses and into the framing members.

Install shim strips for continuous horizontal support behind siding wherever it is notched out above or below openings. Use wooden corner boards at least 1⅛ inches thick or formed metal corners (available from distributors) at all inside and outside corners.

Factory-primed siding should be painted within 60 days after installation. If it is exposed for a longer period, lightly sand the primer, or reprime the siding with a good-quality exterior primer that is compatible with the final finish coat.

Unprimed siding should be finished within 30 days after installation. If the finish will be paint, prime the siding with a good-quality compatible exterior primer.

Nailing Hardboard Lap Siding

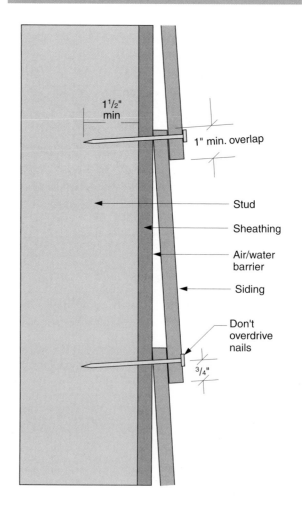

1½" min

1" min. overlap

Stud

Sheathing

Air/water barrier

Siding

Don't overdrive nails

¾"

Hardboard Lap Siding Application Details

ALTERNATE JOINT TREATMENTS

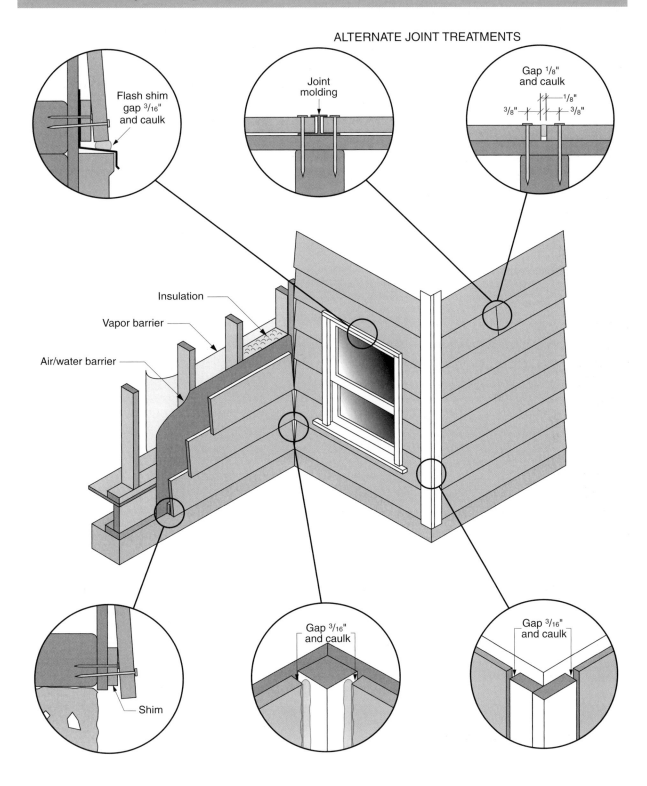

Flash shim gap 3/16" and caulk

Joint molding

Gap 1/8" and caulk

1/8"

3/8"   3/8"

Insulation

Vapor barrier

Air/water barrier

Shim

Gap 3/16" and caulk

Gap 3/16" and caulk

Cedar Shingles

Cedar Shingle Specifications

Grade	Length, in	Butt, in	Bundles Square	Maximum Exposure[1] and Nails Single Course		Double Course	
RED CEDAR							
No. 1 blue label	16	0.40	4	7½	3d	12	5d
(premium grade, 100% heartwood,	18	0.45	4	8½	3d	14	5d
100% clear, 100% edge grain)	24	0.50	4	11½	4d	16	6d
No. 2 red label	16	0.40	4	7½	3d	12	5d
(good grade, 10" clear on 16" shingle,	18	0.45	4	8½	3d	14	5d
16" clear on 24" shingle)	24	0.50	4	11½	4d	16	6d
No. 3 black label	16	0.40	4	7½	3d	12	5d
(utility grade, 6" clear on 16" shingle,	18	0.45	4	8½	3d	14	5d
10" clear on 24" shingle)	24	0.50	4	11½	4d	16	6d
No. 4 undercoursing	16	0.40	2 or 4	7½	5d	–	–
(for bottom course in	18	0.45	2 or 4	8½	5d	–	–
double-coursed walls)							
No. 1 or 2 rebutted-rejoined	16	0.40	1	7½	3d	12	5d
(machine trimmed, square	18	0.45	1	8½	3d	14	5d
edged, top grade)							
WHITE CEDAR							
Extra (perfectly clear)	16	0.40	4	7½	3d	12	5d
1st clear (7" clear, no sapwood)	16	0.40	4	7½	3d	12	5d
2nd clear (sound knots, no sapwood)	16	0.40	4	7½	3d	12	5d
Clear wall (sapwood, curls)	16	0.40	4	7½	3d	12	5d
Utility (undercoursing only)	16	0.40	4	–	3d	–	5d

[1] Exposure given in in.

Cedar Shingle Coverage

Length, in	Coverage[1] of One Square at Exposure, in								
	4	5	6	7	8	9	10	11	12
16	80	100	120	140	160	–	–	–	–
18	72	90	109	127	145	163	–	–	–
24	–	–	80	93	106	120	133	146	160

[1] Coverage given in sq ft.

Cedar Shingle Siding Application Details

CONVENTIONAL

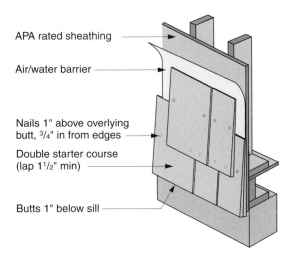

APA rated sheathing

Air/water barrier

Nails 1" above overlying butt, 3/4" in from edges

Double starter course (lap 1 1/2" min)

Butts 1" below sill

WITH RAINSCREEN

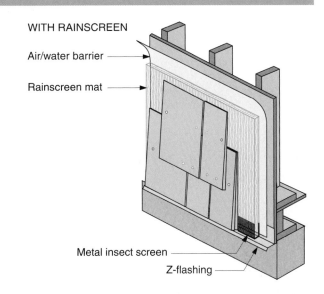

Air/water barrier

Rainscreen mat

Metal insect screen

Z-flashing

CLEARANCE

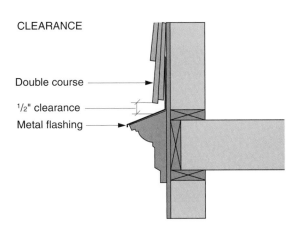

Double course

1/2" clearance

Metal flashing

CLEARANCE

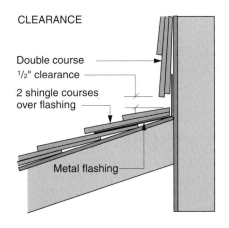

Double course

1/2" clearance

2 shingle courses over flashing

Metal flashing

OUTSIDE CORNER

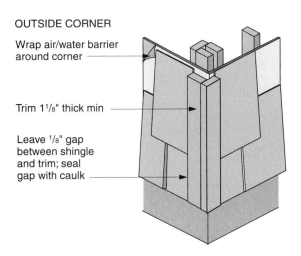

Wrap air/water barrier around corner

Trim 1 1/8" thick min

Leave 1/8" gap between shingle and trim; seal gap with caulk

INSIDE CORNER

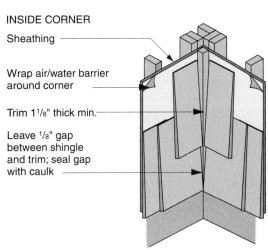

Sheathing

Wrap air/water barrier around corner

Trim 1 1/8" thick min.

Leave 1/8" gap between shingle and trim; seal gap with caulk

Cedar Shingle Coursing

SINGLE COURSING

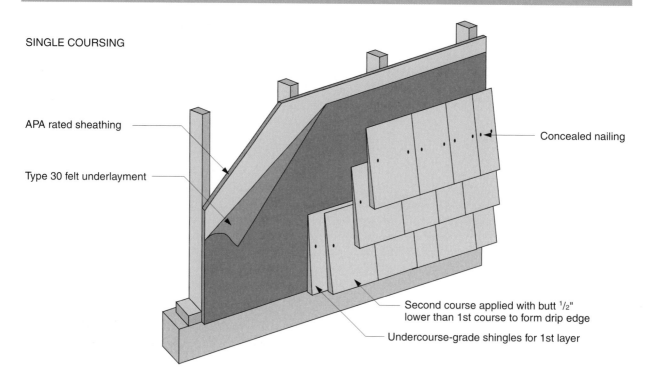

APA rated sheathing

Type 30 felt underlayment

Concealed nailing

Second course applied with butt ¹/₂"
lower than 1st course to form drip edge

Undercourse-grade shingles for 1st layer

DOUBLE COURSING

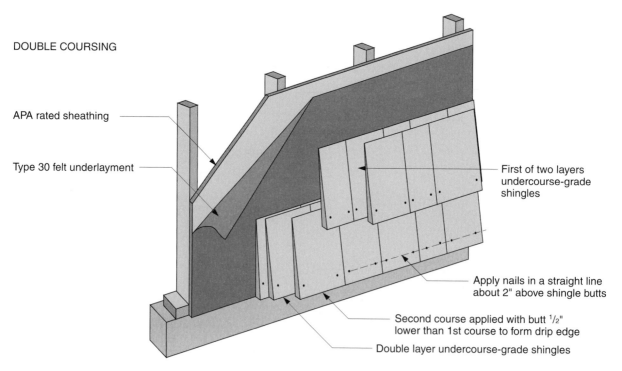

APA rated sheathing

Type 30 felt underlayment

First of two layers
undercourse-grade
shingles

Apply nails in a straight line
about 2" above shingle butts

Second course applied with butt ¹/₂"
lower than 1st course to form drip edge

Double layer undercourse-grade shingles

OVER BEVELED SIDING

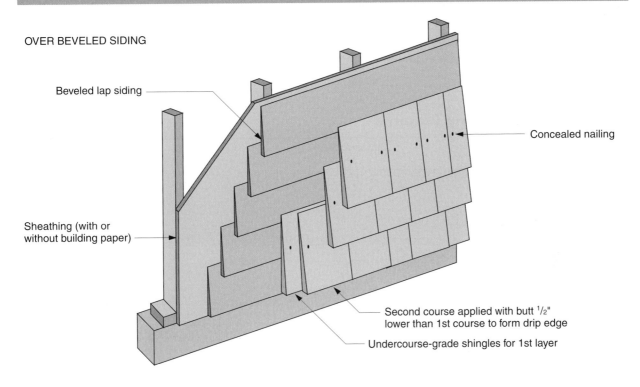

Beveled lap siding

Concealed nailing

Sheathing (with or without building paper)

Second course applied with butt $1/2$" lower than 1st course to form drip edge

Undercourse-grade shingles for 1st layer

OVER STUCCO

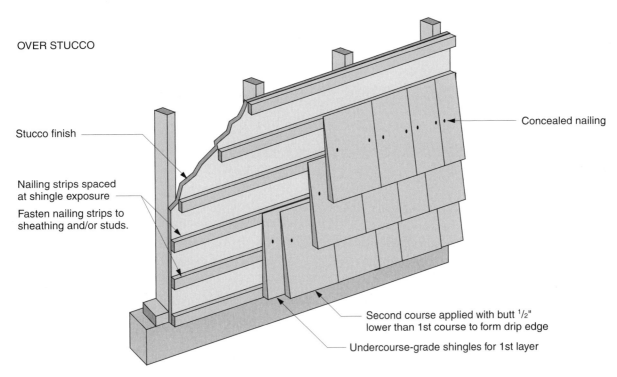

Stucco finish

Concealed nailing

Nailing strips spaced at shingle exposure

Fasten nailing strips to sheathing and/or studs.

Second course applied with butt $1/2$" lower than 1st course to form drip edge

Undercourse-grade shingles for 1st layer

Horizontal Wood

Nails for wood siding should be rust resistant: stainless steel, hot-dipped galvanized, or high-tensile-strength aluminum. Do not use electroplated, galvanized, or bright nails. Recommended penetration into a solid wood base is 1½ inch minimum, or 1¼ inch with ring-shank nails.

The area factors in the table below simplify estimation of the board footage of siding needed for the various patterns and sizes shown. Simply multiply the length and width of the area to be covered by the appropriate area factor. Add a 10-percent allowance for trim and waste to the resulting figure.

Horizontal Wood Siding Patterns

Pattern	Nominal Size, in	Dressed Size, in Total Width	Face Width	Area Factor
 Plain bevel (clapboard)	½ x 4	3½	3½	1.60
	½ x 6	5½	5½	1.33
	¾ x 8	7¼	7¼	1.28
	¾ x 10	9¼	9¼	1.21
 Rabbeted bevel (Dolly Varden)	¾ x 6	5½	5	1.20
	1 x 8	7¼	6¾	1.19
	1 x 10	9¼	8¾	1.18
	1 x 12	11¼	10¾	1.12
 Tongue & groove	1 x 4	3⅜	3⅛	1.28
	1 x 6	5⅜	5⅛	1.17
	1 x 8	7⅛	6⅞	1.16
	1 x 10	9⅛	8⅞	1.13
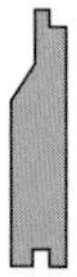 Drop (T&G or shiplap)	1 x 6	5⅜	5⅛	1.17
	1 x 8	7⅛	6¾	1.16
	1 x 10	9⅛	8¾	1.13
	1 x 12	11⅛	10¾	1.10
 Shiplap	1 x 6	5⅜	5	1.17
	1 x 8	7⅛	6¾	1.16
	1 x 10	9⅛	8¾	1.13
	1 x 12	11⅛	10¾	1.10
 Channel shiplap	1 x 6	5⅜	5	1.17
	1 x 8	7⅛	6¾	1.16
	1 x 10	9⅛	8¾	1.13
	1 x 12	11⅛	10¾	1.10
 V - shiplap	1 x 6	5⅜	5	1.17
	1 x 8	7⅛	6¾	1.16
	1 x 10	9⅛	8¾	1.13
	1 x 12	11⅛	10¾	1.10
 Log cabin	1 x 6	5⁷⁄₁₆	4¹⁵⁄₁₆	1.22
	1 x 8	7⅛	6⅝	1.21
	1 x 10	9⅛	8⅝	1.16

Nailing Horizontal Wood Siding

PLAIN BEVEL

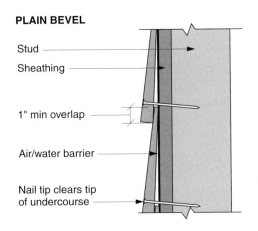

Stud

Sheathing

1" min overlap

Air/water barrier

Nail tip clears tip
of undercourse

RABBETED BEVEL

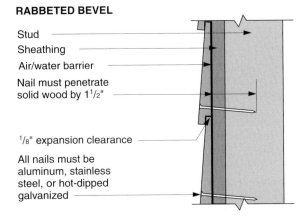

Stud

Sheathing

Air/water barrier

Nail must penetrate
solid wood by $1^1/_2$"

$^1/_8$" expansion clearance

All nails must be
aluminum, stainless
steel, or hot-dipped
galvanized

TONGUE & GROOVE

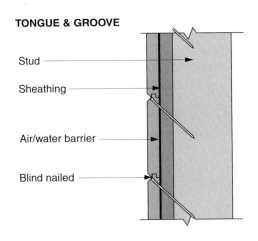

Stud

Sheathing

Air/water barrier

Blind nailed

V - SHIPLAP

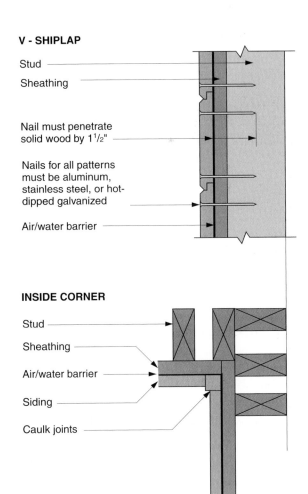

Stud

Sheathing

Nail must penetrate
solid wood by $1^1/_2$"

Nails for all patterns
must be aluminum,
stainless steel, or hot-
dipped galvanized

Air/water barrier

OUTSIDE CORNER

Caulk

Siding

Air/water barrier

Sheathing

Stud

INSIDE CORNER

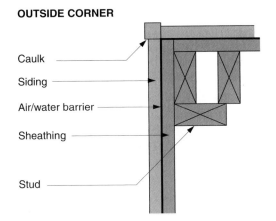

Stud

Sheathing

Air/water barrier

Siding

Caulk joints

Vertical Wood

Wood changes in width and thickness with changes in moisture content. To minimize problems, install siding after it has dried thoroughly and its moisture content has equilibrated with the air. The recommended procedure is this:

- Use as narrow a siding as practical (a rule of thumb is width <8 × thickness).
- Select patterns that allow for movement.
- Treat both sides of siding with a water-repellent exterior finish before installation.

Recommended nailing patterns are shown on the facing page. Nails for applying vertical wood siding should be rust resistant: stainless steel, hot-dipped galvanized, or high-tensile-strength aluminum. Do not use electroplated galvanized or unfinished (bright) nails. Recommended penetration into a solid wood base (either studs or wood sheathing) is 1¼ inches minimum with ring-shank nails. Longer nails are required for installation over other than solid wood sheathing and may require predrilling to avoid splitting the wood.

Joint Treatments in Vertical Wood Sidings

OUTSIDE CORNER

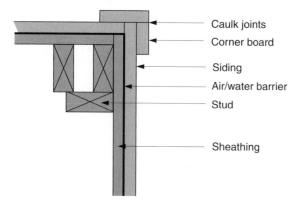

Caulk joints
Corner board
Siding
Air/water barrier
Stud
Sheathing

INSIDE CORNER

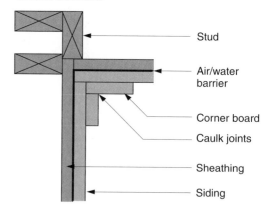

Stud
Air/water barrier
Corner board
Caulk joints
Sheathing
Siding

BELTLINE JOINT

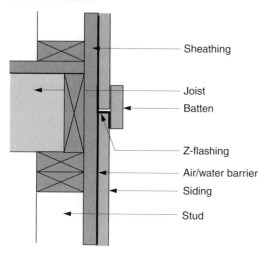

Sheathing
Joist
Batten
Z-flashing
Air/water barrier
Siding
Stud

BEVELED BUTT JOINT

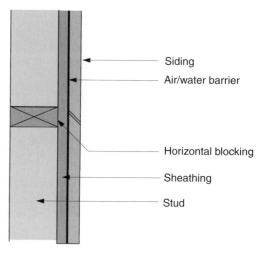

Siding
Air/water barrier
Horizontal blocking
Sheathing
Stud

BOARD & BATTEN

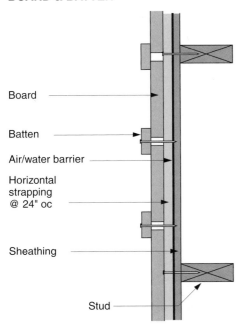

Board

Batten

Air/water barrier

Horizontal
strapping
@ 24" oc

Sheathing

Stud

REVERSE BOARD & BATTEN

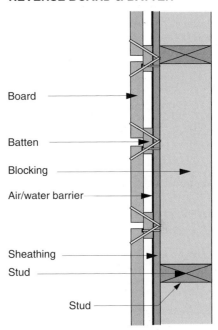

Board

Batten

Blocking

Air/water barrier

Sheathing

Stud

Stud

BOARD & BOARD

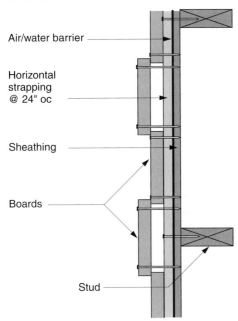

Air/water barrier

Horizontal
strapping
@ 24" oc

Sheathing

Boards

Stud

CHANNEL SHIP LAP

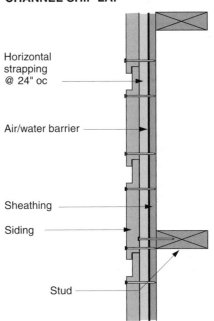

Horizontal
strapping
@ 24" oc

Air/water barrier

Sheathing

Siding

Stud

Plywood

The APA Sturd-I-Wall system consists of APA Rated siding (panel or lap) applied directly to studs or over nonstructural fiberboard, gypsum, or rigid foam insulation sheathing. Nonstructural sheathing is defined as sheathing not recognized by building codes as meeting both bending and racking strength requirements.

A single layer of panel siding, because it is strong and rack resistant, eliminates the cost of installing separate structural sheathing or diagonal wall bracing. Panel sidings are normally installed vertically, but may also be placed horizontally (long dimension across supports) if the horizontal joints are blocked. Maximum stud spacings for both applications are given in the table below.

APA Sturd-I-Wall Construction (Recommendations apply to APA rated siding direct to studs and over nonstructural sheathing)

| | Siding Description[1] | Nominal Thickness (in) or Span Rating, | Max Stud Spacing, (in) | | Nail Size (Use nonstaining box, siding or casing nails)[2,3] | Max Nail Spacing[5], (in) | |
			Strength Axis Vertical	Strength Axis Horizontal		Panel Edges[8]	Intermediate Supports
Panel Siding	APA MDO EXT	$^{11}/_{32}$ & $^{3}/_{8}$	16	24	6d for siding $\leq^{1}/_{2}$" 8d for thicker siding	6[4]	12[6]
		$\geq^{15}/_{32}$	24	24			
	APA RATED SIDING EXT	16 oc (incl. T1-11)	16	16[7]			
		24 oc	24	24			
Lap Siding	APA RATED SIDING–LAP EXT	16 oc	–	16	6d for siding $\leq^{1}/_{2}$"; 8d for thicker siding	16 along bottom edge	–
		24 oc	–	24		24 along edge bottom edge	–

[1] For veneered APA rated siding, including APA 303 siding, recommendations apply to all species groups.

[2] If panel applied over foam insulation sheathing, use next regular nail size. If lap siding installed over rigid foam insulation sheathing up to 1" thick, use 10d (3") nails for $^{3}/_{8}$" or $^{7}/_{16}$" siding, 12d ($3^{1}/_{4}$") nails for $^{15}/_{32}$" or $^{1}/_{2}$" siding, and 16d ($3^{1}/_{2}$") nails for $^{19}/_{32}$" or thicker siding. Use nonstaining box nails for siding installed over foam insulation sheathing.

[3] Hot-dip or hot-tumbled galvanized steel nails are recommended for most siding applications. For best performance, stainless steel nails or aluminum nails should be considered.
Note: Galvanized fasteners may react under wet conditions with the natural extractives of some wood species and may cause staining if left unfinished. Such staining can be minimized if the siding is finished in accordance with APA recommendations, or if the roof overhang protects the siding from direct exposure to moisture and weathering.

[4] For braced wall section with $^{11}/_{32}$" or $^{3}/_{8}$" panel applied horizontally over studs 24" oc, space nails 3" oc along edges.

[5] Recommendations of siding manufacturer may vary.

[6] Where basic wind speed exceeds 90 mph (3-second gust), nails attaching siding to intermediate studs within 10% of the width of the narrow side from wall corners shall be spaced 6" oc.

[7] Stud spacing may be 24" oc for veneer-faced siding panels.

[8] Supported panel joints shall occur approximately along the centerline of framing with a minimum bearing of $^{1}/_{2}$". Fasteners shall be located $^{3}/_{8}$" from panel edges.

APA Sturd-I-Wall Details

VERTICAL PANEL INSTALLATION

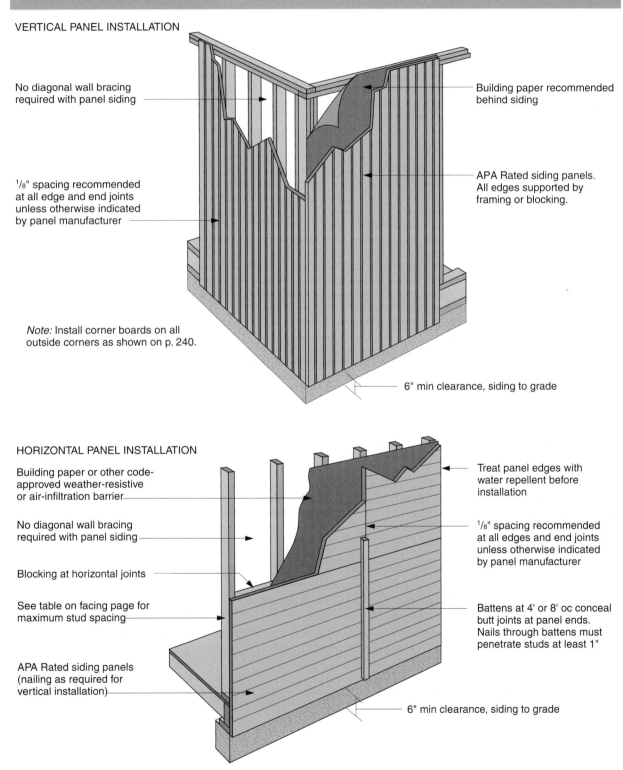

No diagonal wall bracing required with panel siding

$^1/_8$" spacing recommended at all edge and end joints unless otherwise indicated by panel manufacturer

Building paper recommended behind siding

APA Rated siding panels. All edges supported by framing or blocking.

Note: Install corner boards on all outside corners as shown on p. 240.

6" min clearance, siding to grade

HORIZONTAL PANEL INSTALLATION

Building paper or other code-approved weather-resistive or air-infiltration barrier

No diagonal wall bracing required with panel siding

Blocking at horizontal joints

See table on facing page for maximum stud spacing

APA Rated siding panels (nailing as required for vertical installation)

Treat panel edges with water repellent before installation

$^1/_8$" spacing recommended at all edges and end joints unless otherwise indicated by panel manufacturer

Battens at 4' or 8' oc conceal butt joints at panel ends. Nails through battens must penetrate studs at least 1"

6" min clearance, siding to grade

Plywood   **239**

APA Panel Siding Joint Details

VERTICAL WALL JOINTS

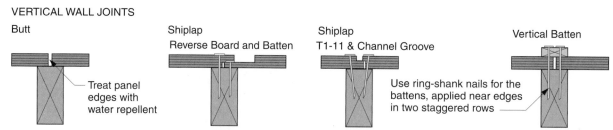

Butt

Treat panel edges with water repellent

Shiplap
Reverse Board and Batten

Shiplap
T1-11 & Channel Groove

Use ring-shank nails for the battens, applied near edges in two staggered rows

Vertical Batten

*Nailing of both panel edges along shiplap joint is recommended.
The "double nailing" is required when wall segment must meet
wall bracing or engineered shear wall requirements.*

VERTICAL INSIDE & OUTSIDE CORNER JOINTS

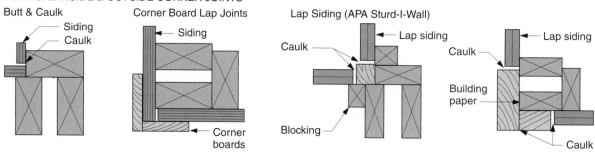

Butt & Caulk
- Siding
- Caulk

Corner Board Lap Joints
- Siding
- Corner boards

Lap Siding (APA Sturd-I-Wall)
- Lap siding
- Caulk
- Blocking

- Lap siding
- Caulk
- Building paper
- Caulk

HORIZONTAL WALL JOINTS

Butt & Flash
- Siding
- Blocking
- Flashing (galvanized or aluminum)

Lap
- Siding
- Blocking
- Lap top panel over bottom panel

Shiplap
- Siding
- Blocking
- Shiplap joint

HORIZONTAL BELTLINE JOINTS

*For multistory buildings, when conventional lumber floor joists and rim boards are used, make provisions
at horizontal joints for shrinkage of framing, especially when applying siding direct to studs.*

Jog Exterior Stud Line

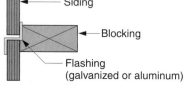

- Floor plate
- Siding
- Band joist
- Stud

Band Board over Panel Filler

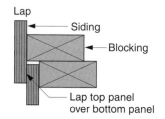

- Siding (4' x 8')
- Alum. or galv. flashing
- Up to 1/2" gap when using lumber floor & rim joists
- Filler
- 2x10 band board
- Siding (4' x 8')

Band Board In Relief

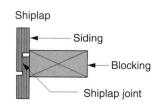

- Siding
- Band board trim
- Galvanized Z flashing
- Galvanized spikes or bolts (countersink)
- Plastic pipe spacer (2" to 6" dia)

APA Panel Wall Sheathing

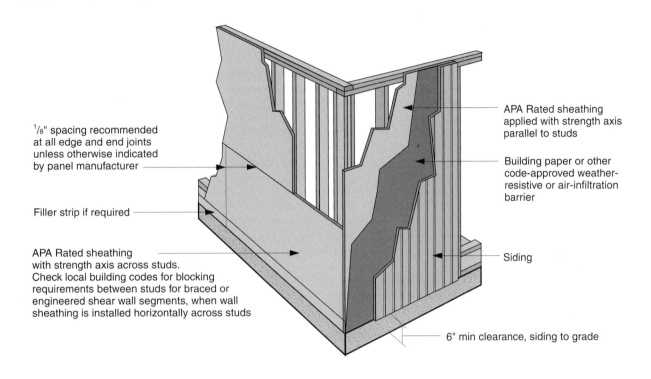

¹/₈" spacing recommended at all edge and end joints unless otherwise indicated by panel manufacturer

Filler strip if required

APA Rated sheathing with strength axis across studs. Check local building codes for blocking requirements between studs for braced or engineered shear wall segments, when wall sheathing is installed horizontally across studs

APA Rated sheathing applied with strength axis parallel to studs

Building paper or other code-approved weather-resistive or air-infiltration barrier

Siding

6" min clearance, siding to grade

APA Panel Wall Sheathing[1] (APA rated sheathing panels continuous over two or more spans)

Panel Span Rating	Maximum Stud Spacing, in	Nail Size[2,3]	Maximum Stud Spacing, in[5]	
			Supported Panel Edges[4]	Intermediate Supports
12/0, 16/0, 20/0 or Wall, 16 oc	16	6d for panels ≤½" 8d for thicker panels	6	12
24/0, 24/16, 32/16 or Wall, 24 oc	24			

[1] See requirements for nailable panel sheathing when exterior covering is to be nailed to sheathing.

[2] Common, smooth, annular, spiral-thread, or galvanized box.

[3] Other code-approved fasteners may be used.

[4] Fasteners shall be located ³/₈" from panel edges.

[5] Increased nail schedules may be required where wall is engineered as a shear wall.

Stucco

Stucco is a mixture of sand, cement, lime, and water. The most common formula is four parts sand to one part portland cement, with a smaller amount of lime. The amount of water is adjusted for workability. A good starting point for the mix is shown in the table below.

Bases

Stucco can be applied over any suitably rigid base. Cast-in-place concrete and concrete masonry block walls are ideal. Wood frame walls can be used, provided they are rigidly braced and covered with metal reinforcement. Metal reinforcement comes in several styles: welded wire, woven wire, and expanded metal lath. The latter consists of sheet metal, slit and deformed to provide an open grid that is usually self-furring (held out from the base wall at a constant distance). If the metal reinforcement is not self-furring, it should be attached and held ¼ inch from the base with special furring nails. The metal reinforcement should be galvanized or otherwise treated to be noncorrosive. The metal reinforcement must be firmly attached and rigid. Joints should overlap a minimum of 1 inch and be made only over a solid backing. For open framing without sheathing, this means at the studs.

Mixes

Achieving the proper mix is the aspect requiring the most experience. (Stucco is not a good candidate for do-it-yourself application.) As in most masonry work, the key is workability. The mix must flow well enough to form a smooth and level coat, but not well enough to sag after application. Also, the amount of sand in the mix influences both strength and susceptibility to later cracking. For convenience, the same mix is used for both the scratch (first) coat and the brown (second) coat, with more sand added to the brown coat. A factory mix is usually used for the finish coat. The manufacturer's recommendations should be strictly followed.

Control Joints

Control joints allow movement without cracking of the stucco due to thermal expansion and contraction, wetting and drying, and slight movements of the underlying structure. Over concrete masonry, control joints in the stucco are only required over the control joints in the masonry. Over wood walls, control joints should be spaced no more than 18 feet apart, but in no case so as to create unjointed panels of over 150 square feet.

Application

The scratch coat should completely fill the metal reinforcement and be scored or scratched horizontally for good bonding. It should be kept moist for a minimum of 12 hours and allowed to set 48 hours before the next coat. The brown coat (if there is one) should be kept moist for 12 hours and allowed to set for 7 days. The finish coat requires wetting for 12 hours. Painting stucco is not recommended, because complete paint removal would be required before repair or recoating of the stucco.

Typical Stucco Mix

Component	Cu Ft	Gal	Lb
Sharp sand	2	15	200
Portland cement	½	3¾	47
Lime	⅓	2½	12
Water	¾	6	48

Optimum Curing Times

Coat	Keep moist, hours	Total set, days
Scratch	12	2
Brown	12	7
Finish	12	2

Stucco Details

OVER CONCRETE MASONRY

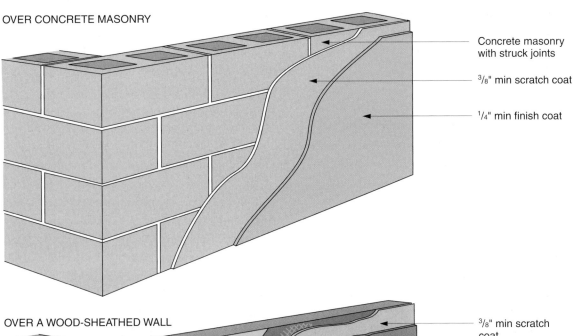

Concrete masonry
with struck joints

$^3/_8$" min scratch coat

$^1/_4$" min finish coat

OVER A WOOD-SHEATHED WALL

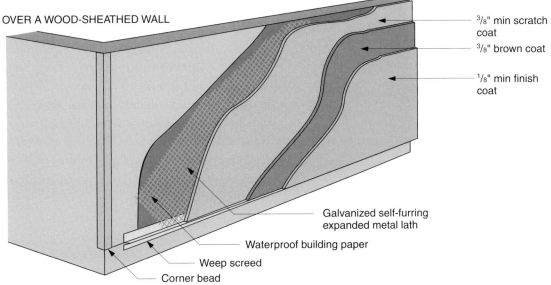

$^3/_8$" min scratch
coat

$^3/_8$" brown coat

$^1/_8$" min finish
coat

Galvanized self-furring
expanded metal lath

Waterproof building paper

Weep screed

Corner bead

INSIDE CORNER

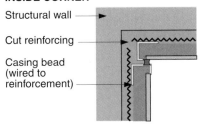

Structural wall

Cut reinforcing

Casing bead
(wired to
reinforcement)

HORIZONTAL

Structure

Reinforcement
cut at joint

Wire control joint
to reinforcement

Waterproof
backing

VERTICAL (EVERY 18' MAX)

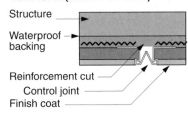

Structure

Waterproof
backing

Reinforcement cut

Control joint

Finish coat

Meet the Code

The following is a partial list of requirements from the *2006 International Residential Code (IRC) for One- and Two-Family Dwellings*. Consult the publication for the full text and additional provisions.

Exterior Covering (R703)

Water-resistive barrier:
- #15 asphalt felt or other approved barrier, free of holes, over studs or sheathing of exterior walls
- applied horizontally and lapped ≥2"
- vertical joints lapped ≥2"
- omission permitted for detached accessory buildings and under paperbacked stucco lath when backing is approved weather-resistive sheathing paper

Panel siding:
- vertical joints to occur over framing members, unless wood or wood structural panel sheathing is used, and be shiplapped or covered with a batten
- horizontal joints lapped ≥1" or shiplapped or be flashed with Z-flashing and occur over solid blocking, wood, or wood structural panel sheathing

Horizontal lap siding:
- lapped ≥1", or ≥½" if rabbeted, with ends caulked, covered with batten, or sealed and installed over strip of flashing

Wood shakes and shingles:
- applied either single-course or double-course over nominal ½" wood-based sheathing or to furring strips over ½" nominal nonwood sheathing
- furring 1×3 or 1×4 fastened to studs with 7d or 8d box nails and spaced at weather exposure
- spacing for expansion between adjacent shingles ≤¼"; for shakes, ≤½"
- offset between joints in courses to be ≥1½"
- weather exposure for shakes and shingles not to exceed that specified in Table R703.5.2
- fastened by 2 hot-dipped, stainless steel, or aluminum nails or staples long enough to penetrate sheathing or furring strips by ≥½"

- staples ≥16 gauge with ≥$\frac{7}{16}$" crown parallel to butt
- fasteners concealed by course above and driven 1" above butt line of next course, ¾" from edges
- In double-course applications, top shake or shingle face-nailed with 2 casing nails, 2" above butt line
- shingles >8" wide to have 2 additional nails 1" apart near center of the shingle
- bottom courses to be doubled

Exterior plaster:
- lath and lath attachments corrosion-resistant
- expanded metal or woven wire lath attached with 1½"-long, 11-gauge nails with $\frac{7}{16}$" head, or $\frac{7}{8}$"-long, 16-gauge staples, spaced ≤6"
- ≥3 coats of portland cement plaster over metal or wire lath or wire lath, and ≥2 coats over masonry, concrete, pressure-preservative-treated wood, decay-resistant wood, or gypsum backing
- ≥2 coats if plaster surface covered by veneer or facing material or completely concealed
- for wood-frame construction with slab-on-grade floor slab, plaster to cover, but not extend below, lath, paper, and screed
- ≥0.019" corrosion-resistant or plastic weep screed, with ≥3½" vertical flange at or below sill plate
- screed ≥4" above earth or 2" above paved areas and allow trapped water to drain to exterior
- exterior lath to cover and terminate on attachment flange of weep screed

Table R703.5.2

Length, in	Maximum Exposure, in	
	Single Course	Double Course
Shingles		
16	7½	12[1]
18	8½	14[2]
24	11½	16
Shakes		
18	8½	14
24	11½	18

[1] 10" for No.2 grade
[2] 11" for No.2 grade

Weather-Resistant Siding Attachment and Minimum Thickness

Siding Material		Nominal Thickness[1], in	Joint Treatment	Support for Siding Material and Fasteners[2,3]					Fastener Number/ Spacing
				Wood/ Structural Sheathing	Fiberboard Sheathing into Stud	Gypsum Sheathing into Stud	Foam Plastic Sheathing into Stud	Direct to Studs	
Hor. alum[4]	no insulation	0.019/.024	Lap	0.120 x 1½ nail	0.120 x 2 nail	0.120 x 2 nail	0.120 nail[14]	Not allowed	Stud spacing
		0.019	Lap	0.120 x 1½ nail	0.120 x 2½ nail	0.120 x 2½ nail	0.120 nail[14]	0.120 x 1½ nail	Stud spacing
	insulation	0.019/.024	Lap ½	0.120 x 1½ nail	0.120 x 2 nail	0.120 x 2 nail	0.120 nail[14]	Not allowed	Stud spacing
Hardboard	vertical panel	7/16	–	7	7	7	7	7	6" at edges 12" interior
	lap siding	7/16	10	9	9	9	9	9	Stud spacing 2 per bearing
Steel		29 ga	Lap	0.113 x 1¾ nail 1¾ staple	0.113 x 2¾ nail 2½ staple	0.113 x 2½ nail 2¾ staple	0.113 nail[14] staple[14]	not allowed	Stud spacing
Particleboard panel		3/8–1/2	–	6d box nail	6d box nail	6d box nail	box nail[14]	6d box nail	6"at edges 12" interior
		5/8	–	6d box nail	8d box nail	8d box nail	6d box nail[14]	6d box nail	
Plywood (exterior) panel[5]		3/8	–	0.099 x 2 nail	0.113 x 2½ nail	0.099 x 2 nail	0.113 x 2½ nail[14]	0.099 x 2 nail	6"at edges 12" interior
Vinyl siding		0.035	Lap	0.120 x 1½ nail 1¾ staple	0.120 x 2 nail 2½ staple	0.120 x 2 nail 2½ staple	0.120 nail[14] staple[14]	Not allowed	Stud spacing
Wood[5]	rustic, drop	3/8 min	Lap	1" fastener penetration into stud				0.113 x 2½ nail	<8" wide— 1 per bearing
	shiplap	19/32 ave	Lap	1" fastener penetration into stud				2 staple	
	bevel	7/16	Lap	1" fastener penetration into stud					≥8" wide—
	butt tip	3/16	Lap	1" fastener penetration into stud					2 per bearing
Fiber cement	panel	5/16	–	6d corrosion-resistant nail[11]	6d corrosion-resistant nail[11]	6d corrosion-resistant nail[11]	6d corrosion-resistant nail[11,14]	4d corrosion-resistant nail[12]	6"at edges 3/8" interior
	lap siding	0.019/.024	–	6d corrosion-resistant nail[11]	6d corrosion-resistant nail[11]	6d corrosion-resistant nail[11]	6d corrosion-resistant nail[11,14]	6d corrosion-resistant nail[13]	13

1. Based on stud spacing of 16 inches on center where studs are spaced 24 inches, siding shall be applied to sheathing approved for that spacing.

2. Nail is a general description and shall be T-head, modified round head, or round head with smooth or deformed shanks.

3. Nails or staples shall be aluminum, galvanized, or rust-preventative coated and shall be driven into the studs for fiberboard or gypsum backing.

4. Aluminum nails to be used to attach aluminum siding.

5. 3/8" vertical plywood not to be applied directly to studs spaced more than 16" oc. Stud spacing not to exceed the panel span rating unless installed with face grain perpendicular to studs or over sheathing approved for stud spacing.

6. Vertical board sidings to be nailed to horizontal nailing strips or blocking set 24" oc. Nails to penetrate 1½" into studs, studs & wood sheathing, or blocking.

7. Minimum shank diameter of 0.092", minimum head diameter of 0.225", and nail length must accommodate sheathing and penetrate framing 1½".

8. When used to resist shear forces, the spacing must be 4" at panel edges and 8" on interior supports.

9. Minimum shank diameter of 0.099", minimum head diameter of 0.240", and nail length must accommodate sheathing and penetrate framing 1½".

10. Vertical end joints to occur at studs and shall be covered with a joint cover or caulked.

11. Minimum 0.102" smooth shank, 0.255" round head.

12. Minimum 0.099" smooth shank, 0.250" round head.

13. Face nailing: 2 nails each stud. Concealed nailing: one 11 gage 1½" galv. roofing nail (0.371" head diameter, 0.120" shank) or 6d galv. box nail each stud.

14. Minimum nail length must accommodate sheathing and penetrate framing 1½".

Roofing

Terms such as *eaves, soffit, fascia,* and *ridge* are referred to throughout this chapter, so before you look up the installation details of your favorite roof, read the first section, *Roofing Terms.*

If you are trying to decide what kind of roofing to install, read the second section, *Roofing Materials.*

The following sections, the real meat of the chapter, describe in words and illustrations how to install ten different types of roofing. They range from *EPDM (rubber membrane),* suitable for flat roofs, through two versions of *roll roofing,* ubiquitous *asphalt shingles,* classic *cedar shingles* and *cedar shakes,* and regional materials such as *slate* and Spanish *tile,* to preformed *metal panel* and *standing-seam* roofing.

Although *ventilation* is not roofing, proper ventilation of space beneath the roofing is imperative for the proper operation and maximum lifetime of the roof. Ventilation removes moisture in winter and heat in summer. It is also absolutely the best way to prevent the destructive buildup of ice dams.

The best time to install, replace, or repair *gutters* is when you are roofing, so a description of the typical gutter system and all of its parts is included, too.

Finally, as usual, we provide a crib sheet to make sure your roofing will *meet the code.*

Roofing Terms

Function of the Roof

The primary function of a roof is the protection of the building beneath from moisture damage, whether from rain, snow, or ice. The primary design characteristics controlling success are pitch (angle) and coverage (overlap) of the roofing material.

Pitch and Slope

The pitch of a roof is the vertical rise divided by the total span. The slope of a roof is vertical rise divided by horizontal run.

Example: A roof peak is 8 feet above the top plate. The span (building width) is 24 feet. The pitch is, therefore, 8/24, or 1/3; The slope, usually expressed as inches rise per 12 inches of run, is 8/12.

Exposure and Coverage

Exposure is the down-slope width of roofing material exposed after installation. Coverage is the number of layers of roofing from surface to underlayment.

Example: A roof is covered with asphalt shingles measuring 12 inches by 36 inches. The bottom 5 inches of each shingle are exposed. Thus, the exposure is 5 inches, and the coverage is double (coverage varies from double to triple, but the least amount is what counts).

Parts of a Roof

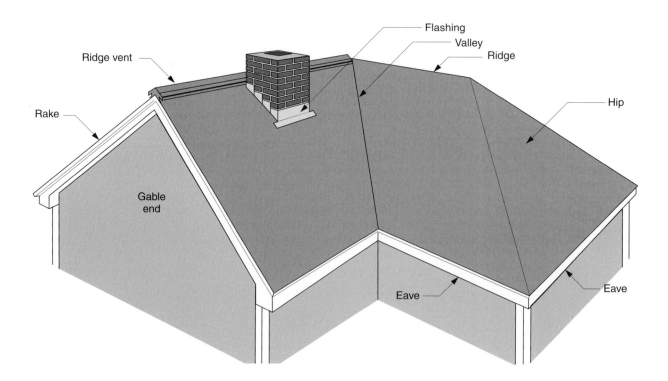

Flashing

Valley

Ridge

Ridge vent

Hip

Rake

Gable end

Eave

Eave

Cornice Terminology

EAVE DETAILS

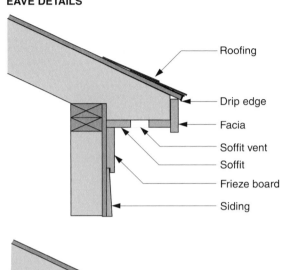

Roofing
Drip edge
Facia
Soffit vent
Soffit
Frieze board
Siding

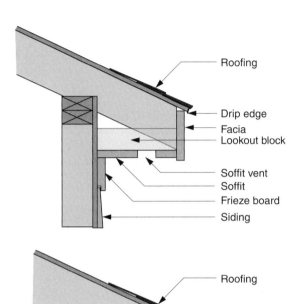

Roofing
Drip edge
Facia
Lookout block
Soffit vent
Soffit
Frieze board
Siding

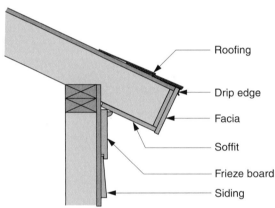

Roofing
Drip edge
Facia
Soffit
Frieze board
Siding

Roofing
Drip edge
Facia
Siding

GABLE END DETAILS

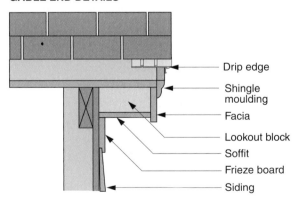

Drip edge
Shingle moulding
Facia
Lookout block
Soffit
Frieze board
Siding

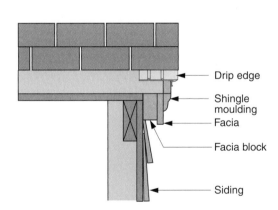

Drip edge
Shingle moulding
Facia
Facia block
Siding

Roofing Materials

The type of roofing material selected is a function of regional architectural style as well as performance. The most common material by far is the ubiquitous asphalt shingle. However, the mark of a top-quality home in Vermont is the slate roof; in much of ski country, standing seam or preformed metal panel; in the Southwest, Spanish tile.

Be aware of rapid changes in the industry. Preformed metal panels have nearly replaced standing-seam, and EPDM (single-ply rubber membranes) are rapidly replacing the old-fashioned built-up roof for flat and low-slope applications.

Roofing Materials Compared

Roofing Type	Minimum Slope	Life, yr	Relative Cost	Weight, lb per 100 sq ft
ASPHALT SHINGLE	4	15–50	Low	200–300
EPDM	0	20	Medium	30–45
PREFORMED METAL	3	30–50	Low–Medium	50
ROLL	2	10	Low	90

ASPHALT SHINGLE — Three-tab / No cutout (NCO)

Roofing Materials Compared — *Continued*

Roofing Type	Minimum Slope	Life, yr	Relative Cost	Weight, lb per 100 sq ft
ASPHALT ROLL	1	15	Low	130
SLATE	5	100	High	800–1,500
SPANISH TILE	4	100	Medium	1,000
STANDING SEAM	3	30–50	Medium	75
WOOD SHAKE	3	50	High	300
WOOD SHINGLE	3	25	Medium	150

EPDM (Rubber Membrane)

Flat and low-slope roofs have always been problematic—until the advent of ethylene propylene diene monomer (EPDM) rubber membranes. The material is available in thicknesses of 45 mil (most common), 60 mil, and 90 mil, and in sheets up to 50 feet wide and 100 feet long, making seams unnecessary for most applications.

Adhering Membrane

The membrane may be adhered to any clean, solid, relatively flat surface. Although self-adhesive versions are available, the use of a bonding adhesive similar to contact cement is recommended.

First make sure the substrate is securely fastened. Rigid foam insulation should be fastened 2 feet on-center using screws or ring-shank nails with fender washers. Before application of the adhesive, the surface must be absolutely dry.

Spread the membrane into position over the roof. The membrane should lap intersecting walls by 8 to 12 inches and overhang the roof edges by 3 inches.

Allow 30 minutes for the membrane to lie flat, then fold the membrane back halfway and wipe the surface with the recommended cleaner. Open the adhesive and stir until uniform.

Using a paint roller, apply the adhesive to the deck and to the back of the membrane. Allow adhesive to dry until just tacky. Very carefully, roll the coated membrane back onto the coated deck. Sweep over the membrane with a push broom to fully adhere the membrane.

Repeat the whole process on the remaining half of the membrane.

Intersecting Wall

The membrane should extend 8 to12 inches up any intersecting wall. Wall siding simply laps over the membrane as if it were roof flashing.

On a masonry (CMU or brick) wall, an aluminum termination bar secures the top edge. First fasten the bar with screws or masonry fasteners. Then trim the membrane flush with the bar, and caulk as shown.

Roof Edges

The membrane laps over the fascia or rake a minimum of 3 inches. Where there is a gutter, lap the membrane over its inside face. The membrane is then fastened to the vertical surface with a termination bar and trimmed even with the bottom of the bar. The top edge of the bar is sealed to the membrane with caulk.

Outside Wall Corners

Cured EPDM membrane has insufficient stretch to make neat outside corners, so patches of easily-stretched uncured EPDM are utilized.

First cut the roof membrane where it meets the corner of the wall down to roof level, and adhere it to the two walls. This leaves a V-shaped gap in the lapped membrane. Two patches of stretchable uncured EPDM (the second larger than the first) are fully adhered over the gap. The top edges of the patches are secured with a termination bar, trimmed flush, and caulked. The remaining exposed edges of the top patch are caulked to the roof membrane.

Roof Penetrations

Prefabricated EPDM boots are available for sealing vent pipes to the roof membrane. Other penetrations may be sealed with patches of uncured EPDM (always doubled) and caulk.

Seams

Sheets of EPDM may be spliced using either a special splicing adhesive or self-adhesive, double-sided seaming tape.

Splicing adhesive is applied to both mating surfaces of a 6-inch overlap and allowed to dry. The seam is then rolled with a hand roller and the exposed edge caulked.

Seaming tape is applied to one face of the seam with the release paper in place. The membranes are overlapped, and the seam is rolled with the hand roller. Finally, the top piece is adhered as the release paper is slowly removed. The exposed edge is then caulked.

Roof Deck Application

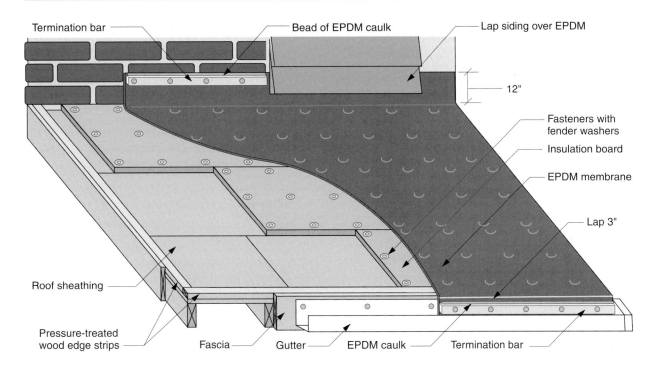

Termination bar

Bead of EPDM caulk

Lap siding over EPDM

12"

Fasteners with fender washers

Insulation board

EPDM membrane

Lap 3"

Roof sheathing

Pressure-treated wood edge strips

Fascia

Gutter

EPDM caulk

Termination bar

Outside Corner

Inside Corner

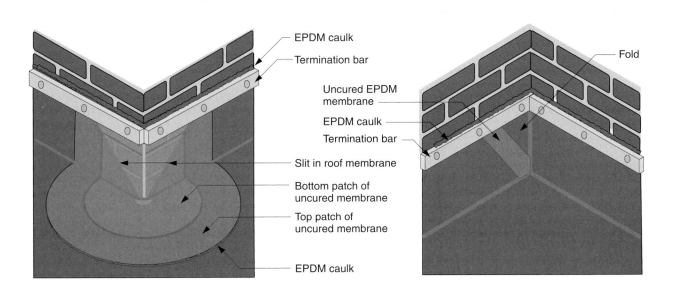

EPDM caulk

Termination bar

Fold

Uncured EPDM membrane

EPDM caulk

Termination bar

Slit in roof membrane

Bottom patch of uncured membrane

Top patch of uncured membrane

EPDM caulk

EPDM (Rubber Membrane)   **253**

Roll Roofing

Roll roofing has a mineral-covered surface just like asphalt shingles, but the material comes in rolls that are 36-in. wide. Roll roofing is best applied in warm weather. If the temperature is below 45°F, the roofing should first be unrolled and laid flat in a warm space. Extreme care must be used in handling the roofing in cold weather to avoid cracking. In warm weather, unroll the roofing, cut it into 12- to 18-foot lengths, and stack it on the roof for several hours or until the top sheet lies flat. This precaution will reduce the tendency of the roofing to ripple during application as it expands and relaxes from its tightly rolled condition.

Proper sealing of lap joints is critical to avoid leaks on low-slope roofs, so use only the plastic cement recommended by the manufacturer. Warm it if necessary to facilitate even spreading. Also, use only the amount recommended, as excess cement tends to bubble.

The illustrations on the facing page shows application parallel to the eaves. Application perpendicular to the eaves is also possible.

Begin by flashing all roof edges as shown. Valleys are flashed with mineral-surfaced roll roofing of the same color. First apply a half strip (18 inches wide), mineral surface down, the full length of the valley, using a minimum number of nails 1 inch from the edges. Next cover that with a full-width sheet, mineral surface up, with minimum nailing 1 inch from the edges.

Next apply 9-inch-wide (one-quarter roll width) strips of roofing to eaves and rakes, nailing them 4 inches on-center 1 inch in from each edge. The strip edges should overhang eaves and rakes by approximately 3/8 inch to form a drip edge.

The first full course of roofing is applied with edges even with those of the underlying edge strips. Nail the top edge 4 inches on-center, taking care that the bottom of the succeeding course will completely cover the nails. If more than one length is required, cement and overlap the next length by 6 inches, then fasten it with a double row of nails 4 inches

on-center. After the top edge is fully nailed, one person lifts the bottom edge while a second fully coats the eaves and rake edge strips with plastic cement, also known as blind nail cement. Thoroughly press the bottom and ends of the sheet into the coated edge strips.

The second and succeeding courses are applied in the same way as the first, except that each course overlaps the preceding by at least 2 inches; 3 inches is better. The sheet is nailed first at the top, allowing for easier correction of ripples, before cementing and nailing of the bottom edge and end laps.

At the valleys and ridges, the sheets are trimmed to butt at the ridge or valley intersections. Chalk lines are snapped 5½ inches to both sides of the intersection, and 2-inch-wide strips of plastic cement are applied. Cut sheets of roofing into 12-inch-wide strips, apply them lengthwise over the intersection, and nail them 3 inches on-center, ¾ inch from the edges.

Edge Flashing and Covering

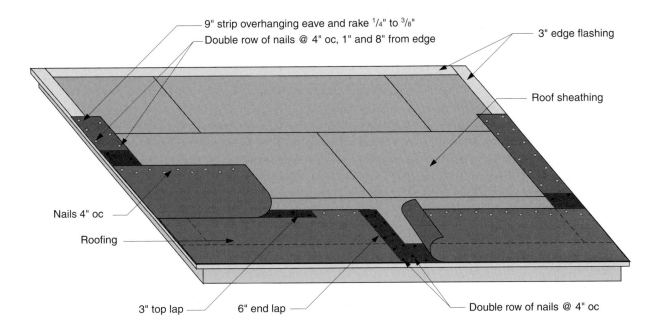

9" strip overhanging eave and rake $^1/_4$" to $^3/_8$"

Double row of nails @ 4" oc, 1" and 8" from edge

3" edge flashing

Roof sheathing

Nails 4" oc

Roofing

3" top lap

6" end lap

Double row of nails @ 4" oc

Valley Flashing

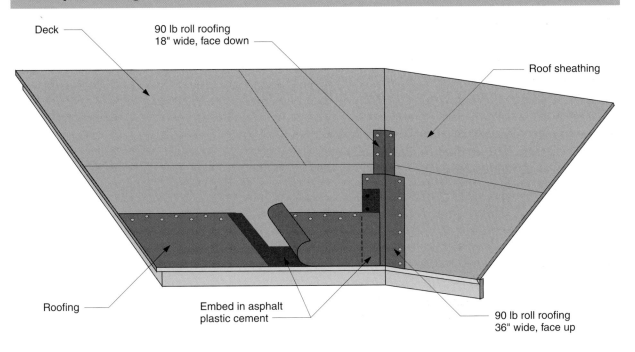

Deck

90 lb roll roofing
18" wide, face down

Roof sheathing

Roofing

Embed in asphalt
plastic cement

90 lb roll roofing
36" wide, face up

Double-Coverage Roll Roofing

Double-coverage roll roofing consists of 17 inches of mineral surfacing, intended for exposure, and 19 inches of selvage (nonmineral-surfaced) to be cemented and lapped. Like the other forms of roll roofing, it is best applied in warm weather in order to avoid cracking and buckling.

In warm weather (over 45°F), unroll the material, cut it into lengths of 12 to 18 feet, and stack it on a flat area of the roof. Allow it to stand until the top sheet lies flat. In cold weather do the same indoors, but be careful not to tear or crack the sheets during transport.

Cementing of the laps is the most critical part of the operation, so use only a plastic cement recommended by the roofing manufacturer, and prewarm the buckets by immersion in warm water if the weather is cold.

The roofing is customarily applied parallel to the eaves, as shown in the illustrations on the facing page. Begin by flashing all roof edges and valleys. Valleys are flashed with mineral-surfaced roll roofing of the same color. First apply a half strip (18 inches wide), mineral surface down, the full length of the valley, using a minimum number of nails 1 inch from the edges. Next cover it with a full-width sheet, mineral surface up, with minimum nailing 1 inch from the edges. The regular courses are then trimmed 3 inches back from the valley intersection, fully cemented to the flashing, and nailed through the selvage portion only.

The starter course is formed by splitting a sheet into a 17-inch-wide mineral-surfaced strip and a 19-inch-wide selvage strip. Put the mineral-surfaced strip aside for the final course, and apply the selvage as a starter strip, overhanging both eaves and rakes by ³⁄₈ inch. Nail the strip 12 inches on-center in two rows: 1 inch above the eaves and 5 inches from the top. Do not cement the starter strip directly to the deck. Coat the entire exposed surface of the starter strip with plastic cement.

The first regular course is a full-width sheet placed with the bottom edge and ends flush with the edges of the starter strip. Press the mineral-surfaced portion of the sheet into the cement (a roller is handy), and nail the selvage portion to the deck in two rows, 5 inches and 13 inches from the top edge. Succeeding courses are applied in the same fashion, except in this order: Nail top sheet, lift bottom of top sheet and apply cement, and press top sheet into cement.

End laps are formed by nailing the surfaced portion of the bottom strip 4 inches on-center and 1 inch from the end, applying a 6-inch-wide band of plastic cement to the entire width and nailing the top strip through the selvage only.

Hips and ridges are finished by covering them with 12-inch-wide strips of roofing. Trim and butt the underlying courses at the intersections. Apply the 12- by 36-inch pieces in exactly the same way as the regular courses, starting with a 12- by 17-inch piece of selvage.

Edge Flashing and Covering

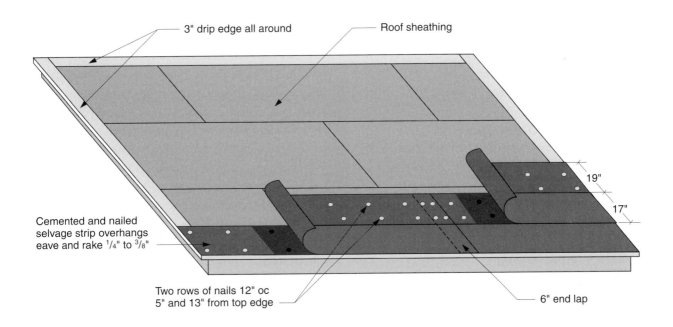

3" drip edge all around

Roof sheathing

19"

17"

Cemented and nailed
selvage strip overhangs
eave and rake $^1/_4$" to $^3/_8$"

Two rows of nails 12" oc
5" and 13" from top edge

6" end lap

Valley Flashing

Embed in asphalt plastic cement

90 lb roll roofing
18" wide, face down

Roof sheathing

19" selvage
strip cemented
and nailed

Embed in asphalt
plastic cement

90 lb roll roofing
36" wide, face up

Double-Coverage Roll Roofing   **257**

Asphalt Shingles

Underlayment and Drip Edges

Begin by installing a drip edge at the eaves. Next apply 15-pound asphalt-saturated felt underlayment, using a minimum number of nails. Take care to align the felt with the eaves so that the lines printed on the felt can serve as guidelines when installing the shingles. Overlap underlayment courses at least 2 inches and end laps 4 inches. Finally, install a drip edge over the underlayment along the rakes.

Eave Flashing

Where there is any possibility of ice dams, install an eave flashing of mineral-surfaced roll roofing or special plastic or rubber ice-shield membrane from the eaves to a point at least 12 inches inside the wall line.

Valley Flashing

Valleys are flashed with mineral-surfaced roll roofing of the same color. First apply a half strip (18 inches wide), mineral surface down, the full length of the valley, using a minimum number of nails 1 inch from the edges. Next cover with a full-width sheet, mineral surface up, with minimum nailing 1 inch from the edges. Shingle courses will be beveled and trimmed along a line 3 inches from the center of the valley.

Shingle Application

Nails should be galvanized or aluminum, 12 gauge, with min ⅜-inch-dia. heads. The length of the nail should be sufficient to penetrate the deck by ¾ inch, and the head of the nail should not penetrate the surface of the shingle.

Begin with a starter strip of shingles from which the mineral-surfaced portion has been removed. Remove 3 inches from the end of the first strip so that the cutouts of the first regular course will not fall over a starter joint. Nail the strip 12 inches on-center 3 inches above the eaves, placing the nails to miss the cutouts of the course to follow.

The first course begins with a full-length shingle strip. Install it with the butts of starter and first course aligned. If there is a dormer, snap vertical chalk lines to both sides of the dormer so that vertical alignment of the interrupted courses can be maintained.

For the most common three-tab shingle, nail it in a line ⅝ inch above the cutouts and 1 inch from each end. With each succeeding course, remove an additional 6-inch width from the first shingle in the row, and line up the butts over the tops of the underlying cutouts. For other types of shingle, follow the manufacturer's directions for nailing.

A less regular effect can be created by removing 4 inches from each succeeding course. The tabs then line up every third course rather than every other course. The disadvantage is the need to measure more often.

For flashing details at pipes, chimneys, and abutting walls, see the following pages.

For further information about all types of asphalt roofing, see the *Residential Asphalt Roofing Manual*, available from the Asphalt Roofing Manufacturer's Association.

Edge Flashing and Covering

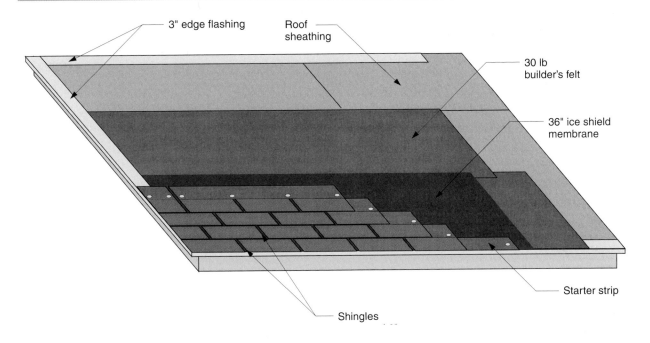

3" edge flashing

Roof sheathing

30 lb builder's felt

36" ice shield membrane

Starter strip

Shingles

Valley Flashing

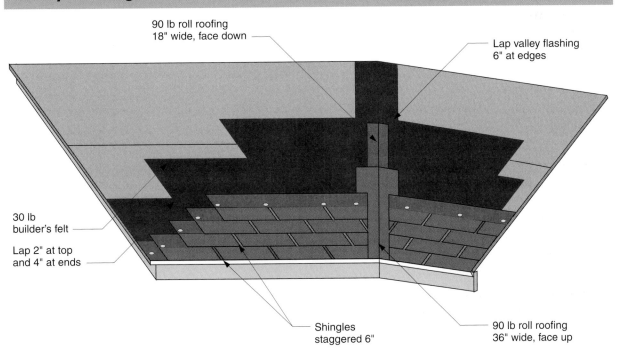

90 lb roll roofing 18" wide, face down

Lap valley flashing 6" at edges

30 lb builder's felt

Lap 2" at top and 4" at ends

Shingles staggered 6"

90 lb roll roofing 36" wide, face up

Asphalt Shingles   **259**

Flashing a Butting Wall

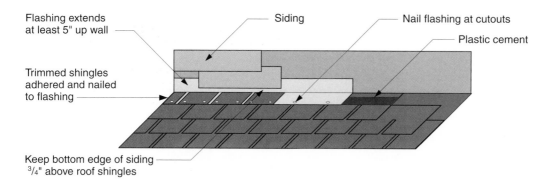

Flashing extends at least 5" up wall

Siding

Nail flashing at cutouts

Plastic cement

Trimmed shingles adhered and nailed to flashing

Keep bottom edge of siding ³/₄" above roof shingles

Flashing a Butting Side Wall

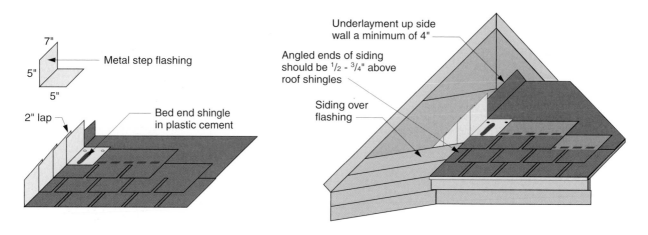

7"

5"

5"

Metal step flashing

2" lap

Bed end shingle in plastic cement

Underlayment up side wall a minimum of 4"

Angled ends of siding should be ¹/₂ - ³/₄" above roof shingles

Siding over flashing

Flashing a Vent Pipe

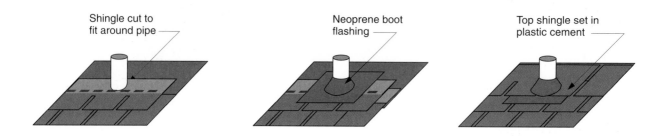

Shingle cut to fit around pipe

Neoprene boot flashing

Top shingle set in plastic cement

STEP 1
Apply asphalt primer to bricks. Apply metal base flashing to front, overlapping shingles 4".

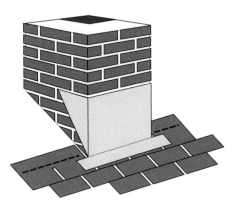

STEP 2
Nail metal step flashing over plastic cement. Bed overlapping shingles in plastic cement.

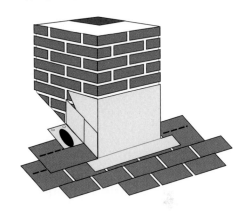

STEP 3
Install wood cricket at rear and shingle to edge. Embed rear corner flashings in cement.

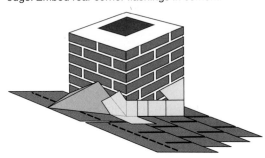

STEP 4
Embed rear base flashing in plastic cement. Nail flashing to deck only.

STEP 5
Set front and side cap flashings 1¹/₂" into raked joints and refill with mortar.

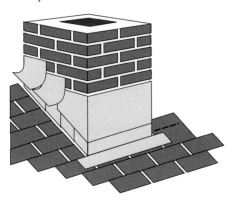

STEP 6
Install rear corner cap flashings, and install rear cap flashing suitable to the situation.

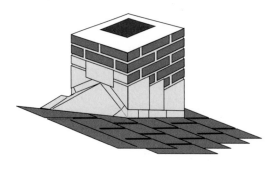

Cedar Shingles

Being wood, cedar shingles periodically become soaked. For the longest life, wood shingles should be applied over a drainage mat material or skip sheathing spaced the same as the exposure of the shingles. To allow for swelling, shingles in the same course should be spaced at least ¼ inch apart, regardless of estimated moisture content.

In areas where ice dams occur, the eaves should be flashed with 30-pound asphalt saturated felt or special ice-shield membrane to at least 24 inches inside the wall line.

The first course should be doubled, with an eaves projection (drip edge) of 1½ inches and joints of succeeding courses offset by at least 1½ inches. Succeeding courses should be laid with exposure and nailing as shown in the table below.

Red Cedar Shingle Specifications

| Shingle Grade | Length, in | Maximum Exposure at Roof Slope, in | | Nails | | Description |
		<4 in 12	>4 in 12	New Roof	Re-roof	
No.1 (blue label)	16	3¾	5	3d	5d	Premium grade of shingle for roofs; 100% heartwood, 100% clear, 100% edge grain
	18	4¼	5½	3d	5d	
	24	5½	7½	4d	6d	
No.2 (red label)	16	3½	4	3d	5d	Good grade; flat grain permitted; 10" clear on 16" shingle; 11" clear on 18" shingle; 16" clear on 24" shingle
	18	4	4½	3d	5d	
	24	5½	6½	4d	6d	
No.3 (black label)	16	3	3½	3d	5d	Utility grade; flat grain permitted; 6" clear on 16" and 18" shingles; 10" clear on 24" shingle
	18	3½	4	3d	5d	
	24	5	5½	4d	6d	

Estimating Coverage

| Shingle Length | Sq-ft Coverage of 4 Bundles (nominal square) at Weather Exposure of | | | | | | | | | |
	3½"	4"	4½"	5"	5½"	6"	7"	8"	9"	10"
16"	70	80	90	100	110	120	140	160		
18"		72	81	90	100	109	127	145	163	
24"						80	93	106	120	133

Source: *Exterior and Interior Product Glossary* (Bellevue, WA: Red Cedar Shingle & Handsplit Shake Bureau, 1980).

Shingle Application

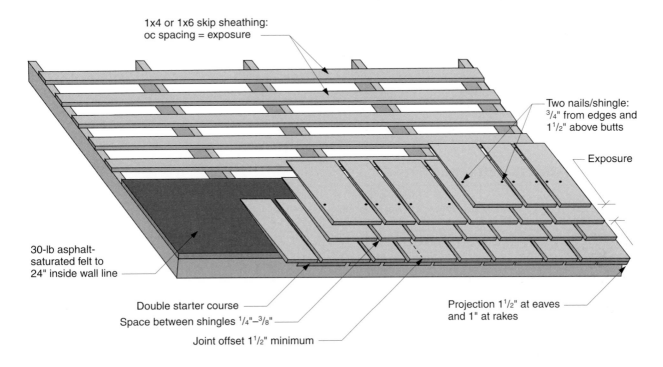

1x4 or 1x6 skip sheathing: oc spacing = exposure

Two nails/shingle: 3/4" from edges and 1 1/2" above butts

Exposure

30-lb asphalt-saturated felt to 24" inside wall line

Double starter course

Space between shingles 1/4"–3/8"

Joint offset 1 1/2" minimum

Projection 1 1/2" at eaves and 1" at rakes

Open-Valley Flashing

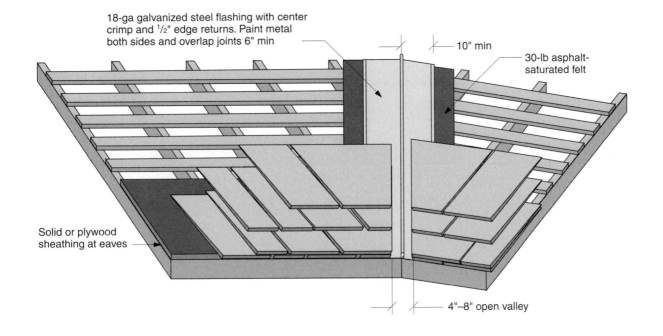

18-ga galvanized steel flashing with center crimp and 1/2" edge returns. Paint metal both sides and overlap joints 6" min

10" min

30-lb asphalt-saturated felt

Solid or plywood sheathing at eaves

4"–8" open valley

Cedar Shakes

For the longest life, shakes should be applied over a drainage mat material or over skip sheathing spaced the same as the exposure of the shakes. To allow for swelling, shakes in the same course should be spaced at least ½ inch apart.

In areas where ice dams occur, eaves should be flashed with 30-pound asphalt-saturated felt to 24 inches inside the wall line.

The first course should be doubled, with an eaves projection of 1 inch and joints spaced 1½ inches minimum. An 18-inch-wide strip of 30-pound asphalt-saturated felt should be applied over the top of each course, twice the exposure above the butt. Use the exposure and nailing listed in the table below.

Cedar Shake Specification

Shake Grade	Length, in	Butt, in	Max Exposure at Roof Slope, in 4 in 12	Nails for New Roof	Nails for Re-roof	Description
No. 1 hand split & resawn	18	½-¾	7½	6d	7d	First split to uniform thickness with steel froe, then sawn to produce two tapered shakes
	18	¾-1¼	7½	7d	8d	
	24	⅜	7	4d	6d	
	24	½-¾	7	4d	6d	
	24	¾-1¼	7	4d	6d	
No. 1 taper split	24	½-⅝	4	6d	7d	Split with steel froe, then reversed and resplit with taper
No. 1 straight split	18	⅜	7½	6d	7d	Same thickness throughout; split with steel froe and mallet
	24	⅜	10	6d	7d	

Estimating Coverage

Shingle Length	Sq-ft Coverage of 4 Bundles (nominal square) at Weather Exposure of									
	3½"	4"	4½"	5"	5½"	6"	7"	8"	9"	10"
16"	70	80	90	100	110	120	140	160		
18"		72	81	90	100	109	127	145	163	
24"						80	93	106	120	133

Source: *Exterior and Interior Product Glossary* (Bellevue, WA: Red Cedar Shingle & Handsplit Shake Bureau, 1980).

Shake Application

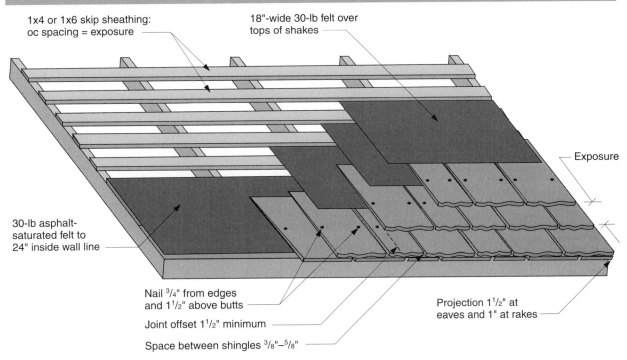

1x4 or 1x6 skip sheathing: oc spacing = exposure

18"-wide 30-lb felt over tops of shakes

Exposure

30-lb asphalt-saturated felt to 24" inside wall line

Nail $^3/_4$" from edges and $1^1/_2$" above butts

Joint offset $1^1/_2$" minimum

Space between shingles $^3/_8$"–$^5/_8$"

Projection $1^1/_2$" at eaves and 1" at rakes

Open-Valley Flashing

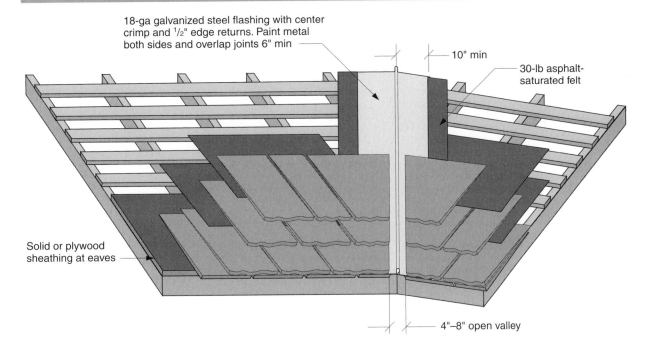

18-ga galvanized steel flashing with center crimp and $^1/_2$" edge returns. Paint metal both sides and overlap joints 6" min

10" min

30-lb asphalt-saturated felt

Solid or plywood sheathing at eaves

4"–8" open valley

Slate

Standard roofing slate is $\frac{3}{16}$ inch thick. With the customary 3-inch lap, a square (100 square feet of roof covered) weighs up to 750 pounds. Thicker slates weigh proportionally more. Thus, the decision to roof with slate should be made before framing the roof. Slate color is usually designated as falling into one of eight groups: black, blue-black, gray, blue-gray, purple, mottled purple and green, green, and red. Application and flashing of slate is similar to that of asphalt shingles (see the sections on asphalt shingles). The differences are described below.

Size

Slates are cut to uniform size, varying in length or depth (in 2-inch increments) from 10 to 26 inches, and width (in 1- and 2-inch increments) from 6 to 14 inches.

Overlap and Exposure

Standard overlap is 3 inches, with 2 inches for slopes over 12/12 and 4 inches for slopes less than 8/12. Exposure is determined by the slate dimension and overlap using this formula:

$$\text{Exposure} = (\text{slate length} - \text{overlap})/2$$

Example: A 16-inch slate with standard 3-inch overlap would be applied with exposure (16 − 3)/2, or 6½ inches.

Joint overlap should be 3 inches minimum and one-half of a slate ideally.

Nailing

Slates come prepunched with nail holes ¼ to ½ inch below the top edge and 1¼ to 2 inches from the edges. Special slate punches or a masonry drill must be used to create additional holes in the field. Most slate failures are due to the use of inferior shingle nails. Use only copper slating nails, available from slate distributors. Use 3d nails for slates up to 18 inches long, 4d for slates over 18 inches, and 6d nails at hips and ridges. Nail length should be twice the slate thickness plus 1 inch for sheathing penetration. Thus, a standard $\frac{3}{16}$-inch slate calls for nails 1¾ inches long.

STARTER COURSE

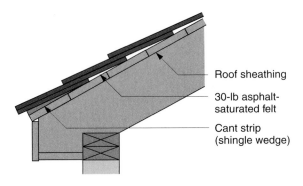

Roof sheathing

30-lb asphalt-saturated felt

Cant strip (shingle wedge)

STARTER COURSE

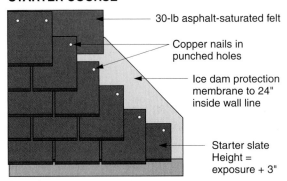

30-lb asphalt-saturated felt

Copper nails in punched holes

Ice dam protection membrane to 24" inside wall line

Starter slate Height = exposure + 3"

SADDLE RIDGE

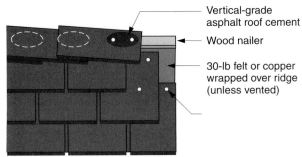

Vertical-grade asphalt roof cement

Wood nailer

30-lb felt or copper wrapped over ridge (unless vented)

STRIP SADDLE RIDGE

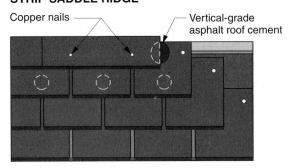

Copper nails

Vertical-grade asphalt roof cement

SADDLE HIP

30-lb asphalt felt

Wood nailer

Plastic cement

Cement edges

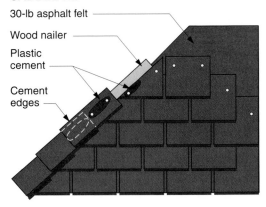

OPEN VALLEY

Prepainted galvanized steel (24-ga) or copper (16 lb) valley flashing

$1/2$" return bend

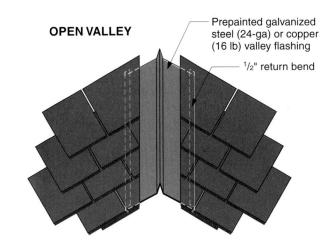

Tile

Roofing tiles generally are made of fired clay or concrete. Aside from being the most architecturally appropriate in certain regions, they have the advantages of nearly zero maintenance and long life (typically 100 years). Disadvantages include weight (90 to 110 psf), high installed cost, and minimum roof slope of 4/12.

Clay Tile

Fired at 2,000°F, the surface particles of the tile fuse, or "vitrify," making undamaged tiles virtually waterproof. Tiles to be installed in cold regions, however, should meet the requirements of ASTM C1167 for freeze–thaw regions.

The color of a clay tile is determined by the color of the clay from which it is made. Colors range from browns through orange to red.

Concrete Tile

Extruded under high pressure and cured under controlled conditions, concrete tiles are impervious to both water and freeze damage.

Concrete tiles come in a wider range of colors than clay tiles. "Color-through" tiles result from dyeing the wet concrete. Other tiles have the color applied only to the surface.

Styles

Both clay tiles and concrete tiles—which imitate the original clay versions—come in three categories of height-to-width ratio: high-profile, low-profile, and flat.

High-profile (H/W >1/5) styles include Spanish (or "S"), Mission, Roman, Greek, and Channeled.

Low-profile (H/W ≤1/5) styles include various interlocking designs.

Flat (top-surface relief <½ inch) styles include flat, interlocking flat, simulated shingle, and simulated shake.

Underlayment

Solid sheathing of at least 1-inch (nominal) boards or $^{15}/_{32}$-inch plywood or OSB is recommended under all tile installations.

For slopes ≥4/12, a double layer of 30-pound, or single layer of 40-pound, asphalt-saturated felt is recommended.

For slopes <4/12, a continuous waterproof membrane is recommended.

Fastening

Tiles may be anchored in one of three ways: nailing, wiring, or setting in adhesive.

Nailing consists of driving annular-ring or hot-dipped galvanized nails through the tile's nailing hole(s) through the underlayment into the sheathing or into 1× strapping over the underlayment.

Wiring consists of attaching individual tiles with twisted wires to a wound pair of 12-gauge wires running from eave to ridge under each vertical run of tiles. The wound pair provide loops every 6 inches through which the twisted wire is threaded. Wiring is recommended in seismic areas because it decouples the tile mass from the roof structure.

Setting in adhesive rigidly bonds the tile to the substrate and is recommended in areas with high winds. Mortar can be used, but a number of special-purpose adhesives are now available.

Typical Spanish Tile Components

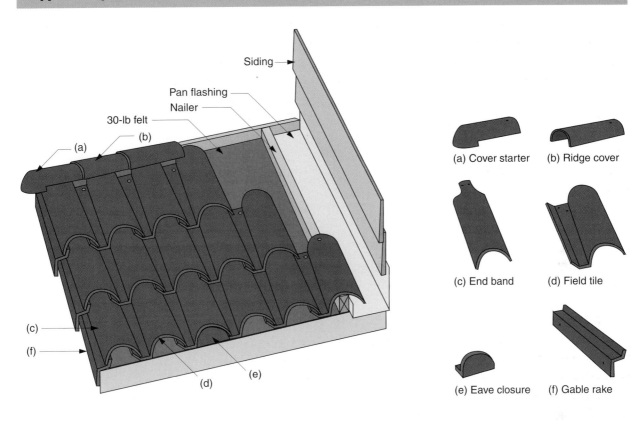

Siding

Pan flashing

Nailer

30-lb felt

(a)

(b)

(c)

(f)

(d)

(e)

(a) Cover starter   (b) Ridge cover

(c) End band   (d) Field tile

(e) Eave closure   (f) Gable rake

Spanish Tile Application

STEP 1
Install right gable-rake
tiles, with first tile
overhanging eave 2";
install eave closures
flush with eave

STEP 2
Lay first field tile in
mastic, covering gable
rake tile nails; space
remaining field tiles
for roof width

STEP 3
Install left gable-rake
tiles; nail a 1x3 on edge
as nailer for end-closure
tiles; set end tiles in
mastic and nail to 1x3

STEP 4
Install a 1x3 ridge nailer;
starting and ending with
cover starter tiles, lay
ridge cover tiles in mastic
tinted to match roof

Metal Panel

Typical Metal Panels and Dimensions

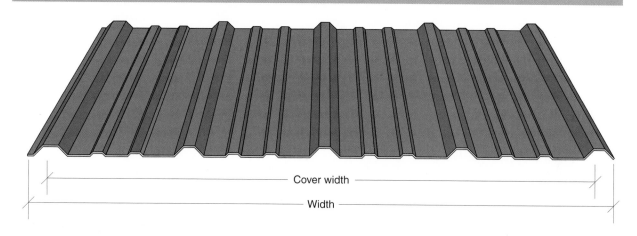

Cover width

Width

Metal Panel Installation

JOINING PANELS

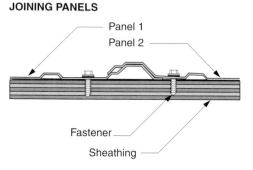

Panel 1

Panel 2

Fastener

Sheathing

RIDGE

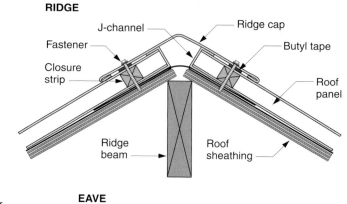

J-channel

Ridge cap

Fastener

Butyl tape

Closure strip

Roof panel

Ridge beam

Roof sheathing

GABLE END

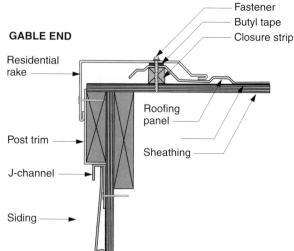

Fastener

Butyl tape

Closure strip

Residential rake

Roofing panel

Post trim

J-channel

Siding

Sheathing

EAVE

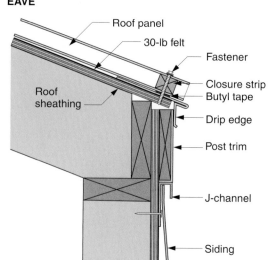

Roof panel

30-lb felt

Fastener

Closure strip

Roof sheathing

Butyl tape

Drip edge

Post trim

J-channel

Siding

Head Wall and Transition Flashing

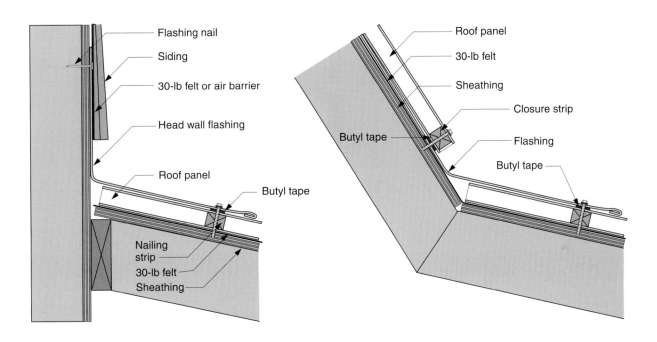

Flashing nail
Siding
30-lb felt or air barrier
Head wall flashing
Roof panel
Butyl tape
Nailing strip
30-lb felt
Sheathing

Roof panel
30-lb felt
Sheathing
Closure strip
Flashing
Butyl tape
Butyl tape

Side Wall Flashing

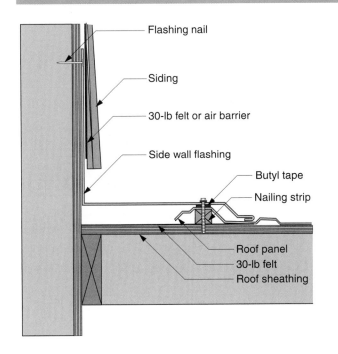

Flashing nail
Siding
30-lb felt or air barrier
Side wall flashing
Butyl tape
Nailing strip
Roof panel
30-lb felt
Roof sheathing

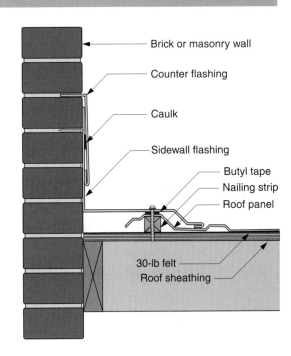

Brick or masonry wall
Counter flashing
Caulk
Sidewall flashing
Butyl tape
Nailing strip
Roof panel
30-lb felt
Roof sheathing

Standing Seam

Typical Standing Seam Panels and Dimensions

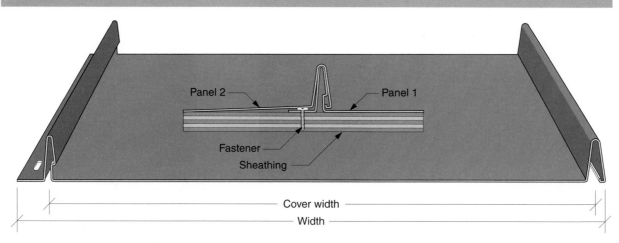

Panel 2
Panel 1
Fastener
Sheathing
Cover width
Width

Standing Seam Panel Installation

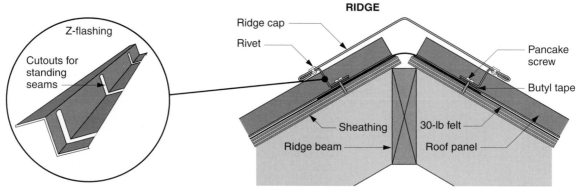

Z-flashing

Cutouts for standing seams

RIDGE

Ridge cap
Rivet
Pancake screw
Butyl tape
Sheathing
30-lb felt
Ridge beam
Roof panel

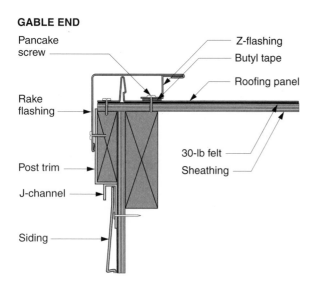

GABLE END

Pancake screw
Z-flashing
Butyl tape
Roofing panel
Rake flashing
30-lb felt
Sheathing
Post trim
J-channel
Siding

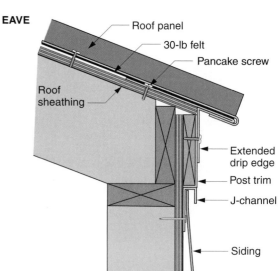

EAVE

Roof panel
30-lb felt
Pancake screw
Roof sheathing
Extended drip edge
Post trim
J-channel
Siding

Head Wall and Transition Flashing

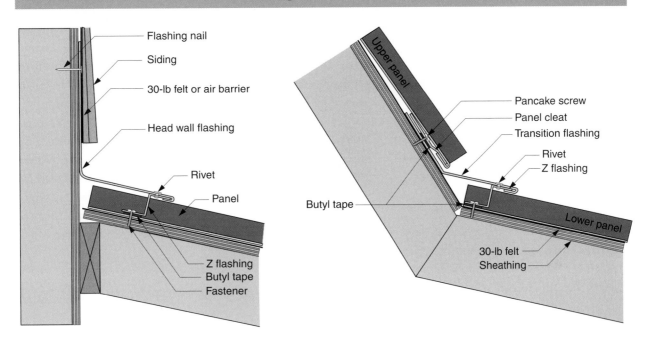

Flashing nail

Siding

30-lb felt or air barrier

Head wall flashing

Rivet

Panel

Z flashing
Butyl tape
Fastener

Upper panel

Pancake screw
Panel cleat
Transition flashing
Rivet
Z flashing

Butyl tape

Lower panel

30-lb felt
Sheathing

Side Wall Flashing

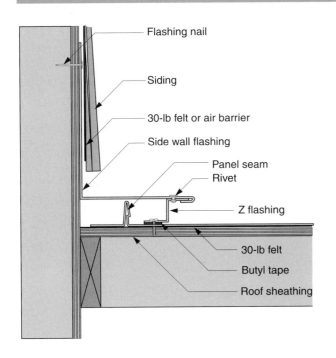

Flashing nail

Siding

30-lb felt or air barrier

Side wall flashing

Panel seam
Rivet

Z flashing

30-lb felt

Butyl tape

Roof sheathing

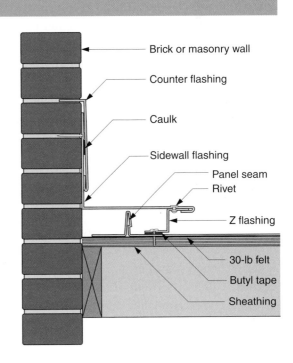

Brick or masonry wall

Counter flashing

Caulk

Sidewall flashing

Panel seam
Rivet

Z flashing

30-lb felt

Butyl tape

Sheathing

Gutters

Gutters are widely available in plain or painted aluminum or plastic. Less widely distributed are galvanized steel or copper. Gutters and downspouts usually come in 10-foot lengths, although some are available in lengths of 26 feet and 33 feet as well.

Several different gutter profiles and hanging systems are available. Your home center or hardware store may offer one style in aluminum and another in plastic. Whatever type you choose, your source will be able to provide all of the accessories needed for a complete installation.

Planning

Use the illustration of a typical system on the facing page to determine the number of each accessory needed for your installation. You would be wise to sketch the dimensions of your house, particularly the profile of the critical roof/eaves/fascia area. An experienced clerk can then verify the pieces needed. Before installation, as a final check, lay out all pieces on the ground in their final relative positions.

Installation

Use a line level (level on a string) to mark the fascia with the proper slope. The slope should be 1 inch per 16 feet minimum from one corner to another on a short building, or from center to both ends on a longer building. If the building is extremely long, intermediate low points and downspouts may be required.

Begin installation at a building corner. Attach end cap, downspout, or corner miter as required before attaching the first length of gutter. If a support molding is planned, install it before the gutter, to facilitate handling of the gutter.

Attach the gutter to the fascia with hangers every 2½ feet on-center. The three most common types of hanger are shown at on the facing page, bottom. Connect sections of gutter with slip joints as you go. PVC slip joints may be glued as you go, Others are caulked after the complete installation with gutter mastic or silicone sealant.

If the downspout discharges into an underground drainage system, install strainers over the inlet of each gutter outlet to prevent clogging of the underground system. If the downspout discharges aboveground, install an elbow and a leader (horizontal section of downspout) leading at least 5 feet away and down-slope from the building foundation.

Finally, if there are trees near your house, install a strainer cap over the gutter outlet to prevent clogging by leaves. Most gutter problems can be avoided by periodic removal of debris. Many gutter failures are due to the freezing of backed-up water, which destroys the mastic seal. Also, the weight of ice can prove more than the gutter hangers can bear.

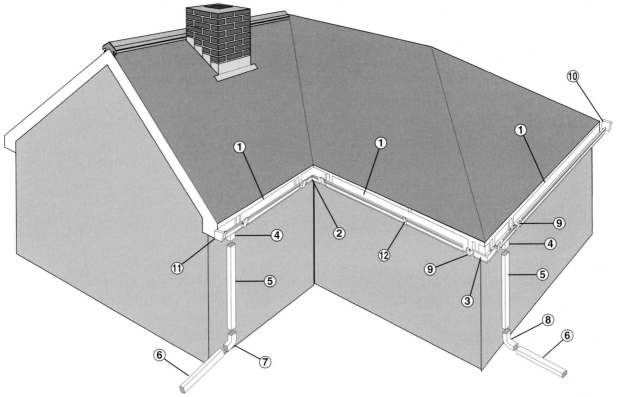

PARTS

1. Gutter
2. Inside corner
3. Outside corner
4. Outlet
5. Downspout
6. Leader
7. Style B elbow
8. Style A elbow
9. Slip connector
10. Right end cap
11. Left end cap
12. Hanger

GUTTER STYLES

Style K   Style D   Half-round

HANGER STYLES

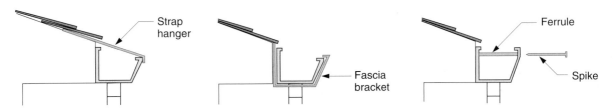

Strap hanger

Fascia bracket

Ferrule

Spike

Meet the Code

The following is a partial list of requirements from the *2006 International Residential Code (IRC) for One- and Two-Family Dwellings.* Consult the publication for the full text and additional provisions.

Roof Drainage (R801.3)

To discharge >5' from foundation or into drain pipe where expansive or collapsible soils exist

Roof Ventilation (R806)

- enclosed attics and rafter spaces to have cross ventilation for each separate space by vents with corrosion-resistant ⅛"–¼" wire mesh
- total net free vent area of ≥1/150 of vented space, except 1/300 if 50%–80% of vent area ≥3' above eave or cornice vents
- 1/300 OK with 1-perm vapor barrier on the warm-in-winter side of ceiling
- ≥1" space between insulation and sheathing at vent for free air flow
- unvented conditioned attics permitted if
  1. no interior vapor retarders installed on the ceiling side (attic floor) of the attic
  2. air-impermeable insulation applied directly to underside of roof deck

Weather Protection (R903)

- flashings required at joints in copings, through moisture permeable materials, and at parapet walls and other roof penetrations
- metal flashings to be corrosion resistant and ≥No. 26 galvanized sheet
- parapet walls to be coped with noncombustible, weatherproof materials of width ≥wall thickness
- drains to be installed at each low point of the roof
- where roof drains required, same-size overflow drains to be installed with inlet line 2" above low point of roof, or overflow scuppers 3× the size of roof drains and with opening height ≥4" to be installed in adjacent parapet walls with inlet flow 2" above low point of roof
- overflow drains not connected to roof drain lines

Roof Coverings (R905)

Asphalt shingles:
- to be fastened to solidly sheathed decks
- to be used only on roof slopes ≥2:12
- dbl underlayment required on slopes 2:12–4:12
- self-seal or interlocking strips required
- fasteners to be galvanized, stainless, aluminum, or copper, ≥12 ga shank and ≥⅜" head, of length to penetrate roofing and ≥¾" into sheathing
- in ice dam areas, an ice barrier of ≥2 layers of underlayment cemented together or of a self-adhering polymer modified bitumen sheet, from roof edge to ≥24" inside exterior wall line
- base and cap flashing of ≥0.019" corrosion-resistant metal or ≥0.77 psf mineral surface roll roofing
- valley flashings permitted:
  1. corrosion-resistant metal ≥24" for open valley
  2. two plies roll roofing, with bottom layer 18" and top layer ≥36" wide for open valley
  3. one-ply smooth roll roofing ≥36" wide or as described in 1 and 2 above for closed valley
  4. alternate materials permitted: 0.0216" cold-rolled copper, 0.0216" lead-coated copper, 0.0162" high-yield copper, 0.0162" lead-coated high-yield copper, 0.024" aluminum, 0.0179" galvanized steel, 28-ga stainless, 0.027" zinc alloy, painted tern
- cricket or saddle required on high side of any chimney or ≥30" wide penetration
- vertical sidewall flashing to be of step-flashing

Clay and concrete tile:
- to be applied over solidly sheathed decks or spaced structural sheathing boards
- to be used only on roof slopes ≥2.5:12
- dbl underlayment required on slopes 2.5:12–4:12
- fasteners to be corrosion resistant, ≥11 ga shank and ≥5/16" head, of length to penetrate ≥¾" into deck
- attaching wire to be ≥0.083"
- perimeter fastening areas to include three tile courses and be ≥36" wide from either side of hips or ridges and edges of eaves and gable rakes
- perimeter tiles fastened with ≥1 fastener per tile

- tiles with installed weight <9 psf require ≥1 fastener per tile regardless of roof slope
- tiles in snow areas to be fastened with ≥2 per tile
- tiles on solid sheathing require 1 fastener per tile
- tiles on spaced sheathing or solid sheathing with battens require no fasteners
- tiles on spaced sheathing with no battens require 1 fastener per tile, except at odd rows if slope <5:12
- flashing and counterflashing to be ≥No. 26 galvanized sheet gauge corrosion-resistant metal
- valley flashing to extend ≥11" from centerline and have a splash diverter rib ≥1" high at flow line
- valley flashings for roof slopes of ≥3:12 to have 36"-wide Type I underlayment the full length of valley
- where the average daily temperature in January is ≤25°F and slope <7:12, metal valley flashing underlayment to be solid-cemented to the roofing underlayment or be self-adhering polymer modified bitumen sheet.

Mineral-surfaced roll roofing:
- to be applied to a solid deck
- not to be installed on roof slopes of <1:12
- in ice dam areas, an ice barrier of ≥2 layers of underlayment cemented together or of a self-adhering polymer modified bitumen sheet, from roof edge to ≥24" inside exterior wall line

Slate and slate-type shingles:
- to be applied to a solid deck
- to be installed on roof slopes of ≥4:12
- in ice dam areas, an ice barrier of ≥2 layers of underlayment cemented together or of a self-adhering polymer modified bitumen sheet, from roof edge to ≥24" inside exterior wall line
- headlap: 4" at <8:12, 3" at 8–20:12, 2" at ≥20:12
- secured to roof with two fasteners per slate.
- flashing and counterflashing of sheet metal
- valley flashing ≥15" wide.
- flashing to be an uncoated thickness of ≥0.0179" zinc coated G90

Wood shingles:
- to be applied to solid deck or 1×4 nominal spaced sheathing spaced at weather exposure
- to be installed on roof slopes of ≥3:12
- solid sheathing required where the average daily temperature in January is ≤25°F
- solid sheathing under an ice barrier
- in ice dam areas, an ice barrier of ≥2 layers of underlayment cemented together or of a self-adhering polymer modified bitumen sheet, from roof edge to ≥24" inside exterior wall line
- laid with a side lap ≥1½" between joints in courses
- no 2 joints in any 3 adjacent courses in alignment
- spacing between shingles to be ¼"–⅜"
- fasteners to be corrosion resistant and penetrate the sheathing ≥½"
- to be attached with two fasteners per shingle, positioned ≥¾" from each edge and ≥1" above the exposure line
- valley flashing ≥No. 26 gauge corrosion-resistant sheet metal and extend 10" from the centerline for slopes <12:12 and 7" from for slopes ≥12:12

Wood shakes (same as wood shingles except):
- where 1×4 spaced sheathing installed 10" oc, additional 1×4 boards to be installed between
- spacing between shakes to be ⅛"–⅝", except ¼"–⅜" for preservative-treated taper-sawn shakes
- fasteners ≤1" from edges and ≤2" above bottom
- to be interlaid with 18" strips of ≥No. 30 felt, the lower edge of each above the butt of the shake it covers a distance equal to twice the weather exposure

Metal roof panels:
- to be applied to solid or spaced sheathing, except where designed to be applied to spaced supports
- min slope for lapped, nonsoldered-seam metal roofs 3:12, except ½:12 with applied lap sealant
- min slope for standing-seam roofs ¼:12
- to be corrosion resistant
- in absence of manufacturer's instructions, fasteners to be galvanized or stainless (300-series for copper roofs)

Windows and Doors

Can you imagine your house without windows? Windows perform more functions than any other component of a house. The more you know about windows, the more they can do for you.

About Windows spells out all of the things windows can do and the types of windows you can buy from a window dealer or home center. Whether you are building a new house or replacing an existing window, you need to know how windows are measured.

With rising energy prices, *window energy performance* is more important than ever. We show you how windows gain and lose energy and how various types compare.

Skylights are not as familiar as windows, but they can light a space twice as efficiently as a window in a wall, so we include a section on a typical skylight product line.

If you are installing a whole wall of windows (for a spectacular view or for a sunspace, for example), you should be interested in *site-built windows*—patio door glazings that can cut your window costs by half.

The second half of this chapter is *About Doors:* their functions, how they are constructed, and how they are installed.

Door installation is an exacting task, so we show the details of both interior and exterior, prehung, and slab-type doors.

There is even a section on doors to the basement. Whether you are building new or converting your basement to a more accessible space, you can find the size of steel *bulkhead door* that will fit your house.

Finally, we provide you with a checklist to make sure your windows and doors *meet the code*.

About Windows

Window Types

The illustration below shows eight generic types of residential windows available from dozens of manufacturers.

Double-hung windows contain two sashes, both of which slide up and down. A variation is the single-hung window, in which the top sash is generally fixed.

Casement windows hinge to one side, which is specified when a unit is ordered. They are very effective at capturing breezes, provided they open toward the prevailing breeze.

Fixed windows are often used in conjunction with operable windows of other styles. Inexpensive "window walls" can be constructed of patio doors and site-built fixed windows utilizing patio door glazing units of the same size.

Awning windows are used for ventilation at low levels, such as in a sun space, or as high windows in bathrooms and kitchens.

Sliding windows are an inexpensive alternative for high windows in bathrooms and kitchens.

Skylights, also known as roof windows, are extremely effective summer exhaust ventilators. They are also more effective in admitting natural daylight than are vertical windows of the same size.

Bay windows add space to rooms (often with window seats) in addition to adding an architectural design feature to an elevation. They most often are assembled from a center fixed unit and two double-hung or casement flankers.

Bow windows are more elegant expressions of the bay. They are often assembled from fixed and casement units of the same unit dimensions.

Common Window Types

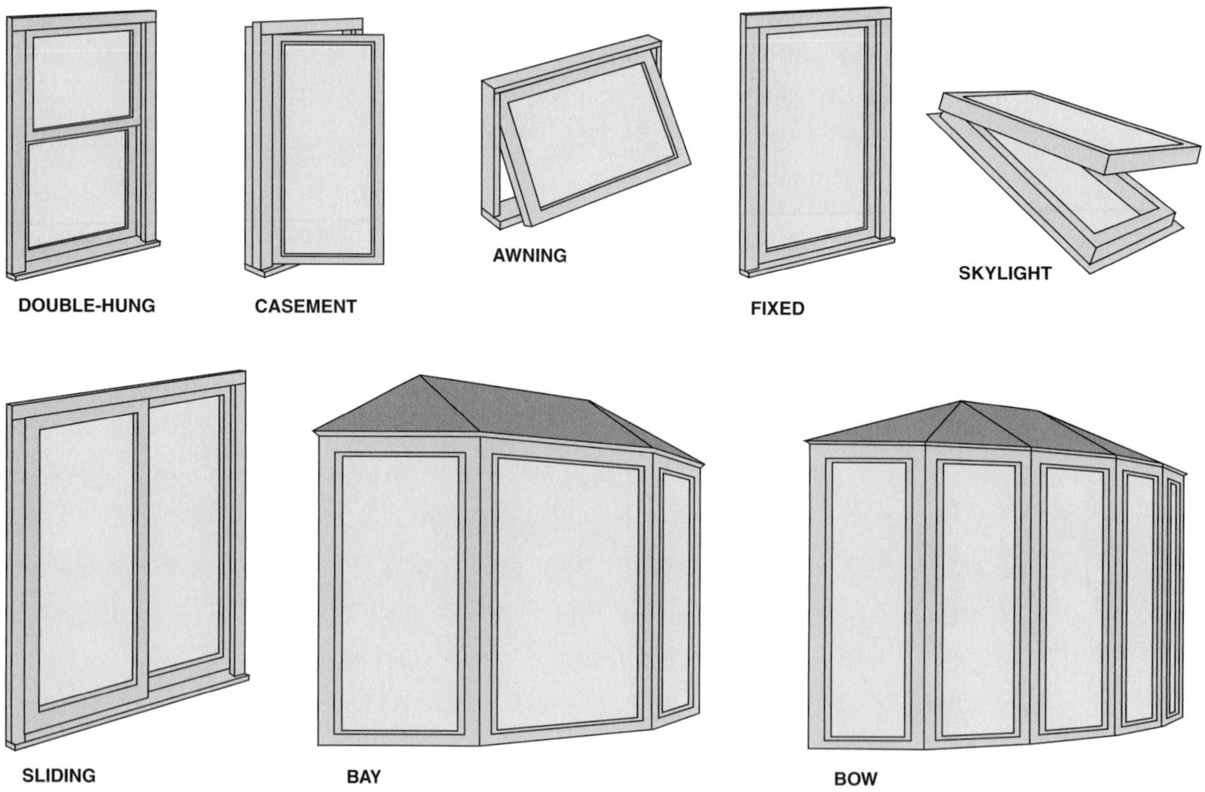

DOUBLE-HUNG   CASEMENT   AWNING   FIXED   SKYLIGHT

SLIDING   BAY   BOW

Anatomy and Measurements

Window manufacturers provide four sets of dimensions (width × height).

Architects require unit size to produce building elevations, glass size for solar gain, and egress opening for the building code. Builders require rough opening, framing sill height, and location on the plan to the center of the unit.

Rough opening is the width and height of the framing opening—generally from ⅜ to ½ inch greater than jamb width and height.

Unit size is the overall size of the window unit, including casing if provided. With a casing, unit dimension will be larger than the rough, or framing, opening. With a nailing flange instead of casing, the unit dimension will be the dimensions of the jambs, or less than the rough opening.

Egress opening is the actual width and height, without removing a sash, of the opening a person might pass through in case of fire.

Glass size is the width and height of the clear portion of glass through which sunlight can pass.

Dimensions of a Typical Double-Hung Window

HORIZONTAL SECTION

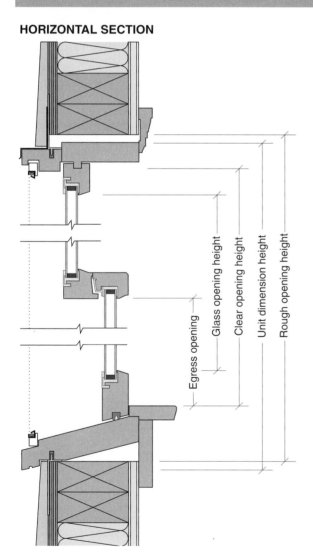

Egress opening | Glass opening height | Clear opening height | Unit dimension height | Rough opening height

VERTICAL SECTION

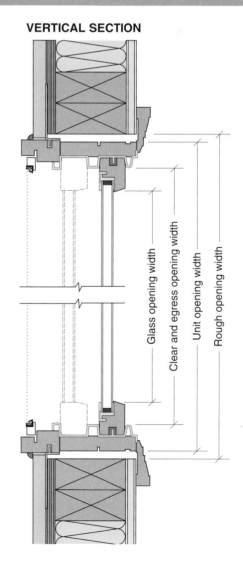

Glass opening width | Clear and egress opening width | Unit opening width | Rough opening width

Window Installation

Modern Double-Hung Window Installation

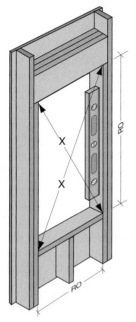

1. Check opening width and height of RO. Diagonals must be within ⅛".

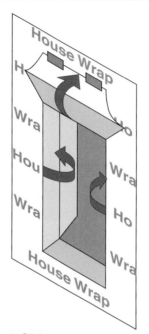

2. Slit house wrap down middle, fold, and staple flaps back. Cut top flap as shown and tape up.

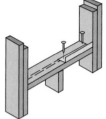

3. Install ¾" back dam.

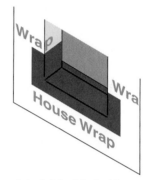

4. Install flexible flashing.

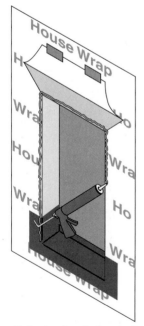

5. Apply a bead of sealant to sides and top (not bottom).

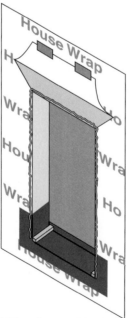

6. Place bottom shims in corners

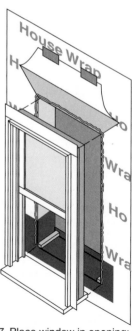

7. Place window in opening; press against sealant.

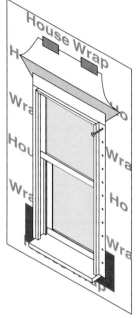

8. Lock the sashes with the sash lock, then fasten a top corner of the nailing flange.

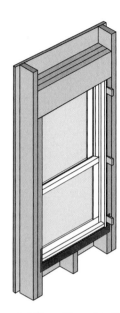

9. Using shims at both sides and the bottom, adjust window frame until diagonals are equal.

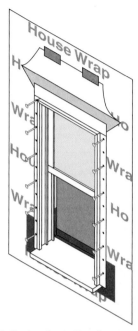

10. Fasten the nailing flange all around by driving nails 6" oc.

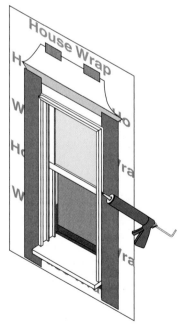

11. Apply flashing strips to both sides, then caulk around sides and top.

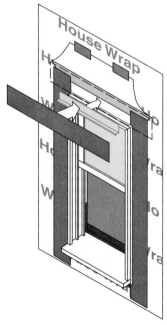

12. Install the top drip cap; cover with a top strip of flashing.

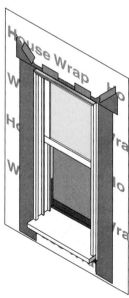

13. Fold house wrap down and tape to top flashing. After siding, caulk siding/window-frame joint.

Window Energy Performance

Window Performance Labels

The National Fenestration Research Council (NFRC) is a non-profit public/private collaboration of manufacturers, builders, designers, specifiers, code officials, consumers, utilities, and regulators that has established a national energy performance rating system for fenestration products. The NFRC system rates a fenestration product's U-factor, solar heat gain coefficient, visible light transmittance, and air leakage, which can be used to determine whether a product meets an energy code.

NFRC labels can be found on all ENERGY STAR window, door, and skylight products, but ENERGY STAR bases its qualification only on U-factor and SHGC ratings.

Performance Factors

Windows, doors, and skylights gain and lose heat in the following ways:

- Conduction through the glazing and frame.
- Radiation from outside (typically from the sun) and from inside from room-temperature objects, such as people, furniture, and interior walls.
- Air leakage.

These properties are measured and rated in the following energy performance characteristics:

U-factor The rate at which the unit conducts non-solar heat flow, expressed in Btu/hr-ft^2-°F. For windows, skylights, and glass doors, a U-factor may refer to just the glazing alone. But National Fenestration Rating Council U-factor ratings represent the entire window performance, including frame and spacer material. The lower the U-factor, the more energy-efficient the window, door, or skylight.

Solar heat gain coefficient (SHGC)
The fraction of solar radiation admitted through the unit—either directly and/or absorbed—and subsequently released as heat inside a home. The lower the SHGC, the less solar heat it transmits and the greater its shading ability. Units with high SHGC

Typical Window Performance Label

World's Best Window Co.

Millenium 2000+
Vinyl-Clad Wood Frame
Double Glazing • Argon Fill • Low E
Product Type: **Vertical Slider**

ENERGY PERFORMANCE RAINGS

U-Factor (U.S./I-P)	Solar Heat Gain Coefficient
0.35	**0.32**

ADDITIONAL PERFORMANCE RAINGS

Visible Transmittance	Air Leakage (U.S./I-P)
0.51	**0.2**

Manufacturer stipulates that these ratings conform to applicable NFRC procedures for determining whole product performance. NFRC ratings are determined for a fixed set of environmental conditions and a specific product size. Consult manufacturer's literature for other product performance information.
www.nfrc.org

ratings are more efficient at collecting solar heat gain during the winter. Units with low SHGC ratings are more effective at reducing cooling loads during the summer by blocking heat gained from the sun. The target SHGC should therefore be determined by factors including climate, orientation, and external shading.

Visible transmittance (VT) The fraction of the visible spectrum of sunlight (380 to 720 nanometers), weighted by the sensitivity of the human eye, transmitted through a unit's glazing. Units with higher VT transmit more visible light. The target VT should be determined by daylighting and interior glare requirements.

Air leakage The rate of air infiltration around or through a unit subjected to a specific pressure difference, in units of cubic feet per minute per square foot of frame area (cfm/ft^2).

Light-to-solar gain (LSG) The ratio of VT to SHGC measures the efficiency of a glazing in transmitting daylight while blocking heat gains. This energy performance rating isn't always provided.

Typical Performance Factors for Window Types

Type of Window	Type of Glazing						
	SG Clear	DG Clear	DG with Bronze/Gray Tint	DG with Hi Solar Gain Low-E, Argon	DG with Mod Solar Gain Low-E, Argon	DG with Low Solar Gain Low-E, Argon	TG with Mod Solar Gain Low-E, Argon
U-FACTOR							
Alum w/thermal break	1.00	0.63	0.63	0.50	0.48	0.47	—
Aluminum	1.16	0.76	0.76	0.61	0.60	0.59	—
Fiberglass	—	0.44	0.44	0.29	0.27	0.26	0.18
Hybrid/Composite	0.84	0.49	0.49	0.37	0.35	0.34	—
Insulated Vinyl	—	0.44	0.44	0.29	0.27	0.26	0.18
Vinyl	0.84	0.49	0.49	0.37	0.35	0.34	—
Wood	0.84	0.49	0.49	0.37	0.35	0.34	—
Wood Clad	0.84	0.49	0.49	0.37	0.35	0.34	0.29
SHGC							
Alum w/thermal break	0.70	0.62	0.52	0.58	0.48	0.33	—
Aluminum	0.76	0.68	0.76	0.64	0.53	0.37	—
Fiberglass	—	0.60	0.49	0.56	0.46	0.31	0.40
Hybrid/Composite	0.64	0.56	0.47	0.53	0.44	0.30	—
Insulated Vinyl	—	0.60	0.49	0.56	0.46	0.31	0.40
Vinyl	0.64	0.56	0.47	0.53	0.44	0.30	—
Wood	0.64	0.56	0.47	0.53	0.44	0.30	—
Wood Clad	0.64	0.56	0.47	0.53	0.44	0.30	0.38
VT							
Alum w/thermal break	0.70	0.63	0.48	0.62	0.65	0.59	—
Aluminum	0.75	0.68	0.51	0.62	0.65	0.59	—
Fiberglass	—	0.63	0.48	0.58	0.60	0.55	0.50
Hybrid/Composite	0.65	0.59	0.44	0.54	0.56	0.52	—
Insulated Vinyl	—	0.63	0.48	0.58	0.60	0.55	0.50
Vinyl	0.65	0.59	0.44	0.54	0.56	0.51	—
Wood	0.65	0.59	0.44	0.54	0.56	0.51	—
Wood Clad	0.65	0.59	0.44	0.54	0.56	0.51	0.47

Data from the Efficient Windows Collaborative, *www.efficientwindows.org*
SG = single glazing
DG = double glazing

Solar/Thermal Properties of Glazings

KEY: ☐ Fraction of visible light transmitted ☐ Fraction of total solar radiation transmitted ☐ Fraction of heat loss compared to SG window

Single Glazed Clear
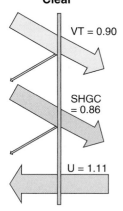
VT = 0.90
SHGC = 0.86
U = 1.11

Single Glazed Bronze Tint
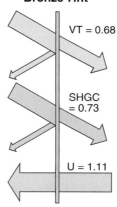
VT = 0.68
SHGC = 0.73
U = 1.11

Double Glazed Clear
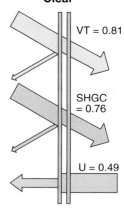
VT = 0.81
SHGC = 0.76
U = 0.49

Double Glazed Bronze Tint
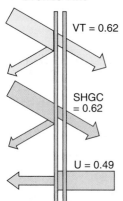
VT = 0.62
SHGC = 0.62
U = 0.49

Double Glazed High Performance Tint
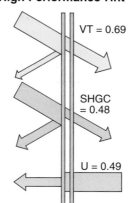
VT = 0.69
SHGC = 0.48
U = 0.49

Double Glazed High Solar Gain Low-E
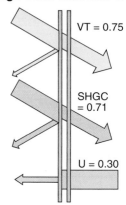
VT = 0.75
SHGC = 0.71
U = 0.30

Double Glazed Mod Solar Gain Low-E
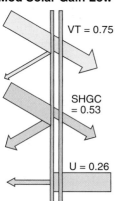
VT = 0.75
SHGC = 0.53
U = 0.26

Double Glazed Low Solar Gain Low-E
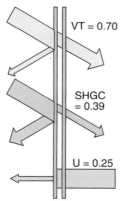
VT = 0.70
SHGC = 0.39
U = 0.25

Triple Glazed Mod Solar Gain Low-E
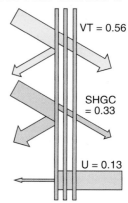
VT = 0.56
SHGC = 0.33
U = 0.13

Regional Performance

The Efficient Windows Collaborative (EWC) is a coalition of window, door, skylight, and component manufacturers, research organizations, federal, state, and local government agencies, and others interested in expanding the market for high-efficiency fenestration products. Among other things, the EWC website includes a *Window Selection Tool*, which allows comparison of heating and cooling costs in nearly 100 U.S. and Canadian cities, as a function of window type.

The calculations are based on a typical new 2,000-square-foot house with windows totaling 15 percent of floor area, distributed equally on all sides, and actual regional energy prices. The results allow one to see, for this average house, the savings resulting from substitution of windows having better energy performance. For those wishing a more precise calculation based on a specific house design, the software used in the calculations (RESFEN) may be downloaded free from *http://windows.lbl.gov/ software/resfen/resfen.html.*

Normalized Calculations

Because the energy prices used in the EWC calculations are likely to change over time, we have normalized the graphs to show heating and cooling costs of differing window types as percentages of those for the least efficient window, generally a single sheet of clear glass in an aluminum frame.

The typical graph at right shows the effect on the heating bill (shaded portion of bars) and cooling bill (white portion of bars) of substituting window types 4, 5, 7, 8, and 9 for the baseline single-glazed, clear window in an aluminum frame (type 1) in Fort Worth, Texas. It is seen that window type 5 (double-glazing with a low-E coating and argon fill in a vinyl/wood frame) would lower the home's total heating and cooling bill by 30 percent.

Graphs for eight other cities are presented on p. 288 and 289.

Window Type Descriptions

1. SG, clear glass, aluminum frame

2. DG, low-E (low solar gain), aluminum frame with thermal break

3. DG, clear glass, vinyl/wood frame

4. DG, low-E (high solar gain), argon fill, vinyl/wood frame

5. DG, low-E (low solar gain), argon fill, vinyl/wood frame

6. TG, low-E (low solar gain), argon fill, vinyl/wood frame

7. SG, tinted, aluminum frame

8. DG, clear, aluminum frame

9. DG, low-E (low solar gain), aluminum frame

10. DG, clear, aluminum frame with thermal break

11. TG, low-E (moderate solar gain), krypton fill, insulated frame

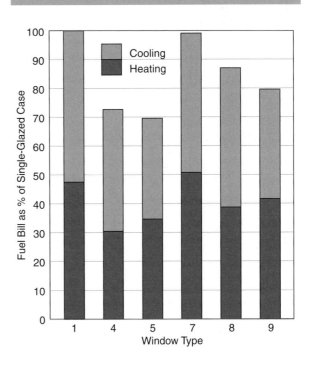

Annual Heating and Cooling Bills vs. Window Type in Ft. Worth, TX

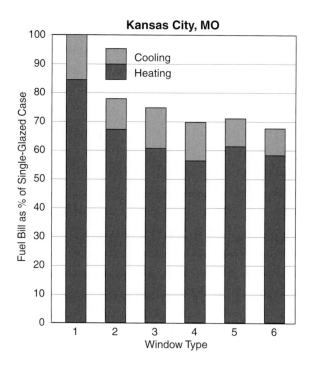

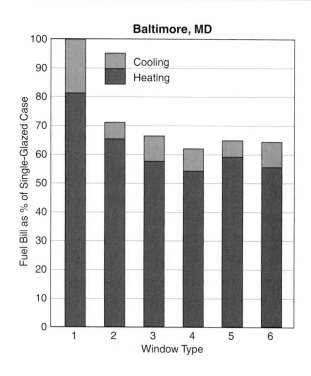

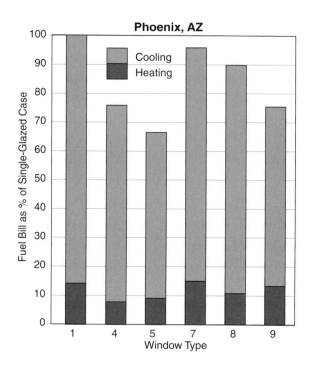

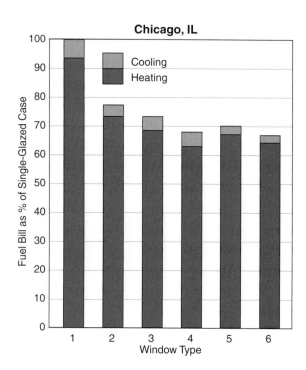

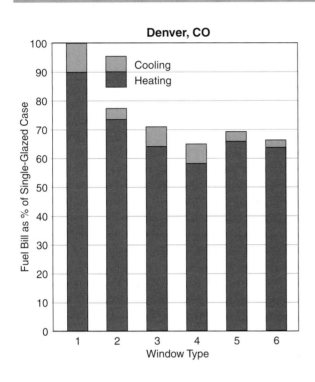

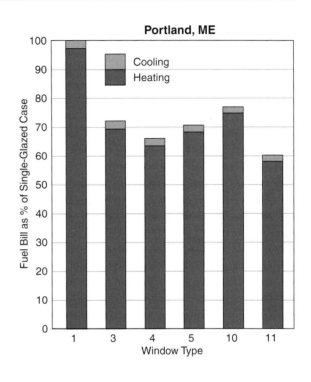

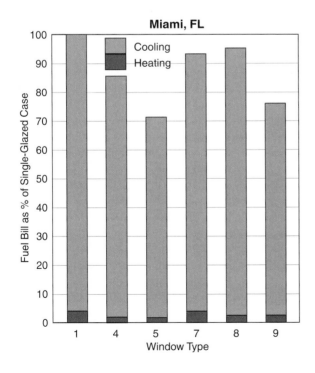

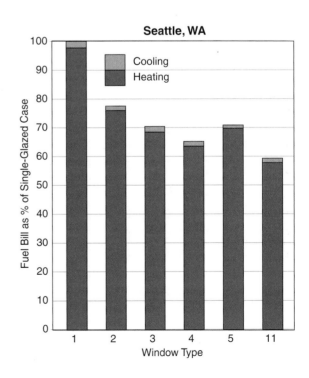

Skylights

The illustrations and table below describe Velux® deck-mounted roof windows and skylights. Roof windows pivot so that both sides may be cleaned. Skylights may be fixed or pivot from the top.

The following models are available:

FS—fixed skylight
FSF—fixed skylight with ventilating flap
VS—ventilating skylight
VSE—electric ventilating skylight
GPL—egress roof window
GDL—balcony roof window

The illustration below at left shows the definitions of unit dimension (outside frame dimensions) and rough opening. Rough opening in the roof sheathing is ½ inch larger than the unit width and height.

The illustration below at right and the table show critical installation measurements for units where sitting and standing views are important.

Several other manufacturers offer skylights and roof windows. Ask for more information at your local building supply center.

Skylight Dimensions

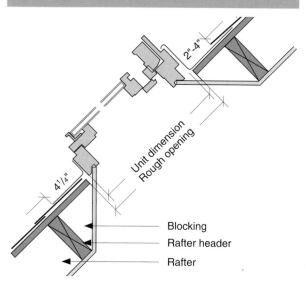

Sitting/Standing View Geometry

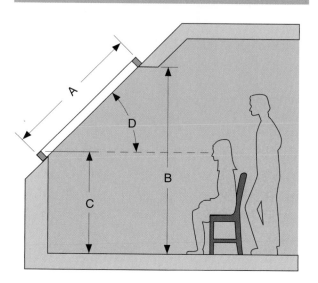

Installation Measurements for Different Roof Pitches, inches

Size Numbers	104, 304				106, 306, 606				108, 308				112			
A	38½				46½				55				70⅞			
B	74	76	78	80	74	76	78	80	74	76	78	80	74	76	78	80
C at D = 30°	60	62	64	66	56	58	60	62	52	54	56	58	44	46	48	50
35°	58	59	62	64	53	55	57	59	48	50	52	54	38	40	42	44
40°	55	57	59	61	50	52	54	56	44	46	48	50	33	35	37	39
45°	52	54	56	58	47	49	51	53	41	43	45	47	30	32	34	36
50°	50	52	54	56	44	46	48	50	37	39	41	43	24	26	28	30

Rough opening	14³/₈"	21¹/₂"	30⁹/₁₆"	44³/₄"
27⁷/₈"		**101** FS FSF VS		**601** FS FSF VS
31"			**302** FS	
38⁷/₈"		**104** FS FSF VS	**304** FS FSF VS	
46³/₄"	**056** FS	**106** FS FSF VS	**306** FS FSF VS	**606** FS FSF VS GPL
55⁷/₁₆"		**108** FS FSF VS	**308** FS FSF VS GPL	
71¹/₄"		**112** FS FSF		

Note: Bold numbers (101, etc.) are sizes; lettered codes (FS, etc.) are models.

Site-Built Windows

When there is no need for a window to open, particularly if there are several such units, installing bare factory-sealed glazing units in the field will save money.

Insulated Glazing Units

Many glass companies manufacture both custom and standard-size patio door replacement units. Due to volume, standard tempered-glass patio door units offer the greatest value. Standard patio door glazing sizes include: 28×76, 33×75, 34×76, 46×75, and 46×76 inches.

Insulated glass units are assembled by bonding two panes of glass to an aluminum spacer. The spacer is filled with a desiccant material, designed to absorb moisture and keep the cavity condensation free for the life of the unit (generally guaranteed for 10 years). The sealant may be one or more of the following: silicone, urethane, polysulfide, or polyisobutylene. If the unit is of patio door size, the glazing will most often be tempered, because building codes require tempered or safety glass in doors, within 10 inches of doors, within 18 inches of the floor, and for overhead or sloped glazings.

The greatest drawback to site-built windows is the high rate of failure of the glass seals. Failure is usually due to one of three causes:

- improper installation, where the unit is subjected to stress.
- sloped installation, where the span is too great for the glass thickness, resulting in shear.
- the use of site sealants that are incompatible with the glazing unit sealant.

As a rule, installation at slopes of greater than 20 degrees from vertical voids manufacturers' warranties. Units can be double-sealed for approximately 20 percent higher cost.

The facing page shows details for installation of glazing direct to framing and within separate frames (jambs). In both cases the keys to success are as follows:

- Float the glazing unit within the frame. All of the weight of the unit should rest on two 4-inch-long strips of neoprene rubber (ask your glass supplier for setting blocks) placed one quarter of the unit width from each bottom corner.
- Don't let the glass surfaces touch wood anywhere. Glazing tape compressed between the unit and the wood stops distributes stresses, allows for seasonal movement, and seals the unit against infiltration.
- Seal against moisture incursion with a compatible sealant. Ask the unit manufacturer for a specific recommendation.
- Provide for moisture drainage. Outside sill and stop must slope away from the unit. Inside sills should also slope away if in a high-humidity environment. Angle 1/8-inch weep holes from both sides of the setting blocks to outside the siding.

The use of pressure-treated lumber for the sills will result in longer life, but be aware that pressure-treated wood does not generally hold paint well until it has aged for about a year.

If the glazing is primarily for solar heat gain, as in a sunspace, read p. 284–289 before selecting the type of glass.

Installation Direct to Framing

JAMB

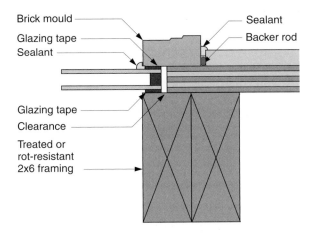

Brick mould
Glazing tape
Sealant

Sealant
Backer rod

Glazing tape
Clearance

Treated or rot-resistant 2x6 framing

MULLION

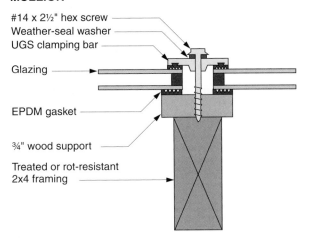

#14 x 2½" hex screw
Weather-seal washer
UGS clamping bar

Glazing

EPDM gasket

¾" wood support

Treated or rot-resistant 2x4 framing

SILL

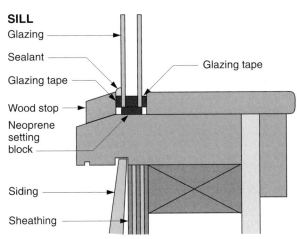

Glazing
Sealant
Glazing tape

Glazing tape

Wood stop
Neoprene setting block

Siding
Sheathing

Installation in Jambs

JAMB

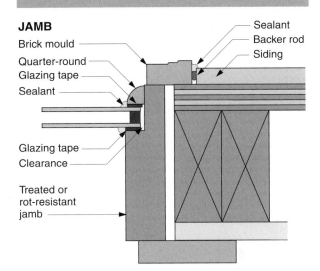

Brick mould
Quarter-round
Glazing tape
Sealant

Sealant
Backer rod
Siding

Glazing tape
Clearance

Treated or rot-resistant jamb

MULLION

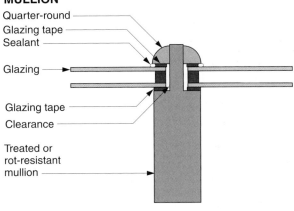

Quarter-round
Glazing tape
Sealant

Glazing

Glazing tape
Clearance

Treated or rot-resistant mullion

SILL

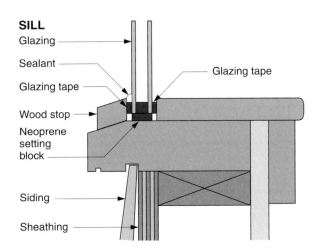

Glazing
Sealant
Glazing tape

Glazing tape

Wood stop
Neoprene setting block

Siding
Sheathing

About Doors

Functions

Exterior doors function in numerous ways:

1. They let people in and out. This is not as trivial as it may seem but relates to the design of a welcoming entryway—an architectural subject by itself.

2. They let large objects in and out. The minimum width for an entry door (and some interior doors as well) should be 3 feet to facilitate moving furniture and appliances.

3. They keep intruders out. All entrance doors should have quality dead-bolt locks as well as the common latch set. In urban areas an additional lock, operated only from the inside, would be worthwhile.

4. They keep out winter wind and cold. Except for custom doors intended for historic preservation, the great majority of exterior doors sold today are steel with foam-insulated cores. These represent a giant advance over the classic wood door, in thermal performance if not appearance. Compared with an R-value of 1.5 for the classic wood-paneled door, the foam-core door has an R-value of 6 to 12, reducing conductive heat loss by 75 to 85 percent. The best metal doors also incorporate magnetic weather strips, virtually eliminating infiltration.

5. They let in summer breezes, winter solar gain, and natural daylight. The original function of the storm door was the same as the storm window: to reduce winter heat loss by conduction and infiltration. These losses have largely been eliminated by the steel door. However, a combination "storm" door may still be desirable for summer ventilation.

Handedness

When ordering a prehung door, you must specify its "handedness." The illustration below shows how handedness is defined.

If a door opens toward you and the door knob is on your left, the door is *left-handed*.

If a door opens toward you and the door knob is on your right, the door is *right-handed*.

Door Handedness

LEFT-HAND DOOR   **RIGHT-HAND DOOR**

Construction

The illustration on the facing page shows how the five most common types of door are constructed. Fiberglass and steel doors are commonly used as entrance doors because of high R-value and dimensional stability. Wood panel doors are used primarily on the interior of classic-styled homes. The hollow-core door is used exclusively on the interior of low-end homes, and the more substantial solid-core door is common in modern, high-end homes.

How Doors Are Constructed

FIBERGLASS OR STEEL DOOR

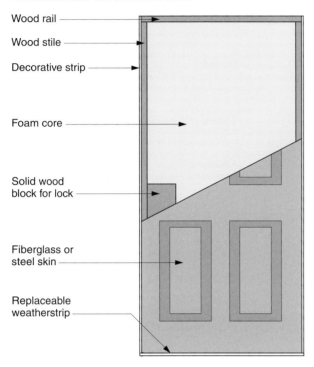

Wood rail

Wood stile

Decorative strip

Foam core

Solid wood
block for lock

Fiberglass or
steel skin

Replaceable
weatherstrip

WOOD PANEL DOOR

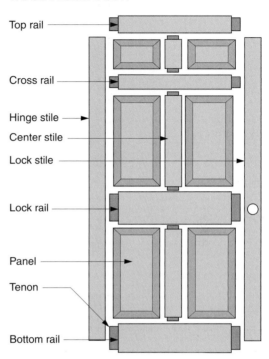

Top rail

Cross rail

Hinge stile

Center stile

Lock stile

Lock rail

Panel

Tenon

Bottom rail

HOLLOW-CORE DOOR

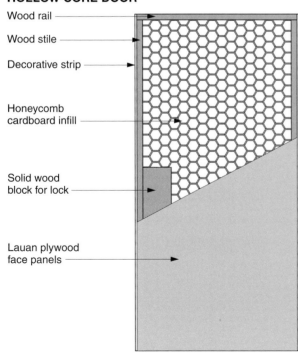

Wood rail

Wood stile

Decorative strip

Honeycomb
cardboard infill

Solid wood
block for lock

Lauan plywood
face panels

SOLID-CORE DOOR

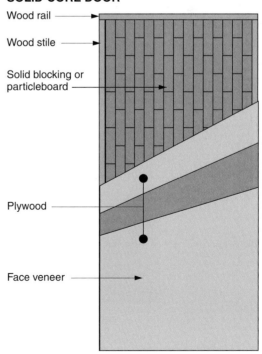

Wood rail

Wood stile

Solid blocking or
particleboard

Plywood

Face veneer

Door Installation

EXTERIOR PREHUNG DOOR

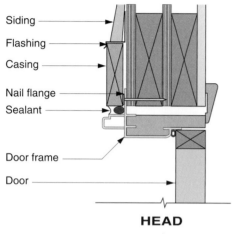

Siding
Flashing
Casing
Nail flange
Sealant
Door frame
Door

HEAD

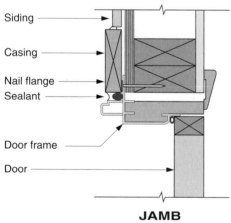

Siding
Casing
Nail flange
Sealant
Door frame
Door

JAMB

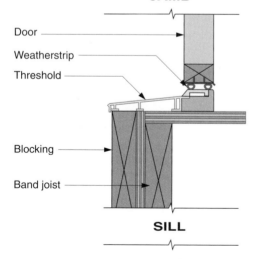

Door
Weatherstrip
Threshold
Blocking
Band joist

SILL

INTERIOR PREHUNG DOOR

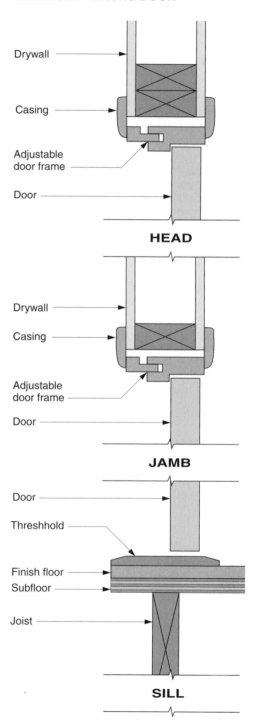

Drywall
Casing
Adjustable door frame
Door

HEAD

Drywall
Casing
Adjustable door frame
Door

JAMB

Door
Threshhold
Finish floor
Subfloor
Joist

SILL

OLDER EXTERIOR DOOR

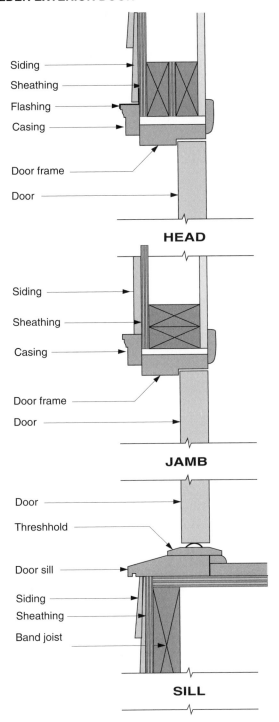

Siding
Sheathing
Flashing
Casing
Door frame
Door

HEAD

Siding
Sheathing
Casing
Door frame
Door

JAMB

Door
Threshhold
Door sill
Siding
Sheathing
Band joist

SILL

OLDER INTERIOR DOOR

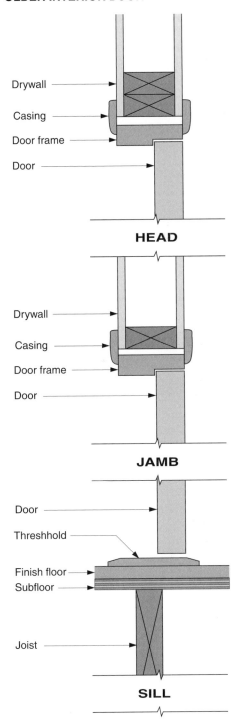

Drywall
Casing
Door frame
Door

HEAD

Drywall
Casing
Door frame
Door

JAMB

Door
Threshhold
Finish floor
Subfloor
Joist

SILL

Bulkhead Doors

The table below and illustrations on the facing page describe steel bulkhead doors and stair stringers available from the Bilco® Company. To design a basement bulkhead installation, take the following steps:

1. Determine the height of grade above the finished basement floor.

2 Find the appropriate height range in the table below.

3. Read across the table to find the dimensions of the concrete areaway (illustration at right) and the recommended sizes (illustrations on the facing page).

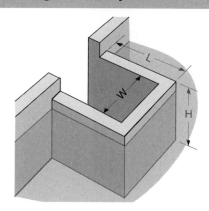

Areaway Dimensions for Bilco Basement Doors

Height of Grade above Floor	H[1]	L	W	Door Style	Extension Required	Stringer Style	Number of Treads
2'8" to 3'3"	3'5¼"	3'4"	3'8"	SL	none	SL	4
3'4" to 3'11" [3]	4'1½"	3'4"	3'8"	SL	none	SL	4
4'0" to 4'7" [2]	4'9¾"	4'6"	3'4"	O	none	O	6
4'8" to 5'4" [2]	5'6"	5'0"	3'8"	B	none	B	7
5'5" to 6'0"	6'2¼"	5'8"	4'0"	C	none	C	8
6'1" to 6'8" [3]	6'10½"	5'8"	4'0"	C	none	C	8
6'1" to 6'8"	6'10½"	6'8"	4'0"	C	12"	O + E	9
6'9" to 7'4" [3]	7'6¾"	6'8"	4'0"	C	12"	O + E	9
6'9" to 7'4"	7'6¾"	7'2"	4'0"	C	18"	B + E	10
7'5" to 8'1" [3]	8'3"	7'2"	4'0"	C	18"	B + E	10
7'5" to 8'1"	8'3"	7'9"	4'0"	C	24"	C + E	11

[1] Height above finished basement floor

[2] Maximum height of ¾ house wall = 7'4"

[3] Requires that one concrete step be added at finished basement floor

Bilco Basement Door Standard Sizes

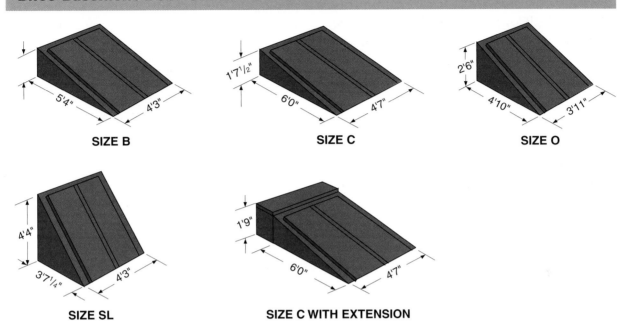

SIZE B

SIZE C

SIZE O

SIZE SL

SIZE C WITH EXTENSION

Typical Installations

STANDARD INSTALLATION

INSTALLATION WITH EXTENSION

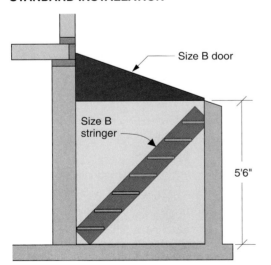

Size B door

Size B stringer

5'6"

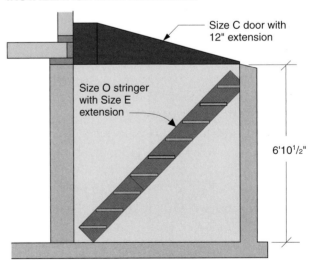

Size C door with 12" extension

Size O stringer with Size E extension

6'10¹/₂"

Meet the Code

The following is a partial list of requirements from the *2006 International Residential Code (IRC) for One- and Two-Family Dwellings*. Consult the publication for the full text and additional provisions.

Light, Ventilation, & Heating (R303)

Habitable rooms:
- habitable rooms to have glazing area of ≥8% of the floor area
- natural ventilation to be through windows, doors, louvers, or other approved openings to outdoor air
- openable area to outdoors ≥4% of floor area

Exceptions:
    1. glazed areas need not be openable with mechanical ventilation of 0.35 ach or 15 cfm per occupant based on 1 occupant/bedroom + 1
    2. no glazing permitted where ventilation and lighting of 6 footcandles @ 30" height provided
    3. sunrooms and patio covers OK if screened only or ≥40% of wall is open

Adjoining rooms:
- Any room may be considered part of adjoining room if ≥50% of common wall open and unobstructed and provides an opening of ≥10% of interior room floor area, but not less than 25 sq ft

Exception: required opening permitted to open into a sunroom addition or patio cover, provided there is an openable area between the spaces of ≥10% of interior room floor area, but not less than 20 sq ft
- Openable area to the outdoors to be based on total floor area ventilated

Bathrooms:
- Bathrooms to have ≥3 sq ft window glazed area, half of which must be openable

Exception: glazed areas need not be openable with mechanical ventilation directly to outside of 50 cfm intermittent or 20 cfm continuous

Glazing (R308)

Identification:
- each pane of glazing in hazardous locations to be provided with a manufacturer's designation visible in the final installation
- designation may be etched, sandblasted, ceramic-fired, laser etched, embossed, or of a type which cannot be removed
- a label permitted in lieu of designation

Exceptions:
    1. except for tempered glass, manufacturer's designations not required provided building official approves other evidence confirming compliance
    2. tempered spandrel glass permitted to be identified by a removable paper designation
- assemblies with individual panes ≤1 sq ft to have at least one pane identified
- regular, float, wired, or patterned glass in jalousies and louvered windows to be ≥nominal 3/16" thick and ≤48" long
- wired glass with wire exposed on long edges shall not be used in jalousies or louvered windows
- glazed areas, including glass mirrors in hazardous locations, must pass the test requirements of CPSC 16 CFR, Part 1201
- hazardous glazing locations include
    1. swinging doors except jalousies
    2. sliding doors and bifold closet doors
    3. storm doors
    4. unframed swinging doors
    5. enclosures for hot tubs, whirlpools, saunas, steam rooms, bathtubs, and showers where bottom exposed edge of glazing is <60" above any standing or walking surface
    6. adjacent to a door where nearest vertical edge is within a 24" arc of the door in a closed position and whose bottom edge is <60" above floor
    7. where an individual pane ≥9 sq ft, bottom edge <18" above the floor, top edge >36" above floor, and walking surface within 36" horizontally

8. in railings

9. in walls and fences enclosing indoor and outdoor swimming pools, hot tubs, and spas where bottom edge ≤60" above floor and within ≤60" horizontally of water

10. next to stairways, landings, and ramps ≤36" horizontally if glazing <60" above walking surface

11. next to stairways ≤60" horizontally of bottom tread if glazing <60" above tread nose

Exceptions: the following products, materials, and uses are exempt from the above hazardous locations:

1. door openings <3" in diameter

2. decorative glass in items 1, 6, or 7

3. glazing in item 6 if an intervening barrier between the door and glazing

4. glazing in items 7 and 10, if protective bar on accessible side(s) of glazing 36" above floor

5. louvered windows and jalousies

6. mirrors and glass panels mounted or hung on a continuous backing support

7. safety glazing in items 10 and 11 not required where a stairway, landing, or ramp has a guardrail or handrail including balusters or in-fill panels, the glass is >18" from the railing, or a solid wall or panel extends from floor to 34"–36" above floor

Egress (R310)

Egress openings:

- basements and every sleeping room to have at least one operable egress opening
- opening to open directly into a public street, public alley, yard, or court
- if basement contains >1 sleeping room, egress openings required in each
- sill height ≤44" above floor
- clear opening height ≥24"
- clear opening height ≥20"
- clear opening dimensions must be obtained by normal operation from inside
- net clear opening ≥5.7 sq ft

Exception: grade floor openings to have clear opening of ≥5 sq ft

- openings operational from the inside room without use of keys, tools, or special knowledge
- openings with sill height below adjacent ground to be provided with a window well

Exception: basements used only to house mechanical equipment and ≤200 sq ft floor area

- horizontal area of window well ≥9 sq ft, with horizontal projection and width ≥36"
- window wells with a vertical depth >44" to be equipped with permanently affixed ladder or steps usable with window in fully open position
- ladders or rungs to have inside width of ≥12", project ≥3" from wall, and be spaced ≤18" oc
- bulkhead enclosures to provide direct access to basement
- bars, grilles, covers, screens, or similar devices permitted over openings, bulkhead enclosures, or window wells that serve openings, provided the minimum clear opening size complies, and are releasable from inside without use of key, tool, special knowledge, or force greater than required for normal operation of the opening
- egress window under deck or porch OK if window can be fully opened and is ≤36" in height to ground

Means of Egress (R310)

- stairways, ramps, exterior egress balconies, hallways, and doors to comply
- at least one exit door, or each dwelling unit
- exit door to provide direct access from habitable portions of dwelling to exterior without travel through a garage
- exit may be by a ramp or a stairway
- exit door side-hinged, ≥3' wide, and ≥6'8" high
- landing required each side of exterior doors
- landing ≤1.5" lower than top of threshold
- landing slope ≤2%
- egress doors readily openable from inside without use of a key or special knowledge or effort

Plumbing

The piping in your basement may seem a maze. Viewing it as three separate systems (cold supply, hot supply, and waste) makes it a lot clearer. That's the approach of this chapter.

First we describe *water wells and pumps* for those who must supply their own water.

The next section looks at the *supply piping*—the pipes that bring water into the building. We look at the materials you are allowed to use and how they are placed in a trench. Then we show how to *size supply pipes* as a function of the loads they carry.

Nothing will gain you more respect at the hardware store than being able to ask for a "drop ell with threaded outlet," instead of a "bent gizmo about 2 inches long with threads at each end," so the next three sections are field guides to *copper, PVC, polyethylene,* and *PEX supply fittings.*

The other half of plumbing is the *drain, waste, and vent (DWV) system.* Instead of relying on water pressure, the DWV system depends on gravity to make its mixture of liquids and solids flow. For this reason, *sizing drainpipe* and *running drainpipe* are both subject to stringent rules.

Because the waste empties into a sewer, the DWV system also includes fixture *traps* to block sewer gas. The "V" in DWV stands for the *venting* system which prevents pressure differences from emptying the traps.

A second field guide illustrates 80 species of *plastic DWV fittings.* Whether you are installing a new system or adapting to a cast-iron system, you'll find just the fittings you'll need.

How do you know where the pipes go before you have the fixtures in hand? The *roughing-in* guide shows you.

A guide to *water treatment* shows you what equipment you need to cure 26 water quality problems.

Finally, we provide you with a checklist to make sure your plumbing installations *meet the code.*

Water Wells and Pumps

Groundwater is water which fills the cracks and pores of rocks and soil beneath the surface of the ground. The soil acts as a filter, so groundwater is usually clean and free from pollution.

Although found in nearly all areas, the quantity available varies widely. Usable amounts might be found by digging just a few feet into soil. On the other hand, a hole might have to be drilled a thousand feet before penetrating an aquifer.

Groundwater, clouds, rain, snow, streams, rivers, lakes, even the ocean are components of the hydrologic cycle (illustration below). Water evaporates from the surfaces of water bodies and vegetation and rises into the atmosphere as water vapor. When it cools to its dewpoint, excess vapor is squeezed out as clouds and precipitation. The precipitation returns to the ground and either percolates into the ground or runs off in streams and rivers into lakes and the ocean. Both evaporation and ground percolation act to return the water to its pure state.

Except in the most remote areas, water from lakes and streams requires treatment. Groundwater, however, is often clean enough to use untreated. The three common methods of tapping groundwater are shown on the facing page.

The Hydrologic Cycle

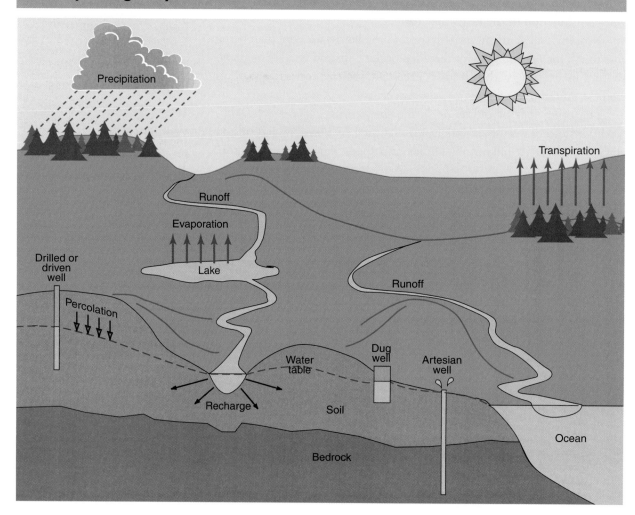

Wells for Tapping Goundwater

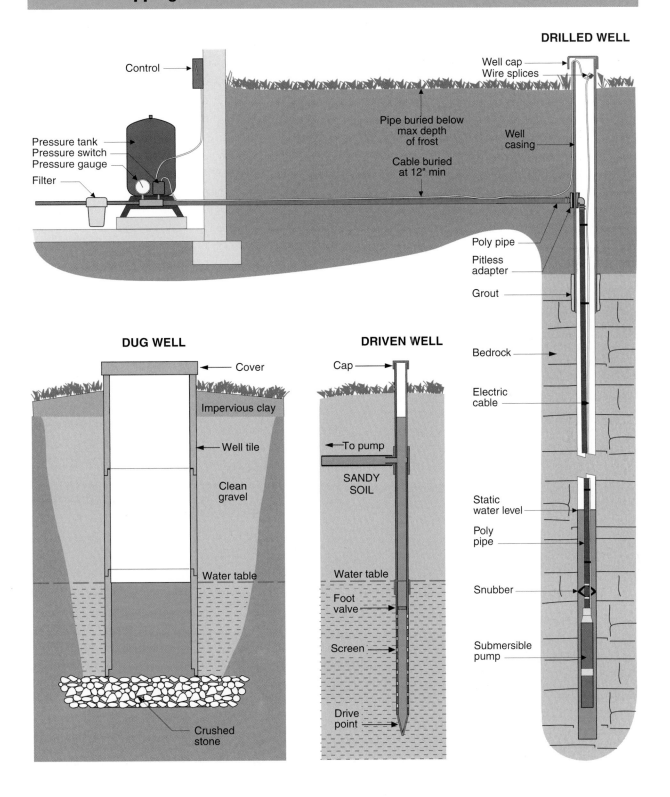

DRILLED WELL

Well cap

Wire splices

Pipe buried below max depth of frost

Cable buried at 12" min

Well casing

Poly pipe

Pitless adapter

Grout

Bedrock

Electric cable

Static water level

Poly pipe

Snubber

Submersible pump

Control

Pressure tank

Pressure switch

Pressure gauge

Filter

DUG WELL

Cover

Impervious clay

Well tile

Clean gravel

Water table

Crushed stone

DRIVEN WELL

Cap

To pump

SANDY SOIL

Water table

Foot valve

Screen

Drive point

Supply Piping

The supply system is the network of piping or tubing that distributes cold and hot water under pressure from the city water main or home well to each fixture in the building. Both the water heater and any water treatment equipment are parts of the distribution system.

Supply water is under pressure of up to 160 pounds per square inch and may be consumed by humans, so the materials allowed are strictly specified by code. Materials allowed under the International Residential Code are listed in the table below.

Allowed Piping Supply Materials

Material	Form	Advantages	Disadvantages
Chlorinated PVC (CPVC)	10', 20' lengths	Approved to 180°F Joined by cement or threading Lightweight	More subject to freeze damage High thermal expansion Better support required
Cross-linked Polyethylene (PEX)	100', 300' coils	Flexible, easy to run Approved to 200°F	Requires special tools

Copper pipe
  Type K (thickest) green
  Type L (medium) blue
  Type M (thin) red
	10', 20' lengths	Easily assembled	Susceptible to freeze damage
			Susceptible to water hammer

Copper tubing
  Type K (thickest) green
  Type L (medium) blue
	30', 60', 100' coils	Requires fewer fittings
		Flare and compression
		fittings may be used
		Withstands a few freezings
			More expensive than pipe
			Susceptible to crushing and crimping

Galvanized steel	21' lengths	Strong	High cost (due to threading) Corroded by soft water Susceptible to scaling Under-slab use only
Polyethylene (PE)	100, 120, 160 psi rated coils	Low cost Long lengths	For cold water only Allowed only to shutoff
Polyvinyl chloride (PVC)	10', 20' lengths	Low cost Joined by cement or threading Can be bent with heat	Approved only to 100°F

Both horizontal and vertical runs of supply and waste pipes are required by code to be supported against gravity. The maximum spacing of supports (see table below) is determined by both the pipe's diameter and its material. In areas of high seismic activity the allowed spacing may be reduced.

The code applies restrictions to service lines running in proximity to waste lines, as shown in the illustrations at right.

Minimum Support Spacing

Pipe Material	Horizontal Spacing	Vertical Spacing
ABS	48"	120"
Cast iron waste		
<10' lengths	60"	180" + base
10' lengths	120"	180" + base
CPVC supply		
≤1"	36"	120"
≥1¼"	48"	120"
PEX supply	32"	120"
PVC	48"	120"
Copper tubing		
≤1¼"	72"	120"
≥1½"	120"	120"
Steel supply		
½"	72"	180"
¾"	96"	180"
1"	96"	180"
≥1¼"	144"	180"
Polyethylene	not allowed	not allowed

Service Lines in Trenches

SEWER AND SUPPLY IN SAME TRENCH

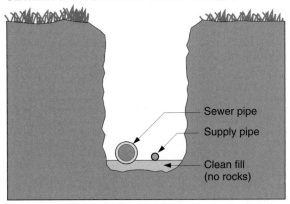

The building sewer and supply pipes may share a trench if both materials are approved for use within the building.

SEWER AND SUPPLY AT DIFFERENT LEVELS

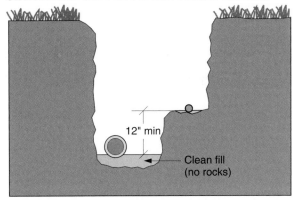

The building sewer and supply pipes may share a trench if the supply runs on a shelf at least 12" above the sewer.

SEWER AND SUPPLY IN SEPARATE TRENCHES

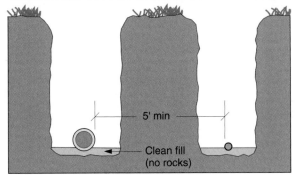

A water supply pipe must be separated at least 5' from a clay sewer pipe.

Supply Pipe Sizing

Supply pipe sizes are a function of demand, pressure, and friction. Follow these steps to calculate the required sizes:

1. Find the service pressure at the outlet of the water meter or pressure-reducing valve.

2. Deduct 0.5 psi for each foot difference in height between the service to the highest fixture.

3. Deduct the pressure loss of equipment such as a water filter or water softener.

4. Find the resulting pressure range in Table 2.

5. "Maximum developed length" is the length of pipe between the service and the furthest fixture, multiplied by 1.2 to compensate for fitting losses.

6. In Table 1, add the combined fixture units for all of the fixtures in the building.

7. Find the size of service pipe and main distribution pipe under the "maximum developed length" column to a fixture unit equal to or greater than the total calculated in Step 6. Read the service pipe in the first column and the main distribution pipe in the second column on the same row.

8. To determine the sizes of branch distribution pipes, repeat Steps 5–7 for the total hot or cold (depending on branch) fixture units and maximum developed length between the main distribution pipe and the most distant fixture.

Table 1. Fixture Units for Plumbing Fixtures and Fixture Groups

Fixture or Fixture Group	Hot	Cold	Combined
Bathtub (with or without shower head)	1.0	1.0	1.4
Clothes washer	1.0	1.0	1.4
Dishwasher	1.4	—	1.4
Full bath group with bathtub or shower stall	1.5	2.7	3.6
Half-bath group (water closet and lavatory)	0.5	2.5	2.6
Hose bibb (sillcock)	—	2.5	2.5
Kitchen group (dishwasher and sink with or without garbage grinder)	1.9	1.0	2.5
Kitchen sink	1.0	1.0	1.4
Laundry group (clothes washer standpipe and laundry tub)	1.8	1.8	2.5
Laundry tub	1.0	1.0	1.4
Lavatory	0.5	0.5	0.7
Shower stall	1.0	1.0	1.4
Water closet (tank type)	—	2.2	2.2

Minimum Fixture Feed Pipe Sizes

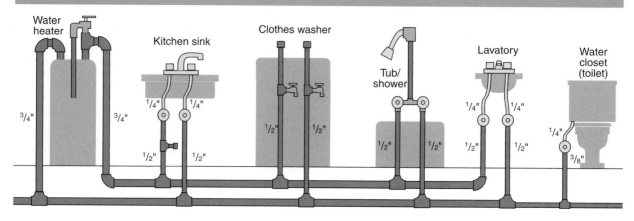

Table 2. Minimum Size of Mains and Distribution Piping (IRC Table P2903.7)

Service Pipe, in	Distribution Pipe, in	Maximum Development Length, ft									
		40	60	80	100	150	200	250	300	400	500
PRESSURE RANGE 30–39 PSI											
¾	½	2.5	2	1.5	1.5	1	1	.5	.5	0	0
¾	¾	9.5	7.5	6	5.5	4	3.5	3	2.5	2	1.5
¾	1	32	25	20	16.5	11	9	7.5	6.5	5.5	4.5
1	1	32	32	27	21	13.5	10	8	7	5.5	5
¾	1¼	32	32	32	32	30	24	20	17	13	10.5
1	1¼	80	80	70	61	45	34	27	22	16	12
1½	1¼	80	80	80	75	54	40	31	25	17.5	13
PRESSURE RANGE 40–49 PSI											
¾	½	3	2.5	2	1.5	1.5	1	1	.5	.5	.5
¾	¾	9.5	9.5	8.5	7	5.5	4.5	3.5	3	2.5	2
¾	1	32	32	32	26	18	13.5	10.5	9	7.5	6
1	1	32	32	32	32	21	15	11.5	9.5	7.5	6.5
¾	1¼	32	32	32	32	32	32	32	27	21	16.5
1	1¼	80	80	80	80	65	52	42	35	26	20
1½	1¼	80	80	80	80	75	59	48	39	28	21
PRESSURE RANGE 50–59 PSI											
¾	½	3	3	2.5	2	1.5	1	1	1	.5	.5
¾	¾	9.5	9.5	9.5	8.5	6.5	5	4.5	4	3	2.5
¾	1	32	32	32	32	25	18.5	14.5	12	9.5	8
1	1	32	32	32	32	30	22	16.5	13	10	8
¾	1¼	32	32	32	32	32	32	32	32	29	24
1	1¼	80	80	80	80	80	68	57	48	35	28
1½	1¼	80	80	80	80	80	75	63	53	39	29
PRESSURE RANGE ≥60 PSI											
¾	½	3	3	3	2.5	2	1.5	1.5	1	1	.5
¾	¾	9.5	9.5	9.5	9.5	7.5	6	5	4.5	3.5	3
¾	1	32	32	32	32	32	24	19.5	15.5	11.5	9.5
1	1	32	32	32	32	32	28	22	17	12	9.5
¾	1¼	32	32	32	32	32	32	32	32	32	30
1	1¼	80	80	80	80	80	80	69	60	46	36
1½	1¼	80	80	80	80	80	80	76	65	50	38

Copper Supply Fittings

Copper Pipe and Fitting Sizes

Matching fittings to copper pipe and tube can be confusing because of the dimensioning conventions. When a plumber refers to the size of either a pipe or a fitting, he is referring to its nominal size, which is, strangely, neither the inside nor the outside diameter! The outside diameter is always the nominal size plus ⅛ inch. The inside diameter is close to the nominal size, but varies with the thickness of the wall. The table at right compares these dimensions.

Type M Copper Pipe Dimensions

Nominal Size	Outside Diameter, in	Inside Diameter, in	Wall Thickness, in
⅜	0.500	0.450	0.025
½	0.625	0.569	0.028
¾	0.875	0.811	0.032
1	1.125	1.055	0.035

Copper Supply Fittings

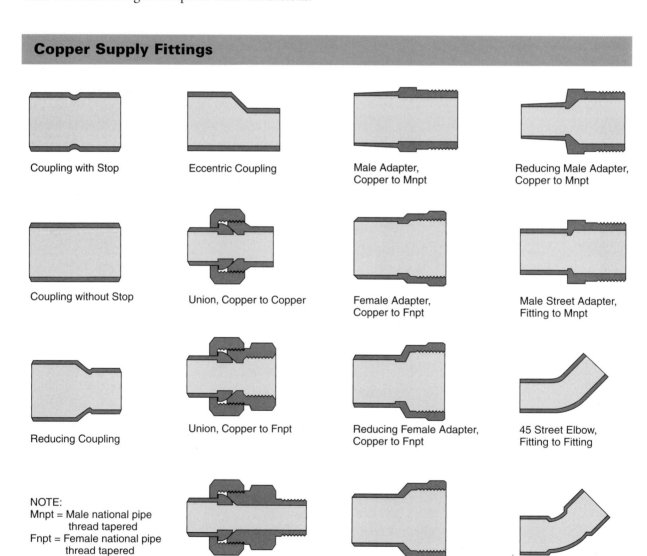

Coupling with Stop

Eccentric Coupling

Male Adapter, Copper to Mnpt

Reducing Male Adapter, Copper to Mnpt

Coupling without Stop

Union, Copper to Copper

Female Adapter, Copper to Fnpt

Male Street Adapter, Fitting to Mnpt

Reducing Coupling

Union, Copper to Fnpt

Reducing Female Adapter, Copper to Fnpt

45 Street Elbow, Fitting to Fitting

NOTE:
Mnpt = Male national pipe thread tapered
Fnpt = Female national pipe thread tapered

Union, Copper to Mnpt

Female Street Adapter, Fitting to Fnpt

45 Street Elbow, Fitting to Copper

45 Street Elbow,
Fitting to Copper

90 Street Elbow,
Fitting to Fitting

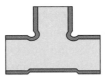
Tee,
All Copper

Cross-Over Coupling,
Copper to Copper

90 Street Elbow,
Fitting to Fitting

90 Elbow-Long Turn,
Copper to Copper

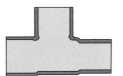
Street Tee,
Copper to Fitting to Copper

Return Bend,
Copper to Copper

90 Elbow,
Copper to Copper

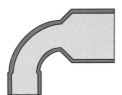
90 Reducing Elbow,
Copper to Copper

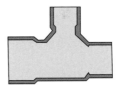
Reducing Tee,
by O.D. Sizes

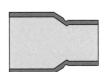
Reducer,
Fitting to Copper

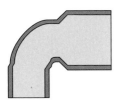
90 Reducing Elbow,
Copper to Copper

90 Street Elbow,
Fitting to Copper

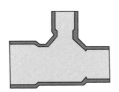
Reducing Tee,
Copper to Copper to Copper

End Plug,
Fitting End

90 Street Elbow,
Copper to Copper

90 Elbow,
Copper to Fnpt

Air Chamber,
Fitting End

Tube Cap,
Tube End

PVC Supply Fittings

PVC Pipe and Fitting Sizes

As is the case with other piping materials, matching PVC and CPVC fittings to pipe can be confusing because of the system of dimensions. The nominal size is neither the inside nor the outside diameter. The outside diameter is the nominal size plus approximately 0.3 inch. The inside diameter is close to the nominal size, but varies with the thickness of the wall. The table at right compares these dimensions.

PVC Schedule 40 Pipe Dimensions

Nominal Size	Outside Diameter, in	Inside Diameter, in	Wall Thickness, in
3/8	0.675	0.483	0.091
1/2	0.840	0.608	0.109
3/4	1.050	0.810	0.113
1	1.315	1.033	0.133

PVC Supply Fittings

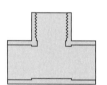

Tee,
Slip x Slip x Slip

Tee,
Slip x Slip x Fipt

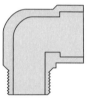

90 Ell Reducing,
Slip x Fipt

90 Street Ell,
Mipt x Slip

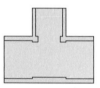

Reducing Tee,
Slip x Slip x Slip

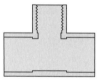

Reducing Tee,
Slip x Slip x Fipt

90 Ell,
Fipt x Fipt

90 Street Ell,
Mipt x Fipt

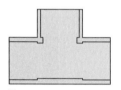

Reducing Tee,
Slip x Slip x Slip

Reducing Tee,
Slip x Slip x Fipt

90 Ell Reducing,
Slip x Fipt

Side Outlet Ell,
Slip x Slip x Fipt

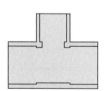

Transition Tee,
Slip x Slip x Insert

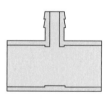

Cross,
Slip x Slip x Slip x Slip

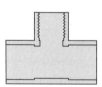

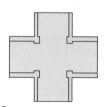

NOTE:
Fipt = Female iron pipe thread
Mipt = Male iron pipe thread
Slip = Slip fitting end
Spig = Spigot fitting end

90 Street Ell,
Spig x Slip

90 Ell,
Slip x Slip

90 Ell,
Fipt x Fipt

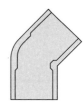

45 Ell,
Slip x Slip

Coupling,
Slip x Slip

Female Adapter,
Slip x Fipt

Deep Coupling

Reducer Bushing,
Spig x Fipt

Reducer Coupling,
Slip x Slip

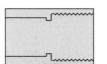

Female Adapter Reducing,
Slip x Fipt

T.T. Bushing,
Mipt x Fipt

Saddle,
Pipe O.D. x Slip

Coupling,
Fipt x Fipt

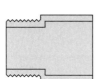

Male Adapter,
Mipt x Slip

IPT Adapter,
Mipt x Fipt

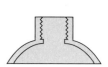

Saddle,
Pipe O.D. x Fipt

IPS to PIP Adapter,
Spig x Slip

Male Adapter Reducing,
Mipt x Slip

Cap,
Slip

Plug,
Spig

Riser Extension,
Fipt x Mipt

Reducer Bushing,
Spig x Slip

Cap,
Fipt

Plug,
Mipt

Polyethylene Supply Fittings

Polyethylene Supply Fittings

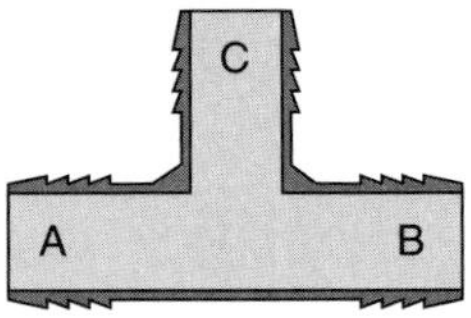

Tee (A x B x C),
Ins x Ins x Ins

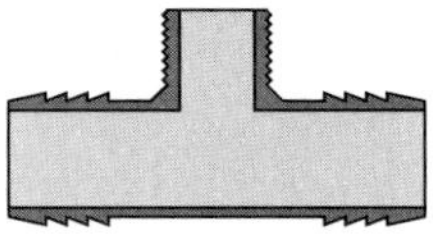

Tee,
Ins x Ins x Mipt

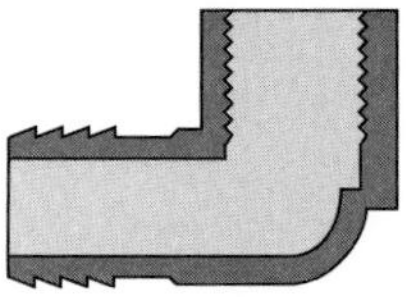

90 Reducing Ell,
Ins x Fipt

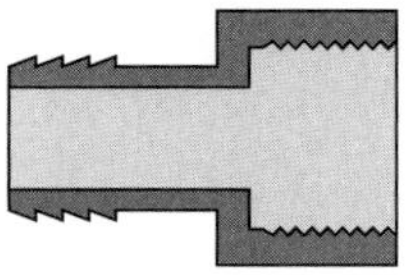

Female Adapter,
Ins x Fipt

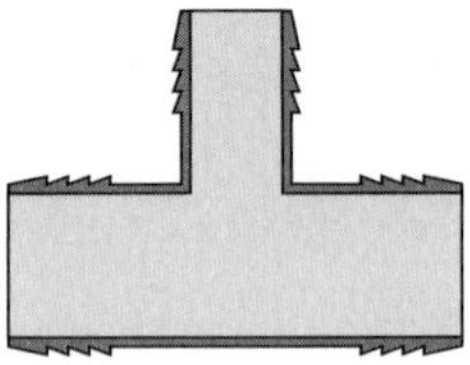

Reducing Tee,
Ins x Ins x Ins

Cross,
Ins x Ins x Ins x Ins

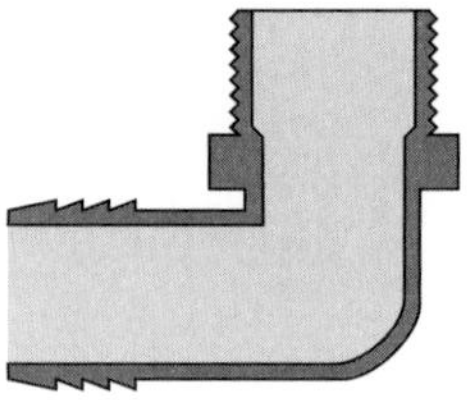

90 Ell,
Ins x Mipt

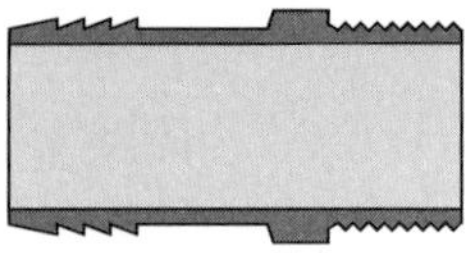

Male Adapter,
Ins x Mipt

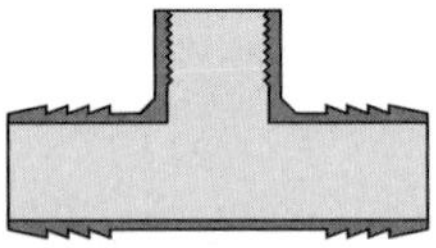

Tee,
Ins x Ins x Fipt

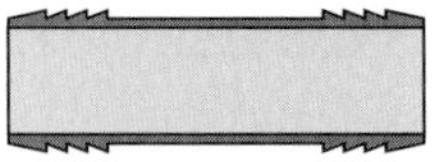

Coupling,
Ins x Ins

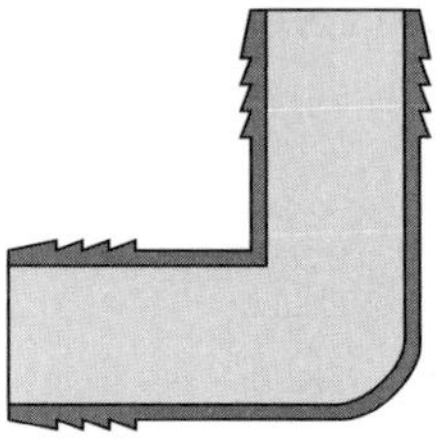

90 Ell,
Ins x Ins

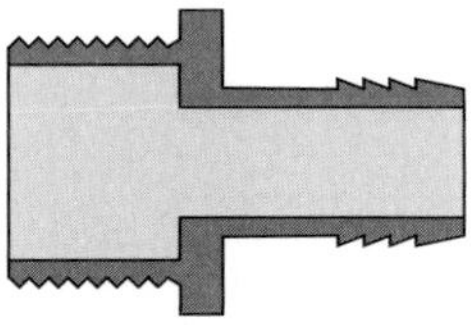

Male Adapter Reducing,
Mipt x Ins

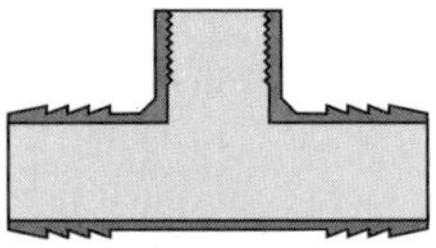

Reducing Tee,
Ins x Ins x Fipt

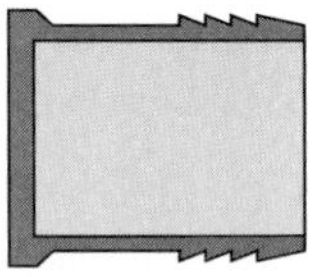

Plug,
Ins

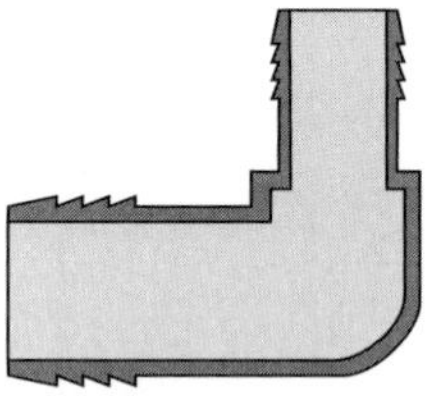

90 Reducing Ell,
Ins x Ins

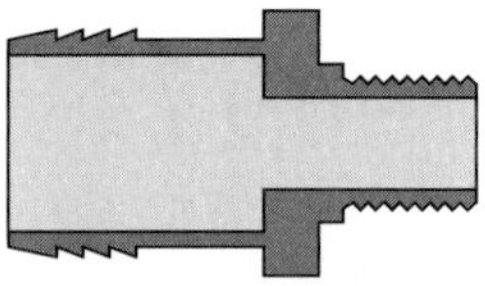

Male Adapter Reducing,
Ins x Mipt

NOTE:
Ins = Insert thread
Fipt = Female iron pipe thread
Mipt = Male iron pipe thread

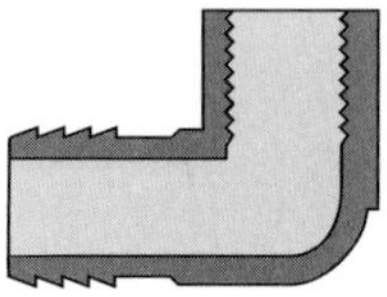

90 Ell,
Ins x Fipt

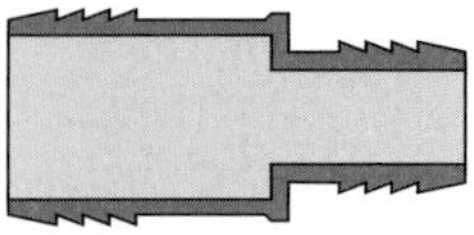

Reducer Coupling,
Ins x Ins

PEX Supply Fittings

PEX Supply Fittings

½" Barb Tee

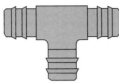

¾" Barb Tee

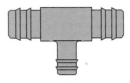

¾" x ¾" x ½" Barb Tee

¾" x ½" x ½" Barb Tee

⅜" Barb Coupling

½" Barb Coupling

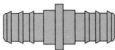

¾" Barb Coupling

¾" x ½" Barb Coupling

½" Barb Elbow

¾" Barb Elbow

¾" x ½" Barb Elbow

½" Barb x ½" Fpt
Swivel Cone Connector

½" Barb x ½" Fpt
Drop Ear Elbow

½" Pex to Poly
Transition Fitting

½" Male Sweat x
½" Barb Brass Sweat

½" Female Sweat x
½" Barb Brass Sweat

½" Barb x ½" Mpt
Adaptor

½" Plug

½" Barb x ¾" Mpt
Adaptor

½" Barb x ½" Fpt
Swivel Cone Connector

½" Barb x ¾" Fpt
Non Swivel Adapter

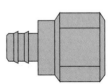

½" Barb x ½" Fpt
Non Swivel Adaptor

¾" Barb x ¾" Fpt
Swivel Cone Connector

¾" Male Sweat x
¾" Barb Brass Sweat

¾" Female Sweat x
¾" Barb Brass Sweat

¾" Barb x ½" Mpt
Adaptor

⅜" Barb x ½" Fpt
Swivel Cone Connector

¾" Male Sweat x... ⅜" Barb x ½" Mpt
Adaptor

Drain, Waste, Vent (DWV) System

Features of the Drain, Waste, Vent System

Waste pipes
Vent pipes

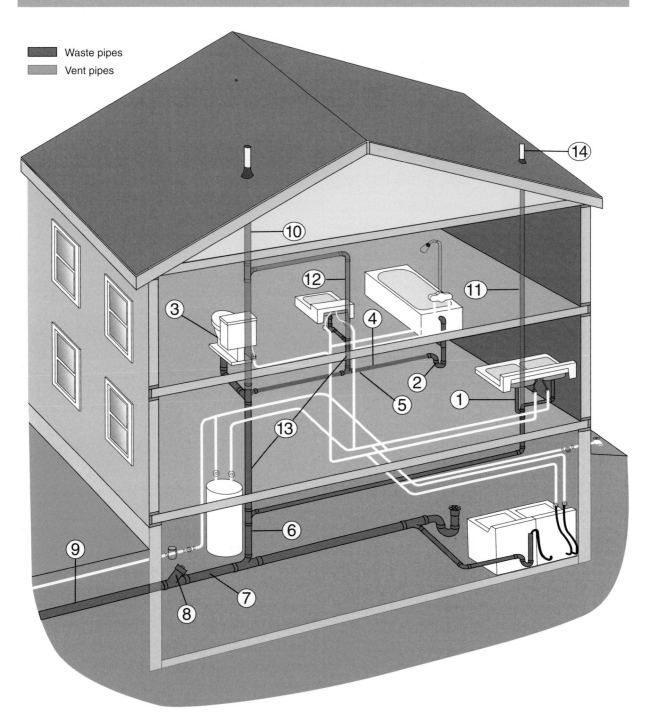

The Waste System

The waste system is the assemblage of pipes that collects and delivers waste (used) water to either the municipal or private sewage system.

1. The pipe that drains away a fixture's waste is its drain. The minimum diameter of the drain is determined by the fixture's rate of discharge.

2. Every fixture drain must be "trapped." A trap passes water, but retains enough water to block noxious sewer gases.

3. Toilets (water closets) have the trap built into the base of the toilet.

4. The horizontal pipe between a trap and the first point of the drain pipe supplied with air is the "trap arm." Code limits trap arm length to prevent siphon action from emptying the trap.

5. Smaller tributary drain pipes that feed into the main "house drain" are called "branches."

6. The largest vertical drain pipe, extending from the lowest point through the roof, and to which the smaller horizontal branch drains connect, is the "soil stack." In a very horizontally extended house, there may be more than one soil stack.

7. The bottom-most horizontal waste pipe is the "house drain." To optimize flow, all horizontal waste pipes must be sloped at ⅛ to ¼ inch per foot.

8. To allow unclogging of drain pipes, "cleanouts" are provided. There is a 4-inch-diameter cleanout where the house drain exits the building. Additional cleanouts are required throughout the waste system for every 100 feet of horizontal run and every cumulative change of direction of 135 degrees.

9. Waste pipe outside the building is termed the "house sewer." It is always at least 4 inches in diameter.

The Vent System

Fixture drains must be kept at atmospheric pressure so the water seals in their traps are not siphoned away. The vent system is the set of pipes that admit air to the drain system.

10. The primary vent is the upper section of the "stack." Below the highest point of waste discharge into it is the "waste stack." Above that point it is the "vent stack." If a waste stack also serves one or more toilets (and it usually does), it is sometimes called the "soil stack." Because it provides direct passage to the sewer, a vent stack must be terminated in the open air. And to keep the sewer gas as far as possible from people, it is usually terminated through the roof.

11. The permitted length of drain pipe from a trap to a vent (the trap arm) is a function of the pipe diameter. If the horizontal run of the drain is too long, a smaller-diameter vent stack may be provided close after the trap.

12. Another solution to a long horizontal drain is breaking it into legal lengths with "revents." A loop vent provides pressure relief by the volume of its contained air. An air check valve allows house air to flow into the drain, but prevents sewer gas from escaping.

13. A vertical vent pipe serving both waste and vent is called a "wet vent."

14. The air in vent pipes is humid. In northern states frost can build up on the inside of exposed vents. To avoid frost blockage, local codes may specify a larger diameter above the roof. In addition, so that snow does not cover the vent pipe, a local code may also call for a vertical extension of the pipe beyond the code minimum of 6 inches.

Sizing Drainpipe

The sizes (diameters) of all drain pipes, including traps, trap arms, branch drains, stacks, and building sewers, are based on the expected maximum rates of flow, measured in drainage fixture units (dfu). One dfu equals one cubic foot of water per minute.

The procedure for determining the size of pipe required at any point is as follows:

1. Draw a plan of the plumbing showing the fixtures and the connecting pipes.

2. Assign dfu figures for each fixture or fixture group using Table 1 below.

3. Starting at the fixture most remote from the building sewer, add the dfu flowing into the pipe. Use the group values wherever possible in order to hold down the total.

4. Use Table 2, below, to determine the sizes of pipes required for the number of accumulated dfu.

5. Use Table 3, below, to determine the required size and slope of the building drain and sewer.

Table 1. Drain Sizes and Fixture Units

Fixture or Fixture Group	Minimum Drain/Trap Size	Drainage Fixture Units[1]
Bar Sink	1¼"	1
Bathtub ½	1½"	2
Bathroom group[2]	3"	6
Half bathroom group[3]	3"	4
1½ Baths	3"	7
2 Baths	3"	8
2½ Baths	3"	9
3 Baths	3"	10
Bidet	1¼"	1
Clothes Washer	2"	2
Dishwasher	1½"	2
Floor drain	2"	2
Kitchen sink	1½"	2
Laundry tub	1½"	2
Laundry group[4]	1½"	2
Lavatory	1¼"	1
Shower[5]	2"	2
Water closet	3"	4

[1] 1 drainage fixture unit (dfu) = 1 cu ft per minute.

[2] Tub or shower, water closet, bidet, and lavatory

[3] Water closet plus lavatory

[4] Clothes washer plus laundry tub

[5] Stand-alone shower stall

Table 2. Maximum Fixture Units Connected to Branches and Stacks

Nominal Pipe Size, in	Any Horizontal Fixture Branch	Any Vertical Stack or Drain
1¼[1]	—	—
1½[2]	3	4
2[2]	6	10
2½[2]	12	20
3	20	48
4	160	240

[1] 1¼ in limited to a single fixture drain or trap arm.

[2] No water closets allowed.

Table 3. Maximum Fixture Units Connected to Building Drain or Sewer

Nominal Pipe Size, in	Slope per Foot		
	⅛ in	¼ in	½ in
1½[1,2]	NA	Note 1	Note 1
2[2]	NA	21	27
2½[2]	NA	24	31
3	36	42	50
4	180	216	250

[1] 1½ in limited to a building drain branch serving not more than two waste fixtures, or not more than one waste fixture if serving a pumped discharge fixture or garbage grinder.

[2] No water closets allowed.

Running Drainpipe

Other than traps (p. 320–321) and vents (p. 322–325), running drain pipes involves four principal issues: slope, direction changes, cleanouts, and physical protection.

Slope

As shown in Table 3 on the facing page, horizontal drain pipes are required to slope between 1/8 and 1/2 inch per foot, the reason being optimal drainage.

Direction Changes

Fittings permitted for changing direction are listed in Table 4 at right and illustrated on p. 326–327. As can be seen from the illustrations, the intent is to create smooth flow and to keep the discharge of one drain from entering another.

Cleanout Requirements

Cleanouts are provided for clearing blockages. To that end, cleanouts must be provided

- every 100 feet horizontally.
- where direction changes >45 degrees, except just one cleanout is required per 40 feet of run.
- at the base of each vertical waste or soil stack.
- near building drain/building sewer junction.
- access without removal of permanent materials.
- front clearance of 18 inches for 3- and 4-inch pipes and 12 inches for smaller pipes.

Protection

Drainlines must be protected, as shown in the illustration at right, from:

- freezing by burial, insulation, or heat tape.
- passing through foundation walls by sleeving with pipe two sizes larger.
- passing under footings by a vertical clearance of 2 inches minimum.
- damage from backfill containing rocks and other construction debris by bedding in sand or fine gravel as shown.

Table 4. Change of Direction

Fitting	Horizontal to Vertical[3]	Vertical to Horizontal	Horizontal to Horizontal
1/16 bend	Y	Y	Y
1/8 bend	Y	Y	Y
1/4 bend	Y	Y[1]	Y[1]
Short sweep	Y	Y[1,2]	Y[1]
Long sweep	Y	Y	Y
Sanitary tee	Y[3]	N	N
Wye	Y	Y	Y
Comb. wye & 1/8 bend	Y	Y	Y

[1] Permitted only for 2-in or smaller fixture drain.

[2] 3 in and larger.

[3] Double sanitary tees not allowed to receive discharge of back-to-back toilets or fixtures with pumped discharge.

Drainline Protection

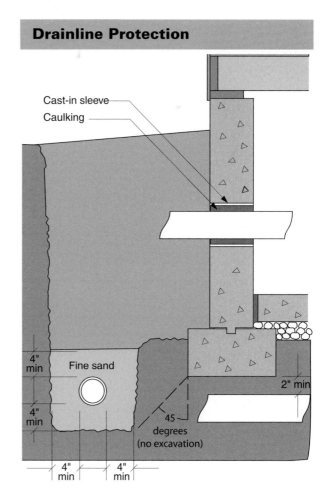

Cast-in sleeve
Caulking
4" min
Fine sand
4" min
2" min
45 degrees (no excavation)
4" min
4" min

Running Drainpipe   **319**

Traps

A trap is a fitting designed to trap a volume of water in order to block the back passage of sewer gas. The illustration at right shows a P-trap.

Trap Failures

Traps can fail in three ways (see numbered illustrations of "Trap Failures" below):

1. If the fixture tailpiece is too long, the falling water may develop enough momentum to carry it past the outlet weir. For this reason the code requires tailpieces to be as short as possible, but in no case longer than 24 inches (except clothes-washer standpipes, which may be between 18 and 42 inches).

2. If the wastewater completely fills the trap and outlet arm to a point below the outlet, the weight of water in the outlet may siphon the water behind it out of the trap.

3. If the trap arm is too long for its diameter, fluid friction may cause the waste to back up until it completely fills the outlet, resulting in siphoning, as in case 2.

The Ubiquitous P-Trap

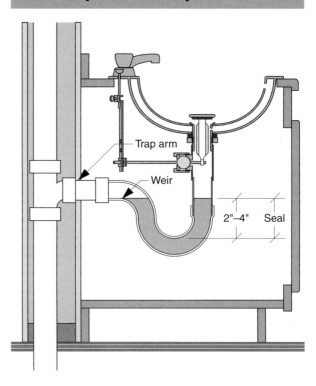

Trap Failures

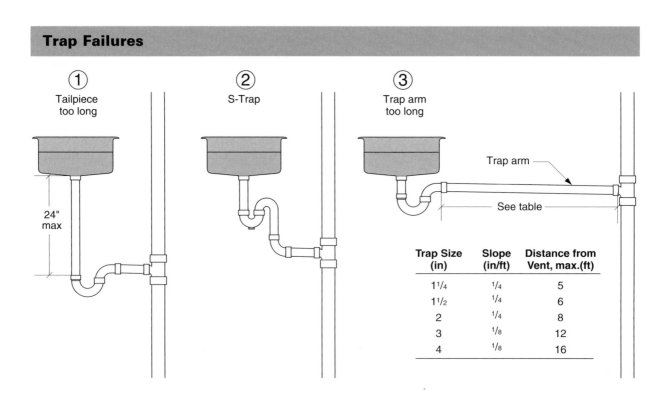

Trap Size (in)	Slope (in/ft)	Distance from Vent, max.(ft)
1¼	¼	5
1½	¼	6
2	¼	8
3	⅛	12
4	⅛	16

Prohibited Traps

S-trap

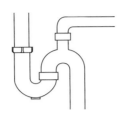

Crown-vented trap

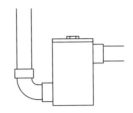

Trap larger than
trap arm (drum trap)

Bell trap

Approved Traps

TUBS & SHOWERS

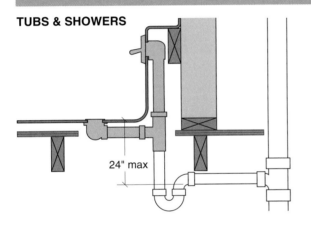

24" max

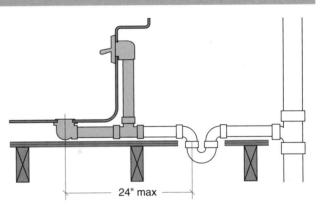

24" max

MULTIPLE SINKS (UP TO 3) ON A SINGLE TRAP

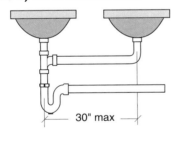

30" max

30" max   30" max

CLOTHES WASHER STANDPIPE

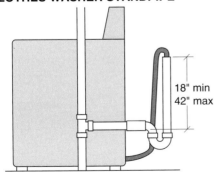

18" min
42" max

INTEGRAL TRAP (WATER CLOSET)

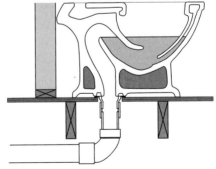

Venting

Every fixture is required to have a trap in order that sewer gas not find its way into the living space. The seal is effected by a slug of water trapped behind the trap's weir. As described on p. 320, the slug of water can be lost if the drain/trap develops a siphon. Vents are designed to introduce air into the drain pipe in order to prevent the siphon.

The most basic vent is one into which individual fixtures drain. The rules for this simple vent are shown in the illustration at right and table below.

Maximum Lengths of Trap Arms

Trap Size, in	Slope, in/ft	Maximum Distance from Vent, ft
1¼	¼	5
1½	¼	6
2	¼	8
3	⅛	12
4	⅛	16

Common Vents

Separate vents through the roof for each and every fixture would be not only expensive but unsightly. The Code therefore specifies a number of ways in which fixtures can share a single vent.

One method is to allow a section of vent pipe to serve either 1) several fixture drains at the same level, or 2) as the vent for one group of fixtures and the drain for a higher group of fixtures, as long as all fixtures are on the same floor of the building and the upper group does not contain a water closet. The section of pipe serving dual purposes is a *wet vent*. Common vent sizes are dictated by the table below.

Common Vent Sizes

Pipe Size, in	Maximum Discharge from Upper Fixture Drain, dfu
1½	1
2	4
2½ to 3	6

Basic Single-Fixture Vent Rules

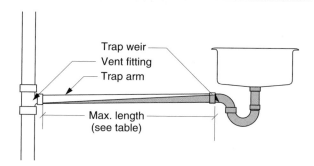

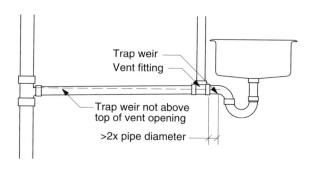

Common Vents

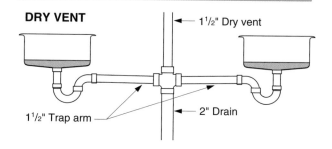

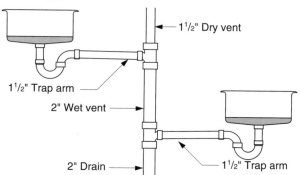

Waste Stack Vents

A vertical pipe can serve as both drain and vent for any number of individual fixture drains, provided:

1. The vertical pipe (waste stack) is sized to the total dfu emptying into it (see table at right).

2. The pipe is straight, with no horizontal offsets between the highest and lowest drains it serves.

3. No water closet or urinal empties into it.

4. The waste stack is vented by a same-size vent stack above the highest fixture drain (offsets are permitted in the vent stack).

Note that the alternative and preferred method, a waste stack plus vent stack, permits water closets and urinals to drain into the waste stack.

Waste Stack Vent Size

Stack Size, in	Total Discharge into One Branch Interval	Total Discharge for Stack, dfu
1½	1	2
2	2	4
2½	No limit	8
3	No limit	24
4	No limit	50

Waste Stacks

WASTE STACK VENT

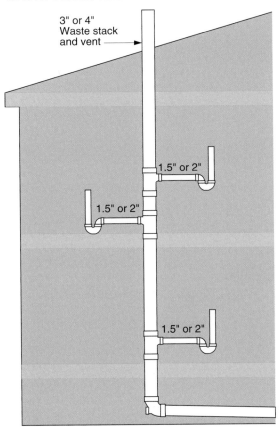

3" or 4" Waste stack and vent

1.5" or 2"

1.5" or 2"

1.5" or 2"

WASTE STACK PLUS VENT STACK

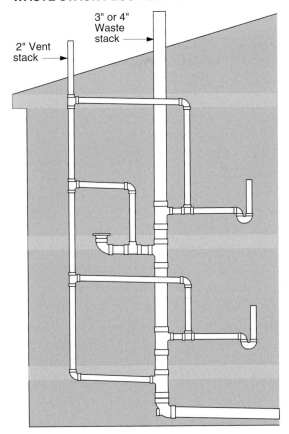

2" Vent stack

3" or 4" Waste stack

Wet Venting

Any number of fixtures in up to two bathrooms on the same floor level are permitted to drain into and be vented by a horizontal vent, provided:

1. The horizontal and vertical wet vents are sized to the dfu emptying into them (see table at right).

2. Each fixture connects horizontally to the horizontal wet vent or has its own dry vent.

3. The dry-vent connection to the wet vent is an individual vent or a combination vent.

4. No more than one fixture drain connects upstream from the dry-vent connection.

Wet-Vent Sizes

Wet Vent Pipe Size, in	Fixture Unit Load, dfu
2	4
2½	6
3	12
4	32

Typical Wet Vent

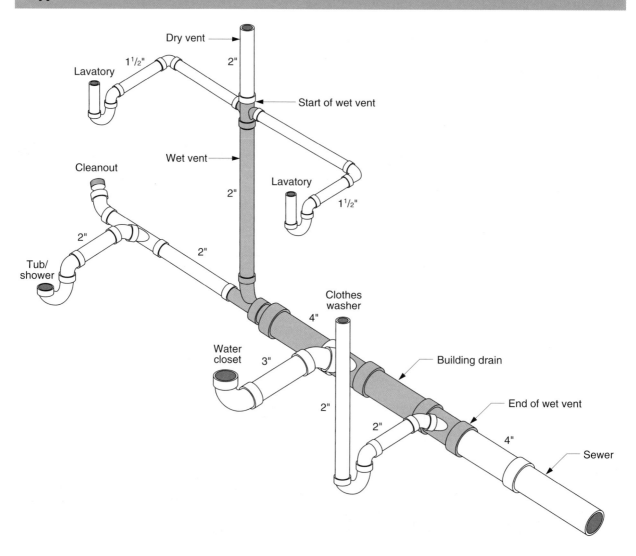

Island Fixture Venting

The Code has special venting provisions for island fixtures, including sinks and dishwashers:

1. A loop vent must rise above its fixture drain.

2. Cleanouts must be provided that permit rodding of every part of the loop vent.

3. Air-admittance valves may only be installed after pressure testing of the DWV system.

4. Air-admittance valves must be at least 4 inches above the fixture drain being vented.

5. Air-admittance valves must be accessible and in a ventilated space.

Venting an Island Sink

LOOP VENT

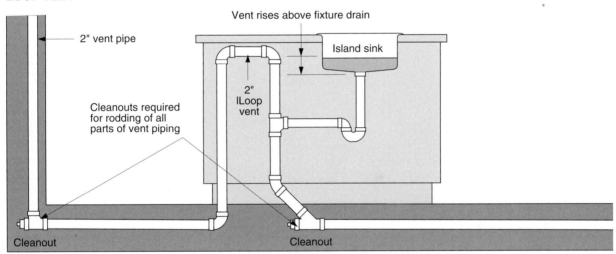

- 2" vent pipe
- Vent rises above fixture drain
- Island sink
- 2" ILoop vent
- Cleanouts required for rodding of all parts of vent piping
- Cleanout
- Cleanout

AIR-ADMITTANCE VALVE

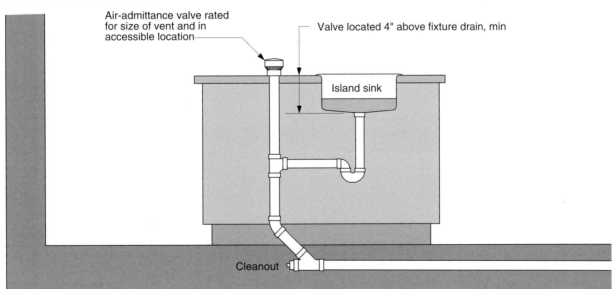

- Air-admittance valve rated for size of vent and in accessible location
- Valve located 4" above fixture drain, min
- Island sink
- Cleanout

Plastic DWV Fittings

PVC/ABS DWV Fittings

90 Ell
P x P

90 Fitting Ell
Fitting x P

P-trap with Cleanout
P x SJ x Cleanout

P-trap with Union
P x SJ

Tee w/ 90 R&L Inlets
P x P x P x P x P

90 Closet Ell
P x P

90 Fitting Closet Ell
Fitting x P

P-trap
P x SJ

P-trap with Union
P x P

Tee with 90 L Inlet
P x P x P x P

90 Long Turn Ell
P x P

90 Fitting Long Turn Ell
Fitting x P

P-trap with Cleanout
P x P x Cleanout

P-trap with Union
P x F

Tee with 90 R Inlet
P x P x P x P

60 Ell
P x P

90 Fitting Vent Ell
Fitting x P

P-trap
P x P

Swivel Drum Trap
P x P x Cleanout

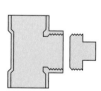
Long Radius TY
P x P x P

45 Ell, P X P

90 Ell
P x F

Return Bend w/ Cleanout
P x P x Cleanout

Ell w/ Hi Heel Inlet
P x P x P

Test Tee
P x P x Cleanout

45 Fitting Ell
Fitting x P

90 Ell with Side Inlet
P x P x P

NOTE:
F = Female
M = Male
P = Plastic Weld
SJ = Slip Joint

90 Vent Ell
P x P

Return Bend
P x P

Ell w/ Lo Heel Inlet
P x P x P

326   PLUMBING

Vent Tee
P x P x P

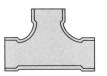

Two-Way Cleanout Tee
P x P x P

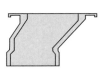

Offset Closet Flange, P

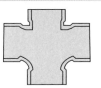

Double Tee
P x P x P x P

Closet Flange, P

Fitting Tee
Fitting x P x P

45 Y
P x P x P

Dbl. Tee w/ 90 Side Inlet
P x P x P x P x P

Double Fixture Tee
P x P x P x P

Adj. Closet Flange, P

Fixture Tee
P x P x F

45 Y
Fitting x P x P

Dbl. Tee w/Two 90 Inlets
P x P x P x P x P x P

Fitting Dbl. Fixture Tee
Fitting x P x P x P

Fitting Adj. Closet
Flange Fitting

Closet Flange, F

Closet Flange, M

Test Tee
P x P x F

Tee
P x P x P

45 Double Y
P x P x P x P

Double Tee
F x F x P x P

Closet Flange with
Knockout Test Plug

45 Y
P x P x F

22½ Ell
P x P

22½ Fitting Ell
Fitting x P

Double Ell
P x P x P

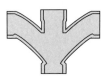

Dbl. Long Turn TY
P x P x P x P

NOTE:
F = Female
M = Male
P = Plastic Weld
SJ = Slip Joint

Sewer & Drain Adapter
P x Sewer & Drain

Fitting Flush Bushing
Fitting x P

Fitting Adapter
Fitting x F

Adapter
P x M

Fitting Cleanout
Fitting x Cleanout

Coupling
P x P

Fitting Trap Adapter
Fitting x SJ

Fitting Flush Adapter
Fitting x F

Fitting Adapter
Fitting x M

Test Cap

Repair Coupling
P x P

Trap Adapter
P x SJ

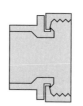

Fitting Swivel Adapter
Fitting x F

Plug, M

Fitting Plug
Fitting

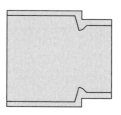

Soil Pipe Adapter
P x Hub

Adapter
P x F

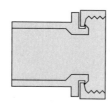

Fitting Swivel Adapter
Fitting x F

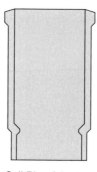

Soil Pipe Adapter
P x Spigot

Cap, F

NOTE:
F = Female
M = Male
P = Plastic Weld
SJ = Slip Joint

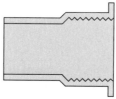

Fitting Tray Plug Adapter
Fitting x NPT Straight

No Hub Soil Pipe Adapt.
P x No Hub

Nipple
M x M

Roughing-In Dimensions

Both supply and DWV piping require cutting holes in floors, walls, and sometimes framing. The cutting of holes and running of pipes prior to installation of fixtures is called roughing-in.

The illustrations at right and below show the normal rough-in dimensions for standard kitchen and bath fixtures. All dimensions are shown as distances from the inside face of framing and vertical distance from the subfloor.

The most variable dimension is distance from the center of the toilet discharge to the wall. Assuming a wall finish of ½-inch drywall, this dimension is normally 12½ inches. For bidets the equivalent distance is 15½ inches.

To play it safe, however, double-check the rough-in dimensions specified by the manufacturer of the fixture before running pipe.

Kitchen Sink (Double) Rough-In

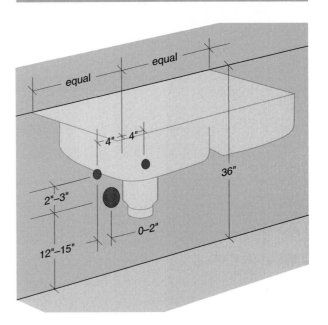

Bathroom Rough-In

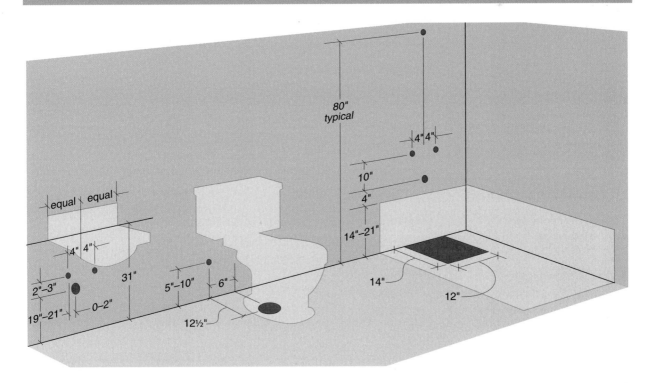

Water Treatment

Water Contaminants and Treatments

Contaminant	Treatment Options
Bacteria	Chlorine, distillation, reverse osmosis
Chloride	Distillation, reverse osmosis
Cloudiness/turbidity/sediments	Particulate filter
Color	
Brown/black stains (manganese)	Water softener (up to 5 milligrams/liter)
Red water (oxidized iron)	particulate filters, water softener (up to 5 milligrams/liter), distillation
Red stains (dissolved iron)	Water softener (up to 5 milligrams/liter), distillation
Fluoride	Distillation, reverse osmosis
Hardness	Water softener, reverse osmosis
Metals	
Arsenic	Distillation, reverse osmosis, carbon filter (with activated alumina added)
Barium	Distillation, reverse osmosis, water softener
Cadmium	Distillation, reverse osmosis, water softener
Chromium	Distillation, reverse osmosis
Copper	Distillation, reverse osmosis
Lead	Distillation, reverse osmosis
Mercury	Distillation, reverse osmosis
Zinc	Distillation, reverse osmosis
Nitrate, nitrite	Anion exchange, distillation, reverse osmosis
Odors	
Chlorine	Carbon filter
Hydrogen sulfide (rotten egg)	Disinfection techniques, iron filter (green sand), ozone generator, pellet chlorinator
Gasoline or chemical solvents	Eliminate source
Musty or earthy odor	Disinfection techniques, ozone generator, pellet chlorinator
Pesticides	Carbon filter, reverse osmosis
High pH (acid)	Limestone neutralizer
Radon	Air stripper
Radium	Distillation, reverse osmosis, water softener
Volatile organic chemicals (VOCs)	Air stripper, carbon filter, reverse osmosis, distillation

Water Treatment Equipment

CARBON CARTRIDGE FILTER

Filtered water travels up the center and out to cold supply line

Untreated water enters top cap

Charcoal core adsorbs chlorine and organic chemicals

Shutoff valves allow cartridge replacement

Water filters thru fiber outer shell, trapping sediment

Cannister unscrews to replace activated charcoal filter cartridge

REVERSE OSMOSIS FILTER

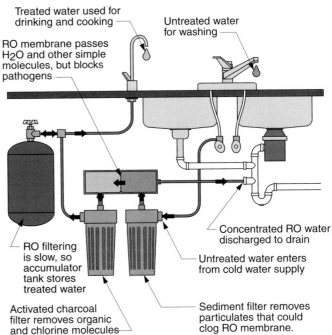

Treated water used for drinking and cooking

Untreated water for washing

RO membrane passes H$_2$O and other simple molecules, but blocks pathogens

RO filtering is slow, so accumulator tank stores treated water

Concentrated RO water discharged to drain

Untreated water enters from cold water supply

Activated charcoal filter removes organic and chlorine molecules

Sediment filter removes particulates that could clog RO membrane.

CARBON WHOLE-HOUSE FILTER

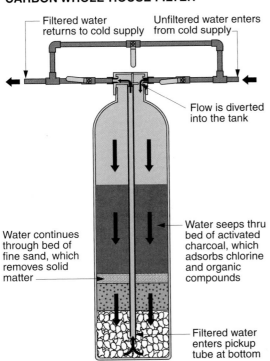

Filtered water returns to cold supply

Unfiltered water enters from cold supply

Flow is diverted into the tank

Water continues through bed of fine sand, which removes solid matter

Water seeps thru bed of activated charcoal, which adsorbs chlorine and organic compounds

Filtered water enters pickup tube at bottom

ION-EXCHANGE WATER SOFTENER

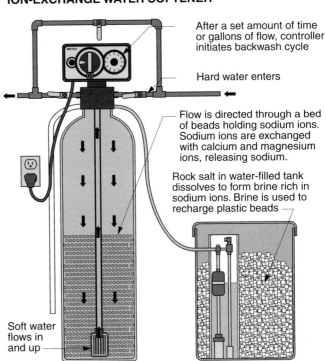

After a set amount of time or gallons of flow, controller initiates backwash cycle

Hard water enters

Flow is directed through a bed of beads holding sodium ions. Sodium ions are exchanged with calcium and magnesium ions, releasing sodium.

Rock salt in water-filled tank dissolves to form brine rich in sodium ions. Brine is used to recharge plastic beads

Soft water flows in and up

Meet the Code

The following is a partial list of requirements from the *2006 International Residential Code (IRC) for One- and Two-Family Dwellings*. Consult the publication for the full text and additional provisions.

Piping Protection (P2603)

Drilling and notching:
- wood structural members not to be drilled, notched, or altered in any structurally unsafe manner
- cutting/notching of flanges and lips of cold-formed steel-framed load-bearing members not permitted
- concealed piping <1½" from edges of studs, joists, or rafters to be protected by ¹⁄₁₆" steel plates

Breakage and corrosion:
- pipes passing through concrete or cinder walls and floors or other corrosive material to be protected by sheathing or wrapping of thickness 0.025" min
- spaces between sleeves and pipes to be filled
- pipe beneath footing or through foundation to be provided with arch or pipe sleeve two sizes greater

Freezing:
- water, soil, or waste pipe not to be installed outside, in exterior walls, attics, or crawl spaces, or in any place subjected to freezing temperature unless protected from freezing by insulation or heat or both
- water service pipe to be installed ≥12" deep and ≥6" below frost line

Trenching and bedding:
- continuous load-bearing support required
- backfill with compacted earth, sand, fine gravel, or similar granular material.
- backfill to be free from rocks for 12" of cover
- trenching parallel to footings not below 45° bearing plane from bottom edge of wall or footing

Support:
- hangers and straps to be of approved material that will not promote galvanic action
- piping to be supported as shown on p. 307

Showers (P2708)

- ≥900 sq in interior area
- ≥30" inside dimension (25" if area ≥1,300 sq in)
- hinged shower doors to open outward
- shower valves to be pressure-balance, thermostatic-mixing, or combination pressure-balance/thermostatic-mixing type set to maximum of 120°F

Protection of Supply (P2902)

- supply system to prevent contamination from nonpotable liquids, solids, or gases
- supply lines and fittings to prevent backflow
- air gap measured from the lowest end of supply outlet to flood level rim of fixture
- air gap to be ≥2x diameter of outlet opening
- dishwashers and clothes washers require air gap devices
- sillcocks and hose bibbs require vacuum breaker

Water Supply System (P2903)

Maximum fixture flow rates:
- lavatory faucet 2.2 gpm at 60 psi
- showerheads 2.5 gpm at 80 psi
- sink faucet 2.2 gpm at 60 psi
- water closet 1.6 gallons per flushing cycle

Pressure:
- minimum 40 psi
- maximum 80 psi
- water-hammer arrestors for quick-closing valves

Service pipe:
- rated at 160 psi at 73°F
- permitted in the same trench with building sewer if sewer of material listed for use within building. If not, service pipe to be separated horizontally by ≥5' earth or on a ledge ≥12" above sewer

Distribution pipe:
- hot-water pipe rated 100 psi at 180°F min
- plastic piping under slabs rated 100 psi at 180°F min

Drainage System (P3005)

Drainage fittings and connections:
- fittings for changes in direction (see p. 319)
- dfu for future fixture rough-ins to be included in determining required drain sizes
- size of the drainage piping shall not be reduced in size in the direction of the flow

Cleanouts:
- must be brass or plastic
- spaced ≤100' in horizontal lines
- at each horizontal fitting with direction change >45°
    Exception: only one cleanout required in 40'
- 3" and 4" cleanouts require 18" clearance
- <3" cleanouts require 12" clearance
- required near bases of vertical waste or soil stacks
- required near building drain and sewer junction

Horizontal drainage piping slope:
- uniform ≥⅛" per 12" for ≥3" piping
- uniform ≥¼" per 12" for ≤2½" piping

Drain pipe sizing: see procedure on p. 318

Vent Terminals (P3103)

- termination ≥6" above roof or snow accumulation
- termination ≥7' where roof is used
- ≥3" diameter where design min temp. ≤0°F
- prohibited <4' beneath door, opening window, or air intake, plus <10' horizontal from such opening unless ≥2' above
- wall terminals to terminate ≥10' from lot line and ≥10' above any point within 10' horizontally
- wall terminals prohibited under roof overhangs with soffit vents

Connections and Grades (P3104)

- vent pipes to drain back to soil or waste pipe
- dry vents to connect above centerline of a horizontal drain pipe
- dry vents to rise ≥6" above flood level rim of highest trap or trapped fixture being vented

Fixture Vents (P3105)

- trap arm length (see p. 322)
- total fall in a fixture drain <pipe diameter
- no vent <two pipe diameters from trap weir

Common Vent (P3107)

- individual vent permitted to vent two traps on the same floor level
- where two drains connect at different levels, vent to connect as an extension of the vertical drain
- upper fixture cannot be a water closet

Wet Venting (P3108)

- any fixture combination in two same-floor bathroom groups may be vented by a horizontal wet vent
- each fixture drain to connect horizontally to the horizontal branch being wet vented or have a dry vent
- dry vent connections to wet vent to be individual or common vent to lavatory, bidet, shower, or bathtub
- upstream fixture drain in vertical wet-vent system to be a dry-vented fixture drain connection
- in horizontal wet-vent systems, only one wet-vented fixture drain can discharge upstream of the dry-vented fixture drain connection
- wet-vent sizing (see p. 324)

Waste Stack Vent P3109)

- vertical between lowest and highest fixture drain
- not to receive water closets or urinals
- stack vent size ≥size of waste stack
- offsets permitted in stack vent ≥6" above flood level of highest fixture

Circuit Venting (P3110)

- maximum of 8 fixtures to be circuit vented.
- connection to be located between the two most upstream fixture drains
- circuit vent pipe to not receive any soil or waste
- slope ≤1 unit vertical in 12 units horizontal
- individually or common-vented fixtures other than circuit-vented fixtures permitted to discharge to horizontal branch if located on the same floor

Wiring

As with most things in life, wiring is scary only if you don't understand it. That is why this chapter begins with a simple analogy between an *electrical circuit* and water in a hose. The theory is simple, but it explains the functions of all of the elements in a typical residential system: *service drop*, *grounding*, *panels and subpanels*, receptacles, and switches.

The code is very particular about how electricity gets from the utility pole to your service entrance box. *Service Drops* illustrates the six possible methods, from temporary service during construction to underground service.

Next we give you an overview of *required circuits* in the code. *Kitchen circuits* and *bathroom circuits* deserve, and get, special attention.

Load Calculations explains how to determine the size of the service entrance your home needs.

Wire and Cable and *Electrical Boxes* explain the color code for wire insulation, the current-carrying capacity of each wire and cable size, and the number of wires electrical boxes are allowed to contain.

Running Cable and *Running Conduit* illustrate the code requirements for the two common ways of getting electricity around the building.

Whether you are adding circuits or troubleshooting a defective circuit, you should find the illustrations in *Wiring Switches, Receptacles, and Lights* a clear guide to which wire goes where.

Finally, we provide you with a checklist to make sure your wiring techniques *meet the code*.

Electrical Circuit

Volts, Amps, and Ohms

A useful analogy can be made between the flow of water and electric current. In the illustration below, the pump creates water pressure in the pipe; the faucet turns the flow on and off; the energy in the falling water is converted to work in the paddle wheel; and the spent (zero-energy) water flows back to the pump intake.

Similarly, in an electrical circuit, a generator creates an electrical pressure (measured in volts); a switch turns the current of electrons (measured in amps) on and off; the current flowing through the motor is converted to physical work; and the spent (zero-energy) current flows back to the generator.

All of the useful theory in residential wiring can be summed up in two simple relationships:

Watts = volts × amps (the power formula)

Amps = volts/ohms (Ohm's law)

The first relationship, the power formula, allows us to convert wattage ratings, found on electric devices such as lights and appliances, to amps of current draw. We need amps because this is the way wires and circuits are sized.

The second relationship, Ohm's law, allows us to understand why lights and appliances may draw different amperage even though connected to the same voltage.

A Water/Electricity Analogy

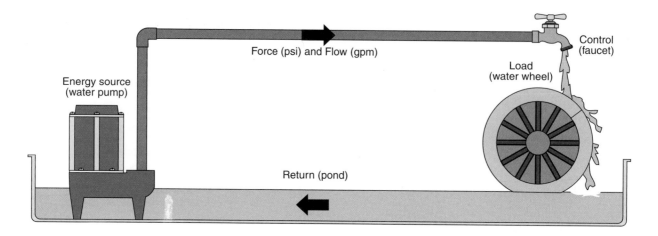

Force (psi) and Flow (gpm)

Energy source (water pump)

Control (faucet)

Load (water wheel)

Return (pond)

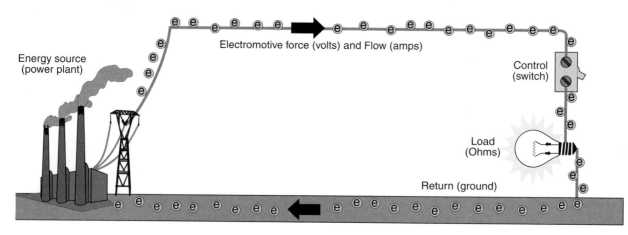

Electromotive force (volts) and Flow (amps)

Energy source (power plant)

Control (switch)

Load (Ohms)

Return (ground)

An Actual Circuit

The utility power lines actually terminate in the home's breaker panel. From there, electricity is distributed to individual circuits, each protected by circuit breakers against overload.

This 120 VAC (volts alternating current) circuit serves multiple loads, of which two are shown in the illustration below.

The first load is a 60-watt lamp having an electrical resistance of 240 Ohms. By Ohm's law, the lamp draws 0.5 amps

Amps = 120V/240 Ohms = 0.5

The switch connects the lamp into or out of the circuit, thereby turning the lamp on or off.

The second load is a 1,200-watt toaster (which can be read from the label under the appliance). From the power formula on the facing page, we can calculate the current the toaster draws:

Amps = Watts/volts = 1,200/120 = 10

The receptacle provides a convenient way to connect a portable load—here the toaster—into a circuit.

The number of receptacles and loads in a circuit is limited only by the total current drawn.

A Simple Electrical Circuit

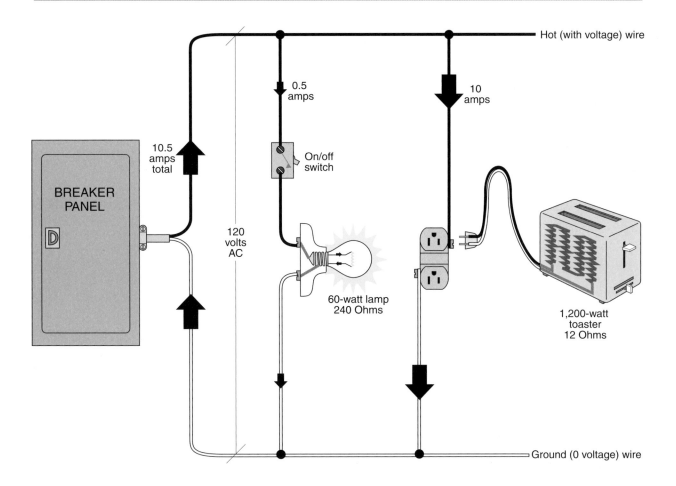

Service Drops

The *service drop* is the portion of wiring from the electric utility company's secondary distribution system (generally overhead wires on poles) to the first point of attachment on the building.

The *service entrance conductors* are the wires extending from the point of attachment of the service drop to the building's *service entrance equipment* (service entrance box).

The information presented here is based on the National Electrical Code. All local utilities adhere to the code, but some have even stricter requirements. So check with your local utility before installing a service drop or entrance.

The type of service installed depends on capacity (maximum amps), height of the building, type of exterior building surface, and whether the owner or zoning calls for underground service.

The illustrations on the following pages show the specifications for various types of servIce:

Temporary Service is used while a building is under construction. It generally ceases as soon as the building's service entrance equipment has been installed and inspected.

Cable Service is commonly used on wood-sided buildings when the building height is sufficient to provide the required clearance above the ground.

Conduit Service is used for capacities over 200 amps and for buildings with metal, stucco, or masonry siding. The conduit may be made of steel, aluminum, or PVC plastic.

Rigid Steel Masts are used when the building is too low to provide clearance for the service drop.

Mobile-Home Service is used when the building (in most cases a mobile home) is temporary, subject to excessive movement, or structurally inadequate to support a rigid steel mast.

Underground service is provided at the owner's discretion (and added cost sometimes) or to comply with local zoning.

Minimum clearances for all service drops are as follows:

- 10 feet above ground.
- 10 feet above sidewalks.
- 15 feet above residential driveways.
- 18 feet above public ways (streets).

A 120/240 VAC Service Drop

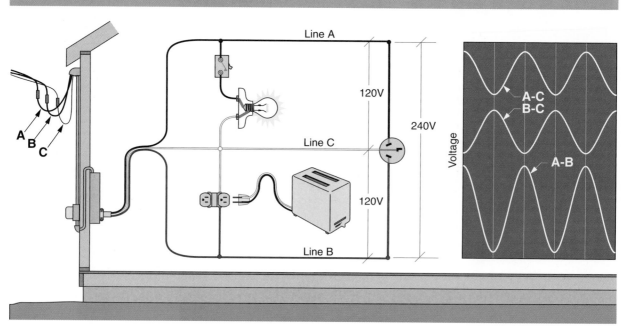

Temporary Service

Suitable tree or building may be substituted for pole

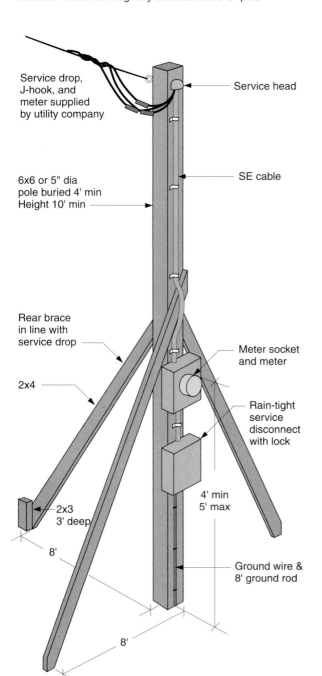

Service drop, J-hook, and meter supplied by utility company

Service head

6x6 or 5" dia pole buried 4' min Height 10' min

SE cable

Rear brace in line with service drop

2x4

Meter socket and meter

Rain-tight service disconnect with lock

2x3 3' deep

8'

4' min 5' max

Ground wire & 8' ground rod

8'

Cable Service to 200 Amps

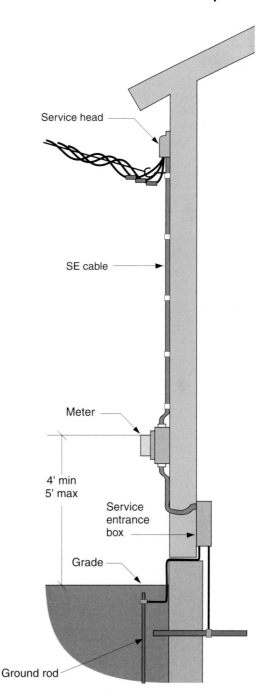

Service head

SE cable

Meter

4' min 5' max

Service entrance box

Grade

Ground rod

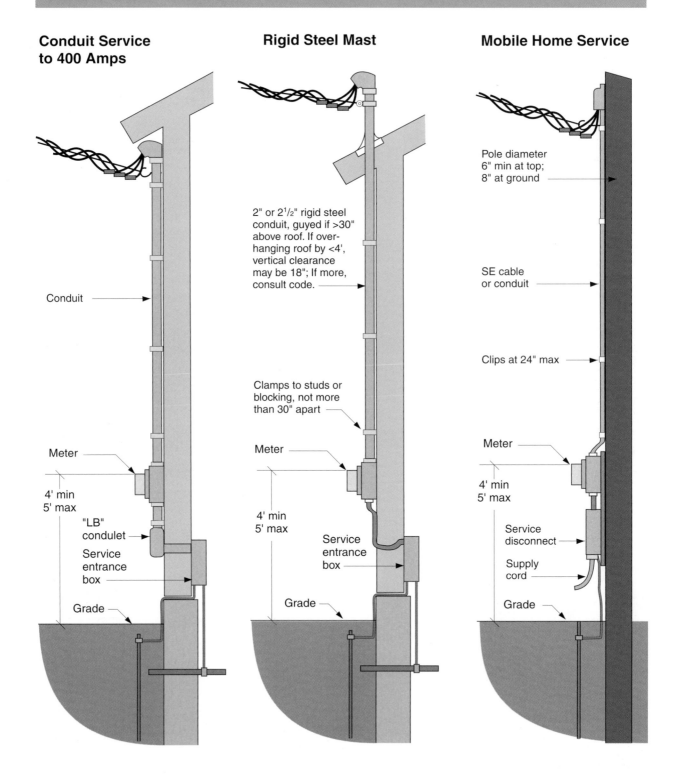

Conduit Service to 400 Amps

Conduit

Meter

4' min
5' max

"LB" condulet

Service entrance box

Grade

Rigid Steel Mast

2" or 2¹/₂" rigid steel conduit, guyed if >30" above roof. If over-hanging roof by <4', vertical clearance may be 18"; If more, consult code.

Clamps to studs or blocking, not more than 30" apart

Meter

4' min
5' max

Service entrance box

Grade

Mobile Home Service

Pole diameter 6" min at top; 8" at ground

SE cable or conduit

Clips at 24" max

Meter

4' min
5' max

Service disconnect

Supply cord

Grade

Underground Service to 400 Amps

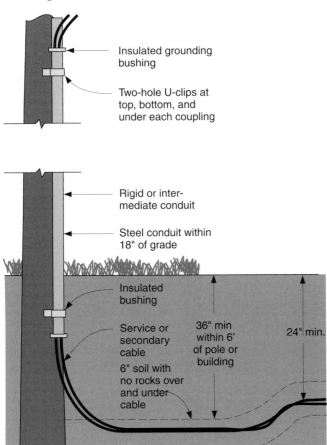

Insulated grounding bushing

Two-hole U-clips at top, bottom, and under each coupling

Rigid or inter-mediate conduit

Steel conduit within 18" of grade

Insulated bushing

Service or secondary cable

36" min within 6' of pole or building

6" soil with no rocks over and under cable

24" min.

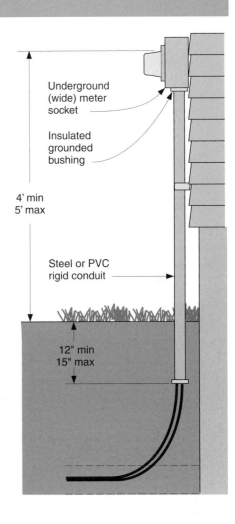

Underground (wide) meter socket

Insulated grounded bushing

4' min
5' max

Steel or PVC rigid conduit

12" min
15" max

PRIMARY CABLE (OVER 240 VOLTS)

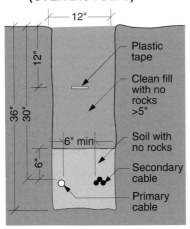

12"

12"

36"
30"

6" min

6"

Plastic tape

Clean fill with no rocks >5"

Soil with no rocks

Secondary cable

Primary cable

SECONDARY CABLE (UP TO 240 VOLTS)

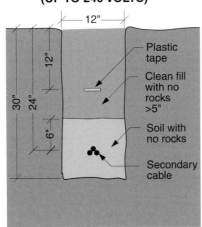

12"

12"

30"
24"

6"

Plastic tape

Clean fill with no rocks >5"

Soil with no rocks

Secondary cable

JOINT ELECTRIC AND TELEPHONE

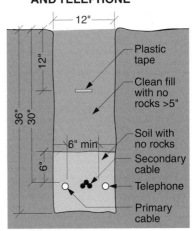

12"

12"

36"
30"

6" min

6"

Plastic tape

Clean fill with no rocks >5"

Soil with no rocks

Secondary cable

Telephone

Primary cable

Grounding

Because the electrical system uses the earth as its return path, and because the human body is quite electrically conductive (due to its salt content), a person standing on the ground and touching a live wire may serve as a current path. If the current is great enough, it can cause the heart muscle to spasm and possibly lead to death.

The current is especially dangerous when it flows through the chest from arm to arm. Current flow is also greater when shoes are absent or wet and when the ground (including a concrete slab-on-grade) is wet. For these reasons electricians are careful to wear rubber-soled shoes, stand on a dry surface, and sometimes work with one hand behind their backs.

The better solution, however, is the grounded circuit, as shown on the facing page.

An Ungrounded Circuit Poses Risk of Electrocution

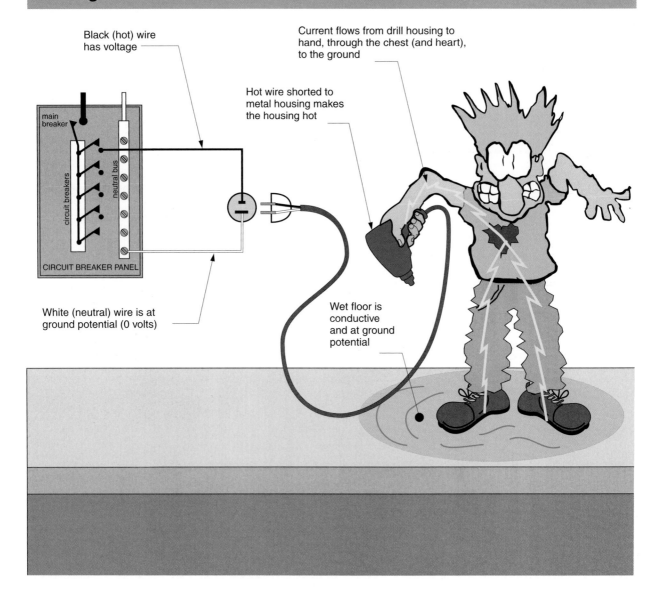

Black (hot) wire has voltage

Current flows from drill housing to hand, through the chest (and heart), to the ground

Hot wire shorted to metal housing makes the housing hot

main breaker

circuit breakers

neutral bus

CIRCUIT BREAKER PANEL

White (neutral) wire is at ground potential (0 volts)

Wet floor is conductive and at ground potential

Grounding a circuit consists of adding a bare or green "grounding wire" to the black (hot) and white (neutral) wires.

The grounding wire and the neutral wire connect, in the service entrance box, to a neutral bus bar, which is further connected to either an underground metal water pipe or a metal rod driven into the ground.

Connected to the metal cabinet or housing of appliances and tools, the grounding wire provides a path to ground in case the housing becomes live.

In the illustration below, the drill housing is connected directly to ground through the grounding wire, so short-circuit current now flows safely to ground through it rather than through the operator's body.

Grounded, the Same Circuit Is Safe

A bare (sometimes green) grounding wire provides a safe path to ground for the metallic housings of fixtures, tools, and appliances

Drill housing connected to ground through grounding wire, so short-circuit current flows to ground instead of operator's body

main breaker

circuit breakers

neutral bus

Grounding and neutral wires connected to neutral bus, then to a metal water pipe or ground rod

Panels

The main distribution panel provides a single, convenient location for controlling all of the electricity usage in a building. This is an important safety consideration for anyone working on the wiring anywhere downstream of the main circuit breaker.

Main Distribution Panel

One bare (neutral) and two black (hot) wires (the SE cable) enter from the meter and service-disconnect box outside the building

SE Cable

Double-pole main breaker disconnects all power

200A

One hot wire feeds Bus A; the other feeds Bus B

Bus A

Bus B

Circuit breakers plug into either Bus A or Bus B

Alternating prongs mean that adjacent breakers are on different buses

20
20
15
20
20
15
20

ON ON ON ON ON ON ON

ON ON ON ON ON ON ON

30
30
20
15
20
20
20

240-VAC circuits created with double-pole breakers plugged into both bus bars

15 amp or 20 amp circuits

Neutral and grounding wires connect to neutral bus bars

Neutral buses

Jumper cable or strap connects the two neutral buses

Ground cable from neutral bus connects to metal water pipe or metal rod in ground

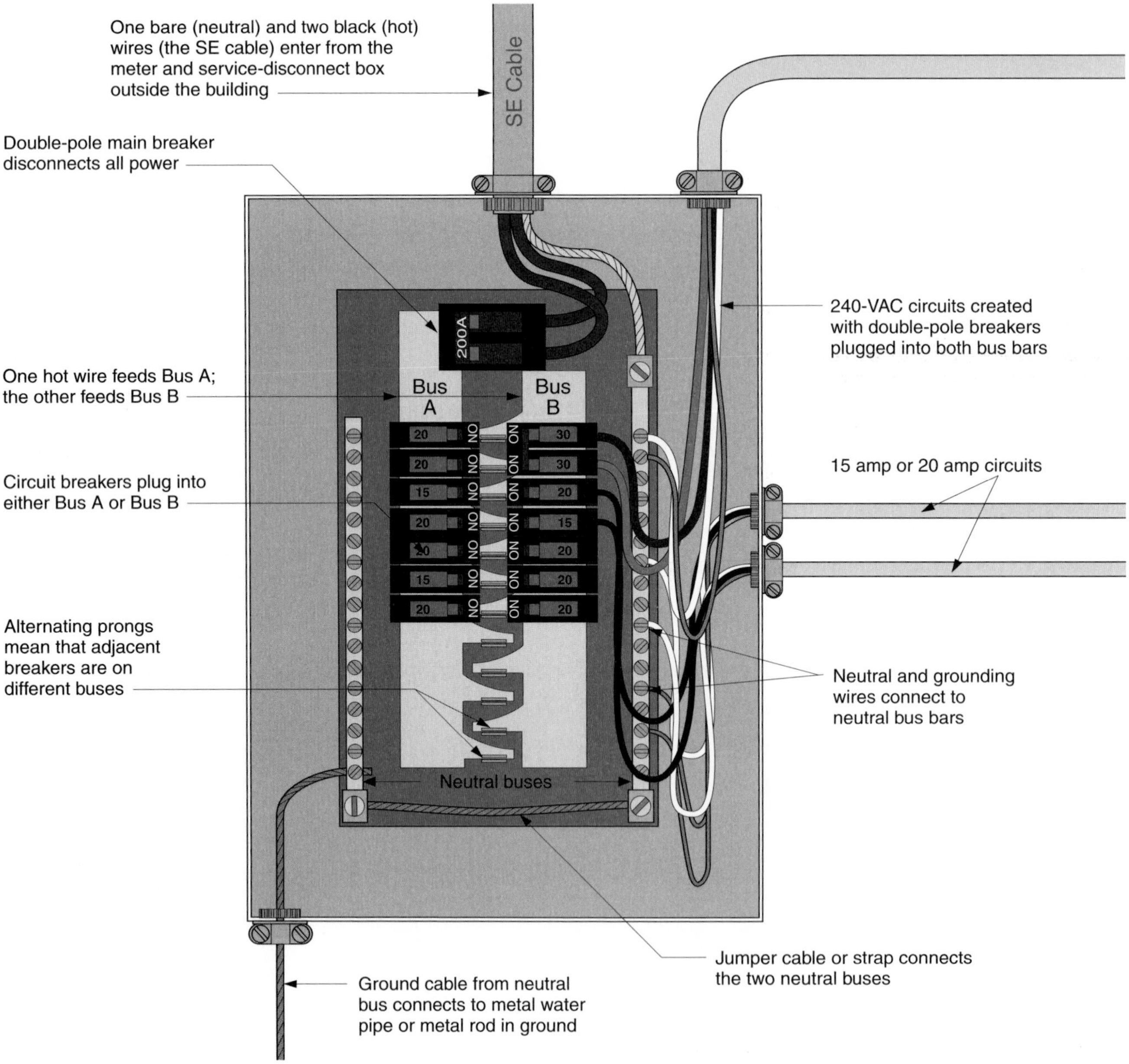

Subpanels (there may be any number) reduce the cost of wiring by eliminating long runs for individual circuits back to the main panel. They also provide the safety feature of being able to turn off all of the circuits in the area they serve, such as a workshop, a separate apartment, or an outbuilding.

Subpanel (Fed by Main Panel at Left)

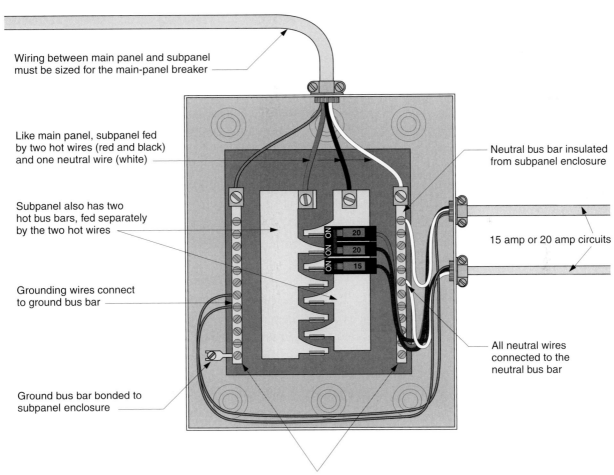

Wiring between main panel and subpanel must be sized for the main-panel breaker

Like main panel, subpanel fed by two hot wires (red and black) and one neutral wire (white)

Neutral bus bar insulated from subpanel enclosure

Subpanel also has two hot bus bars, fed separately by the two hot wires

15 amp or 20 amp circuits

Grounding wires connect to ground bus bar

All neutral wires connected to the neutral bus bar

Ground bus bar bonded to subpanel enclosure

In subpanel, the ground bus bar, fed by a bare grounding wire from the main panel, is not connected to the neutral bus bar

Required Circuits

The IRC requires breaking a building's load into several categories and many individual breaker-protected circuits.

Lighting

The Code requires a lighting allowance of 3 watts per square foot of living space. A 15A circuit can carry 15A ×120V, or 1,800 watts. The requirement is thus one 15A circuit for every 600 square feet.

Because much lighting is with lamps plugged into receptacles, "lighting circuits" may also include the general-purpose receptacles in a room. In any habitable room, no point along a wall may be further than 6 feet horizontally from a receptacle. This includes any wall 2 feet or more in width, peninsulas, islands, and freestanding railings.

Small Appliances

Small kitchen-type appliances draw more power than lamps and radios, so the Code requires two 20A circuits in the area of kitchen, pantry, and dining room. Except for a kitchen clock and the oven light/ignition system of a gas range, no lighting may be on these circuits. Although the circuits are rated 20A, receptacles may be rated either 15A or 20A.

Individual Appliances

Larger, power-hungry appliances should be served by separate circuits. These include clothes washer, clothes dryer, dishwasher, waste disposer, water heater, water pump, electric range, electric wall oven, electric cooktop, oil burner, furnace blower, any permanently connected appliance over 1,000 watts, and any permanently connected motor over ⅛ horsepower.

Safety

In locations where water, metal plumbing, or earth make electric shock potentially more lethal, receptacles are required to be protected by GFCI (grand fault circuit interrupter) circuit breakers. A GFCI can protect just one receptacle (at the point of use) or a whole circuit (installed in the service box).

The Code specifies the following GFCI locations: kitchen counters within 6 feet of a sink, bathrooms, garages (whether attached or separate), unfinished basements, crawl spaces, around swimming pools, and outdoor decks, patios, and porches. At a minimum, protected exterior receptacles are required at both front and rear of the house.

As a safety precaution against fire, all receptacles in sleeping areas (bedrooms) must now be protected by arc-fault circuit breakers.

Room Lighting and Receptacles

Kitchen The kitchen requires two separate 20A small-appliance receptacle circuits. Receptacles should be located 6 to 10 inches above counter surfaces so that no point of the counter is more than 24 inches from a receptacle. Peninsulas and islands are exceptions, requiring just one receptacle each. Remember that receptacles within 6 feet of a sink must be GFCI-protected. Lighting in a kitchen should be both general (one or more overhead fixtures) and task (under wall cabinets or spots from ceiling) to illuminate work surfaces. If there are two entrances to the kitchen the overhead lights should be controlled by a pair of three-way switches.

Dining Room and Pantry At least one of the two kitchen small-appliance circuits must make an appearance in any adjacent dining room, breakfast area, or pantry.

Bathrooms A GFCI-protected receptacle must be provided within 36 inches of all lavatories (bathroom sinks). A switch-operated ceiling fixture and lights to either side of each lavatory generally provide effective lighting. An important, but often overlooked, prohibition is ceiling fixtures and ceiling fans within 3 feet horizontally and 8 feet vertically of tubs and showers.

Living Rooms The "no more than 6 feet from a receptacle" rule applies here. Plan to ensure that receptacles don't fall behind couches and that there will always be a convenient receptacle for vacuuming. Living room lighting can be provided

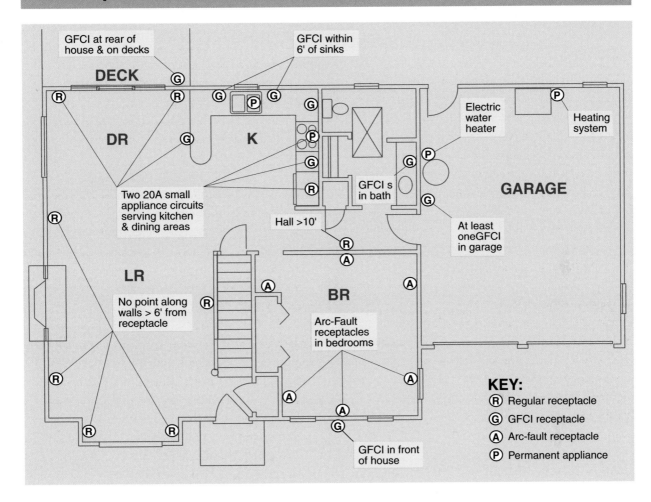

GFCI at rear of house & on decks

GFCI within 6' of sinks

DECK

DR

K

Two 20A small appliance circuits serving kitchen & dining areas

GFCI s in bath

Hall >10'

Electric water heater

Heating system

GARAGE

At least oneGFCI in garage

LR

No point along walls > 6' from receptacle

BR

Arc-Fault receptacles in bedrooms

GFCI in front of house

KEY:
- (R) Regular receptacle
- (G) GFCI receptacle
- (A) Arc-fault receptacle
- (P) Permanent appliance

either by a switch-controlled ceiling light, or by switch-controlled receptacles into which lamps are plugged. A common practice is to switch just the top or bottom halves of several lighting receptacles. Again, if the room has more than one entrance, use three-way switches so the lights can be switched on and off again as you pass through the room.

Bedrooms Again, the 6-foot rule for receptacles, except this time they must be protected by arc-fault circuit breakers. Lighting should be as in living rooms.

Closets There should be a light in every closet, but incandescent bulbs must be enclosed in fixtures (bare fluorescent bulbs are OK). In any case, the light fixture must be separated from stored clothes and other objects by a minimum of 12 inches horizontally and vertically. Separation may be reduced to 6 inches for recessed fixtures.

Stairways For safety's sake, make sure every step is illuminated. Stairway lights should, without exception, be controlled by three-way switches at top and bottom landings.

Garages The Code requires garage receptacles, except for garage-door openers and those dedicated to appliances, to be GFCI-protected (a minimum of one). At least one switch-controlled light should be provided, preferably three-way-controlled from both the house and the entrance door to the garage.

Kitchen Circuits

Placement of Kitchen Receptacles

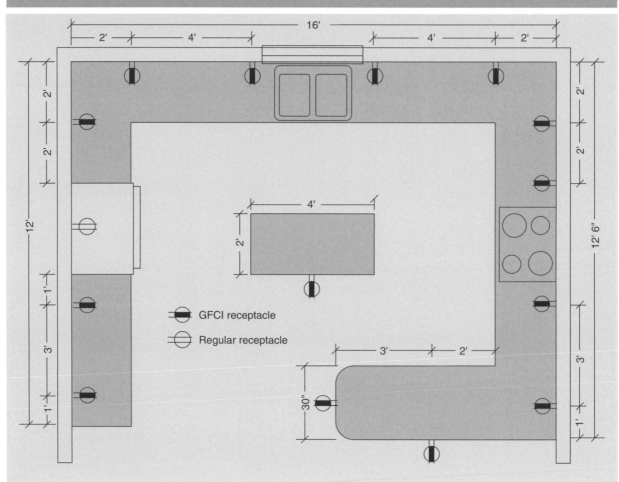

GFCI receptacle

Regular receptacle

ISLANDS AND PENINSULAS

1. Face-up receptacles prohibited
2. Prohibited if A >12"
3. OK
4. Prohibited if B > 6"
5. Prohibited if C > 20"
6. Prohibited where above-counter mounting is possible

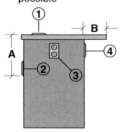

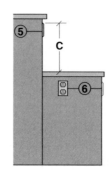

COUNTER BEHIND SINKS

7. Receptacle required within 24"
8. Receptacle not required if D < 18"
9. Receptacle not required if E < 12"

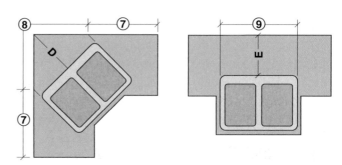

Bathroom Circuits

Dedicated GFCI-Protected Circuit

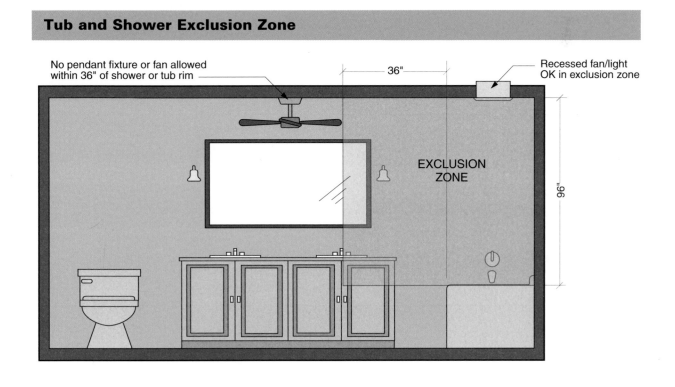

GFCI feeds all fixtures and receptacles in bathroom only

Dedicated branch circuit serves bathroom only

Tub and Shower Exclusion Zone

No pendant fixture or fan allowed within 36" of shower or tub rim

Recessed fan/light OK in exclusion zone

36"

EXCLUSION ZONE

96"

Load Calculations

The IRC specifies a method for computing a *building's electrical load*, which then determines the required capacity of the service entrance and service entrance cable:

1. Compute the *heating, ventilating, and air-conditioning (HVAC) load*, which is the larger of 65 percent of central electric heating (not including electric baseboards) or 100 percent of air conditioning (AC).

2. List and total the *other loads*: baseboard or radiant electric heating, general lighting at 3 watts per square foot, small-appliance circuits at 1,500 watts each, and the other remaining major appliances.

3. Compute the *total derated load*, which is 10,000 watts, plus 40 percent of the total of other loads less 10,000 watts, plus the HVAC load.

4. Find the required service entrance amperage by dividing total derated load by 240 volts.

The example below demonstrates the method for a typical electrically heated house.

Appliance wattages are always listed on the equipment nameplate, which is usually found on the back or the bottom of the appliance. Alternatively, use the figures from the table on the facing page.

Example Building-Load Calculation

Load		Calculation	Watts
HVAC	65% of central electric heat (none)	0.65	0
	100% of 35,000 Btu/hr AC (5,000 watts)	1.00 × 5,000	5,000
		Total HVAC Load	5,000
Other Loads	Electric baseboard, 70 lin ft	70 × 250 watts/ft	17,500
	General lighting for 2,000 sq ft	2,000 sq ft × 3 watts/sq ft	6,000
	Small appliances, 2 circuits	2 × 1,500 watts	3,000
	Laundry circuit	1 × 1,500 watts	1,500
	Clothes dryer		5,800
	Water heater		4,500
	Range/oven		12,000
		Total Other Loads	50,300
Derated Load	10,000 watts		10,000
	0.40 × (Total Other Loads – 10,000 watts)	0.40 × 40,300	16,120
	Total HVAC Load		5,000
		Total Derated Load	31,120

Service amps = Total Derated Load ÷ 240 volts

= 31,120 ÷ 240

= 130 amps (150-amp service entrance)

Typical Appliance Wattages

Appliance	Spacing	Watts		Appliance	Spacing	Watts
Air conditioner	Room, 7,000 Btu/hr	800		Humidifier	Portable	80
	Central, 35,000 Btu/hr	5,000		Iron		1,100
Aquarium	Small	100		Light bulb		wattage
	Large	500		Microwave	smallest	800
Blender		375			medium	1,200
Clothes dryer	Electric	5,000			largest	1,800
	Gas	500		Mixer		200
Clothes washer		500		Motor, running	¼ hp	600
Coffee maker		1,000			⅓ hp	660
Computer	CPU	100			½ hp	840
	monitor	150			¾ hp	1,140
	Laptop	50			1 hp	1,320
Copy machine		1,500			1½ hp	1,820
Dehumidifier	25 pint/day	575			2 hp	2,400
Dishwasher		1,200			3 hp	3,360
DVD player		25		Projector	Slide	500
Electric blanket	Single	60			LCD	300
	Double	100		Range	Electric	12,000
Electric heat	Baseboard/foot	250			Gas	100
Fan	Attic	500		Refrigerator	Frost-free	350
	Bath	100			Regular	300
	Kitchen	250		Sewing machine		90
	Ceiling	50		Stereo	40 watts/channel	225
	Window, 20-in	275		Sunlamp		275
Freezer		500		Television	21-in CRT	120
Fryer, deep fat		1,500			32-in LCD	140
Frying pan		1,200			40-in plasma	300
Furnace	Blower	1,000			50-in plasma	400
	Burner	300		Toaster oven		1,200
Garbage disposer		400		Vacuum cleaner		650
Hair curler		1,200		Waffle iron	Single	600
Hair dryer		1,200			Double	1,200
Heat lamp		250		Water bed	Heater/no cover	200
Heater	Portable radiant	1,500		Water heater		4,500
Heating pad		75		Water pump	Shallow	660
Hot plate	Per burner	800			Deep	1,320

Wire and Cable

Color Code

The Code specifies the colors of wire insulation so that it is obvious which wires serve which functions (hot, neutral, or grounding):

Black—hot; connects to the darkest terminal screw on a receptacle or switch

Red—second hot wire when there are two, as in a 240-volt circuit

White—neutral wire; connects to the silver terminal screw on a receptacle or switch

Bar or green—grounding wire; connects to the green-tinted screw on a receptacle, switch, fixture, or appliance.

The Code allows a white wire to be used as a black wire if its end is visibly painted or taped black.

Wire and Cable Types

All wire insulation must also be labeled, identifying the type of insulation:

H—heat resistant

R—rubber

T—thermoplastic

W—water resistant

All wire insulation must also be labeled, identifying the type of insulation:

AC—armored (metal jacket) cable

C—corrosion resistant

F—feeder

NM—nonmetallic

U—underground

SE—service entrance

Wire (Single-Lead) Labels

Wire Type	Label	Specifications
Thermoplastic vinyl	T	General purpose to 140°F (60°C)
	TW	General purpose to 140°F (60°C) and water resistant
	THW	General purpose to 167°F (75°C) and water resistant
Rubber	R	General purpose indoor-only to 140°F (60°C)
	RW	General purpose indoor-only to 140°F (60°C) and water resistant
Rubber and cotton braid	RH	General purpose to 167°F (75°C)
	RHH	General purpose to 194°F (90°C)
	RHW	General purpose to 167°F (75°C) and water resistant
	RH/RW	General purpose to 167°F (75°C) dry and 140°F (60°C) wet
Cotton braid	WP	Weatherproof for overhead outdoors

Cable (Multiple-Lead) Labels

Wire Type	Label	Specifications
Thermoplastic vinyl	T	General purpose to 140°F (60°C)
	TW	General purpose to 140°F (60°C) and water resistant
	THW	General purpose to 167°F (75°C) and water resistant
Rubber	R	General purpose indoor-only to 140°F (60°C)
	RW	General purpose indoor-only to 140°F (60°C) and water resistant
Rubber and cotton braid	RH	General purpose to 167°F (75°C)
Cotton braid	WP	Weatherproof for overhead outdoors

Ampacity

Because all wire has electrical resistance, the flow of electrons (current) generates heat and raises the temperature of the conductor, posing a fire danger. The IRC specifies the current-carrying capacity (ampacity) of wires depending on their size, insulation type, and temperature rating, as shown in the table below.

Ampacity of Copper Wire in Cable and Conduit

	Conductor Temperature Rating					
	60°C	75°C	90°C	60°C	75°C	90°C
		RHW. THHW THW, THWN, XHHW, USE	RHW-2, THHN, THHW THW-2, THWN-2 XHHW, XHHW-2, USE-2		RHW. THHW THW, THWN, XHHW, USE	RHW-2, THHN, THHW THW-2, THWN-2 XHHW, XHHW-2, USE-2
	TW, UF			TW, UF		
Size, AWG	Copper			Aluminum or Copper-Clad Aluminum		
18	—	—	14	—	—	—
16	—	—	18	—	—	—
14	20	20	25	—	—	—
12	25	25	30	20	20	25
10	30	35	40	25	30	35
8	40	50	55	30	40	45
6	55	65	75	40	50	60
4	70	85	95	55	65	75
3	85	100	110	65	75	85
2	95	115	130	75	90	100
1	110	130	150	85	100	115
1/0	125	150	170	100	120	135
2/0	145	175	195	115	135	150
3/0	165	200	225	130	155	175
4/0	195	230	260	150	180	205

Recommended Maximum Length of Branch Circuits, Ft

| | Circuit Amperage | | | | | | |
Size, AWG	5	10	15	20	30	40	50
14	234	117	78	—	—	—	—
12	517	187	124	93	—	—	—
10	595	298	198	149	99	—	—
8	—	—	—	236	157	118	—
6	—	—	—	—	—	183	146
4	—	—	—	—	—	—	234

Electrical Boxes

All wire connections, whether to switches, receptacles, and light fixtures or as junctions between branch circuits, must be made within a code-approved box having an approved cover plate. The code specifies the number of conductors allowed on the basis of box volume.

By conductor, the code means anything that occupies an equivalent volume. To arrive at the number of conductors, add the following:

- each wire terminating in the box.
- each wire running unbroken through the box.
- each device, such as a switch or receptacle.
- each cable clamp or fixture stud.
- all grounding wires lumped as one.

Box volume is usually stamped on the box. If not, compute the volume from the inside dimensions. Box extensions and covers having volume add to the total volume.

The table below lists the conductor capacities of most available boxes.

Maximum Number of Conductors in Metal Boxes

Box Dimensions, in	Capacity, cu in	Maximum Number of Conductors[1]						
		No. 18	No. 16	No. 14	No. 12	No. 10	No. 8	No. 6
4 × 1¼ round or octagonal	12.5	8	7	6	5	5	4	2
4 × 1½ round or octagonal	15.5	10	8	7	6	6	5	3
4 × 2⅛ round or octagonal	21.5	14	12	10	9	8	7	4
4 × 1¼ square	18.0	12	10	9	8	7	6	3
4 × 1½ square	21.0	14	12	10	9	8	7	4
4 × 2⅛ square	30.3	20	17	15	13	12	10	6
4¹¹⁄₁₆ × 1¼ square	25.5	17	14	12	11	10	8	5
4¹¹⁄₁₆ × 1½ square	29.5	19	16	14	13	11	9	5
4¹¹⁄₁₆ × 2⅛ square	42.0	28	24	21	18	16	14	8
3 × 2 × 1½ device	7.5	5	4	3	3	3	2	1
3 × 2 × 2 device	10.0	6	5	5	4	4	3	2
3 × 2 × 2¼ device	10.5	7	6	5	4	4	3	2
3 × 2 × 2½ device	12.5	8	7	6	5	5	4	2
3 × 2 × 1¾ device	14.0	9	8	7	6	5	4	2
3 × 2 × 3½ device	18.0	12	10	9	8	7	6	3
4 × 2⅛ × 1½ device	10.3	6	5	5	4	4	3	2
4 × 2⅛ × 1⅞ device	13.0	8	7	6	5	5	4	2
4 × 2⅛ × 2⅛ device	14.5	9	8	7	6	5	4	2
3¾ × 2 × 2½ masonry box/gang	14.0	9	8	7	6	5	4	2
3¾ × 2 × 3½ masonry box/gang	21.0	14	12	10	9	8	7	4

[1]Where no volume allowances are made for clamps, fixture studs, hickeys, etc. as described in IRC Sections E3805.12.2.2 through E3805.12.2.5.

Common Electrical Boxes

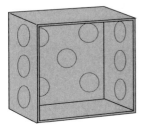

Square

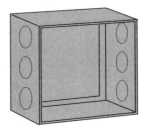

Square extender

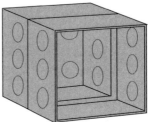

Square box with extender

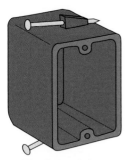

Plastic handy box

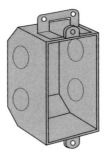

Bevelled switch

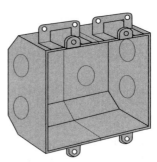

Ganged bevelled switch

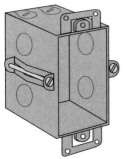

Box with ears and clamps

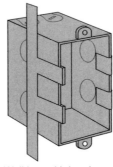

Wall box with brackets

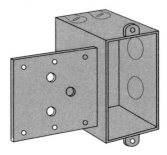

Box with side bracket

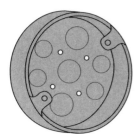

Round pancake

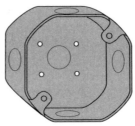

Octagon box

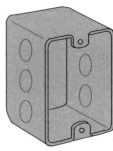

Metal handy box

Running Cable

With nonmetallic (NM) cable and plastic boxes, running cable through walls and ceilings is fairly simple. The more difficult part is fitting batt insulation around the cable and boxes.

The illustration below shows the key provisions in the International Residential Code:

- staple within 8 inches of a plastic box.
- staple within 12 inches of a metal box.

- staple every 4 feet 6 inches minimum along framing.
- bore holes in middle of framing.
- cable within 1¼ inches of stud face to be protected by 18 gauge metal plate.
- radius of cable bends 5 × cable diameter, minimum.

Rules for ceilings and floors are illustrated on the facing page.

Running NM Cable in Walls

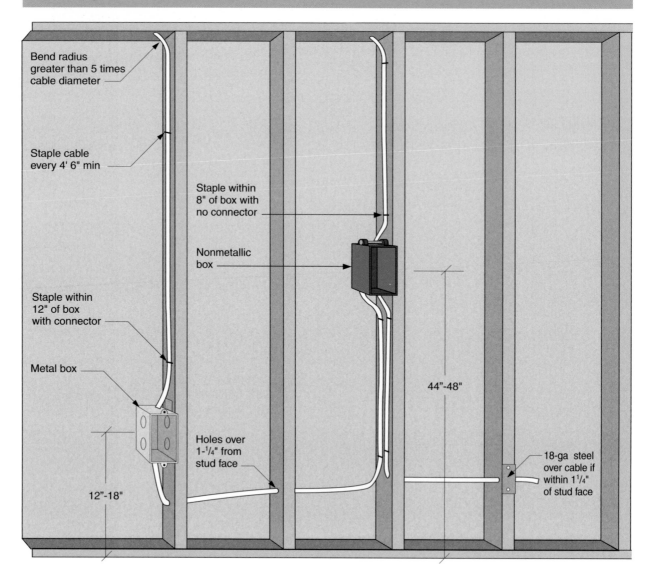

Bend radius greater than 5 times cable diameter

Staple cable every 4' 6" min

Staple within 8" of box with no connector

Nonmetallic box

Staple within 12" of box with connector

Metal box

Holes over 1-¼" from stud face

44"-48"

12"-18"

18-ga steel over cable if within 1¼" of stud face

Running NM Cable in Floors and Ceilings

UNFINISHED BASEMENT CEILING

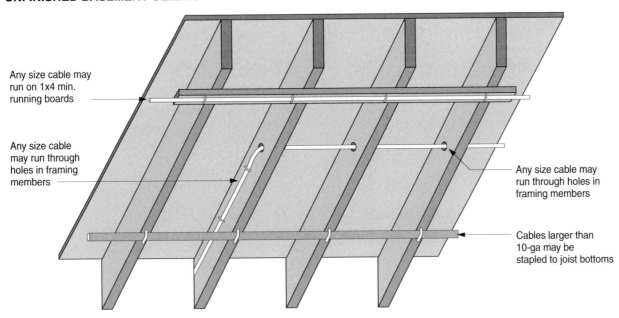

Any size cable may run on 1x4 min. running boards

Any size cable may run through holes in framing members

Any size cable may run through holes in framing members

Cables larger than 10-ga may be stapled to joist bottoms

ATTIC FLOOR WITHOUT LADDER OR STAIRS

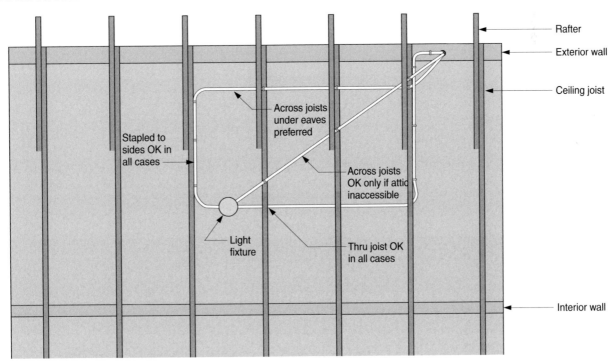

Rafter

Exterior wall

Ceiling joist

Stapled to sides OK in all cases

Across joists under eaves preferred

Across joists OK only if attic inaccessible

Light fixture

Thru joist OK in all cases

Interior wall

Running Conduit

The International Residential Code calls for wires to be protected by conduit when run through concrete or when otherwise exposed to physical damage. Two types of conduit predominate in residential construction: electrical metallic tubing (EMT) and Schedule 80 PVC rigid nonmetallic conduit (RNC).

EMT is the easiest to use and the most common. All conduit comes in straight 10-foot lengths and must be connected using only fittings appropriate for the application. Fittings (see the illustrations on the facing page) are designed for either dry inside locations or wet outside locations. Outside fittings may be used either inside or outside.

Rules for Running Conduit

- Conduit is always run before the wire it will contain. Wires are pulled though the conduit one section at a time, using a special pulling wire.
- A special pulling fitting must be provided for every 360 degrees of accumulated bend in the conduit.

- Metal conduit is grounded, so no separate grounding wire is required; the white grounded-neutral wire is required, however.
- The size of a conduit is dictated by the number and type of wires it contains (see tables below).

Bending EMT

Always use a conduit bender specifically designed for the size conduit being installed. The illustration on the facing page show the operation of bending conduit:

1. Measure half the desired finished distance of the bend. This is usually the distance to a wall.

2. For $\frac{1}{2}$-inch conduit, add $2\frac{1}{4}$ inches to the finished distance and mark the conduit. For other sizes see the markings on the conduit bender.

3. Line up the mark with the arrow on the bender, and pull back until the conduit makes a 90 degree angle with no pull on the bender handle.

Maximum Number of Conductors in Electrical Metallic Tubing (EMT)

Wire Type	Size, AWG	$\frac{1}{2}$	$\frac{3}{4}$	1	Trade Size, in $1\frac{1}{4}$	$1\frac{1}{2}$	2
TW 1/2	14	8	15	25	43	58	96
	12	6	11	19	33	45	74
	10	5	8	14	24	33	55
	8	2	5	8	13	18	30
	6	1	3	4	8	11	18
	4	1	1	3	6	8	13
	2	1	1	2	4	6	10
	1	1	1	1	3	4	7
THW	14	6	10	16	28	39	64
	12	4	8	13	23	31	51
	10	3	6	10	18	24	40
	8	1	4	6	10	14	24
	6	1	3	4	8	11	18
	4	1	1	3	6	8	13
	2	1	1	2	4	6	10
	1	1	1	1	3	4	7

Conduit Fittings

INSIDE (DRY) USE ONLY

Coupling

90° bushed elbow

Set-screw connector

LB condulet

Offset connector

Pulling elbow

OUTSIDE (WET) USE

Coupling

90° connector

Connector

LB condulet

Offset connector

LL or LR condulet

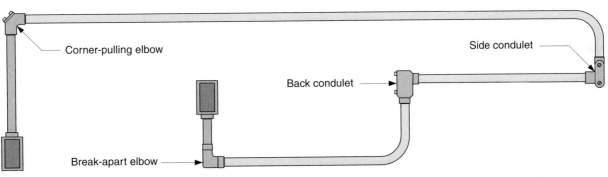

Corner-pulling elbow

Side condulet

Back condulet

Break-apart elbow

Bending Conduit

BENDING CONDUIT

Length required

Length + 2¼"
(for ½" EMT)

Finished length

MAKING A KICKBEND (OFFSET)

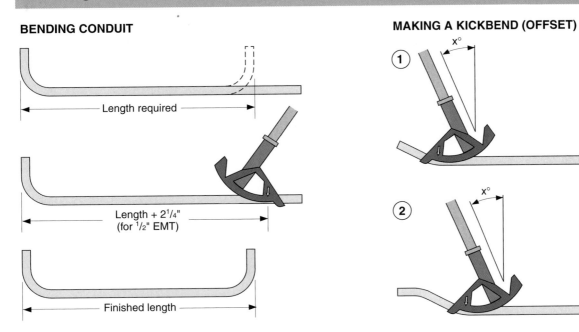

① x°

② x°

Receptacles

Receptacle Types

120 VAC RECEPTACLE

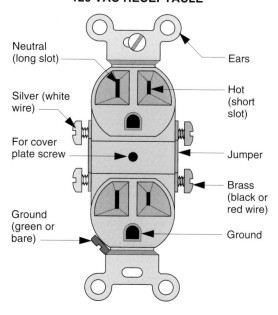

Neutral (long slot)

Ears

Silver (white wire)

Hot (short slot)

For cover plate screw

Jumper

Brass (black or red wire)

Ground (green or bare)

Ground

GROUND FAULT (GFCI) RECEPTACLE

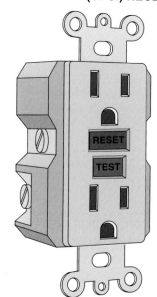

RESET

TEST

OTHER COMMON RECEPTACLES

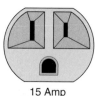

15 Amp
120 Volt

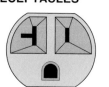

20 Amp
120 Volt

20 Amp
240 Volt

30 Amp
240 Volt

30 Amp
120/240 Volt

50 Amp
120/240 Volt

HOW THE GFCI WORKS

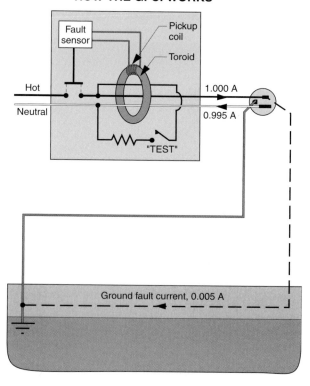

Fault sensor

Pickup coil

Toroid

Hot

1.000 A

Neutral

0.995 A

"TEST"

Ground fault current, 0.005 A

Switches

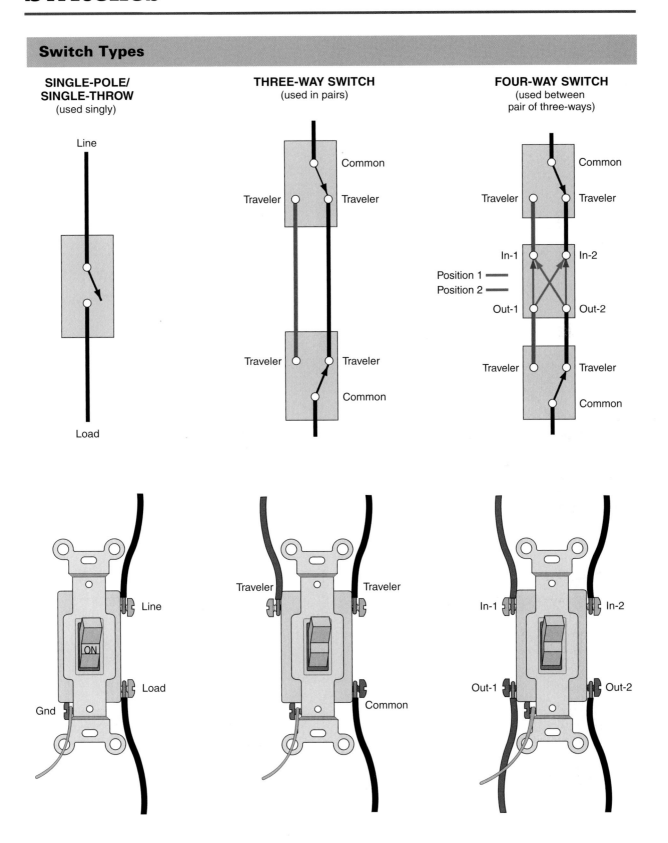

**SINGLE-POLE/
SINGLE-THROW**
(used singly)

Line

Load

THREE-WAY SWITCH
(used in pairs)

Common

Traveler   Traveler

Traveler   Traveler

Common

FOUR-WAY SWITCH
(used between
pair of three-ways)

Common

Traveler   Traveler

In-1   In-2

Position 1
Position 2

Out-1   Out-2

Traveler   Traveler

Common

Line

ON

Load

Gnd

Traveler   Traveler

Common

In-1   In-2

Out-1   Out-2

Wiring Switches, Receptacles, and Lights

What to Do with the Grounding Conductor

PLASTIC BOX, END OF CIRCUIT

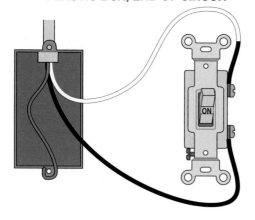

PLASTIC BOX, MID-CIRCUIT

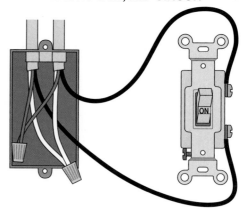

PLASTIC BOX, END OF CIRCUIT

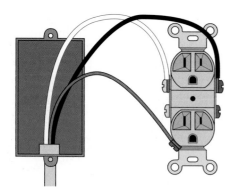

PLASTIC BOX, MID-CIRCUIT

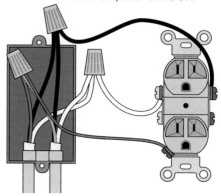

METAL BOX, END OF CIRCUIT

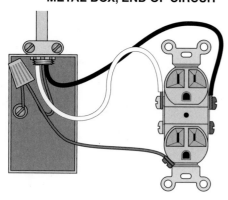

METAL BOX, MID-CIRCUIT

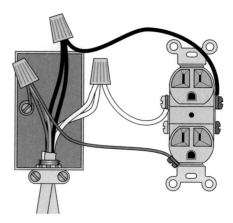

SERIES OF RECEPTACLES

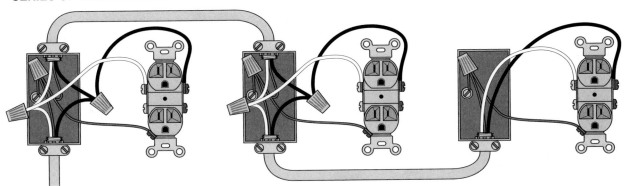

SPLIT-SWITCHED RECEPTACLE
(top receptacle switched)

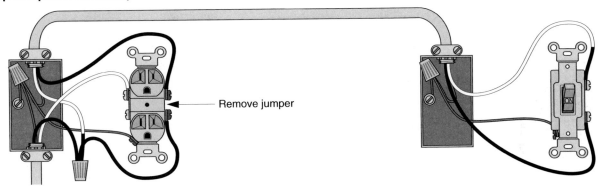

Remove jumper

SPLIT-CIRCUIT RECEPTACLE
(two separate circuits)

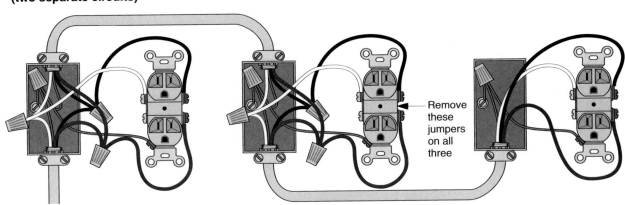

Remove these jumpers on all three

SPLIT-CIRCUIT RECEPTACLE

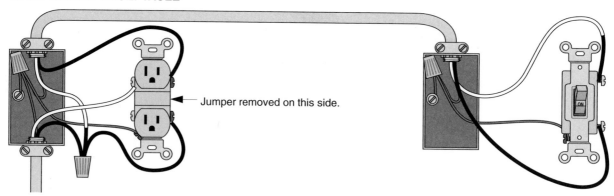

Jumper removed on this side.

LIGHT IN MIDDLE OF CIRCUIT

Note: white wires may be used instead of black wires, but only if the ends are taped or painted black.

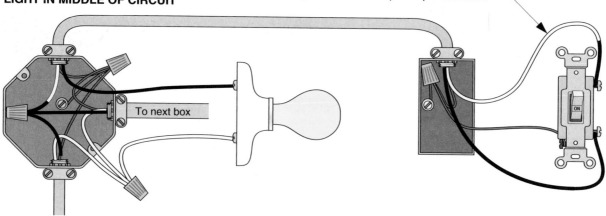

To next box

LIGHT AT END OF CIRCUIT

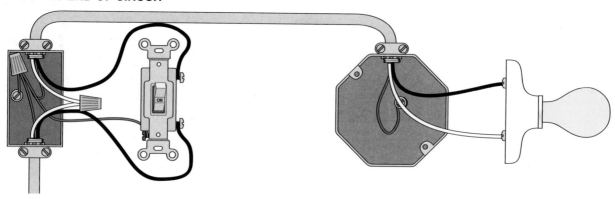

LIGHT IN MIDDLE OF 3-WAY SWITCHES

LIGHT AT END OF 3-WAY SWITCHES

4-WAY SWITCH

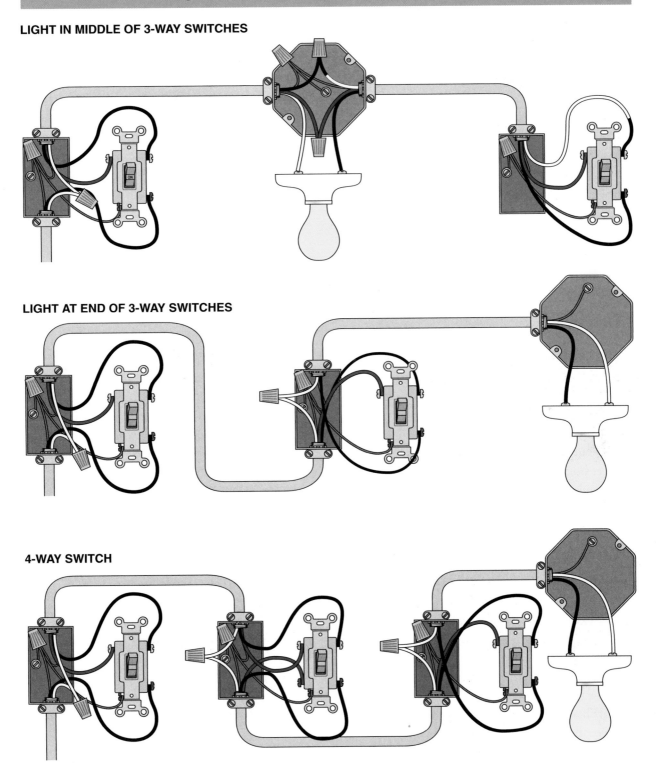

Meet the Code

The following is a partial list of requirements from the *2006 International Residential Code (IRC) for One- and Two-Family Dwellings.* Consult the publication for the full text and additional provisions.

Equipment Location (E3305)

Working space and clearances for panels:
- ≥36" in front
- ≥30" wide
- ≥width of equipment
- from floor or platform to a height of 6½'

Location:
- not in clothes closets or bathrooms
- artificial illumination to be provided indoors
- working space headroom ≥6½'

Conductors/Connections (E3306)

- dissimilar metals not allowed where physical contact occurs except where device is listed for purpose
- inhibitors/compounds to be suitable for application
- terminals to not damage conductors
- terminals for more than one conductor and for aluminum conductors to be identified
- splicing devices to be listed for the purpose
- splices and conductor ends to be insulated
- direct burial splices to be listed for such use
- continuity of grounded conductor not to be through devices such as receptacles
- removal of a receptacle from box to not interrupt grounding continuity
- ≥6" of free conductor to be provided at boxes
- conductors to extend ≥3" outside box opening

General Services (E3501)

- 1- and 2-family dwellings supplied by 1 service
- service conductors not to pass through interior of another building
- service disconnects to be marked
- individual meter enclosures not service equipment
- service disconnect to be accessible outside or inside nearest point of entry of the service conductors

Service Size (E3502)

- for 1-family dwellings, ampacity ≥100A, 3-wire
- for other installations, ampacity ≥60A
- load to be computed as shown on page 350

Service Drop (E3504)

Clearances on buildings:
- ≥3' from sides of doors, porches, decks, stairs, ladders, fire escapes, and balconies, and from sides and bottom of windows that open
- ≥8' above roof surface and 3' from edge of roof.

Exceptions:
1. clearance above roof subject to pedestrian traffic to be same as that above grade
2. ≥3' for roof slope ≥4" in 12"
- ≥10' at service entrance to building, at lowest point of drip loop, and above pedestrian areas
- ≥12' over residential property and driveways
- ≥18' over public streets, alleys, roads, or parking areas subject to truck traffic

System Grounding (E3507)

- grounding electrode conductor to be connected to grounded service conductor from load end of service drop to terminal or bus to which grounded service conductor is connected at service disconnect
- structures supplied by feeder(s) or branch circuit(s) to have grounding electrode. Exception: where one branch circuit supplies the structure and the branch circuit includes grounding conductor
- equipment grounding conductor to be run with supply conductors and connected to structure disconnecting means and grounding electrode(s)
- main bonding jumper to connect equipment grounding conductor and service-disconnect enclosure to the grounded conductor within enclosure
- a metal underground water pipe in direct contact with earth ≥10', including a well casing, to be considered a grounding electrode
- continuity of bonding connection to interior piping not to rely on water meters, filtering devices, and similar equipment

Branch Circuit Ratings (E3602)

- overcurrent device determines circuit rating
- rating of any plug-connected equipment not fastened in place ≤80% of branch-circuit rating
- total rating of fixed equipment, other than lighting, to be ≤50% of branch-circuit rating where lighting, plug-connected equipment not fastened in place, or both are also supplied
- circuits serving a single motor to have ampacity ≥125% of motor full-load current rating
- for circuits with ballasts, calculated load based on total ampere ratings, not on the total watts
- branch-circuit load for a countertop unit and not more than 2 wall-mounted ovens in same room is sum the nameplate ratings of the appliances
- marked rating of a plug-connected room AC to be ≤50% of the branch circuit rating where lighting or other appliances are also supplied

Required Branch Circuits (E3603)

- central heating, fixed AC equipment, and auxiliary associated equipment
- at least two 20A receptacle circuits in kitchen, pantry, breakfast, and dining areas
- one 20A receptacle circuit for laundry area
- at least one 20A receptacle circuit for bathrooms
- lighting and general receptacle load of 3 watts/sq ft based on outside dimensions (excluding open porches, garages, and spaces not adaptable for future use)

Wiring Methods (E3701)

- guard strips required for cable crossing framing members within 7' in attics with permanent access
- guard strips required only for cable within 6' of edges of attic entrances
- no protection required for cable through or parallel to framing
- cable exposed to damage to be protected by conduit
- cable exposed to direct sun be listed "sunlight resistant" or covered with approved material
- SE 6/2 and 8/3 OK across joist bottoms
- inner bend radius ≥5× diameter of NM&SE cable

Required Receptacles (E3801)

- no point along wall >6' from a receptacle, where wall is defined as:
1. ≥2' unbroken
2. panels in exterior walls, excluding sliding panels
3. room dividers, railings, and freestanding counters
- one for countertops ≥12" wide
(no point along countertop >24" from a receptacle)
- one for island counters ≥12"×24" (counters divided by sinks and ranges are separate)
- face-up countertop receptacles prohibited
- receptacles ≤20" above and 12" below countertops
- one ≤36" from lavatory in bathroom
- one front and back of dwelling ≤6'6" above grade
- one for basement in addition to that for laundry
- one in attached garage
- one in detached garage having electricity
- one in hallways ≥10' long
- ≤25' of HVAC equipment, not on same circuit

Required GFCI/AFCIs (E3802)

- all bathroom receptacles
- all countertop receptacles
- all 15A and 20A receptacles ≤6' from a laundry sink
- accessible receptacles in garages and grade-level unfinished storage or work buildings
- outdoor receptacles
- crawl space receptacles
- accessible receptacles in unfinished basement, except those serving normally stationary appliances
- electrically heated floors in bathrooms
- AFCI-protected receptacle circuits in bedrooms

Switched Lighting (E3803)

- all habitable rooms and bathrooms
- switched receptacles OK except in kitchen and bath
- hallways, stairways, and garages with power
- on exterior of outdoor egress doors at grade level, including garages
- all storage and equipment spaces
- a switch at each floor level of stairs with ≥6 risers
- automatic light OK at egress doors, halls, and stairs

The Thermal Envelope

13

Sealing your house against both winter heat loss and summer heat gain requires the creation of what building scientists call the *thermal envelope.* Just as a knowledge of wood or fiberglass is required in order to construct a watertight boat, an *understanding of R-values* is required to construct an energy-efficient home.

Walls, floors, and ceilings consist of building materials, air spaces, and insulations. So you'll find tables of *building material R-values, surface and air-space R-values*, and R-values of insulation materials.
R-value, however, is not the only important quality of an insulation.

Some insulations can be used only in walls and attics, some can be used under roofing shingles, some can be buried between the foundation wall and the earth. A table of the characteristics of *insulation materials* will help you select the right one for every application.

You'll learn how to calculate the actual R-value of a construction. But to save you some calculation, this chapter includes an extensive illustrated table of the *R-values of walls, roofs, and floors.*

Of course, insulation is not the only component of a tight house. You will learn about the recent discoveries regarding air/vapor barriers: why and where they are needed and how they work.

Moisture is the enemy of both insulation and wood construction, robbing fibrous insulation of R-value and a wood frame of structural integrity. For these reasons we cover vapor barriers used for *moisture control.* A second defense against moisture is ventilation: *attic and roof ventilation* and *crawl space ventilation.*

Even a well-insulated home can be air-leaky, however, and suffer from infiltration. We therefore provide a guide to *envelope air leaks* and discuss techniques for *sealing envelope air leaks.*

Structural insulated panels (SIPs) minimize framing and building joints, and thereby reduce envelope air leaks by 90 percent.

In addition to vapor-barrier and air-barrier membranes, penetrations and joints in the envelope require caulks and sealants, so we provide a field guide to *caulking and sealing techniques.*

Finally, doors and windows represent moveable joints in the envelope. To seal these we offer *weather strips.*

The Thermal Envelope

The thermal envelope is the set of building surfaces separating the conditioned (heated and cooled) interior of a building from the outdoors and the earth. It often includes roofs, ceilings, exterior walls, foundation walls, floors, windows, and doors.

A useful analogy can be made between a thermal envelope and a hot air balloon. Both contain a volume of hot (or at least warm) air, and just as a hole in the balloon will allow the hot air to escape, so will a gap in the thermal envelope.

To be maximally effective, the thermal envelope must meet the following conditions:

- Every surface must be insulated to the R-value (thermal resistance) appropriate to the climate.
- The entire envelope must be sealed on its warm side by a vapor barrier.
- The envelope must be relatively air tight.
- Doors and windows must be caulked and weatherstripped against infiltration.

This chapter describes the creation of thermal envelopes for a heating climate. Cooling-climate techniques are identical, except the warm-side vapor barriers are now placed on the outside.

A Building Thermal Envelope

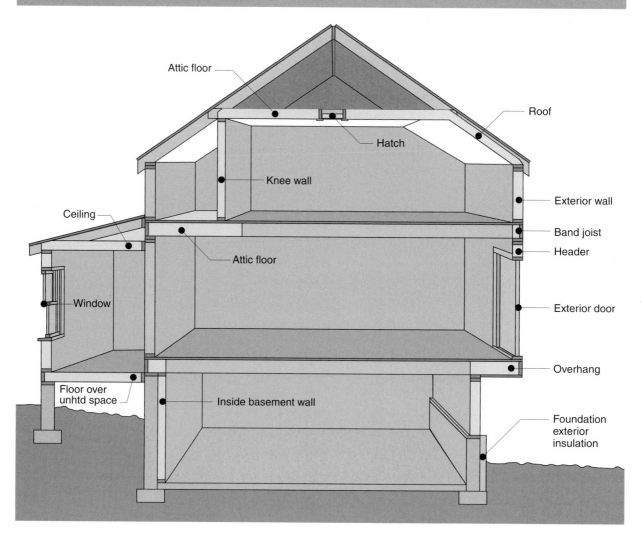

Understanding R-Values

The Conduction Equation

Heat flow (either loss or gain) through a building component is described by the conduction equation (illustration at right).

$$H = A \times \Delta T / R$$

where: H = British thermal units (Btu) per hour through the component surface

A = Area of the surface in square feet

ΔT = Difference in temperature, °F, on opposite sides of the component

R = R-value of the component

Adding R-Values

Most building constructions consider of a number of component parts, each with differing thickness and R-value. The illustration below shows how R-values add through the construction. Component R-values, including those for air spaces and surfaces, are listed in tables on the following pages.

Conductive Heat Flow

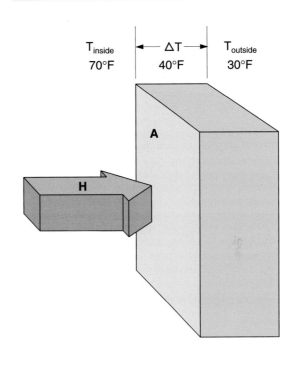

T_{inside}	$\leftarrow \Delta T \rightarrow$	$T_{outside}$
70°F	40°F	30°F

Calculating Total R-Value

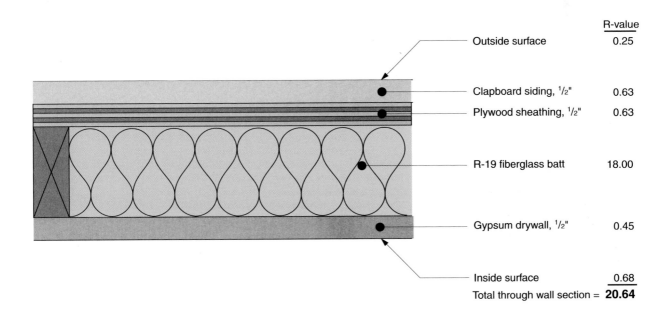

	R-value
Outside surface	0.25
Clapboard siding, 1/2"	0.63
Plywood sheathing, 1/2"	0.63
R-19 fiberglass batt	18.00
Gypsum drywall, 1/2"	0.45
Inside surface	0.68
Total through wall section =	**20.64**

Building Material R-Values

Building Material R-Values

Material	R/in	R-value
Boards and Panels		
Gypsum drywall, ½"	0.90	0.45
⅜"	0.90	0.34
½"	0.90	0.45
⅝"	0.90	0.56
Hardboard		
Medium density	1.37	
High-density underlay	1.22	
High-density tempered	1.00	
Laminated paperboard	2.00	
Particleboard		
Low density	1.41	
Medium density	1.06	
High density	0.85	
Underlayment	1.31	
Plywood, fir	1.25	
Fiberboard	2.64	
Wood		
Hardwoods	0.90	
Softwoods	1.25	
Doors		
Hollow-core flush lauan, 1¾"		1.80
Solid-core flush, 1¾"		2.17
Urethane-filled, steel or fiberglass		5.30
Storm door		
aluminum, 50% glazed		1.00
wood, 50% glazed		1.25
Flooring		
Carpet with fibrous pad		2.08
Carpet with foam rubber pad		1.23
Cork tile, ⅛"	2.24	0.28
Terrazzo	0.08	
Tile, linoleum or vinyl, ⅛"	0.40	0.05
Wood		
Hardwood	0.90	
Softwood	1.25	

Material	R/in	R-value
Framing Lumber		
2" nominal (1½")	1.25	1.88
4" nominal (3½")	1.25	4.38
6" nominal (5½")	1.25	6.88
8" nominal (7¼")	1.25	9.06
10" nominal (9¼")	1.25	11.56
12" nominal (11¼")	1.25	14.06
Carpet with foam rubber pad		1.23
Cork tile, ⅛"	2.24	0.28
Masonry		
Cement mortar	0.20	
Gypsum fiber concrete	0.60	
Sand and gravel aggregate	0.09	
Lightweight aggregate		
120 lb/cu ft	0.09–0.18	
80 lb/cu ft	0.29–0.40	
40 lb/cu ft	0.90–1.08	
20 lb/cu ft	1.43	
Perlite, expanded	1.08	
Stucco	0.20	
Masonry Units		
Brick		
90 lb/cu ft	0.20	
120 lb/cu ft	0.11	
Clay tile, hollow		
One-cell, 3"		0.80
One-cell, 4"		1.11
Two-cell, 6"		1.52
Two-cell, 8"		1.85
Two-cell, 10"		2.22
Three-cell, 12"		2.50
Concrete block, normal weight		
8" empty cores		0.97–1.11
8" perlite cores		2.00
8" vermiculite cores		1.37–1.92
12" empty cores		1.23

Building Material R-Values *(Continued)*

Material	R/in	R-value
Concrete block, medium weight		
8" empty cores		1.28–1.71
8" perlite cores		2.3–3.7
8" vermiculite cores		3.3
8" expanded polystyrene beads		3.2
Concrete block, medium weight		
6" empty cores		1.65–1.93
6" perlite cores		4.2
6" vermiculite cores		3.0
8" empty cores		1.9–3.2
8" perlite cores		4.4–6.8
8" vermiculite cores		3.9–5.3
8" expanded polystyrene beads		4.8
12" empty cores		2.3–2.6
12" perlite cores		6.3–9.2
12" vermiculite cores		5.8
Stone	0.08	
Metals	negligible	
Plasters		
Cement, sand aggregate	0.64	
Plasters		
Cement, sand aggregate	0.64	
Gypsum		
Lightweight aggregate	0.20	
Perlite aggregate	0.67	
Sand aggregate	0.18	
Vermiculite aggregate	0.59	
Roofing		
Asbestos-cement shingle		0.21
Asphalt roll (90 lb)		0.15
Asphalt shingle		0.44
Built-up asphalt, 3/8"		0.33
Slate, 1/2"		0.05
Wood shingles (not furred)		0.94

Material	R/in	R-value
Sheathing, Plywood or OSB		
1/4" panel	1.25	0.31
3/8" panel	1.25	0.47
1/2" panel	1.25	0.63
5/8" panel	1.25	0.77
3/4" panel	1.25	0.94
Siding		
Shingles		
Asbestos-cement		0.21
Wood, 16" (7" exposure)		0.87
Wood		
Drop, 1" x 8"		0.79
Bevel, 1/2" x 8"		0.81
Bevel, 3/4" x 10"		1.05
Aluminum or steel		
Hollow		0.61
With 3/8" backer		1.82
With 3/8" backer and foil		2.96
Windows (Use window ratings values if available)		
Single ordinary glazing		0.91
Single glazing plus storm panel		2.00
Double-glazed		
3/16" air space		1.61
1/4" air space		1.69
1/2" air space		2.04
3/4" air space		2.38
1/2" Low-E		3.13
Suspended film plus Low-E		4.05
Triple-glazed		
1/4" air spaces		2.56
1/2" air spaces		3.23

Surface and Air-Space R-Values

R-Values of Building Surfaces

Surface	Heat Flow Direction	Type of Surface	
		Nonreflective	Foil-Faced
STILL AIR			
Horizontal	Upward	0.61	1.32
Sloped 45	Upward	0.62	1.37
Vertical	Horizontal	0.68	1.70
Sloped 45	Upward	0.61	1.32
Horizontal	Upward	0.62	1.37
MOVING AIR, ANY ORIENTATION			
7.5 mph wind	Any	0.25	—
15 mph wind	Any	0.17	—

Source: *Handbook of Fundamentals* (Atlanta: American Society of Heating, Refrigeration, and Air-Conditioning Engineers, 1977).

R-Values of Trapped Air Spaces

Thickness, in	Heat Flow	Season	Type of Surface	
			Nonreflective	One Foil-Faced
HORIZONTAL				
3/4	Upward	Winter	0.87	2.23
3/4	Downward	Winter	1.02	3.55
4	Upward	Winter	0.94	2.73
4	Downward	Winter	1.23	8.94
SLOPED 45°				
3/4	Upward	Winter	0.94	2.78
3/4	Downward	Summer	0.84	3.24
4	Upward	Winter	0.96	3.00
4	Downward	Summer	0.90	4.36
HORIZONTAL				
3/4	Outward	Winter	1.01	3.48
3/4	Inward	Summer	0.84	3.28
4	Outward	Winter	1.01	3.45
4	Inward	Summer	0.91	3.44

Source: *Handbook of Fundamentals* (Atlanta: American Society of Heating, Refrigeration, and Air-Conditioning Engineers, 1977).

Insulation Materials

Characteristics of Insulation Materials

Type of Insulation	Rated R/in	Max Temp., °F	Vapor Barrier	Resistance to Water Absorption	Moisture Damage	Direct Sunlight	Fire
Roll, Blanket, or Batt							
Fiberglass	3.17 (3.0–3.8)	180	unfaced: P	G	E	E	G
Rock wool	3.17 (3.0–3.7)	>500	unfaced: P	G	E	E	E
Loose Fill							
Fiberglass	2.2 (2.2–4.0)	180	P	G	E	E	G
Rock wool	3.1 (2.8–3.7)	>500	P	G	E	G	G
Cellulose	3.2 (3.1–3.7)	180	P	P	P	G	F
Perlite	3.0 (2.8–3.7)	200	P	F	G	E	G
Vermiculite	2.4	>500	P	G	E	E	G
Rigid Board							
Expanded polystyrene	4.0 (3.6–4.4)	165	P	P	G	P	P
Extruded polystyrene	5.0	165	G	E	E	P	P
Polyurethane	6.2 (5.8–6.8)	165	G	E	E	P	P
Polyisocyanurate	6.0 (5.6–7.7)	200	G	G	E	P	P
Fiberglass board	4.4 (3.8–4.8)	180	F	G	E	E	G
Sprayed in Place							
Cellulose	3.5 (3.0–3.7)	165	P	P	F	G	F
Fiberglass, high-density	4.0	180	P	G	E	E	G
Icynene	3.6	200	G	E	E	P	F
Foamed in Place							
Phenolic	4.8	300	G	G	E	E	P
Urethane	6.2 (5.8–6.8)	165	E	E	E	P	P

Note: E = excellent; G = good; F = fair; P = poor

Floor, Wall, and Roof Total R-Values

In the pages that follow, a variety of walls, roofs, ceilings, and floors are shown, along with their calculated average R-values. Note that the average R-values of the assemblies are often less than the R-values of the insulations alone. This is due to the greater conductivity (lower R-value) of the framing material. For this reason, staggered framing is sometimes used.

The average R-values listed were calculated as shown in the example below, using component R-values from the tables in the previous pages.

Wherever foam is shown, an average R-value of 6.0/inch is assumed. Correction factors for other R-values are listed in the table at right.

R-value Correction Factors for Rigid Foam Insulations

Type of Foam	R/in	Correction Factor/in
Expanded polystyrene	4.0	-2.0
Extruded polystyrene	5.0	-1.0
Polyurethane	6.0	0.0
Polyisocyanurate	6.0	0.0
Fiberglass board	4.0	-2.0

Calculating Average R-Value of a Building Section

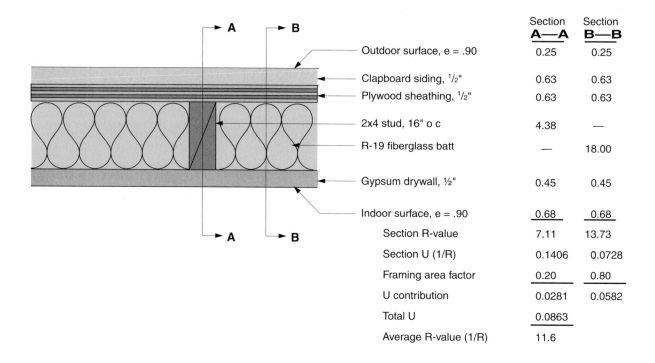

	Section A—A	Section B—B
Outdoor surface, e = .90	0.25	0.25
Clapboard siding, 1/2"	0.63	0.63
Plywood sheathing, 1/2"	0.63	0.63
2x4 stud, 16" o c	4.38	—
R-19 fiberglass batt	—	18.00
Gypsum drywall, ½"	0.45	0.45
Indoor surface, e = .90	0.68	0.68
Section R-value	7.11	13.73
Section U (1/R)	0.1406	0.0728
Framing area factor	0.20	0.80
U contribution	0.0281	0.0582
Total U	0.0863	
Average R-value (1/R)	11.6	

Average R-Values of Frame Walls

FRAMED, CAVITY INSULATION

2x4 studs / R-11 batt   **R-11.6**

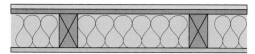

Full 4" cavity blown   **R-13.4**
with cellulose

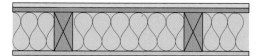

Blown cavity plus 1" urethane foam   **R-19.9**

2x6 studs / R-19 batt   **R-17.2**

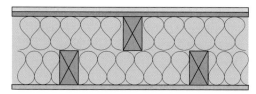

Double 2x4 studs / R-11 batts   **R-20.7**

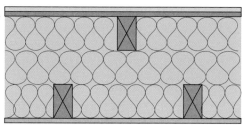

2x4 studs / R-11 batts   **R-31.7**

FRAMED, CAVITY and FOAM INSULATION

2x4 studs with R-11 batt plus   **R-15.6**
¾" urethane foam sheathing

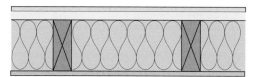

Full 4" cavity blown with cellulose,   **R-19.4**
plus 1" urethane foam

2x6 studs with R-11 batt plus   **R-23.2**
1" urethane foam sheathing

STRUCTURAL INSULATED PANEL (SIP)
⁷/₁₆" OSB FACES, EPS CORE

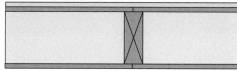

SIP with 3⁵/₈" EPS core   **R-16.6**

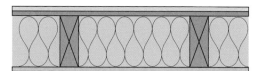

SIP with 5⁵/₈" EPS core   **R-26.3**

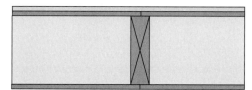

SIP with 7³/₈" EPS core   **R-32.3**

MASONRY WALLS

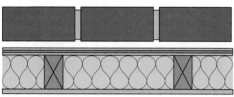

Brick veneer with 2x4
studs and R-11 batt   **R-12.1**

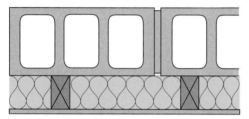

8" masonry block with
2x4 studs and R-11 batt   **R-12.8**

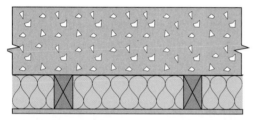

8" solid masonry with
2x4 studs and R-11 batt   **R-12.3**

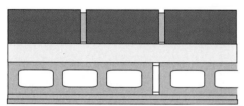

Brick, 2" expanded polystyrene foam,   **R-15.3**
4" block, and strapping

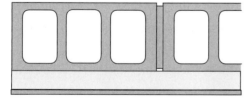

8" masonry block and 2" expanded   **R-14.4**
polystyrene foam

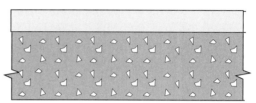

8" solid masonry and 3" foam   **R-14.9**

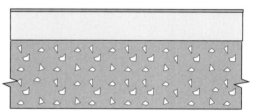

8" solid masonry with 4" expanded   **R-18.9**
polystyrene foam and stucco finish

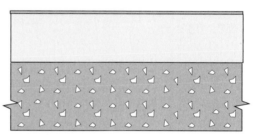

8" solid masonry with 6" expanded   **R-26.9**
polystyrene foam and stucco finish

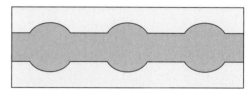

9¼" ICF (insulated concrete forms)   **R-18.7**
and EPS foam

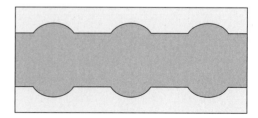

11½" ICF and expanded   **R-21.0**
polystyrene foam

Average R-Values of Attic Floors

ATTIC FLOORS

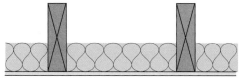

R-11 batt   **R-9.8**

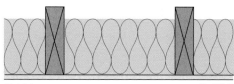

R-19 batt   **R-16.5**

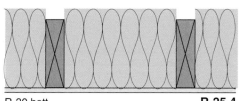

R-30 batt   **R-25.4**

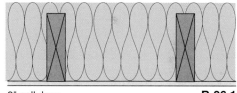

Two R-19 batts   **R-35.5**

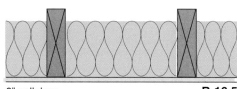

6" cellulose   **R-16.5**

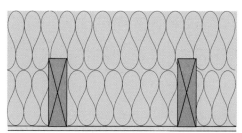

9" cellulose   **R-26.1**

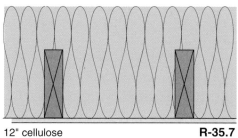

12" cellulose   **R-35.7**

R-19 batt plus 6" cellulose   **R-35.7**

Average R-Values of Roofs and Ceilings

ROOFS AND CEILINGS

Vented ceiling with R-11 batt   **R-9.8**

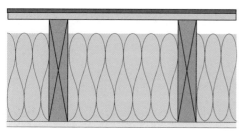

Vented ceiling with R-30 batt   **R-25.4**

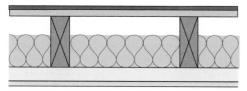

Vented ceiling with R-11   **R-18.8**
batt and 1¹/₂" urethane foam

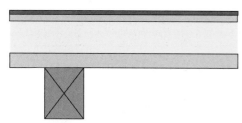

Cathedral ceiling with 1¹/₂"-thick   **R-25.3**
wood boards and 3¹/₂" urethane foam

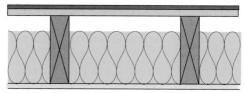

Vented ceiling with R-19 batt   **R-16.5**

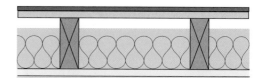

Vented ceiling with R-11   **R-14.3**
batt and ³/₄" urethane foam

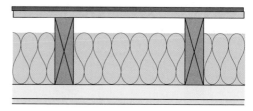

Vented ceiling with R-19   **R-25.5**
batt and 1¹/₂" urethane foam

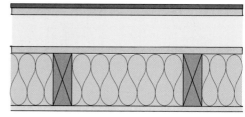

Unvented roof with R-19   **R-38.2**
batt and 3¹/₂" urethane foam

FLOORS

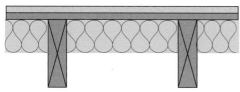

R-11 batt over crawlspace
or basement **R-13.9**

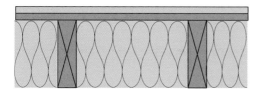

R-19 batt over crawlspace
or basement **R-20.9**

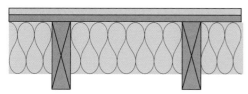

R-30 batt over crawlspace
or basement **R-30.6**

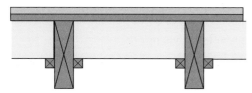

Open to air beneath
4" urethane foam **R-22.1**

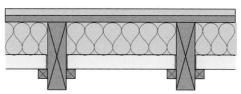

Open to air beneath R-11 batt
and 1¹/₂" urethane foam **R-21.8**

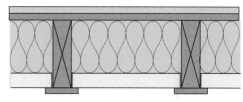

Open to air beneath R-19 batt
and 1¹/₂" urethane foam **R-28.8**

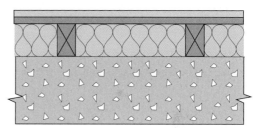

2x4 sleepers and
R-11 batt over slab **adds R-10.4 to R of slab**

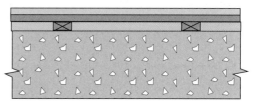

³/₄" sleepers and ³/₄" extruded
polystyrene foam over slab **adds R-3.7 to R of slab**

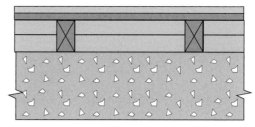

2x4 sleepers and 3¹/₂" extruded
polystyrene foam over slab **adds R-14.2 to R of slab**

Moisture Control

Humidity and Condensation

Unfortunately, stopping infiltration is not as simple as wrapping a building in plastic. Such an approach might lead to moisture problems within the building and its materials. To understand why, we need to understand the behavior of moisture in air.

The illustration at right (a form of the psychrometric chart) describes the behavior of the gaseous form of water, *water vapor*, in ordinary air. The horizontal scale is air temperature; the vertical scale is humidity, expressed as pounds of water vapor in a pound of air. The moisture condition of air can always be described by a single point on the chart. Point A, for example, represents air at 70°F and a certain moisture content.

One of the properties of a mixture of air and water vapor is saturation: Like a sponge, air can hold only a limited amount of water vapor before becoming saturated. The warmer the air, the more water vapor it can hold. This phenomenon is demonstrated by the chart's uppermost curve, known as the *saturation curve*. Air at any point along the saturation curve contains 100 percent of the possible water vapor for that temperature. Air anywhere else (such as at point A) contains a percentage of the saturation amount. This percentage is known as the *relative humidity* of the air. Thus, the air at point A is characterized as having a temperature of 70°F and relative humidity of 40 percent.

The air at point A is typical of the air in a building in winter. To illustrate the potentially damaging behavior of moist air in winter, let the air at point A flow into a cooler space such as an unheated attic. No water vapor is added or removed as the air flows; only the temperature changes as the air loses heat to its new surroundings. On the psychrometric chart, this parcel of air simply moves horizontally to the left until it strikes the saturation curve (its *dew point*) at point B. As the air cools further, it slides down the saturation curve, forcing water vapor out as liquid (water) or solid (ice), which is typically deposited on the coldest solid surface, the underside of the roof sheathing.

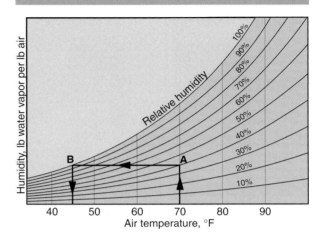

Psychrometric Chart

Sources of Moisture

The air in buildings in winter is often said to be *dry*, which means it has low relative humidity. Actually, interior winter air usually contains more water vapor than the outside air. The table (below) lists the amounts of water vapor (in liquid equivalents) evaporated into building air from typical sources, including the activities of a family of four.

Possible Sources of Water Vapor

Source	Quarts/Day
Construction materials, first year	40
Standing water in basement	30
Damp basement or crawl space	25
Greenhouse connected to house	25
Humidifier, cabinet size	20
Drying 1 cord of firewood	16
Clothes dryer vented to inside	13
Respiration and perspiration, 4 occupants	4.7
Clothes washing	2.1
Unvented gas range	1.3
Cooking without pot lids	1.0
Houseplants, average number	0.5
Dish washing	0.5
Showering/bathing	0.3

Moisture Transfer

As shown in the illustration at right, water vapor can move from warm living spaces to cooler spaces (wall, ceiling, and floor cavities and attics) in two different ways:

1. *convection*—the bulk motion of air, of which water vapor is but a component

2. *diffusion*—movement of water vapor molecules alone as they spread by random motion from an area of higher concentration (inside) to an area of lower concentration (the cavity or outdoors).

Permeance of Building Materials

Material placed on the warm side of a building surface to retard diffusion of water vapor is called a *vapor barrier*. Material intended to retard convection is called an *air barrier*. A material qualifies as a vapor barrier if its permeance is 1.0 perm or less.

Perm Ratings of Common Materials

Type	Material	Perms
Masonry	Concrete block, 8"	2.4
	Brick masonry, 4"	0.8
Exterior wall	Plywood, ½"	0.7
	T&G pine, ¾"	4.5
	Clapboards	8.0
Interior wall	Gypsum drywall, ½"	40
Insulation	Extruded polystyrene, 1"	1.2
	Expanded polystyrene, 1"	2.0–5.8
	Fibrous batt, unfaced	116
Vapor barrier	Polyethylene, 4-mil	0.08
	Aluminum foil, 1-mil	0.0
	Foil facing on batt insulation	0.5
	Kraft facing on batt insulation	1.0
Paint and	Latex primer sealer, 1 coat	6.3
wallpaper	"Vapor barrier" paint, 1 coat	0.6
	Paper wallpaper	20
	Vinyl wallpaper	1.0
Housewrap	15-lb building felt	5.6
	Air barrier, Tyvek, etc.	10–40

CONVECTION THROUGH HOLES

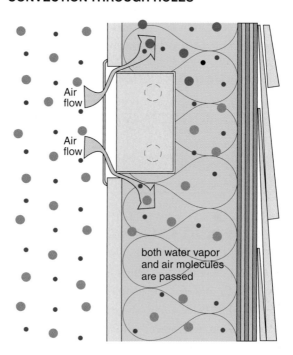

Air flow

Air flow

both water vapor and air molecules are passed

DIFFUSION THROUGH SURFACE

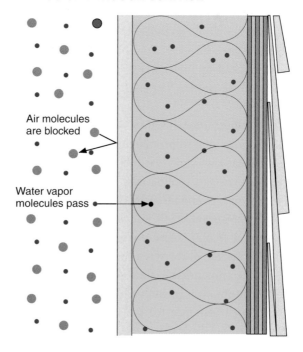

Air molecules are blocked

Water vapor molecules pass

Attic and Roof Ventilation

The International Residential Code requires both open attics and ceilings with closed rafter spaces to have net free ventilation openings of 1/300 of the ceiling area. Ceilings without vapor barriers require a ventilation ratio of 1/150. Louvers and screens reduce net free areas by the factors in the table below.

Ventilating Area Reduction Factors

Vent Covering	Factor
⅛" mesh screen	1.25
1/16" mesh screen	2.00
Louvers plus ⅛" screen	2.25
Louvers plus 1/16" screen	3.00

Cause and Cure of Ice Dams

Ice dams are not inevitable. Understanding the cause points to the cure. The illustration at right shows an ice dam in action. The attic floor is well insulated, but so is the roof, due to the insulating action of the snow. With insufficient attic ventilation, the attic temperature falls somewhere between that of the living space below and the air outside. Water from melting snow flows downward toward the eaves. The roofing at the eaves is closer to ambient air temperature, however, so the meltwater refreezes. As the ice builds up, it creates a dam for further meltwater. If the backed-up meltwater extends beyond the coverage of the roofing material, the water penetrates the roofing.

The illustration at right shows the most common cure: continuous soffit and ridge vents with insulation baffles providing a minimum 1-inch air channel. Attic air and roofing now track the ambient air temperature, eliminating the melting and refreezing of the snow cover. The "hot roof" shown on p. 386 provides a second solution where the roof temperature is constant all the way to the eave.

A recommended backup solution is installation of a continuous 36-inch-wide waterproof membrane, such as Grace Ice & Water Shield®, under the starter course at the eaves.

Example: What is the required total gross vent opening for attic vents with louvers and ⅛-inch screen in a 25 by 40-foot house?

Ceiling area = 25' × 40' = 1,000 sq ft

Vent factor = 2.25

Gross area = 2.25 × 1/300 × 1,000 sq ft = 7.5 sq ft

The gross vent area should be split between inlets at the eaves and higher outlets. The most effective combination—because it has the greatest difference in height and, therefore, stack effect—is soffit strips and ridge vents. Second most effective is a combination of soffit vents and gable end vents. Powered roof vents are generally less effective.

Ice Dam Prevention

INSUFFICIENT VENTILATION

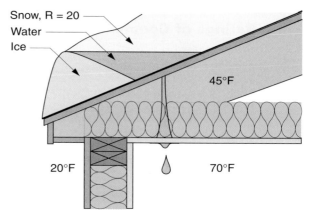

PROPER VENTILATION

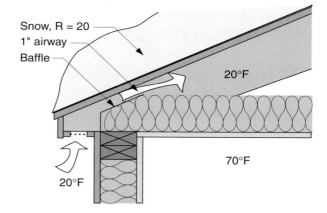

A Variety of Properly Vented Roofs

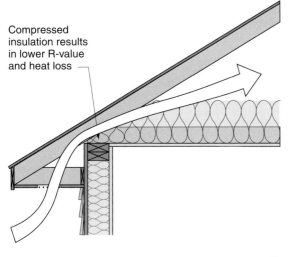

Compressed insulation results in lower R-value and heat loss

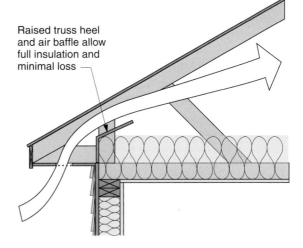

Raised truss heel and air baffle allow full insulation and minimal loss

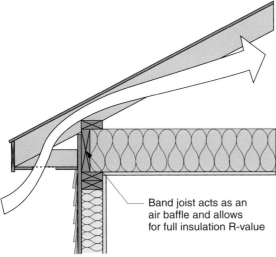

Band joist acts as an air baffle and allows for full insulation R-value

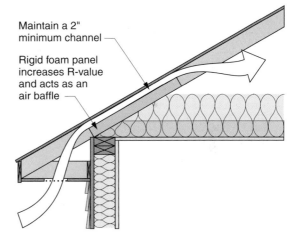

Maintain a 2" minimum channel

Rigid foam panel increases R-value and acts as an air baffle

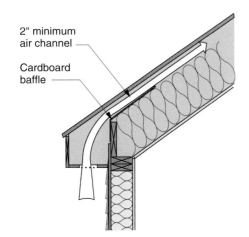

2" minimum air channel

Cardboard baffle

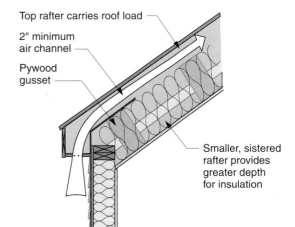

Top rafter carries roof load

2" minimum air channel

Pywood gusset

Smaller, sistered rafter provides greater depth for insulation

Venting a Roof Abutting a Wall

Venting a roof which abuts a wall poses a difficult problem. Two solutions are as follows:

1) the vented wall shown here

2) the "hot roof" shown in the illustration below

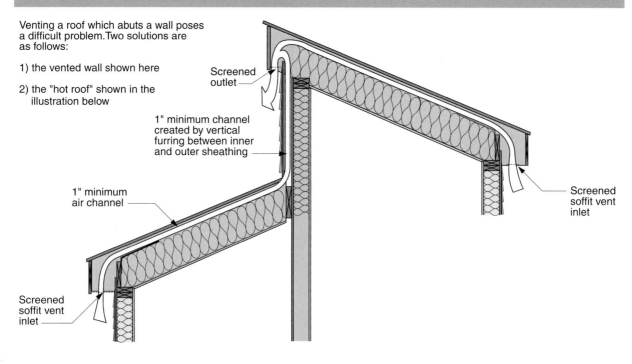

Screened outlet

1" minimum channel created by vertical furring between inner and outer sheathing

1" minimum air channel

Screened soffit vent inlet

Screened soffit vent inlet

Hot Roofs

EXPOSED RAFTER CEILING

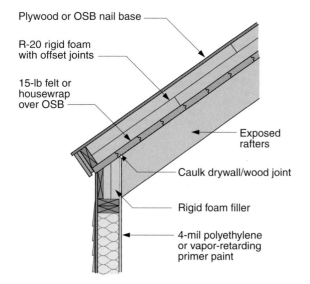

Plywood or OSB nail base

R-20 rigid foam with offset joints

15-lb felt or housewrap over OSB

Exposed rafters

Caulk drywall/wood joint

Rigid foam filler

4-mil polyethylene or vapor-retarding primer paint

CONVENTIONAL SLOPED CEILING

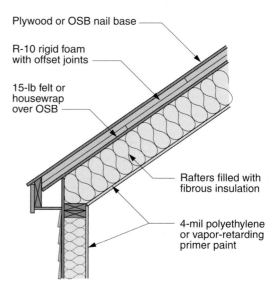

Plywood or OSB nail base

R-10 rigid foam with offset joints

15-lb felt or housewrap over OSB

Rafters filled with fibrous insulation

4-mil polyethylene or vapor-retarding primer paint

Crawl Space Ventilation

Vented Crawl Space

The IRC requires unconditioned crawl spaces to be ventilated to prevent moisture buildup. Vents are required no farther than 3 feet from each corner. The net free (open) area of all vents must total no less than 1/150 of the floor area. The vent openings must be screened, with the smallest opening not exceeding ¼ inch.

An access opening must also be provided with minimum dimensions of 16 inches by 24 inches.

A Vented Crawl Space

Protective coating

Slope away from wall 6" in 10'

Rigid foam insulation

Sealant

Seam lapped and sealed

Treated cleat

Vapor-retarding ground cover

Screened vent , 3' from each corner

The Unvented Option

Building scientists now believe crawl spaces should be included in the building envelope. The IRC allows unvented crawl spaces, assuming that:

1. A continuous vapor-retarding ground cover, with seams lapped 6 inches and sealed, and perimeter seams sealed and fastened to the foundation walls.

2. Mechanical circulation of air between crawl space and conditioned spaces at the rate of 1 cfm per 50 square feet. The ventilation air can be returned to the building through floor leaks or a plenum. In both cases the foundation walls must be insulated.

The Unvented Crawl Space Option

Protective coating

Slope away from wall 6" in 10'

Rigid foam insulation

Return

Sealant

Seam lapped and sealed

Treated cleat

Mechanical ventilation of 1 cfm/50 sq ft

Vapor-retarding ground cover

Envelope Air Leaks

Heated homes in winter are hot air balloons. Their warm, buoyant, interior air volumes push upward, looking for holes (heat leaks) in the upper surfaces. Air that does escape is replaced by cold air flowing in at lower levels.

The illustration below and the table on the facing page identify air leaks (holes and cracks) found in most homes built prior to 1990. Although any one leak seems inconsequential, adding up the individual areas listed in the table shows that the net effect is comparable to leaving a double-hung window open all winter!

Building science has determined that an energy-efficient home must address three issues:

1. The conditioned interior must be thermally isolated from the exterior by a complete insulated thermal envelope (see pp. 370–381).

2. The construction must be protected against harmful condensation of moisture by a vapor-diffusion retarder (see pp. 382–387).

3. The envelope surfaces must be sealed against air flow by an air-flow retarder (pp. 388–391).

Hidden Heat Leaks in a Building Thermal Envelope

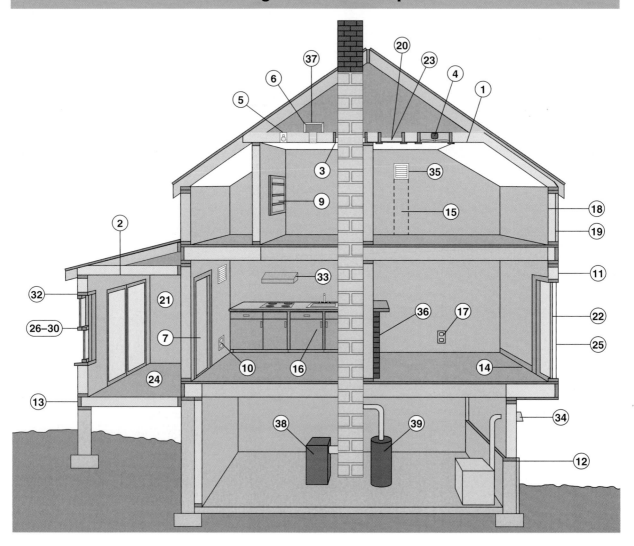

Air Leakage in Buildings

Heat Leak	Area, sq in
Ceiling	
1. General, per 100 sq ft	0.05
2. Dropped ceiling, per 100 sq ft, no poly VB	78
With poly vapor retarder	8
3. Framing around chimney	12
Sealed off	1
4. Whole-house fan, louvers closed	8
Covered with weatherstripped box	0.6
5. Ceiling fixture, surface or sealed recessed	0.3
Recessed, not air-tight	4
6. Pipe or duct through ceiling	1
Caulked at ceiling	0.2
Interior Walls	
7. Pocket door	5
8. Pipe or HVAC duct in wall cavity	2
9. Recessed cabinet	0.8
10. Electrical switch or receptacle	0.2
With foam cover plate gasket	0.03
Exterior Walls	
11. General, per 100 sq ft	0.8
12. Sill on masonry foundation	65
Caulked	13
13. Box sill	65
Caulked	13
14. Floor/wall joint	27
Caulked	7
15. HVAC Duct in wall	9
16. Vent pipe in wall	2
17. Electrical switch or receptacle	0.2
With foam cover plate gasket	0.05
18. Polyethylene vapor retarder (deduct for)	-30
19. Extruded polystyrene sheathing (deduct for)	-15
Doors	
20. Attic fold down	17
Weatherstripped	8
Insulated and weatherstripped cover	2

Heat Leak	Area, sq in
21. Patio sliding	16
22. Entrance	8
Weatherstripped	6
Magnetic seal	4
23. Attic hatch	6
Weatherstripped	3
24. Air-lock entry (deduct for)	-4
25. Storm door (deduct for)	-3
Windows (all weatherstripped)	
26. Double-hung	0.8
27. Horizontal slider	0.6
28. Awning	0.2
29. Casement	0.2
30. Fixed	0.2
Door and Window Frames	
31. Masonry wall	2
Caulked	0.4
32. Wood wall	0.6
Caulked	0.1
Vents	
33. Range hood vent, damper open	9
Damper closed	2
34. Clothes dryer vent, damper open	4
Damper closed	1
35. Bathroom fan, damper open	3
Damper closed	1
36. Fireplace, damper open	54
Average damper closed	9
Stove insert with cover plate	2
Heat and Hot Water	
37. Ducts in unheated space	56
Joints caulked and taped	28
38. Furnace, with retention head burner	12
With stack damper	12
With retention head and stack damper	9
39. Gas/oil boiler or water heater	8

Sealing Envelope Air Leaks

Polyethylene placed on the interior can serve the dual function of vapor diffusion barrier and air flow barrier. It should not be used in cooling climates, however, due to being on the wrong side of the wall.

To be effective, all penetrations (such as switches and receptacles) of the polyethylene must be taped or otherwise sealed.

Interior drywall finish can serve as an air-flow retarder, provided all openings are sealed. When primed with a vapor-retarding paint, it can also serve as a heating-climate vapor-diffusion retarder.

An exterior housewrap should also be used in order to reduce heat-robbing air wash of the cavity insulation from the exterior.

Interior Polyethylene Air Barrier

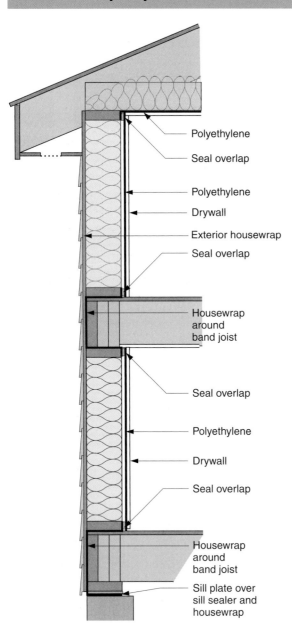

- Polyethylene
- Seal overlap
- Polyethylene
- Drywall
- Exterior housewrap
- Seal overlap
- Housewrap around band joist
- Seal overlap
- Polyethylene
- Drywall
- Seal overlap
- Housewrap around band joist
- Sill plate over sill sealer and housewrap

Drywall Air Barrier

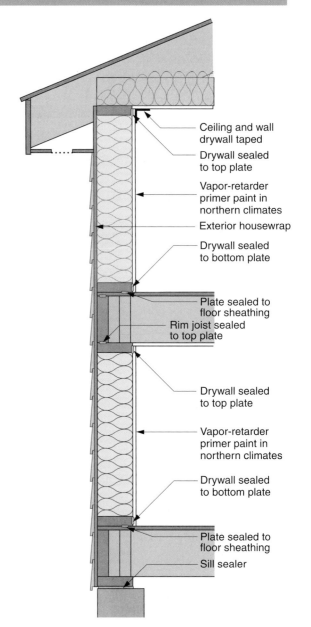

- Ceiling and wall drywall taped
- Drywall sealed to top plate
- Vapor-retarder primer paint in northern climates
- Exterior housewrap
- Drywall sealed to bottom plate
- Plate sealed to floor sheathing
- Rim joist sealed to top plate
- Drywall sealed to top plate
- Vapor-retarder primer paint in northern climates
- Drywall sealed to bottom plate
- Plate sealed to floor sheathing
- Sill sealer

In all but the coldest climates (above 8,000 heating degree days) closed-cell or foil-faced foam wall sheathing can provide an air-flow barrier. Though the foam is a vapor barrier on the wrong side for heating climates, the R-value of a sufficiently thick foam will result in the vapor dew point falling within the impermeable foam.

Housewrap is an inexpensive and effective air-flow barrier, which accounts for its popularity. Too often, however, it is applied early and haphazardly as an obligatory gesture toward energy efficiency. To be maximally effective, it must wrap around top plate and sill. Additionally, in heating climates the drywall should be primed with vapor-retarding paint.

Exterior Foam Sheathing Air Barrier

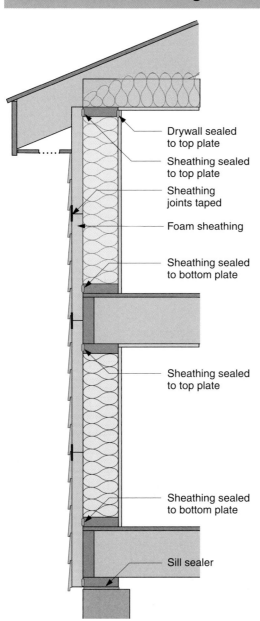

- Drywall sealed to top plate
- Sheathing sealed to top plate
- Sheathing joints taped
- Foam sheathing
- Sheathing sealed to bottom plate
- Sheathing sealed to top plate
- Sheathing sealed to bottom plate
- Sill sealer

Exterior Housewrap Air Barrier

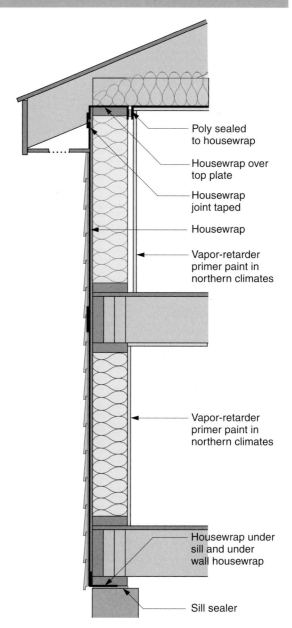

- Poly sealed to housewrap
- Housewrap over top plate
- Housewrap joint taped
- Housewrap
- Vapor-retarder primer paint in northern climates
- Vapor-retarder primer paint in northern climates
- Housewrap under sill and under wall housewrap
- Sill sealer

Structural Insulated Panels (SIPs)

Structural insulated panels (SIPs) consist of rigid foam insulation between two wood structural panels, most often OSB (oriented strand board). The foam may be expanded polystyrene, extruded polystyrene, polyurethane, or polyisocyanurate. Standard panel sizes range from 4 by 8 feet to 8 by 24 feet. Thicknesses range from 4½ inches to 12¼ inches. CAD drawings generate panel sizes, cutouts, wiring chases and other details.

A SIP's foam core provides continuous high-R insulation and enables structures to be assembled with minimal framing. A typical stick-framed wall has a framing factor (percentage of thermal-bridging solid wood) of 15 to 25 percent; a SIP wall has only 3 percent. As a result, a 4-inch-thick SIP wall commonly outperforms a 6-inch-thick stick-framed wall.

SIPs also require fewer joints to be sealed, resulting in 90 percent less leakage than in their stick-framed equivalents.

SIP Connection Details

DOOR AND WINDOW FRAMING

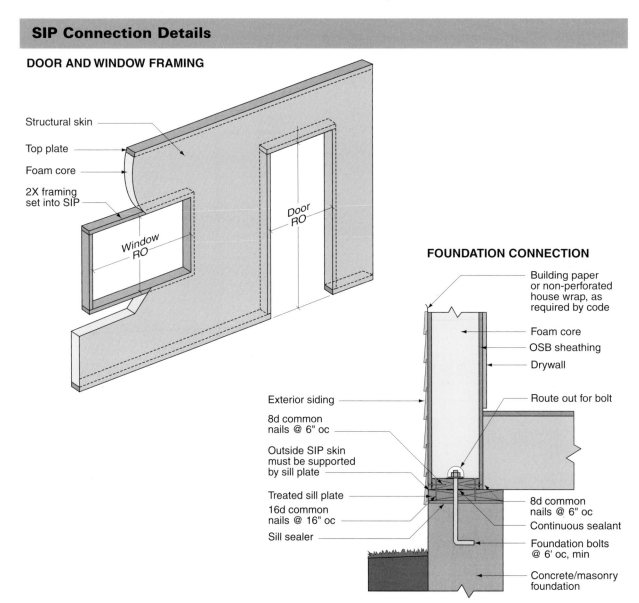

Structural skin

Top plate

Foam core

2X framing set into SIP

Window RO

Door RO

FOUNDATION CONNECTION

Building paper or non-perforated house wrap, as required by code

Foam core

OSB sheathing

Drywall

Route out for bolt

Exterior siding

8d common nails @ 6" oc

Outside SIP skin must be supported by sill plate

Treated sill plate

16d common nails @ 16" oc

Sill sealer

8d common nails @ 6" oc

Continuous sealant

Foundation bolts @ 6' oc, min

Concrete/masonry foundation

EAVES CONNECTION

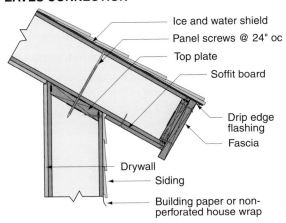

- Ice and water shield
- Panel screws @ 24" oc
- Top plate
- Soffit board
- Drip edge flashing
- Fascia
- Drywall
- Siding
- Building paper or non-perforated house wrap

RIDGE CONNECTION

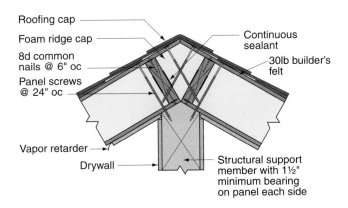

- Roofing cap
- Foam ridge cap
- 8d common nails @ 6" oc
- Panel screws @ 24" oc
- Vapor retarder
- Drywall
- Continuous sealant
- 30lb builder's felt
- Structural support member with 1½" minimum bearing on panel each side

WALL CONNECTION WITH SIP BLOCK SPLINE

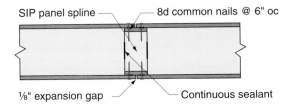

- SIP panel spline
- 8d common nails @ 6" oc
- ⅛" expansion gap
- Continuous sealant

WALL CONNECTION WITH DIMENSION LUMBER SPLINE

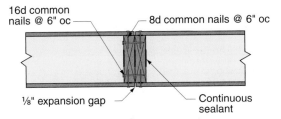

- 16d common nails @ 6" oc
- 8d common nails @ 6" oc
- ⅛" expansion gap
- Continuous sealant

SECOND FLOOR CONNECTION WITH HANGING FLOOR

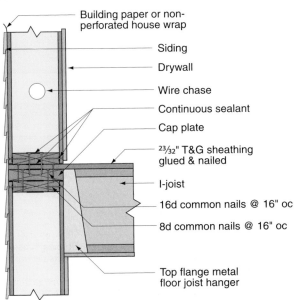

- Building paper or non-perforated house wrap
- Siding
- Drywall
- Wire chase
- Continuous sealant
- Cap plate
- 23⁄32" T&G sheathing glued & nailed
- I-joist
- 16d common nails @ 16" oc
- 8d common nails @ 16" oc
- Top flange metal floor joist hanger

SECOND FLOOR CONNECTION WITH RIM JOIST

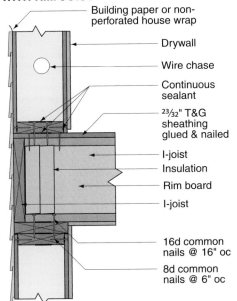

- Building paper or non-perforated house wrap
- Drywall
- Wire chase
- Continuous sealant
- 23⁄32" T&G sheathing glued & nailed
- I-joist
- Insulation
- Rim board
- I-joist
- 16d common nails @ 16" oc
- 8d common nails @ 6" oc

Caulking and Sealing Techniques

Successful sealing involves three steps:

1. Selection of the best caulk or sealant for the intended purpose.

2. Preparation of surfaces exactly as recommended by the caulk or sealant manufacturer. Note that products—even products from the same manufacturer—can vary in formulation and surface preparation.

3. Application of the product with the proper techniques, as shown in the illustrations here.

Surprisingly, joints fail more often from use of too much rather than too little caulk or sealant. For narrow joints, push rather than drag the tip. For wide joints, first install foam backer rod, in order to limit the depth of the joint.

Application Technique

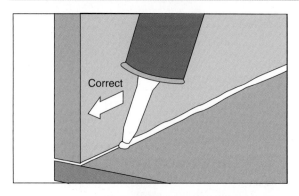

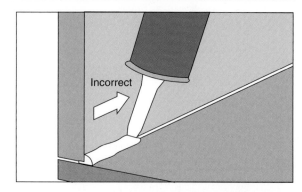

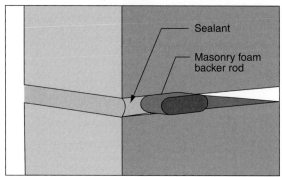

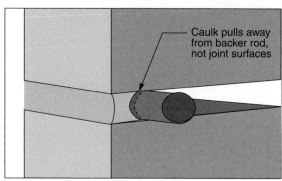

Wall Penetrations

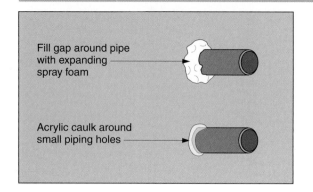

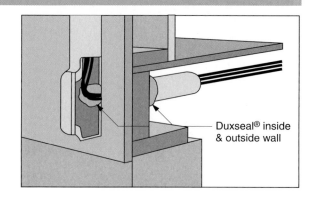

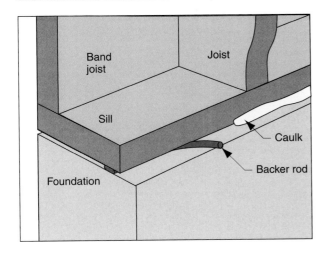

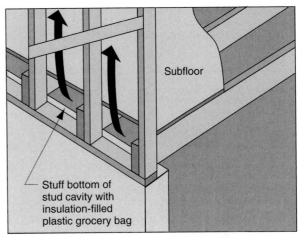

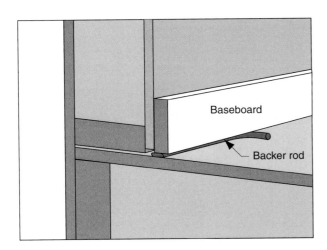

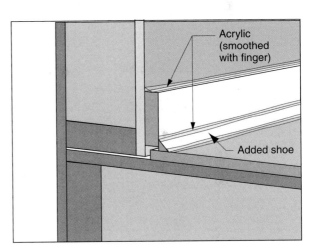

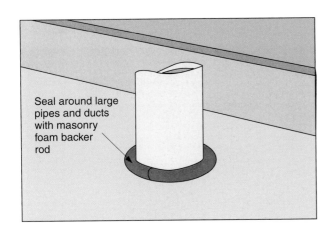

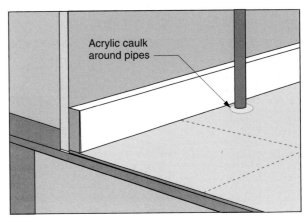

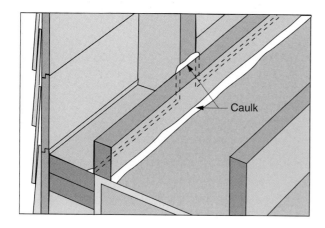

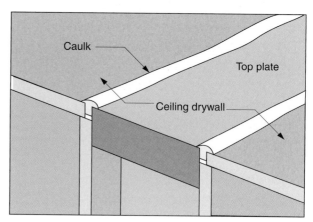

Caulk

Top plate

Ceiling drywall

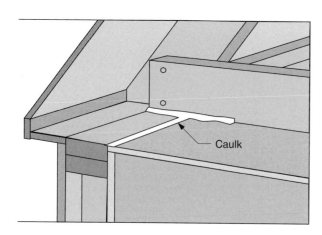

Caulk

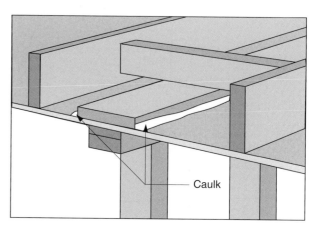

Caulk

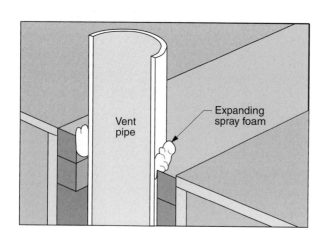

Vent pipe

Expanding spray foam

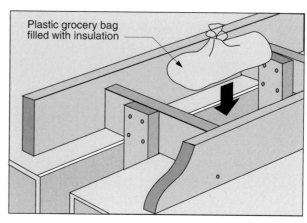

Plastic grocery bag filled with insulation

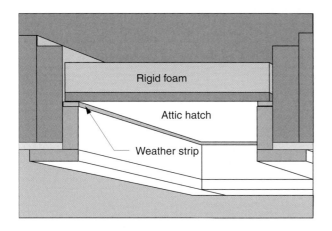

Rigid foam

Attic hatch

Weather strip

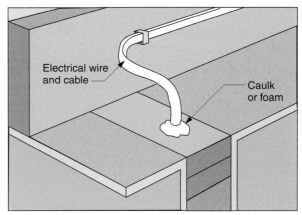

Electrical wire
and cable

Caulk
or foam

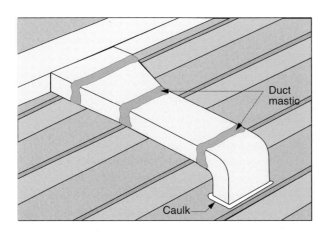

Duct
mastic

Caulk

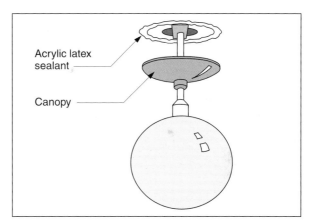

Acrylic latex
sealant

Canopy

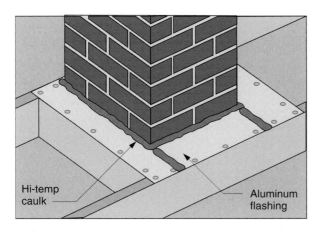

Hi-temp
caulk

Aluminum
flashing

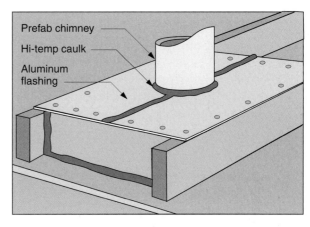

Prefab chimney

Hi-temp caulk

Aluminum
flashing

Weather Strips

Whereas caulks and sealants are designed to seal cracks and joints with limited movement, weather strips are designed to seal operable joints around windows and doors. The table below describes the most effective commonly available strips. Note that weather strips should *never be painted*.

Common Weather Strips Compared

	Type	Cost	Comments
	Foam on wood	Medium	• Seals well on doors and windows; installed by nailing attachment strip to window or door jamb • Operation of window or door may be hindered if installed too tight • Not for sliding windows or doors
	Closed-cell rubber	Low	• Effective when under compression (doors, hinged windows, clamped attic hatches, etc.) • Does not work with large gap variation • Installation simple but relies on effective adhesion
	Hollow/foam-filled tube	Low to medium	• Good provided properly installed • Does not require significant pressure to create seal
	Plastic V-shape	Low to medium	• Effective and versatile for use throughout house • Strips may be supplied with self-adhesive backing • Protection against failure of adhesive backing may be supplied by stapling through back edge

Weather Strips for Retrofitting Windows

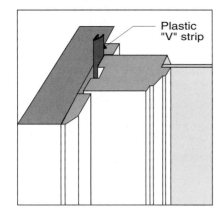

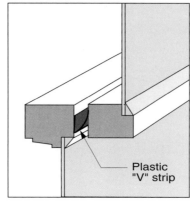

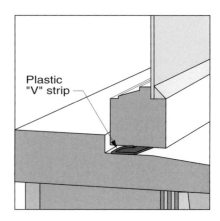

398   **THERMAL ENVELOPE**

Weather Strips for Retrofitting Doors

LOCKING EDGE OF DOOR

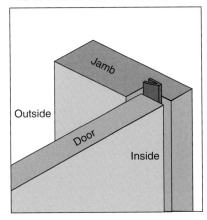

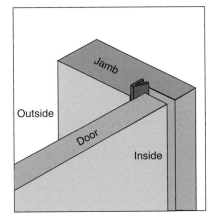

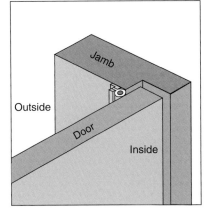

HINGE EDGE OF DOOR

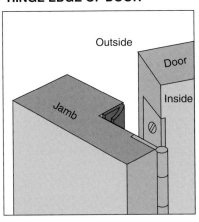

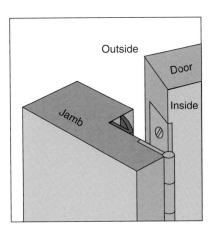

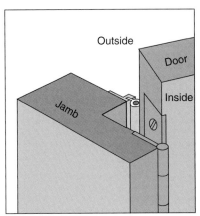

BOTTOM OF DOOR

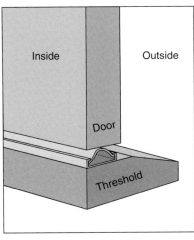

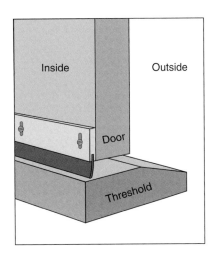

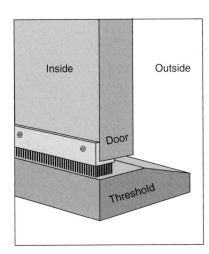

Floors, Walls, and Ceilings

14

Floors, walls, and ceilings are the surfaces we live with. It's important to select the best material and to install it properly to achieve long-term performance.

This chapter starts at the bottom, with *carpeting* and *resilient flooring*. It shows you the differences between carpet materials and weaves, and which are best for which room. Using proper tile setting materials assures long-lasting applications. Our tables of *standard tile sizes* and comprehensive illustration of common *tile patterns* allows preplanning of room layouts.

Hardwood flooring is also a hallmark of a quality home. Today you can buy unfinished or prefinished hardwood flooring in three styles: strip, plank, and parquet. This section shows you interesting parquet patterns, how to estimate coverage, and how to install wood flooring over concrete or wood subfloor.

Gypsum wallboard is one of the most popular of all homeowner projects. In this section you'll find the variety of wallboards, how to estimate all of the materials needed to finish a room, and techniques from a professional manual.

A section on solid *wood paneling* shows the patterns commonly available, how to estimate quantities, and installation.

Suspended ceilings are inexpensive solutions for hiding basement pipes and wires or lowering high ceilings. Provided are step-by-step procedures for installing this engineered system.

Most people blame the manufacturer when *exterior finishes* and *interior paints* fail. But more often, the problem lies elsewhere. *Diagnosing paint failures* will help you avoid that mistake and find out what went wrong the first time.

Our nearly complete collection of standard *wood moldings*, along with suggestions for *built-up wood moldings*, will help you create a truly finished look.

Carpeting

Carpet

Most wall-to-wall carpeting is produced by looping yarns through a coarse-fiber backing, binding the backs of the loops with latex, then applying a second backing for strength and dimensional stability. Finally, the loops may be left uncut for a tough, nubby surface or cut for a soft, plush surface. The quality of carpeting is determined mostly by its *face weight*, defined as ounces of yarn (pile) per square yard.

Installation

There are two basic carpet installation methods:

Padded and Stretched carpeting is stretched over a separate pad and mechanically fastened at joints and the perimeter. Soft foam pads are inexpensive and give the carpet a soft, luxurious feel. The more expensive jute and felt pads give better support and dimensional stability and make the carpet last longer.

Glued-Down carpets are usually used in areas such as offices and stores, where carpets are subjected to heavily loaded wheel traffic. They are usually glued down with carpet adhesive with a pad. This minimizes destructive flexing of the backing and prevents rippling.

Fiber Materials

Manufacturers prefer to specify the trade names of their yarns rather than chemical type, because they all claim to have variations with superior qualities. However, the general characteristics are as shown below.

Carpet Materials

Fiber	Advantages	Disadvantages
Acrylic	Resembles wool	Not very tough Attracts oily dirt
Nylon (most popular)	Very tough Resists dirt Resembles wool Low static buildup	None
Polyester deep pile	Soft, luxurious	Less resilient Attracts oily dirt
Polypropylene indoor/outdoor	Waterproof Resists fading Resists stains Easily cleaned	Crushes easily
Wool	Most durable Easy to clean Feels good Easily dyed	Most expensive

Carpet Pile Types

UNCUT LEVEL LOOP

Good for offices and high-wear areas

UNCUT UNEVEN LOOP

Good for offices and high-wear areas

CUT YARN, MINIMUM TWIST

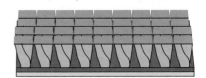

Good for living rooms and bedrooms

CUT YARN, TIGHT TWIST

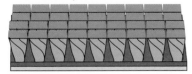

Good for living rooms and bedrooms

CUT YARN AND UNCUT LOOP

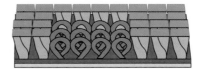

Good for family and children's rooms

CUT YARN (SHAG)

Entries, family and children's rooms

Resilient Flooring

Resilient Flooring

No-wax cushion vinyl is the most popular type of resilient flooring, mainly because of its economical price, ease of installation, and variety of patterns and styles. However, linoleum flooring is making a comeback because it offers similar advantages without any of the adverse environmental impact of vinyl products. Vinyl is made with petroleum products and can produce toxic fumes when it burns. Linoleum is made from natural materials.

Available as 12-foot-wide rolls and as 9-by-9-inch and 12-by-12-inch tiles, cushion vinyl consists of a shiny (no-wax) clear vinyl coating, colored vinyl substrate, high-density vinyl foam, and a felt back. The roll material may be loose-laid, with double-sided tape or joint adhesive only at seams, or it may be fully glued down. Tiles are meant to be glued down. Some are self-sticking; others are applied over vinyl adhesive.

The primary measure of quality and longevity is the thickness of the clear no-wax wear layer. When the wear layer is worn through, the flooring has to be replaced or periodically treated with a vinyl dressing or wax.

All resilient flooring must be applied over a solid, smooth base. If the base is not smooth, the vinyl will appear wavy. If the base is not solid (plywood with a missing knot, for example), women's heels or other heavily loaded objects may punch through.

The table at right describes adequate bases for resilient flooring. However, plywood is recommended as the best underlayment by most resilient-flooring manufacturers.

Plywood Underlayment

Underlayment grades of plywood have a solid, sanded surface and solid inner plies for resistance to indentation and punctures from concentrated loads. APA underlayment-rated plywood is also dimensionally stable and eliminates swelling, buckling, and humps around nails. Where floors may be subject to moisture, use panels with an Exterior exposure rating.

Ordinary sanded plywood grades such as A-C or B-C Exterior and C-D Plugged Exposure 1 plywood are not adequate substitutes for underlayment grade, because they do not insure equivalent resistance to indentation or puncture.

The thickness of plywood underlayment required over uneven floors depends on floor roughness and expected loads. Usually a minimum thickness of $^{11}/_{32}$ inch, although ¼ inch is acceptable for underlayment over smooth subfloors, especially in remodeling work. Thicker plywood underlayment, which is stiffer and more dimensionally stable, is recommended for large floor areas where sidelighting across long expanses of flooring tends to highlight any floor surface irregularities.

Plywood underlayment also provides a smooth surface for installation of adhered carpet flooring.

Concentrated loads from wheel traffic may cause deterioration of the plywood underlayment face beneath resilient floor covering. For such applications, smooth, tempered hardboard underlayment may be more appropriate.

Bases for Resilient Flooring

Existing Floor	Cover or Repairs
Plywood subfloor, not rated as underlayment	Hardboard or plywood underlayment
Plywood rated as underlayment	None needed
OSB rated as underlayment	None needed
Single-layer board subfloor	Plywood underlayment, 5/8" minimum
Subfloor plus finish floor of strips less than 3" wide	Replace damaged strips; renail loose spots; sand smooth
Subfloor plus finish floor of strips more than 3" wide	Hardboard or plywood underlayment
Concrete	None needed, but clean thoroughly by degreasing and wire brushing

Ceramic Tile

Tile Varieties

The word tile generally means any hard-wearing material used to cover floors, walls, and roofs. In building we are most interested in six categories of tile intended to cover floors and walls

Glazed Wall Tile is intended for decorative interior applications. The most popular size is 4½ by 4½ inches, but many other rectangular, hexagonal, octagonal sizes are available.

Mosaic Tile is premounted and spaced on a fabric backing. All mosaics come with ¹⁄₁₆-inch joints.

Paver Tile is formed by compressing clay dust. Most pavers are rectangular, but hexagons and Spanish patterns are also available.

Floor Tile (Porcelain) is made of highly refined clay and fired at extreme temperatures, resulting in a floor surface which wears well and is water- and frost-resistant.

Quarry Tile is an extremely hard, wear-resistant, unglazed, moderately-priced tile which is ideal for floors.

Natural Stone, usually cut to standard sizes, is also used as a flooring tile. Granite, marble, and slate are the most popular, with the granite and marble usually polished to a mirror finish.

Floor Tile Ratings

Floor tiles, unlike wall tiles, are subject to wear and freezing, and must not be slippery underfoot. The most important ratings to consider are as follows:

Coefficient of Friction (ASTM C 1028) tells how slippery the tile is when dry and when wet. It is thus vital when trying to avoid slip and fall injuries. The American Disabilities Act (ADA) requires ratings of ≥0.6 for level floors and ≥0.8 for ramps.

Water Absorption (ASTM C 373) tells the maximum amount of water the tile can absorb as a percentage by weight. It is important if exposed to freeze–thaw cycles. *Non-vitreous* absorbs >7 percent water, *semi-vitreous* absorbs 3 to 7 percent water, *vitreous* absorbs .5 to 3 percent water, and *impervious* absorbs <0.5 percent water.

Abrasive Hardness (ASTM C 501) Measures the resistance to abrasion of the tile surface. The higher the number, the harder the tile surface:

1. walls only.
2. low-traffic residential.
3. residential and medium interior commercial.
4. heavy interior commercial.
5. extra-heavy interior or exterior commercial.

Modular Ceramic Tile Sizes

Type	Thickness	Shape	Dimensions, inches
Glazed Wall	⁵⁄₁₆	rectangular	3x6, 4¼x4¼, 6x4¼, 6x6, 6x8, 8x10
Mosaic	¼	rectangular	1x1, 1x2, 2x2
	¼	hexagonal	1x1, 2x2
Paver	³⁄₈	rectangular	4x4, 4x8, 6x6
	½	rectangular	4x4, 4x8, 6x6
Floor	³⁄₈	rectangular	6x6, 6x12, 12x12, 13x13, 16x16
Quarry	½	rectangular	3x3, 3x6, 4x4, 4x8, 6x6, 8x8
	¾	rectangular	4x8, 6x6

Tile Setting Materials

Cement Backerboard

Other than concrete, the best base for setting tiles is cement backerboard, a fiberglass-reinforced cement panel which is rigid and water-resistant. It comes in panel sizes of 3×5 feet, 4×4 feet, and 4×8 feet and thicknesses of ¼ and ½ inches.

Fasten the backerboard in place using 1¼-inch (1½-inch for ½-inch board) No. 8 galvanized, wafer-head, self-countersinking screws, available where backerboard is sold.

Mortars and Adhesives

A wide variety of materials is available for setting tiles. The choice depends on the application (wet or dry, freezing or not) and the skill level of the tile setter.

Organic mastics are used exclusively for wall tiles up to 6 by 6 inches which are not subject to loads. They are convenient in that they are supplied premixed in a can.

Thin-set mortars consist of premixed sand and portland cement. A latex additive improves bonding, water resistance, and flexibility. The latex version is recommended over all wood substrates.

Grout

Grout (for filling the joints between tiles) may be identical to the tile-setting material, except that organic mastic may be used only for setting tile. More commonly the grout is of finer consistency and contains dye to match or complement the color(s) of the tile. Latex grout, like latex-additive mortar, improves bonding, water resistance, and flexibility.

Tile-Setting Materials

Material	Form	Bed, in	Advantages	Disadvantages
Organic adhesive	Ready-set mastic	1/16	Easy application Low cost Flexible bond	Interior only Immersion resistance
Epoxy mortar	2 or 3 parts mixed on site	1/16–1/8	Excellent resistance to water and chemicals Very strong bond	Limited working time Difficult application
Thin-set mortar	Dry mix of portland cement, sand, and latex	¼	Immersion resistance Freeze resistance	Requirement of being kept moist for 3 days before grouting
Portland cement mortar	Portland cement, sand, and water mixed on site	¾ walls 1¼ floors	Allowance for slight leveling of uneven surfaces	Presoaking of tiles required; metal lath reinforcement recommended

Standard Tile Sizes

FIELD TILE (thickness ⁵⁄₁₆")

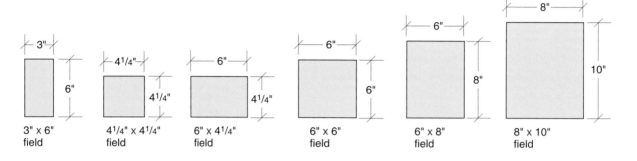

3" x 6"
field

4¹/₄" x 4¹/₄"
field

6" x 4¹/₄"
field

6" x 6"
field

6" x 8"
field

8" x 10"
field

TRIM SECTIONS (thickness ⁵⁄₁₆")

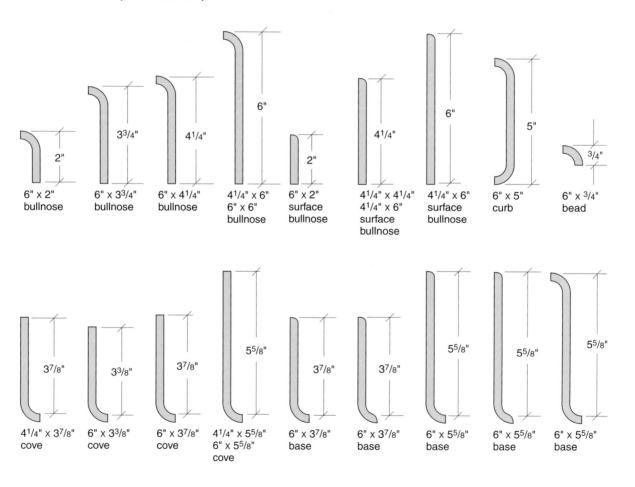

6" x 2"
bullnose

6" x 3³/₄"
bullnose

6" x 4¹/₄"
bullnose

4¹/₄" x 6"
6" x 6"
bullnose

6" x 2"
surface
bullnose

4¹/₄" x 4¹/₄"
4¹/₄" x 6"
surface
bullnose

4¹/₄" x 6"
surface
bullnose

6" x 5"
curb

6" x ³/₄"
bead

4¹/₄" x 3⁷/₈"
cove

6" x 3³/₈"
cove

6" x 3⁷/₈"
cove

4¹/₄" x 5⁵/₈"
6" x 5⁵/₈"
cove

6" x 3⁷/₈"
base

6" x 3⁷/₈"
base

6" x 5⁵/₈"
base

6" x 5⁵/₈"
base

6" x 5⁵/₈"
base

Mosaic Tile

FIELD TILE (thickness ¼")

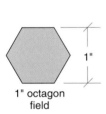

1" x 1"
field

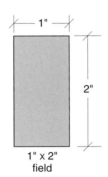

1" x 2"
field

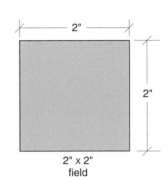

2" x 2"
field

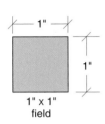

1" octagon
field

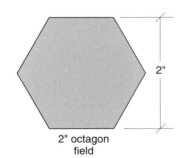

2" octagon
field

TRIM SECTIONS (thickness ¼")

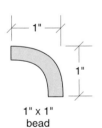

1" x 1"
bead

2" x 1"
bead

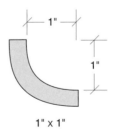

1" x 1"
cove

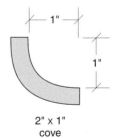

2" x 1"
cove

1" x 1"
surface
bullnose

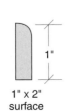

1" x 2"
surface
bullnose

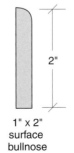

1" x 2"
surface
bullnose

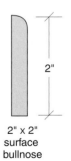

2" x 2"
surface
bullnose

PAVER FIELD TILE
(both ½" and ⅜" thick)

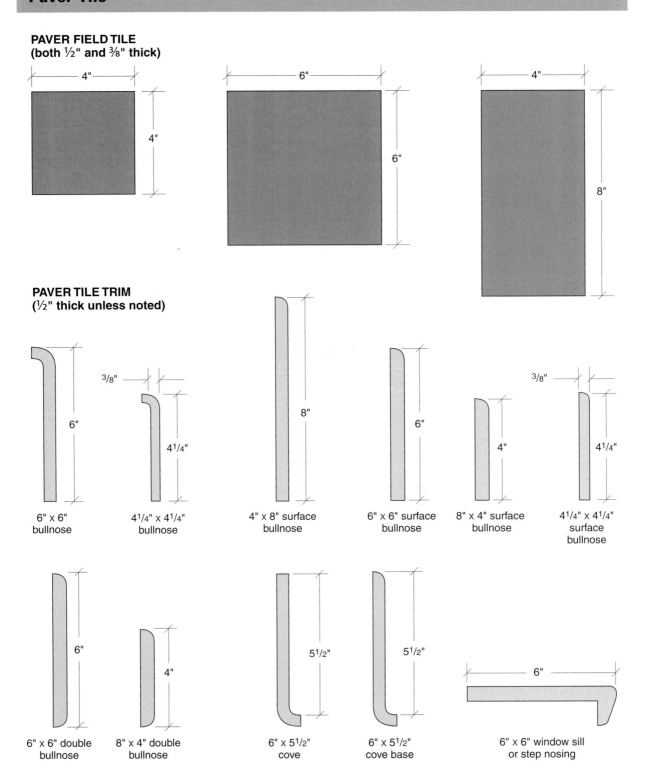

PAVER TILE TRIM
(½" thick unless noted)

4"

6"

4"

4"

6"

8"

6" x 6"
bullnose

4¼" x 4¼"
bullnose

4" x 8" surface
bullnose

6" x 6" surface
bullnose

8" x 4" surface
bullnose

4¼" x 4¼"
surface
bullnose

6" x 6" double
bullnose

8" x 4" double
bullnose

6" x 5½"
cove

6" x 5½"
cove base

6" x 6" window sill
or step nosing

Quarry Tile

FIELD TILES (thickness ½")

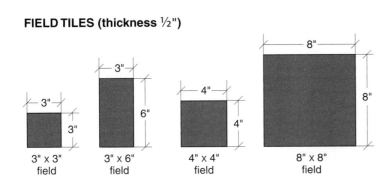

3" x 3"
field

3" x 6"
field

4" x 4"
field

8" x 8"
field

FIELD TILES (thickness ½" & ¾")

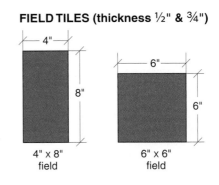

4" x 8"
field

6" x 6"
field

QUARRY TILE TRIM

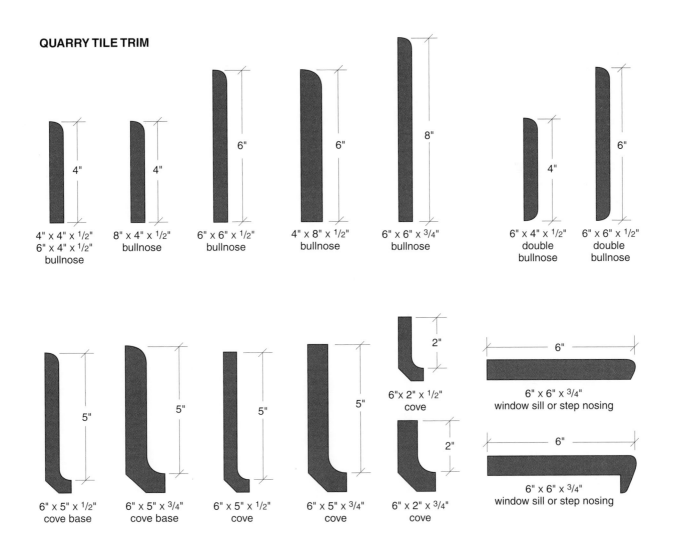

4" x 4" x ½"
6" x 4" x ½"
bullnose

8" x 4" x ½"
bullnose

6" x 6" x ½"
bullnose

4" x 8" x ½"
bullnose

6" x 6" x ¾"
bullnose

6" x 4" x ½"
double
bullnose

6" x 6" x ½"
double
bullnose

6" x 5" x ½"
cove base

6" x 5" x ¾"
cove base

6" x 5" x ½"
cove

6" x 5" x ¾"
cove

6" x 2" x ¾"
cove

6" x 2" x ½"
cove

6" x 6" x ¾"
window sill or step nosing

6" x 6" x ¾"
window sill or step nosing

Tile Patterns

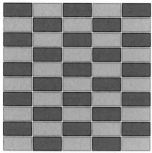

Dark rectangle 50%
Light rectangle 50%

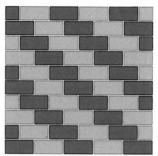

Dark rectangle 50%
Light rectangle 50%

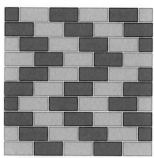

Dark rectangle 50%
Light rectangle 50%

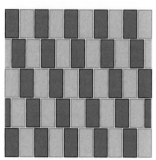

Dark rectangle 50%
Light rectangle 50%

Dark rectangle 67%
Light rectangle 33%

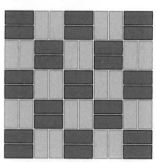

Dark rectangle 50%
Light rectangle 50%

Dark rectangle 50%
Light rectangle 50%

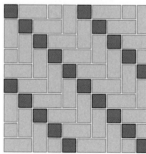

Dark square 20%
Light rectangle 80%

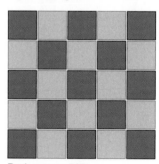

Dark square 50%
Light square 50%

Dark rectangle 50%
Light rectangle 50%

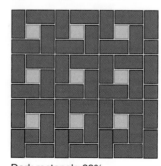

Dark rectangle 89%
Light square 11%

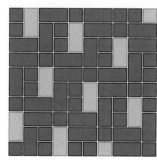

Dark rectangle 58%   Dark square 25%
Light rectangle 17%

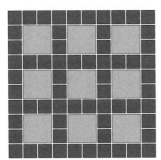

Dark square 56%
Light square 44%

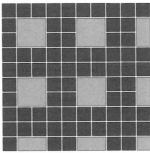

Dark square 75%
Light square 25%

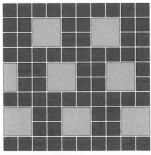

Dark square 67%
Light square 33%

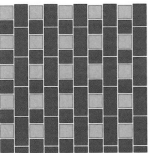

Dark square 25%   Dark rectangle 50%
Light square 25%

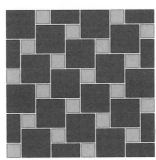

Dark square 80%
Light square 20%

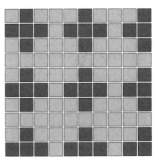

Dark square 31%
Light square 69%

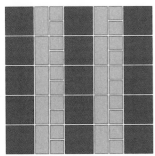

Dark square 50%   Light rectangle 25%
Light square 25%

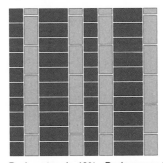

Dark rectangle 40%   Dark square 20%
Light rectangle 40%

Small light square 4%   Dark rectangle 32%
Large light square 64%

Small light square 33%   Light rectangle 33%
Large dark square 33%

Dark square 50%
Light square 50%

Dark square 20%
Light rectangle 80%

Hardwood Flooring

Hardwood flooring is available in three styles: strip, plank, and parquet.

Strip Flooring

Strip flooring is tongue-and-grooved on all four edges, making for a very secure installation without visible nails. Lengths vary by grade. The table below shows the standard cross-sectional sizes (thickness by width) and the board feet to order to cover a specified floor area. The table assumes a 5-percent cutting-waste factor.

Plank Flooring

Plank flooring is the same as strip flooring, except widths range from 3 to 8 inches. Because of its greater width, plank flooring is subject to more swelling and shrinkage with change in humidity. Standard planks should be installed with a gap the thickness of a putty knife. Laminated plank is also available in three-ply construction. Because plank flooring is sold by the square footage of its face dimensions, simply multiply the floor area by 1.05 to allow for waste.

Estimating Hardwood Strip Flooring (board ft, assuming 5% waste)

Floor Area, sq ft	3/4 x 1 1/2	3/4 x 2 1/4	3/4 x 3 1/4	Cross-Sectional Size, in 1/2 x 1 1/2	1/2 x 2	3/8 x 1 1/2	3/8 x 2
5	8	7	6	7	7	7	7
10	16	14	13	14	13	14	13
20	31	28	26	28	26	28	26
30	47	42	39	42	39	42	39
40	62	55	52	55	52	55	52
50	78	69	65	69	65	69	65
60	93	83	77	83	78	83	78
70	109	97	90	97	91	97	91
80	124	111	103	111	104	111	104
90	140	125	116	125	117	125	117
100	155	138	129	138	130	138	130
200	310	277	258	277	260	277	260
300	465	415	387	415	390	415	390
400	620	553	516	553	520	553	520
500	775	691	645	691	650	691	650

Parquet Flooring

Parquet flooring consists of either slats (precisely milled short strips) or blocks (strips preassembled into square units). Slats are usually square edged. Blocks may be square edged or, more commonly, tongue-and-grooved on all four sides. Most blocks are ⁵⁄₁₆-inch thick.

Face dimensions vary with manufacturer but are usually 6 by 6, 8 by 8, 9 by 9, 10 by 10, or 12 by 12 inches. The illustrations below show a few of the dozens of parquet patterns which can be either purchased as blocks or assembled from strips.

Parquet Patterns

BRICK

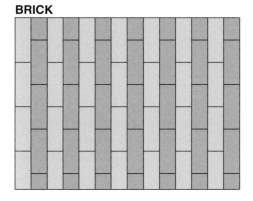

HERRINGBONE

FOURSQUARE

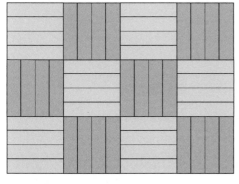

FOURSQUARE LAID DIAGONALLY

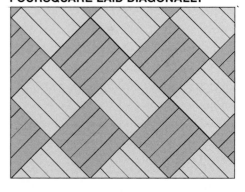

FINGER

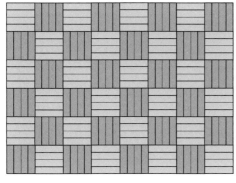

FINGER LAID DIAGONALLY

Strip Flooring Installation

Solid wood flooring is subject to dimensional change when its moisture content changes. Make sure the flooring never gets wet, is stored in a dry location, and is allowed to equilibrate for at least five days at the building site prior to installation.

When flooring is installed over a concrete slab with plywood subfloor (illustration at right), the slab must be dry and must not be located below grade. Tape a 1-square-foot piece of clear polyethylene to the slab for 24 hours; if no condensation appears, the slab is dry.

Apply cold cut-back asphalt mastic with a fine-tooth, 100-square-foot-per-gallon trowel. After it dries 1½ hours minimum, unroll 6-mil polyethylene over the entire area with 6-inch overlaps. Walk on the entire surface to make sure the mastic makes contact. (Small bubbles may be punctured.)

Nail ¾-inch sheathing or underlayment-grade plywood to the slab, leaving ¾-inch spaces at walls and ¼ inch between panels. Nail or cement finish flooring to the plywood per manufacturer's instructions.

Strip flooring may also be installed over a slab and wood sleepers. Lay pressure-treated 18- to 48-inch random-cut 2×4 sleepers 12 inches on-center in asphalt mastic (enough for 100 percent contact). Stagger and overlap the sleepers at least 4 inches. Leave ¾ inch at walls. Cover with polyethylene, lapping joints at sleepers.

With conventional wood joist construction over a basement or crawl space, either outside cross ventilation must be provided or the crawl space must be unvented and supplied with conditioned air (see p. 387). In either case, the crawl space earth must be covered with polyethylene. The subfloor should be either ⅝-inch or thicker performance-rated exterior or underlayment plywood or ¾-inch square-edge, group I dense softwood boards laid diagonally on joists with ¼-inch spaces. Plywood must be laid with the face veneer across joists.

Slab with Plywood Subfloor

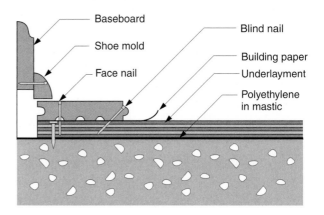

- Baseboard
- Shoe mold
- Face nail
- Blind nail
- Building paper
- Underlayment
- Polyethylene in mastic

Slab with Wood Sleepers

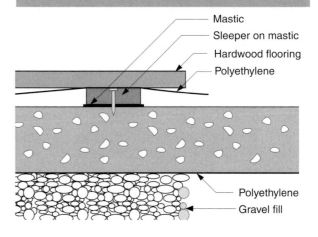

- Mastic
- Sleeper on mastic
- Hardwood flooring
- Polyethylene
- Polyethylene
- Gravel fill

Over Crawl Space

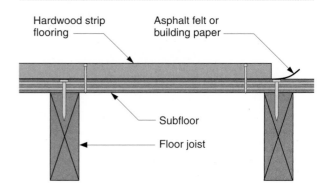

- Hardwood strip flooring
- Asphalt felt or building paper
- Subfloor
- Floor joist

Plank Flooring Installation

Sealing the backs of planks greater than 4 inches wide is recommended to minimize cupping with moisture changes.

Random-width planks are installed in the same way as strip flooring, except for a combination of edge nails and countersunk and plugged face screws, as shown in the illustration at right. The general practice is to blind nail through the tongue as with conventional strip flooring. Pairs of flat-head or drywall screws at the ends of the planks hold the ends securely and are aesthetically pleasing. The countersunk screws are then covered with wood plugs glued into the holes.

Use 1-inch screws for flooring laid over ¾-inch plywood on a slab. Use 1- to 1¼-inch screws for planks over screeds or wood joists. Some manufacturers recommend leaving an expansion crack the thickness of a putty knife between planks.

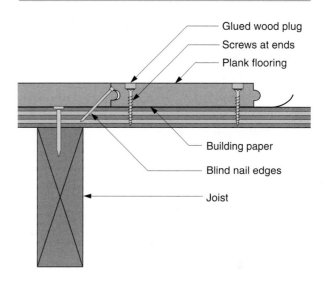

Fasteners for Plank Flooring

- Glued wood plug
- Screws at ends
- Plank flooring
- Building paper
- Blind nail edges
- Joist

Nailing Schedule

Flooring	Fasteners	Spacing
¾"-THICK T&G		
1½", 2¼", 3¼" strip	2" barbed flooring cleat 7d or 8d flooring nail 7d or 8d casing nail 2" 15-ga staples with ½" crowns	8"–12"
4"–8" plank	2" barbed flooring cleat 7d or 8d flooring nail 2" 15-ga staples with ½" crowns	8"
½"-THICK T&G		
1½", 2" wide	1½" barbed flooring cleat 5d screw cut steel or wire casing nail	10"
⅜"-THICK T&G		
1½", 2" wide	1¼" barbed flooring cleat 4d bright wire casing nail	8"
⁵⁄₁₆"-THICK SQUARE EDGE		
1½", 2" wide	1" 15-ga fully barbed flooring brad	2 nails every 7"
1⅓" wide	1" 15-ga barbed flooring brad	1 nail every 5" alternate sides

Notes: 1. T&G flooring blind nailed on tongue edge. 2. Face nailing required on starting and ending strips. 3. Hard species may require predrilling to avoid splits. 4. Always follow manufacturer's specific fastening instructions.

Gypsum Wallboard

Gypsum Wallboard Types

Gypsum wallboard, due to its low cost, ease of application, ease of finishing, and superior fire and acoustic properties, is the most common wall material. The table below shows the readily available types and sizes of gypsum wallboard and their applications.

Gypsum Drywall Products

Type	Application	Edge Types	Thicknesses, in	Lengths, ft
Regular	Usual wall and ceiling applications in dry locations where special fire rating not required	Tapered, square, rounded	¼ ⅜ ½ ⅝	6, 8, 10, 12
Foil-backed	Same as regular, but with aluminum foil back face suitable as vapor barrier	Tapered, rounded, square	⅜ ½ ⅝	6, 8, 10, 12, 14, 16
Water-resistant (type W)	Moist areas such as bathrooms; As base for ceramic tile	Tapered	½ ⅝	8, 11, 12
Fire-rated (type X)	Walls and ceilings with increased fire rating	Tapered, rounded, square	½ ⅝	6, 8, 10, 12, 14, 16

Fasteners

Various specialized fasteners have been developed specifically for gypsum drywall (see the table below). The appropriate type depends not on the type of drywall, but on the type of substrate being fastened to. The drywall screw has proven so technically superior in wood-to-wood applications, as well, that it is now available in lengths to 4 inches.

Fasteners for Gypsum Wallboard

Type	Common Length	Application	Base Penetration
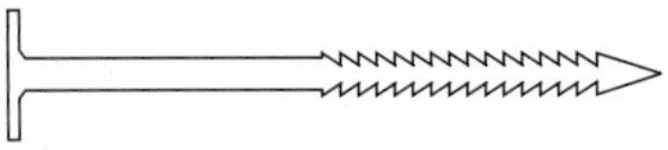 RING-SHANK NAIL	1¼"	Single layer of wallboard to wood framing or furring	¾"
 TYPE W SCREW	1¼"	Single layer of wallboard to wood framing or furring	⅝"
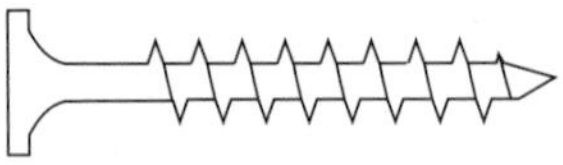 TYPE S SCREW	1"	Single layer of wallboard to sheet-metal studs and furring	⅜"
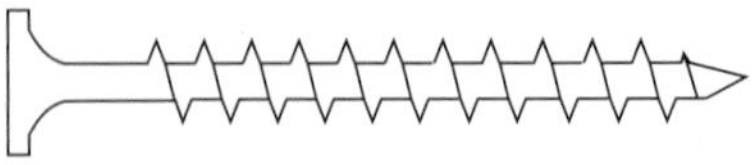 TYPE G SCREW	1⅝"	Wallboard to gypsum wallboard or wood framing	½"

Achieving Fire Ratings

Walls with 45-minute and 1-hour fire ratings are often required in residential construction. For example, the International Residential Code requires a 1-hour rating for the wall separating a dwelling from an attached garage and, unless that wall extends to the roof, a 45-minute rating for the garage ceiling.

Commercial buildings may require even greater fire ratings. Gypsum drywall is ideally suited to fire-rated construction because the material of which it is formed contains chemically bound water in the ratio of 1 quart to 10 pounds of drywall. The temperature of the drywall and the framing that it protects cannot rise much above 212°F until all of the water has been converted to steam and driven off.

The illustration below shows drywall constructions that achieve fire ratings of 1 to 4 hours. The framing material can be either wood or steel.

Fire-Rated Constructions

45-MINUTE RATING

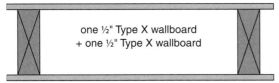

one ½" Type X wallboard
+ one ½" Type X wallboard

1-HOUR RATING

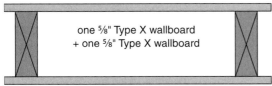

one ⅝" Type X wallboard
+ one ⅝" Type X wallboard

1.5-HOUR RATING

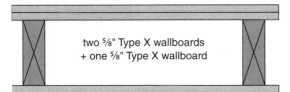

two ⅝" Type X wallboards
+ one ⅝" Type X wallboard

2-HOUR RATING

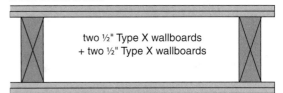

two ½" Type X wallboards
+ two ½" Type X wallboards

3-HOUR RATING (estimated)

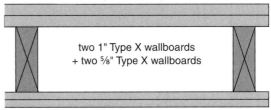

two 1" Type X wallboards
+ two ⅝" Type X wallboards

4-HOUR RATING (estimated)

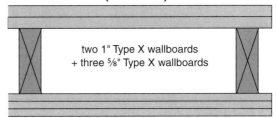

two 1" Type X wallboards
+ three ⅝" Type X wallboards

Fastening Schedule

The illustration below shows the maximum recommended fastener spacing. Select fastener lengths as shown at right for adequate framing penetration:

- ring-shank nails — ¾ inch into wood
- type W screws — ⅝ inch into wood
- type S screws — ⅜ inch into metal
- type G screws — ½ inch into gypsum

Gypsum Drywall Fastener Spacing

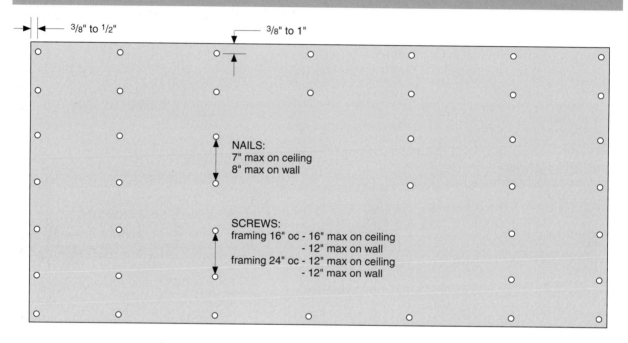

3/8" to 1/2"   3/8" to 1"

NAILS:
7" max on ceiling
8" max on wall

SCREWS:
framing 16" oc - 16" max on ceiling
- 12" max on wall
framing 24" oc - 12" max on ceiling
- 12" max on wall

Metal Trim Accessories

The illustration below shows a selection of commonly used trim accessories designed to protect exposed drywall edges from mechanical damage and produce in combination with drywall compound.

Plastic and lightweight steel versions of these profiles are available; both materials cut easily with tin snips. The best results on corner and L-beads are obtained when the trim is bedded and nailed into joint compound, then finished unlike a taped joint (see p. 421).

Drywall Trim Accessories

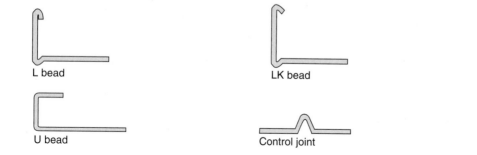
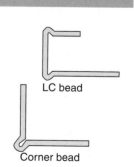

L bead

LK bead

LC bead

U bead

Control joint

Corner bead

Floating Corner Techniques

The cracking of ceiling/wall joints and room corners is minimized by a technique known as floating. Drywall is always applied to the ceiling first, then the wall panels are shoved up tightly beneath.

Where the ceiling/wall joint runs parallel to the ceiling framing (see the illustration at top right), the ceiling panel is nailed or screwed at its edge, and the wall panel is not.

Where the ceiling/wall joint is perpendicular to the ceiling framing (see the illustration at middle right) neither edge is fastened.

At room corner joints (see the illustration at bottom right), the edge of the underlying, or first-applied, sheet floats.

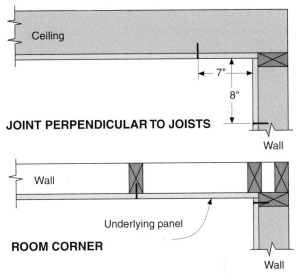

Gypsum Drywall Corner Fastening

Ceiling

Underlying panel — 8"

JOINT PARALLEL TO JOISTS

Wall

Ceiling

7"

8"

JOINT PERPENDICULAR TO JOISTS

Wall

Wall

Underlying panel

ROOM CORNER

Wall

Fastener Pops

Fastener pops are most often the result of high-moisture-content framing drying and shrinking after drywalling. As shown in the illustration, the midpoint of the engaged threads of the fastener remain in place while the dimension between the midpoint and the framing edge shrinks by as much as 5 percent. If the drywall follows the framing (it usually does), the compound covering the fastener head pops out.

Delay repairing pops until the end of the heating season when the framing is finished shrinking. Press the gypsum board into firm contact with the framing, then drive the popped fasteners to just below the surface of the drywall. Remove loose material and fill the depressions with low-shrinkage spackling compound.

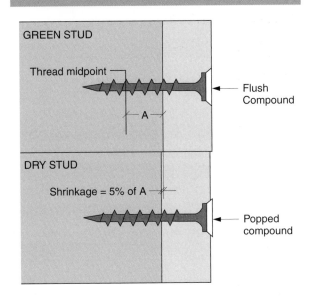

Why Drywall Fasteners "Pop"

GREEN STUD

Thread midpoint

Flush Compound

A

DRY STUD

Shrinkage = 5% of A

Popped compound

Estimating Drywall Materials

The illustration at right and table below allow simple estimation of the materials required to finish walls and ceilings:

1. Measure the room's length, L, width, W, and height, H, in feet.

2. Calculate ceiling area: $A_c = L \times W$.

3. Calculate wall area: $A_w = 2H(L + W)$

4. Total ceiling and wall areas: $A_t = A_c + A_w$.

5. Calculate net area, A_n, by deducting from A_t for each of the items below:

- windows, 8 square feet
- doors, 11 square feet
- fireplace, 16 square feet
- patio door or bay window, 22 square feet.

6. Using A_n, find the required quantities of drywall, tape, joint compound, and screws or nails in the table below.

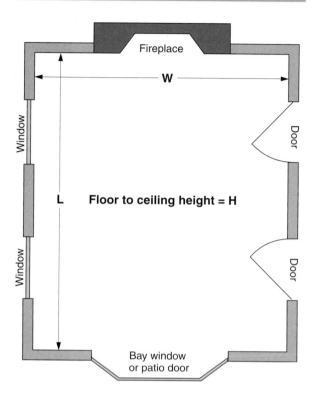

Room Dimensions for Estimating

Fireplace

W

Window

Door

L

Floor to ceiling height = H

Window

Door

Bay window or patio door

Estimating Drywall Materials

Area, A_n, sq ft	Wallboard Size			Joint Compound, lb	Joint Tape, ft	Drywall Nails	Drywall Screws
	4 x 8	4 x 10	4 x 12				
100	4	3	3	14	35	168	90
200	7	5	5	28	70	294	150
300	10	8	7	42	105	420	240
400	13	10	9	56	140	546	300
500	16	13	11	70	175	672	390
600	19	15	13	84	210	798	456
700	22	18	15	98	245	924	528
800	25	20	17	112	280	1,050	600
900	29	23	19	126	315	1,218	696
1000	32	25	21	140	350	1,344	768
2000	63	50	42	280	700	2,646	1,512
3000	94	75	63	420	1,050	3,948	2,256
4000	125	100	84	560	1,400	5,250	3,000

Joint Taping

Joints between sheets of gypsum drywall are taped and covered with joint compound. Tapered-edge boards have the two longer edges tapered to facilitate the process. Drywall should be applied either horizontally or vertically, in the manner which minimizes the number of square-edge joints, which require a much wider application of compound.

1. Fill the tapered area with compound, using a 6-inch trowel. Apply reinforcing tape, and press the tape firmly into the compound. Remove excess compound.

2. After the compound has dried completely, apply a second coat 8 inches wide, at square-edge joints, 12 to 16 inches wide.

3. After the second coat has dried, lightly sand or wipe with a damp sponge to remove and ridges or bumps. Apply a 12-inch-wide final coat. Lightly sand before painting.

4. Apply 2 inches of compound to both sides of inside corners. Fold the tape and press into the corner. Remove excess compound, leaving just enough under the tape for adhesion. Apply a finish coat to one side of the corner. Allow to dry, then apply a

Gypsum Drywall Taping

DRYWALL JOINT TAPING

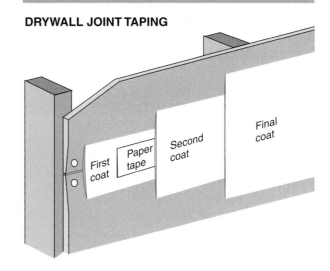

finish coat to the other side of the corner. After the finish coat is dry, lightly sand and prime.

5. Install metal cornerbead over outside corners. Apply compound over the cornerbead 4 inches wide, then 6 inches wide, then 10 inches wide on either side of the corner, allowing each layer to first dry. After the finish coat is dry, lightly sand and prime.

Estimated Drying Time for Taped Joints

Relative Humidity	Temperature, °F						
	32	40	50	60	70	80	100
0%	38 hours	28 hours	19 hours	13 hours	9 hours	6 hours	3 hours
20%	48 hours	34 hours	23 hours	16 hours	11 hours	8 hours	4 hours
30%	2.2 days	39 hours	26 hours	18 hours	12 hours	9 hours	5 hours
40%	2.5 days	44 hours	29 hours	20 hours	14 hours	10 hours	5 hours
50%	3 days	2 days	36 hours	24 hours	17 hours	12 hours	6 hours
60%	3.5 days	2.5 days	42 hours	29 hours	20 hours	14 hours	8 hours
70%	4.5 days	3.5 days	2.2 days	38 hours	26 hours	19 hours	10 hours
80%	7 days	4.5 days	3.2 days	2.2 days	38 hours	27 hours	14 hours
90%	13 days	9 days	6 days	4.5 days	3 days	2 days	26 hours
98%	53 days	37 days	26 days	18 days	12 days	9 days	5 days

Wood Paneling

Nothing beats the warmth of genuine wood paneling, whether it be of irreplaceable old walnut, wide old-growth clear pine, or inexpensive knotty pine. The table below, from the Western Wood Products Association, provides area factors to help estimate of the number of board feet required to cover walls:

1. Calculate the gross area by multiplying ceiling height by room perimeter, in feet.

2. Deduct the areas of windows, doors, and other non-paneled areas to get net area.

3. Multiply net area by the appropriate area factor in the table, and add 10 percent for waste.

Wood Paneling Coverage

Paneling Style	Nominal Size, in	Width Total, in	Width Face, in	Area Factor
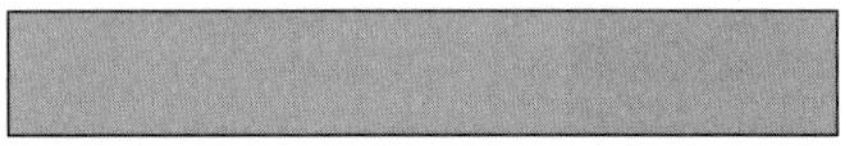 **SQUARE-EDGE BOARD**	1x4	3½	3½	1.14
	1x6	5½	5½	1.09
	1x8	7¼	7¼	1.10
	1x10	9¼	9¼	1.08
	1x12	11¼	11¼	1.07
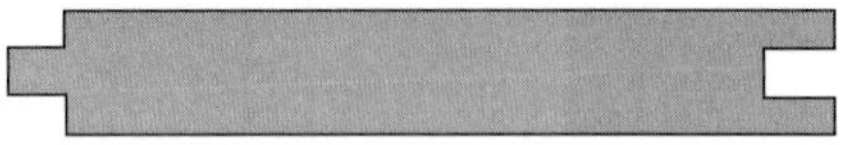 **TONGUE & GROOVE**	1x4	3⅜	3⅛	1.28
	1x6	5⅜	5⅛	1.17
	1x8	7⅛	6⅞	1.16
	1x10	9⅛	8⅞	1.13
	1x12	11⅛	10⅞	1.10
 **PROFILE PATTERN (various)**	1x6	5⁷⁄₁₆	5¹⁄₁₆	1.19
	1x8	7⅛	6¾	1.19
	1x10	9⅛	8¾	1.14
	1x12	11⅛	10¾	1.12
 **V-JOINT RUSTIC**	1x6	5⅜	5	1.20
	1x8	7⅛	6¾	1.19
	1x10	9⅛	8¾	1.14
	1x12	11⅛	10¾	1.12
 **CHANNEL RUSTIC**	1x6	5⅜	4⅞	1.23
	1x8	7⅛	6⅝	1.21
	1x10	9⅛	8⅝	1.16
	1x12	11⅛	10⅝	1.13

Paneling over Masonry

Over a masonry wall (see drawing at right), 1×4 strapping should be fastened with either masonry nails or construction adhesive 36 inches on-center maximum. If the masonry wall is below grade, first apply a 6-mil vapor barrier, stapling it to the sill plate. Then install 1×4 furring, 36 inches on-center maximum, with masonry nails. An alternative is to install a stud wall and then wire and insulate between the studs before paneling.

Trim

If the paneling has relief, baseboards will look better installed flush than installed over the paneling. Flush baseboards may be installed over furring strips, as in the illustration at right, or over 2×4 blocking between the studs. There should be sufficient blocking to catch not only the baseboard, but the bottom of the paneling as well.

The second and third illustrations at right apply to either door or window trim.

If the paneling is applied directly to the existing wall surface, simply remove the existing door and window trim and replace them with square-edge strips of the same thickness and species as the paneling.

If the paneling is furred out, use jamb extenders to bring the jambs out to the finish wall surface, and apply casing over the joint.

Electrical switch and receptacle boxes can be left in place with convenient extension collars, available from electrical suppliers and larger hardware stores.

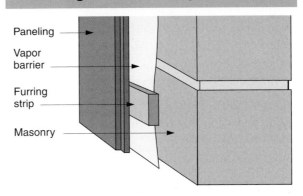

Paneling over Masonry

- Paneling
- Vapor barrier
- Furring strip
- Masonry

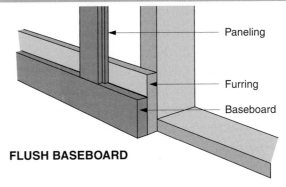

Trim Details

- Paneling
- Furring
- Baseboard

FLUSH BASEBOARD

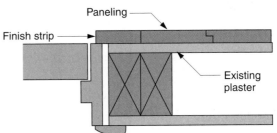

- Finish strip
- Paneling
- Existing plaster

PANELING OVER EXISTING PLASTER

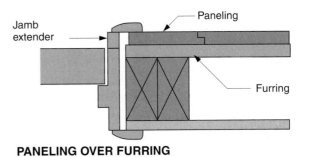

- Jamb extender
- Paneling
- Furring

PANELING OVER FURRING

Suspended Ceilings

A suspended ceiling is a simple and inexpensive way to achieve a level ceiling beneath an existing ceiling or roof, whether flat or not. A strong point is the convenience of "dropping in" fluorescent fixtures at any point. A weakness is a commercial look, not appropriate to residences except in utilitarian rooms such as laundries, game rooms, or workshops.

Installation

Install a suspended ceiling as follows:

1. Plot the dimensions of the room on a large piece of 8 by 8-inch graph paper. Let each square represent either 3 or 6 inches. On the plot, draw a 2 by 4-foot grid so that the spaces next to the perimeter are symmetric and as large as possible (see the illustration on the facing page).

2. If the original ceiling is flat and level, measure down to the level of the new ceiling (allowing 6 inches minimum for recessed light fixtures), and snap a chalk line around the perimeter of the room. If the ceiling is not level, establish a level perimeter with a laser level or a line level.

3. Fasten sections of wall angle with the bottom flanges at the level of the perimeter line. Nail them into studs if possible. Don't be shy about poking holes in the wall to find stud locations—as long as the holes are above the suspended-ceiling level where they will be out of sight.

4. Stretch strings along the positions of the main tees. Use a plumb bob or level to mark the locations where the string intersects the ceiling joists overhead. Again, don't be afraid to poke holes to find the joist locations: They'll never be seen.

5. Cut suspension wires 12 inches longer than the distance between the old ceiling or ceiling joists and the wall angle, and fasten a wire at each marked intersection. After fastening, make a right-angle bend in the wire at the level of the stretched string.

6. Determine, from the layout sketch, the distance from the wall to the first intersection with a cross tee (1 foot 6 inches in the layout example on the facing page).

Measure this distance from the end of a main tee and select the slot just beyond. From the slot, measure back toward the original end, and mark. Cut the main tee ⅛ inch shorter than the mark, which allows for the thickness of the wall angle.

7. Install all of the main tees, repeating step 6 each time. Main tees are 12 feet long, but splice fittings are available if required.

8. Install the cross tees by snapping the end tongues into the main tee slots. Cross tees at the perimeter will have to be cut to fit.

9. Install the wiring for any recessed light fixtures.

10. Install the ceiling panels, cutting perimeter panels as necessary with a utility knife and straightedge.

Cutting a Main Tee

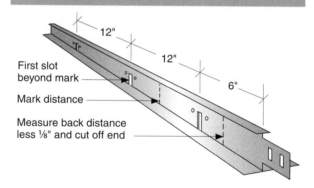

First slot beyond mark

Mark distance

Measure back distance less ⅛" and cut off end

12" 12" 6"

Installing Cross Tees

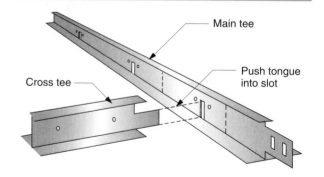

Main tee

Push tongue into slot

Cross tee

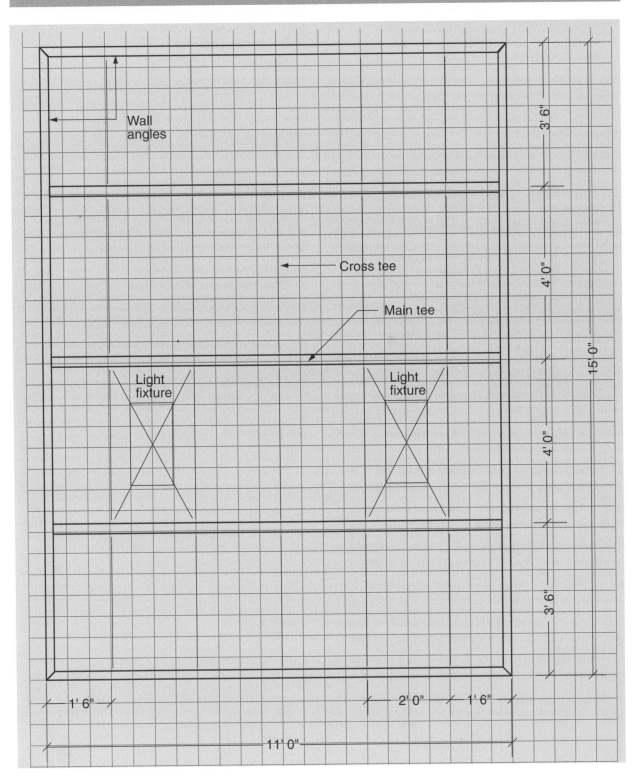

Exterior Finishes

When it comes to finishing newly applied siding, there are six basic choices: no finish at all, water-repellent preservatives, semitransparent stains, paint, solid-color stains, and transparent coatings.

No Finish It should be noted that paints and stains do not necessarily preserve wood. If protected from excessive running water, such as by a moderate to large roof overhang, wood beveled siding and shingles may last a century or more. More specifically, paint and stain preserve an appearance. The decision is a tough one because, once painted, exterior wood requires some sort of recoating every 5 to 10 years at best.

Water-Repellent Preservatives These keep water out of wood and thus reduce the mechanical stresses of swelling and shrinking. The addition of a preservative chemical prevents mildew and dry rot in horizontal members such as deck joists and window sills. Preservatives usually have no color of their own but darken natural wood somewhat. The very large drawback is that they need to be reapplied every few years, an expensive prospect for the average home.

Semitransparent Stains These are most often water-repellent preservatives with light pigmentation. In addition to supplying the positive qualities of a repellent and preservative, the stains penetrate the wood surface without forming a skin. Thus, they impart color but cannot fail by peeling. These treatments must be applied over unpainted wood. Service life is greatest when applied to rough-sawn or already weathered natural wood, due to greater absorption.

Paint For the best overall job of protecting wood outdoors, paint forms a protective coating. Oil-based paint seals out moisture better, but latex paint is more flexible and less likely to fail by cracking and peeling. Latex paint has become increasingly popular, especially with amateur painters, because it is easier to apply, dries quicker than oil-based paint, and cleans up with water. Cleanup for oil paints requires mineral spirits. A proper application of latex or oil paint lasts as long as 10 years. The disadvantage of paint and other film-forming finishes, such as solid stains, is that recoating causes a buildup that eventually has to be laboriously removed.

Solid-Color Stains Like paint, solid-color stains completely obscure the natural color and grain of the wood. They can be latex or oil-based. They have much more pigment than other stains. As a result, they form a film like paint and can even peel as paint does. Solid-color stains can be used over old paint or stain, and in fact, these stains are quite similar to thinned paint. The film layers can build up, but because the stain is thinner than paint, the surface can be recoated many more times before it needs to be stripped. Solid-color stains are not recommended for areas that will be walked on.

Transparent Coatings Forget transparent urethanes, shellacs, and varnishes for exterior use! No matter what the manufacturer claims, the finish will crack and peel within a few years, requiring total removal, or at least extensive sanding before recoating. What fails is not the coating, but the wood beneath. Because the finish is transparent, UV rays from the sun penetrate to the wood substrate, destroying the wood fibers. The fibers turn to powder, leaving the finish coat nothing to adhere to, so the finish lifts.

Performance of Exterior Coatings

Type of Exterior Wood Surface	Water-Repellent Preservative Suitability	Life, yr	Semitransparent Stain Suitability	Life, yr	Paints and Solid Stains Suitability	Life, yr
SIDING						
Cedar and Redwood						
Smooth (vertical grain)	Good	1–2	Fair	2–4	Good	4–6
Rough-sawn or weathered	Good	2–3	Excellent	5–8	Fair	3–5
Pine, Fir, Spruce, etc.						
Smooth (flat grain)	Good	1–2	Poor	2–3	Fair	3–5
Rough (flat grain)	Good	2–3	Good	4–7	Fair	3–5
Shingles						
Sawn	Good	2–3	Excellent	4–8	Fair	3–5
Split	Good	1–2	Excellent	4–8	NA	NA
Plywood (Douglas fir & southern pine)						
Sanded	Poor	1–2	Fair	2–4	Fair	3–5
Rough-sawn	Poor	2–3	Good	4–8	Fair	3–5
Medium-density overlay (MDO)	NA	NA	NA	NA	Excellent	6–8
Plywood (cedar and redwood)						
Sanded	Poor	1–2	Fair	2–4	Fair	3–5
Rough-sawn	Poor	2–3	Excellent	5–8	Fair	3–5
HARDBOARD (MEDIUM DENSITY)						
Smooth						
Unfinished	NA	NA	NA	NA	Good	4–6
Preprimed	NA	NA	NA	NA	Good	4–6
Textured						
Unfinished	NA	NA	NA	NA	Good	4–6
Preprimed	NA	NA	NA	NA	Good	4–6
MILLWORK (USUALLY PINE)						
Windows, doors, trim	Good	NA	Fair	2–3	Good	3–6
DECKING						
New (smooth)	Good	1–2	Fair	2–3	Poor	2–3
Weathered (rough)	Good	2–3	Good	3–6	Poor	2–3
GLUED LAMINATED MEMBERS						
Smooth	Good	1–2	Fair	3–4	Fair	3–4
Rough	Good	2–3	Good	6–8	Fair	3–4
WAFERBOARD	NA	NA	Poor	1–3	Fair	2–4

Interior Paints

Practically speaking, there are three types of interior primer and two types of interior paint:

Shellac-based primer-sealer This primer is designed to prevent bleedthrough of wood resin contained in knots and pitch pockets. It's a good idea to apply at least two coats to knots in wood before painting.

All-purpose latex primer These formulations come close to covering all materials, including gypsum wallboard, plaster, paint and bare wood. But make sure to read the instructions on the can regarding surface preparation.

Alkyd primer Alkyd primer is just the opposite of latex primer: Alkyd primer is the best first coat over raw wood but should not be used on wallboard or masonry.

Latex paint Latex paint is the most popular interior finish because it cleans up with water (warm, soapy water works best). It can be applied over gypsum wallboard, plaster, and masonry. Bare wood should be primed first. Latex also adheres to latex and flat oils. Avoid gloss oils and alkyds other than primers.

Alkyd paint Alkyd paint has nearly replaced natural oil paint. It has the same good qualities as natural oil such as linseed, but it is nearly odor free. Alkyd can be applied over any other paint or bare wood. It should not be applied to bare gypsum wallboard, plaster, or masonry.

The table below compares the advantages and disadvantages of the interior paints.

Interior Primers and Paints

Materials	Advantages	Disadvantages
Shellac-based primer-sealer	Stops bleeding of knots Dries extremely quickly	Stains white; must be painted Requires alcohol for cleanup
All-purpose latex primer	Cleans up with water Dries quickly unless humid Relatively odor-free	Not good on wood
Alkyd primer	Excellent wood primer Suitable primer under all paint types	Not good on gypsum wallboard Requires paint thinner for cleanup
Latex paint	Cleans up with water Dries quickly Relatively odor-free Inexpensive	Requires primer over wood Not as tough as alkyd Adheres poorly to gloss finishes Wets and loosens wallpaper
Alkyd paint	Provides tough finish Relatively odor-free Adheres to all other paints	Dries relatively slowly Requires paint thinner for cleanup Requires primer over masonry, plaster, and gypsum wallboard

Diagnosing Paint Failures

We blame the manufacturer when paints fails prematurely. Ninety percent of paint failures, however are due to either moisture problems or inadequate preparation of the surface. Use the table below to find out what went wrong and what can be done to correct the problem.

Causes and Cures of Paint Failures

Symptom		Possible Causes	Suggested Cures
Alligating	Top layer only	Second coat applied before first coat dry	Remove down to bare wood
	To wood	Paint too thick; lost flexibility	Remove down to bare wood
Blistering	Top layer only	Paint applied in hot sun	Paint on cloudy days
		Surface oily or dirty	Wash surface with detergent; rinse
		Latex applied over heavily chalked paint	Wash, scrub, rinse
	To wood	Moisture driving paint off (from roof leak, ice dam, impervious sheathing, excess humidity, gutter leak)	Eliminate source of moisture / Apply siding over strapping / Insert wedges under siding
Checking of plywood		Expansion, contraction, and delamination of plywood veneers	Sand plywood and paint / Replace plywood
Cracking	Top layer only	Inflexible paint	Scrape and wire brush / Use latex paint
	To wood	Inflexible paint	Remove down to bare wood / Use primer and latex
Flaking off masonry surface		Inadequate preparation of masonry	Wire brush loose paint / Apply masonry conditioner / Apply two coats exterior latex
Mildew/mold	Inside	Cold wall or ceiling due to no insulation	Treat with bleach, insulate
		Lack of air movement	Leave closet doors open
	Outside	Warm, humid outside air with no direct sunlight	Scrub with ½ cup bleach/gallon water, rinse, prime / Use mildew-resistant paint
Peeling inside		Inadequate moisture storage of sheathing	Install fiberboard or wood sheathing
		Rain wicking under siding	Apply siding over strapping
Rust stains		Steel siding nails	Sand all rust, set nails ⅛", prime, fill with caulk, paint
Wrinkling and sagging		Too cold at application (below 50°F) / Second coat applied too soon / Too much paint	Sand smooth, paint over

Wood Moldings

Wood moldings are strips of wood milled with flat or curved surfaces continuous over their lengths. The name molding derives from the fact that they are so perfectly smooth, they appear to be molded of plaster. In fact, they were first intended to be painted to resemble the stone carvings found on classical Greek and Roman buildings. The purposes of moldings include decoration (such as edging for paneling), protection (such as chair rails), and concealment (such as base and cove moldings):

Crown, Bed, and Cove Moldings are milled from thin stock but installed at an angle at the wall/ceiling intersection. This allows the molding to be wide, yet follow irregularities in the wall and ceiling.

Quarter-Rounds are designed to both cover and reinforce the joint between paneling and a frame.

Base Shoes are used alone or on top of regular board stock to cover the wall/floor joint and to protect the base of the wall.

Astragals cover panel joints and sometimes simply add decorative relief.

Screen Moldings are used to fasten and cover the edges of screening material in door and window frames.

Casings visually frame windows and doors and cover the joint between the door or window frame and the plaster or drywall finish. They are hollow on the back side in order to still lie flat despite possible cupping.

Brick Moldings provide casings for doors and windows in masonry walls.

Drip Caps are designed to shed water over doors and windows but have been mostly replaced by metal flashings.

Stops are used on both door and window frames to stop or constrain the motion of the door or sash.

Panel Strips and Mullion Casings are used to join large sections of paneling or to join several window units together.

The most common species of wood used in moldings is pine. Other species used in significant quantities are alder, poplar, cherry, maple, mahogany; red oak, sugar pine, fir, larch, cedar, and hemlock. Clear wood in long lengths is increasingly more expensive, so manufacturers have turned to finger jointing to eliminate defects. As large, clear-wood moldings become more expensive, some manufacturers have begun to offer the most popular moldings in medium-density fiberboard (MDF), polystyrene foam, and polyurethane foam.

The Moulding and Millwork Producers Association (MMPA) provides a comprehensive selection of molding profiles. The illustrations that follow contain *full-scale* sections of the most popular profiles. Regional millwork distributors generally offer selections of these profiles, customized to local demand.

Standard moldings may be combined to create a nearly infinite number of custom moldings. P. 438 and 439 contain a dozen examples of what might easily be created on-site.

Crown Moldings (full scale)

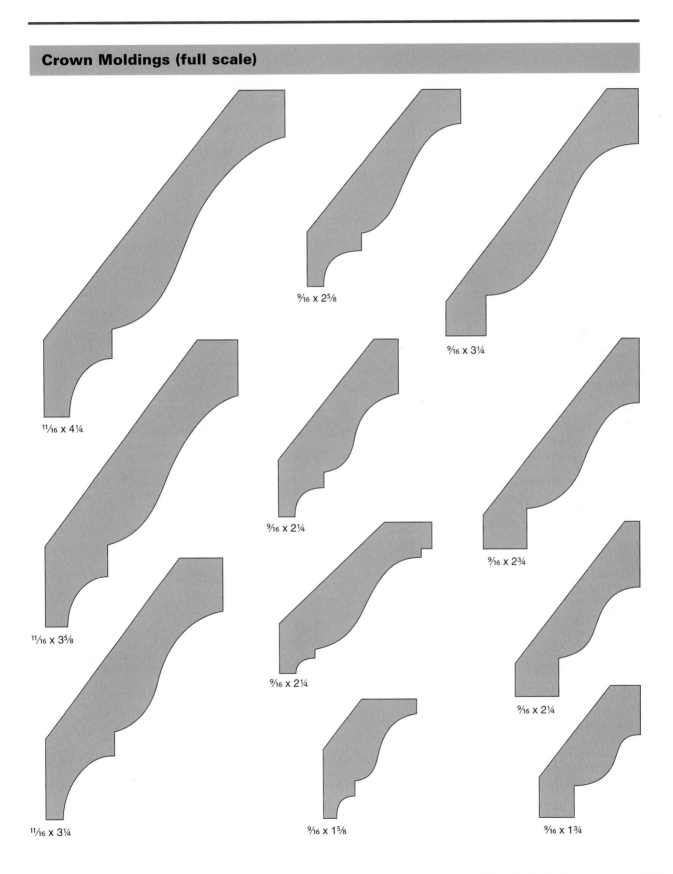

⁹⁄₁₆ x 2⁵⁄₈

⁹⁄₁₆ x 3¼

¹¹⁄₁₆ x 4¼

⁹⁄₁₆ x 2¼

¹¹⁄₁₆ x 3⁵⁄₈

⁹⁄₁₆ x 2¾

⁹⁄₁₆ x 2¼

⁹⁄₁₆ x 2¼

¹¹⁄₁₆ x 3¼

⁹⁄₁₆ x 1⁵⁄₈

⁹⁄₁₆ x 1¾

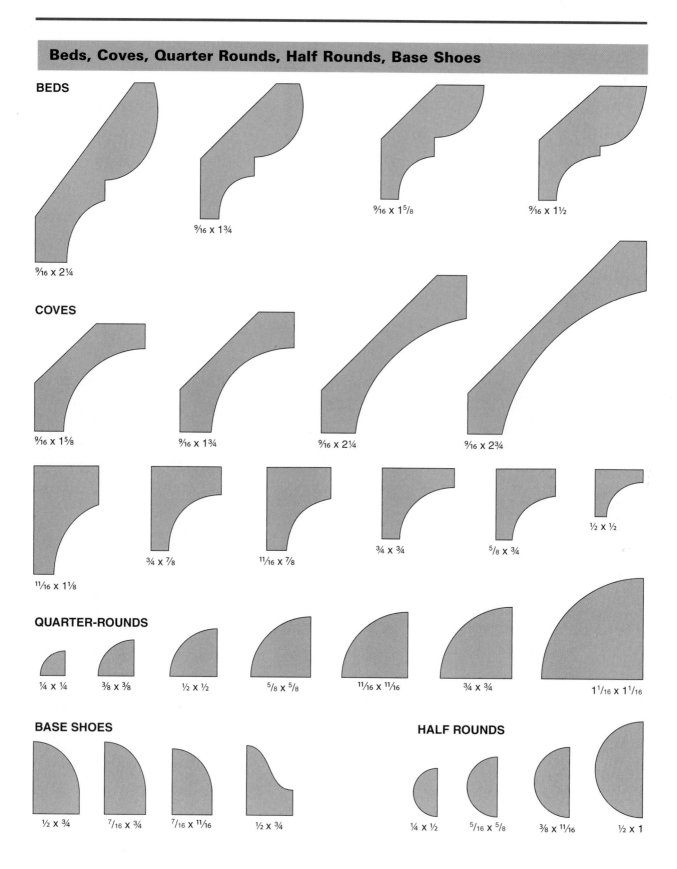

Beds, Coves, Quarter Rounds, Half Rounds, Base Shoes

BEDS

9/16 x 2¼

9/16 x 1¾

9/16 x 1⅝

9/16 x 1½

COVES

9/16 x 1⅝

9/16 x 1¾

9/16 x 2¼

9/16 x 2¾

11/16 x 1⅛

¾ x ⅞

11/16 x ⅞

¾ x ¾

⅝ x ¾

½ x ½

QUARTER-ROUNDS

¼ x ¼

⅜ x ⅜

½ x ½

⅝ x ⅝

11/16 x 11/16

¾ x ¾

1 1/16 x 1 1/16

BASE SHOES

½ x ¾

7/16 x ¾

7/16 x 11/16

½ x ¾

HALF ROUNDS

¼ x ½

5/16 x ⅝

⅜ x 11/16

½ x 1

Chair Rails, Corner Guards, Picture Mouldings, Back Bands, Plycap

CHAIR RAILS

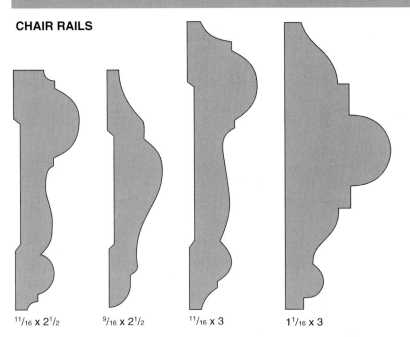

$^{11}/_{16}$ x 2$^1/_2$

$^9/_{16}$ x 2$^1/_2$

$^{11}/_{16}$ x 3

1$^1/_{16}$ x 3

CORNER GUARDS

1 x 1

$^3/_4$ x $^3/_4$

PICTURE MOULDINGS

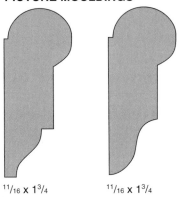

$^{11}/_{16}$ x 1$^3/_4$

$^{11}/_{16}$ x 1$^3/_4$

BACK BANDS

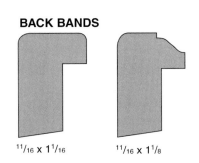

$^{11}/_{16}$ x 1$^1/_{16}$

$^{11}/_{16}$ x 1$^1/_8$

CORNER GUARDS

$^3/_4$ x $^3/_4$

1$^1/_8$ x 1$^1/_8$

1$^5/_{16}$ x 1$^5/_{16}$

CORNER GUARDS

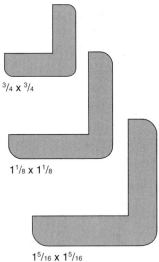

$^3/_4$ x $^3/_4$

1$^1/_8$ x 1$^1/_8$

1$^5/_{16}$ x 1$^5/_{16}$

WAINSCOT / PLYCAP MOULDINGS

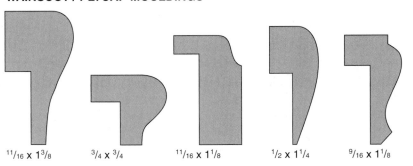

$^{11}/_{16}$ x 1$^3/_8$

$^3/_4$ x $^3/_4$

$^{11}/_{16}$ x 1$^1/_8$

$^1/_2$ x 1$^1/_4$

$^9/_{16}$ x 1$^1/_8$

Stops, Shingle and Panel Mouldings, Battens

STOPS

$^7/_{16}$ x $1^3/_8$
other widths: $^7/_8$, $1^1/_8$,
$1^1/_4$, $1^5/_8$, $1^3/_4$, $2^1/_4$

$^3/_8$ x $1^3/_8$
other widths: $^3/_4$, $^7/_8$, $1^1/_8$,
$1^1/_4$, $1^5/_8$, $1^3/_4$, $2^1/_4$

$^7/_{16}$ x $1^3/_8$
other widths: $^3/_4$, $^7/_8$, $1^1/_8$,
$1^1/_4$, $1^5/_8$, $1^3/_4$, $2^1/_4$

$^3/_8$ x $1^3/_8$
other widths: $^3/_4$, $^7/_8$, $1^1/_8$,
$1^1/_4$, $1^5/_8$, $1^3/_4$, $2^1/_4$

$^7/_{16}$ x $1^3/_8$
other widths: $^3/_4$, $^7/_8$, $1^1/_8$,
$1^1/_4$, $1^5/_8$, $1^3/_4$, $2^1/_4$

$^3/_8$ x $1^3/_8$
other widths: $^3/_4$, $^7/_8$, $1^1/_8$,
$1^1/_4$, $1^5/_8$, $1^3/_4$, $2^1/_4$

$^7/_{16}$ x specified widths

$^3/_8$ x specified widths

$^7/_{16}$ x $1^3/_8$
other widths: $^3/_4$, $^7/_8$, $1^1/_8$,
$1^1/_4$, $1^5/_8$, $1^3/_4$, $2^1/_4$

$^3/_8$ x $1^3/_8$
other widths: $^3/_4$, $^7/_8$, $1^1/_8$,
$1^1/_4$, $1^5/_8$, $1^3/_4$, $2^1/_4$

$^7/_{16}$ x $1^3/_8$
other widths: $^3/_4$, $^7/_8$, $1^1/_8$,
$1^1/_4$, $1^5/_8$, $1^3/_4$, $2^1/_4$

$^3/_8$ x $1^3/_8$
other widths: $^3/_4$, $^7/_8$, $1^1/_8$,
$1^1/_4$, $1^5/_8$, $1^3/_4$, $2^1/_4$

$^7/_{16}$ x $1^3/_8$
other widths: $^3/_4$, $^7/_8$, $1^1/_8$,
$1^1/_4$, $1^5/_8$, $1^3/_4$, $2^1/_4$

$^3/_8$ x $1^3/_8$
other widths: $^3/_4$, $^7/_8$, $1^1/_8$,
$1^1/_4$, $1^5/_8$, $1^3/_4$, $2^1/_4$

$^7/_{16}$ x $1^3/_8$
other widths: $^3/_4$, $^7/_8$, $1^1/_8$,
$1^1/_4$, $1^5/_8$, $1^3/_4$, $2^1/_4$

$^3/_8$ x $1^3/_8$
other widths: $^3/_4$, $^7/_8$, $1^1/_8$,
$1^1/_4$, $1^5/_8$, $1^3/_4$, $2^1/_4$

SHINGLE AND PANEL MOULDINGS   BATTENS

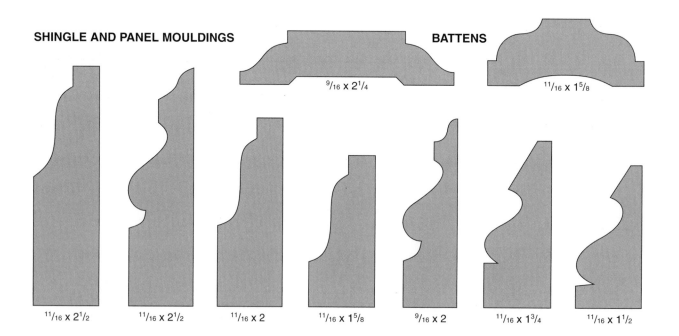

$^9/_{16}$ x $2^1/_4$

$^{11}/_{16}$ x $1^5/_8$

$^{11}/_{16}$ x $2^1/_2$ $^{11}/_{16}$ x $2^1/_2$ $^{11}/_{16}$ x 2 $^{11}/_{16}$ x $1^5/_8$ $^9/_{16}$ x 2 $^{11}/_{16}$ x $1^3/_4$ $^{11}/_{16}$ x $1^1/_2$

Panel Strips, Mullion Casings, Rabbeted Stools, Astragals, Panel Mouldings

PANEL STRIPS AND MULLION CASINGS

$^3/_8$ x 1$^3/_4$, 2, 2$^1/_4$

$^3/_8$ x 1$^3/_4$, 2, 2$^1/_4$

$^3/_8$ x 1$^3/_4$, 2, 2$^1/_4$

$^3/_8$ x 1$^3/_4$, 2, 2$^1/_4$

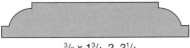

$^3/_8$ x 1$^3/_4$, 2, 2$^1/_4$

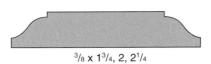

$^3/_8$ x 1$^3/_4$, 2, 2$^1/_4$

$^3/_8$ x 1$^3/_4$, 2, 2$^1/_4$

RABBETED STOOLS

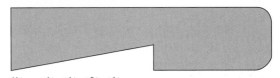

$^{11}/_{16}$ x 2$^1/_4$, 2$^1/_2$, 2$^3/_4$, 3$^1/_4$

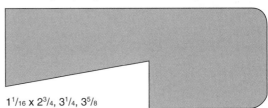

1$^1/_{16}$ x 2$^3/_4$, 3$^1/_4$, 3$^5/_8$

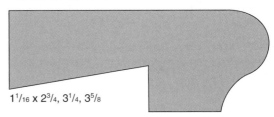

$^{11}/_{16}$ x 2$^1/_4$, 2$^1/_2$, 2$^3/_4$, 3$^1/_4$

1$^1/_{16}$ x 2$^3/_4$, 3$^1/_4$, 3$^5/_8$

FLAT STOOLS

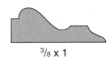

$^{11}/_{16}$ x specified widths

FLAT ASTRAGALS

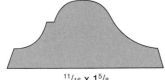

$^{11}/_{16}$ x 1$^3/_4$

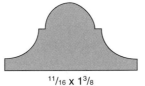

$^{11}/_{16}$ x 1$^3/_8$

$^7/_{16}$ x $^3/_4$

PANEL MOLDINGS

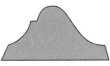

$^{11}/_{16}$ x 1$^5/_8$

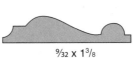

$^9/_{16}$ x 1$^1/_8$

$^9/_{32}$ x 1$^3/_8$

$^3/_8$ x 1

Built-Up Wood Moldings

Built-Up Crown Moldings

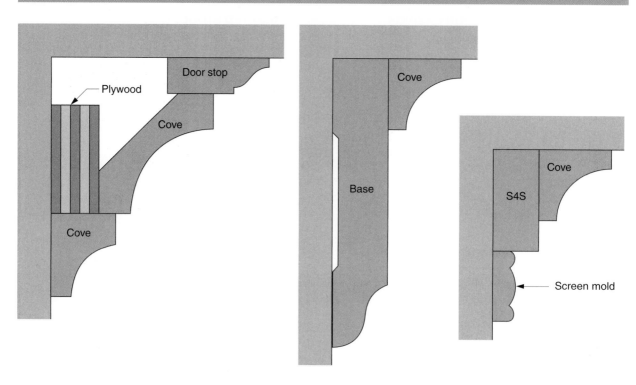

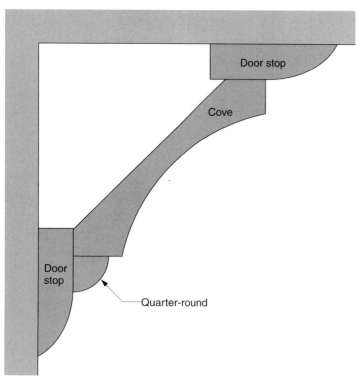

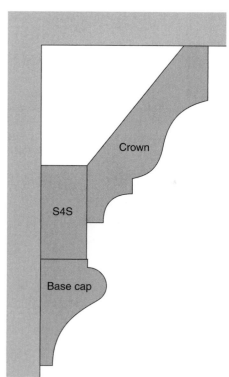

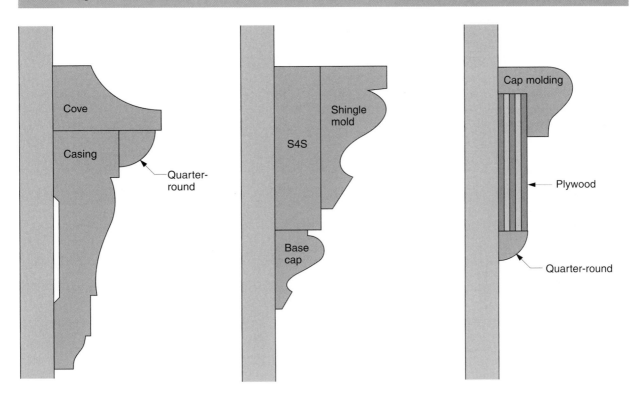

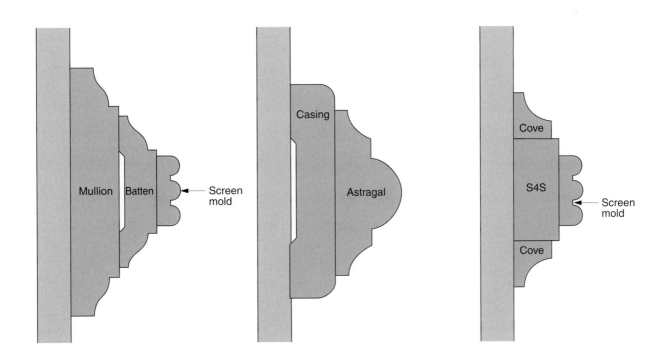

Storage

Homes today, if anything, have too many rooms and too much space. But regardless of floor area, they never seem to have enough storage for the acquisitive families that occupy them. Instead of building a storage barn or even a new home, we'll show you how you can increase the effectiveness of the space that you already have.

We start with *bath cabinetry*. In the old days, with pedestal-mounted sinks, about the only storage in the bathroom was the medicine cabinet. Replace that old sink with one or more lavatories in a multidrawer vanity.

One of the most popular remodels is the kitchen. Today's kitchens are as much about fashion as utility. If you feel a kitchen remodel coming up, get to your local home center to check out the vast array of options in *kitchen cabinetry*. We offer here a generic catalog of the cabinets you will find.

If you feel your present home is bulging at the seams and impossibly cluttered, go to a boat show for inspiration. Yacht designers, particularly those of sailboats, have developed the art of *finding more storage* to the ultimate degree. We offer a field guide to the possibilities you may discover in your non-floating home.

The most common, least expensive form of storage is plain *shelving*. We offer solutions to the two most common questions: how to support the shelves, and what distances they can span without sagging.

Bedrooms in many older homes are plenty large, but have no closets. *Adding a closet* to an empty room corner is a project well within the capabilities of the average handyperson.

Even if your bedroom already has them, *organizing closets* for maximum space efficiency is one of the least expensive and most gratifying projects you can tackle.

Bath Cabinetry

Most cabinet manufacturers offer comprehensive lines of both bath and kitchen cabinets. Some offer both lines in the standard kitchen-cabinet height (without counter top) of 34½ inches so that cabinet types can be combined. Most, however, offer bath cabinets (vanities) with heights of either 32 or 33½ inches.

Most manufacturers also offer vanities with depths (front to back of frame) of both 18 and 21 inches. When combining vanity modules and when ordering vanity tops, double check the vanity depths.

Typical Modular Bath Cabinetry

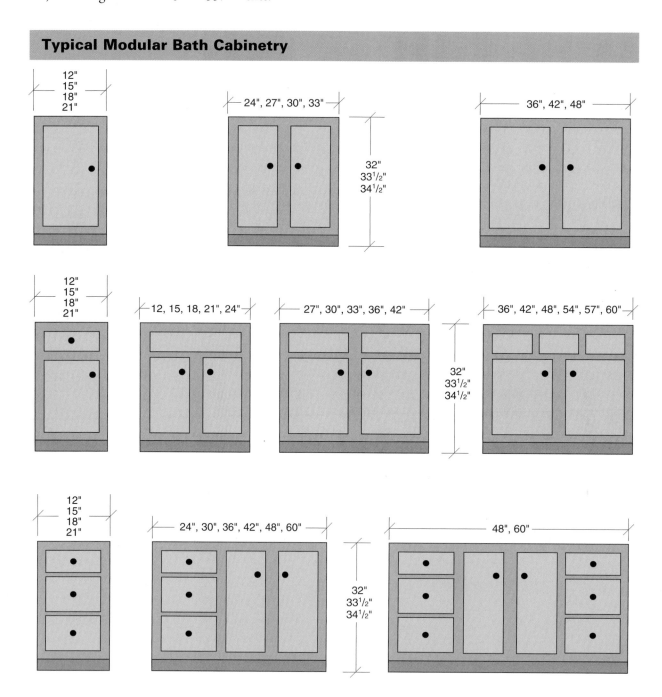

Kitchen Cabinetry

Unless you special order or build your own, chances are your cabinetry will be of standard dimensions. The only choice open to you is the height of the wall cabinets above the counter.

Low wall cabinets make wall shelving more accessible. On the other hand, if you plan to hang a microwave oven and a cookbook shelf under the wall cabinets, you will need greater height for a useful counter surface.

The countertop frontages shown are the minimum. Cooks who use lots of pots and pans or who entertain a lot will appreciate 36 inches to the left of the sink and a separate 24- by 48-inch work surface, such as the island shown.

Recessed counter surfaces on inside corners do not count toward either frontage or surface area.

Recommended Kitchen Cabinetry Dimensions

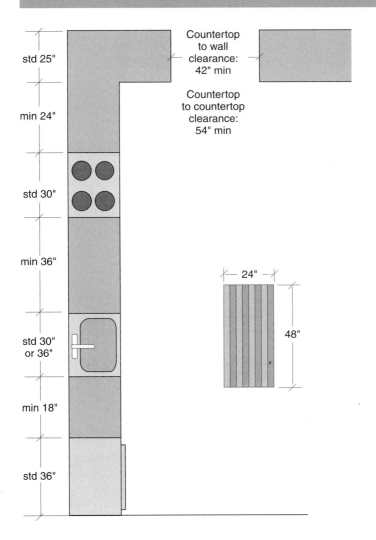

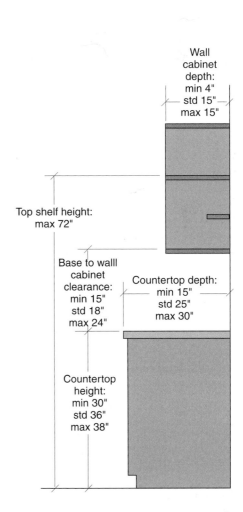

Standard modular kitchen cabinets are available in a wide range of styles and prices.

Standard base cabinet height is 34½ inches, assuming a 1½-inch countertop and 36-inch counter surface height. Cabinet height can be raised or lowered by adding to or removing from the kick space.

Ideal counter height is considered to be the bottom of a bent elbow less 3 inches, but modifying counter heights should be taken seriously because it decreases the home's resale value.

Cabinet widths range from 9 to 36 inches in 3-inch increments, and 36 to 48 inches in 6-inch increments. Exact fit is made by trimming standard 3- and 6-inch filler strips.

Typical modular kitchen cabinets are shown below and on the opposite page.

Typical Modular Kitchen Base Cabinets

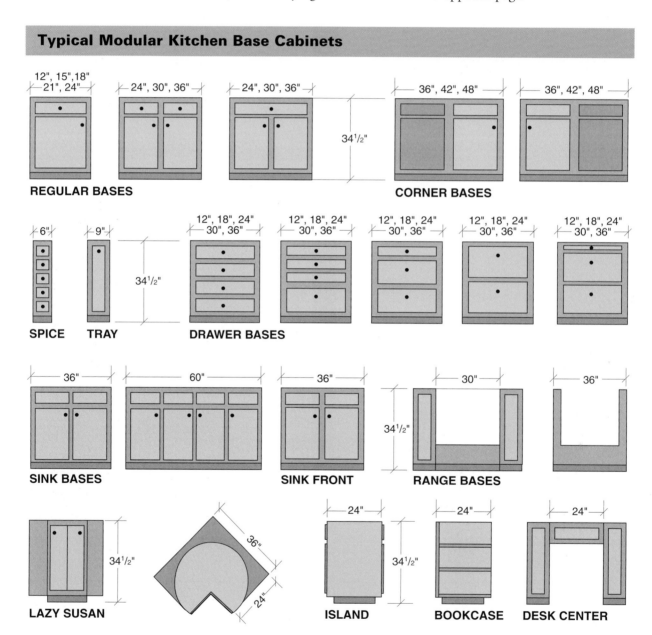

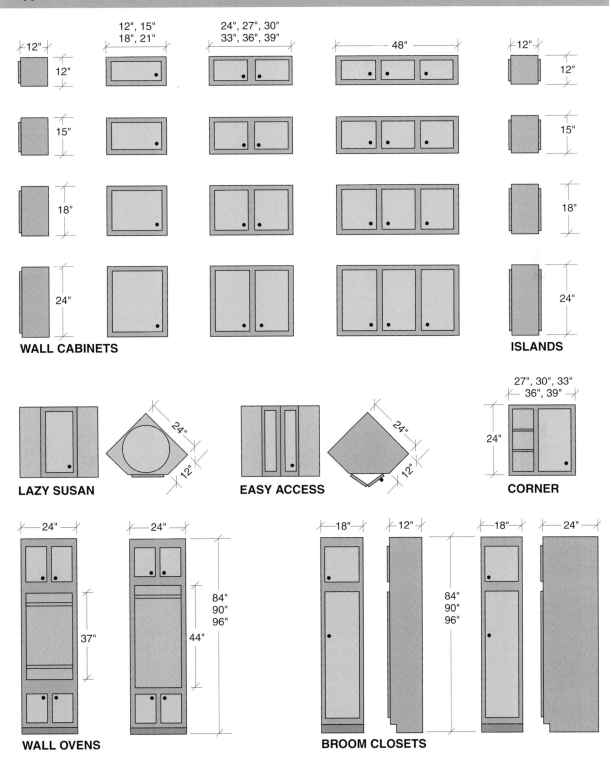

12", 15"
18", 21"

24", 27", 30"
33", 36", 39"

48"

12"

12"

12"

15"

15"

18"

18"

24"

24"

WALL CABINETS

ISLANDS

27", 30", 33"
36", 39"

24"

24"

24"

12"

24"

12"

LAZY SUSAN

EASY ACCESS

CORNER

24"

24"

18"

12"

18"

24"

37"

44"

84"
90"
96"

84"
90"
96"

WALL OVENS

BROOM CLOSETS

Finding Space

The single most common complaint about houses is lack of storage space. Of course, just as "nature abhors a vacuum," so do our possessions rapidly fill all available space. Short of holding an annual garage sale, however, we can increase, or at least improve, the built-in storage capacities of our homes. The illustration on the facing page points to storage possibilities you may have overlooked:

1. The space behind a knee wall is perfect for either built-in bookshelves or (as shown) drawers. Note that to preserve the home's thermal envelope, the insulation must be between the rafters.

2. Heated or unheated, attics offer huge unused storage spaces. If the insulation is between the rafters, install a plywood or OSB floor. If the insulation is between the joists, suspend a platform from the rafters.

3. The spaces under most beds store nothing more than shoes and dust bunnies. Placing the mattress on a platform allows for pull-out drawers perfect for storage of sheets and blankets.

4. Dual-lavatory vanities often contain enough undercounter space for a half-dozen drawers. If that is not enough, add a hanging wall cabinet to any blank wall in a large bathroom.

5. Walk-in closets are a must for both him and her. Extra depth can be used for storage shelves, as well as one or two closet poles.

6. You can never have too much cabinet space in a kitchen. Utilize every inch of wall space for both undercounter and wall cabinets.

7. A room between an attached garage and the kitchen can serve double duty as both a mud room and a pantry. Pantries are especially useful because their open shelving allows one to see contents at a glance.

8. A linen closet can often be tucked into a left-over nook or cranny. They don't have to be very large to store the linens for the average home.

9. An entrance closet solves the problem of where to hang guest overcoats and umbrellas. Find a place close to the entrance door so that wet and muddy apparel don't penetrate too far into your home.

10. Walls on either or both sides of a fireplace are the perfect places for built-in shelves and bookcases. Use them for a sound system, family photos, and interesting objects d'art, as well as your prized collection of books.

11. A window bay is a perfect place for a window seat, whether for you or the family cat. Hinge the seat, and you will have a perfect place to store games and toys for the grandchildren.

12. Garages offer a wealth of storage opportunities. A space beyond the automobiles at the end may be perfect for a built-in workshop. Placing the workbench on top of kitchen base cabinets provides drawers for storage of tools and supplies. Use kitchen wall cabinets for storage of paints, stains, adhesives, and chemicals. Install pegboard, or plywood with screws and nails, on the wall beneath the cabinets for hanging tools.

13. A wide garage may provide space along one side for wall racks to hold bicycles, canoes, kayaks, etc. The walls of even the narrowest garage can be used to hang garden tools.

INTERIORS

KNEE WALLS

③

①

④

④

⑤

⑥

⑦

⑪

⑧

⑤

⑫

⑤

⑩

⑬

⑩

⑬

⑨

ATTICS

②   ②

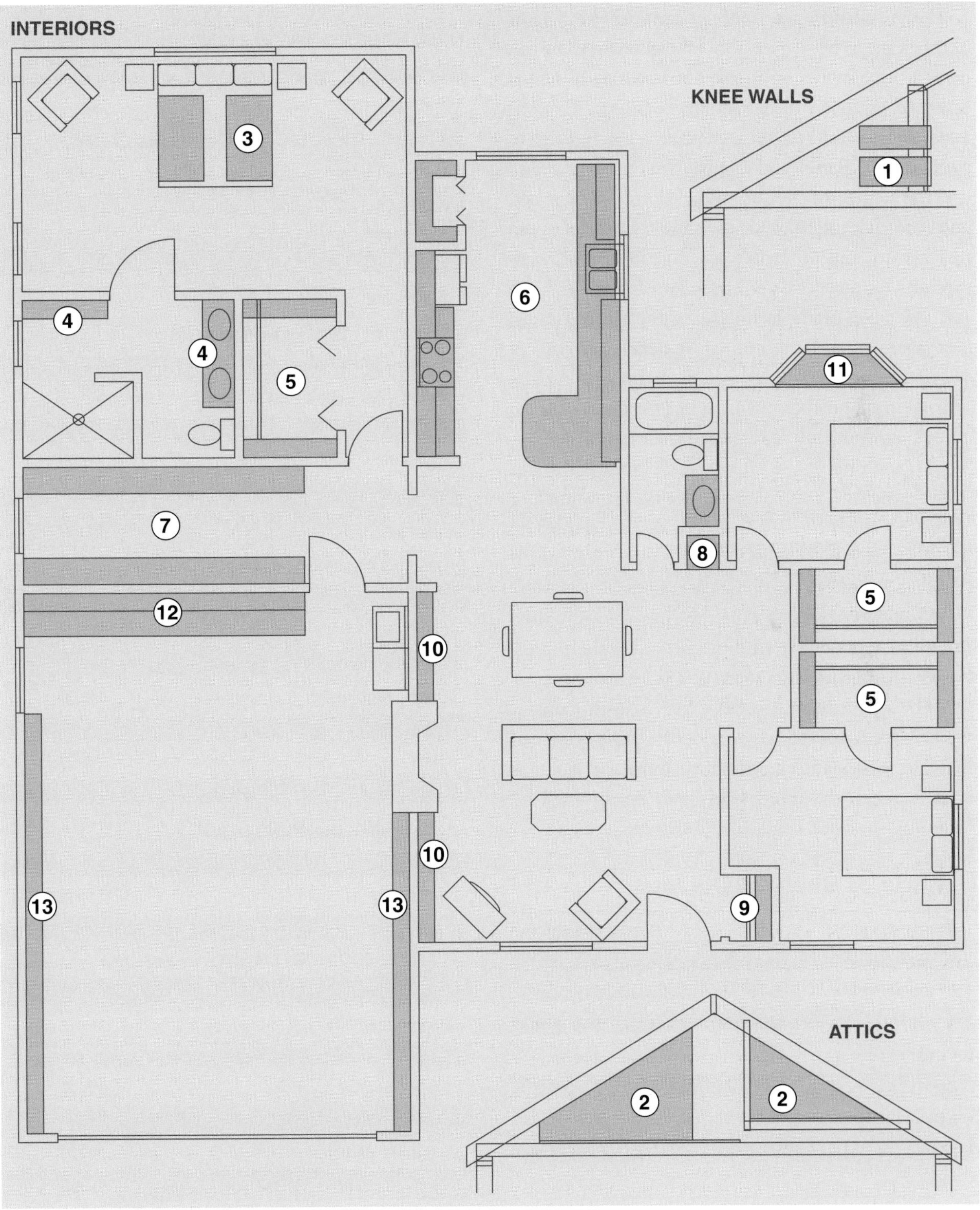

Shelving

No residence or office ever has enough shelving, whether for books, DVDs, clothes, or items for display.

For fixed shelving, carefully consider the heights of the items to be shelved. Book heights, for example, range from 8 inches for small paperbacks to 16 inches or more for oversize coffee-table editions. Use the tables below and at right to calculate the spacing of your shelves. Better yet, sort your items by size, and use the actual maximum dimensions. Remember, however, that the height is the clear distance between shelves, not the on-center spacing. If you are very careful, you may just squeeze in an extra shelf.

The tables on the facing page show the maximum clear spans of shelving limited by deflection (sag) of 1/240 of the shelf length (1 inch in 240 inches, ½ inch in 120 inches, ⅒ inch in 24 inches, etc.) for a range of uniformly-distributed shelf loads.

To use one of the tables, weigh on a bathroom scale a typical load you plan to place on a running foot of shelf. If the shelf is 12 inches deep, that is the load in psf (pounds per square foot) of the first column. If the shelf is 6 inches deep, the psf is doubled.

Find the nearest psf in the first column, then run across the table to find the allowable shelf spans for the listed shelving materials and thicknesses.

The deflection ratio of 1/240 is quite conservative. For a more saggy ratio of 1/180, you can increase shelf loads by one-third. If the shelving has a back panel, the listed spans may be doubled by fastening the back edges of the shelves.

Heights of Shelved Objects

Item	Typical Height, in
Audio cassette	5
Book, hardback	11
Book, oversized hardback	15
Book, paperback	8
Book, oversized paperback	16
CDs and DVDs	5
Slide carousel	10
Videotape	8

Dimensions of Closet Storage Items

Item	Dimensions, in
LINEN (LENGTH × WIDTH × HEIGHT)	
Bath mat	9×10×3
Bath towel	13×14×2
Blanket	22×27×4
Dish towel	10×16×1
Fitted sheet	11×18×2
Flat sheet	14×15×2
Hand towel	6×10×1
Pillowcase	7×15×1
MEN'S CLOTHING (HANGING HEIGHT)	
Pants, folded	22×27
Pants, unfolded	11×18
Shirt	22×27
Suit	22×27
Tie	11×18
Topcoat	22×27
WOMEN'S CLOTHING (HANGING HEIGHT)	
Blouse	22×27
Coat	11×18
Dress, long	22×27
Dress, regular	22×27
Robe	11×18
Skirt	22×27
Suit	22×27
ACCESSORIES (HANGING HEIGHT)	
Garment bag	22×27
Shoe bag	11×18
Umbrella	22×27
CLEANING EQUIPMENT (WIDTH × HEIGHT)	
Broom, push	22×27
Broom, regular	11×18
Carpet sweeper	22×27
Floor polisher	22×27
Scrub bucket	11×18
Vacuum, canister	22×27
Vacuum, upright	11×18

Maximum Shelf Span, Shelves Freely Supported at Ends

Load, psf	Particleboard			Medium Density Fiberboard			AC Plywood		E. White Pine		Red Oak	
	½"	⅝"	¾"	½"	⅝"	¾"	⅝"	¾"	¾"	1"	¾"	1"
10	23	31	37	25	32	38	31	38	55	74	63	84
15	20	27	32	22	28	33	27	33	48	67	54	73
20	18	22	27	20	25	30	24	30	44	61	49	66
25	17	21	25	19	23	28	23	28	41	57	46	62
30	16	20	23	18	22	26	21	26	38	53	43	58
35	15	19	22	17	21	25	20	25	36	51	41	55
40	15	18	21	16	20	24	19	24	35	49	39	53
45	14	18	21	16	19	23	18	23	33	47	38	51
50	13	17	20	15	19	22	18	22	32	45	36	48

Maximum Allowable Span, in

Notes: Shelf ends not fastened in any way.

Maximum span limited by deflection of 1/240 (deflection = length between supports divided by 240).

Assumed Moduli of Elasticity: Particleboard = 0.32×10^6, Medium Density Fiberboard = 0.35×10^6, AC Plywood = 0.33×10^6, Eastern White Pine = 1.1×10^6, Red Oak = 1.6×10^6.

Maximum Shelf Span, Shelves Supported at Ends and Midpoint

Load, psf	Particleboard			Medium Density Fiberboard			AC Plywood		White Pine		Red Oak	
	½"	⅝"	¾"	½"	⅝"	¾"	⅝"	¾"	¾"	1"	¾"	1"
10	30	38	45	34	39	46	37	46	67	90	77	102
15	25	32	39	29	34	40	33	40	58	82	66	89
20	22	27	33	27	33	36	29	36	53	74	60	80
25	19	24	29	25	31	34	28	34	50	69	56	75
30	18	22	27	23	29	32	25	31	46	64	52	70
35	16	20	24	22	28	31	24	30	44	62	50	67
40	15	19	23	21	26	30	23	29	42	60	47	64
45	14	18	22	21	25	28	22	28	40	57	46	62
50	13	17	20	20	25	27	22	27	39	55	44	58

Maximum Allowable Span, in

Notes: Shelves freely supported at ends and at midpoint. Span refers to distance between an end and the midpoint, not the total shelf length.

Maximum span limited by deflection of 1/240 (deflection = length between supports divided by 240).

Assumed Moduli of Elasticity: Particleboard = 0.32×10^6, Medium Density Fiberboard = 0.35×10^6, AC Plywood = 0.33×10^6, Eastern White Pine = 1.1×10^6, Red Oak = 1.6×10^6.

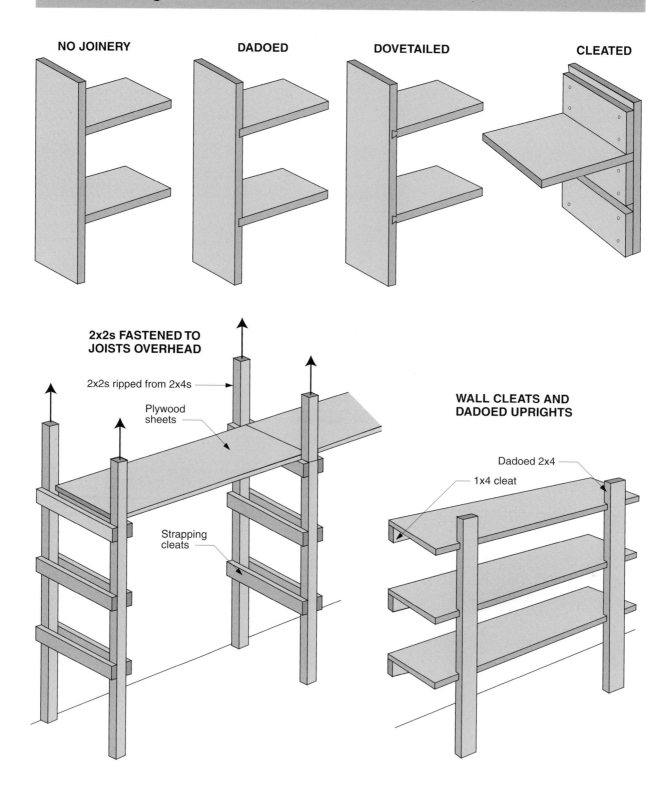

NO JOINERY

DADOED

DOVETAILED

CLEATED

2x2s FASTENED TO JOISTS OVERHEAD

2x2s ripped from 2x4s

Plywood sheets

Strapping cleats

WALL CLEATS AND DADOED UPRIGHTS

Dadoed 2x4

1x4 cleat

45° AND 90° KERFS

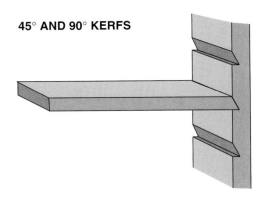

SPLIT 2x4 WITH ⁷/₈" HOLES

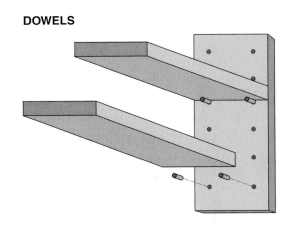

SHELF SUPPORTS

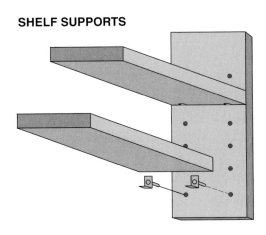

DOWELS

STANDARD AND BRACKETS

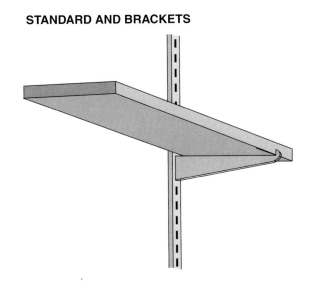

PILASTERS AND CLIPS

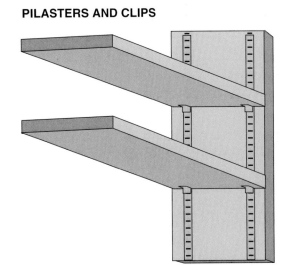

Adding a Closet

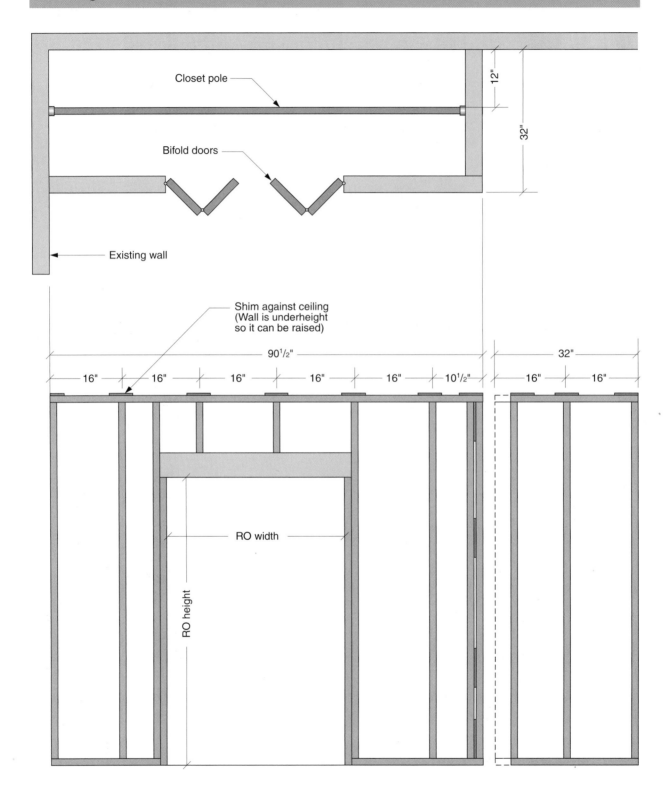

Closet pole

12"

32"

Bifold doors

Existing wall

Shim against ceiling
(Wall is underheight
so it can be raised)

90½"

32"

16"   16"   16"   16"   16"   10½"   16"   16"

RO width

RO height

Organizing Closets

A well-organized closet will hold twice the clothing of an unorganized one. Reorganizing an existing closet can be a one-day project using standard materials.

Home centers usually offer several lines of modular, wire-frame systems, as well as whole books on the subject. Below are several ideas for reorganizing your closets for either dual- or single-occupancy, using standard bathroom drawer units, closet poles, and shelving.

Note that vanity drawer units come in a variety of widths, from 12 to 27 inches. Mix and match the widths to fit your existing space.

Organizing Closets for One and Two Persons

ONE-PERSON CLOSETS

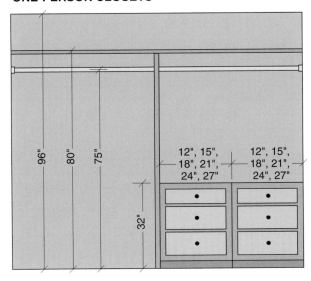

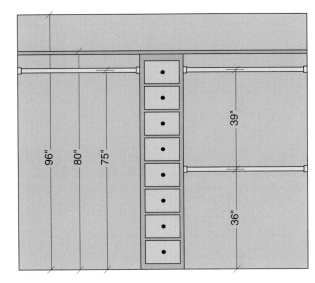

TWO-PERSON CLOSETS

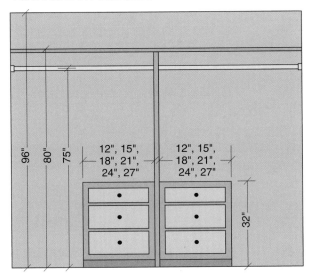

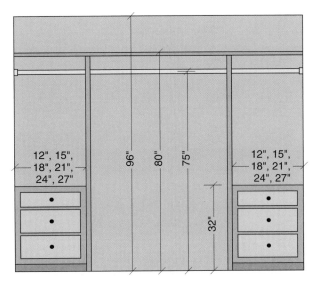

Heating

16

Americans have learned that energy supplies can no longer be taken for granted. No longer is the heating system a neglected, mysterious object in the nether regions of our homes that we try not to think about. Winter comfort requires that we have the right type of heating system, properly sized to the *building heat load*.

This chapter begins with a simple form for calculating heat loads, both for the coldest day of winter and for the entire winter. We supply the *heating climate data* specific to your location.

Next, you'll learn how the various *heat sources* and *distribution systems* work and the pros and cons of each.

Most of us have considered switching fuels at some time. Some of us supplement our main heating systems with wood stoves. *Fuels and Efficiencies* gives you a simple method for comparing the cost per delivered Btu of all fuels and a chart that shows the fuel savings you can expect if you install a more efficient system.

If you are going to have a fireplace anyway, why not make it as fuel-efficient as possible? We show detailed, energy-efficient plans for both *standard fireplaces* and the more efficient *Rumford fireplaces*.

For others, a wood stove is a more practical alternative to the fireplace. *Wood Stove Installation* and *Stovepipe Installation* show the fire-code requirements for stove and stovepipe clearances. It also shows how to vent a wood stove into an existing fireplace.

If you don't already have a sound and safe masonry flue, the section on *metal prefabricated chimneys* will be helpful, showing every detail of six typical installations.

Finally, we provide you with a checklist to make sure you *meet the IRC code*.

Building Heat Loads

In designing a building and its equipment, we are interested in two types of heat load (rate of heat loss):

Design Heat Load This is the rate at which heat is lost from the building in British thermal units (Btu) per hour on that coldest night when the outside temperature is at the design minimum temperature (DMT) for the location. The number is used to size the heating system.

Annual Heat Load This is the annual heat load, the total heat loss in Btu over the entire heating season. The quantity can be used to estimate the annual heating bill in dollars.

Use the work sheet on the facing page to estimate both of these loads for your home. A completed example work sheet follows on pp. 458-459.

Work Sheet Instructions

Line 1. Use line 1 if you have an unheated attic. Find the R-value in Chapter 13, or use a value of 3.0 if the attic is totally uninsulated.

Line 2. Use line 2 if the ceiling is also the underside of the roof. Get the R-value from Chapter 13, or use 3.0 if the roof is uninsulated.

Line 3. Get the wall R-values from Chapter 13, or use 4.0 if the wall is uninsulated. If there are different wall constructions, use a different line for each type. Subtract window and door areas from each wall section.

Line 4. The area of most exterior doors is 20 square feet. Use an R-value of 2.0 for solid wood doors, 3.0 for a wood door plus storm door, and 6.0 for an insulated door.

Line 5. Window area is the area of the sash, not just the glazing. A window's R-value is simply 1/U, where U is the window's U-value. Find your windows' U-values from the very complete table of tested U-values on p. 285.

Line 6. Use this line if your home, or a portion of it, sits on piers or over a ventilated crawl space. Get the floor R-values from Chapter 13, or use 5.0 if the floor is uninsulated.

Line 7. Use this line if your home sits on a concrete slab. Use an R-value of 20 if the slab is uninsulated. Add the insulation R-value as shown on p. 381 if it is insulated.

Line 8. Use this line if your home has a basement. Use an R-value of 5.0 if the foundation is uninsulated. Add the insulation R-value (from Chapter 13) if the walls are insulated.

Line 9. For air changes per hour, use 1.5 for an older drafty house, 0.75 for a typical 10- to 30-year-old house, 0.50 for an average new house, and 0.25 for a new "green" or "energy-efficient" house. Heated volume is 8× the heated floor area.

Line 10. Add up all of the numbers appearing in the right-hand column above this line.

Line 11. First enter the sum from line 10. Next enter 65 minus the design minimum temperature (DMT 97.5%) from the table on p. 460. Multiply the entries and enter the result in the right column. Your heating contractor can use this result to properly size your heating system.

Line 12. Enter the sum from line 10. Next find heating degree-days, base 65°F (HDD 65), from either the table of climate data on p. 460 or the map on page 461. Multiply the entries. The result is the total annual heat loss.

To estimate the amount of fuel used, divide this number by 100,000 for gallons of oil; 70,000 per hundred cubic feet of gas; 3,410 for kilowatt-hours (kwhr) of electric-resistance heat; and 6,830 for an electric heat pump. (You will see how to adjust for other heating system efficiencies on p. 472.)

HDD 65 is used with the assumption that the house requires heat when the daily average outdoor temperature drops below 65°F. If your house generates a lot of internal heat, or retains internal heat gains well, the heat may not come on until the outdoor temperature drops to 55°F, for example. In that case, use HDD 55 from the table.

Work Sheet for Heat Loads

Surface	Area, sq ft	÷	R-value	=	Result
1. Ceiling under attic #1	_____	÷	_____	=	_____
Ceiling under attic #2	_____	÷	_____	=	_____
2. Cathedral ceiling or roof #1	_____	÷	_____	=	_____
Cathedral ceiling or roof #2	_____	÷	_____	=	_____
3. Exterior wall #1	_____	÷	_____	=	_____
Exterior wall #2	_____	÷	_____	=	_____
Exterior wall #3	_____	÷	_____	=	_____
Exterior wall #4	_____	÷	_____	=	_____
Exterior wall #5	_____	÷	_____	=	_____
Exterior wall #6	_____	÷	_____	=	_____
4. Exterior door #1	_____	÷	_____	=	_____
Exterior door #2	_____	÷	_____	=	_____
Exterior door #3	_____	÷	_____	=	_____
5. Window type #1	_____	÷	_____	=	_____
Window type #2	_____	÷	_____	=	_____
Window type #3	_____	÷	_____	=	_____
Window type #4	_____	÷	_____	=	_____
6. Floor over crawl space	_____	÷	_____	=	_____
7. Slab on-grade	_____	÷	_____	=	_____
8. Foundation wall	_____	÷	_____	=	_____
9. Air changes per hour _____ x 0.018 x heated volume in cu ft			_____	=	_____

10. Sum of results of all lines above = _____

11. Design heat load: Line 10 _____ × _____ (65°F–DMT) = _____ Btu/hr

12. Annual heat load: Line 10 _____ × 24 × _____ HDD_{65} = _____ Btu/yr

The facing page contains an example work sheet showing the calculations for design heat load and annual heat load for a small house in Boston, Massachusetts, shown below.

The house is deliberately kept simple in order to clarify the calculations. Many homes will have more than one type of exterior wall, foundation, or window, and they will require multiple entries for these items.

Line 1. The ceiling measures 30 by 40 feet, so its area is 1,200 square feet. Chapter 13 gives an R-value of 35.5 for its two R-19 batts.

Line 3. After the areas of windows and doors are deducted, the remaining area of exterior wall is 996 square feet. The 2×6 wall with R-19 batts has an R-value of 17.2.

Line 4. The first exterior door is solid wood with storm and has a combined R-value of 3.0. The second has an insulated core and R-value of 6.0.

Line 5. All of the windows are double glazed without storm windows (total R-value of 2.0). The total area of window sash is 84 square feet.

Line 6. The house sits on a crawl space that is ventilated in winter and is insulated with R-19 batts between the joists. Chapter 13 gives this type of floor an R-value of 20.9.

Line 9. The house is a recently built tract home, so its air change rate is about 0.50 changes per hour. The heated volume is the floor area times the ceiling height, 8 feet.

Line 10. The sum of all of the results in the right-hand column is 287.5.

Line 11. From the table following the example work sheet, DMT 97.5% is 9°F for Boston. The result for this line is a design heat load at 9°F of 16,100 Btu per hour.

Line 12. From the same table, for Boston the HDD 65 is 5,630. The result of multiplying the three numbers on line 12 is the annual heat load: 38,847,000 Btu.

If the house were heated with oil, the approximate winter fuel consumption would be the annual heat load divided by 100,000, or 388 gallons of oil.

Example House for Heat Load Calculation

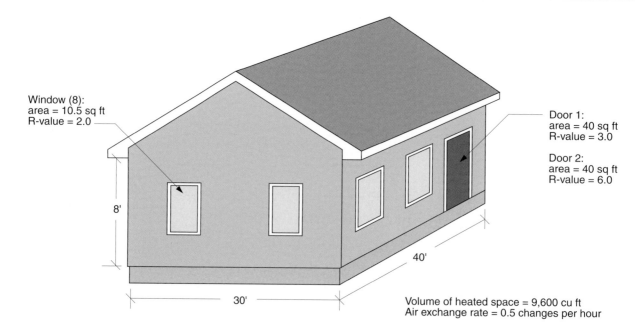

Window (8):
area = 10.5 sq ft
R-value = 2.0

Door 1:
area = 40 sq ft
R-value = 3.0

Door 2:
area = 40 sq ft
R-value = 6.0

8'

40'

30'

Volume of heated space = 9,600 cu ft
Air exchange rate = 0.5 changes per hour

Work Sheet for Heat Loads

Surface	Area, sq ft	÷	R-value	=	Result
1. Ceiling under attic #1	1,200	÷	35.5	=	33.8
Ceiling under attic #2		÷		=	
2. Cathedral ceiling or roof #1		÷		=	
Cathedral ceiling or roof #2		÷		=	
3. Exterior wall #1	996	÷	17.2	=	57.9
Exterior wall #2		÷		=	
Exterior wall #3		÷		=	
Exterior wall #4		÷		=	
Exterior wall #5		÷		=	
Exterior wall #6		÷		=	
4. Exterior door #1	20	÷	3.0	=	6.7
Exterior door #2	20	÷	6.0	=	3.3
Exterior door #3		÷		=	
5. Window type #1	84	÷	2.0	=	42.0
Window type #2		÷		=	
Window type #3		÷		=	
Window type #4		÷		=	
6. Floor over crawl space	1,200	÷	20.9	=	57.4
7. Slab on-grade		÷		=	
8. Foundation wall		÷		=	

9. Air changes per hr   0.50   x 0.018 x heated volume in cu ft   9,600   =   86.4

10. Sum of results of all lines above   =   287.5

11. **Design heat load:** Line 10   287.5   ×   56   (65°F–DMT)   =   16,100   Btu/hr

12. **Annual heat load:** Line 10   287.5   × 24 ×   5,630   HDD$_{65}$ =   38,847,000   Btu/yr

Heating Climate Data

Climate Data for North American Cities

City	DMT$_{97.5\%}$	HDD$_{55}$	HDD$_{65}$	City	DMT$_{97.5\%}$	HDD$_{55}$	HDD$_{65}$
Alabama, Birmingham	21	1,293	2,823	Nevada, Reno	11	3,086	5,600
Alaska, Fairbanks	-47	10,836	13,980	New Hampshire, Concord	-3	4,858	7,478
Alaska, Juneau	1	5,154	8,574	New Jersey, Newark	14	2,727	4,843
Arizona, Flagstaff	4	5,185	8,340	New Mexico, Albuquerque	16	2,277	4,281
Arizona, Phoenix	34	174	1,125	New Mexico, Santa Fe	10	3,593	6,073
Arkansas, Little Rock	20	1,512	3,084	New York, New York City	15	2,659	4,754
California, Los Angeles	43	88	1,274	New York, Syracuse	2	4,172	6,803
Colorado, Denver	1	3,701	6,128	North Carolina, Greensboro	18	1,972	3,848
Colorado, Fort Collins	-4	3,734	6,238	North Dakota, Bismarck	-19	6,157	8,802
Connecticut, Hartford	7	3,772	6,121	Ohio, Columbus	5	3,356	5,492
Delaware, Wilmington	14	2,774	4,888	Oklahoma, Tulsa	13	1,957	3,642
DC, Washington	17	2,869	5,010	Oregon, Bend	4	4,058	7,042
Florida, Miami	47	16	149	Oregon, Salem	23	2,175	4,784
Florida, Orlando	38	121	580	Pennsylvania, Philadelphia	14	2,687	4,759
Georgia, Atlanta	22	1,289	2,827	Pennsylvania, Pittsburgh	5	3,545	5,829
Idaho, Boise	10	3,370	5,727	Rhode Island, Providence	9	3,397	5,754
Illinois, Chicago	0	3,861	6,083	South Carolina, Columbia	24	1,127	2,594
Indiana, Indianapolis	2	3,389	5,521	South Dakota, Rapid City	-7	4,679	7,211
Iowa, Des Moines	-5	4,206	6,436	Tennessee, Nashville	14	1,914	3,677
Kansas, Topeka	4	3,175	5,225	Texas, Austin	28	614	1,648
Kentucky, Louisville	10	2,451	4,352	Texas, Brownsville	39	150	644
Louisiana, Baton Rouge	29	602	1,689	Texas, Dallas	22	943	2,290
Maine, Caribou	-13	6,638	9,560	Texas, Houston	33	532	1,528
Maine, Portland	-1	4,637	7,318	Utah, Salt Lake City	8	3,299	5,631
Maryland, Baltimore	13	2,007	3,807	Vermont, Burlington	-7	5,091	7,665
Massachusetts, Boston	9	3,299	5,630	Virginia, Norfolk	22	1,608	3,368
Massachusetts, Springfield	0	3,754	6,104	Virginia, Richmond	17	2,021	3,919
Michigan, Detroit	6	3,657	5,898	Washington, Seattle	26	2,112	4,797
Michigan, Sault Ste. Marie	-12	6,262	9,224	West Virginia, Charleston	11	2,584	4,644
Minnesota, Duluth	-16	6,816	9,724	Wisconsin, Madison	-7	4,993	7,493
Minnesota, Int'l Falls	-25	7,422	10,269	Wyoming, Casper	-5	4,898	7,571
Mississippi, Jackson	25	1,027	2,401	Alberta, Edmonton	-25	7,563	10,650
Missouri, St. Louis	6	2,830	4,758	British Columbia, Vancouver	19'	2,781	5,588
Montana, Great Falls	-15	4,932	7,828	Manitoba, Winnipeg	-27	8,062	10,790
Montana, Missoula	-6	4,795	7,622	Nova Scotia, Halifax	5	4,500	7,211
Nebraska, North Platte	-4	4,361	6,766	Ontario, Ottawa	-13	5,965	8,529
Nevada, Las Vegas	28	832	2,239	Quebec, Quebec City	-14	8,308	11,376

Heating Degree Days, Base 65°F

Contour Interval: 500

MOUNTAINTOP STATION	HDD
HALEAKALA RES STN 338	4235
HAWAII VOL NP HDQTR 54	1609
KANALOHULUHULU 1075	2315
KULANI CAMP 79	3450
MAUNA LOA SLOPE OBSERVATORY	7428

MOST HDD VALUES ARE LESS THAN 100

Heat Sources

The hydronic, or forced-hot-water, system heats water in a gas or oil boiler and circulates it through loops of pipe to distribute heat to separate heating zones. Annual fuel utilization efficiencies (AFUEs) are similar to those of furnaces: about 85 percent for high-efficiency models and about 90 percent for condensing boilers. Pros include even heating, ease of zoning with separate thermostats, and small, easy-to-conceal pipes. Cons include no air cleaning or humidification and no sharing of ducts with central air conditioning.

Oil-Fired Hydronic Boiler

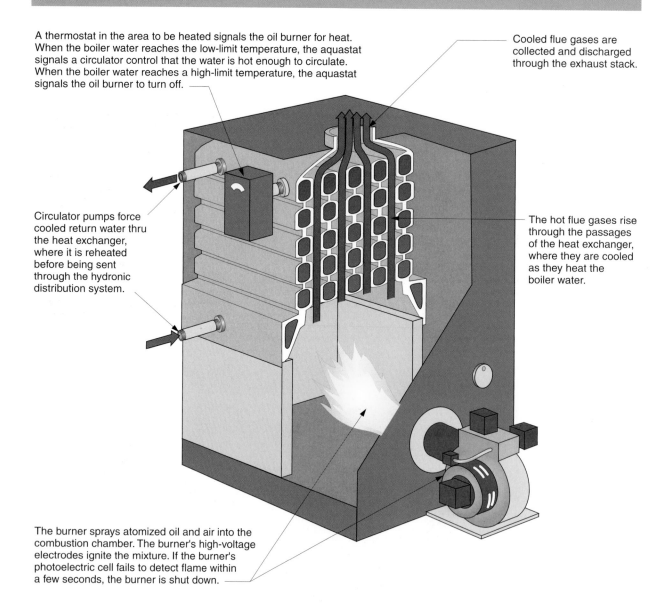

A thermostat in the area to be heated signals the oil burner for heat. When the boiler water reaches the low-limit temperature, the aquastat signals a circulator control that the water is hot enough to circulate. When the boiler water reaches a high-limit temperature, the aquastat signals the oil burner to turn off.

Cooled flue gases are collected and discharged through the exhaust stack.

Circulator pumps force cooled return water thru the heat exchanger, where it is reheated before being sent through the hydronic distribution system.

The hot flue gases rise through the passages of the heat exchanger, where they are cooled as they heat the boiler water.

The burner sprays atomized oil and air into the combustion chamber. The burner's high-voltage electrodes ignite the mixture. If the burner's photoelectric cell fails to detect flame within a few seconds, the burner is shut down.

The first furnaces distributed heat by natural convection of buoyant heated air through large ducts. The modern warm-air furnace is a great improvement. Heat is produced by clean and efficient combustion of gas or oil, and the warm air is distributed evenly throughout the building by a blower, supply and return ducts, and registers. AFUEs average about 84 percent for high-efficiency furnaces and 93 percent for condensing furnaces. Pros include circulation and filtration of air, humidification and dehumidification, possible integration with heat exchangers, and ductwork that can be shared with air-conditioning. Cons include bulky, hard-to-conceal ducts, noise at high air velocity, and sound transmission between rooms.

Gas Warm-Air Furnace

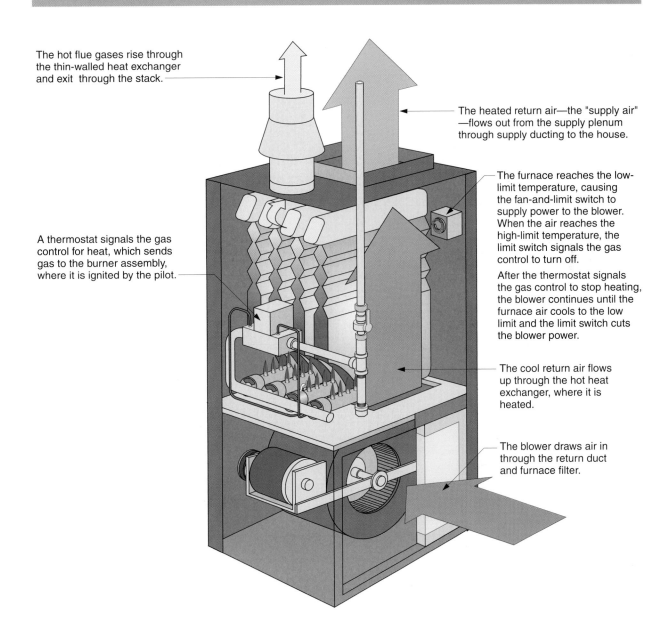

The hot flue gases rise through the thin-walled heat exchanger and exit through the stack.

The heated return air—the "supply air"—flows out from the supply plenum through supply ducting to the house.

The furnace reaches the low-limit temperature, causing the fan-and-limit switch to supply power to the blower. When the air reaches the high-limit temperature, the limit switch signals the gas control to turn off.

After the thermostat signals the gas control to stop heating, the blower continues until the furnace air cools to the low limit and the limit switch cuts the blower power.

A thermostat signals the gas control for heat, which sends gas to the burner assembly, where it is ignited by the pilot.

The cool return air flows up through the hot heat exchanger, where it is heated.

The blower draws air in through the return duct and furnace filter.

The direct-vent heater takes its name from the fact that, due to small size and high efficiency, its combustion gases are cool enough to be safely vented directly through the wall. Both propane and kerosene versions are available. Air return and supply are directly into and out of the unit, eliminating ductwork, as well.

The savings due to elimination of chimney, ducts, and pipes result in a relatively low installation cost. Pros include both a low installation cost and a low operating cost. Cons are a small output (about 50,000 Btu/hr maximum) and a lack of ducts, limiting direct-vent heaters to relatively small, open spaces and superinsulated buildings.

Direct-Vent Gas Fireplace

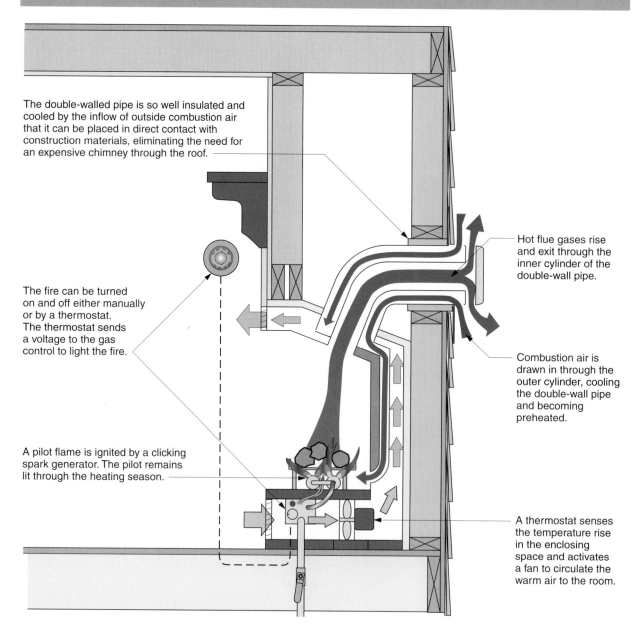

The double-walled pipe is so well insulated and cooled by the inflow of outside combustion air that it can be placed in direct contact with construction materials, eliminating the need for an expensive chimney through the roof.

The fire can be turned on and off either manually or by a thermostat. The thermostat sends a voltage to the gas control to light the fire.

A pilot flame is ignited by a clicking spark generator. The pilot remains lit through the heating season.

Hot flue gases rise and exit through the inner cylinder of the double-wall pipe.

Combustion air is drawn in through the outer cylinder, cooling the double-wall pipe and becoming preheated.

A thermostat senses the temperature rise in the enclosing space and activates a fan to circulate the warm air to the room.

Heat pumps operate on the same principle as refrigerators. By compressing and expanding a gas they can extract heat from a cooler *source* and deliver it to a warmer *sink*. By reversing the pump, you can cool, as well as heat, a house.

Most heat pumps extract heat from outside air. These air-source heat pumps are most cost effective in warm regions where air temperature rarely dips below 45°F. For more northern areas, consider more expensive, but more efficient, water-source and ground-source heat pumps. Pros include circulation and filtration of air, humidification and dehumidification, and combined heating and air conditioning. The single disadvantage is high installation cost.

Air-Source Heat Pump

HEATING MODE

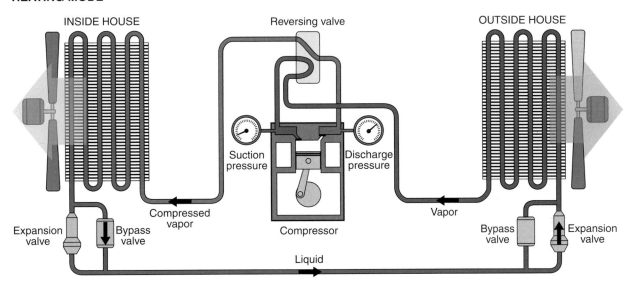

COOLING MODE

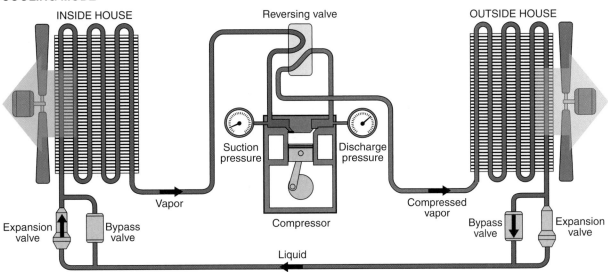

Electric-resistance baseboards convert electricity to heat with 100-percent efficiency because no heat goes up a flue along with products of combustion. However, 100-percent conversion efficiency is misleading. The generation of electricity from fossil fuels is 40-percent efficient at best, making electricity a very expensive "fuel." A possible exception would be a regionally lower electricity price due to geothermal power or hydropower.

Pros include the least expensive installation cost of all, room-by-room thermostatic control, and freedom from pipes and ducts. Cons include the highest operating cost and a lack of air cleaning and humidification.

Electric-Resistance Baseboard Heater

The louver at the top may be adjusted to control the flow of warm air.

Cool room air is drawn in at floor level, is heated by the fins, and rises out at the top.

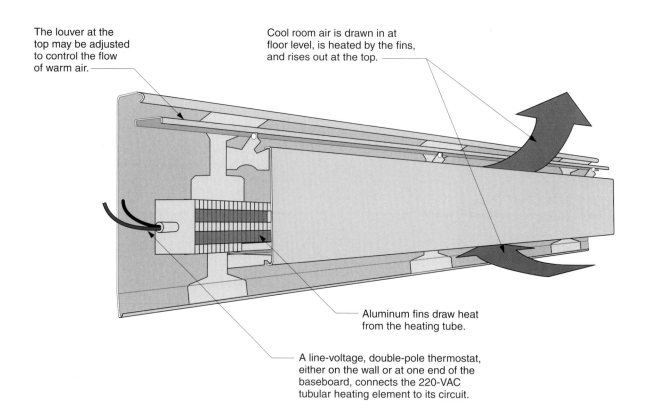

Aluminum fins draw heat from the heating tube.

A line-voltage, double-pole thermostat, either on the wall or at one end of the baseboard, connects the 220-VAC tubular heating element to its circuit.

Solid-fuel (wood, wood pellet, and coal) stoves heat both by radiation to the immediate surroundings and by natural convection of warmed air. Most new stoves also include a blower option for circulating the warmed air more effectively.

Pros include relatively inexpensive fuel and a psychologically comforting radiant heat that defines a social space. Cons are smoke and pollution, dangerous creosote deposits in the chimney, no thermostatic control, and the labor involved in carrying the fuel, tending the stove, and cleaning up.

Air-Tight Wood Stove with and without Catalytic Converter

NON-CATALYTIC WOOD STOVE

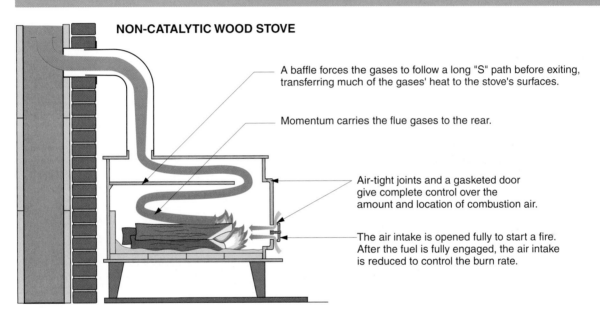

A baffle forces the gases to follow a long "S" path before exiting, transferring much of the gases' heat to the stove's surfaces.

Momentum carries the flue gases to the rear.

Air-tight joints and a gasketed door give complete control over the amount and location of combustion air.

The air intake is opened fully to start a fire. After the fuel is fully engaged, the air intake is reduced to control the burn rate.

CATALYTIC WOOD STOVE

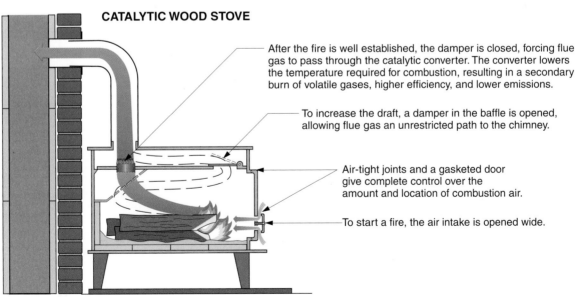

After the fire is well established, the damper is closed, forcing flue gas to pass through the catalytic converter. The converter lowers the temperature required for combustion, resulting in a secondary burn of volatile gases, higher efficiency, and lower emissions.

To increase the draft, a damper in the baffle is opened, allowing flue gas an unrestricted path to the chimney.

Air-tight joints and a gasketed door give complete control over the amount and location of combustion air.

To start a fire, the air intake is opened wide.

Distribution Systems

Warm-air furnaces are popular because they provide a single system of ducts which can be used for four purposes: heating, cooling, humidity control, and air purification.

A past drawback has been the size of the ducts, but there has recently been a trend toward the use of small, high-speed PVC piping for air delivery. The airspeed is reduced at the points of discharge by diffusers.

A future advantage of the warm-air system is the possibility of replacing an original gas or oil furnace with a more efficient heat pump, and of incorporating an air-to-air heat exchanger into the ductwork.

Warm-Air Distribution

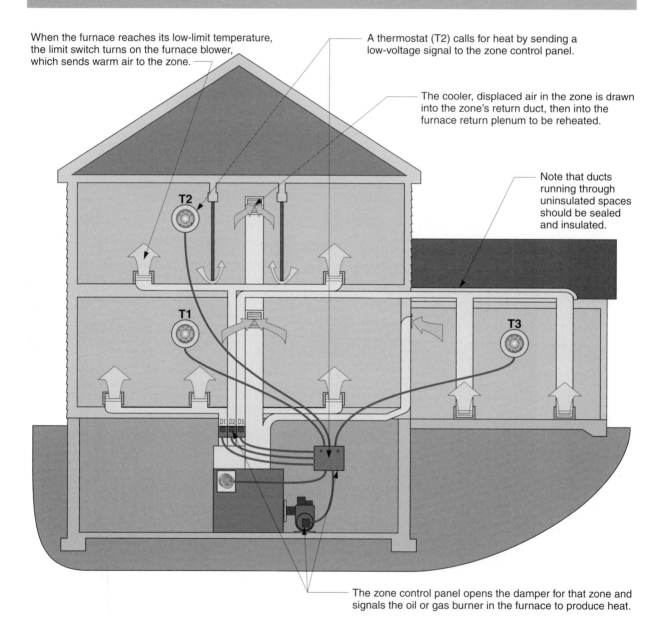

When the furnace reaches its low-limit temperature, the limit switch turns on the furnace blower, which sends warm air to the zone.

A thermostat (T2) calls for heat by sending a low-voltage signal to the zone control panel.

The cooler, displaced air in the zone is drawn into the zone's return duct, then into the furnace return plenum to be reheated.

Note that ducts running through uninsulated spaces should be sealed and insulated.

The zone control panel opens the damper for that zone and signals the oil or gas burner in the furnace to produce heat.

In the era of wood and coal stoves—even the first wood and coal furnaces—heat was distributed by natural convection: simply warm air rising and cooler air falling. The advent of controlled distribution, made possible by forced-warm-air and forced-hot-water (hydronic) systems, made temperature control much more manageable.

However, two changes are bringing natural convection back:

1. Increased insulation and air-tightness, resulting in smaller temperature differences through the house.

2. Very efficient wood and wood pellet direct-vent heaters with built-in air circulation.

Natural Convection

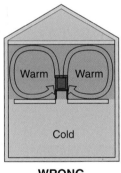

RIGHT

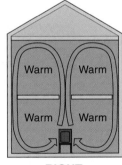

WRONG

RIGHT

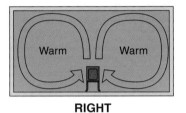

WRONG

RIGHT

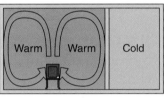

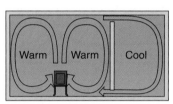

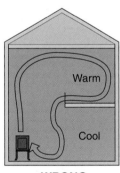

WRONG

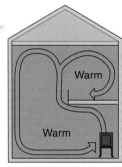

RIGHT

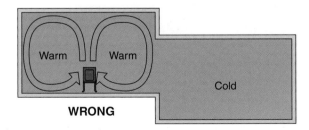

WRONG

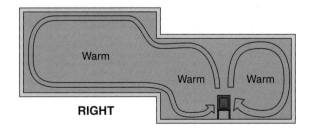

RIGHT

Hydronic heating systems are popular because of the ease (relative to warm-air ductwork) of running the delivery and return piping. Creating a separate temperature zone requires only the addition of a thermostat and a small circulator pump.

A recent energy-efficiency improvement is the addition of an indirect water heater (BoilerMate®) as a zone. The highly insulated, stand-alone tank with heat exchanger reduces both the standby loss of the common water heater and the cycling of boilers incorporating tankless coils.

Hydronic Distribution

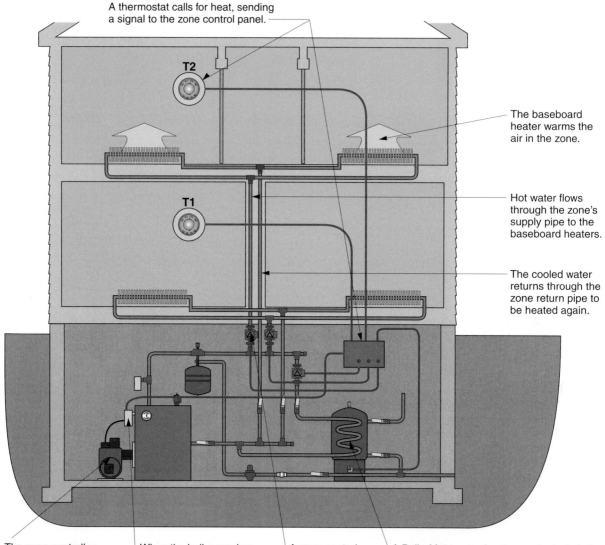

A thermostat calls for heat, sending a signal to the zone control panel.

T2

T1

The baseboard heater warms the air in the zone.

Hot water flows through the zone's supply pipe to the baseboard heaters.

The cooled water returns through the zone return pipe to be heated again.

The zone controller signals the boiler's oil or gas burner to produce heat.

When the boiler reaches its low-limit temperature, the aquastat signals the zone controller.

A zone control turns on the zone circulator pump.

A BoilerMate water heater can be installed as a separate heating zone, or the boiler may be tankless, having a domestic water heating coil within the boiler itself.

Anyone who has heated with a wood stove realizes that heat travels by radiation, as well as by conduction and convection. Because radiative heat transfer is independent of air temperature, a person receiving radiant heat can feel comfortable at a lower temperature (think of the effect of the sun).

Proponents of radiant heat cite the energy savings resulting from a lowered thermostat and a much more uniform heat distribution.

Radiant heat tubing can be installed in a wood-framed ceiling or floor, or buried in a concrete slab. Slabs have long thermal lag times.

Radiant Distribution

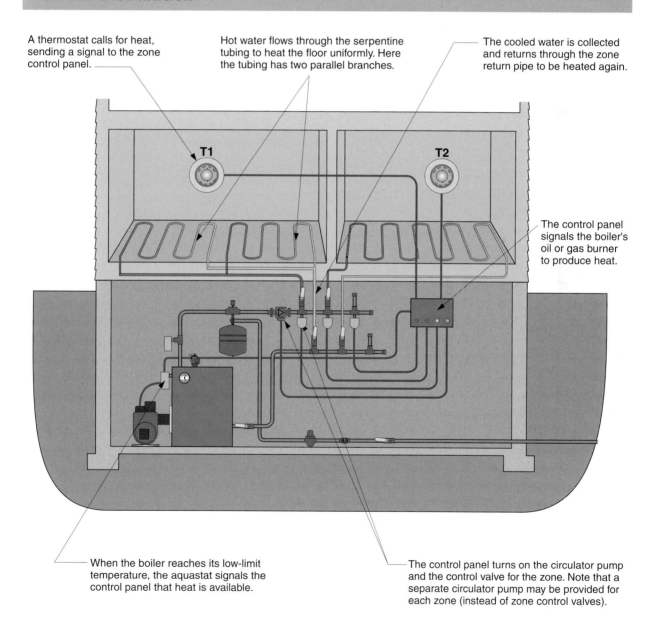

A thermostat calls for heat, sending a signal to the zone control panel.

Hot water flows through the serpentine tubing to heat the floor uniformly. Here the tubing has two parallel branches.

The cooled water is collected and returns through the zone return pipe to be heated again.

The control panel signals the boiler's oil or gas burner to produce heat.

When the boiler reaches its low-limit temperature, the aquastat signals the control panel that heat is available.

The control panel turns on the circulator pump and the control valve for the zone. Note that a separate circulator pump may be provided for each zone (instead of zone control valves).

Fuels and Efficiencies

The only way to compare heating costs is on an apple-to-apple basis, in this case cost per million Btu of delivered heat:

$$\text{Cost per million } (10^6) \text{ Btu} = \frac{10^8 \times P}{F \times \text{AFUE}}$$

where:

P = price of a unit of fuel, $

F = Btu content of the same unit of fuel

AFUE = annual fuel utilization efficiency, percentage

The table at right lists the Btu contents of fuels in their usual unit quantities. Wood pellets are packaged in 40-pound bags, but are most often sold by the 50-bag pallet weighing 1 ton.

To simplify calculations even further, the table below shows cost per 10^6 Btu as a function of fuel price only.

Cost per Million Btu Delivered Heat

Fuel	Unit	System AFUE	Price Multiplier
Coal, anthracite	ton	80%	0.042
Electricity			
baseboard or furnace	kwhr	100%	293
heat pump, air-source	kwhr	230%	127
heat pump, ground-source	kwhr	330%	89
Gas, natural			
average, new furnace/boiler	ccf	80%	12.1
condensing furnace/boiler	ccf	93%	10.4
Gas, propane			
average, new furnace/boiler	gal	80%	13.6
condensing furnace/boiler	gal	93%	11.7
Oil			
average, new furnace/boiler	gal	80%	9.0
high-efficiency furnace/boiler	gal	84%	8.6
Wood[1]			
older stove, non-air-tight	cord	40%	0.104
Non-catalytic air-tight	cord	60%	0.069
Catalytic air-tight	cord	70%	0.059
Pellet stove	lb	80%	0.052

[1] Assuming average hardwood at 24.0 × 10⁶ Btu per cord.

Energy Content of Fuels

Fuel		Btu per	Unit
Coal	Anthracite	30 × 10⁶	ton
	Bituminous	26 × 10⁶	ton
	Cannel	22 × 10⁶	ton
	Lignite	22 × 10⁶	ton
Electricity		3,412	kwhr
Gas	Natural	1,030	cu ft
		103,000	ccf
	Propane	91,600	gal
Oil	#1 (kerosene)	134,000	gal
	#2 (residential)	139,000	gal
	#4 (industrial)	150,000	gal
	#6 (industrial)	153,000	gal
Wood, pellets[1,2]	any species	17.0 × 10⁶	ton
Wood, air-dried[3]	Alder	18.9 × 10⁶	cord
	Ash	25.0 × 10⁶	cord
	Aspen	17.5 × 10⁶	cord
	Beech	29.5 × 10⁶	cord
	Birch, white	23.4 × 10⁶	cord
	Birch, yellow	25.8 × 10⁶	cord
	Cedar, red	18.9 × 10⁶	cord
	Cedar, western red	16.4 × 10⁶	cord
	Fir, Douglas	25.0 × 10⁶	cord
	Hemlock, eastern	18.5 × 10⁶	cord
	Hickory	30.6 × 10⁶	cord
	Maple, red	24.0 × 10⁶	cord
	Maple, sugar	29.0 × 10⁶	cord
	Oak, red	24.0 × 10⁶	cord
	Oak, white	30.6 × 10⁶	cord
	Pine, pitch	22.8 × 10⁶	cord
	Pine, white	15.8 × 10⁶	cord
	Poplar	17.4 × 10⁶	cord
	Spruce	17.5 × 10⁶	cord
	Tamarack	23.1 × 10⁶	cord
	Walnut	25.2 × 10⁶	cord

[1] Energy content depends on local wood species.

[2] Moisture content 4%.

[3] "Air-dried" moisture content 12%.

The cost-per-million Btu formula on the previous page can also be used to calculate the savings realized from increasing heating-system efficiency. Provided the type of fuel remains the same, the table below is more convenient because it shows the projected reduction in annual heating bill as a percentage of the existing bill.

Example 1: What savings would be realized on a heating bill of $2,000 by installing a new gas furnace if the AFUE is increased from 65 to 80 percent? From the table below, the annual savings would be 18.8 percent of $2,000, or $376.

Example 2: How long would it take for a flame-retention-head burner replacement to pay back its cost if the burner increases the estimated annual efficiency of a boiler from 60 to 75 percent? The present fuel bill is $2,400 per year, and the new burner costs $600. From the table below, the annual savings would be 20 percent of $2,400, or $480. The $600 cost would be paid back in $600/$480 = 1.25 years. This is equivalent to receiving 80 percent interest on the $600 investment.

Example 3: How long would it take for an $8,500 air-source heat pump to pay for itself if replacing electric baseboard heat, where the present heating bill is $3,200 per year? Consulting the left table on the previous page, we see that the present AFUE (electricity, baseboard) is 100 percent and the proposed AFUE (electricity, air-source heat pump) is typically 230 percent. From the table below we find that the savings are between 50 and 60 percent, which is between $1,600 and $1,920. Using an average savings of $1,760, the payback will occur in $8,500/$1,760 = 4.8 years.

Percentage Fuel Savings from Increased Efficiency

From AFUE, %	to AFUE, %												
	60	65	70	75	80	85	90	95	100	150	200	250	300
30	50.0	53.8	57.1	60.0	62.5	64.7	66.7	68.4	70.0	80.0	85.0	88.0	90.0
35	41.7	46.2	50.0	53.3	56.3	58.8	61.1	63.2	65.0	76.7	82.5	86.0	88.3
40	33.3	38.5	42.9	46.7	50	52.9	55.6	57.9	60.0	73.3	80.0	84.0	86.7
45	25.0	30.8	35.7	40.0	43.8	47.1	50.0	52.6	55.0	70.0	77.5	82.0	85.0
50	16.7	23.1	28.6	33.3	37.5	41.2	44.4	47.4	50.0	66.7	75.0	80.0	83.3
55	8.3	15.4	21.4	26.7	31.3	35.3	38.9	42.1	45.0	63.3	72.5	78.0	81.7
60	0.0	7.7	14.3	20.0	25.0	29.4	33.3	36.8	40.0	60.0	70.0	76.0	80.0
65	—	0.0	7.1	13.3	18.8	23.5	27.8	31.6	35.0	56.7	67.5	74.0	78.3
70	—	—	0.0	6.7	12.5	17.6	22.2	26.3	30.0	53.3	65.0	72.0	76.7
75	—	—	—	0.0	6.3	11.8	16.7	21.1	25.0	50.0	62.5	70.0	75.0
80	—	—	—	—	0.0	5.9	11.1	15.8	20.0	46.7	60.0	68.0	73.3
85	—	—	—	—	—	0.0	5.6	10.5	15.0	43.3	57.5	66.0	71.7
90	—	—	—	—	—	—	0.0	5.3	10.0	40.0	55.0	64.0	70.0
95	—	—	—	—	—	—	—	0.0	5.0	36.7	52.5	62.0	68.3
100	—	—	—	—	—	—	—	—	0.0	33.3	50.0	60.0	66.7

Standard Fireplaces

The energy-efficient conventional fireplace design, illustrated on the following page, offers two key advantages over older designs: It uses outside air for combustion, and it cuts down on infiltration of cold air caused by replacement of warm air used for combustion. Both factors increase heating efficiency. To reduce infiltration when the fireplace is not in operation, tight-fitting dampers, louvers, and glass screens should be used.

Air Intake

Combustion air may be drawn from the outside or from any unheated area of the building, such as a crawl space. Building codes may restrict the location of the air intake, however. For example, codes usually prohibit air being drawn from a garage to prevent the introduction of exhaust gases from automobiles into the house. Regardless of the location of the air intake, it requires a screened closable louver, preferably one that can be operated from inside the house.

To ensure sufficient air, the passageway should have a cross-sectional area of at least 55 square inches. The insulated passageway can be built into the base of the fireplace assembly or channeled between joists in the floor.

The inlet brings the outside air into the firebox. A damper is required for volume and direction control. The damper is located in the front of the firebox, and although its dimensions may vary, most openings will be about 4½ by 13 inches.

The air intake pit, located directly below the inlet, should have the same dimensions and should be about 13 inches deep.

Lintel and Damper

Both the steel lintel and the cast-iron damper assembly should be installed with precautions against thermal expansion damaging the masonry. To this end, a compressible, non-combustible material, such as fiberglass insulation, should be placed between the ends of the lintel and the masonry. Similarly, the damper should not be embedded or bonded to the masonry, but rest on a level mortar setting bed so it is free to expand.

Conventional Fireplace Dimensions, in

Finished Fireplace Opening							Rough Brickwork				Flue Size	Steel Angle
A	B	C	D	E	F	G	H	I	J	K	L × M	N
24	24	16	11	14	16	8¾	32	21	19	10	8 × 12	A-36
26	24	16	13	14	18	8¾	34	21	21	11	8 × 12	A-36
28	24	16	15	14	18	8¾	36	21	21	12	8 × 12	A-36
30	29	16	17	14	23	8¾	38	21	24	13	12 × 12	A-42
32	29	16	19	14	23	8¾	40	21	24	14	12 × 12	A-42
36	29	16	23	14	23	8¾	44	21	27	16	12 × 12	A-48
40	29	16	27	14	23	8¾	48	21	29	16	12 × 12	A-48
42	32	16	29	16	24	8¾	50	21	32	17	12 × 16	B-54
48	32	18	33	16	24	8¾	56	23	37	20	12 × 16	B-60
54	37	20	37	16	29	13	68	25	45	26	16 × 16	B-66
60	40	22	42	18	30	13	72	27	45	26	16 × 20	B-72
72	40	22	54	18	30	13	84	27	56	32	20 × 20	C-84

Conventional Fireplace with Outside Air Supply

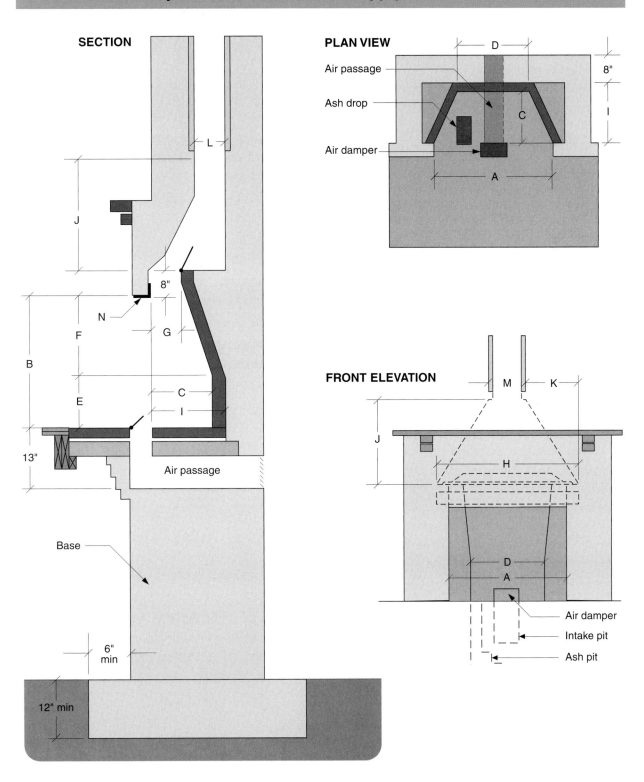

SECTION

L

J

8"

N

F

B

E

13"

G

C

I

Air passage

Base

6" min

12" min

PLAN VIEW

D

8"

Air passage

Ash drop

I

C

Air damper

A

FRONT ELEVATION

M   K

J

H

D

A

Air damper

Intake pit

Ash pit

Rumford Fireplaces

Most of the heat that can be gotten from a fireplace is radiated heat. The amount of heat an object—in this case a fire—can radiate depends on three principal variables:

1. The size of the fire.

2. The temperature of the flame or coals to the fourth power (the Stefan-Boltzmann Law).

3. The solid (two-dimensional) angle of the space into which the fire radiates.

If the fire were suspended in space, it could radiate in all directions; built in the middle of a floor, it can radiate into half as much space; located at the junction of a wall and a floor, it would be limited to one-quarter of space; and located deep inside a fireplace, it would be constrained even further.

There is a particular class of fireplace design, featuring shallow fireboxes with obliquely flared sides and backs, that produces the maximum amount of radiated heat. This design is called the *Rumford fireplace*. The design rules below and the illustration on the facing page provide details and dimensions for a Rumford fireplace and guidance on how it should be designed and built.

Combining this data with the information on p. 474 on outside combustion air, you can achieve the maximum in energy-efficient fireplace design. A Rumford fireplace, with exterior air supply and glass screens for the opening, will provide the most radiated heat, the least infiltration, and the best all-around energy performance to be found in true (noninsert) fireplaces.

Rumford Design Rules

1. The width of the firebox (D) must equal the depth (C).

2. The vertical portion of the firebox (E) must equal the width (D).

3. The thickness of the firebox (I minus C) should be at least 2¼ inches.

4. The area of the fireplace opening (A × B) must not exceed ten times the flue opening area.

5. The width of the fireplace opening (A) and its height (B) should each be two to three times the depth of the firebox (C).

6. The opening height (B) should not be larger than the width (A).

7. The throat (G) should be not less than 3 nor more than 4 inches.

8. The centerline of the throat must align with the center of the firebox.

9. The smoke shelf (R) should be 4 inches wide.

10. The width of the lintel (O) should be not less than 4 nor more than 5 inches.

11. The vertical distance from lintel to throat (P) must be at least 12 inches.

12. A flat plate damper is required at the throat and must open toward the smoke shelf.

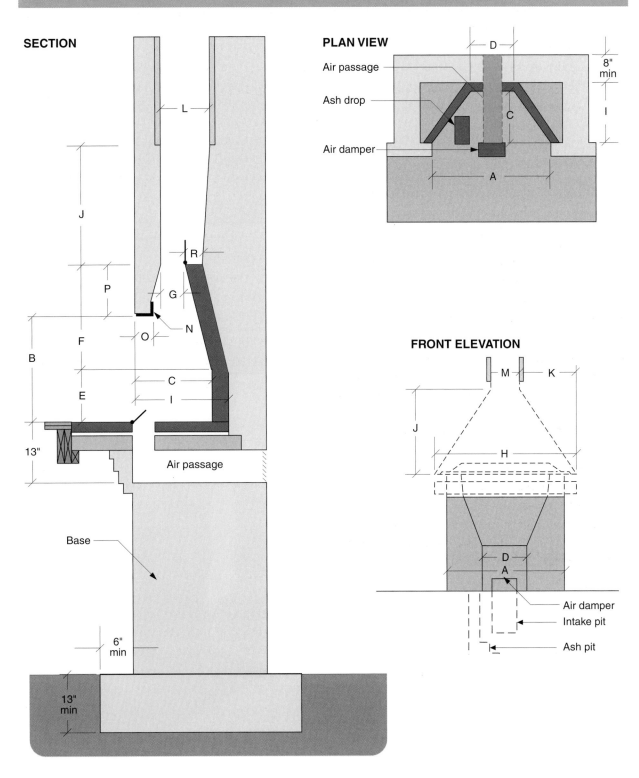

SECTION

L

J

P

R

G

N

O

F

B

E

C

I

13"

Air passage

Base

6"
min

13"
min

PLAN VIEW

Air passage

Ash drop

Air damper

D

8"
min

I

C

A

FRONT ELEVATION

M

K

J

H

D

A

Air damper

Intake pit

Ash pit

Wood Stove Installation

Wood and coal stoves are classified as circulating, radiant, or cookstove. A circulating stove has two walls: an inner wall surrounding the firebox, and an outer wall. Heated air rises, drawing cool air from the floor into the space between the inner and outer walls. Because the air circulates, clearances for this type of stove are less than those needed for a radiant stove.

Much of the heat from the single-walled radiant stove is in the form of infrared radiation. Clearances are greater because the infrared radiation heats combustible materials and changes their composition, lowering the temperature at which they can spontaneously combust. Because the changes are not always evident, proper clearances should be maintained to prevent the possibility of fire.

Stovepipes ordinarily run cooler than the stoves to which they are connected. However, in case of a chimney fire, the stovepipe may temporarily become much hotter than the stove. Significant clearances are therefore specified for stovepipes as well.

Combustible materials include anything that can burn. Examples are the wood box, magazine racks, furniture, draperies, and wood paneling. Even a gypsum-drywalled or plastered wall is combustible because the wood studs behind the surface can burn.

The illustrations below show minimum side and rear clearances for radiant stoves and single-walled stovepipes, both with and without protection of combustible surfaces.

The tables below and on the facing page list more detailed specifications.

Floor Clearances

Stove Leg	Floor Clearance and Protection
<2"	Fire-resistant floor
2"–6"	Combustible floor protection by 4" of hollow masonry, laid to provide circulation through the masonry layer, covered by 24-ga sheet metal
>6"	Combustible floor protected by 2" thick masonry, placed over a sheet of 24-ga sheet metal

Radiant Stove, No Rear Protection

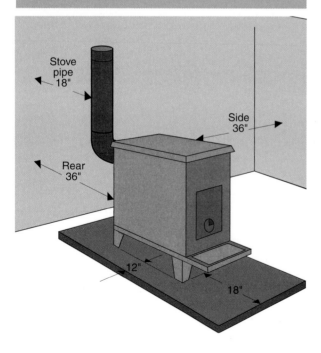

Radiant Stove with Rear Protection

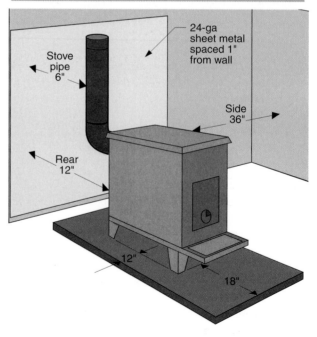

Minimum Clearances from Wood Burning Stoves to Combustible Surfaces with No Added Protection

Surface	Radiant	System Circulating	Cookstove Clay-Lined Firepot	Cookstove Unlined Firepot	Single-Wall Stovepipe
Ceiling	36″	36″	30″	30″	18″
Front	36″	24″	—	—	18″
Firing Side	36″	12″	24″	36″	18″
Opposite Side	36″	12″	18″	18″	18″
Rear	36″	12″	24″	36″	18″

Minimum Clearances from Wood Burning Stoves with Specified Forms of Protection, in

	Where Required Clearance with No Protection Is									
	36		18		12		9		6	
	Use Col.1 above appliance or horizontal connector. Use Col. 2 for clearance from appliance, vertical pipe, and single-wall pipe.									
Type of Protection	Above Col. 1	Sides & Rear Col. 2	Above Col. 1	Sides & Rear Col. 2	Above Col. 1	Sides & Rear Col. 2	Above Col. 1	Sides & Rear Col. 2	Above Col. 1	Sides & Rear Col. 2
3½″ masonry wall without ventilated air space	—	24	—	12	—	9	—	6	—	5
½″-thick insulation board over 1″ glass fiber or mineral wool batts	24	18	12	9	9	6	6	5	4	3
24-ga sheet metal over glass/wool batts, wire-reinforced, with ventilated air space	18	12	9	6	6	4	5	3	3	3
3½″ masonry wall with ventilated air space	—	12	—	6	—	6	—	6	—	6
24-ga sheet metal with ventilated air space	18	12	9	6	6	4	5	3	3	2
½″-thick insulation board with ventilated air space	18	12	9	6	6	4	5	3	3	3
24-ga sheet metal with vented space over 24-ga sheet metal with ventilated air space	18	12	9	6	6	4	5	3	3	3
1″ glass/wool batts between two sheets 24-ga sheet metal with vented air space	18	12	9	6	6	4	5	3	3	3

Notes: Reduction of clearances shall not interfere with combustion air, draft hood clearance and relief, and accessibility of servicing.

Clearances measured from surface of combustible material to nearest point on the surface of the appliance.

Spacers and ties to be of noncombustible material. No spacer or tie to be used directly opposite an appliance or connector.

For all clearance-reduction systems using a ventilated airspace, adequate provision for air circulation shall be provided.

There shall be at least 1″ between the appliance and the protector.

All clearances and thicknesses are minimum; larger clearances and thicknesses are acceptable.

Stovepipe Installation

Proper installation of the stovepipe connecting a stove to its chimney is important for both safety and performance. Make sure you observe the following rules:

1. The stovepipe should be as short as possible. Horizontal runs should be no longer than 75 percent of the vertical chimney height above the connecting thimble.

2. The stovepipe should be as straight as possible. No more than two 90-degree bends should be used. Additional bends could cause creosote to collect in the stovepipe or chimney, block flue gas flow, and increase the potential for fire.

3. Use a stovepipe that has a diameter as large as the collar where the pipe joins the stove.

4. Horizontal runs should rise ¼ inch per foot, with the highest point at the thimble.

5. When joining stovepipe, overlap the joint at least 2 inches, with the crimped end pointing down to prevent creosote leaks. Secure each joint with three sheet metal screws. A fireproof sealant (furnace cement) may be used as well.

6. All pipe joints should fit snugly, including connections with the stove and thimble. The pipe should not project into the chimney and hinder the draft.

7. The stovepipe should not pass through ceilings. Factory-built, listed, all-fuel chimney should be used for passing through ceilings. Follow the manufacturer's directions.

8. A stovepipe passing through walls must be supported and spaced by vented thimbles of three times the diameter of the pipe. An alternative is a section of factory-built, listed, all-fuel chimney installed as directed.

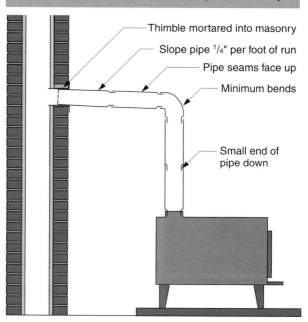

Connecting to a Masonry Chimney

- Thimble mortared into masonry
- Slope pipe ¼" per foot of run
- Pipe seams face up
- Minimum bends
- Small end of pipe down

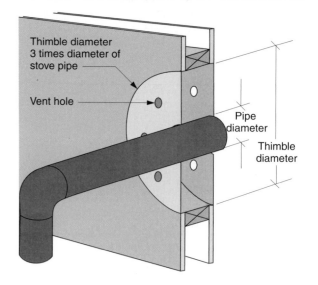

Passing through a Combustible Wall

- Thimble diameter 3 times diameter of stove pipe
- Vent hole
- Pipe diameter
- Thimble diameter

Metal Prefabricated Chimneys

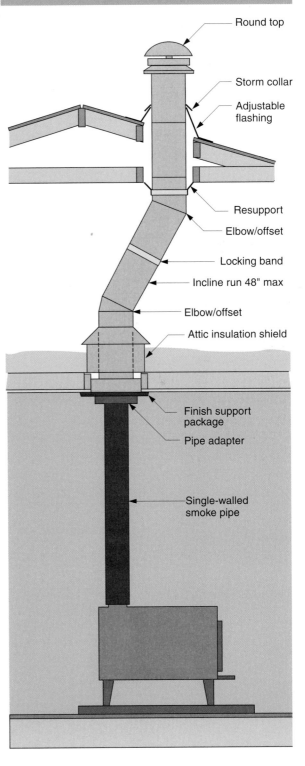

Through Attic Insulation

Round top

Storm collar

Adjustable flashing

Chimney pipe

Attic insulation shield

Finish support package

Pipe adapter

Smoke pipe

Attic Offset to Avoid Ridge

Round top

Storm collar

Adjustable flashing

Resupport

Elbow/offset

Locking band

Incline run 48" max

Elbow/offset

Attic insulation shield

Finish support package

Pipe adapter

Single-walled smoke pipe

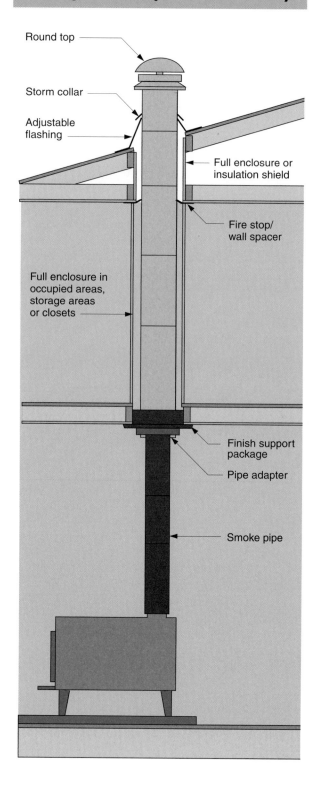

Round top

Roof brace

2' min

High-pitch
flashing

Roof support
under flashing

Pitched ceiling plate

Suspended length long
enough to provide 18"
min clearance

Chimney pipe adapter

Smoke pipe,
all sections secured
with three screws

Round top

Storm collar

Adjustable
flashing

Full enclosure or
insulation shield

Fire stop/
wall spacer

Full enclosure in
occupied areas,
storage areas
or closets

Finish support
package

Pipe adapter

Smoke pipe

Chimney for a Fireplace

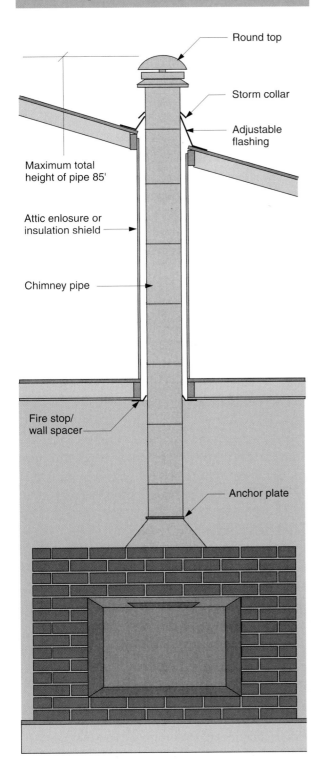

Round top

Storm collar

Adjustable flashing

Maximum total height of pipe 85'

Attic enlosure or insulation shield

Chimney pipe

Fire stop/ wall spacer

Anchor plate

Tee-Supported Outside Chimney

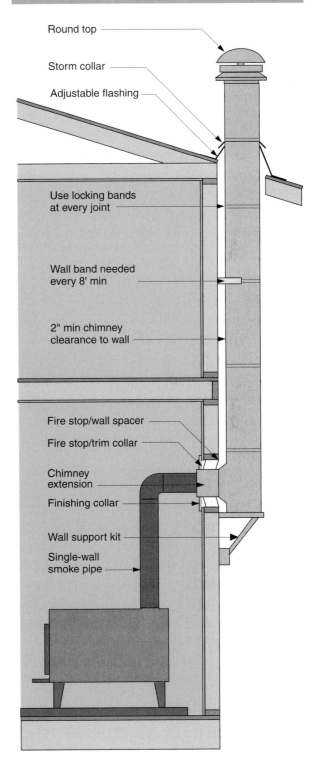

Round top

Storm collar

Adjustable flashing

Use locking bands at every joint

Wall band needed every 8' min

2" min chimney clearance to wall

Fire stop/wall spacer

Fire stop/trim collar

Chimney extension

Finishing collar

Wall support kit

Single-wall smoke pipe

Meet the Code

The following is a partial list of requirements from the *2006 International Residential Code (IRC) for One- and Two-Family Dwellings.* Consult the publication for the full text and additional provisions.

Masonry Fireplaces (R1001)

Footings and foundations:
- of concrete or solid masonry ≥12" thick
- to extend ≥6" beyond face of fireplace on all sides
- on undisturbed earth or engineered fill below frost

Firebox dimensions:
- depth ≥20"
- throat ≥8" above fireplace opening and ≥4" deep
- passageway above firebox, including throat, damper, and smoke chamber, ≥cross-sectional area of flue

Exception—Rumford fireplaces:
- depth ≥12" and ≥⅓ width of opening
- throat ≥12" above lintel
- throat opening ≥1/20 fireplace opening

Lintel, throat, and damper:
- noncombustible lintel over opening required
- throat or damper to be ≥8" above lintel
- ferrous metal damper ≥8" above opening required
- damper installed in fireplace or chimney
- damper operable from room containing fireplace

Hearth and extensions:
- of concrete or masonry, supported by noncombustible material, and reinforced for imposed loads
- no combustible material against the underside of hearths and hearth extensions after construction
- hearth thickness ≥4"; extension thickness ≥2"

Exception: if firebox opening ≥8" above hearth extension, extension thickness ≥3/8" permitted
- extensions to extend ≥16" front and ≥8" sides; where opening ≥6 sq ft, ≥20" front and ≥12" sides

Fireplace clearance:
- ≥2" from the front faces and sides
- ≥4" from the back faces

Masonry Chimneys (R1003)

- inlets to have thimble to prevent connector from pulling out or from extending beyond liner
- cleanout opening ≤6" of base of each flue

Exception: flues serving fireplaces
- spaces between chimneys and floors and ceilings to be fireblocked with noncombustible material
- chimneys ≥30" parallel to ridge to have crickets

Factory-Built Chimneys (R1005)

- in dwelling units with solid-fuel-burning appliances to comply with the Type HT requirements of UL 103

Exterior Air Supply (R1006)

- combustion air ducts for factory-built fireplaces to be a listed component of the fireplace
- exterior air intake capable of supplying all combustion air from exterior or from spaces ventilated with outside air such as vented crawl or attic spaces
- intake not to be located in a garage or basement
- intake not to be located higher than firebox
- intake covered with corrosion-resistant ¼" mesh.
- passageway ≥6 and ≤55 sq in except constructed according to the fireplace manufacturer's instructions
- outlet to be in back or sides of firebox or within 24" of the firebox opening on or near the floor

Connectors (M1803)

- connectors for oil and solid-fuel-burning appliances to be of factory-built chimney material, Type L vent material, or single-wall metal of thicknesses: diameter <6" —0.019", 6–10"—.024", >10"—.029"
- as short and straight as possible
- installed with a slope of ≥¼" rise per 12" of run
- joints fastened with sheet-metal screws or rivets
- not to pass through floor or ceiling
- not to pass through wall unless listed or routed through a device listed for wall pass-through
- connectors for oil-fired appliances listed for Type

L vents, passing through walls, to be installed with listed clearances to combustible material.

- single-wall metal pipe through walls to be through a ventilated metal thimble ≥4" larger in diameter, and with ≥6" clearance to combustibles.
- horizontal run of uninsulated connector to natural draft chimney ≤75% of height of chimney above
- horizontal run of a listed connector to natural draft chimney ≤100% of height of chimney above
- connector diameter to be ≥ that of flue collar

Termination (M1804)

- vents for natural draft appliances to terminate ≥5' above highest connected appliance
- natural draft gas vents for wall furnaces to terminate ≥12' above bottom of furnace.
- Type L vents to terminate ≥2' above roof and ≥2' above any portion of the building within 10'
- direct-vent terminal to be installed in accordance with the manufacturer's installation instructions

Mechanical draft systems:
- vent terminal ≥3' above forced-air inlet within 10'
- vent terminal ≥4' below, ≥4' horizontally from, and ≥1' above door, window, or air inlet into a dwelling
- vent terminal ≥4' to an interior corner formed by two walls perpendicular to each other
- bottom of vent terminal ≥12" above grade
- vent terminal not directly above or ≤3' horizontally from oil tank vent or gas meter
- power exhaust terminations to be located ≥10' from lot lines and adjacent buildings

Chimney Flues:
- effective area of a natural draft flue for one appliance to be ≥area of the connector to the appliance
- area of flues connected to more than one appliance to be ≥area of the largest connector plus 50% of areas of additional connectors
- area of flue connected to a solid-fuel-burning appliance to be ≥area of the flue collar or connector, and ≤3 times area of the flue collar

Gas Piping Installation (G2415)

Prohibited locations:
- in air duct, clothes chute, chimney or gas vent, dumbwaiter, or elevator shaft
- through any townhouse unit other than the unit served by such piping
- in solid partitions/walls, unless in a chase or casing

In concealed locations:
- no unions, tubing fittings, right and left couplings, bushings, compression couplings, and swing joints made by combinations of fittings
- *Exceptions*: brazed joints, listed fittings

Underground piping:
- in protective sleeve through foundation walls
- space between piping and sleeve to be sealed

Protective shield plates:
- where <1.5" from edge of concealed framing
- to be minimum 1/16"-thick steel
- to extend ≥4" above sole plates, below top plates, and to each side of framing member
- *Exceptions*: black iron pipe, galvanized steel pipe

Above-ground piping outdoors:
- ≥3½" above ground and roof surface
- securely supported and located where it will be protected from physical damage
- passing through an outside wall, piping protected against corrosion by coating or wrapping

Gas Shutoff Valves (G2420)

- not in concealed locations and furnace plenums
- access for operation and protected from damage
- on the supply side of every gas meter
- immediately ahead of each MP regulator
- in same room and ≤6' from each appliance
Exception: valves for vented decorative appliances may be remote from appliance if provided with ready access
Exception: in the firebox of a fireplace if installed according to manufacturer's instructions

Cooling

The object of this chapter is to help you achieve cool comfort for the lowest possible cost. You'll find there are numerous techniques you can employ before resorting to mechanical air conditioning. To understand how and why these other techniques work, the chapter begins by explaining the relationship between *cooling and comfort.*

Inexpensive *attic radiant barriers* have been shown to result in dramatic cooling savings in southern states.

A high percentage of summer heat gain is from the sun. *Solar radiation charts* for summer and winter show just how much heat is received in both summer and winter.

Everyone knows that it is cooler in the shade in summer, but this chapter shows you exactly how much you will save using different *window shading strategies.*

We also show how to select and size the right type of *fan* for your cooling needs, from a small oscillating fan in the kitchen, to an old-fashioned but surprisingly effective ceiling fan, to large window and whole-house fans.

If you live in a dry climate, chances are excellent that you can cool air by 20 degrees or more with an economical *evaporative cooler.* Here you'll find a table listing the evaporative cooling potential for your area and a formula for estimating the size of cooler for your home.

If all of the above fail to cool you sufficiently, use the work sheet provided for calculating the amount of *air conditioning* needed to cool either a single room or the whole house.

Cooling and Comfort

Many people think of temperature as the only variable affecting their comfort. In fact, as the human comfort chart below illustrates, humidity, air movement, and radiation all strongly affect our comfort:

Relative Humidity Relative humidity affects the rate of evaporation from the skin. Because evaporation of perspiration absorbs heat, it lowers the temperature of the skin. Thus, at high temperatures, we are more comfortable at lower relative humidities.

Air Movement Air movement across the body increases heat loss from the body and allows us to feel comfortable at higher temperatures. In a 6 mph breeze, for example, the average person would feel comfortable at up to 87°F at 60 percent relative humidity (Point A), and up to 93°F at 20 percent relative humidity (Point B).

Radiation Radiation adds heat to the body. The chart below shows that radiation of 250 Btu/h-sq ft (approximately the level of midday winter solar radiation) allows the average person, dressed in normal clothing, to be comfortable down to a temperature of 50°F!

The Human Comfort Zone

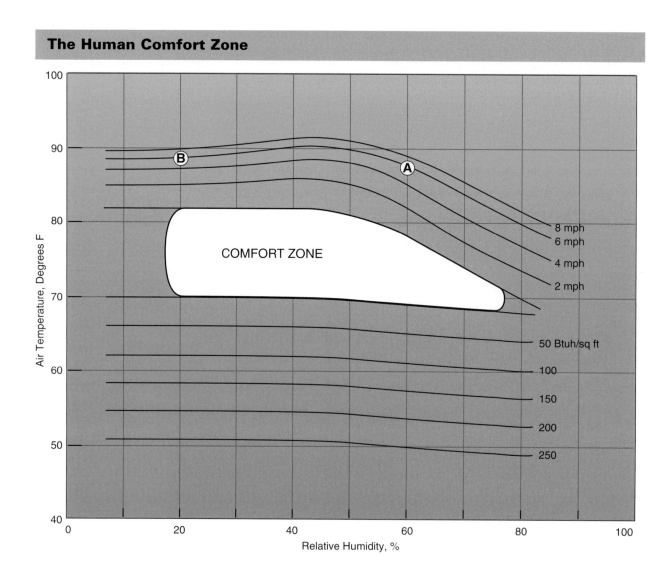

Attic Radiant Barriers

A radiant barrier is a layer of aluminum foil installed in an interior space to block radiant heat transfer from a heat-radiating surface (such as a hot roof) to a heat-absorbing surface (such as conventional attic insulation). Radiant barriers are used predominately in attics in southern states, where they have proven effective in lowering cooling bills.

A radiant barrier is not insulation. It does not block *conducted heat*, as insulation does. You can pick up a foam cup of hot coffee because the foam is retarding the conduction of heat from the inside of the cup to the outside. But you'd have a rough time drinking hot coffee from an aluminum beer can. The heat would conduct right through to your skin.

Radiant heat consists of rays of energy that travel through air or space and don't turn into heat until they strike an object. An aluminum foil barrier works because it is capable of reflecting 95 to 98 percent of the radiant heat that strikes it. But because aluminum is a good heat conductor, there must be an air space between the radiating surface and the surface to be shielded from radiant energy. As a result, there are two recommended ways to install a radiant barrier in an attic:

Under Roof Sheathing Under the sheathing is the simplest and cheapest method for new construction. The barrier, usually consisting of aluminum foil backed by a tear-resistant material, is rolled out on top of the rafters before the sheathing is installed.

To Rafter Bottoms Attached to the bottom edges of the rafters is the easiest, most effective method for existing houses. Simply staple the material to the underside of the rafters.

Whichever method you use, install the barrier with the foil facing down into the attic space. At first, the foil would work equally well facing up or down. However, dust would eventually collect on upward-facing foil, reducing the effectiveness of the barrier.

This dust problem also makes it ineffective to install the barrier over attic floor insulation, facing up.

Note that small tears or gaps in the radiant barrier will not significantly reduce overall performance.

Attic Section with Alternative Radiant Barrier Locations

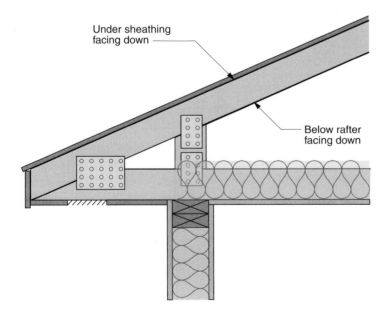

Under sheathing facing down

Below rafter facing down

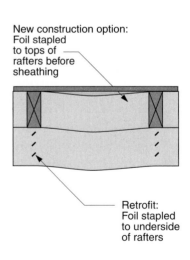

New construction option: Foil stapled to tops of rafters before sheathing

Retrofit: Foil stapled to underside of rafters

Solar Radiation Charts

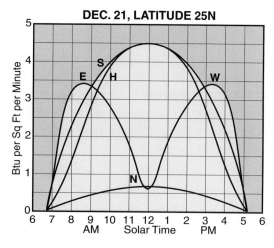

DEC. 21, LATITUDE 25N

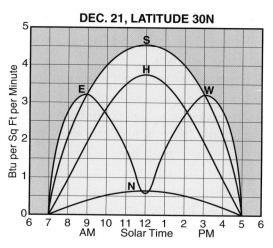

DEC. 21, LATITUDE 30N

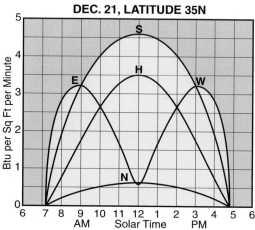

DEC. 21, LATITUDE 35N

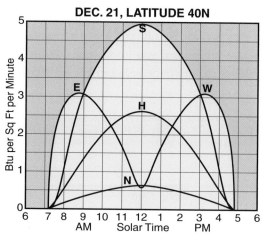

DEC. 21, LATITUDE 40N

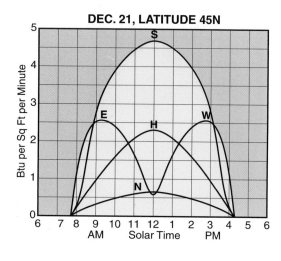

DEC. 21, LATITUDE 45N

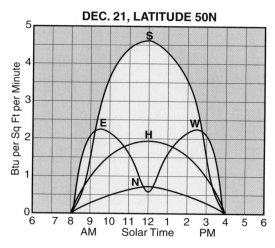

DEC. 21, LATITUDE 50N

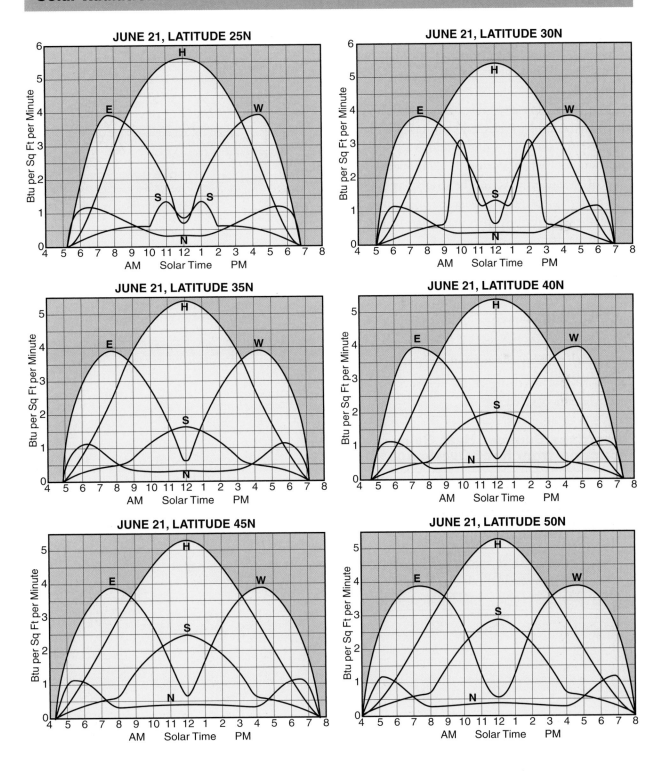

Window Shading Strategies

A high percentage of summer heat gain comes through windows as solar radiation. Much of the radiation is diffuse or reflected, and not directly from the sun. As a result, it pays to shade all windows, regardless of the direction they face. The single exception is passive solar glazings in northern states, which should have calculated overhangs, as shown in Chapter 18.

The illustration and table below show the percentage reductions in heat gain through the entire cooling season for 4- by 4-foot windows at 30 degree north latitude, when shaded by continuous overhangs of various lengths, L. The reductions are seen to be nearly independent of window orientation. Of course, there are reasons other than solar shading for building overhangs:

1. A 2-foot overhang protects siding, windows, and doors from the weathering effects of rain. In addition, windows can be left open without worrying about sudden showers.

2. A 6- to 8-foot overhang is common for porch roofs, which are very common in the South.

3. A 10-foot overhang could be provided by a carport or vine-covered patio.

Sun's Path in Winter and Summer

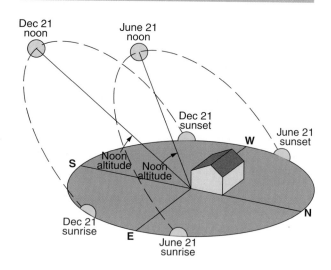

Overhang Geometry for Table

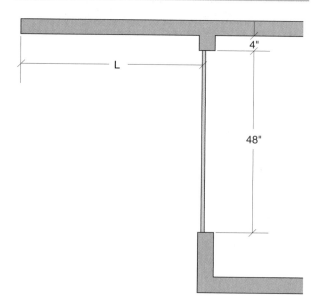

Percentage Summer Heat Gain Reduction from Roof Overhangs

Window Facing	Width of Overhang (L), ft					
	1	2	3	4	6	10
North	16	32	44	54	66	78
East	14	32	47	58	72	84
South	17	35	47	56	67	79
West	15	32	47	58	71	83
Average	16	33	46	57	69	81

The illustration at right shows an adjustable opaque window awning with side panels. Both the awnings and windows measure 4 feet by 4 feet, so at a 90 degree slope, the awning would completely cover the window. The table below the illustration shows the cooling-season reductions in heat gain to be expected through single-glazed windows with different shading strategies.

As the slope of a shading device increases, visibility from the window decreases until, at 90-degree slope, nothing can be seen. Fortunately, much of the shading benefit is achieved with a slope of only 30 degrees, at which point the top half of the view is blocked.

Canvas awnings can be rolled up, but the other shading options would be difficult or impossible to adjust in different seasons. We therefore need to know for each the net effect, or cooling-season savings less reduction in winter solar gain.

Both cooling and heating bills vary with latitude. As latitude increases, cooling bills decrease and heating bills increase. Net savings from fixed shading devices therefore vary with latitude. In the South, net savings are positive; in the North they can be negative.

The table at right shows how strongly net savings can vary. Savings in Miami (virtually zero winter heating load) are nearly three times those in Jacksonville, only 4.5 degrees to the north. For example, permanent charcoal-colored screens over 100 square feet of uniformly distributed glazing would save 1,000 kwhr in Miami, but only 350 kwhr in Jacksonville.

Shading devices above 30 degrees north latitude should be of the adjustable variety in order to maximize both summer and winter savings.

Adjustable Awning with Sides

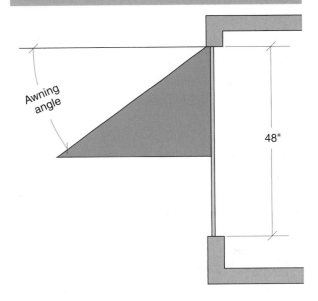

Net Savings from Awnings, kwhr/sq ft-yr

Window Facing	Tinted Glass	Silver Film	Charcoal Screen	Awning No Side	Awning & Sides
Jacksonville, FL, 30.5° N Latitude					
North	1.5	3.6	3.8	2.9	4.2
East	1.5	3.4	3.6	4.1	4.5
South	0.4	0.9	1.0	0.4	0.9
West	2.3	5.4	5.6	5.6	6.8
Average	1.4	3.3	3.5	3.3	4.1
Miami, FL, 26° N Latitude					
North	3.1	7.4	7.7	5.8	8.6
East	4.5	10.5	11.0	10.2	13.1
South	17	35	47	67	79
West	15	32	47	71	83
Average	16	33	46	69	81

Fans

During the cooling season in hot, humid regions of the United States, air-conditioning costs are the largest part of the monthly utility bill. In Florida, for example, air-conditioning accounts for about 30 percent of the total annual electric bill in an all-electric home. To a large extent, fans can reduce the need for air conditioning by raising the upper limit of the comfort zone.

Powered attic vent fans ventilate an attic but not the house. Research has shown that attics with recommended natural ventilation and insulation levels do not require attic vent fans. Such vent fans typically cost more to operate than they save in cooling bills. Instead, install the recommended R-value of attic insulation (see Chapter 13) with an attic radiant barrier as described on p. 489. For effective natural attic ventilation, use continuous soffit vents at the eaves plus ridge vents at the peak.

There are three generic types of fans:

- ceiling, cooling by air motion.
- window, cooling by air exchange.
- whole-house, cooling by air exchange.

The cooling effect of a breeze depends on its velocity. Air velocity can be approximated if you know the total area through which the breeze is blowing (such as total open area of inlet windows) and the fan rating in cfm. The chart below shows ranges of fan cfm versus fan size for the fans discussed in this chapter, as well as their approximate efficiencies in cfm per watt of electrical consumption. Note that ceiling fans are at least three times more efficient than any other type.

Fan Efficiencies

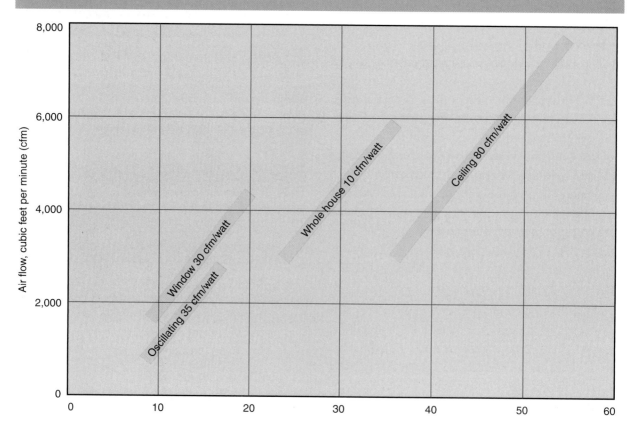

494   COOLING

Ceiling Fans

Air-circulating fans include oscillating, box, and ceiling fans. The breezes they create can easily allow air conditioner setbacks of 5°F to 10°F, lowering cooling bills by 40 to 80 percent. Portable fans are best at cooling small areas, such as people sitting at desks or working in the kitchen. Larger box fans can be placed in doorways to move large volumes of air between rooms. The quietest and most efficient, however, are ceiling fans. A ceiling fixture can usually be easily converted to a ceiling fan plus light. The illustration at right shows required clearances and proper fan size.

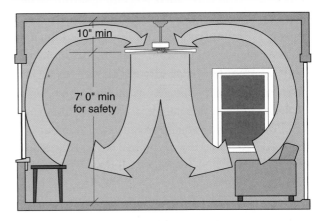

Ceiling Fan Operation

Window Fans

Whole-house fans are effective, but they are also expensive, difficult to retrofit, and power hungry (500 to 700 watts). Operated properly, a window fan can be nearly as effective:

1. Place the fan to blow out in a room far from the cooled rooms.

2. Locate the specific areas you wish to cool, such as the two bedrooms below and open those windows.

3. Close all other windows.

Get ready to enjoy a cooling breeze through your bedroom window without the noise of a fan.

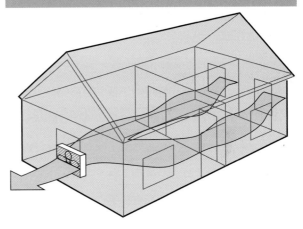

Window Fan Operation

Whole-House Fans

As the illustration at right shows, a centrally located whole-house fan can pull air from every room in which there is an open window. The total open window area should be three times the fan intake area. Similarly, the total attic vent area should be three times the fan intake, assuming screened vents.

The fan should be sized to replace one-third of the house air every minute. For example, a 1,500-square-foot house with 8-foot ceiling contains 12,000 cubic feet. The fan should therefore be rated at $\frac{1}{3} \times 12,000 = 4,000$ cubic feet per minute. If the fan's rating is for "free air," increase the cfm by 20 percent.

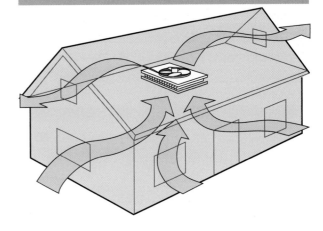

Whole-House Fan Operation

Evaporative Cooling

When water evaporates, it absorbs heat. This is why you feel so cool when you emerge from swimming on a dry, breezy day. Evaporative coolers (also known as swamp coolers) utilize this phenomenon to lower air temperature. As the illustration on the facing page shows, hot, dry air blown through a water-soaked pad emerges as humid, but much cooler, air. The temperature drop can be predicted from the following equation:

Temperature drop = E × (DB − WB)
where E = cooler efficiency, percentage
       DB = intake air dry bulb temperature
       WB = intake air wet bulb temperature

Evaporative coolers are recommended wherever the temperature drop (DB − WB) is over 20°F and the cooled air would be below 79°F. The table below lists these criteria for selected cities. Cities which meet both criteria appear in italics. To size an evaporative cooler, follow these steps:

1. Compute the volume of house air.

2. Find the recommended minutes per air change for your location.

3. Divide the house volume by minutes to find the recommended cooler capacity in cfm.

4. If your home is very energy efficient, divide cfm by 2; if not insulated, multiply by 2.

Potential for Evaporative Cooling

Location	DB °F	WB °F	Temp Drop °F	Cooled Temp °F	Minutes per Air Change
AL, Birmingham	96	74	18	78	NR[1]
AR, Little Rock	99	76	18	81	NR
AZ, Phoenix	109	71	30	79	2
CA, Los Angeles	93	70	18	75	2
CO, Denver	93	59	27	66	4
CT, Hartford	91	74	14	77	NR
DC, Washington	93	75	14	79	NR
DE, Wilmington	92	74	14	78	NR
FL, Orlando	94	76	14	80	NR
GA, Atlanta	94	74	16	78	NR
IA, Des Moines	94	75	15	79	NR
ID, Boise	96	65	25	71	4
IL, Chicago	94	75	15	79	NR
IN, Indianapolis	92	74	14	78	NR
KS, Topeka	99	75	20	79	2
KY, Louisville	95	74	17	78	NR
LA, Baton Rouge	95	77	14	81	NR
MA, Boston	91	73	14	77	NR
MI, Detroit	91	73	14	77	NR
MO, St. Louis	98	75	18	80	NR
MS, Jackson	97	76	17	80	NR

Location	DB °F	WB °F	Temp Drop °F	Cooled Temp °F	Minutes per Air Change
MT, Great Falls	91	60	25	66	3
NC, Greensboro	93	74	15	78	NR
ND, Bismarck	95	68	22	73	3
NE, North Platte	97	69	22	75	3
NV, Las Vegas	108	66	34	74	3
NH, Concord	90	72	14	76	NR
NJ, Newark	94	74	16	78	NR
NM, Albuquerque	96	61	28	68	3
NY, Syracuse	90	73	14	76	NR
OH, Columbus	92	73	15	77	NR
OK, Tulsa	101	74	22	79	1
OR, Portland	89	68	17	72	NR
PA, Pittsburgh	91	72	15	76	NR
RI, Providence	89	73	13	76	NR
SC, Columbia	97	76	17	80	NR
SD, Rapid City	95	66	23	72	3
TN, Nashville	97	75	18	79	NR
TX, Dallas	102	75	22	80	2
UT, Salt Lake City	97	62	28	69	4
VA, Richmond	95	76	15	80	NR
WY, Casper	92	58	27	65	4

[1] NR = Not Recommended

How an Evaporative Cooler (Swamp Cooler) Works

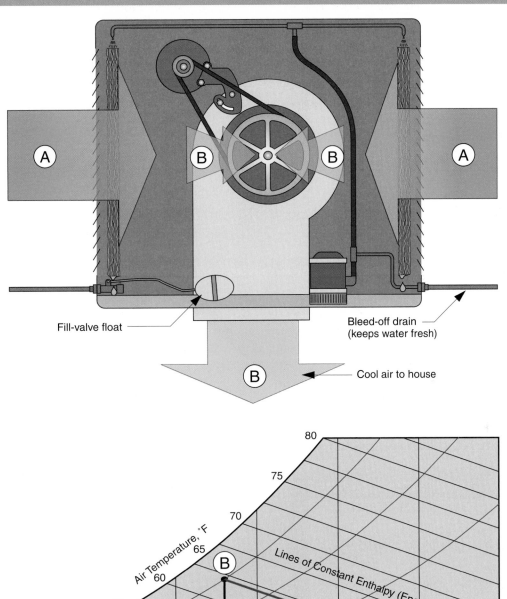

Fill-valve float

Bleed-off drain
(keeps water fresh)

Ⓑ Cool air to house

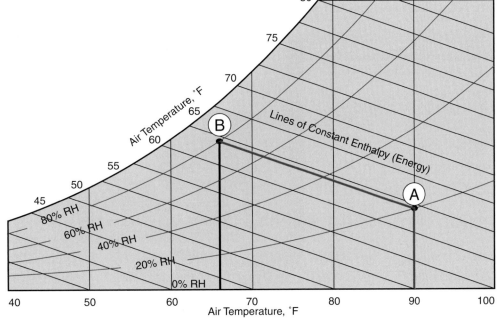

Air Conditioning

How Air Conditioners Work

ROOM AIR CONDITIONER

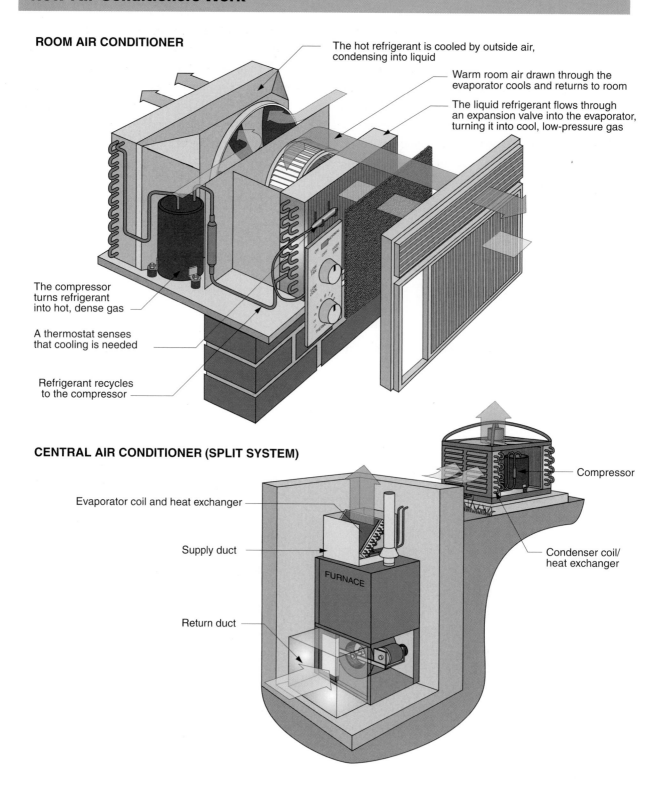

The hot refrigerant is cooled by outside air, condensing into liquid

Warm room air drawn through the evaporator cools and returns to room

The liquid refrigerant flows through an expansion valve into the evaporator, turning it into cool, low-pressure gas

The compressor turns refrigerant into hot, dense gas

A thermostat senses that cooling is needed

Refrigerant recycles to the compressor

CENTRAL AIR CONDITIONER (SPLIT SYSTEM)

Evaporator coil and heat exchanger

Supply duct

FURNACE

Return duct

Compressor

Condenser coil/ heat exchanger

If all else fails to cool you into the comfort zone, you have no choice but to air-condition. Air conditioners, powerful but expensive tools, lower humidity as well as temperature.

What you need first is an estimate of your peak cooling load, the number of Btus per hour that need to be removed under the worst conditions of the cooling season. The work sheet and tables that follow allow you to find that load, whether you are cooling just a bedroom or the entire house, no matter where you live in the United States.

You may wish to photocopy the work sheet so that you will be able to calculate the peak cooling load for a second room.

Read the instructions carefully for each line before entering any numbers. An example calculation follows the work sheet.

When you are done, go to the Energy Star site *www.energystar.gov*. There you will find an up-to-date list of all air conditioners, with their *rated cooling capacities* and *energy efficiency ratios* (EER). Look for models with the highest EER (the ratio of Btus removed to watts of electricity consumed) that also closely match your load. The most efficient air conditioner for your purpose will be one that is just capable of supplying the load.

Cooling Factors for Air Conditioner Work Sheet, Line 9

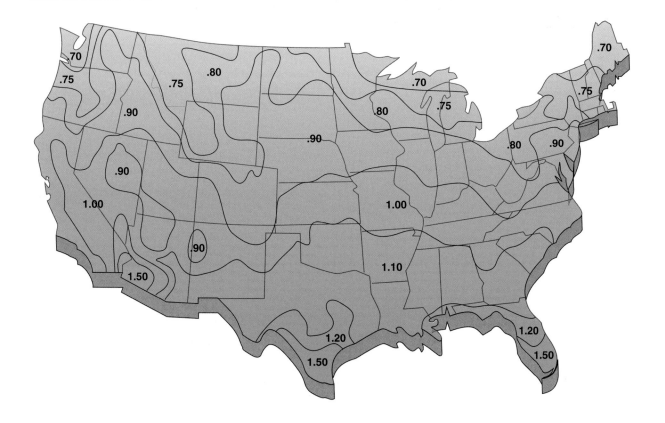

Instructions for Work Sheet

Lines 1 and 2. Use line 1 if your house has a well-ventilated attic; otherwise use line 2. Find the shading factor in column 1 of Table 1. The insulation factor is 0.8 times the nominal R-value of the attic insulation. (See Chapter 13 for insulation R-values.) Use the value 2.4 if there is no insulation present.

Line 3. Follow the same instructions as for lines 1 and 2. Exterior walls are those facing the outdoors. Enter doors as exterior walls. Do not include windows, as they will be entered below.

Line 4. Interior walls are those that separate the cooled space from unconditioned spaces. If you are cooling the entire house, there will be no interior walls. The insulation factor is 0.8 times the nominal R-value of the wall insulation (see Chapter 13 for insulation R-values), or 2.4 if there is none.

Line 5. Get the floor factor from Table 2; the insulation factor is as in line 4.

Line 6. Enter the total floor area of the cooled space. Estimate air changes per hour as 0.4 for the tightest possible house to 1.3 for a drafty one.

Line 7. Calculate window areas as height times width of the sash (the frames holding the glass). Get the glazing factors from Table 3.

Line 8. Get the shading factors from Table 1 and the glazing factors from Table 3.

Line 9. Add the results from lines 1 through 8 and multiply by the cooling factor for your geographic area, shown on the map on p. 499.

Line 10. Multiply your average monthly spring or fall kilowatt-hours (get these from your utility bills or by calling your electric utility) by 1.4. For the average home the result should be about 600 kwhr/month.

Line 11. Enter the average number of people occupying the cooled space during the hot months.

Line 12. Add lines 9, 10, and 11, then multiply the result by the mass factor from Table 4.

Table 1. Shading Factors

Degree of Shading	Roof, Wall, Ceiling	Windows
Unshaded areas	1.00	1.00
Fully shaded areas	0.70	0.20
Partially shaded by awning overhang, or small trees	0.90	0.65
Shaded inside by window shades, drapes, films		0.45

Table 2. Floor Factors

Floor Above	Factor
Open crawl space	1.0
Closed crawl space	0.0
Full basement	0.0
Unconditioned room	0.9
Ground (slab-on-grade)	0.1

Table 3. Glazing Factors

Type of Glazing	Line 7	Line 8
Single-glazed window	1.0	1.0
Double-glazed window	0.5	0.8
Triple-glazed window	0.33	0.65

Table 4. Thermal Mass Factors

Building Construction	Factor
Light wood frame	1.00
Solid masonry or wood frame with exterior masonry veneer	0.90
Wood frame with masonry interior walls, floors, or other mass	0.80
Earth-sheltered (underground) walls and roof	0.50

Work Sheet for Sizing Air Conditioners

Source of Heat Gain	Calculations	Results
1. Roof over ventilated attic	_____ sq ft x 44 x _____ shading factor /_____ insulation factor =	_____
2. Cathedral ceiling or roof over unventilated attic	_____ sq ft x 48 x _____ shading factor /_____ insulation factor =	_____
3. Exterior wall facing: North	_____ sq ft x 18 x _____ shading factor /_____ insulation factor =	_____
East	_____ sq ft x 28 x _____ shading factor /_____ insulation factor =	_____
South	_____ sq ft x 24 x _____ shading factor /_____ insulation factor =	_____
West	_____ sq ft x 28 x _____ shading factor /_____ insulation factor =	_____
4. Interior walls facing unconditioned rooms	_____ sq ft x 12 /_____ insulation factor =	_____
5. Floors over unconditioned spaces	_____ sq ft x 20 x _____ floor factor /_____ insulation factor =	_____
6. Infiltration: area of living space	_____ sq ft x _____ air changes/hour x 1.6 =	_____
7. Window conduction	_____ sq ft x 16 x _____ glazing factor =	_____
8. Window solar gain: North	_____ sq ft x 16 x _____ shading factor /_____ glazing factor =	_____
East, South, Southeast	_____ sq ft x 80 x _____ shading factor /_____ glazing factor =	_____
West, Southwest, Northwest	_____ sq ft x 140 x _____ shading factor /_____ glazing factor =	_____
Northeast	_____ sq ft x 50 x _____ shading factor /_____ glazing factor =	_____
9. Sum of lines 1 – 8	_____ x _____ cooling factor from map on p. 499 =	_____
10. Utility gain	_____ watts being consumed in space x 3.4 =	_____
11. People gain	_____ number of people in space x 600 =	_____
12. Peak cooling load, Btu/hour: sum of lines 9 – 11 x _____ thermal mass factor =		_____

Cooling Load Example

The facing page contains a completed form showing the calculations for the required capacity of a central air conditioner for a small house in Boston, Massachusetts, shown at right.

The house is deliberately kept simple in order to clarify the calculations. Many homes will have more than one type of exterior wall, foundation, or window, and they will require multiple entries for these line items.

Line 1. The ceiling measures 30 by 40 feet, so its area is 1,200 square feet. The roof, however, is pitched 30 degrees, so its area is 1,386 square feet. (If you don't know how to do this calculation, see the relationships between the sides of a triangle in Chapter 24.) The unshaded roof has a shading factor of 1.00, from column 1 of Table 1. The insulation factor is 0.8 times the nominal R-value of 38.

Line 3. The north and south walls are each 320 square feet, less the window area of 21 square feet, or 299 square feet. The east and west walls measure 219 square feet by the same process. The west wall is fully shaded, so its shading factor (Table 1) is 0.70. The rest are unshaded, so their shading factors are 1.00. The nominal R-values of 19 are multiplied by 0.8 to get insulation factors of 15.2.

Line 4. The entire house is air-conditioned, so the interior walls have no effect and are left blank.

Line 5. The house sits on a vented (open) crawl space, so the floor factor is 1.0.

Line 6. The house is quite air-tight, so there are estimated to be 0.50 air changes per hour.

Line 7. The glazing factor, from column 1 of Table 3, for double-glazed windows is 0.5.

Line 8. Both east and south windows are entered on a single line. The shading factors are the same as for the walls in line 3. The glazing factor of 0.8 is found in column 2 of Table 3.

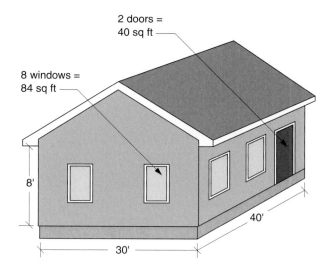

Air exchange rate = 0.5 changes per hour

Ceiling R-38, walls R-19, floor R-19 over vented crawlspace

Windows 21 sq ft each facing N, S, E, and W

West wall fully shaded; other walls and roof unshaded

Spring and fall utility bills average 350 kwhr/month

Three occupants in summer months

Line 9. The sum of the results column for all of the lines above is 13,921. Boston's cooling factor of 0.75 is found from the map on p. 499.

Line 10. The electric utility bills for the spring and fall months show an average consumption of 350 kilowatt-hours per month.

Line 11. There are three occupants of the home during the cooling season.

Line 12. The thermal mass factor for a light wood frame house (1.00) is found in Table 4. The sum of lines 9 through 11 is 13,906, so the peak cooling load is 13,906 Btu per hour. This is a small cooling load for a house and could be satisfied easily by two 7,000 Btu/hr room air conditioners.

Work Sheet for Sizing Air Conditioners

Source of Heat Gain	Calculations	Results
1. Roof over ventilated attic	_1,386_ sq ft x 44 x _1.00_ shading factor / _30.4_ insulation factor =	_2,006_
2. Cathedral ceiling or roof over unventilated attic	_____ sq ft x 48 x _____ shading factor / _____ insulation factor =	_____
3. Exterior wall facing: North	_299_ sq ft x 18 x _1.00_ shading factor / _15.2_ insulation factor =	_354_
East	_219_ sq ft x 28 x _1.00_ shading factor / _15.2_ insulation factor =	_403_
South	_299_ sq ft x 24 x _1.00_ shading factor / _15.2_ insulation factor =	_472_
West	_219_ sq ft x 28 x _0.70_ shading factor / _15.2_ insulation factor =	_282_
4. Interior walls facing unconditioned rooms	_____ sq ft x 12 / _____ insulation factor =	_____
5. Floors over unconditioned spaces	_1,200_ sq ft x 20 x _1.0_ floor factor / _15.2_ insulation factor =	_1,579_
6. Infiltration: area of living space	_1,200_ sq ft x _0.5_ air changes/hour x 1.6 =	_960_
7. Window conduction	_84_ sq ft x 16 x _0.5_ glazing factor =	_672_
8. Window solar gain: North	_21_ sq ft x 16 x _1.00_ shading factor / _0.8_ glazing factor =	_420_
East, South, Southeast	_42_ sq ft x 80 x _1.00_ shading factor / _0.8_ glazing factor =	_4,200_
West, Southwest, Northwest	_21_ sq ft x 140 x _0.70_ shading factor / _0.8_ glazing factor =	_2,573_
Northeast	_____ sq ft x 50 x _____ shading factor / _____ glazing factor =	_____
9. Sum of lines 1 – 8	_13,921_ x _0.75_ cooling factor from map on p. 499 =	_10,440_
10. Utility gain	_350_ x _1.4 = 490_ watts being consumed in space x 3.4 =	_1,666_
11. People gain	_3_ number of people in space x 600 =	_1,800_
12. Peak cooling load, Btu/hour: sum of lines 9 – 11 x _1.00_ thermal mass factor =		_13,906_

Passive Solar

Since man constructed the first rudimentary shelter, he has always instinctively utilized free energy from the sun. What are our *passive solar possibilities* today? First you have to determine whether, and to what degree, your site has enough direct sun (solar access). To *determine solar access*, we utilize *solar path charts*, or maps of the sun's path at different seasons and latitudes.

Next we look at the effects of *glazing orientation and tilt*. We find that good passive solar performance requires placing a high percentage of glazing (windows) on the south wall and little or none on the north. We also discover that ordinary vertical windows perform as well or better than tilted windows when the ground is covered with snow.

Of course windows which gather the sun's heat in winter can also gain heat in the summer, so we look at techniques for *summer shading*.

If we want to get a high percentage of our heat from the sun, we have to take in as much radiation as possible while the sun is shining. In order that the building not overheat and that we have heat to carry us through the sunless night, we need some form of *heat storage*.

Utilizing all of the tricks above, we are able to predict the solar performance of our design using *a passive solar design procedure*. Many ordinary building materials have significant ability to store heat. We show how to calculate the required surface areas of various heat-storing building materials in five different *thermal mass patterns*.

Passive Solar Possibilities

What Is Passive Solar?

There are many techniques for reducing energy consumption in buildings. Techniques such as increasing insulation, caulking and weather-stripping, and using high-performance windows and doors have been described in previous chapters. These energy conservation techniques are primarily buffers against cold climates, reducing the rate of escape of interior heat.

There are, however, techniques that capture free energy from the sun, reducing, and in some cases eliminating, the need for conventional central heating sources. These solar techniques can be roughly divided into two categories: active and passive solar heating. Passive techniques rely upon the interrelationship of solar radiation, mass of the building, and siting; with these they capture, store, and release solar energy. With little if any increased cost, and with no noisy equipment to maintain, passive solar has become the technique of choice.

During the past 25 years, designers have learned a lot about the actual performance of passive solar structures. This chapter contains a condensation of that knowledge in the form of a design procedure with simple graphs and tables that allow the design of near-optimum residential passive solar buildings anywhere in North America.

Passive solar, of course, is no substitute for standard energy conservation techniques. An underlying assumption for all that follows is a very high level of energy conservation. State and local energy standards should be considered the minimum for any passive solar design.

Conservation Requirements

Guidelines for energy conservation in conjunction with passive solar design include the following:

• Insulate walls, roofs, and floors one step beyond the local norm; i.e., if the code calls for R-19 walls, make them R-25.

• Select triple-glazed, low-E, or Heat Mirror windows, and insulated doors.

• Reduce air infiltration through the use of continuous air/vapor barriers and caulking and weatherstripping of all openings.

• Reduce the area of windows and doors on the north side of the building.

• Orient the building and openings to maximize the effects of cooling summer breezes and minimize the effects of winter winds.

• Utilize landscape elements to provide summer shade and to block winter winds.

• If natural deciduous shading is not possible, provide overhangs and projections to shade glazings during the cooling season.

• Ventilate roofs and attics to avoid condensation damage and summer overheating.

Direct Gain

Of all the passive solar types, direct gain is the easiest to understand, because it is a simple variation from an ordinary house with south-facing windows. A direct-gain design is one in which the solar radiation directly enters and heats the living spaces. The building itself is the solar collector.

In the heating season during daylight hours, sunlight enters through south-facing windows, patio doors, clerestories, or skylights. The radiation strikes and is absorbed by floors, walls, ceilings, and furnishings. As anyone who has ever been in a south-facing room in winter realizes, some of the heat is transferred to the air immediately, warming the room. Some of the heat is absorbed into the structure and objects in the room, to be released slowly during the night, filling some of the overnight heating requirement. In extreme designs, increased surface absorptivities and increased amounts of mass allow capture and storage of a full day's heat supply.

Although ceilings can be designed to store heat, common direct-gain storage materials are most easily incorporated into floors and walls, which frequently serve a structural purpose as well. Two very simple but effective storage masses that can be incorporated into any home are a masonry, tile, or slate floor, and walls with double layers of gypsum drywall.

Open floor plans are recommended, to allow distribution of the released heat throughout the house by natural air circulation.

Isolated Sun Space

Attached sun spaces are frequently constructed as extensions to homes. They are generally considered secondary-use spaces, in which heat is either collected and vented directly to the living space or is stored for later use, The energy collected is generally used to heat both the sun space and the adjacent living space.

Sun spaces are designed for one of two basic modes of operation. In the first, the sun space is isolated from the living space (illustration at middle right) by an insulated wall and doors which may be closed. As a result of this isolation, the sun space is not treated as part of the conditioned space, and its temperature is allowed to fluctuate beyond the range of human comfort.

Integrated Sun Space

In the second case, the sun space is integrated with the living space (illustration at bottom right), and its temperature is controlled with auxiliary heat or heat from the main living areas.

Integration is desirable when the space is primarily a living space. Isolation is desirable when the sun space is used primarily as a greenhouse, generating more water vapor than the house can safely absorb without causing condensation and mildew.

Sun-space glazings are often tilted for maximum light penetration and collection, but this exposes the glazings to increased summer heat gain. Two solutions are deciduous shade trees to block direct summer sun and ventilating windows and doors left open during the summer.

In northern areas sun-space glazings should either be of a high-performance type (double-glazed with high-solar-gain low-E coating) or covered at night with a form of movable window insulation.

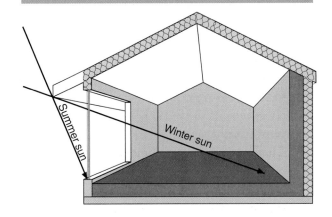

Direct Gain

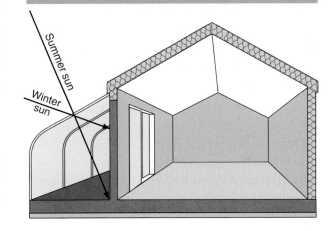

Isolated Sun Space

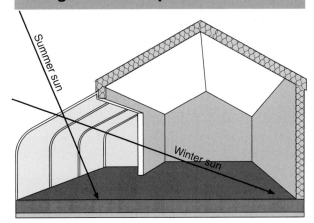

Integrated Sun Space

Determining Solar Access

The amount of solar heat that reaches glazing is affected by its orientation to the sun and the fraction of the sky blocked by permanent objects such as trees and buildings. Optimum solar access permits no shading between the hours of 8 AM and 4 PM from September 21 through March 21. These hours and seasons are represented by the darker yellow area in the charts on the facing page.

In planning glazing, you can plot solar access on a sun chart, a map of the sky viewed from the location of the glazing. In the pages that follow, you'll find sun charts for latitudes in the United States and southern Canada.

Measuring Altitude and Azimuth

On the charts, the height scale, from 0 to 90 degrees represents *altitude*, the angle of the sun above the horizon; the horizontal scale represents *azimuth*, the number of degrees east or west of true south. To plot obstructions on your sun chart, you need to determine their azimuths and altitudes.

To find altitude, sight the top of an object along the straight edge of a protractor, as shown in the illustration at top right, and read altitude where the string crosses the outside of the scale.

To find azimuth, first find true north–south as described on p. 38. Then, simply use a protractor and a piece of string as shown in the illustration at bottom right. Standing at the proposed location of the glazing, point the zero on the protractor to true south and the string toward the object. The string will lie on the azimuth reading.

Take as many readings as you need to plot the outlines of all obstructing objects on the sun chart, as shown in the "Good Solar Access" and "Poor Solar Access" examples on the facing page.

Measuring the Sun's Altitude

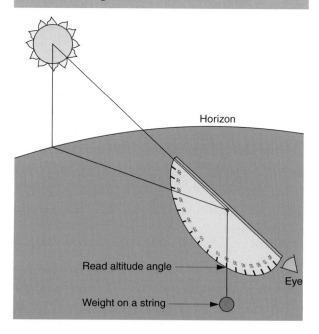

Measuring the Sun's Azimuth

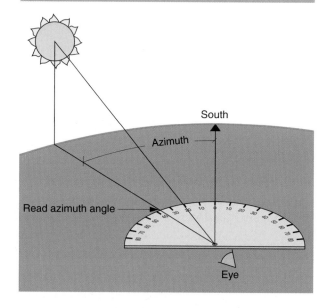

An Example of Good Solar Access

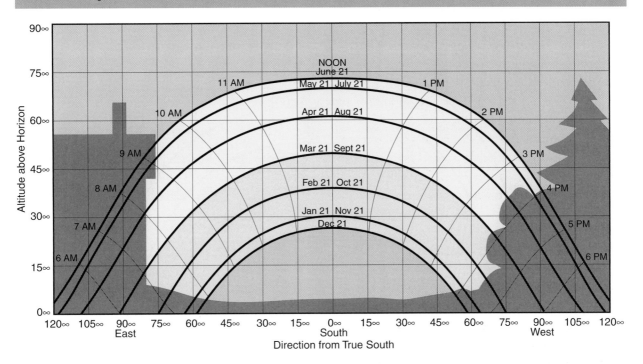

An Example of Poor Solar Access

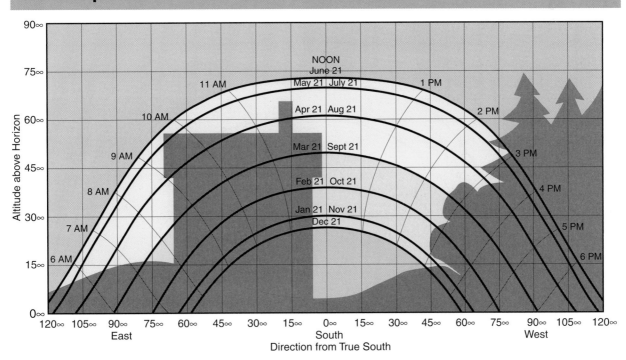

Solar Path Charts

Sun Chart for 24° N Latitude

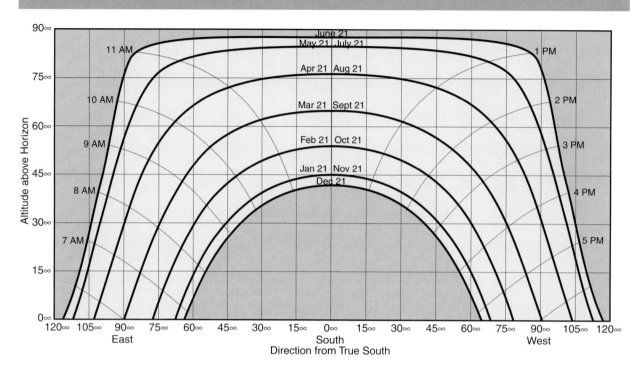

Sun Chart for 28° N Latitude

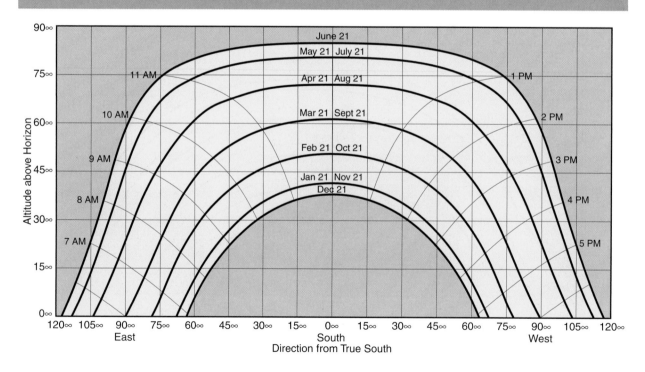

Sun Chart for 32° N Latitude

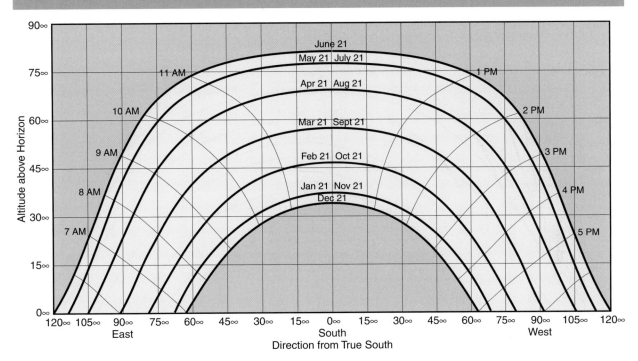

Sun Chart for 36° N Latitude

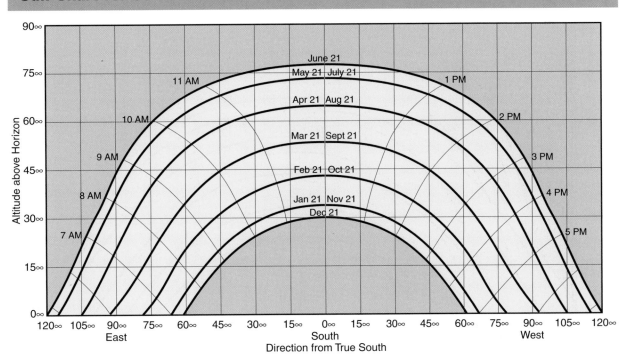

Sun Chart for 40° N Latitude

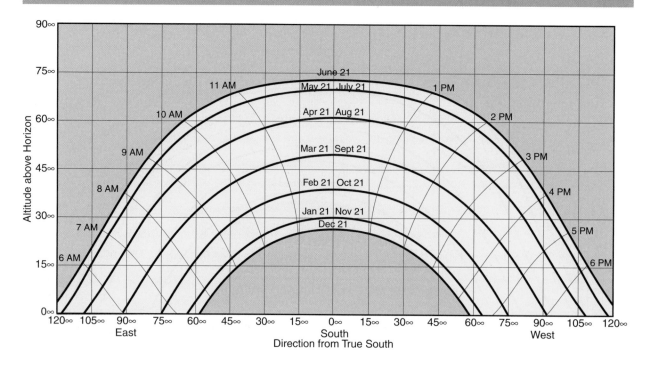

Sun Chart for 44° N Latitude

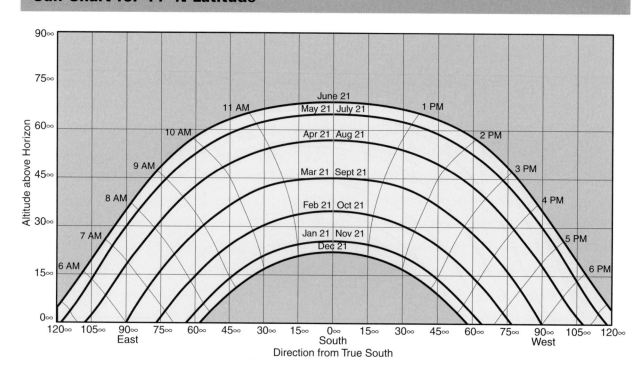

Sun Chart for 48° N Latitude

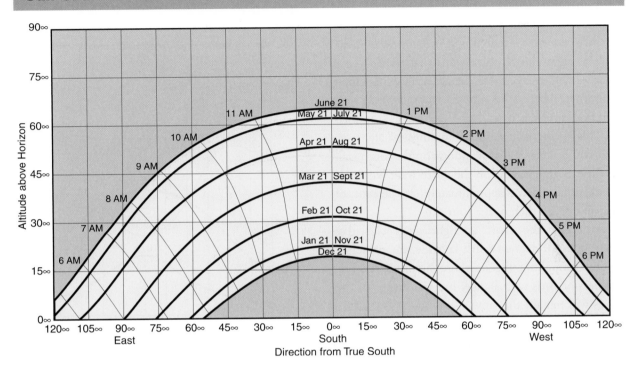

Sun Chart for 52° N Latitude

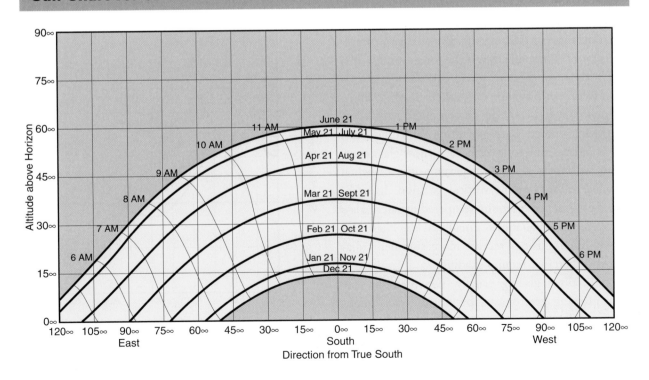

Glazing Orientation and Tilt

Glazing Orientation

A key circumstance that makes passive solar heating possible is the fact that the sun is lower in the southern sky in the winter than it is in the summer. As the graph at right shows, this means that south-facing windows will receive more solar heat in winter than in summer, whereas for north, east, and west exposures, the reverse is true.

This is why passive solar buildings usually have 50 to 100 percent of their windows on the south wall and little, if any, glazing on the north wall. Nonsolar houses usually have approximately 25 percent of their glazing on each of the four sides.

Although the chart at right gives clear-day radiation at 40 degrees north latitude, the principle applies throughout the northern hemisphere. The numbers of Btus will change, but the shapes of the curves will remain the same.

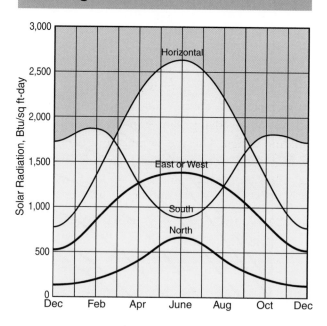

Clear-Day Radiation on Vertical Glazings at 40° N

Glazing Tilt

Over the years, there has been controversy over the proper tilt for solar glazing. As the graph at right shows, tilted glazing receives slightly more *direct* radiation than vertical glazing. But vertical surfaces receive more *total* radiation if the foreground is covered with snow. The net effect is that tilt has little effect upon performance. Moreover, tilted glazing has practical disadvantages as compared with vertical glazing. Tilted glazing is more difficult to seal and is more prone to leak. In fact, most glass companies will not guarantee the glazing-unit seal when installed in any but the vertical position. In addition, building codes require tempered or safety glass for overhead installations. Finally, as the chart also shows, tilted glazings receive more summer radiation and therefore require shading.

Still, tilted glazing usually is favored for true plant-growing greenhouses because direct sunlight is needed throughout the structure.

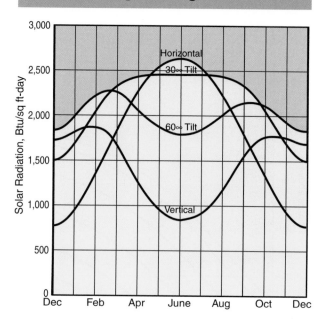

Clear-Day Radiation on Tilted South-Facing Glazings at 40° N

Summer Shading

As explained in Chapter 17, south vertical glazings must be shaded to prevent summer overheating. You can use a variety of awnings and inside or outside shades and shutters. But the most practical, attractive, and maintenance-free ways to provide shade are deciduous trees and roof overhangs.

Save existing shade trees and incorporate them into the siting of the building. If trees prove insufficient, roof overhangs can be incorporated into the building design. Use the formula and table below to find the proper overhang projection from the latitude of the site and the height of the eaves above the window sill. Use the May 10 to August 1 shade factor in the table if you have no shade trees on the south side of the house.

$$OH = H \times F$$

where:
OH = overhang's horizontal projection
H   = height from eaves to window sill
F   = factor found in the table below

Example: What is the required horizontal projection of eaves (beyond the plane of the glazing) to fully shade, on June 21, a south-facing window located at 40 degrees north latitude if the window sill is 7 feet 2 inches lower than the eaves?

H   = 7'2"
    = 86"
F   = 0.29
OH = 86" × 0.29
    = 25"

Roof overhangs are not practical for shading windows facing east or west or for tilted south-facing windows.

South Overhang Geometry

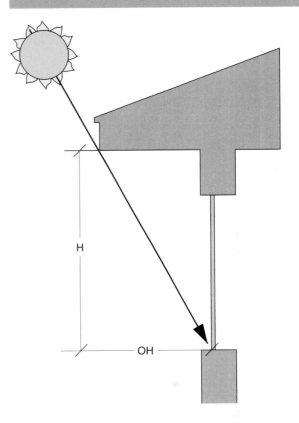

Factors for South-Facing Overhangs

North Latitude	For 100% Shading	
	June 21 Only	May 10–Aug 1
28	0.09	0.18
32	0.16	0.25
36	0.22	0.33
40	0.29	0.40
44	0.37	0.50
48	0.45	0.59

Heat Storage

Solar Absorptance

Once through the glazing, transmitted solar energy striking an interior surface can do one of two things:

1. be reflected to another room surface or back through the glazing.

2. be absorbed (converted from radiant energy to sensible heat) by the surface.

The fraction not reflected, but converted to heat, is termed the *absorptance* of the surface. The choice of absorptances of room surfaces is more complicated than one might at first assume. If all light were absorbed, room lighting conditions would be poor, with all of the light coming from a single direction. If little of the light were absorbed in the first several reflections, much of the radiation could escape back through the windows. And light absorbed by light-weight surfaces results in heated air and little thermal storage.

Solar designers recommend the following rules of thumb:

• Lightweight objects should be light in color to avoid overheating of the room air, promote more even light distribution, and reflect radiation onto more massive surfaces.

• Surfaces of massive objects, such as concrete slabs and fireplaces, should be dark in color and be placed to receive direct sunlight in order to efficiently collect and store heat.

• Ceilings should be white, and deep rooms should have light-colored back walls to diffuse light more evenly.

• Masonry floors receiving direct sun should not be covered with rugs or wall-to-wall carpeting.

Example: A room has both wood-paneled and brick walls. Make the paneled walls light in color and the brick walls dark.

Example: A combined living/kitchen space has both wood and slate floors. You may carpet the wood floor, but leave the slate floor uncovered.

Solar Absorptance of Surfaces

Material	Solar Absorptance
Flat black paint	0.95
Water	0.94
Gloss black paint	0.92
Black concrete	0.91
Gloss dark blue paint	0.91
Stafford blue bricks	0.90
Dark gray slate	0.90
Dark olive drab paint	0.89
Dark brown paint	0.88
Dark blue-gray paint	0.88
Dark green lacquer	0.88
Brown concrete	0.85
Medium brown paint	0.84
Silver gray slate	0.80
Medium light brown paint	0.80
Medium rust paint	0.78
Light gray oil paint	0.75
Red oil paint	0.74
Red brick	0.70
Uncolored concrete	0.65
Light buff bricks	0.60
Medium dull green paint	0.59
Medium orange paint	0.58
Medium yellow paint	0.57
Medium blue paint	0.51
Kelly green paint	0.51
Light green paint	0.47
White semigloss paint	0.30
White gloss paint	0.25
White unpainted plaster	0.07
Aluminum foil	0.03

Heat Storage Capacity of Building Materials

Thermal mass is the amount of heat absorbed by a material as its temperature rises, expressed as Btu/°F. The specific heat of a material is its thermal mass per pound. Note that the *specific heat* of water is, by definition, exactly 1.00, coincidentally the highest of all natural materials.

As shown in the graph at right, the benefit of building thermal mass into a house is that the house becomes less responsive to outdoor temperature swings. This means the house won't get as hot during the day or as cold at night as it would without the added mass. In the graph, the outdoor temperature swings from an overnight low of 60°F to a daytime high of 80°F. An ordinary well-insulated house's interior temperature might swing from 65°F to 75°F, but the same house with added mass would swing only from 68°F to 72°F. The wider the outdoor temperature swing, the more beneficial the mass.

The table at right shows that there is little reason to turn to exotic materials. Masonry floors and walls, exposed wood, and extra-thick gypsum drywall can all be used effectively as storage masses. Water has been included in the table and in the design procedures at the end of the chapter, in case you wish to go supersolar.

You have already seen how material and color can affect the effectiveness of thermal mass. A third factor is thickness. When it comes to thermal mass, thicker is not necessarily better. If a wall is too thick, it always remains too cool to become a heat source. If too thin, it warms too quickly and begins returning heat before evening, when it is most needed.

Optimum thicknesses for common heat storage materials are as follows:

- adobe   8 to 12 inches
- brick   10 to 14 inches
- concrete   12 to 18 inches
- water   6 or more inches

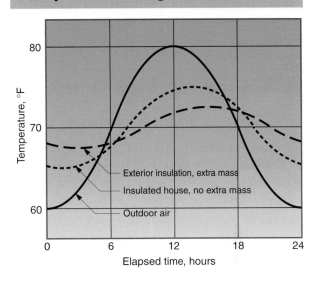

Temperature Swing vs. Thermal Mass

Exterior insulation, extra mass
Insulated house, no extra mass
Outdoor air

Heat Capacities of Materials

North Material	Specific Heat Btu/lb-°F	Density lb/cu ft	Heat Capacity Btu/cu ft-°F
Air (at 75°F)	0.24	0.075	0.018
Asphalt	0.22	132	29.0
Brick	0.20	123	24.6
Cement	0.16	120	19.2
Clay	0.22	63	13.9
Concrete	0.22	144	31.7
Copper	0.09	556	51.2
Glass	0.18	154	27.7
Gypsum drywall	0.26	78	20.2
Iron	0.12	450	54.0
Limestone	0.22	103	22.4
Marble	0.21	162	34.0
Sand	0.19	94.6	18.1
Steel	0.12	489	58.7
Water	1.00	62.4	62.4
White oak	0.57	47	26.8
White pine	0.67	27	18.1

A Passive Solar Design Procedure

The tables in this section provide a simple method for the preliminary design of passive solar buildings. Initial sizing of both window area and storage mass can be quickly achieved knowing only location, floor area, building insulation level, and window R-value.

The procedure yields the area of south-facing windows, amount and placement of storage mass, and estimated reduction in winter heating bills.

Glazed Area and Fuel Saving

Extensive computer simulations have been performed by researchers at Los Alamos Laboratory for passive solar homes in the cities listed in the table on the facing page. Interpretation of the table is simple:

"A south-facing window area of between X1 and X2 percent of the floor area can be expected to reduce the winter fuel bill of a home by Y1 to Y2 percent."

The smaller window area and fuel-saving percentages (X1 and Y1) correspond to ordinary homes with ordinary window areas, with the exception that the windows have all been moved to the south wall. The larger figures (X2 and Y2) give the maximum recommended target percentages for the location.

The predicted fuel saving depends on the type of window: double-glazed (DG), triple-glazed or equivalent R-3 glazing such as Low-E (TG), or double-glazed with R-9 night insulation (DG+R9).

Example: In Boston, Massachusetts, a south-facing window area of 15 to 29 percent of floor area can be expected to reduce the winter fuel bill by 17 to 25 percent if double glazed, 26 to 39 percent if triple glazed, or 40 to 64 percent if double glazed with R-9 night window insulation.

Assumed Heat Loss

The predictions assume a building heat loss of 6 Btu per degree-day per square foot of floor area. This corresponds roughly to R-19 walls, R-38 ceilings, double glazing, and an infiltration rate of ¾ air change per hour. If your home's insulation levels are different, the table values may be adjusted proportionally. For example, if your home has R-28 walls, R-57 ceilings, triple glazing, and ½ air change per hour (one and a half times as much insulation and two-thirds as much heat loss as the standard), you can reduce your window areas by one-third and still achieve the same percentage fuel saving.

Typical Solar Savings for Passive Solar Heating, Percentage

■ >80	□ 40–50
■ 70–80	■ 30–40
■ 60–70	■ 20–30
□ 50–60	■ <20

Glazed Area vs. Solar Savings

City	Glazed Area[1] X1–X2	Percentage Savings[2] for DG Y1–Y2	TG Y1–Y2	DG+R9 Y1–Y2
AL, Birmingham	9–18	22–37	34–58	34–58
AR, Little Rock	10–19	23–38	28v47	37–62
AZ, Phoenix	6–12	37–60	41–66	48–75
CA, Los Angeles	5–9	36–58	39–63	44–72
CO, Denver	12–23	27–43	34–54	47–74
DC, Washington	12–23	18–28	25–40	37–61
DE, Wilmington	15–29	19–30	26–42	39–63
FL, Orlando	3–6	30–52	33–56	37–63
GA, Atlanta	8–17	22–36	26–44	34–58
IA, Des Moines	21–43	19–25	30–44	50–75
ID, Boise	14–28	27–38	35–50	48–71
IL, Chicago	17–35	17–23	27–39	43–67
IN, Indianapolis	14–28	15–21	23–35	37–60
KS, Topeka	14–28	24–35	32–48	45–71
KY, Louisville	13–27	18–27	24–39	35–59
LA, Baton Rouge	6–12	26–43	29–49	34–59
MA, Boston	15–29	17–25	26–39	40–64
ME, Portland	17–34	14–17	25–36	45–69
MI, Detroit	17–34	13–17	23–33	39–61
MN, Duluth	25–50	Not Rec	24–33	50–70
MS, Jackson	8–15	24–40	28–47	34–59
MO, St. Louis	15–29	21–33	28–45	41–65
MT, Great Falls	18–37	23–28	35–46	56–77
NC, Greensboro	10–20	23–37	28–47	37–63
ND, Bismarck	25–50	Not Rec	27–36	56–77
NE, North Platte	17–34	25–36	34–51	50–76
NH, Concord	17–34	13–15	25–35	45–68
NJ, Newark	13–25	19–29	26–42	39–64

City	Glazed Area[1] X1–X2	Percentage Savings[2] for DG Y1–Y2	TG Y1–Y2	DG+R9 Y1–Y2
NM, Albuquerque	11–22	29–47	35–57	46–73
NV, Las Vegas	9–18	35–56	40–63	48–75
NY, Syracuse	19–38	Not Rec	20–29	37–59
OH, Columbus	14–28	13–18	21–32	35–57
OK, Tulsa	11–22	24–38	30–49	41–67
OR, Salem	12–24	21–32	27–33	37–59
PA, Pittsburgh	14–28	12–16	20–30	33–55
RI, Providence	15–30	17–24	26–40	40–64
SC, Columbia	8–17	25–41	29–48	36–61
SD, Pierre	22–43	21–33	35–44	58–80
TN, Nashville	10–21	19–30	24–39	33–55
TX, Dallas	8–17	27–44	31–51	38–64
UT, Salt Lake City	13–26	27–39	31–51	48–72
VA, Richmond	11–22	21–34	27–44	37–61
VT, Burlington	22–43	Not Rec	23–33	46–68
WA, Seattle	11–22	21–30	28–41	39–59
WI, Madison	20–40	15–17	28–38	51–74
WV, Charleston	13–25	16–24	22–35	32–54
WY, Caper	13–26	27–39	38–53	53–78
AB, Edmonton	25–50	Not Rec	26–34	54–72
BC, Vancouver	13–26	20–28	27–40	40–60
MB, Winnipeg	25–50	Not Rec	26–34	54–74
NS, Dartmouth	14–28	17–24	27–41	45–70
ON, Ottawa	25–50	Not Rec	28–37	59–80
QC, Normandin	25–50	Not Rec	26–35	54–74

[1] Glazed area as percentage of heated floor area.

[2] Percentage reduction in annual heating bill from that of an equivalent house having uniform distribution of windows of area totaling 15 percent of heated floor area.

Thermal Mass Patterns

Sizing and Placing Storage Mass

All buildings have mass in their floors, walls, ceilings, and furnishings. If they didn't, they'd all overheat on sunny days. The table below shows the approximate areas of south-facing windows in average-insulated and well-insulated wood frame homes before overheating occurs.

South Glazing Area Limits
(glazed area as percentage of floor area)

Degree-Days[1]	Ave Jan. Temp, °F	Average House[2]	Well-Insulated House[3]
4,000	40	11	6
5,000	30	13	6
6,000	25	13	7
7,000	20	14	7

[1] See Chapter 16 for heating degree days, base 65°F.

[2] R-11 walls, R-19 ceiling, double-glazed windows.

[3] R-25 walls, R-38 ceiling, triple-glazed windows.

Example: With no additional mass, what is the maximum allowable area of south-facing windows for a 1,800-square-foot home in Boston (6,000 DD_{65}) constructed with R-25 walls, R-49 ceiling, and R-3 windows? The energy efficiency of the home is close to the well-insulated house in the table, so the appropriate percentage is 7, and the maximum glazed area is $0.07 \times 1,800 = 126$ square feet.

The example above was a typical nonsolar home. To realize the higher fuel savings listed in the table on p. 519, however, a much greater window area is required. For example, the suggested window percentage for Boston is 15 to 29 percent, or two to four times the percentage in the example. Such a home will require additional storage mass.

Adding Mass

In the pages that follow, five distinctly different storage mass patterns are shown. For each, an accompanying table specifies the material, thickness, and surface area of mass required for each square foot of glazing in excess of the norm.

Example: Assuming you wish to achieve 25 percent solar savings for the home in Boston, you will need about 15 percent of the floor area in south glazing. You therefore need additional thermal mass to compensate for (15 percent minus 7 percent equals) 8 percent of the floor area, or 144 square feet of glazing. Using Pattern 1 and assuming a bare 6-inch concrete slab as the mass, you'll find you need 3×144 square feet, or 432 square feet of slab in direct sunlight. If you don't have the required area of slab, you'll have to add mass from other patterns.

The Mass Patterns

Pattern 1 corresponds to a home with a masonry floor. The floor may be a concrete slab-on-grade, or it may consist of a masonry veneer over a wood or concrete base.

Pattern 2 might represent a home with one or more exposed masonry walls or a home with extra-thick plaster or drywall.

Pattern 3 might occur when a building is remodeled, exposing an interior masonry party wall. It could also represent a very large masonry fireplace.

Pattern 4 typically represents a sun space with a masonry rear wall.

Pattern 5 is not very common but accounts for any massive structure in direct sunlight that does not reach the ceiling. A masonry planter/room divider would fall into Pattern 5.

Pattern 1

Pattern 1 is defined as thermal storage mass with one surface exposed to the living space and in direct sun for at least 6 hours a day. Architecturally, this pattern combined with Pattern 2 is useful for direct-gain passive solar rooms.

The mass can be either a directly irradiated floor slab, as shown, or a directly irradiated outside wall (inside walls are considered in Pattern 3). As with Patterns 2 and 3, the mass element is single-sided; that is, heat enters and exits the mass from the same surface.

Example: The design procedure has called for 100 square feet of south-facing glass in a room with 200 square feet of floor and 380 square feet of windowless wall. Does a 4-inch concrete slab provide enough thermal mass to prevent overheating?

According to the table, you should provide 4 square feet of 4-inch concrete slab for each square

Mass Sizing for Floors and Walls in Direct Sun

Mass Thickness	Sq Ft of Mass per Sq Ft of Glazing				
	Concrete	Brick	Drywall	Oak	Pine
½″	—	—	76	—	—
1″	14	17	38	17	21
1½″	—	—	26	—	—
2″	7	8	20	10	12
3″	5	6	—	10	12
4″	4	5	—	11	12
6″	3	5	—	11	13
8″	3	5	—	11	13

foot of glazing. That would require 400 square feet of slab. Increasing the slab thickness to 6 inches would still require 300 square feet of slab. Therefore you must either reduce the glazed area or add further mass, utilizing one of the other four mass patterns.

Thermal Mass Pattern 1

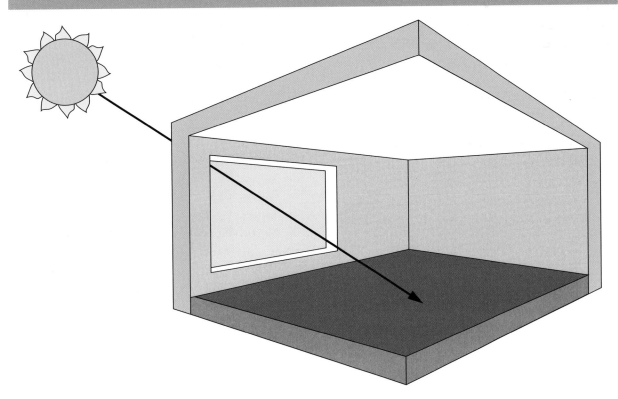

Pattern 2

The mass in Pattern 2 is like that in Pattern 1, that is, the mass is single-sided and insulated on the back side. The distinction here is that the mass is receiving not direct radiation, but reflected sun.

In a simple direct-gain space, some of the mass will be of Pattern 1 (a floor slab near the solar glazing, for example), and some mass will be of Pattern 2 (the ceiling, for example). Much of the mass in such a space will be directly irradiated some of the time and indirectly irradiated the rest of the day. In these cases, an interpolation between Pattern 1 and Pattern 2 must be carried out, as described in Pattern 1.

Example: You have decided to use an 8-inch concrete slab for the room described in mass Pattern 1. This leaves 33 square feet of glazing to provide mass for. How many square feet of 8-inch brick wall will be required to provide the mass?

Mass Sizing for Floor, Wall, or Ceiling in Indirect Sun

| Mass Thickness | Sq Ft of Mass per Sq Ft of Glazing | | | | |
	Concrete	Brick	Drywall	Oak	Pine
½″	—	—	114	—	—
1″	25	30	57	28	36
1½″	—	—	39	—	—
2″	12	15	31	17	21
3″	8	11	—	17	20
4″	7	9	—	19	21
6″	5	9	—	19	22
8″	5	10	—	19	22

According to the table above, 10 square feet of 8-inch brick wall is required to balance each square foot of glazing. You therefore need 330 square feet of brick wall. Because the total wall area is 380 square feet, this is a practical solution.

Thermal Mass Pattern 2

Pattern 3

As in Patterns 1 and 2, the mass in this pattern is one-sided. The difference is that the mass receives neither direct radiation nor reflected radiation. It is instead heated by the room air that is warmed as a result of solar gains elsewhere in the building.

This pattern is useful for mass deeper within a passive building. However, solar-heated air must reach the remote mass either by natural or forced air circulation. Judgment is required here—a hallway open to a south room could be included, a back room closed off from the solar-heated space should be excluded.

Example: Your remodeling plan calls for removing half of a wood-framed gypsum wall to open the south-facing kitchen to the living room. The remaining wall has an 80-square-foot fireplace of 8-inch brick on the living room side. You plan to add a south-facing window in the kitchen. How many square feet of window will the mass of the fireplace balance?

According to the table, the fireplace alone will account for only 4 square feet of window. You must look elsewhere for thermal mass.

Mass Sizing for Floor, Wall, or Ceiling Remote from Sun

Mass Thickness	Sq Ft of Mass per Sq Ft of Glazing				
	Concrete	Brick	Drywall	Oak	Pine
½"	—	—	114	—	—
1"	27	32	57	32	39
1½"	—	—	42	—	—
2"	17	20	35	24	27
3"	15	17	—	26	28
4"	14	17	—	24	30
6"	14	18	—	28	31
8"	15	19	—	28	31

Thermal Mass Pattern 3

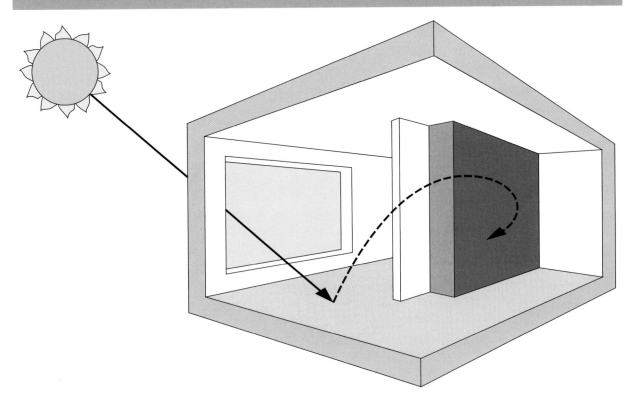

Pattern 4

Pattern 4 is defined as a floor-to-ceiling wall of massive material that receives direct sun on one side and is exposed to the living space on the other side. In other words, the sunlit side is isolated from the living space.

This pattern is useful for isolated sun spaces and greenhouses. The storage wall may have high and low vents or be unvented, as shown, without affecting the values in the table.

The performance of the wall improves with thickness up to about 18 inches but is not very sensitive to variations in thickness within normal buildable ranges. For brick walls, higher density bricks (with water absorption of less than 6 percent) are recommended over bricks of lower density. Note that the mass surface area refers to the area of the sunlit side only.

Mass Sizing for Mass Wall or Water Wall in Direct Sun

Material and Thickness	Sq Ft of Mass Surface per Sq Ft of Glazing
8″-thick brick	1
12″-thick brick	1
8″-thick water wall	1

Example: You are considering adding an attached solar greenhouse. The primary purpose of the greenhouse will be growing plants. The greenhouse structure should therefore be isolated to avoid excess humidity in the living space.

As the table shows, 1 square foot of 8-inch brick, 12-inch concrete, or 8-inch water wall (water containers) for each square foot of glazing will conveniently provide all of the required thermal mass.

Thermal Mass Pattern 4

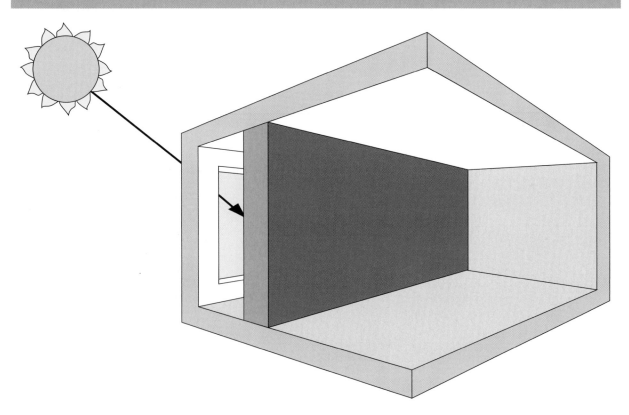

Pattern 5

Similar to Pattern 4, mass in this pattern is sunlit on one side and exposed to the living space on the other side. The distinction is that there is free air circulation around this mass material so that heat may be gained by the living space from either side of the partial wall or from all sides of the water containers.

This pattern may represent a freestanding masonry wall or a series of water containers.

The mass is assumed to be in full sun for at least 6 hours. As with Pattern 4, the wall thicknesses listed are not very sensitive to variations, and the wall surface area listed is for one side of the wall only. Water containers are listed in the table at right as gallons per square foot of glazing.

Example: You plan to add a sun space with 160 square feet of south-facing glazing. Unlike the example in Pattern 4, however, you plan to use the space for liv-

Mass Sizing for Partial Mass Wall or Water Containers in Direct Sun

Material and Thickness	Sq Ft of Mass Surface per Sq Ft of Glazing
8"-thick brick	2
6"-thick concrete	2
Water containers	7 gal per sq ft of glazing

ing rather than growing. You'd like the sun space to be open to the adjacent kitchen. Will a 3-foot high by 20-foot-long room divider constructed of 8-inch brick provide sufficient thermal mass?

The area of the room divider exposed to direct sunlight is 60 square feet. According to the table, the room divider alone will account for only 30 square feet of glazing. You will probably need to employ a Pattern 1 brick floor as well.

Thermal Mass Pattern 5

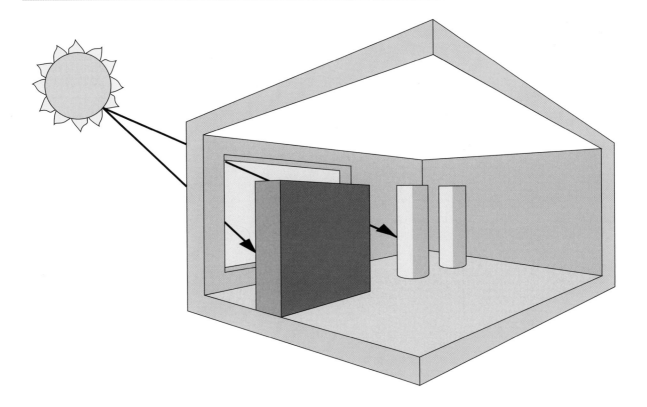

Lighting

Proper lighting around the home is important for safety, for reading, for working, for atmosphere, for the long-term health of your eyes, and now for economy and the environment. In order to understand why different light sources and intensities are recommended for different applications, you need to understand the relationships between *light and seeing.*

Light Sources lists the efficiencies and color characteristics of more than 30 incandescent, fluorescent, high-intensity-discharge, and light-emitting diode (LED) lamps for use in and around the home.

Lamp Shapes and Bases illustrates the incredible variety of bulb shapes and bases available today.

Perhaps the most useful section in this chapter is *Residential Lighting Guidelines,* adapted from a publication of the California Lighting Technology Center, designed to aid builders in complying with California's rigorous 2005 energy code.

Finally, we provide you with a checklist to make sure your lighting design and techniques *meet the code.*

Light and Seeing

Light Units

The relationship between lighting units is displayed in the illustration at right. A point light source with a strength (candlepower) of 1 candela results in an *illuminance* of 1 *foot-candle*, or 1 lumen per square foot. Because a sphere of radius 1 foot has a surface area of 12.57 square feet, the total light output is 12.57 *lumens*.

Illumination levels are usually given in foot-candles, although lumens per square foot is equivalent. Total lamp output is always given in lumens.

The intensity of light falling on a surface is the illuminance. The intensity of light given off or reflected by a surface is its *luminance*. For non-light-emitting surfaces,

Luminance = illuminance × *reflectivity*

Example: What is the luminance of a surface of reflectivity 0.50 when illuminated at an intensity of 100 foot-candles? Luminance = illuminance × reflectivity = 100 footcandles × 0.50 = 50 footcandles

Visual Acuity

As shown in the illustration at right, the human eye can detect light from nearly an entire half sphere (radius 90 degrees). The ability to discriminate among small details, however, is limited to a radius of about 1 degree, the *central field*. The area surrounding the central field is the *surround*.

The ability of the eye to discern the small details of a task within the central field is determined by four factors:

- size of the field.
- contrast between detail and background.
- time (eye fatigue).
- brightness of the task.

The size of a task can be magnified by a lens. In the case of printed material, contrast is maximized by printing black on white. Luminance is a function of both illumination and task reflectance. Deficiencies in size, contrast, and time can all be compensated to a degree by an increase in illumination.

Light Measurements

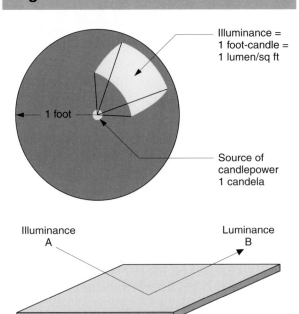

Illuminance =
1 foot-candle =
1 lumen/sq ft

1 foot

Source of candlepower 1 candela

Illuminance A

Luminance B

Surface reflectivity = R
B = R x A

The Visual Field of a Human

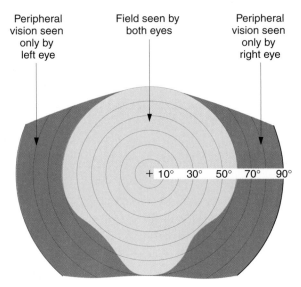

Peripheral vision seen only by left eye

Field seen by both eyes

Peripheral vision seen only by right eye

+ 10° 30° 50° 70° 90°

Angles are from straight ahead

Glare

An area within the visual field that has sufficient luminance to cause either discomfort or a reduction in visual acuity is an area of *glare*. Direct glare is illumination direct from a light source, such as a window or exposed lamp. Reflected glare is light which has been reflected from a shiny or glossy surface, usually within the task area. For optimum visual comfort, the luminance of the task should be slightly greater than the luminance of the surround. The table at right lists maximum recommended luminance ratios.

Color

Most objects simply reflect incident light received from a light source. The perceived color of an object is determined by the color (energy content at different wavelengths) of the light source and the reflectivity of the object at the corresponding wavelengths.

Objects which reflect all wavelengths equally are termed *white*, and light sources which emit light of all frequencies are termed *white lights*. Not all wavelengths are emitted equally, however, even from white lights. The graphs at right show the distribution of power with frequency (spectral power curves) of various common lamps.

A measure of peak emission wavelength is the color-correlated temperature (CCT) of the source. Direct light from the sun is at a color temperature of about 6,000°Kelvin (K). The color-correlated temperatures of incandescent sources range from about 2,400 to 3,100°K. Most fluorescent lamps have color-correlated temperatures between 3,000°K (warm white) and 4,200°K (cool white).

Incandescent lamps emit light at all wavelengths. Fluorescent and other gas-discharge lamps emit light only at specific wavelengths. Color rendition may therefore be different between incandescent and gas-discharge lamps even though their color-correlated temperatures may be the same. The color-rendering index (CRI) compares lamp output with natural daylight at all frequencies, with a CRI of 100 indicating a perfect match.

Glare Guidelines

Compared Areas	Luminance Ratio, Max
Task to adjacent area	3 to 1
Task to a remote dark surface	10 to 1
Task to a remote light surface	0.1 to 1
Window to adjacent wall	20 to 1
Task to any area within visual field	40 to 1

Spectral Power Curves of Lamps

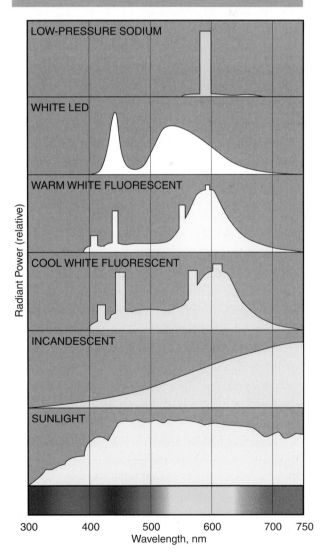

Light Sources

Electrical lamps fall into one of four categories, depending on the way in which they convert electricity to light:

Incandescent lamps emit light from filaments heated to incandescence by an electric current. Efficiencies range from about 10 to 20 lumens per watt. Quartz-halogen lamps achieve higher efficiencies, of up to 24 lumens per watt, through the use of higher-temperature filaments. Strong points include a wide range of bulb styles, a wide range of available output for the same base style and bulb size, and ability to concentrate the light beam, Weak points are relatively low efficiency and short lives. Due to their low efficiency, most versions are slated for phase-out starting in 2012.

Fluorescent lamps emit light from phosphor coatings stimulated by high-voltage discharge through the mercury-vapor-filled bulbs. Rare earth phosphor additives modify color output. Ballasts are required to limit the arc current. Excluding the tiniest lamps, efficiencies range from about 70 to 90 lumens per watt, including ballast power. Strong points include long lamp life, low operating cost, and low operating temperature. Compact fluorescent lamps (CFLs) are rapidly replacing incandescent lamps in residential applications.

High-intensity discharge (HID) lamps emit light directly from electric arcs through metal vapor. Color rendition is inappropriate for residential applications, but efficiencies range up to 144 lumens per watt.

Light-emitting diode (LED) A light-emitting diode is a semiconductor diode emitting narrow-spectrum light when electrically biased in the forward direction of the p-n junction.

Individual LEDs are tiny and emit light from a flat surface. Most often they are encapsulated in a plastic lens to shape the radiation pattern. LEDs have long been used as small indicator lights on electronic devices and increasingly in applications such as flashlights. It is expected that they will ultimately replace fluorescent lamps.

Efficiencies of Light Sources

Light Source	Type	Efficacy, Lumens/W
Incandescent	5W tungsten	5.0
	40W tungsten	12.6
	100W tungsten	16.8
	100W tungsten halogen	16.7
	2.6W tungsten halogen (5V)	19.2
	Quartz tungsten halogen (12V)	24
Fluorescent	5W to 24W compact bulb	45–60
	34W, T-12 tube	50
	32W, T-8 tube	60
	36W, T-8 tube	to 93
	28W, T-5 tube	104
HID	Xenon	30–50
	Mercury-xenon	50–55
	High-pressure sodium	150
	Low-pressure sodium	183–200
	1,400W sulfur	100
LED	White, available	10–90
	White, experimental	to 150

Lamp Efficiencies

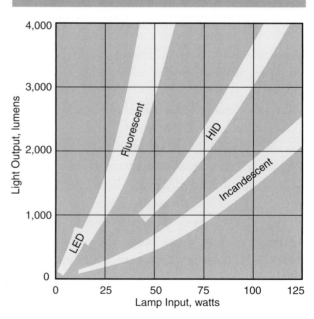

Characteristics of Some Commercially Available Lamps

Type	Description	Color Temp, °K	CRI	Output, Lumens	Power, Watts	Lumens per Watt
Incandescent	A19, frosted, 25 watt	2,900	—	357	25	14
	A19, frosted, 40 watt	2,900	—	460	40	12
	A19, frosted, 60 watt	2,950	—	890	60	15
	A19, frosted, 75 watt	3,000	—	1,210	75	16
	A19, frosted, 100 watt	3,050	—	2,850	150	18
	12V quartz-halogen, 20 watt	2,900	—	300	19.4	15
	12V quartz-halogen, 45 watt	3,100	—	980	44.5	22
Fluorescent	Dulux® EL, 11 watt	3,000	82	600	11	54
	Dulux EL, 19 watt	3,000	82	1,200	19	63
	Deluxe warm white	2,950	74	1,550	30	52
	Warm white	3,000	52	2,360	30	79
	Designer 3000K	3,000	67	3,300	40	83
	Royal white	3,000	80	2,400	30	80
	Octron® 3100K	3,100	75	3,650	40	91
	White	3,450	57	1,900	30	63
	Octron 3500K	3,500	75	3,650	40	91
	Natural white	3,600	86	3,050	55	55
	Designer 4100K	4,100	67	8,800	95	93
	Octron 4100K	4,100	75	3,650	40	91
	Deluxe cool white	4,100	89	2,100	40	53
	Lite white	4,150	48	4,300	60	72
	Cool white	4,200	62	3,150	40	79
	Design 50	5,000	90	1,610	30	54
	Daylight	6,300	76	1,900	30	63
HID	Mercury, Warmtone	3,300	52	3,700	100	37
	Mercury, Brite White Deluxe	4,000	45	3,650	100	37
	Mercury, clear	5,900	22	3,380	100	34
	Metal halide, clear	3,200	65	6,800	100	68
	Metal halide, coated	3,900	70	16,000	250	64
	High-pressure sodium, Lumalox	2,000	22	8,850	100	89
	High-pressure sodium, Unalox	1,900	20	11,700	150	78
LED	A19, warm white	3,000	—	43	1.3	33
	A19, cool white	8,000	—	42	1.3	32
	PAR38, warm white	3,000	—	182	4.5	40
	PAR38, pure white	5,500	—	230	5.0	46
	Chandelier, warm white	3,000	—	52	2.4	22

Lamp Shapes and Bases

Standard Lamp Shapes

COMPACT FLUORESCENT (CFL)

Mini-Twist | Twist | Triple twin | Double twin | Double twin | Twin | Classic | Classic | Candelabra | Globe | Reflector | Circline

FLUORESCENT

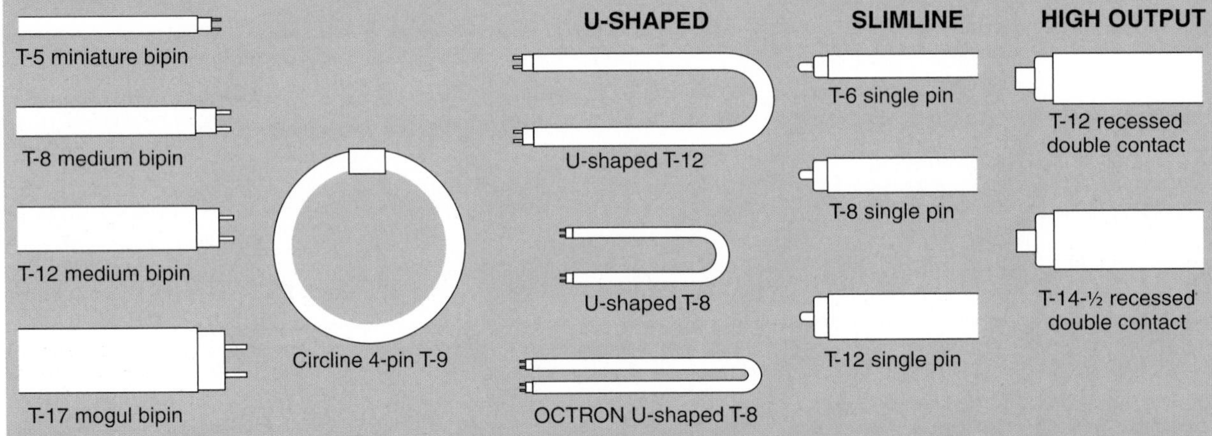

T-5 miniature bipin

T-8 medium bipin

T-12 medium bipin

T-17 mogul bipin

Circline 4-pin T-9

U-SHAPED

U-shaped T-12

U-shaped T-8

OCTRON U-shaped T-8

SLIMLINE

T-6 single pin

T-8 single pin

T-12 single pin

HIGH OUTPUT

T-12 recessed double contact

T-14-½ recessed double contact

INCANDESCENT

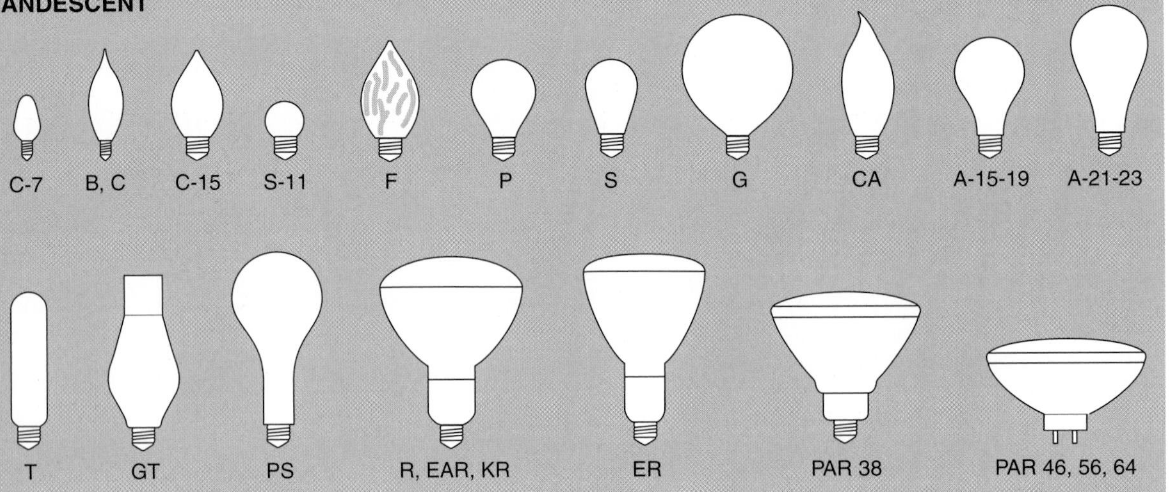

C-7 | B, C | C-15 | S-11 | F | P | S | G | CA | A-15-19 | A-21-23

T | GT | PS | R, EAR, KR | ER | PAR 38 | PAR 46, 56, 64

Standard Lamp Bases

Single-contact bayonet

Double-contact bayonet

Mini screw

Mini-can screw

Candelabra

Intermediate

3 kon-tact medium

Medium

Admedium skirted

Medium skirted

Medium skirted

Position oriented mogul

Mogul

3 contact mogul

Mogul prefocus

Mogul bipost

Single pin T-12

Single pin T-8

Single pin T-6

Single-ended bipin, 7 & 9 Watt

Single-ended bipin, 13 Watt

Mogul bipin

Medium 2 pin

Medium bipost

Medium bipin T-8 lamp

Medium bipin T-12 lamp

Miniature bipin

Recessed double contact

Candelabra prefocus

4 pin circline

Medium side prong

Medium prefocus

Residential Lighting Guidelines

As the old saying goes, "A picture is worth a thousand words." By "picture" we mean, of course, a wiring plan.

In the next four pages we present wiring plans demonstrating a variety of ways of satisfying the energy code—specifically the 2005 California Energy Code. Because no state is more stringent than California, the ideas should work in your state as well.

Bathrooms

MASTER BATH

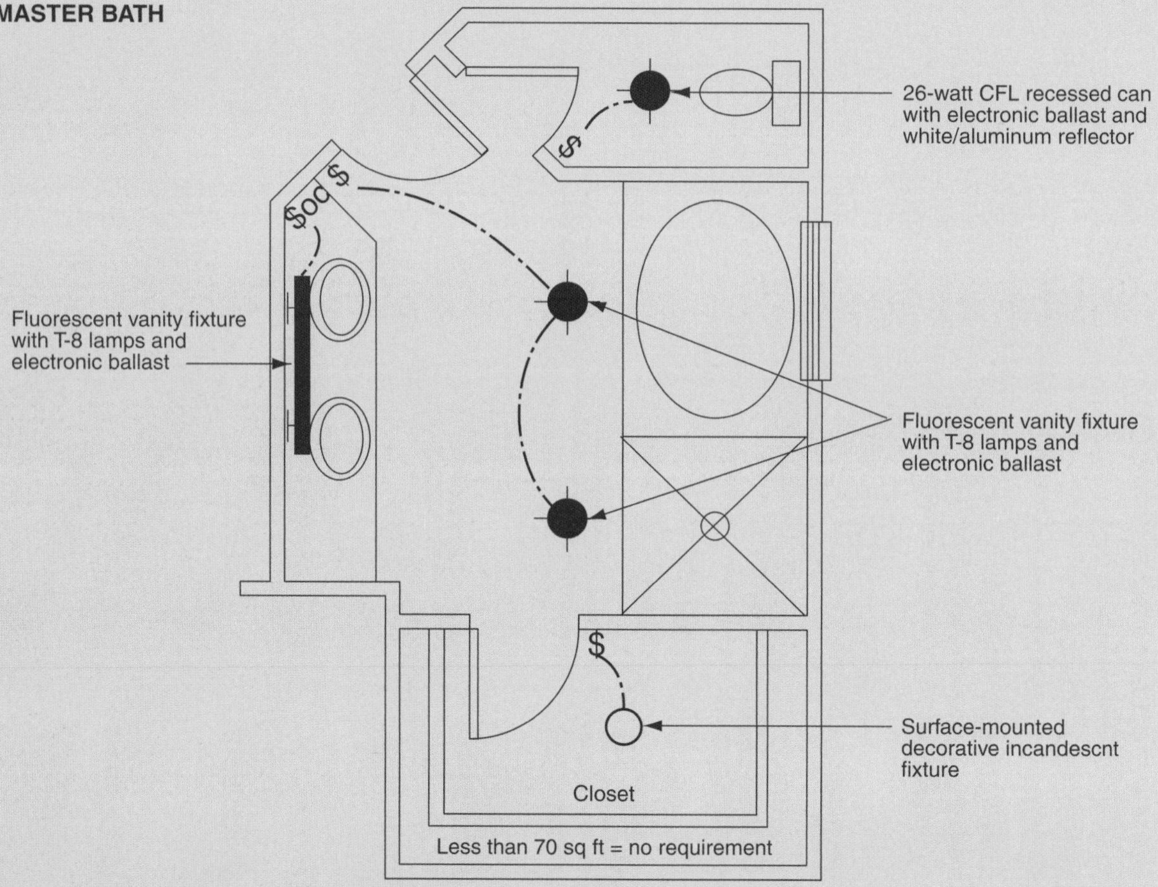

26-watt CFL recessed can with electronic ballast and white/aluminum reflector

Fluorescent vanity fixture with T-8 lamps and electronic ballast

Fluorescent vanity fixture with T-8 lamps and electronic ballast

Surface-mounted decorative incandescnt fixture

Closet

Less than 70 sq ft = no requirement

STANDARD BATH

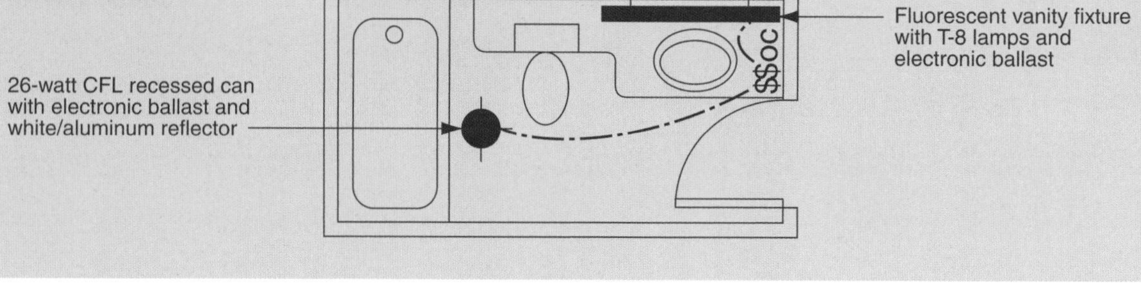

Fluorescent vanity fixture with T-8 lamps and electronic ballast

26-watt CFL recessed can with electronic ballast and white/aluminum reflector

OPTION 1: RECESSED CEILING FIXTURES

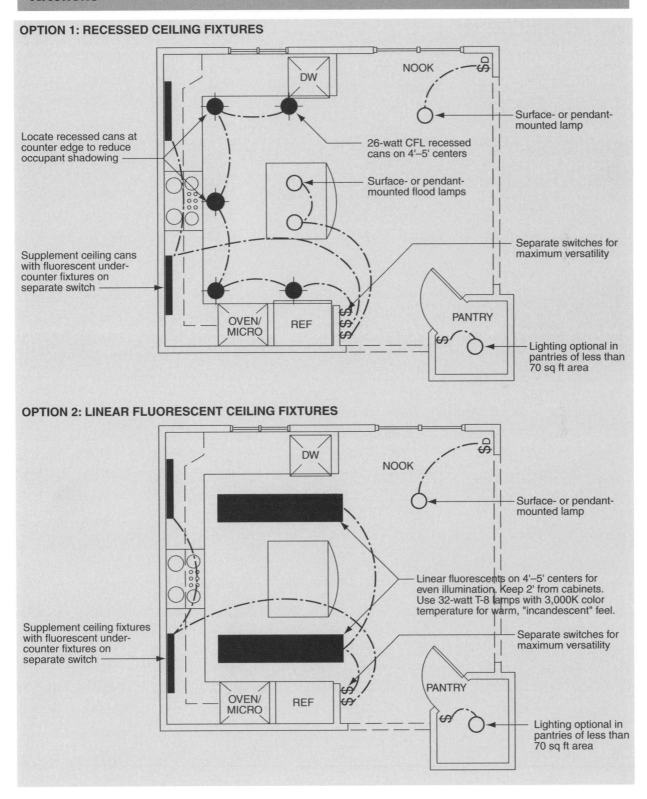

NOOK

Surface- or pendant-
mounted lamp

Locate recessed cans at
counter edge to reduce
occupant shadowing

26-watt CFL recessed
cans on 4'–5' centers

Surface- or pendant-
mounted flood lamps

Separate switches for
maximum versatility

Supplement ceiling cans
with fluorescent under-
counter fixtures on
separate switch

DW

OVEN/
MICRO

REF

PANTRY

Lighting optional in
pantries of less than
70 sq ft area

OPTION 2: LINEAR FLUORESCENT CEILING FIXTURES

DW

NOOK

Surface- or pendant-
mounted lamp

Linear fluorescents on 4'–5' centers for
even illumination. Keep 2' from cabinets.
Use 32-watt T-8 lamps with 3,000K color
temperature for warm, "incandescent" feel.

Separate switches for
maximum versatility

Supplement ceiling fixtures
with fluorescent under-
counter fixtures on
separate switch

OVEN/
MICRO

REF

PANTRY

Lighting optional in
pantries of less than
70 sq ft area

Dining Rooms and Living Rooms

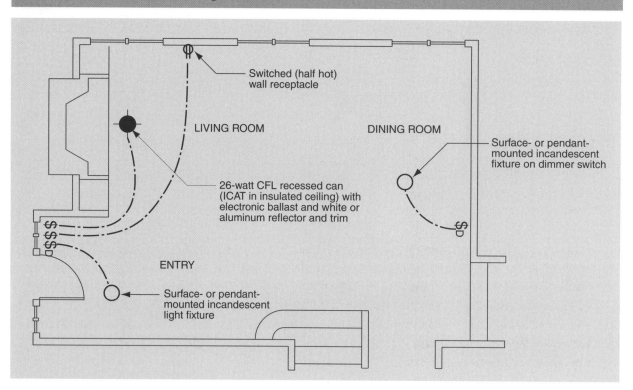

Switched (half hot) wall receptacle

LIVING ROOM

DINING ROOM

Surface- or pendant-mounted incandescent fixture on dimmer switch

26-watt CFL recessed can (ICAT in insulated ceiling) with electronic ballast and white or aluminum reflector and trim

ENTRY

Surface- or pendant-mounted incandescent light fixture

Bedrooms

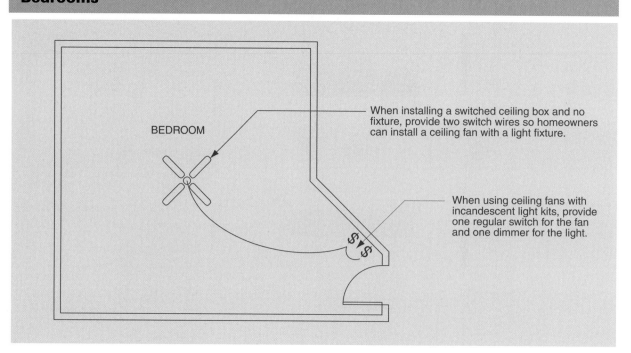

BEDROOM

When installing a switched ceiling box and no fixture, provide two switch wires so homeowners can install a ceiling fan with a light fixture.

When using ceiling fans with incandescent light kits, provide one regular switch for the fan and one dimmer for the light.

Entry Areas, Foyers, and Hallways

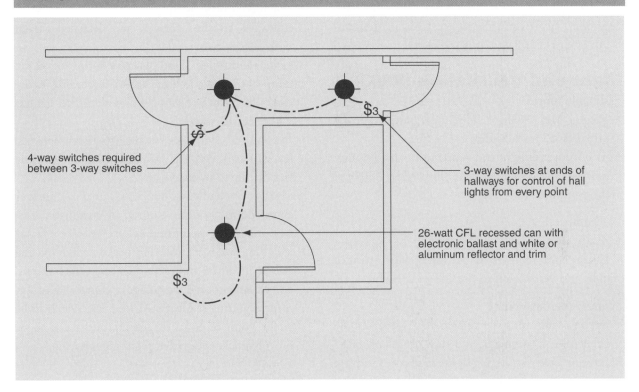

4-way switches required
between 3-way switches

3-way switches at ends of
hallways for control of hall
lights from every point

26-watt CFL recessed can with
electronic ballast and white or
aluminum reflector and trim

Porches

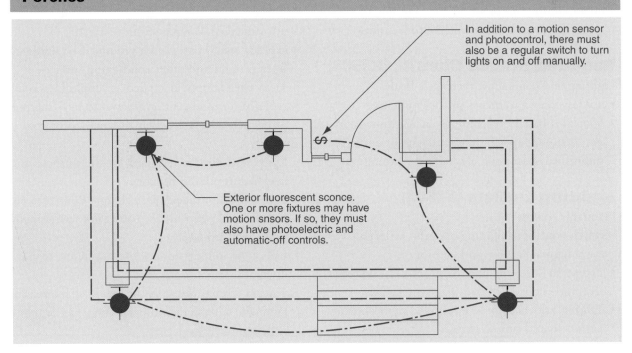

In addition to a motion sensor
and photocontrol, there must
also be a regular switch to turn
lights on and off manually.

Exterior fluorescent sconce.
One or more fixtures may have
motion snsors. If so, they must
also have photoelectric and
automatic-off controls.

Meet the Code

The following is a partial list of requirements from the *2006 International Residential Code (IRC) for One- and Two-Family Dwellings*. Consult the publication for the full text and additional provisions.

Light and Ventilation (R303)

Habitable rooms:
- glazing area ≥8% of floor area unless lighting provides ≥6 foot-candles
- for purposes of light and ventilation, an adjoining room is considered part of a room when ≥50% of the common wall is open

Bathrooms:
- glazing area ≥3 sq ft, half openable
- glazing not required if provided with artificial light and ventilation to outside of ≥50 cfm

Stairway Illumination:
- interior stairs must be lighted to ≥1 foot-candle either at each landing or over each section of stairs
- exterior stairs must be lighted at top landing; basement bulkhead stairs at lower landing
- lighting for interior stairways of ≥6 stairs must be controllable from both levels
- unless continuous or automatic, lighting for exterior stairs must be controllable from inside

Required Branch Circuits (E3603)

Lighting and general use receptacle loads:
- not less than 3 watts per sq ft of floor area
- floor area based on building outside dimensions, not including open porches, garages, or unused or unfinished spaces not adaptable for future use

Lighting Outlets (E3803)

Habitable rooms:
- switch-controlled lighting outlet to be installed in every habitable room and bathroom
- except in kitchens and bathrooms, a switched receptacle controlled by a wall switch OK
- lighting outlets may be controlled by occupancy sensors in addition to manual wall switches

Additional locations:
- switch-controlled lighting to be installed in hallways, stairways, attached garages, and detached garages with electric power
- switch-controlled lighting on exterior of egress door having grade-level access, including egress doors for attached garages and detached garages with electric power
- for interior stairways having ≥6 risers between levels, a wall switch at each floor level and landing that includes an entryway

Exception: in hallways, stairways, and at outdoor egress doors, remote, central, or automatic control of lighting permitted
- a lighting outlet controlled by wall switch or integral switch in attics, underfloor spaces, utility rooms, and basements used for storage or containing equipment requiring servicing. At least one switch to be at the point of entry. A lighting outlet also to be provided near equipment requiring servicing.

Fixtures (E3903)

- luminaires, lampholders, lamps, and receptacles not to have energized parts exposed
- luminaires installed so that combustible material not subjected to temperatures >194°F
- exposed metal parts to be grounded or insulated from ground and other conducting surfaces
- screw-shell lampholders used as lampholders only
- recessed incandescent luminaires to have thermal protection and be listed as thermally protected

Exceptions:
1. recessed luminaires listed for the purpose and installed in poured concrete
2. recessed luminaires with design, construction, and thermal performance equivalent to thermally protected luminaires
- ballast of indoor fluorescent luminaire to have integral thermal protection

Exception: simple reactance ballast in a fluorescent luminaire with straight tubular lamps not required to be thermally protected

- recessed high-intensity luminaires to have thermal protection and be identified as thermally protected.

Exceptions:

1. recessed luminaires listed for purpose and installed in poured concrete
2. recessed luminaires equivalent to thermally protected luminaires

Wet Locations:

- luminaires to be installed so that water cannot enter or accumulate in wiring compartments, lampholders, or other electrical parts.
- luminaires in wet locations to be marked SUITABLE FOR WET LOCATIONS
- luminaires in damp locations to be marked SUITABLE FOR WET LOCATIONS or SUITABLE FOR DAMP LOCATIONS
- lampholders to be weatherproof
- cord-connected luminaires, chain-, cable-, or cord-suspended-luminaires, lighting track, pendants, and ceiling fans to have no parts within 3' horizontally and 8' vertically from top of a bathtub rim or shower stall threshold. Luminaires located in this zone to be listed for damp locations and, where subject to shower spray, listed for wet locations.

Clothes Closets:

- luminaires limited to surface-mounted or recessed incandescent with completely enclosed lamps, and surface-mounted or recessed fluorescent

Installation:

- Surface-mounted incandescent luminaires to be installed on wall above door or on ceiling, with clearance of ≥12" between fixture and storage space
- Surface-mounted and recessed fluorescent luminaires and recessed incandescent luminaires with completely enclosed lamps to be installed on wall above door or on ceiling, with clearance of ≥6" between fixture and storage space
- luminaires to be wired so screwshells of lampholders connected to same luminaire or circuit conductor or terminal. The grounded conductor to be connected to the screw shell.

Luminaire Installation (E3904)

- outlet boxes to have covers except where covered by canopy, lampholder, or device with faceplate.
- combustible finish exposed between edge of a canopy or pan and outlet box to be covered with a noncombustible material
- connections between luminaire conductors and circuit conductors to be accessible without disconnection
- luminaires >6 lb or exceeding 16" in any dimension may not be supported by screwshell of a lampholder
- luminaires with exposed ballasts or transformers to be installed so ballasts or transformers not in contact with combustible material
- surface-mounted luminaires with ballasts on combustible low-density cellulose fiberboard must be listed for the purpose or spaced ≥1.5" from surface
- recessed luminaires not identified for contact with insulation (Type IC) to have all recessed parts spaced ≥0.5" from combustibles, except points of support and finish trim parts
- no thermal insulation above a recessed luminaire or <3" from enclosure, wiring compartment, or ballast except where identified for contact with insulation, Type IC

Track Lighting (E3905)

- track to be permanently installed and connected to a circuit with rating ≤ that of track
- fittings for track to be designed specifically for the track
- electrical load on track not to exceed track rating
- track not to be installed in the following locations:
    1. subjected to physical damage
    2. wet or damp locations
    3. subject to corrosive vapors
    4. storage battery rooms
    5. hazardous locations
    6. concealed
    7. extended through walls or partitions
    8. <5' above floor except where protected from damage or track operates at <30 volts rms

Sound

The *quality of sound* in our homes has a great effect on the quality of our lives. When we play music or engage in conversation, we want to hear clearly and hear well. On the other hand, when junior is playing what teenagers call music, or the neighbors upstairs are fighting, we don't want to hear at all.

In this chapter you'll see how to achieve quality sound in a room and what to do about a room that either rings or is acoustically flat.

You'll also find guidelines for acceptable levels of *sound transmission* between rooms and between floors. Tables of *sound transmission classes of walls* and *sound transmission classes and impact insulation classes of floor-ceilings* show specific construction techniques for reducing sound transmission to almost any level.

Quality of Sound

Sound is the sensation produced when pressure waves in the acoustic range of frequencies strike the eardrum. Typically, a young person can hear sound over the range of 20 to 20,000 cycles per second, or hertz (Hz).

Sound quality involves sound source intensity, absorption, echo, standing-wave amplification, and reverberation time.

Intensity

Sound intensity is measured in decibels (db). The 0 db level is defined as a sound energy level of 10^{-16} watts per square centimeter and corresponds roughly to the smallest sound detectable by the human ear. Perceived intensity, or sound "volume," is logarithmic; that is, a 10-db increase in intensity is an increase of 10 times the power of the sound wave, but is perceived as a doubling of volume. The table at right lists characteristic sound intensities of everyday sources.

Absorption

The fraction of energy absorbed by a surface is its absorption coefficient, α. Gypsum drywall is highly reflective (α = 0.05 at 500 Hz), whereas heavy carpet is highly absorptive (α = 0.57 at 500 Hz). One unit of absorption is equivalent to an area of one square foot of perfect (α = 1.00) absorption.

High absorption does not reduce the intensity of sound received directly from a source, but reduces the buildup of reflected sound. It thus reduces the total intensity of sound in a space.

Absorption is measured at 125, 250, 500, 1,000, 2,000, and 4,000 Hz. In order to give a material a single absorption figure, the noise-reduction coefficient (NRC) is defined as the average of coefficients at 250, 500, 1,000, and 2,000 Hz. The table on the facing page lists typical NRCs for surfaces in the home.

Sound Intensities

Intensity, db	Sound Source
0	Threshold of hearing
10	Rustling leaves
20	Rural background
30	Bedroom conversation
40	Living room conversation
50	Large office activity
60	Face-to-face conversation
70	Auto interior at 55 mph
80	Face-to-face shouting
90	Downtown traffic
100	Tablesaw
110	Symphony orchestra maximum
120	Elevated train from platform
130	Threshold of pain (rock concert)
140	Jet engine

Sound Reflection and Absorption

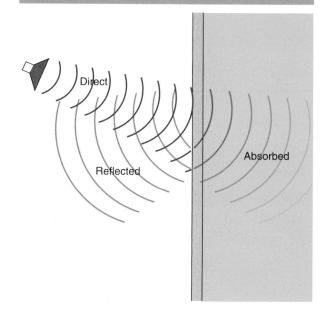

Noise-Reduction Coefficients

Typical Noise Reduction Coefficients (NRCs)

Material		Absorption Coefficient at, Hz				
		250	500	1,000	2,000	NRC
Brick	Bare	0.03	0.03	0.04	0.05	0.04
	Painted	0.01	0.02	0.02	0.02	0.02
Carpet, Heavy	On slab	0.06	0.14	0.37	0.60	0.29
	On 40-oz foam pad	0.24	0.57	0.69	0.71	0.55
	On foam with latex backing	0.27	0.39	0.34	0.48	0.37
Concrete Block	Bare	0.44	0.31	0.29	0.39	0.36
	Painted	0.05	0.06	0.07	0.09	0.07
Fabric	10-oz velour hung straight	0.04	0.11	0.17	0.24	0.14
	14-oz velour pleated double	0.31	0.49	0.75	0.70	0.56
	18-oz velour pleated double	0.35	0.55	0.72	0.70	0.58
Floor	Bare concrete	0.01	0.02	0.02	0.02	0.02
	Resilient on concrete	0.03	0.03	0.03	0.03	0.03
	Bare wood	0.11	0.10	0.07	0.06	0.09
	Parquet on concrete	0.04	0.07	0.06	0.06	0.06
Furniture	Bare wood	0.04	0.05	0.07	0.07	0.06
	Metal	0.04	0.05	0.07	0.07	0.06
	Upholstered with plastic	0.45	0.50	0.55	0.50	0.50
	Upholstered with fabric	0.37	0.56	0.67	0.61	0.55
Glass	Plate	0.06	0.04	0.03	0.02	0.04
	Double strength	0.25	0.18	0.12	0.07	0.16
Wall	½" gypsum drywall	0.10	0.05	0.04	0.07	0.07
	Marble	0.01	0.01	0.01	0.02	0.01
	Glazed tile	0.01	0.01	0.01	0.01	0.01
	Plywood paneling	0.22	0.17	0.09	0.10	0.15
Plaster	Smooth finish on brick	0.02	0.02	0.03	0.04	0.03
	Smooth finish on lath	0.03	0.04	0.05	0.04	0.04
	Rough finish on lath	0.02	0.03	0.04	0.04	0.04
Cellulose Fiber	Sprayed ⅝" on solid backing	0.16	0.44	0.79	0.90	0.42
	Sprayed 1" on solid backing	0.29	0.75	0.98	0.93	0.74
	Sprayed 1" on timber lath	0.90	1.00	1.00	1.00	0.98
	Sprayed 1¼" on solid backing	0.30	0.73	0.92	0.98	0.73
	Sprayed 3" on solid backing	0.95	1.00	0.85	0.85	0.91

Absorption and Reverberation

Echo

An echo is a sound reflection. To be perceived as a distinct sound, the reflected wave must arrive at least ¹⁄₁₇th of a second after the direct wave. Because sound travels at about 1,000 feet per second, an echo must have travelled at least 60 feet further than the direct sound. Thus, echoes occur only in rooms more than 30 feet deep. Echoes are stronger when the reflecting surface is highly reflective and is concave toward the listener (focussing the reflected wave toward the listener).

Standing Waves

When the dimensions of a room are a multiple of the wavelength of a sound, the sound wave is reinforced by reflection. Frequencies are thus selectively amplified, distorting the original, direct sound. The problem is made worse by reflective room surfaces, parallel room surfaces, and room dimensions in simple ratios, such as 1:4, 1:3, etc.

Reverberation Time

The length of time required for the intensity of sound in a space to diminish by 60 db is the *reverberation time* of the space. A room with too short a reverberation time is acoustically dead; too long a reverberation time confuses sounds. Reverberation time can be calculated as

$$T = V/20A$$

where

T = reverberation time in seconds
V = volume of room in cubic feet
A = total absorption of the room

The procedure is as follows:

1. Calculate the areas of all surfaces, including furnishings.

2. Multiply each surface area by its 500-Hz absorption coefficient.

3. Sum the products to get total absorption, A.

4. Calculate reverberation time, T = V/20A.

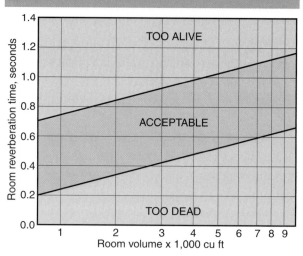

Acceptable Reverberation Times

Example: What is the 500-Hz reverberation time of a 12- by 15- × 8-foot room having a bare wood floor, gypsum drywall ceiling, smooth plaster walls, two 3- by 5-foot windows covered by pleated 14-oz velour drapes, and 40 square feet (floor area) of fabric-upholstered furniture?

Surface	Area, sq ft	α at 500 Hz	Product
Floor	140	0.10	14.0
Ceiling	180	0.05	9.0
Wall	402	0.04	16.1
Drapes	30	0.49	14.7
Furniture	40	0.56	22.4

Total room absorption, A = 76.2

Reverberation time = 1,440/(20 × 76.2) = 0.94 seconds

The volume of the room in question is 12 × 15 × 8 feet = 1,440 cubic feet. Referring to the graph of acceptable reverberation times. you find 0.3 to 0.8 seconds for a room of this volume. Thus, the computed reverberation time falls outside the acceptable range. Carpeting the floor (carpet on foam pad, α = 0.57) would increase he total room absorption to 142 and bring the reverberation time down to an acceptable 0.51 seconds.

Transmission of Sound

Sound can be transmitted through a wall, floor, or ceiling in three ways, as seen in the illustration at right:

Leaks or openings allow sound to propagate as though the wall, floor, or ceiling didn't exist. Examples are the space under a door, back-to-back electrical fixtures, rough-in holes for pipes, and heating ducts connecting rooms.

Airborne sounds set a building surface into vibration. The vibration is carried through the rigidly attached wall studs to the opposite surface, causing it in turn to reradiate to the other side, much like the two heads of a drum.

Impact of an object falling on a floor causes the ceiling attached to the same floor joists to radiate sound to the room below.

Walls and floor-ceilings are rated by their abilities to reduce sound transmission. The reduction is measured in decibels, where 10 db corresponds to a factor-of-10 difference in sound energy and a factor-of-2 difference in sound loudness (volume). The table at middle right shows the effects on hearing of various levels of sound reduction between spaces.

Walls are rated by *sound transmission class* (STC), roughly the sound reduction at 500 Hz, but taking into consideration frequencies from 125 to 4,000 Hz as well. Floor-ceilings are rated by both STC and impact insulation class (IIC), a measure of the noise transmitted when objects are dropped on the floor above.

The table at bottom right, from the U.S. Department of Housing and Urban Development (HUD) Minimum Property Standards, serves as a guide to minimum acceptable STCs and IICs for residential construction. Walls and ceilings with higher ratings are desirable in a quality home, especially one with children.

Further, the International Residential Code requires, for walls and floor-ceilings separating dwelling units, values of at least STC 45 and IIC 45.

Types of Sound Transmission

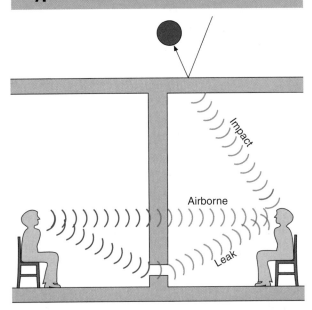

Effectiveness of Sound Reduction

Reduction	Effect on Hearing
25 db	Little effect, normal speech heard clearly
30 db	Loud speech understood fairly well
35 db	Loud speech audible but not understood
40 db	Loud speech heard as a murmur
45 db	Loud speech a strain to hear
50 db	Loud speech not heard at all

Recommended Residential STC and IIC

STC	IIC	Effect on Hearing
45	—	Wall separating living space from living space or public space, such as corridor
50	—	Wall separating living space from commercial space or high-noise service space such as boiler or mechanical room
45	45	Floor-ceiling separating living space from living space or public space, such as corridor
50	50	Floor-ceiling separating living space from commercial space or high-noise service space

STCs of Walls

The STC rating of a wall can be increased by three principal techniques:

• Increasing the mass of the wall (installing a second layer of drywall, for example).

• Decoupling the opposing surfaces (by staggering the studs, for example).

• Including sound-absorbing materials (filling stud cavities with fibrous insulation, for example).

Sound Transmission Classes of Wall Constructions

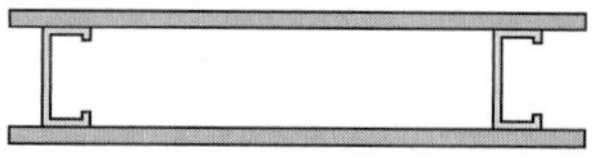

STC 42

5/8" fire-rated gypsum wallboard screw-attached horizontally to both sides of 35/8" screw studs, 24" oc. All wallboard joints staggered. Note that rating of 42 is below HUD and IRC minimums.

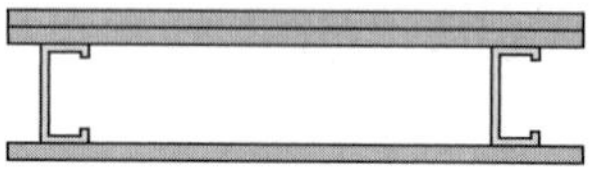

STC 44

5/8" fire-rated gypsum wallboard screw-attached vertically to both sides of 35/8" screw studs, 24" oc. Second layer laminated vertically and screwed to one side only.

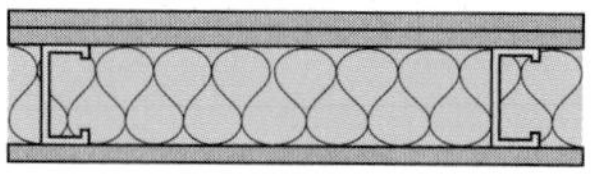

STC 47

5/8" fire-rated gypsum wallboard screw-attached horizontally to both sides of 35/8" screw studs, 24" oc. Second layer laminated vertically and screwed to one side only. 31/2" fiberglass or mineral wool in cavity.

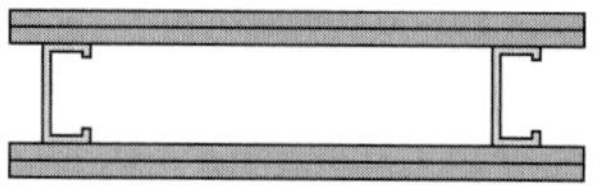

STC 49

First layer 5/8" fire-rated gypsum wallboard screw-attached vertically to both sides of 35/8" screw studs, 24" oc. Second layer laminated vertically to both sides.

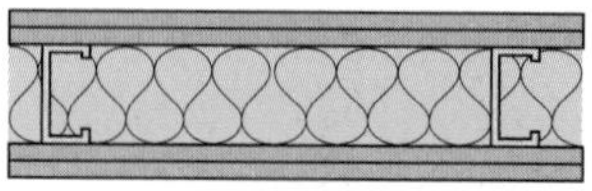

STC 56

First layer 5/8" fire-rated gypsum wallboard screw-attached vertically to both sides of 35/8" screw studs, 24" oc. Second layer laminated or screw-attached vertically to both sides. 3" fiberglass in cavity.

STC 35

⁵/₈" fire-rated gypsum wallboard nailed to both sides of 2x4 wood studs, 16" oc.

STC 40

⁵/₈" fire-rated gypsum wallboard. Base layer nail-applied to 2x4 wood studs, spaced 24" oc. Face layer nail-applied.

STC 43

⁵/₈" fire-rated gypsum wallboard. One side screw-applied to resilient furring channel, spaced 24" oc, on 2x4 studs spaced 16" oc. Other side nailed direct to studs.

STC 46

⁵/₈" fire-rated gypsum wallboard nailed on both sides to staggered 2x4 wood studs, 16" oc, on single 6" plate.

STC 50

⁵/₈" fire-rated gypsum wallboard. One side screw-applied to resilient furring channel, spaced 24" oc, on 2x4 studs spaced 16" oc. Other side nailed to studs. 3¹/₂" fiberglass in stud cavity.

STC 50

Two layers of ⁵/₈" fire-rated gypsum wallboard. One side screw-applied to resilient furring channel, spaced 24" oc, on 2x4 studs spaced 16" oc. Other side nailed direct to studs.

STC 51

Two layers of ⁵/₈" fire-rated gypsum wallboard screw-attached horizontally to both sides of 3⁵/₈" screw studs, 24" oc.
All wallboard nailed on both sides to staggered 2x4 wood studs, 16" oc, on single 6" plate.

STC 58

⁵/₈" fire-rated gypsum wallboard. Base layer applied vertically, nailed 6" oc. Face layer applied horizontally, nailed 8" oc. Nailed to double row of wood studs 16" oc on separate plates. 3½" fiberglass in cavity.

STCs and IICs of Floor-Ceilings

Both STC and IIC ratings of floor-ceilings are increased by the same three measures used in walls: increasing mass, decoupling surfaces, and incorporating absorption materials. In addition, IICs are dramatically increased by installation of impact-absorbing flooring materials such as carpets and pads.

As with walls, ratings higher than minimum HUD and IRC standards are desirable in quality homes.

Sound and Impact Transmission Classes of Ceiling Constructions

STC 37
IIC 34

1/8" vinyl tile on 1/2" plywood underlayment, over 5/8" plywood subfloor on 2x joists at 16" oc. Ceiling 1/2" gypsum drywall nailed to joists.

STC 37
IIC 56

1/4" foam rubber pad and 3/8" nylon carpet on 1/2" plywood underlayment, over 5/8" plywood subfloor on 2x joists at 16" oc. Ceiling 1/2" gypsum drywall nailed to joists.

STC 46
IIC 44

0.075" vinyl sheet on 3/8" plywood underlayment, over 5/8" plywood subfloor on 2x joists at 16" oc with 3" fiberglass batts. Ceiling 5/8" gypsum drywall screwed to resilient channels.

STC 48
IIC 45

1/16" vinyl sheet on 19/32" T&G Sturd-I-Floor on 2x joists at 16" oc with 3" fiberglass batts. Ceiling 5/8" gypsum drywall screwed to resilient channels.

STC 51
IIC 80

44-oz carpet and 40-oz pad on 1 1/8" T&G Sturd-I-Floor on 2x joists at 16" oc with 3" fiberglass batts. Ceiling 5/8" gypsum drywall nailed to separate joists.

STC 56
IIC 78

44-oz carpet and 40-oz pad on 19/32" T&G Sturd-I-Floor, nailed to 2x3 sleepers, glued between joists to 1/2" insulation board, stapled to 1/2" plywood on 2x joists at 16" oc with 3" fiberglass batts. Ceiling 5/8" gypsum drywall screwed to resilient channels.

STC 53
IIC 51

$^{25}/_{32}$" wood strip flooring nailed to 2x3 sleepers, glued between joists to $^{1}/_{2}$" insulation board, stapled to $^{1}/_{2}$" plywood on 2x joists at 16" oc with 3" fiberglass batts. Ceiling $^{5}/_{8}$" gypsum drywall screwed to resilient channels.

STC 53
IIC 45

$^{25}/_{32}$" wood strip flooring on $^{1}/_{2}$" plywood subfloor on 2x joists at 16" oc with 3" fiberglass batts. Ceiling $^{5}/_{8}$" gypsum drywall nailed to separate joists.

STC 53
IIC 74

44-oz carpet and 40-oz pad on $1^{5}/_{8}$" of 75 pcf perlite/sand concrete over $^{5}/_{8}$" plywood subfloor on 2x joists at 16" oc. Ceiling $^{5}/_{8}$" gypsum drywall nailed to separate joists.

STC 54
IIC 50

$^{25}/_{32}$" wood strip flooring nailed to 2x3 sleepers, glued to 3"-wide strips of $^{1}/_{2}$" insulation board, nailed above the floor joists to $^{1}/_{2}$" plywood on 2x joists at 16" oc. Ceiling $^{5}/_{8}$" gypsum drywall nailed to separate joists. 3" and $1^{1}/_{2}$" fiberglass batts between joists and sleepers.

STC 54
IIC 51

$^{5}/_{16}$" wood block flooring glued to $^{1}/_{2}$" plywood underlayment, glued to $^{1}/_{2}$" soundboard over $^{1}/_{2}$" plywood subfloor on 2x joists at 16" oc. Ceiling $^{5}/_{8}$" gypsum drywall screwed to resilient channels with 3" fiberglass between joists.

STC 55
IIC 72

Carpet and pad on $^{1}/_{2}$" plywood underlayment, glued to $^{1}/_{2}$" soundboard over $^{5}/_{8}$" subfloor on 2x joists at 16" oc. Ceiling $^{5}/_{8}$" gypsum drywall screwed to resilient channels with 3" fiberglass between joists.

STC 57
IIC 56

Vinyl flooring glued to $^{1}/_{2}$" plywood underlayment over 1x3 furring strips between joists, on top of $^{1}/_{2}$" soundboard, over $^{5}/_{8}$" plywood subfloor on 2x joists at 16" oc. Ceiling $^{5}/_{8}$" gypsum drywall screwed to resilient channels with 3" fiberglass between joists.

STC 58
IIC 55

Vinyl flooring on $^{1}/_{2}$" plywood underlayment, over $^{1}/_{2}$" soundboard over $^{5}/_{8}$" subfloor on 2x joists at 16" oc. Ceiling $^{5}/_{8}$" gypsum drywall screwed to resilient channels with 3" fiberglass between joists.

Fasteners

Houses consist of thousands of pieces, held together by what seems like millions of fasteners. What is the right type, how long should it be, how much will it hold, and how many should I use? These are the questions that must be answered every day on a construction project. And these are the answers this chapter provides.

Nails provides a field guide to 38 types of nails and 52 different applications. It shows you the relationship between pennyweight (d) and nail length. It lists the type, size, and number of nails to use in every step of residential construction. It even contains tables showing you exactly how much force you can expect a single nail to resist, in 32 species of wood.

Wood Screws shows how to drill just the right pilot hole for each size of screw. It also contains tables of allowable holding power for screws.

Screws and Bolts contains illustrations of screws, bolts, screw heads, and washers.

Metal framing aids are a boon to both contractors and do-it-yourselfers, resulting in stronger fastening in less time than required using more traditional methods of nailing. Illustrated are dozens of these useful aids.

Finally, modern chemistry has produced nothing more amazing than the variety of *adhesives* you can buy at your local building supply store. Unfortunately, they all claim to be the best for every application. Hopefully, the adhesives guide will clear up the confusion.

Nails

Nails and Their Uses

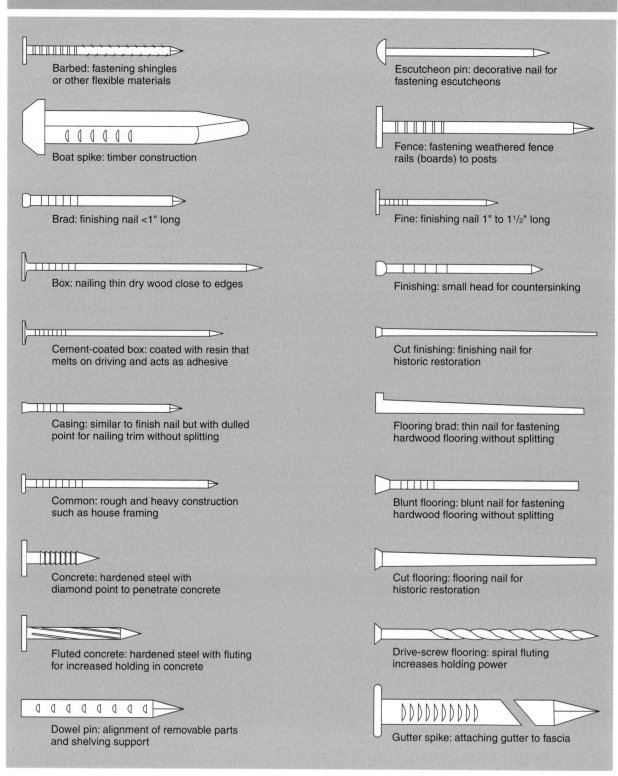

Barbed: fastening shingles or other flexible materials

Boat spike: timber construction

Brad: finishing nail <1" long

Box: nailing thin dry wood close to edges

Cement-coated box: coated with resin that melts on driving and acts as adhesive

Casing: similar to finish nail but with dulled point for nailing trim without splitting

Common: rough and heavy construction such as house framing

Concrete: hardened steel with diamond point to penetrate concrete

Fluted concrete: hardened steel with fluting for increased holding in concrete

Dowel pin: alignment of removable parts and shelving support

Escutcheon pin: decorative nail for fastening escutcheons

Fence: fastening weathered fence rails (boards) to posts

Fine: finishing nail 1" to 1½" long

Finishing: small head for countersinking

Cut finishing: finishing nail for historic restoration

Flooring brad: thin nail for fastening hardwood flooring without splitting

Blunt flooring: blunt nail for fastening hardwood flooring without splitting

Cut flooring: flooring nail for historic restoration

Drive-screw flooring: spiral fluting increases holding power

Gutter spike: attaching gutter to fascia

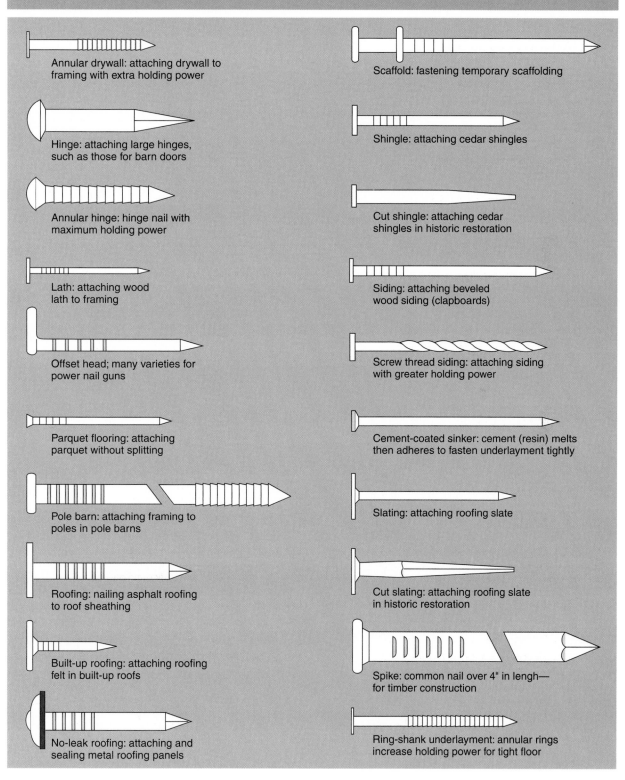

Annular drywall: attaching drywall to framing with extra holding power

Hinge: attaching large hinges, such as those for barn doors

Annular hinge: hinge nail with maximum holding power

Lath: attaching wood lath to framing

Offset head; many varieties for power nail guns

Parquet flooring: attaching parquet without splitting

Pole barn: attaching framing to poles in pole barns

Roofing: nailing asphalt roofing to roof sheathing

Built-up roofing: attaching roofing felt in built-up roofs

No-leak roofing: attaching and sealing metal roofing panels

Scaffold: fastening temporary scaffolding

Shingle: attaching cedar shingles

Cut shingle: attaching cedar shingles in historic restoration

Siding: attaching beveled wood siding (clapboards)

Screw thread siding: attaching siding with greater holding power

Cement-coated sinker: cement (resin) melts then adheres to fasten underlayment tightly

Slating: attaching roofing slate

Cut slating: attaching roofing slate in historic restoration

Spike: common nail over 4" in lengh— for timber construction

Ring-shank underlayment: annular rings increase holding power for tight floor

Nailing Schedule for Light Construction

Table R602.3(1). IRC Fastener Schedule for Structural Members

Description of Building Elements	Number and Type of Fastener[1,2,3]	Spacing of Fasteners
Joist to sill or girder, toenail	3-8d (2½" × 0.113")	—
1x6 subfloor or less to each joist, face nail	2-8d (2½" × 0.113") 2 staples, 1¾"	— —
2" subfloor to joist or girder, blind and face nail	2-16d (3½" × 0.135")	—
Sole plate to joist or blocking, face nail	16d (3½" × 0.135")	16" oc
Top or sole plate to stud, end nail	2-16d (3½" × 0.135")	—
Stud to sole plate, toenail	3-8d (2½" × 0.113") or 2-16d (3½" × 0.135")	— —
Double studs, face nail	10d (3" × 0.128")	24" oc
Double top plates, face nail	10d (3" × 0.128")	24" oc
Sole plate to joist or blocking at braced wall panels	3-16d (3½" × 0.135")	16" oc
Double top plates, minimum 24" offset of end joints, face nail in lapped area	8-16d (3½" × 0.135")	—
Blocking between joists or rafters to top plate, toenail	3-8d (2½" × 0.113")	—
Rim joist to top plate, toenail	8d (2½" × 0.113")	6" oc
Top plates, laps at corners and intersections, face nail	2-10d (3" × 0.128")	—
Built-up header, two pieces with ½" spacer	16d (3½" × 0.135")	16" oc along each edge
Continued header, two pieces	16d (3½" × 0.135")	16" oc along each edge
Ceiling joists to plate, toenail	3-8d (2½" × 0.113")	—
Continuous header to stud, toenail	4-8d (2½" × 0.113")	—
Ceiling joist, laps over partitions, face nail	3-10d (3" × 0.128")	—
Ceiling parallel rafters, face nail	3-10d (3" × 0.128")	—
Rafter to plate, toenail	2-16d (3½" × 0.135")	—
1" brace to each stud and plate, face nail	2-8d (2½" × 0.113") 2 staples, 1¾"	— —
1×6 sheathing to each bearing, face nail	2-8d (2½" × 0.113") 2 staples, 1¾"	— —
1×8 sheathing to each bearing, face nail	2-8d (2½" × 0.113") 3 staples, 1¾"	— —
Wider than 1×8 sheathing to each bearing, face nail	3-8d (2½" × 0.113") 4 staples, 1¾"	— —
Built-up corner studs	10d (3" × 0.128")	24" oc
Built-up girders and beams, 2" lumber layers	10d (3" × 0.128")	Nail each layer 32" oc at top and bottom and staggered. Two nails at ends and splices.
2" planks	2-16d (3½" × 0.135")	At each bearing
Roof rafters to ridge, valley or hip rafters, toenail	4-16d (3½" × 0.135")	—
face nail	3-16d (3½" × 0.135")	—
Rafter ties to rafters, face nail	3-8d (2½" × 0.113")	—
Collar tie to rafter, face nail, or 1¼" × 20-ga ridge strap	3-10d (3" × 0.128")	—

Table R602.3(1). IRC Fastener Schedule for Structural Members—*Continued*

Description of Building Materials	Number and Type of Fastener[1,2,3]	Spacing of Fasteners	
		Edges, in[8]	Intermediate Supports, in[3]
Wood structural panels, subfloor, roof and wall sheathing to framing, and particleboard wall sheathing to framing			
5/16" – 1/2"	6d common (2" × 0.113") nail (subfloor, wall) 8d common (2½" × 0.131") nail (roof)[5]	6	12[6]
19/32" – 1"	8d common (2½" × 0.131")	6	12[6]
1⅛" – 1¼"	10d common (3" × 0.148") nail or 8d (2½" × 0.131") deformed nail	6	12
Other wall sheathing[7]			
½" structural cellulosic fiberboard sheathing	1½" galvanized roofing nail 8d common (2½" × 0.131") nail; staple 16 ga, 1½" long	3	6
25/32" structural cellulosic fiberboard sheathing	1¾" galvanized roofing nail 8d common (2½" × 0.131") nail; staple 16 ga, 1¾" long	3	6
½" gypsum sheathing[4]	1½" galvanized roofing nail 6d common (2" × 0.113") nail; staple galvanized 1½" long; 1¼" screws, Type W or S	4	8
5/8" gypsum sheathing[4]	1¾" galvanized roofing nail 8d common (2½" × 0.131") nail; staple galvanized 1⅝" long; 1⅝" screws, Type W or S	4	8
Wood structural panels, combination subfloor underlayment to framing			
¾" and less	6d deformed (2" × 0.120") nail or 8d common (2½" × 0.131") nail	6	12
7/8" – 1"	8d deformed (2½" × 0.120") nail or 8d common (2½" × 0.131") nail	6	12
1⅛" – 1¼"	8d deformed (2½" × 0.120") nail or 10d common (3" × 0.148") nail	6	12

1. All nails are smooth-common, box, or deformed shanks except where otherwise stated. Nails used for framing and sheathing connections shall have minimum average bending yield strengths as shown: 80 ksi for shank diameter of 0.192" (20d common nail), 90 ksi for shank diameters larger than 0.142" but not larger than 0.177", and 100 ksi for shank diameters of 0.142" or less.

2. Staples are 16-ga wire and have a minimum 7/16" on diameter crown width.

3. Nails shall be spaced at not more than 6" on center at all supports where spans are 48" or greater.

4. 4' by 8' or 4' by 9' panels shall be applied vertically.

5. For regions having basic wind speed of 110 mph or greater, 8d deformed (2½" x 0.120") nails shall be used for attaching plywood and wood structural panel roof sheathing to framing within minimum 48" distance from gable end walls, if mean roof height is more than 25', up to 35' maximum.

6. For regions having basic wind speed of 100 mph or less, nails for attaching wood structural panel roof sheathing to gable end wall framing shall be spaced 6" oc. When basic wind speed is greater than 100 mph, nails for attaching panel roof sheathing to intermediate supports shall be spaced 6" oc for minimum 48" distance from ridges, eaves and gable end walls; and 4" oc to gable end wall framing.

7. Gypsum sheathing shall conform to ASTM C 79 and shall be installed in accordance with GA 253. Fiberboard sheathing shall conform to ASTM C 208.

8. Spacing of fasteners on floor sheathing panel edges applies to panel edges supported by framing members and required blocking and at all floor perimeters only. Spacing of fasteners on roof sheathing panel edges applies to panel edges supported by framing members and required blocking. Blocking of roof or floor sheathing panel edges perpendicular to the framing members need not be provided except as required by other provisions of this code. Floor perimeters shall be supported by framing members or solid blocking.

Estimating Nail Requirements

Use the table below and the residential nailing schedule on pp. 554–555 to estimate your requirements, in pounds, for the most common residential building nails. Note that special coatings such as electroplating, etching, and resin add significantly to nail weight. Hot-dip galvanizing, in particular, can increase weight by 20 percent. You should also allow 5 percent for waste.

Example: How many pounds of nails are required to fasten the floor joists to the sills for a 24- by 40-foot floor? The IRC nailing schedule specifies toenailing three 8d common nails at each joint. Counting the doubled joists at the ends, there are 33 joists, so you need 3 nails × 33 joists × 2 connections = 198 nails. In the table below, you will find there are 106 8d common nails in a pound, so you need 1.77 pounds. Adding 20 percent weight for galvanized finish and an additional 5 percent for waste, you should allow 2.3 pounds.

Nails per Pound

Length, in	Penny weight, d	Type of Nail							
		Box	Casing	Common	Drywall	Finishing	Roofing	Siding	Spike
1	2	—	—	876	—	1351	255	—	—
1¼	3	635	—	568	375	807	210	—	—
1½	4	473	473	316	329	584	180	—	—
1¾	5	406	406	271	289	500	150	—	—
2	6	236	236	181	248	309	138	236	—
2¼	7	210	—	161	—	238	—	236	—
2½	8	145	145	106	—	189	118	210	—
3	10	94	94	69	—	121	—	94	—
3¼	12	87	—	63	—	—	—	—	—
3½	16	71	71	49	—	90	—	—	—
4	20	52	—	31	—	62	—	—	—
4½	30	—	—	24	—	—	—	—	—
5	40	—	—	18	—	—	—	—	—
5½	50	—	—	18	—	—	—	—	—
6	60	—	—	14	—	—	—	—	—
7		—	—	11	—	—	—	—	6
8		—	—	—	—	—	—	—	5
10		—	—	—	—	—	—	—	3
12		—	—	—	—	—	—	—	3

Note: Sinkers up to 12d are ⅛″ shorter than common nails of the same penny size. Sinker of 16d and larger are ¼″ shorter than common nails of the same penny size.

Holding Power of Common Nails

The tables below show the lateral (sideways) resistance and the withdrawal (pulling out) resistance of common nails driven perpendicular to wood grain.

Holding power depends on species group and dry specific gravity (see table at right). Holding power can also be increased by

- surface etching or coating.
- annular or spiral threads.
- clinching (hammering tips over).

Specific Gravities of Wood Species

Species Group	Specific Gravity	Wood Species
I	0.67	Oak, red and white
II	0.55	Southern pine
	0.51	Douglas fir-larch
III	0.45	Eastern Hemlock
	0.42	Hem-fir, Spruce-pine-fir
IV	0.38	Eastern white pine
	0.31	Northern white cedar

Allowable Lateral Loads for Common Nails (lb and in penetration)

Species Group	Common Nail Size, d								
	6	8	10	12	16	20	30	40	60
I	77 (1.2)	97 (1.4)	116 (1.5)	116 (1.5)	133 (1.7)	172 (2.0)	192 (2.1)	218 (2.3)	275 (2.7)
II	63 (1.3)	78 (1.5)	94 (1.7)	94 (1.7)	108 (1.8)	139 (2.2)	155 (2.3)	176 (2.5)	223 (2.9)
III	51 (1.5)	64 (1.7)	77 (2.0)	77 (2.0)	88 (2.2)	114 (2.5)	127 (2.7)	144 (3.0)	182 (3.5)
IV	41 (1.6)	51 (1.9)	61 (2.1)	61 (2.1)	70 (2.3)	91 (2.7)	102 (2.9)	115 (3.2)	146 (3.7)

Allowable Withdrawal Loads[1] for Common Nails (lb)

Specific Gravity[2]	Common Nail Size, d								
	6	8	10	12	16	20	30	40	60
0.75	76	88	99	99	109	129	139	151	177
0.68	59	69	78	78	86	101	109	118	138
0.66	55	64	72	72	79	94	101	110	128
0.62	47	55	62	62	68	80	86	94	110
0.55	35	41	46	46	50	59	64	70	81
0.51	29	34	38	38	42	49	53	58	67
0.47	24	27	31	31	34	40	43	47	55
0.45	21	25	28	28	30	36	39	42	49
0.43	19	22	25	25	27	32	35	38	44
0.41	17	19	22	22	24	29	31	33	39
0.39	15	17	19	19	21	25	27	29	34
0.37	13	15	17	17	19	22	24	26	30
0.33	10	11	13	13	14	17	18	19	23
0.31	8	10	11	11	12	14	15	17	19

[1] Loads are per inch of penetration into member holding point.

[2] Based on oven-dry weight and volume.

Wood Screws

Wood-screw size is specified by diameter gauge (see illustration at bottom) and by length from tip to plane of the wood surface.

Screws are designed to draw two pieces together. For maximum effectiveness, the first piece is drilled out to the diameter of the screw body or shank, while the receiving piece is drilled just large enough to prevent splitting. Drill sizes for pilot holes are listed in the table below.

Maximum wood-screw loads for different wood species are listed in the tables on the facing page.

Pilot Holes for Wood Screws

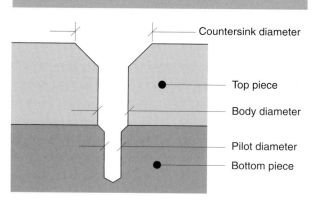

- Countersink diameter
- Top piece
- Body diameter
- Pilot diameter
- Bottom piece

Wood-Screw Pilot Hole Dimensions

Hole	Screw Size									
	2	3	4	5	6	8	10	12	14	16
Body diameter, in	5/64	3/32	7/64	1/8	9/64	5/32	3/16	7/32	15/64	17/64
Pilot Drill: Softwood	#65	#58	1/16	5/64	5/64	3/32	7/64	1/8	11/64	3/16
Hardwood	#56	#54	5/64	3/32	3/32	7/64	1/8	5/32	7/32	15/64
Body Drill	#42	#37	1/8	9/64	9/64	11/64	3/16	7/32	1/4	9/32
Countersink diameter, in	5/32	3/16	7/32	1/4	9/32	11/32	3/8	7/16	15/32	11/16

Wood-Screw Gauges (actual sizes)

20 18 16 14 12 11 10 9 8 7 6 5 4 3 2

Holding Power of Wood Screws

The tables below show the lateral (sideways) resistance and the withdrawal (pulling out) resistance of flathead wood screws driven perpendicular to wood grain.

Holding power depends on species group and dry specific gravity (see table at right). Although the representative wood species for the holding power of common nails on p. 557 are those commonly used in framing, the wood species for screws in the table at right are those commonly used in millwork and cabinetry.

Specific Gravities of Wood Species

Species Group	Specific Gravity	Wood Species
I	0.67	Oak, red and white
	0.63	Sugar maple
II	0.55	Black walnut, teak
	0.50	Black cherry
III	0.45	Honduras mahogany
IV	0.38	Eastern white pine
	0.31	Northern white cedar

Allowable Lateral Loads for Wood Screws (lb and in penetration)

Group	Wood-Screw Size							
	6	8	10	12	14	16	18	20
I	91 (0.97)	129 (1.15)	173 (1.33)	224 (1.51)	281 (1.69)	345 (1.88)	415 (2.06)	492 (2.24)
II	75 (0.97)	106 (1.15)	143 (1.33)	185 (1.51)	232 (1.69)	284 (1.88)	342 (2.06)	406 (2.24)
III	62 (0.97)	87 (1.15)	117 (1.33)	151 (1.51)	190 (1.69)	233 (1.88)	280 (2.06)	332 (2.24)
IV	48 (0.97)	68 (1.15)	91 (1.33)	118 (1.51)	148 (1.69)	181 (1.88)	218 (2.06)	258 (2.24)

Allowable Withdrawal Loads[1] for Wood Screws (lb)

Specific Gravity[2]	Wood-Screw Size							
	6	8	10	12	14	16	18	20
0.75	220	262	304	345	387	428	470	511
0.68	181	215	250	284	318	352	386	420
0.66	171	203	235	267	299	332	364	396
0.62	151	179	207	236	264	293	321	349
0.55	119	141	163	186	208	230	253	275
0.51	102	121	140	160	179	198	217	236
0.47	87	103	119	136	152	168	184	201
0.45	79	94	109	124	139	154	169	184
0.43	72	86	100	113	127	141	154	168
0.41	66	78	91	103	116	128	140	153
0.39	60	71	82	93	105	116	127	138
0.37	54	64	74	84	94	104	114	124
0.33	43	51	59	67	75	83	91	99
0.31	38	45	52	59	66	73	80	87

[1] Loads are per inch of penetration into member holding point.

[2] Based on oven-dry weight and volume.

Screws and Bolts

Screws

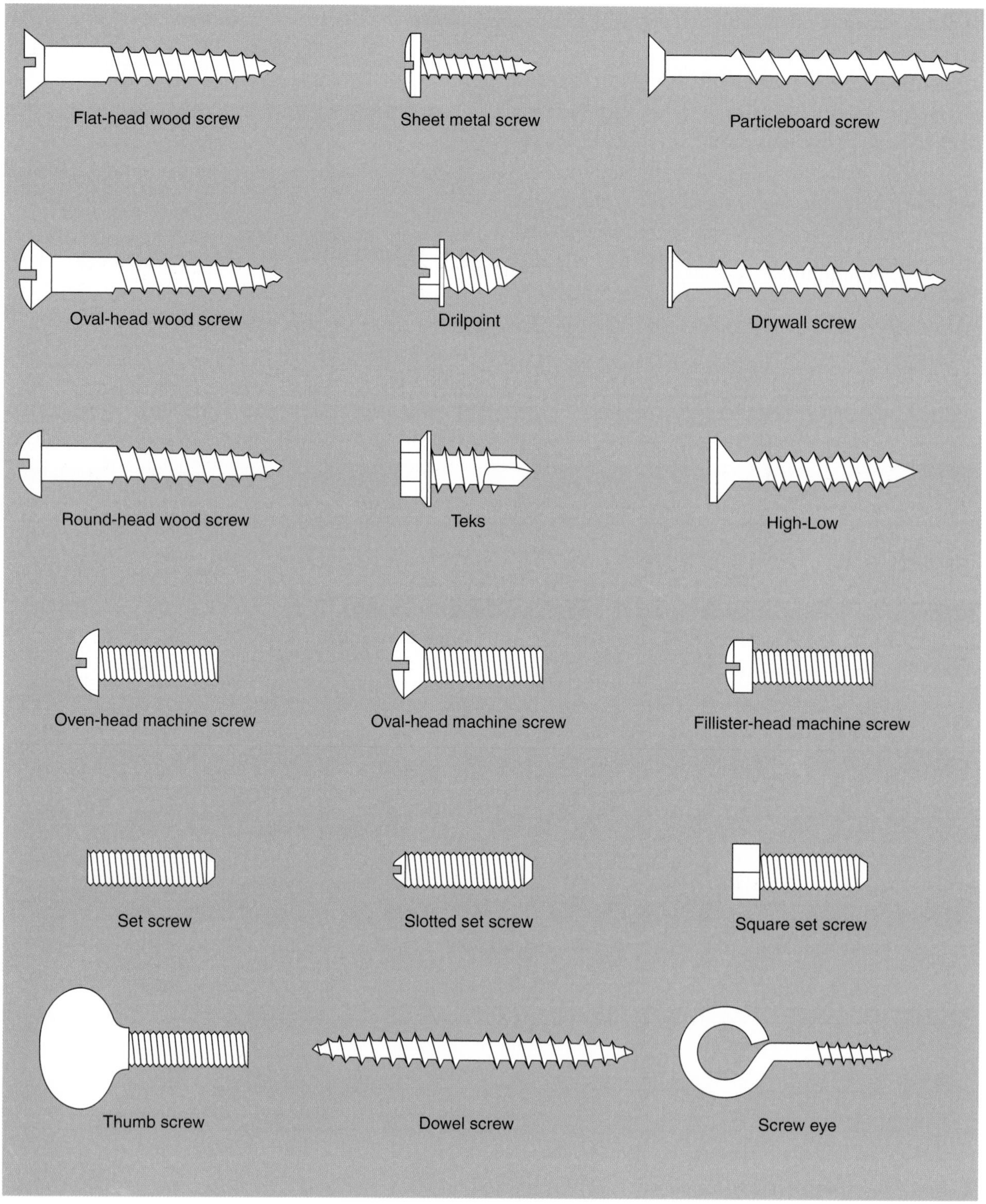

Flat-head wood screw

Sheet metal screw

Particleboard screw

Oval-head wood screw

Drilpoint

Drywall screw

Round-head wood screw

Teks

High-Low

Oven-head machine screw

Oval-head machine screw

Fillister-head machine screw

Set screw

Slotted set screw

Square set screw

Thumb screw

Dowel screw

Screw eye

Bolts

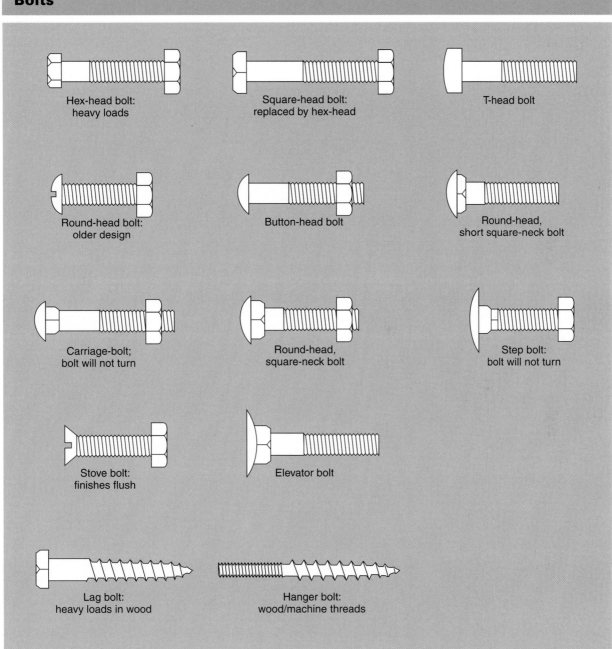

Hex-head bolt:
heavy loads

Square-head bolt:
replaced by hex-head

T-head bolt

Round-head bolt:
older design

Button-head bolt

Round-head,
short square-neck bolt

Carriage-bolt;
bolt will not turn

Round-head,
square-neck bolt

Step bolt:
bolt will not turn

Stove bolt:
finishes flush

Elevator bolt

Lag bolt:
heavy loads in wood

Hanger bolt:
wood/machine threads

Drives

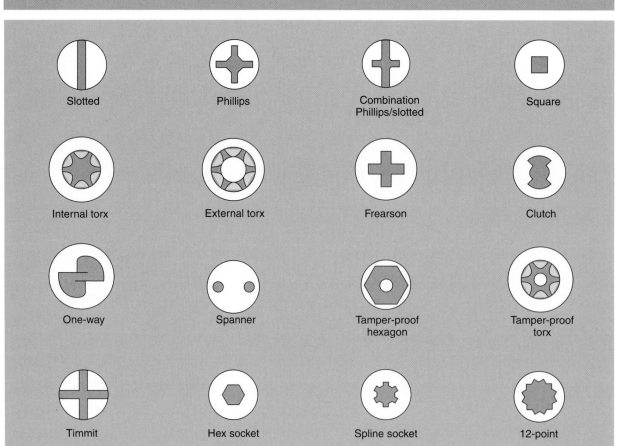

Slotted

Phillips

Combination Phillips/slotted

Square

Internal torx

External torx

Frearson

Clutch

One-way

Spanner

Tamper-proof hexagon

Tamper-proof torx

Timmit

Hex socket

Spline socket

12-point

Washers

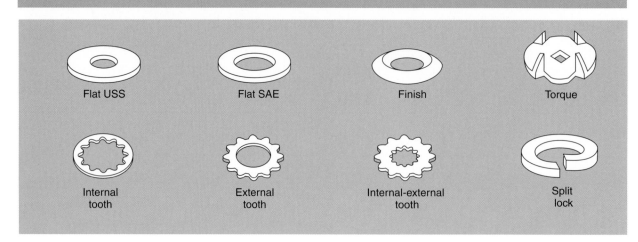

Flat USS

Flat SAE

Finish

Torque

Internal tooth

External tooth

Internal-external tooth

Split lock

Nuts

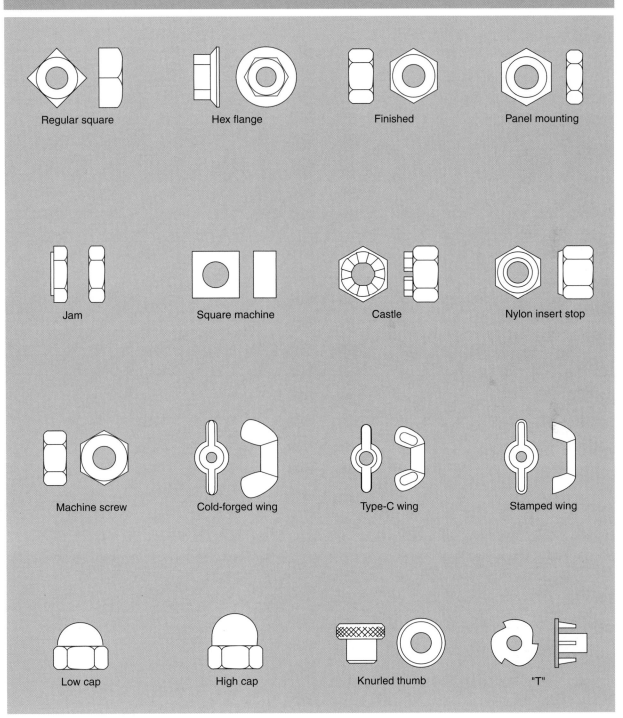

Regular square

Hex flange

Finished

Panel mounting

Jam

Square machine

Castle

Nylon insert stop

Machine screw

Cold-forged wing

Type-C wing

Stamped wing

Low cap

High cap

Knurled thumb

"T"

Metal Framing Connectors—Simpson Strong-Tie

Post and Column Bases

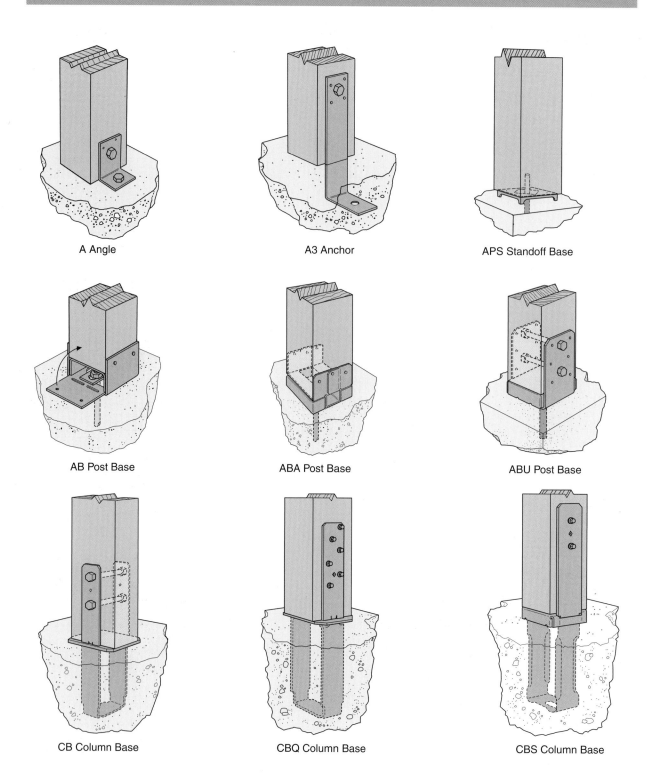

A Angle

A3 Anchor

APS Standoff Base

AB Post Base

ABA Post Base

ABU Post Base

CB Column Base

CBQ Column Base

CBS Column Base

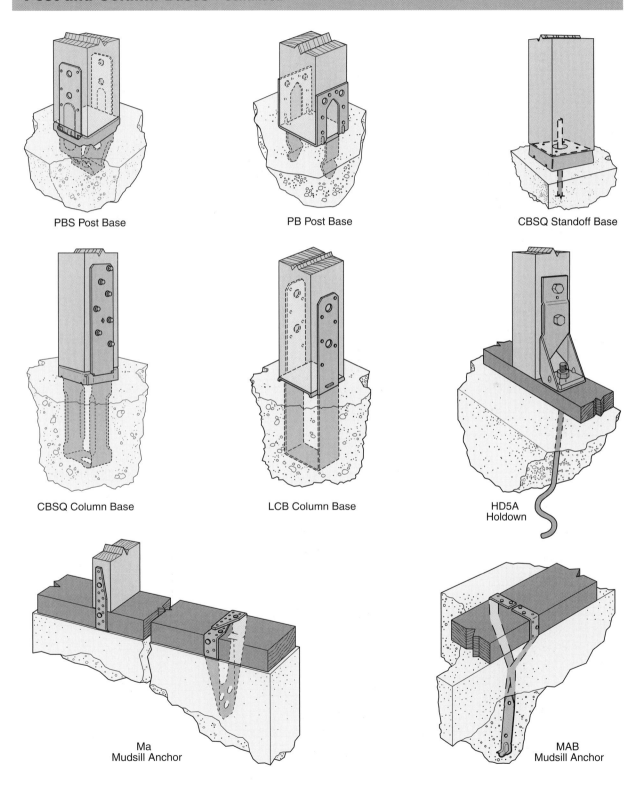

PBS Post Base

PB Post Base

CBSQ Standoff Base

CBSQ Column Base

LCB Column Base

HD5A
Holdown

Ma
Mudsill Anchor

MAB
Mudsill Anchor

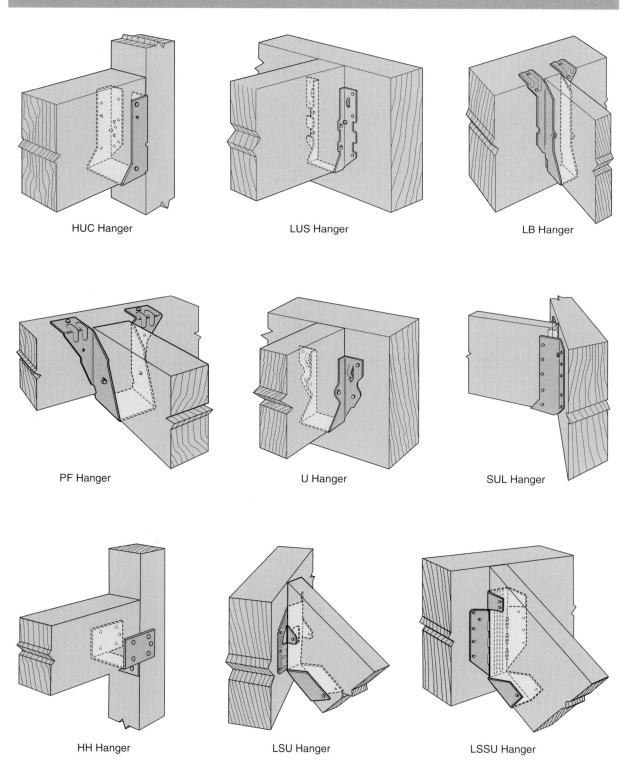

HUC Hanger

LUS Hanger

LB Hanger

PF Hanger

U Hanger

SUL Hanger

HH Hanger

LSU Hanger

LSSU Hanger

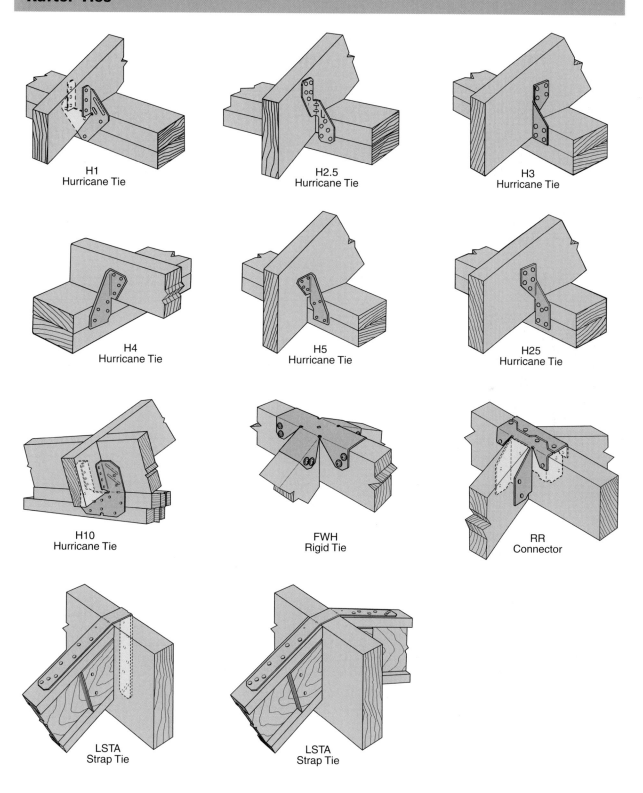

H1
Hurricane Tie

H2.5
Hurricane Tie

H3
Hurricane Tie

H4
Hurricane Tie

H5
Hurricane Tie

H25
Hurricane Tie

H10
Hurricane Tie

FWH
Rigid Tie

RR
Connector

LSTA
Strap Tie

LSTA
Strap Tie

Angles

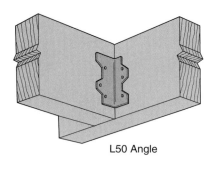

L50 Angle

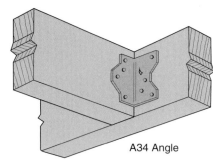

A34 Angle

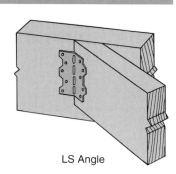

LS Angle

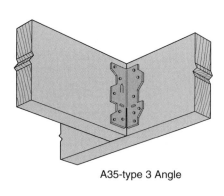

A35-type 3 Angle

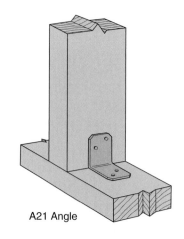

A21 Angle

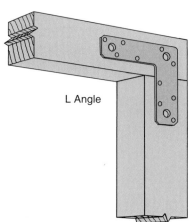

L Angle

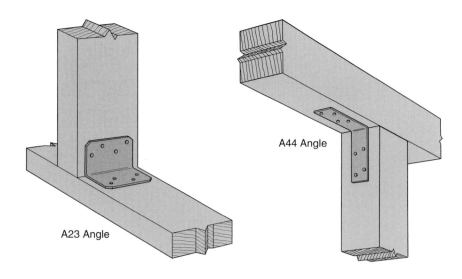

A23 Angle

A44 Angle

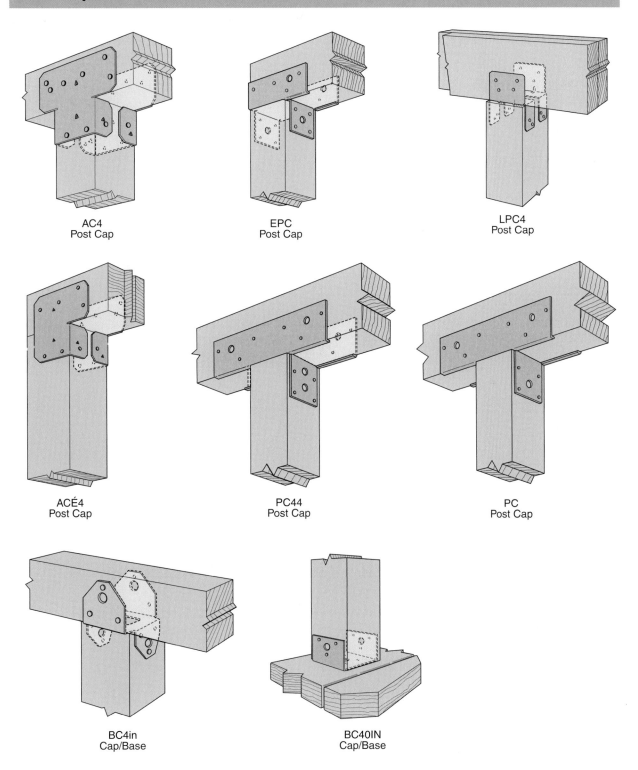

AC4
Post Cap

EPC
Post Cap

LPC4
Post Cap

ACÉ4
Post Cap

PC44
Post Cap

PC
Post Cap

BC4in
Cap/Base

BC40IN
Cap/Base

Ties and Braces

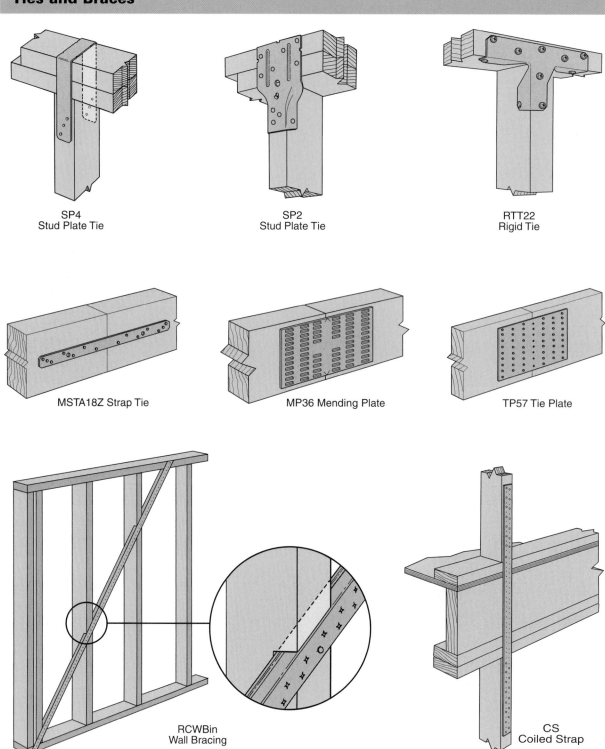

SP4
Stud Plate Tie

SP2
Stud Plate Tie

RTT22
Rigid Tie

MSTA18Z Strap Tie

MP36 Mending Plate

TP57 Tie Plate

RCWBin
Wall Bracing

CS
Coiled Strap

Deck Ties and Fence Brackets

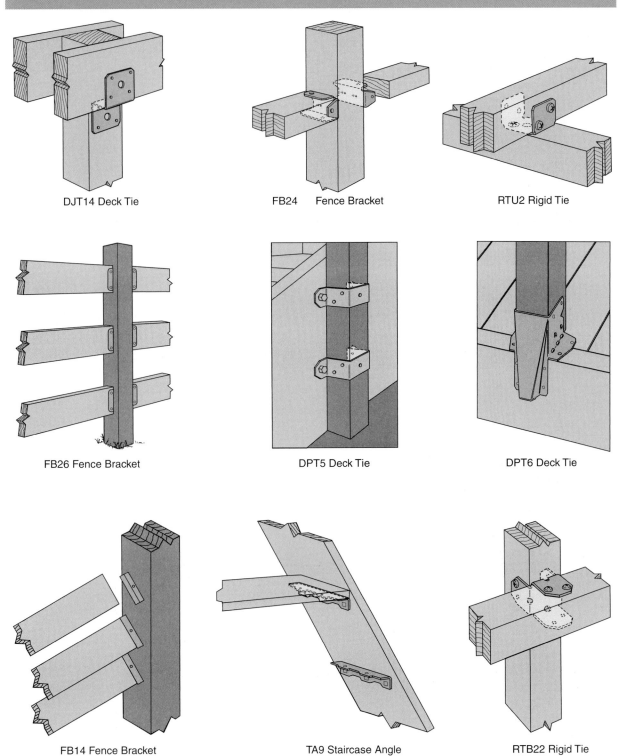

DJT14 Deck Tie

FB24　Fence Bracket

RTU2 Rigid Tie

FB26 Fence Bracket

DPT5 Deck Tie

DPT6 Deck Tie

FB14 Fence Bracket

TA9 Staircase Angle

RTB22 Rigid Tie

Adhesives

	Ceramic	Fabric	Glass	Leather	Metal
Ceramic	Krazy Glue® Super Glue™ Zap®	3M®77	Loctite® 349 GE® Silicone II Weldbond®	Household Goop® 3M 77	LePage® Metal Epoxy J-B Weld® Faststeel® Epoxy Putty
Fabric	3M 77 Elmer's Carpenter's LePage Bondfast	Sobo® Rhoplex™ 3M 77	3M 77 Weldbond Hot Glue	Barge 3M 77 Sobo	3M 77
Glass	Loctite 349 Impruv GE Silicone II Weldbond	3M 77 Weldbond Hot Glue	Locktite Impruv Household Goop Krazy Glue	GE Silicone II Seal-All Household Goop	Loctite Impruv J-B Weld
Leather	Household Goop 3M 77	Barge 3M 77 Sobo	GE Silicone II Seal-All Household Goop	Barge	Household Goop
Metal	LePage Metal Epoxy J-B Weld Faststeel Epoxy Putty	3M 77	Loctite Impruv J-B Weld	Household Goop	LePage Metal Epoxy J-B Weld Faststeel Epoxy Putty
Paper	3M 77	Sobo Rhoplex 3M 77	3M 77 Weldbond Hot Glue	3M 77 Sobo Yamato Sticking Paste	LePage Metal Epoxy J-B Weld Faststeel Epoxy Putty
Plastic	Household Goop	3M 80 3M 77	Loctite Impruv Household Goop Weldbond	Barge	LePage Metal Epoxy J-B Weld Faststeel Epoxy Putty
Rubber	Household Goop Hot Glue	Barge 3M 77	GE Silicone II Seal-All	Barge 3M 80	Household Goop 3M 80
Polystyrene	LePage Reg. Epoxy Hot Glue Weldbond	Hot Glue Weldbond 3M 77	LePage Reg. Epoxy 3M 77 Weldbond	Hot Glue LePage Press-Tite	LePage Metal Epoxy J-B Weld Faststeel Epoxy Putty
Vinyl	Household Goop 3M 80	Sobo Rhoplex Barge	GE Silicone II Seal-All	Barge 3M 80	Household Goop 3M 80
Wood	LePage 5-min Epoxy	LePage Bulldog Grip	GE Silicone II Weldbond Hot Glue	Barge LePage Press-Tite 3M Fastbond® 30NF	LePage Metal Epoxy LePage Press-Tite 3M Fastbond 30NF

Paper	Plastic	Rubber	Polystyrene	Vinyl	Wood
3M 77	Household Goop	Household Goop Hot Glue 3M 80	LePage's Regular Epoxy Hot Glue Weldbond	Household Goop 3M 80	LePage's 5 Min Epoxy LePage's Bulldog Grip
Sobo Rhoplex Elmer's Carpenter's	3M 80 3M 77	Barge 3M 77	Hot Glue Weldbond 3M 77	Sobo Rhoplex Barge	3M 77 Elmer's Carpenter's LePage Bondfast
3M 77 Weldbond Hot Glue	Loctite Impruv Household Goop Weldbond	GE Silicone II Seal-All	LePage Reg Epoxy 3M 77 Weldwood	GE Silicone II Seal-All	GE Silicone II Weldbond Hot Glue
3M 77 Sobo Rhoplex	Barge	Barge 3M 80	Hot Glue LePage Press-Tite	Barge 3M 80	Barge LePage Press-Tite 3M Fastbond 30NF
LePage Metal Epoxy Faststeel Epoxy Putty 3M 77 (large areas)	LePage Metal Epoxy J-B Weld Faststeel Epoxy Putty	Household Goop 3M 80	LePage Metal Epoxy J-B Weld Faststeel Epoxy Putty	Household Goop 3M 80	LePage Metal Epoxy Faststeel Epoxy Putty 3M Fastbond 30NF
Uhu® Glue Sobo Rhoplex	3M 80 3M 77	Barge 3M 77	3M 77 Weldbond Hot Glue	Barge 3M 77	3M 77 Yamato Sticking Paste
3M 80 3M 77	PVC Adhesive Household Goop LePage 5-min Epoxy	Barge 3M 80 LePage Press-Tite	Lepage Reg. Epoxy Hot Glue	3M 80 Hot Glue	Household Goop LePage 5-min Epoxy
Barge 3M 77	Barge 3M 80 LePage Press-Tite	3M 80 Barge	LePage PL-200 3M 77	LePage Press-Tite Barge 3M 80	Barge LePage Press-Tite 3M Fastbond 30N
3M 77 Weldbond Hot Glue	Lepage Reg. Epoxy Hot Glue	LePage PL-200 3M 77	Weldbond LePage Press-Tite 3M 77	Hot Glue 3M 77	Elmer's Polyurethane LePage Universal Gorilla Glue®
Barge 3M 77	3M 80 Hot Glue Household Goop	LePage Press-Tite Barge 3M 80	Hot Glue 3M 77	LePage Press-Tite 3M Fastbond 30NF Sobo	Elmer's Carpenter LePage Press-Tite 3M Fastbond 30NF
3M 77 Yamato Sticking Paste	Household Goop LePage 5-min Epoxy LePage Press-Tite	Barge LePage Press-Tite 3M Fastbond 30NF	Elmer's Polyurethane LePage Universal Gorilla Glue	Elmer's Carpenter LePage Press-Tite 3M Fastbond 30NF	Elmer's Carpenter LePage Outdoor Wood Tite-Bond

Decks

Good residential design incorporates outdoor spaces into the overall plan. Decks can provide graceful transitions from enclosed living/dining areas to the outdoors.

After settling on a design, the first task is the *layout* of the deck's outside frame dimensions. This allows for precise location of the *foundation*.

Framing consists of connecting the posts, beams, and joists. A wide variety of metal framing aids (see Chapter 21, "Fasteners") make assembling the frame simpler than ever.

Grade level changes allow for interesting *level changes* in the deck itself. Visual interest can also be increased by varying the *decking patterns*.

Rails and guards are required whenever a deck is more than 30 inches above the ground, whereas *stairs* provide access to ground-level spaces.

No matter how ambitious your design, you will find that complex decks are really nothing more than combinations of simple deck designs, We include three *design examples* of varying complexity to get you started.

Layout and Foundation

Establishing a square-cornered layout

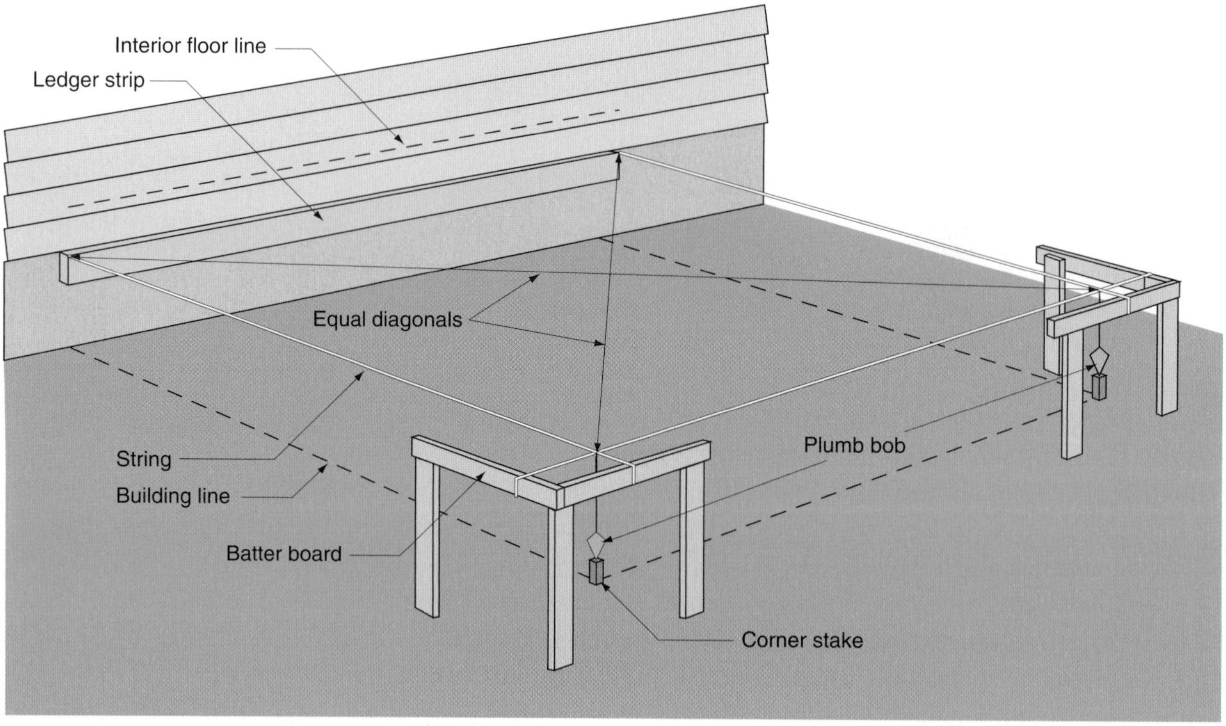

Interior floor line
Ledger strip
Equal diagonals
String
Building line
Batter board
Plumb bob
Corner stake

Setting the Posts

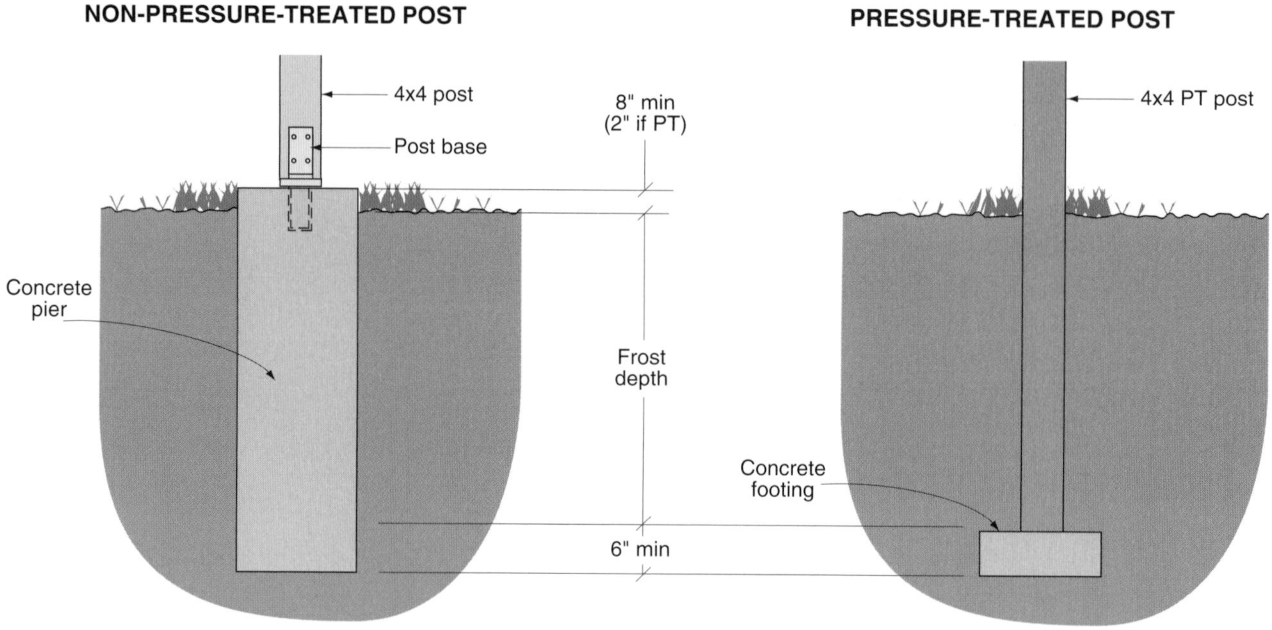

NON-PRESSURE-TREATED POST

4x4 post
Post base
8" min (2" if PT)
Concrete pier
Frost depth
6" min

PRESSURE-TREATED POST

4x4 PT post
Concrete footing

Framing

ATTACHING TO BUILDING

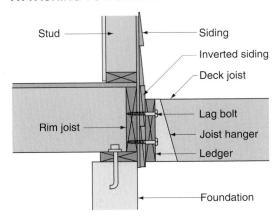

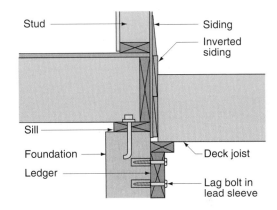

POSTS AND BEAMS

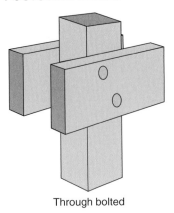

Through bolted

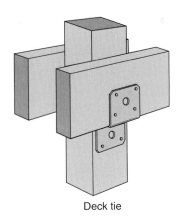

Deck tie

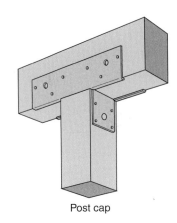

Post cap

BEAMS AND JOISTS

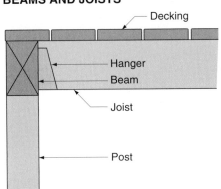

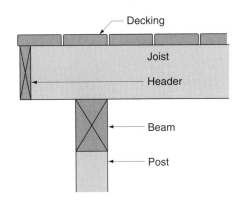

Level Changes

A Variety of Methods for Making Elevation Changes

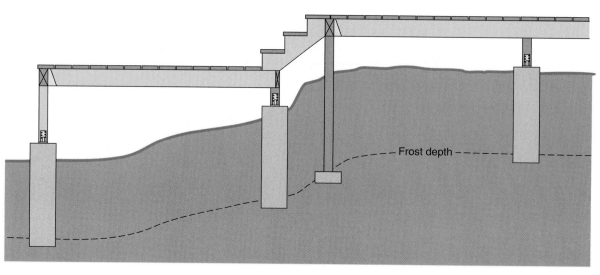

Post base

Frost depth

Frost depth

Frost depth

Frost depth

Decking Patterns

DIAGONAL

HERRINGBONE

CURVED

ANGLED

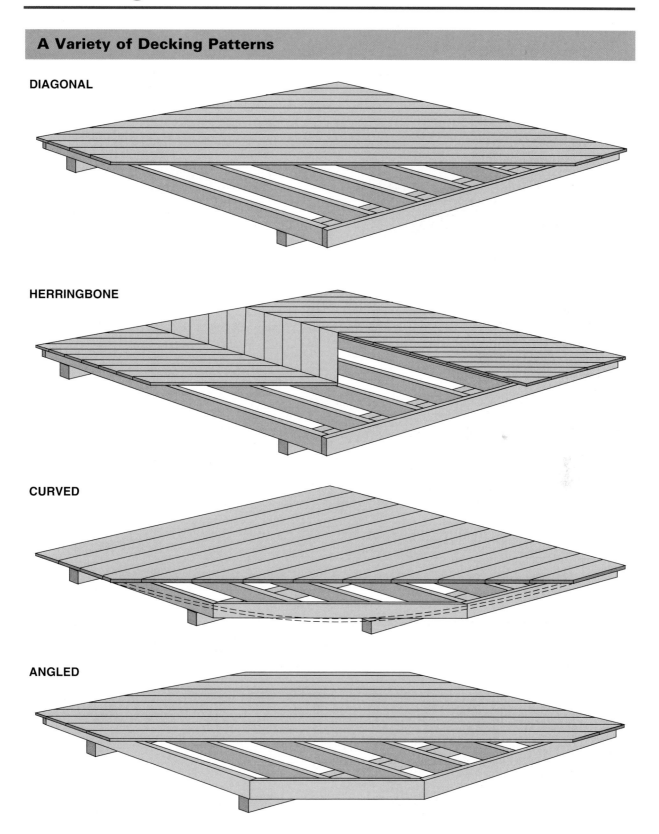

Rails and Guards

OUTSIDE HORIZONTAL RAILS

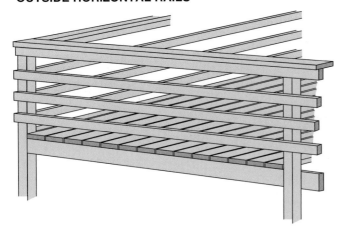

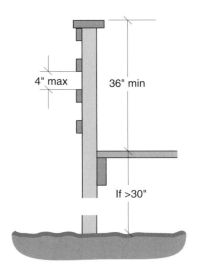

INSIDE HORIZONTAL RAILS

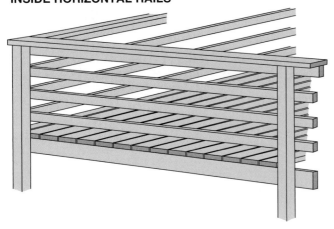

OUTSIDE BALUSTERS

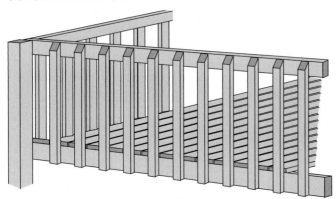

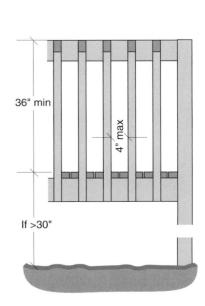

Stairs

FIGURING RISE AND RUN

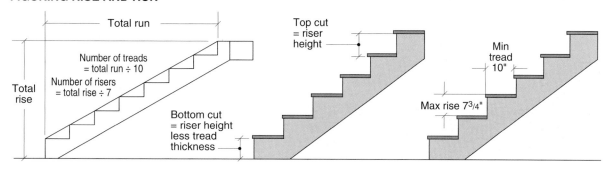

Total run

Number of treads = total run ÷ 10

Number of risers = total rise ÷ 7

Total rise

Bottom cut = riser height less tread thickness

Top cut = riser height

Min tread 10"

Max rise 7³/4"

HUNG STRINGERS

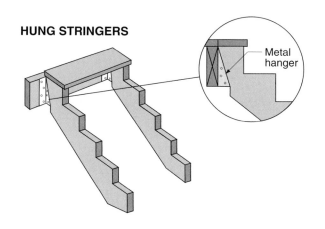

Metal hanger

BOLTED STRINGERS

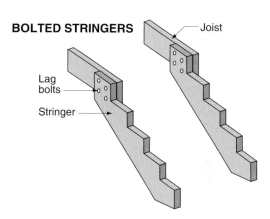

Joist

Lag bolts

Stringer

OPEN TREAD

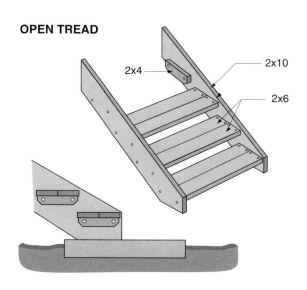

2x4

2x10

2x6

CLOSED TREAD

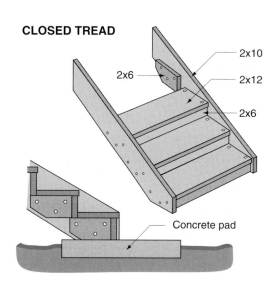

2x10

2x6

2x12

2x6

Concrete pad

Design Examples

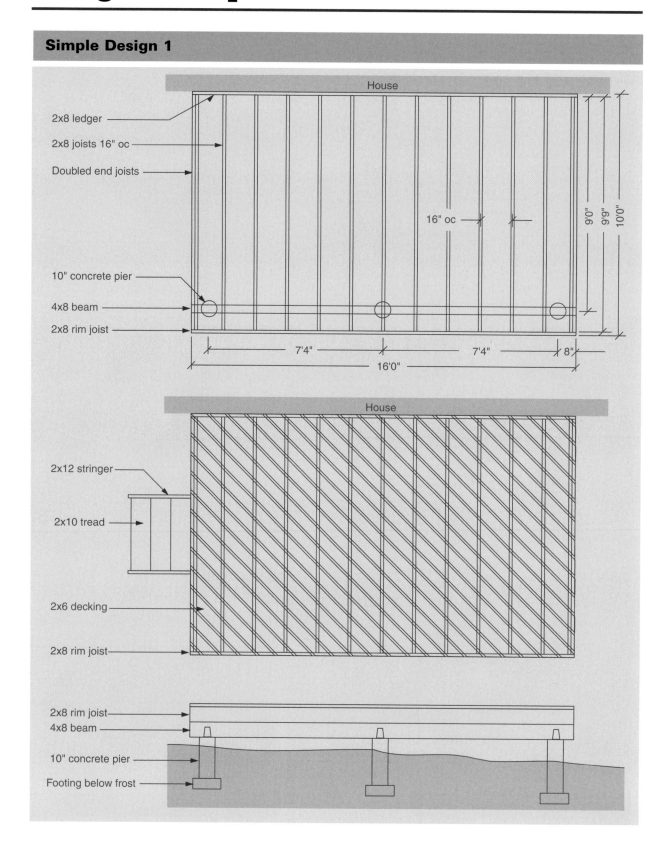

- 2x8 ledger
- 2x8 joists 16" oc
- Doubled end joists
- 16" oc
- 9'0"
- 9'9"
- 10'0"
- 10" concrete pier
- 4x8 beam
- 2x8 rim joist
- 7'4"
- 7'4"
- 8"
- 16'0"
- House
- 2x12 stringer
- 2x10 tread
- 2x6 decking
- 2x8 rim joist
- House
- 2x8 rim joist
- 4x8 beam
- 10" concrete pier
- Footing below frost

582   DECKS

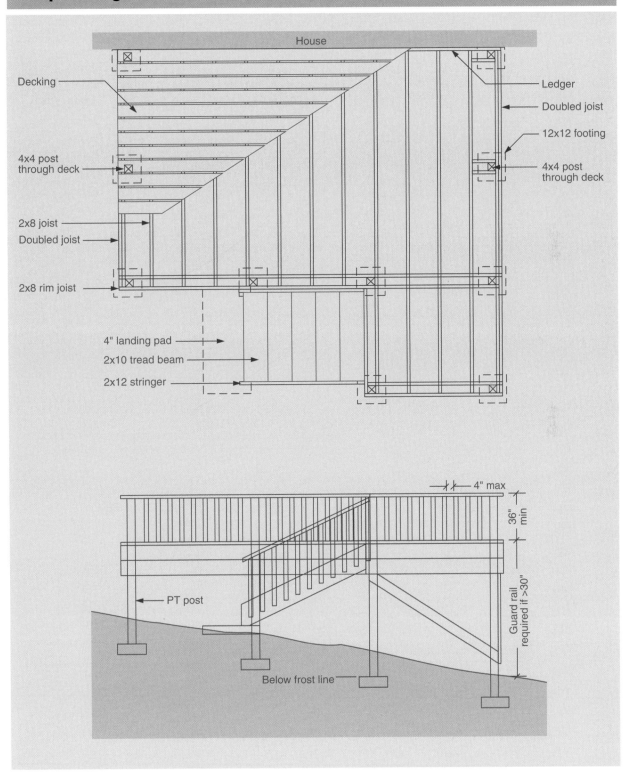

House

Decking

Ledger

Doubled joist

12x12 footing

4x4 post
through deck

4x4 post
through deck

2x8 joist

Doubled joist

2x8 rim joist

4" landing pad

2x10 tread beam

2x12 stringer

4" max

36"
min

Guard rail
required if >30"

PT post

Below frost line

Multilevel Design

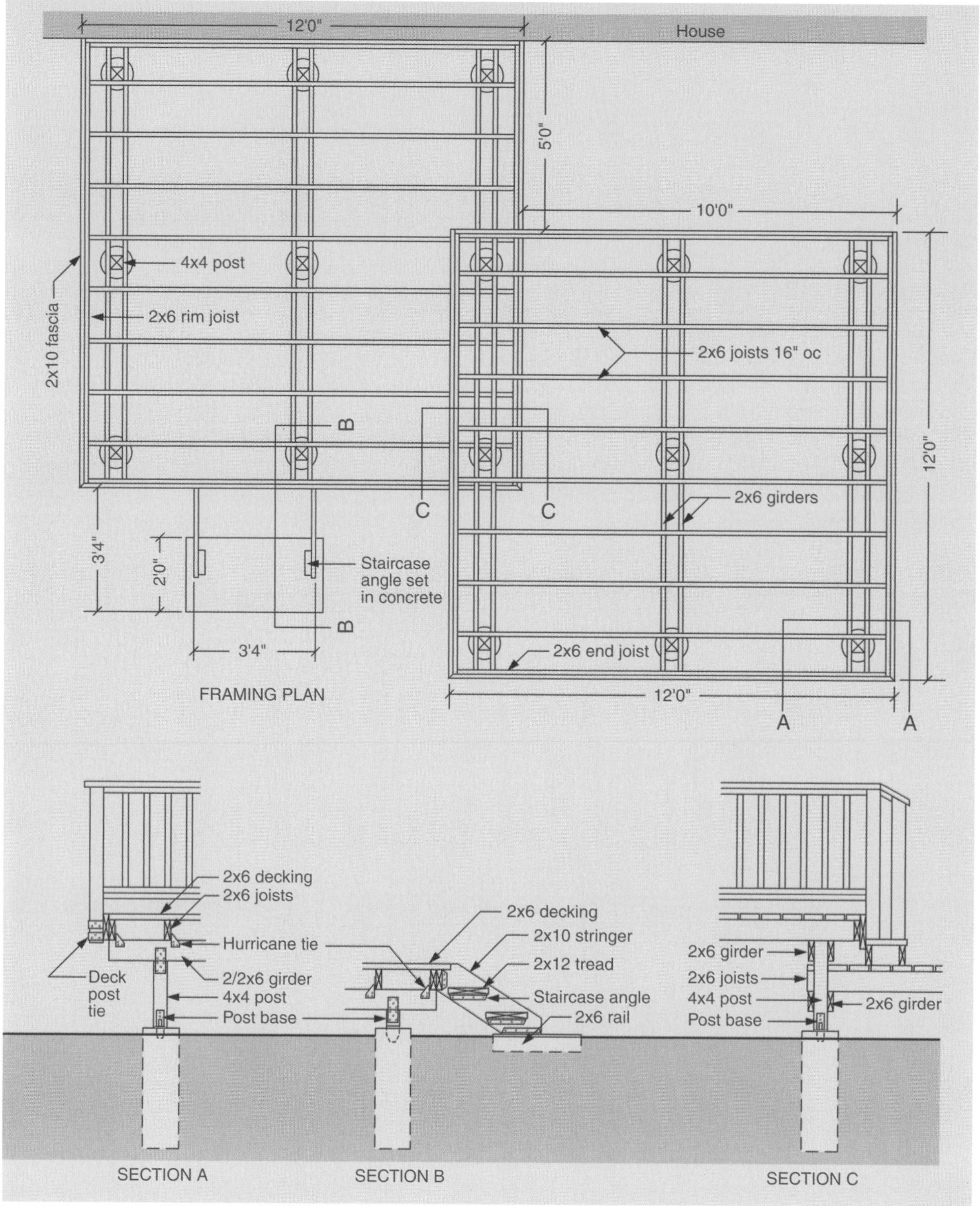

12'0"
House
5'0"
10'0"
4x4 post
2x10 fascia
2x6 rim joist
2x6 joists 16" oc
B
C
C
2x6 girders
12'0"
3'4"
2'0"
Staircase angle set in concrete
B
3'4"
2x6 end joist
FRAMING PLAN
12'0"
A
A
2x6 decking
2x6 joists
Hurricane tie
Deck post tie
2/2x6 girder
4x4 post
Post base
2x6 decking
2x10 stringer
2x12 tread
Staircase angle
2x6 rail
2x6 girder
2x6 joists
4x4 post
2x6 girder
Post base
SECTION A
SECTION B
SECTION C

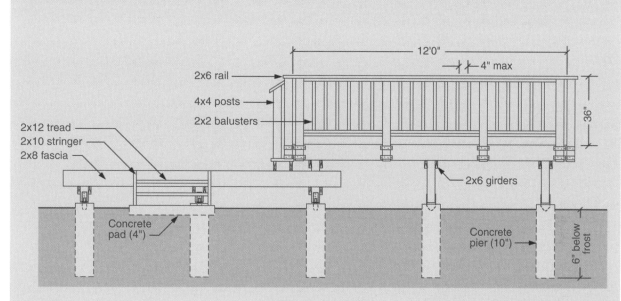

2x6 rail

4x4 posts

2x2 balusters

12'0"

4" max

36"

2x12 tread
2x10 stringer
2x8 fascia

2x6 girders

Concrete
pad (4")

Concrete
pier (10")

6" below
frost

FRONT ELEVATION

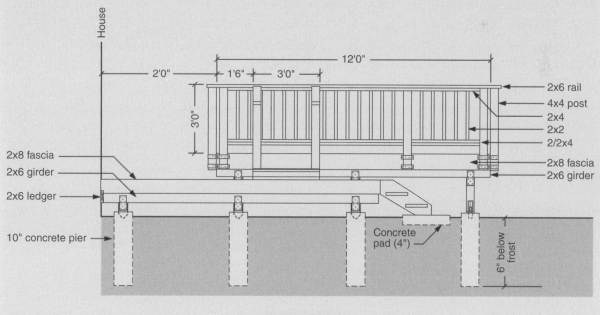

House

2'0"

1'6"

3'0"

12'0"

3'0"

2x6 rail
4x4 post
2x4
2x2
2/2x4

2x8 fascia
2x6 girder

2x8 fascia
2x6 girder
2x6 ledger

10" concrete pier

Concrete
pad (4")

6" below
frost

LEFT ELEVATION

Sustainable Building

Sustainable, or "green," building implies reducing the environmental impact (global warming, consumption of nonrenewable resources, destruction of natural habitats) of our built environment. It also implies protecting occupant health through improved air quality. Thus it involves nearly every aspect of building. In this chapter we will identify the most salient issues.

As has been true since the cave, your building *site* will have considerable influence on your use (and possible production) of energy. And you may be surprised at the important roles the *foundation* plays in annual heating and cooling costs and indoor air quality.

In sustainable building the *frame* plays a dual role in conserving natural resources (wood) and energy (through its insulation). But the frame is just the skeleton for the all-important *thermal envelope*, the key to maintaining a healthy, dry, warm, or cool environment.

Special elements in the envelope are the *windows*. No longer is a window just a piece of glass in a frame. Today's high-tech glazings should be matched to orientation and climate.

No matter how tight the envelope, the building will require systems for supplemental *heating and cooling*. We show how to minimize the cost of installing and operating both.

No areas of electrical use offer greater potential for savings than *lights and appliances*, and most of these savings can be as easily achieved in existing homes as in new.

In some areas *water* is of as great concern as energy. We discuss the conservation of both water and the energy used in heating it.

Although an energy-saving envelope is necessarily an air-tight envelope, we don't have to suffer poor interior *air quality*. We show how, in many cases, to make the air inside your home healthier than the air outside.

Once we have created an optimally efficient structure, we are in a good position to supply much, if not most, of our heating, cooling, and electrical needs from *renewable energies*.

The Site

Architects say, "You can't build a good house on a bad site." This is especially true of a "green" house. If you wish to take advantage of free energy from the sun, the free shade offered by deciduous trees, free ventilating and cooling breezes, and clean air, the site must provide them.

Site for Natural Drainage

Water runs downhill. It also seeks its own level, which in spring is the natural seasonal high-water table. A full in-the-ground basement in soil having a high water table is little more than a dug well. Therefore, build either in well-drained soil (see p. 37) having a low water table or into a sloping hillside.

Build on a Southern Slope

You have probably noticed that spring seems to arrive earlier on south-sloping ground. That is because a square foot of ground tilted ten degrees toward the noon sun receives the same intensity of solar radiation as a square foot of level ground located ten degrees (690 miles) to the south. The opposite is, of course, true of building on a northern slope. Imagine—a difference of nearly 1,400 miles in solar ground warming just by moving from a north slope to a south slope!

A second powerful reason for building on a slope is "cold ponding." On clear nights the ground radiates infrared energy toward the cold of deep space. The result can be seen as dew or frost on your automobile and lawn. Not seen is the layer of chilled air in contact with the ground. Being more dense, this chilled air flows downward and accumulates in low spots. If you build in such a low spot, on clear nights your house may be immersed in a pond of air 10°F–20°F colder than average.

Verify Solar Access

Radiation from the sun is the only totally free heat source. There is a lot of kinetic energy in wind, but an expensive wind turbine is required to convert it to electricity before we can use the energy. All you

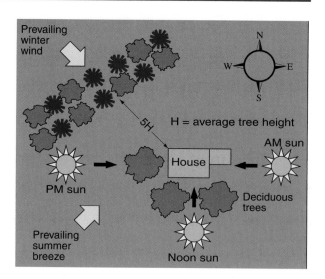

have to do to capture solar heat is face your windows toward the sun. The key is whether the sun's rays have a clear path or whether they are blocked by neighboring buildings or trees (see pp. 506–507).

Utilize Existing Trees

Developers often make the mistake of clear-cutting a site before building. From their standpoint, trees are nothing more than obstacles complicating material deliveries and landscaping. Mature trees may, however, have a great influence on the microclimate of the site (see illustration and pp. 46–47). As a shelterbelt they may block the prevailing winter wind and channel cooling summer breezes. Mature deciduous trees, such as maple and oak, may provide all of the summer shading needed to prevent a passive solar structure from overheating, while admitting the desired winter radiation.

Yes, such trees may be planted after construction, but they won't become fully effective for at least forty years. Can you wait that long?

Locate Upwind of Pollution

This should be a no-brainer. If you have no choice but to locate in an area with sources of pollution (pig farm, anyone?), consult the local weather office or the maps on p. 45 to better your chances of being upwind most of the time.

The Foundation

The very word says it best. The *foundation*, that upon which all else rests or depends, is the single most important part of a building. Unfortunately, its mass—its "concreteness"—leads us to ignore many issues which must be addressed if it is to serve as the foundation of a truly sustainable building.

Moistureproof the Foundation

Concrete is, to a small degree, porous. Liquid water on one side of a concrete floor or wall will find its way out the opposite surface in the form of water vapor or as liquid water through joints and cracks. Builders have long applied asphalt-based coatings to the outside of walls to seal against moisture, but a combination of a rubber-based sealant, or 6-mil black polyethylene, and a drainage pad is much more effective.

Manage Rainwater Runoff

Without gutters, rainwater falling on the roof ends up in the worst possible place, next to the foundation. A combination of grading the soil away from the foundation and gutters with leaders (see pp. 274–275) to discharge the water far from the foundation can eliminate this large source of moisture.

Install Perimeter Drains

Even if all roof and surface water is disposed of, a soil water table higher than the foundation footing can turn a basement or crawl space into a shallow well. Perimeter drains (see illustration and pp. 84–93) around the outside of the footings lower the water table to their own level; i.e., below the level of the floor.

Where available, discharge the perimeter drains into city storm sewers. If the site slopes sufficiently, run the underground drain downslope so that it breaks ground below floor level. If neither is possible, install both exterior and interior perimeter drains and discharge them into a sump pit. Discharge the sump pump far away from the foundation, and provide a backup battery or generator in case of power outages.

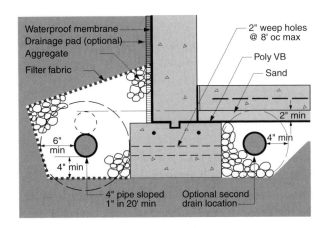

Insulate the Foundation

In an otherwise well-insulated house, an uninsulated foundation can account for 25 percent of total heat loss. In fact, because the R-value of an 8-inch concrete wall is 1.4, homes with uninsulated crawl spaces and basements effectively sit on about 200 square feet of window. And because soil is not much better as an insulator, even slabs on grade lose heat.

The great mass of a concrete foundation makes it a significant thermal mass. Enclosing the concrete within the thermal envelope (see p. 370) by placing the insulation on the exterior, we make a building less susceptible to ambient temperature swings.

Being tough and completely waterproof, extruded polystyrene (see p. 375) is the insulation of choice for exterior application. Follow the recommendations on p. 82 (basements), p. 90 (crawl spaces), and p. 96 (slabs on grade) for R-values and depths.

Where exterior application is prohibited by code (local codes may ban it due to termites), interior application is possible. If your code bans exterior foam, point out to the code official that termites can be stopped by sheet metal sandwiched between the concrete and foam and the building sill.

Because below-grade concrete is generally cooler than interior air both winter and summer, mold-promoting moisture may condense on the concrete surface. Therefore, cover the concrete with at least one inch of closed-cell foam before adding any fibrous insulation.

Consider a Frost-Protected Slab

Much of the cost and material savings of a slab-on-grade foundation may be negated by the requirement of a stem wall extending below the depth of frost. In northern areas, frost depths can be 6 feet or more. A green solution is the well-documented and proven frost-protected slab (see top illustration and p. 97). The combination of horizontal perimeter insulation and heat from the earth and from under the slab prevents frost from reaching under the grade beam.

Do Not Vent a Crawl Space

Building codes previously insisted on crawl spaces being ventilated to avoid condensation during summer months. A minimum of four vents, one on each wall, located no farther than 3 feet from each corner were specified for rectangular crawl spaces.

Things have changed. Unless the building is on posts, allowing free flow of air under the building, it is now considered better to seal and insulate the perimeter walls and treat the space as part of the conditioned space. The IRC calls for a continuous vapor-retarder ground cover of either 6-mil polyethylene or 45-mil EPDM. The retarder sheets must overlap by at least 6 inches and be sealed or taped, and the retarder must extend at least 6 inches up the foundation walls and be fastened and sealed to the wall. In addition, the crawl space must either serve as a heat-distribution plenum or be provided a minimum of 1 cfm per 50 square feet of forced ventilating air.

Specify Fly-Ash Concrete

The combustion of coal produces two pollutants: carbon dioxide, the chief cause of global warming, and fly ash, the solid mineral residue. Every ton of coal burned pushes 2.7 tons of carbon dioxide into the atmosphere and leaves behind about 300 pounds of fly ash. Altogether, about 130 million tons of fly ash pile up every year.

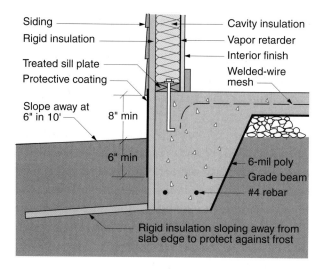

In addition, manufacturing cement, which mainly consists of heating limestone to drive off the hydrated water, is responsible for about 8 percent of all carbon dioxide production.

Here is the good news: Waste fly ash can be used as a partial substitute for cement in concrete. Fly-ash concrete is a win-win sustainable product: 1) a use is found for waste which otherwise clogs landfills, 2) the concrete requires 15 to 50 percent less cement, and 3) the resulting concrete is actually stronger and more crack-resistant than standard concrete.

The Frame

Although timber framing results in beautiful "feel-good" buildings, it requires the use of large timbers. Unless you are lucky enough to find sufficient salvaged timber or FSC-certified timber, you may be violating the principle of sustainability of natural resources.

But timber frames account for a very small percentage of lumber usage today, not because of the sustainability issue, but because of the relatively high cost of the timbers and the skilled labor required for the joinery. As the availability of long lengths of relatively clear logs has diminished, the wood industry has responded with increasing types and quantities of "engineered lumber."

Use Engineered Lumber

The manufacture of engineered lumber consists of taking a log apart, removing knots and other defects, and regluing it in a way that maximizes its strength. An I-Joist, for example, consists of a thin web of OSB separating upper and lower 2×2 solid wood chords. The engineered joist is twice as strong, yet uses half as much wood fiber. Its use reduces not only the consumption of wood, but the overall cost of construction, as well.

Use Advanced (OVE) Framing

Advanced, or optimum-value-engineered, framing uses engineered lumber wherever possible and eliminates components of the standard platform frame wherever not required for structural integrity. By this double-barreled approach, the system reduces the amount of wood fiber in the frame by as much as 40 percent.

Treat the Frame and Insulation as a System

Coincidentally, advanced framing also reduces the amount of thermal bridging—the thermal short-circuiting of insulation by relatively conductive framing members. Advanced framing also fits windows into the regular openings between studs, eliminating

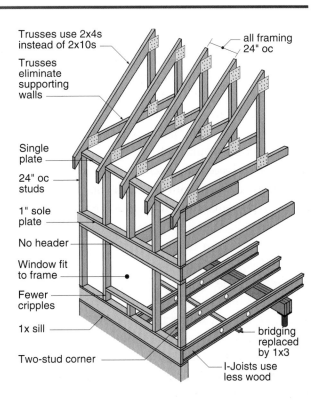

most of the need for jacks and headers. Rather than cutting and fitting fiberglass batts into numerous odd-dimensioned stud spaces, the 24-inch on-center frame and 24-inch batts now work as a system.

Consider SIPs

Structural insulated panels (SIPS) (see pp. 392–393) take a further step toward the insulation ideal. Consisting of foam insulation sandwiched between OSB structural panels, they completely eliminate the thermal bridging of framing members. Precut in the factory and assembled on-site by factory-trained workers, SIPs enclose a building quickly, and the resulting thermal envelope is tighter than its stick-built equivalent.

Specify FSC-Certified Lumber

One of the basic principles of sustainable building is to avoid the destruction of diminishing natural forest habitats and old-growth timber. Purchasing only Forest Stewardship Council (FSC) certified lumber is the best way to assure you are doing your part.

The Thermal Envelope

The primary function of the thermal envelope is easily understood: to conserve energy by keeping heat inside the house in winter and outside the house in summer. Think of the envelope as a thermos bottle. A hot liquid placed in the thermos will remain warm, if not hot, for many hours. Similarly, a cold liquid will remain cold, even in a warm environment. The way in which the thermos is constructed resists heat flow either into or out of the interior to a remarkable degree.

This is what we desire of our home's thermal envelope. However, the devil is in the details. Here are the design principles for creating a sustainable thermal envelope.

Define the Thermal Envelope

The thermal envelope (see illustration at right and pp. 369–399) is defined as the complete assemblage of surfaces separating the conditioned (heated and/or cooled) interior spaces from the outside environment. The operative term is *complete*. Ignoring holes, cracks, and seemingly unimportant surfaces—such as basement walls—defeats the goal.

Define the Air Barrier

Because air contains heat energy, a key requirement of the envelope is to prevent air movement ("infiltration"), both into and out of the conditioned space. Thus, we must identify exactly where the air barrier—the "line in the sand"—will be created.

Create a Moisture Barrier

As air cools, its ability to contain water vapor (the gaseous form of water) diminishes. Cool it enough (to its dew point) and water will be forced out as a liquid. If this occurs inside a building cavity, there is potential for wood rot and mold. Thus, the envelope must include a (water) vapor barrier to prevent movement of water vapor from warmer to cooler areas. In predominately heating climates, this means on the interior side of an insulated floor, wall, roof, or ceiling; in cooling climates just the opposite.

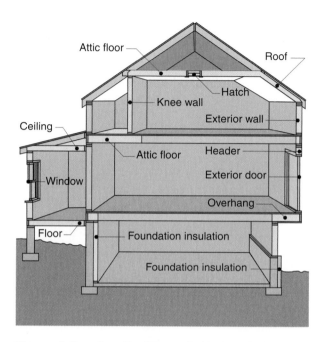

Provide Attic/Roof Ventilation

A perfect ceiling moisture barrier (also a perfect air barrier, because air contains water vapor) will guarantee no condensation and resulting mold and rot in the attic or rafter cavities. However, it will do nothing to prevent an entirely unrelated problem with roofs in heating climates: the dreaded ice dam.

For those who have never experienced an ice dam, here is what typically happens. A heavy snowfall occurs. All is cozy inside the well-insulated home when, a day or two later, water starts dripping from the ceiling near the intersection of ceiling and wall. When the dripping stops you are left with an ugly brown stain on the ceiling and sometimes peeling wallpaper. If this happens often enough or for long enough, you may find black mold growing in the ceiling drywall or plaster. This is *not* sustainable building. Until you find and rectify the cause, you will be replacing drywall forever.

What is going on? Outside you see icicles and a thick layer of ice at the eave of the roof. The rest of the roof still carries a thick layer of snow, but at the eave it is all ice. The illustration at top right on the facing page (see also pp. 384–386) shows the sequence of events leading to water dripping from your ceiling.

The attic floor is covered with insulation, but so is the roof, because dry snow has an R-value of nearly 2.0/inch. With insufficient attic ventilation, the attic temperature warms to an average of the living space (70°F) and the outdoor air (20°F). Water from melting snow flows downslope to the eave. The roofing of the uninsulated eave is close to ambient air temperature, however, so the meltwater refreezes. As the ice builds up, it creates a dammed pond of meltwater. Eventually the water makes its way under the roofing and leaks into the attic through holes or cracks.

The lower illustration shows a common solution: continuous soffit and ridge vents with baffles providing an air channel above the insulation. The attic and roof now track the outdoor air temperature, eliminating the sequential melting and refreezing.

Another solution is the "hot roof" (see p. 386). Here a thick layer of foam insulation extends all the way to the edge of the roof so that meltwater is never exposed to freezing temperatures until it is ready to drop. Icicles may form, but no dam.

In either case, as a precaution, install a 36-inch-wide waterproof membrane, such as Grace Ice and Water Shield®, under the starter course at the eaves.

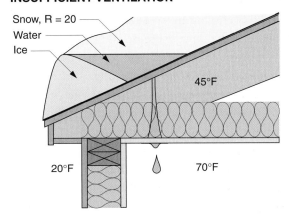

INSUFFICIENT VENTILATION

Snow, R = 20
Water
Ice
45°F
20°F
70°F

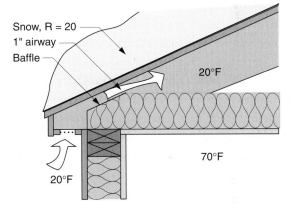

PROPER VENTILATION

Snow, R = 20
1" airway
Baffle
20°F
70°F
20°F

Sheath Walls with Foam

Replacing plywood or OSB wall sheathing with a minimum of 1 inch of rigid foam improves the performance of the envelope in several ways:
• total wall R-value is increased.
• infiltration is reduced.
• Stud cavity temperature is increased, reducing the chance of condensation and mold.

Foam does not have the rigidity and nailholding power of wood, so metal corner bracing must be installed, and some sidings (shingles and clapboards) will require strapping.

Insulate Beyond the Standard

An open attic invites unlimited insulation and R-value. However, I-joists used as studs, foam sheathing, and SIPS offer simple ways to increase wall R-values, as well. It is far less expensive to add insulation in new construction than as a retrofit. Therefore, increase the R-values of your envelope beyond the standard DOE recommended values.

Install Durable Roofing

If you look at a detailed reroofing estimate, you will be struck by the small fraction of the total the roofing material represents. Reroofing can involve removing and disposing of one or more layers of old shingles, replacing a portion of damaged sheathing, and replacing all edge, vent pipe, skylight, and chimney flashing—all before installing the new shingles.

A core principle of sustainable building is minimizing waste. Install the most durable roofing material you can afford.

Windows

Windows perform a remarkable number of functions, from letting us see out, to admitting fresh air, to lighting the interior of our homes, but the things they historically do least well is save energy. New glazings and a new way of thinking about windows, however, can change them from net energy losers to energy savers, even net energy producers. For that to happen we have to do the following:

Read the Performance Labels

All of the information needed to predict the energy gain and loss of a window is contained in the little black and white window performance label (p. 284) affixed to the glazing of every new window. Use this information in selecting and sizing the windows for your energy-efficient thermal envelope.

Design for Your Climate

We want windows to do different things in different climates: block solar heat gain in cooling climates, but admit solar heat gain and block conductive heat loss in heating climates. Amazingly, with a variety of special coatings, the new windows can do that (see illustration at top right and pp. 286–289). Go to *www.efficientwindows.org* to find the right glazings for your location.

Use South Glazings for Gain

Solar heat gain can reduce building energy consumption in heating climates. A glance at the chart on p. 515 will convince you that most of the glazed area should face south and as little as possible face north. Chapter 18 will show you how to calculate the optimum area of south glazing.

Consider Frame Performance

When considering the thermal performance of a window, don't overlook the frame. The table on p. 285 compares performance factors for the whole window for seven glazings and eight frame materials. You can see that U-factor (1/R-factor) can differ by 50 percent between the best and worst frames.

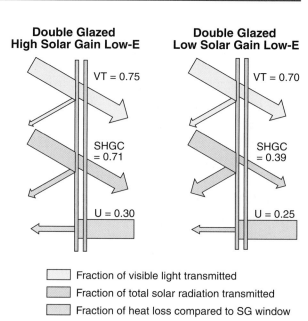

Double Glazed High Solar Gain Low-E
VT = 0.75
SHGC = 0.71
U = 0.30

Double Glazed Low Solar Gain Low-E
VT = 0.70
SHGC = 0.39
U = 0.25

☐ Fraction of visible light transmitted
☐ Fraction of total solar radiation transmitted
☐ Fraction of heat loss compared to SG window

Consider Window Insulation

After the sun goes down we no longer need either its light or heat. Therefore, consider modifying your windows diurnally with moveable insulation. During the day the insulation is moved out of the way, but at night it can cover the glazing and add to the R-value. Many commercial insulating shades are available, whereas instructions for constructing side-hinged shutters are available in several books.

A critical quality is the ability to seal the space between the insulation and the glazing tightly. Otherwise, the now colder glass may condense moisture from convecting air and damage the window sill.

Consider Tubular Skylights

Skylights are more effective for natural daylighting than windows because they 1) receive more light, 2) receive light from above, and therefore more uniformly, and 3) can light rooms having no exterior walls. On the negative side, they lose a lot of heat, and they only work on the uppermost floor.

Tubular skylights gather light at roof level and transmit it to remote locations by way of insulated and highly reflective tubes. They lose less heat and can deliver free daylight to otherwise dark interior spaces.

Heating and Cooling

Heating and cooling account for more than half of the energy consumption of homes. Sustainable building dictates three goals: 1) Design the building to minimize its maximum (design) heating and cooling loads, in Btu/hour, 2) utilize energy sources which are renewable, and 3) design the heating and cooling systems to convert and deliver that energy as efficiently as possible. Here is how:

Minimize the Heating Load

This is accomplished by 1) designing the thermal envelope (pp. 592–593 and pp. 369–399) with R-values of 150 percent those of the DOE standards or as determined by life-cycle cost analysis, and 2) installing a central heat recovery ventilation system.

Minimize the Cooling Load

The cooling load may be reduced by many factors other than thermal envelope R-values: 1) increased interior thermal mass, 2) glazings with low solar heat gain coefficients, 3) external shading of windows and walls, and 4) use of ceiling fans.

Compute the Sizes of Systems

Residential heating and cooling equipment installers have a penchant for oversizing, often by a factor of 1.5 to 2 times. This is not because the larger equipment costs more, but because they fear being blamed for undersizing. But efficiency is highest when systems run continuously. The answer is to calculate the maximum heating and cooling loads using the Air Conditioning Contractors of America (ACCA) *Manual J* or an equivalent.

Use Life-Cycle Costing

Don't select either heating or cooling equipment based solely on efficiency, installed cost, or both. The true cost is the life-cycle cost, the total of all costs associated with the equipment and its operation for the *life of the equipment*. This includes the costs of the original equipment, installation, maintenance, finance, and fuel.

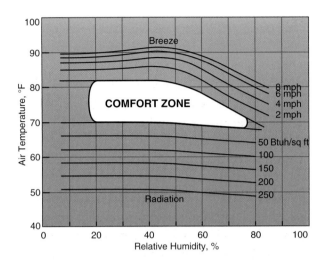

Avoid Electric Resistance Heat

Electric resistance heating is 100-percent efficient at converting electricity to heat. However, when compared to the energy content of the coal or gas consumed in generating the electricity, it is 30-percent efficient at best. Therefore, use electricity only to power heat pumps, the blowers and pumps of furnaces and boilers, and spot heaters.

Run Ducts in Conditioned Space

Running heating ducts containing 120°F–200°F air through a 20°F attic or crawl space makes no more sense than running cooling ducts full of 60°F air through a 120°F attic. Keeping ducts inside the thermal envelope reduces losses to zero.

Use Fans as Much as Possible

As the illustration above shows, an 8-mph breeze can raise your comfort zone by as much as 10°F. Studies show that raising the cooling setpoint on the thermostat lowers cooling bills by 6–8 percent per °F. Do the math. Just raising the thermostat by 7°F, from 78°F to 85°F, will likely reduce your cooling bill by 50 percent!

Install a ceiling fan (or two if the room is large) in the living room, dining room, kitchen, study, family room or media room, and every bedroom, including those for guests.

Lights and Appliances

Not much attention was paid to the efficiency of lighting fixtures and appliances until the advent of compact fluorescent lamps (CFLs) and the government's Energy Star Program. CFLs use 75 percent less energy and last 10 times as long as incandescent lamps. Now "warm white" versions are available, and at nearly the same price as incandescents. Note: coming soon are light emitting diode (LED) lamps, which use 60 percent less energy and last 10 times as long as CFLs (see pp. 528–529).

Design for Daylighting

Locate the rooms most occupied during the day on the east, south, and west to capitalize on free daylighting. Place windows on two or more walls, if possible, for more natural lighting. To illuminate deep rooms, window height needs to be at least 40 percent of the depth. And consider energy-efficient tubular skylights (see p. 594) for areas and rooms remote from windows.

Provide Task Lighting

Reading, sewing, and hobbies requiring assembling small parts all require intense light. Illuminating the entire room at the highest level is wasteful. Much electricity can be saved even in kitchens (see illustration) by concentrating lighting just on the areas where work is performed. So provide task lighting at every location where work is going on (see pp.534–537).

Install Intelligent Switches

Perhaps "intelligent" is too strong a word, but there are many types of wall switches which can reduce waste in lighting. Dimmer switches reduce lighting levels to create a more intimate mood while saving energy at the same time. (Yes, there are dimmer switches that work with CFLs.) Other switches detect motion and turn on and off automatically when a person enters or leaves a room. Still other switches contain timers that will turn off room lights after an interval you control. No longer should you have to roam the house, turning off the unneeded lights.

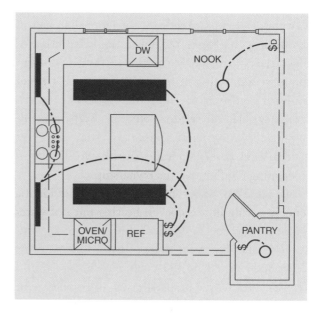

Avoid Recessed Fixtures

Recessed lighting fixtures are attractive in that the light seems to come from nowhere. Efficiency relative to other incandescent fixtures is not the issue; recessed fixtures contain reflectors which direct a high percentage of the light downward. The issue is air leakage. Unless the fixture is rated "IC" to allow contact with thermal insulation, the heat generated by the lamp is purposely vented upward into the joist cavity or, in the case of an upper story, the attic.

Incandescent fixtures generate 10 percent light and 90 percent heat; CFLs generate 20 percent light and 80 percent heat. Installing surface-mounted fixtures keeps all of that expensive heat inside the thermal envelope.

Use Appliance Life-Cycle Costs

The DOE Energy Star program (*www.energystar.gov*) has been effective in getting manufacturers to improve appliance efficiencies. Only appliances earning the Energy Star rating should be considered. However, take your research further and calculate life-cycle cost: the initial purchase price plus the cost of electricity consumed over the expected life of the appliance. Assuming electric rates will rise at the rate of inflation, this will be simply the annual kwhr usage × cost per kwhr × years of life.

Water

Water is a sustainability issue for two reasons: availability and energy consumed in heating it. Technically, as the illustration of the hydrologic cycle shows, water is a renewable resource. It is not, however, unlimited. Ninety-seven percent is saline ocean water, and two percent is locked up in ice, leaving just one percent usable by humans. That one percent is very unevenly distributed, leading to increasing conflict over its ownership.

In addition, about fifteen percent of residential energy consumption goes to heating our hot water. Here is what you can do to help:

Install Low-Flow Fixtures

We all love the sensation of showering under a torrent of hot water. To do so, however, is akin to commuting in a Hummer. Installing low-flow shower heads and faucet aerators will reduce hot water consumption by 25 to 50 percent. Not all shower heads are the same. Flow rates vary from 1.3 to 2.75 gallons per minute, compared to 5 gallons per minute or more for standard heads. In addition, some shower heads maintain pressure and the impression of full flow by aerating. Others restrict the size and numbers of orifices to create a forceful spray.

Buy Water-Saving Appliances

Top-loading clothes washers use about 40 gallons per wash. With settings of hot wash and warm rinse, heating that 40 gallons electrically requires about 5 kwhr. A front-loading washer would save 65 percent of that water and electricity. Switching to cold/cold settings would further reduce your electrical consumption by 95 percent—and your clothes would last longer!

Use Heater Life-Cycle Costs

Water heaters are famous for failing one month after their warranties expire. These warranties are typically for 6, 9, or 12 years. If it costs $500 to install a 6-year heater and $600 for a 12-year model, over 12 years the cheaper model will cost $1,000, the "more expensive" one $600. In addition, the 12-year model is usually better insulated, leading to further savings.

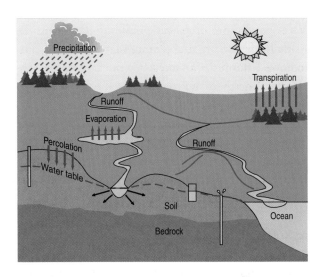

Minimize Hot Water Pipe Loss

A ¾-inch hot water supply pipe contains 0.023 gallon/foot (a ½-inch pipe, 0.01 gallon/foot). If a lavatory where you wash your hands is 50 feet from your water heater, a gallon of hot water will have to fill the pipe before reaching you. After the tap is shut off, all of the heat in the gallon remaining in the pipe will be lost. Even were the supply line insulated, the heat would be lost within several hours. Therefore: 1) locate bathrooms, kitchen, laundry, and the water heater in a way that minimizes hot water supply runs, 2) use ½- or even ⅜-inch pipe where practical, and 3) insulate all hot water pipes.

Xeriscape

Americans spend $25 billion per year to maintain green lawns. About $1 billion of that pays for 67 million pounds of pesticide. Most of the expenditure is due to the fact that we are trying to maintain something unnatural. Governments and homeowners in dry regions are beginning to realize that lush green lawns are no longer sustainable.

A new ethic is spreading: xeriscaping (*xeros*—Greek, meaning "dry"—plus *landscaping*). The principle is to landscape primarily with plants which occur naturally in the local climate and don't, therefore, require irrigation.

Air Quality

We spend more time inside buildings than outside. Aside from moving to a remote island or mountaintop, we have little control over the atmosphere we breathe, but there are many actions we can take to maintain clean air inside our homes.

The most dangerous pollutant, mold, cannot be avoided. It grows wherever there is moisture, organic matter, and above-freezing temperatures. It spreads by sending microscopic spores into the air, so simply opening a door or window will let it in.

Most people tolerate the natural background concentration of mold. Trouble starts when your home's relative humidity exceeds 60 percent, or when a roof leak, plumbing leak, or wet basement results in damp wallpaper, ceiling tiles, or even unfinished wood.

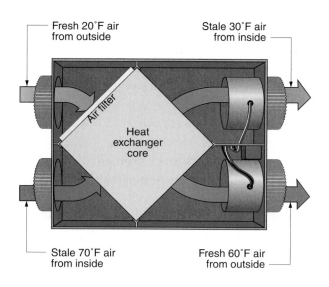

Fresh 20°F air from outside

Stale 30°F air from inside

Air filter

Heat exchanger core

Stale 70°F air from inside

Fresh 60°F air from outside

Design a Dry Foundation

The most common source of moisture in a home, by far, is a full basement. In "Moisture Sources in Houses," the National Research Council of Canada states, "A house basement should be compared to a warm sponge on wet ground." As much as 80 percent of the moisture in a home may be generated by the concrete walls and floor of a basement or the dirt floor of a crawl space. Therefore, implement the moisture-control steps discussed on pp. 100–101.

Control Humidity

Bathing, showering, cooking, watering house plants, and even breathing contribute large quantities of water vapor. Make sure that kitchen and bathrooms are equipped with vent fans to exhaust moist air. Also, control the relative humidity within the ideal range of 40–60 percent with an energy-efficient dehumidifier.

Use a HEPA Air Cleaner

High-efficiency particulate air (HEPA) filters remove 99.97 percent of airborne particles 0.3 micrometers (0.000012 inch) in diameter. Coupled with an ultraviolet light source, an air cleaner can remove or kill pollen, dust-mite feces, bacteria, and viruses.

Isolate the Garage

During the heating season homes are under negative pressure. Air will be drawn from an attached garage through any breach in the common wall. An automobile can be a potent source of CO. Therefore, seal the common wall as if it were an exterior wall.

Install CO Alarms

Carbon monoxide (CO) gas is insidious because it is odorless and deadly. Sources of CO can be the automobile in the garage, running a generator in the basement, or a poorly adjusted, backdrafting furnace, boiler, or water heater. Protect your family with inexpensive CO alarms.

Avoid Off-Gassing Materials

"New carpet smell" (butylated hydroxytoluene) and "new car smell" (phthalates) are just two indicators that something is off-gassing. If you can smell it, either don't install it, or stay out of the house until the smell disappears.

Consider a Central-Air HRV

After you have done all you can to eliminate indoor pollutants, exchange indoor and outdoor air (but without giving up all of the expensive heat) with a heat recovery ventilation system (see illustration above).

Renewable Energies

Not all solar heating is rocket science. The ancient Greeks laid out their cities so that the streets lined up with the noon sun, giving every home access to the warming rays. The Romans were the first to employ the "greenhouse effect" by enclosing the south walls of greenhouses with mica or glass to trap the heat of the sun. Simple passive solar heating is still the most cost-effective technique for reducing both home and hot water heating bills.

Check the Winter Solar Access

The sun comes up every day, but will it shine on your site—more specifically will it shine unshaded directly on your windows and/or water heater and/or photovoltaic panels? Determining your solar access (pp. 508–513) is an absolute must before considering solar heating of any kind.

Design for Passive Solar Heat

Thousands of passive (no fans or pumps) solar structures have been built. Many have been monitored and computer-modeled, so that the principles and rules-of-thumb for success are now well-established. Follow the simple design procedures on pp. 518–525 to achieve the heating savings shown on the above map.

Preplumb and Wire for Solar

Installing a solar water heater or photovoltaic panels while a house is under construction is a relatively simple matter because the special plumbing and wiring can be installed at the same time and by the same workers as the main plumbing and electrical systems. If you think you may someday want to add solar but are not quite ready to take the plunge, at least spend the modest amounts to preplumb and prewire.

Install a Solar Water Heater

Anyone who has ever tried drinking from a hose that has been lying in the sun can see how simple solar water heating can be. Provided you have good solar access (see pp. 508–513) and that you use an average amount of hot water, a solar domestic water heater

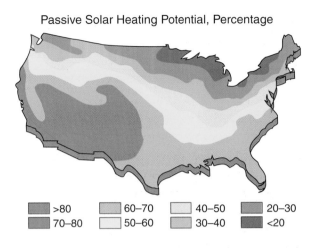

Passive Solar Heating Potential, Percentage

>80 | 60–70 | 40–50 | 20–30
70–80 | 50–60 | 30–40 | <20

should drop your water heating bills by 50 to 80 percent. Including the cost in a 30-year mortgage adds $12 to $20 to the monthly payment, but the federal mortgage interest deduction reduces that to just $9 to $15 per month. The hot water bill for the average home is about $80/month, so the solar saving should be $40 to $64 per month. A solar water heater would thus yield an immediate and substantial net saving.

Photovoltaics and Wind

An estimated 200,000 U.S. homes are now off the utility grid. The usual reason is the high cost of extending utility lines to remote sites. However, with government tax incentives and the spread of feed-in tariffs (wherein the utility pays the homeowner above-market prices for excess fed-back power), everyone building a new home should investigate the feasibility of photovoltaic and/or wind power generation.

The subject is too complex to be dealt with adequately here. Further, output of both solar and wind systems depend strongly on site variables, so professional surveys and analyses are recommended. However, a simple calculator for estimating PV cost and performance can be found at the American Solar Energy Society website: *www.findsolar.com*.

As a rule of thumb, residential wind turbines require an annual average wind speed of >12 mph. For a rough estimate of average wind speeds at your site, go to *www.awstruewind.com*.

Measuring and Finance

24

$\mathbf{F}$ew building projects are paid for with cash; usually somebody must obtain a mortgage. This chapter contains a guide to *home mortgage types* that will let you in on what the banker and the real estate broker are talking about. The table of *interest on loans* will help you calculate the monthly payments.

Geometric figures and *trigonometry* may bring back bad memories, but sooner or later you'll find it useful or even necessary to compute the volume of a space, an area of carpeting, or the angle of a saw cut. This chapter contains the formulae for all of the shapes you could think of.

How many square feet are there in an acre, how many ounces in a kilogram, what is the decimal value of 3 feet 4⁵⁄₁₆ inches? The answers to these and a hundred more building questions are all contained in *Units and Conversion Factors*.

Home Mortgage Types

Loan Type	How Loan Works	Pros and Cons
Adjustable-rate (ARM)	Interest rate tied to published financial index such as prime lending rate. Most have annual and lifetime caps.	Interest rate lower initially. Interest and payments usually increase over time.
Assumable	Buyer takes over seller's mortgage.	Mortgage usually fixed-rate at below-market interest rate.
Balloon	Payments based on long term (usually 30 years), but entire principle due in short term (usually 3 to 5 years).	Refinancing required at unknown interest rate at time of balloon payment.
Buy-down	Seller pays part of interest for first years.	Loan more affordable for buyer whose income is expected to rise.
Fixed-rate (FRM)	Interest rate and monthly payments constant for life of loan (usually 30 years).	Interest rate usually higher. Equity grows slowly in early years.
Graduated-payment (GPM)	Payments increase for first few years, then remain constant. Interest rate may vary.	Loan more affordable for buyer whose income is expected to rise.
Growing-equity (GEM)	Payments increase annually, with increase applied to principle. Interest rate usually constant.	Buyer equity increases rapidly, but buyer must be able to make increased payments.
Interest-only	Entire payment goes toward interest only. Principle remains at original amount.	Requires lowest payments. Owner equity consists of down payment plus appreciation.
Owner-financed (seller take back)	Seller holds either first or second mortgage.	Interest rate may be higher than market rate.
Renegotiable (rollover)	Same as adjustable-rate mortgage, but interest rate adjusted less often.	Interest rate and monthly payment variable, but fixed for longer periods.
Reverse annuity (reverse mortgage)	Lender makes monthly payments to borrower. Debt increases over time to maximum percentage of appraised value of property.	Provides monthly income to borrower but decreases equity.
Shared-appreciation (SAM)	Lender charges less interest in exchange for share of appreciation when property sold.	Makes property more affordable. Reduces owner's gain upon sale.
Wraparound (blended-rate)	Existing lower-interest loan combined with new additional loan for single loan with intermediate interest rate.	Decreases interest rate.
Zero-interest (no-interest)	No interest charged. Fixed monthly payments usually over short term.	Sale price usually inflated. One-time fee may be charged. No tax deduction allowed.

Interest on Loans

Monthly Payment

The table below shows monthly payments for each $1,000 borrowed for fixed-interest rates from 0 to 18 percent and for periods from 1 to 40 years. Monthly payments at other interest rates can be accurately interpolated using the figures in the table.

Example: What are the monthly payments on a 10-year, $1,000 loan at 11 percent interest? From the table, the payments at 10 and 12 percent are $13.22 and $14.35. Because 11 percent is the average of 10 and 12 percent, the monthly payment is ($13.22 + $14.35) ÷ 2 = $13.78 for each $1,000 borrowed.

Total Interest Paid

Knowing the monthly payment, it is easy to find the total interest paid over the life of a loan. Total interest is the difference between the sum of the payments over life and the original amount.

Example: For a 30-year, 12-percent, $100,000 mortgage, what is the total interest paid? From the table, the monthly payment for each $1,000 is $10.29. Therefore, the total lifetime payment is 100 × 12 months × 30 years × $10.29 = $370,440. Because the original loan is for $100,000, the total interest paid is the difference: $270,440.

Monthly Payments for Fixed-Rate Loans ($ for each $1,000)

Rate %	\multicolumn{10}{c}{Life of Loan, years}

Rate %	1	2	3	4	5	10	15	20	30	40
0	83.33	41.67	27.78	20.83	16.67	8.33	5.56	4.17	2.78	2.08
1	83.79	42.10	28.21	21.26	17.09	8.76	5.98	4.60	3.22	2.53
2	84.24	42.54	28.64	21.70	17.53	9.20	6.44	5.06	3.70	3.03
3	84.69	42.98	29.08	22.13	17.97	9.66	6.91	5.55	4.22	3.58
4	85.15	43.42	29.52	22.58	18.42	10.12	7.40	6.06	4.77	4.18
5	85.61	43.88	29.98	23.03	18.88	10.61	7.91	6.60	5.37	4.83
6	86.07	44.33	30.43	23.49	19.34	11.11	8.44	7.17	6.00	5.51
7	86.53	44.78	30.88	23.95	19.81	11.62	8.99	7.76	6.66	6.22
8	86.99	45.23	31.34	24.42	20.28	12.14	9.56	8.37	7.34	6.96
9	87.46	45.69	31.80	24.89	20.76	12.67	10.15	9.00	8.05	7.72
10	87.92	46.15	32.27	25.37	21.25	13.22	10.75	9.66	8.78	8.50
11	88.38	46.60	32.73	25.84	21.74	13.77	11.36	10.32	9.52	9.28
12	88.85	47.08	33.22	26.34	22.25	14.35	12.01	11.02	10.29	10.09
13	89.31	47.54	33.69	26.82	22.75	14.93	12.65	11.71	11.06	10.89
14	89.79	48.02	34.18	27.33	23.27	15.53	13.32	12.44	11.85	11.72
15	90.25	48.48	34.66	27.83	23.78	16.13	13.99	13.16	12.64	12.53
16	90.74	48.97	35.16	28.35	24.32	16.76	14.69	13.92	13.45	13.36
17	91.20	49.44	35.65	28.85	24.85	17.37	15.39	14.66	14.25	14.18
18	91.68	49.93	36.16	29.38	25.40	18.02	16.11	15.44	15.08	15.02
19	92.15	50.40	36.65	29.90	25.94	18.66	16.82	16.20	15.88	15.84
20	92.63	50.89	37.16	30.43	26.49	19.32	17.56	16.98	16.71	16.67

Geometric Figures

TRIANGLE
Area = bh/2
Perimeter = a + b + c

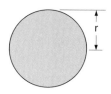

CIRCLE
Area = πr^2
Perimeter = $2\pi r$

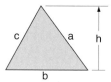

SQUARE
Area = ab
Perimeter = 4a

CIRCULAR SECTOR
Area = $\pi r/360$
Perimeter = 0.01745rA°

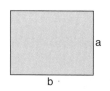

RECTANGLE
Area = ab
Perimeter = 2a + 2b

CIRCULAR SEGMENT
Area = $r^2(\pi A° - \sin A°)/360$
Perimeter = 2r sinA°/2

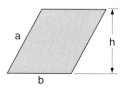

PARALLELOGRAM
Area = bh
Perimeter = 2a + 2b

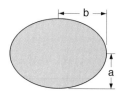

ELLIPSE
Area = πab
Perimeter = $\pi\sqrt{2(a^2 + b^2)}$

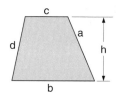

TRAPEZOID
Area = h(b + c)/2
Perimeter = a + b + c + d

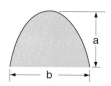

PARABOLA
Area = 2ab/3
Perimeter = $b(1 + 8a^2/3b^2)$

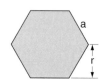

N-SIDED POLYGON
Area = N(ra)/2
Perimeter = a + b + c

CIRCLE/SQUARE
Area = $0.2146a^2$
Perimeter = $2a + \pi a/2$

Areas and Volumes of Three-Dimensional Bodies

CUBE
Area = $6a^2$
Volume = a^3

CYLINDER
Area = $2\pi r^2 + 2\pi rh$
Volume = $\pi r^2 h$

RECTANGULAR PRISM
Area = $2(ab + ac + bc)$
Volume = abc

CONE
Area = $\pi r\sqrt{r^2 + h^3} + \pi r^2$
Volume = $\pi r^2 h/3$

SPHERE
Area = $4\pi r^2$
Volume = $4\pi r^3/3$

SPHERICAL SEGMENT
Area = $2\pi ra$
Volume = $\pi a^2(3r - a)/3$

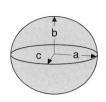

ELLIPSOID
Volume = $\pi abc/3$

PARABOLOID
Volume = $\pi r^2 h/2$

Trigonometry

Right Triangles

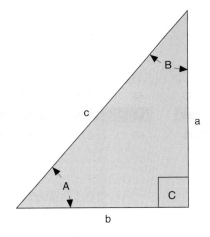

Ratios of Sides (Trig Functions)

$\sin A = a/c$	$\sin B = b/c$	$\sin C = 1$
$\cos A = b/c$	$\cos B = a/c$	$\cos C = 0$
$\tan A = a/b$	$\tan B = b/a$	$\tan C = \infty$

Pythagorean Theorem

$$a^2 + b^2 = c^2$$

$$c = \sqrt{a^2 + b^2}$$

Any Triangle

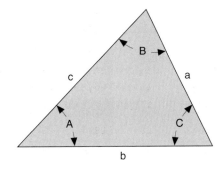

Law of Cosines

$a^2 = b^2 + c^2 - 2bc \cos A$ $\cos A = (b^2 + c^2 - a^2)/2bc$

$b^2 = a^2 + c^2 - 2ac \cos B$ $\cos B = (a^2 + c^2 - b^2)/2ac$

$c^2 = a^2 + b^2 - 2ab \cos C$ $\cos C = (a^2 + b^2 - c^2)/2ab$

Law of Sines

$a/\sin A = b/\sin B = c/\sin C$

$a/b = \sin A/\sin B$, etc.

Trigonometry Tables

Deg	Sin	Cos	Tan	Deg	Sin	Cos	Tan	Deg	Sin	Cos	Tan
1	.0175	.9998	.0175	31	.5150	.8572	.6009	61	.8746	.4848	1.8040
2	.0349	.9994	.0349	32	.5299	.8480	.6249	62	.8829	.4695	1.8807
3	.0523	.9986	.0524	33	.5446	.8387	.6494	63	.8910	.4540	1.9626
4	.0698	.9976	.0699	34	.5592	.8290	.6745	64	.8988	.4384	2.0503
5	.0872	.9962	.0875	35	.5736	.8192	.7002	65	.9063	.4226	2.1445
6	.1045	.9945	.1051	36	.5878	.8090	.7265	66	.9135	.4067	2.2460
7	.1219	.9925	.1228	37	.6018	.7986	.7536	67	.9205	.3907	2.3559
8	.1392	.9903	.1405	38	.6157	.7880	.7813	68	.9272	.3746	2.4751
9	.1564	.9877	.1584	39	.6293	.7771	.8098	69	.9336	.3584	2.6051
10	.1736	.9848	.1763	40	.6428	.7660	.8391	70	.9397	.3420	2.7475
11	.1908	.9816	.1944	41	.6561	.7547	.8693	71	.9455	.3256	2.9042
12	.2079	.9781	.2126	42	.6691	.7431	.9004	72	.9511	.3090	3.0777
13	.2250	.9744	.2309	43	.6820	.7314	.9325	73	.9563	.2924	3.2709
14	.2419	.9703	.2493	44	.6947	.7193	.9657	74	.9613	.2756	3.4874
15	.2588	.9659	.2679	45	.7071	.7071	1.0000	75	.9659	.2588	3.7321
16	.2756	.9613	.2867	46	.7193	.6947	1.0355	76	.9703	.2419	4.0108
17	2924	.9563	.3057	47	.7314	.6820	1.0724	77	.9744	.2250	4.3315
18	.3090	.9511	.3249	48	.7431	.6691	1.1106	78	.9781	.2079	4.7046
19	.3256	.9455	.3443	49	.7547	.6561	1.1504	79	.9816	.1908	5.1446
20	.3420	.9397	.3640	50	.7660	.6428	1.1918	80	.9848	.1736	5.6713
21	.3584	.9336	.3839	51	.7771	.6293	1.2349	81	.9877	.1564	6.3138
22	.3746	.9272	.4040	52	.7880	.6157	1.2799	82	.9903	.1392	7.1154
23	.3907	.9205	.4245	53	.7986	.6018	1.3270	83	.9925	.1219	8.1443
24	.4067	.9135	.4452	54	.8090	.5878	1.3764	84	.9945	.1045	9.5144
25	.4226	.9063	.4663	55	.8192	.5736	1.4281	85	.9962	.0872	11.4301
26	.4384	.8988	.4877	56	.8290	.5592	1.4826	86	.9976	.0698	14.3007
27	.4540	.8910	.5095	57	.8387	.5446	1.5399	87	.9986	.0523	19.0811
28	.4695	.8829	.5317	58	.8480	.5299	1.6003	88	.9994	.0349	28.6363
29	.4848	.8746	.5543	59	.8572	.5150	1.6643	89	.9998	.0175	57.2900
30	.5000	.8660	.5774	60	.8660	.5000	1.7321	90	1.000	.0000	∞

Units and Conversion Factors

Multiply	By	To Get
LENGTH		
Centimeter	0.3937	Inches
Centimeter	10	Millimeters
Centimeter	0.01	Meters
Inch	2.54	Centimeters
Inch	0.0833	Feet
Inch	0.0278	Yards
Foot	30.48	Centimeters
Foot	0.3048	Meters
Foot	12	Inches
Foot	0.3333	Yards
Yard	91.44	Centimeters
Yard	0.9144	Meters
Yard	36	Inches
Yard	3	Feet
Meter	39.37	Inches
Meter	3.281	Feet
Meter	1.094	Yards
Meter	100	Centimeters
Meter	0.001	Kilometers
Kilometer	3,281	Feet
Kilometer	1,094	Yards
Kilometer	0.6214	Miles
Kilometer	1,000	Meters
Mile	5,280	Feet
Mile	1,760	Yards
Mile	1,609	Meters
Mile	1.609	Kilometers
AREA		
Square centimeter	0.1550	Square inches
Square centimeter	100	Square millimeters
Square centimeter	0.0001	Square meters
Square inch	6.4516	Square centimeters
Square inch	0.0069	Square feet
Square inch	7.72×10^{-4}	Square yards
Square foot	929	Square centimeters
Square foot	0.0929	Square meters
Square foot	144	Square inches

Multiply	By	To Get
Square foot	0.1111	Square yards
Square yard	8,361	Square centimeters
Square yard	0.8361	Square meters
Square yard	1,296	Square inches
Square yard	9	Square feet
Square meter	1,550	Square inches
Square meter	10.765	Square feet
Square meter	1.1968	Square yards
Square meter	10,000	Square centimeters
Square meter	1.0×10^{-6}	Square kilometers
Square kilometer	1.076×10^{7}	Square feet
Square kilometer	1.197×10^{6}	Square yards
Square kilometer	0.3861	Square miles
Square kilometer	1.0×10^{6}	Square meters
Square mile	2.788×10^{7}	Square feet
Square mile	3.098×10^{6}	Square yards
Square mile	640	Acres
Square mile	2.590	Square kilometers
SURVEYOR'S MEASURE		
Link	7.92	Inches
Rod	16.5	Feet
Chain	4	Rods
Rood	40	Square rods
Acre	160	Square rods
Acre	43,560	Square feet
Square mile	640	Acres
Township	36	Square miles
VOLUME		
Cubic centimeter	0.0610	Cubic inches
Cubic centimeter	1,000	Cubic millimeters
Cubic centimeter	1.0×10^{-6}	Cubic meters
Cubic inch	16.387	Cubic centimeters
Cubic inch	5.787×10^{-4}	Cubic feet
Liter	0.2642	Gallons, US
Liter	1.0568	Quarts
Liter	1,000	Cubic centimeters
Gallon, US	0.0238	Barrels (42 gallon)
Gallon, US	4	Quarts

Multiply	By	To Get
Gallon, US	231	Cubic inches
Gallon, US	3,785	Cubic centimeters
Cubic foot	2.832×10^4	Cubic centimeters
Cubic foot	0.0283	Cubic meters
Cubic foot	1,728	Cubic inches
Cubic foot	0.0370	Cubic yards
Cubic yard	7.646×10^5	Cubic centimeters
Cubic yard	0.7646	Cubic meters
Cubic yard	4.667×10^4	Cubic inches
Cubic yard	27	Cubic feet
Cubic meter	6.102×10^4	Cubic inches
Cubic meter	35.320	Cubic feet
Cubic meter	1.3093	Cubic yards
Cubic meter	1.0×10^6	Cubic centimeters
Cubic meter	1,000	Liters

ENERGY

Multiply	By	To Get
Erg	1.0×10^{-7}	Joules
Joule	1	Newton-meters
Joule	1.0×10^7	Ergs
Joule	0.2389	Calories
Joule	9.48×10^{-4}	British thermal units
Joule	0.7376	Foot-pounds
Calorie	3.97×10^{-3}	British thermal units
Btu/hour	0.293	Joules/second
Btu/hour	252	Calories/hour

TEMPERATURE

A temperature change of 1 C degree is equivalent to a change of 1.8 F degrees

A temperature change of 1 F degree is equivalent to a change of 0.5556 C degrees

A temperature change of 1 K degree is equivalent to a change of 1 C degrees

Degrees F=1.8 (Degrees C+32)

Degrees C =0.556 (Degrees F-32)

Degrees C=Degrees K-273

MASS

Multiply	By	To Get
Pound	4.448	Newtons
Pound	32.17	Poundals
Ton, US short	2,000	Pounds
Ton, US long	2,240	Pounds
Ton, metric	2,205	Pounds
Ton, metric	1,000	Kilograms
Gram	0.0353	Ounces
Gram	2.205×10^{-3}	Pounds
Gram	0.001	Kilograms
Gram	15.432	Grains
Ounce	28.35	Grams
Ounce	0.0284	Kilograms
Ounce	0.0625	Pounds
Pound	453.6	Grams
Pound	0.4536	Kilograms
Pound	16	Ounces
Kilogram	35.28	Ounces
Kilogram	2.205	Pounds
Kilogram	1,000	Grams
Ton, US	0.9070	Tons metric
Ton, US	907	Kilograms
Ton, US	2,000	Pounds
Ton, metric	1.102	Tons, US
Ton, metric	2,205	Pounds
Ton, metric	1,000	Kilograms

LIGHT

Multiply	By	To Get
Lux meter	1	Lumens/square
Lux foot	0.0929	Lumens/square
Lux	0.0929	Foot-candles
Footcandle	10.76	Lux
Lumen/square foot	10.76	Lux

Abbreviations

AASHO: American Association of State Highway Officials

ABS: acrylonitrile-butadienes-tyrene

AC: armored cable

ACA: ammoniacal copper arsenate

ACCA: Air Conditioning Contractors of America

ACZA: ammoniacal copper zinc arsenate

ADA: Americans with Disabilities Act

ADA: airtight drywall approach

AF&PA: American Forest & Paper Association

AFUE: annual fuel utilization efficiency

ag: above grade

amp: ampere

ANSI: American National Standards Institute

APA: The Engineered Wood Association (formerly known as the American Plywood Association)

ARM: adjustable-rate mortgage

ARMA: Asphalt Roofing Manufacturers Association

ASHRAE: American Society of Heating, Refrigerating and Air Conditioning Engineers

ASTM: American Society for Testing and Materials

avg: average

AWPB: American Wood Preservers Bureau

BIA: Brick Institute of America

b: breadth

bg: below grade

Btu: British thermal unit

Btuh: British thermal unit per hour

BUR: built-up roof

BX: armored cable (interchangeable with AC)

C: centigrade; corrosion resistant

CABO: Council of American Building Officials

CCA: chromated copper arsenate

CCF: hundred cubic feet

CCT: color-correlated temperature

Co: duration of load factor

CDD: cooling degree-day

C_F: size factor

CFL: compact fluorescent lamp

cfm: cubic feet per minute

CFR: Code of Federal Regulations

C_H: horizontal shear adjustment

CMU: concrete masonry unit

CO: carbon monoxide

CPSC: Consumer Product Safety Commission

CPVC: chlorinated polyvinyl chloride

C_r: repetitive member factor

CRI: color-rendering index

cu ft: cubic foot

d: depth; pennyweight

D: deciduous

db: decibel

dbl: double

DD_{65}: base 65°F degree day

dfu: drainage fixture unit

dia: diagonal; diameter

DMT: design minimum temperature

DOE: Department of Energy

DS: double-strength

DWV: drain, waste, and vent

E: east; modulus of elasticity; evergreen; excellent

EER: energy efficiency ratio

EMC: equilibrium moisture content

EMT: thin-wall metal conduit

EPA: U.S. Environmental Protection Agency

EPDM: ethylene propylene diene monomer

EWC: Efficient Windows Collaborative

EWS: Engineered Wood Society

Exp 1: exposure 1

EXT: exterior

F: Fahrenheit; fair; feeder; female

Fb: extreme fiber stress in bending

Fc: compression parallel to grain

FHA: Federal Housing Administration

fipt: female iron pipe thread

fnpt: female national pipe thread tapered

FRM: fixed-rate mortgage

FSC: Forest Stewardship Council

FSEC: Florida Solar Energy Center

Ft: fiber stress in tension

Fv: horizontal shear stress

G: good

ga: gauge

gal: gallon

GEM: growing-equity mortgage

GFCI: ground fault circuit interrupter

GPM: graduated-payment mortgage; gallon per minute

H: heat-resistant; height; run

HDD: heating degree-day

HDO: high-density overlay
HEPA: High-efficiency particulate air
HID: high-intensity discharge
hp: horsepower
hr: hour
HUD: U.S. Department of Housing and Urban Development
HVAC: heating, ventilating, and air-conditioning
Hz: hertz
ICC: International Code Council
ICF: insulated concrete form
ID: internal diameter
IIC: impact insulation class
IJC: I-Joist Compatible
IMC: intermediate metal conduit
ins: insert thread
INT: interior
IRC: International Residential Code
IRMA: insulated roof membrane assembly
K: Kelvin
kwhr: kilowatt-hour
L: left; length
lb: pound
LED: light-emitting diode
lin ft: linear feet
LSG: light-to-solar gain
M: male
max: maximum
MC: moisture content
MDF: medium-density fiberboard
MDO: medium-density overlay
min: minimum; minute
mipt: male iron pipe thread
mnpt: male national pipe thread tapered
mph: miles per hour

MW: moderate weather
N: north
NAHB: National Association of Home Builders
NCMA: National Concrete Masonry Association
NFRC: National Fenestration Research Council
NKBA: National Kitchen & Bath Association
NM: nonmetallic (cable)
NRC: noise-reduction coefficient
NWWDA: National Wood Window and Door Association
oc: on-center
OD: outside diameter
ORNL: Oak Ridge National Laboratory
OSB: oriented strand board
OVE: Optimum-Value Engineering
oz: ounce
P: perennial; plasticweld; poor
PB: polybutylene
PE: polyethylene
perm: measure of permeability
PRI: Performance Rated I-Joist
PS: product standard
psf: pounds per square foot
psi: pounds per square inch
PT: pressure treated
PVC: polyvinyl chloride
R: right; riser; rubber
rec: recommended
Ref: reference point
RMC: rigid metal conduit
RNC: rigid nonmetallic conduit
RO: rough opening
R-value: thermal resistance
S: south

SAM: shared-appreciation mortgage
SCL: Structural Composite Lumber
SE: service entrance
sel str: select structural
SHGC: solar heat gain coefficient
SIP: structural insulated panel
sgl: single(s)
SJ: slip joint
slip: slip fitting end
SMA: Stairway Manufacturers' Association
spig: spigot fitting end
sq ft: square foot
sq in: square inch
STC: sound transmission class
std: standard
SW: severe weather
S1S: surfaced one side
S4S: surfaced four sides
T: texture; thermoplastic; tread
T&G: tongue-and-groove
TCE: trichloroethylene
THM: trihalomethane
U: underground
UF: underground feeder
USDA: U.S. Department of Agriculture
U-value: thermal conductance
V: rise; volt
VAC: volts alternating current
VB: vapor barrier
VT: visible transmittance
W: water-resistant; watt; west; width
WM: Wood Moulding and Millwork Producers Association
WWPA: Western Wood Products Association
yr: year

Glossary

Absorptance: ratio of energy absorbed by a surface to the amount striking it.

Absorption: weight of water absorbed, expressed as percentage of dry weight; interception of radiant energy or sound waves.

Absorptivity: (see absorptance).

Accelerator: chemical added to concrete to speed setting.

Active solar collector: mechanical system for collecting solar heat.

Admixture: substance added to mortar to change its properties.

Aggregate: granular materials used in masonry.

Air barrier: material or surface designed to prevent passage of air but not water vapor.

Air-entrained concrete: concrete containing microscopic air bubbles to make it less susceptible to freeze damage.

Alkyd: synthetic resin paint base. Alkyd resin has replaced linseed oil.

Alternating current: electrical current which reverses direction regularly (60 hertz, or cycles per second, in the U.S.).

Altitude: vertical angle of the sun above the horizon.

Ampacity: ampere-carrying capacity of a wire.

Ampere: unit of electrical current. Often abbreviated *amp*.

Anchor bolt: bolt set into a foundation to fasten it to the building sill.

Apron: vertical panel below the window sill.

Ash drop: opening in the floor of a fireplace for ash disposal.

Ashlar: one of several masonry patterns, consisting of large rectangular units of cut stone.

Asphalt: waterproof organic liquid used to waterproof.

Asphalt plastic cement: asphalt used to seal roofing materials together.

Awning: shading device mounted above a window.

Awning window: single window sash hinged at the top and swinging outward.

Azimuth angle: direction to the sun, usually measured from true north. Solar azimuth is measured east or west from true south.

Backer rod: foam rope used to fill large gaps before caulking.

Backfill: material used to fill excavation around a foundation.

Balloon frame: wood frame in which studs are continuous from the sill to the top plate of the top floor.

Baluster: vertical member under railing.

Baseboard: horizontal molding at the base of a wall. Also known as *mopboard*.

Batten: thin molding of rectangular section used to cover a joint.

Bay window: window that projects from a wall.

Beam: horizontal structural member designed to support loads in bending.

Bearing wall: wall that supports load from above.

Bevel cut: wood cut made at any angle other than 0° or 90°.

Bitumin: substance containing oil or coal-based compounds; asphalt.

Blocking: short member bracing between two longer framing members.

Boiler: central heating appliance that generates either hot water or steam.

Bond: strength of adhesion. Also one of several patterns in which masonry units may be laid.

Bow window: same as a bay window, except the projection approximates a circular arc.

Braced frame: heavy-timber frame braced in the corners by lighter members.

Branch circuit: one of several circuits in a building, originating at the service entrance panel and protected by a separate circuit breaker or fuse.

Brick: rectangular masonry unit hardened by firing in a kiln.

Brick mold: standard wood molding used as outside casing around doors and windows.

Brick veneer: brick facing over wood or masonry.

Bridging: bracing between floor joists to prevent twist.

British thermal unit (Btu): amount of heat required to raise the temperature of 1 pound of water 1°F.

Brown coat: next-to-last plaster or stucco coat.

Building code: rules adopted by a government for the regulation of building.

Built-up roof: roofing consisting of many alternating layers of asphalt and felt.

Bull nose: rounded masonry unit for use in corners.

Bundle: package of shingles.

Bus bar: rectangular metal (usually copper) bar for carrying large electrical current.

Butt: bottom edge of a roof shingle.

Butt joint: joint in which two members meet without overlap or miter.

Calcium chloride: concrete accelerator.

Cant strip: beveled strip around the perimeter of a roof.

Capillarity: movement of water through small gaps due to adhesion and surface tension.

Casement window: window hinged on the side and opening outward.

Casing: inside or outside molding which covers space between a window or door jamb and a wall.

Caulk: material used to fill building joints and cracks.

Cavity wall: masonry wall with a continuous space between the inside and outside bricks that acts as a capillary break.

Cellulose insulation: loose-fill insulation consisting of shredded and treated newspaper.

Ceramic mosaic: sheet of small ceramic tiles.

Chalk line: straight line made by snapping a taut string coated by colored chalk.

Check: cracks in the surface of wood resulting from drying (and shrinking) of the surface faster than of the interior.

Chimney: vertical tube for venting flue gases by natural convection.

Chimney fire: burning of creosote and other deposits within a chimney.

Circuit: two or more wires carrying electricity to lights, receptacles, switches, or appliances.

Circuit breaker: electromechanical device that opens when the current exceeds its rating.

Clapboard: board for overlapping as horizontal siding.

Closed valley: roof valley where the shingles extend in an unbroken line across the valley intersection.

Collar: preformed vent pipe flashing. Also the part of an appliance that connects to a stove or vent pipe.

Collar tie: rafter tie beam.

Column: structural member designed to carry a vertical load in compression.

Common nail: large-diameter nail for rough framing.

Compression: action of forces to squeeze or compact.

Concealed-nail roofing: method of applying asphalt roll roofing where all nails are in the underlying layer and the top layer is attached by asphalt cement only.

Concrete: hardened mixture of portland cement, sand, gravel, and water.

Condensation: process of water vapor turning to liquid water.

Conduction: transfer of heat through an opaque material. Also the transfer of electrons (current) through a material.

Conductor: wire intended to carry electric current.

Conduit: metal or plastic pipe that surrounds electrical wires and protects them from physical damage.

Control joint: groove in concrete to control the location of cracking.

Convection: heat transfer through either the natural or forced movement of air.

Corner bead: strip of metal designed to provide protection of a plaster or drywall corner.

Corner board: vertical board at a wall intersection for butting siding.

Corner bracing: diagonal boards, metal strips, or rigid panels used at building corners to prevent racking.

Cornice: top, projecting molding of the entablature.

Countersink: to sink a nail or screw below the surface.

Course: row of roofing or siding.

Cove molding: popular molding (trim) for ceiling/wall intersections.

Coverage: minimum number of layers of roofing at any section.

Crawl space: space beneath a building not high enough for a person to stand in.

Cricket: small roof for diverting water.

Curing: process of hardening of concrete over time.

Cut-in brace: corner brace of framing lumber cut into studs.

Cutout: space between tabs in a roofing shingle.

Cycle: one complete reversal of electrical current and voltage. Cycles per second are called hertz.

Dado: rectangular groove cut across the grain of wood.

Damper: valve designed to control the flow of air or smoke.

Damp-proofing: treating a masonry surface to retard capillary action.

Dead load: load imposed on a structure by the weight of the building materials only.

Decay: deterioration of wood from attack by fungi or insects.

Decibel: logarithmic measure of sound intensity. An increase of 6 db is the same as doubling the sound pressure.

Deciduous plant: one that loses its leaves in winter.

Deck: roof surface to which roofing is applied.

Deflection: distance moved upon application of a specified load on a structural member.

Deflection ratio: ratio of clear span to deflection at design load.

Degree-day: difference between the average of daily high and low temperatures and a fixed temperature —usually 65°F.

Dew point: air temperature at which water vapor begins to condense as either water or ice (frost).

Diffuse radiation: solar energy received from a direction different from that of the sun.

Dimension lumber: framing lumber 2 to 5 inches in nominal thickness and up to 12 inches in nominal width.

Direct current: electrical current that flows in a single direction.

Direct gain: heating system in which energy received from the sun directly enters and heats the living spaces.

Dormer: vertical window projecting from a roof. Gabled dormers have peaked roofs; shed dormers have shed roofs.

Double coverage: result of applying asphalt roll roofing with sufficient overlap to get a double layer. See *coverage*.

Double-hung window: window with vertically sliding upper and lower sash. If the upper sash is fixed, the window becomes single-hung.

Double-strength glass: sheet glass of nominal thickness 0.125 inch.

Dovetail: flared mortise and tenon that form a locking joint.

Downspout: vertical section of pipe in a gutter system.

Draft: air pressure difference between the inside and outside of a chimney. Also the rate of flue gas or combustion airflow.

Drip cap: molding at the top of a window or door.

Drip edge: material designed to force water to drip from roof rakes and eaves.

Drywall: interior finish material in large sheets. Plywood paneling and gypsum drywall are two examples.

Drywall nail: special, ringed nail for fastening drywall.

Duct: enclosure for distributing heated or cooled air.

Eaves: lower edge of a sloped roof.

Eaves flashing: flashing at eaves designed to prevent leaking from an ice dam.

Egress window: window whose clear dimensions are large enough that it can serve as a fire exit.

Elastic modulus: ratio of stress to strain in a material. Also known as the modulus of elasticity.

Elbow: right-angle bend in stovepipe.

Elevation: view of a vertical face of a building.

Ell: L-shaped pipe fitting.

Envelope: collection of building surfaces that separate the building interior from the outside; i.e., roof, walls, floor, windows, and doors.

Exposed-nail roofing: mineral-surfaced roll roofing where nails are exposed.

Exposure: portion of roofing or siding material exposed after installation.

Extension jamb: addition to a door or window jamb to bring the jamb up to full wall thickness. Also known as a jamb extender.

Face: side of a masonry unit or wood panel intended to be exposed.

Face brick: brick intended to be used in an exposed surface.

Face nailing: nailing perpendicular to the face or surface. Also called direct nailing.

Fahrenheit: temperature scale defined by the freezing (32°) and boiling (212°) points of water.

Fascia: vertical flat board at a cornice. Also spelled *facia*.

Fastener: any device for connecting two members.

Felt: fibrous sheet material for roofing.

Finger joint: wood joint formed by interlocking fingers.

Finish coat: final coat of a material.

Finish grade: final ground level around a building.

Finish nail: thin nail intended to be driven flush or countersunk.

Fire-stop: framing member designed to block the spread of fire within a framing cavity.

Flashing: material used to prevent leaks at intersections and penetrations of a roof.

Float glass: glass formed by floating molten glass on molten tin.

Flue: passage in a chimney for the venting of flue gases or products of combustion.

Flue gases: mixture of air and the products of combustion.

Fluorescent light: lamp that emits light when an electric discharge excites a phosphor coating.

Footing: bottom section of a foundation that rests directly on the soil.

Forced-air system: heat transfer system using a blower.

Foundation: section of a building that transfers the building load to the earth.

Frame: assemblage of structural support members.

Frieze: middle section of an entablature, between the architrave below and the cornice above. In wood construction, the horizontal board between the top of the siding and the soffit. Also a decorative band near the top of a wall.

Frost heave: expansion of the earth due to freezing of interstitial water.

Frost line: maximum depth of freezing in the soil.

Fuel efficiency: percentage of energy in fuel that is converted to useful energy.

Furnace: appliance that generates hot air.

Furring: strip of wood that provides space for insulation or that levels an uneven surface.

Gable: upper, triangular portion of an end wall.

Gable roof: roof having gables at opposite ends, each equally pitched.

Gasket: elastic strip that forms a seal between two parts.

Girder: main supporting beam.

Girt: horizontal beam framed into the posts.

Glare: excessive contrast in lighting.

Glass: transparent material composed of silica (sand), soda (sodium carbonate), lime (calcium carbonate), and small quantities of other minerals.

Glass block: glass molded into hollow blocks that serve to support loads and pass light.

Glazing: glass or other transparent material used for windows.

Gloss paint: paint with a high percentage of resin that dries to a highly reflective finish.

Grade: level of the ground.

Ground: any metal object that is connected to and serves as the earth in an electrical system.

Grounded wire: wire in a circuit that is connected to the ground and serves to return current from the hot wire back to the ground. Identified by a white insulation jacket.

Ground fault circuit interrupter (GFCI): circuit breaker that trips on leakage of current.

Grounding wire: bare or green wire in a circuit that connects metal components, such as appliance cabinets, to the ground.

Grout: very thin mortar applied to masonry joints.

Gusset: flat plate used on either side of a wood joint to aid in connection.

Gutter: horizontal trough for collecting rain water from a roof.

Gypsum: calcium sulfate, a naturally occurring mineral.

Gypsum drywall: rigid paper-faced board made from hydrated gypsum and used as a substitute for plaster and lath.

Handrail: top rail in a balustrade.

Hard water: calcium-rich water.

Hardwood: wood from a deciduous tree.

Head: top element in many structures.

Header: beam over a door or window for supporting the load from above. Also any beam which crosses and supports the ends of other beams. Also a brick placed to tie two adjacent wythes together.

Heartwood: portion of the tree from the pith (center) to the sapwood.

Heat-absorbing glass: glass containing additives that absorb light in order to reduce glare, brightness, and solar heat gain.

Heat capacity: quantity of heat required to raise the temperature of 1 cubic foot of a material 1°F.

Heat Mirror®: trade name for a plastic film treated with selective coating.

Heat pump: mechanical device that transfers heat from a cooler to a warmer medium.

Hip: convex intersection of two roof planes, running from eaves to ridge.

Hip shingle: shingle covering a hip.

Hot roof: roof with no ventilating air beneath the sheathing.

Hot wire: current-carrying wire that is not connected to the ground.

Humidifier: appliance for adding water vapor to the air.

Hydrated lime: quicklime and water combined. Also called *slaked lime*.

Hydronic: method of distributing heat by hot water.

I-beam: steel beam whose section resembles the letter I.

Ice dam: ridge of ice at roof eaves.

Incandescent: heated to the point of giving off light.

Infiltration: incursion of outdoor air through cracks, holes, and joints.

Infrared radiation: radiation of a wavelength longer than that of red light. Also known as heat radiation.

Inside sill: window stool.

Insulated Concrete Form: concrete form which doubles as form for concrete pour and wall insulation.

Insulating glass: factory-sealed double or triple glazing.

Insulation: material with high resistance to heat flow.

Insulation board: wood fiber board available in ½-inch and $^{25}/_{32}$-inch thicknesses.

Jamb: top and sides of a door or window.

Jamb depth: width of a window frame.

Jamb extender: same as an extension jamb.

Joint compound: material used to finish joints in gypsum drywall. Also known as *mud*.

Joist: repetitive narrow beam supporting the floor load.

Kiln-dried: lumber dried in a kiln at elevated temperatures. The process removes cellular water.

Kilowatt: 1,000 watts. Abbreviated *kw*.

Kilowatt-hour: unit of electrical energy consumed. One thousand watts of power for a 1-hour duration. Abbreviated *kwhr*.

Knot: section of the base of a branch enclosed in the stem from which it arises. Found in lumber such as pine.

Landing: platform between or at the ends of stairways.

Latex paint: water-based paint.

Lath: perforated base for application of plaster. Formerly wood, now usually metal.

Lattice: framework of crossed strips of wood, plastic, or metal.

Leader: horizontal section of downspout.

Ledger strip: strip of wood forming a ledge on a girder or sill for supporting the bottoms of joists.

Let-in brace: corner brace of 1×4 lumber cut into studs.

Lime: calcium carbonate. When heated, it becomes quicklime.

Linseed oil: oil from the seed of the flax plant.

Lintel: solid member above a door or window that carries the load above.

Live load: temporary load imposed on a building by occupancy and the environment.

Lookout: wood member supporting the end of an overhanging rafter.

Louver: slanted slat of wood, plastic, or metal. Used to admit air but block rain and visibility.

Lumen: measure of total light output. A wax candle gives off about 13 lumens, a 100-watt incandescent bulb about 1,200 lumens.

Masonry: construction consisting of stone, brick, or concrete block.

Masonry cement: cement to which water and sand must be added.

Masonry primer: asphalt primer for bonding asphalt-based products to masonry.

Mastic: thick-bodied adhesive or sealant.

Membrane roof: roofing consisting of a single waterproof sheet.

Metal lath: sheet metal slit and formed into a mesh for use as a plaster base.

Mil: one-thousandth of an inch.

Millwork: building components manufactured in a woodworking plant.

Mineral spirits: petroleum-base solvent for oil-based paint and varnish.

Miter: to cut at an angle other than 90°.

Miter joint: joint where each member is mitered at equal angles.

Module: repeated dimension.

Modulus of elasticity: (see *elastic*).

Moisture barrier: material or surface with the purpose of blocking the diffusion of water vapor. The same as a vapor barrier.

Moisture content: amount of moisture in a material, expressed as the percentage of dry weight.

Mortar: plastic mixture of cement, sand, and water.

Mortise: hole into which a tenon (tongue) fits.

Movable window insulation: shutter or shade for insulating a window against heat loss.

Natural finish: wood finish that does not greatly alter the unfinished color.

Natural ventilation: air movement in a building due only to natural pressure differences caused by air temperatures.

Neoprene: synthetic rubber.

Neutral wire: grounded wire.

Nonbearing wall: wall or partition that does not carry a load from above.

Nosing: projection of a stair tread beyond the riser; the amount by which the actual tread is wider than the mathematical tread.

Ohm: measure of resistance to electric current.

On-center: framing measurement from the center of one member to the center of the other.

Open valley: roof valley where shingles do not cross the valley intersection; flashing does.

Orientation: placement relative to the sun, wind, view, and so forth.

Overhang: portion of a roof extending beyond the wall line.

Overload: excessive electric current in a conductor. The danger is from overheating. Circuit breakers interrupt circuits upon detecting overloads.

Pane: piece of glass that, when installed in a window, becomes a light.

Panel: thin, flat piece.

Parget: a surface coat of cement over masonry. Also known as *parge*.

Parquet: thin strips of wood applied in geometric patterns on floors and furniture.

Partition wall: nonbearing wall.

Party wall: common wall that separates two properties.

Passive solar collector: system for collecting solar energy without use of mechanical devices such as fans or pumps.

Penetrating finish: finish that sinks into wood grain and does not leave a hard skin.

Penny: formerly the price in pennies of 100 nails of a certain size; now a measure of length. A 6-penny (6d) nail is 2 inches long.

Perlite: expanded volcanic glass. Used as an insulator and as a lightweight additive to concrete.

Perm: 1 grain of water vapor per square foot per hour per inch of mercury difference in water vapor pressure.

Permeability: ability to transmit water vapor, measured in perms.

Picture window: large fixed window.

Pier: isolated masonry column.

Pigment: powdered dye added to stain or paint.

Pitch: ratio of roof rise to span.

Pith: soft core of a tree that represents the original shoot.

Plaster: mortar-like material that hardens after application. Stucco is simply exterior plaster.

Plasterboard: term for gypsum drywall.

Plate: horizontal member at the top or bottom of a wall. The top plate supports the rafter ends. The bottom or sill plate supports studs and posts.

Plenum: ductwork chamber that serves as a distribution point.

Plumb: vertical.

Plywood: wood panel made of three or more veneers of wood alternating in direction of grain.

Pocket door: door that slides into a wall.

Pores: large-diameter wood cells that open to the surface.

Portland cement: strong, water-resistant cement consisting of silica, lime, and alumina.

Preservative: water-repellent liquid containing fungicide.

Pressure-treated wood: wood that has been injected with preservative under pressure.

Primer: first coating, applied prior to regular paint.

Psychrometric chart: graph showing the properties of water vapor in air.

Purlin: a horizontal member perpendicular to, and supporting, rafters.

Quarter-round: molding whose section is that of a quarter of a circle.

Rabbet: a rectangular shape consisting of two surfaces cut along the edge or end of a board.

Racking: distortion of a building surface from the rectangular in its plane.

Radiant heating: method of heating whereby much of the heat transfer is accomplished by radiation through space from warm building surfaces such as floors, walls, or ceilings.

Rafter: roof beam running in the direction of the slope.

Rail: horizontal member of a door or window sash. Also the top member of a balustrade.

Rebar: abbreviation for reinforcing bar. Usually applied to steel bars used in concrete.

Receptacle: electrical device into which a plug may be connected.

Reflectance: decimal fraction of light incident on a surface reflected and not absorbed. Absorptance equals 1 minus reflectance.

Reflective glass: glass treated to reflect a fraction (the reflectance) of incident light.

Reflectivity: (see reflectance).

Register: grill or grate covering the outlet of a duct.

Reinforcement: (see rebar).

Relative humidity: amount of water vapor in air compared with the maximum amount possible, expressed as a percentage.

Resorcinol glue: plastic resin glue that withstands water.

Retrofit: to upgrade a structure using modern materials.

Return: general term for a right-angle turn.

Reverberation time: measure of the length of time a sound wave will bounce around a space before being absorbed.

Ribbon: horizontal strip (usually 1×4) let into studs to support joist ends. Also called a *ribband*.

Ridge: junction of the top of opposing roof planes.

Ridge board: vertical board between the upper ends of rafters.

Ridge vent: continuous, prefabricated outlet ventilator placed over an opening at the ridge.

Rise: vertical increase in one step of a stair. Also the total vertical span of a stairway from landing to landing, or any vertical change.

Riser: vertical board between stair treads. Also a vertical pipe.

Roll roofing: low-cost asphalt roofing in roll form.

Roof overhang: horizontal projection of the roof beyond the wall.

Run: horizontal span of a flight of stairs.

R-value: measure of resistance to heat flow.

Saddle: pitched section of roof hind a chimney or between a roof and the wall toward which it slopes. Its purpose is to avoid trapped water.

Safety glass: one of a number of types of glass that have been strengthened or reinforced for safety.

Sapwood: wood between the heartwood and the bark, in which the sap runs.

Sash: frame holding the panes of glass in a window or door.

Saturated felt: felt impregnated with asphalt in order to make it water resistant.

Scratch coat: first coat of plaster. It is scratched to provide better bonding with the next coat.

Screen molding: thin wood molding for covering the edge of screening.

Sealant: compressible material used to seal building joints, etc.

Sealed glass: panes of glass with a sealed air space between.

Sealer: liquid applied to unfinished wood to seal the surface.

Selvage: portion of roll roofing meant to be overlapped by the succeeding course.

Sensible heat: heat required to raise the temperature of a material without changing its form.

Service drop: wiring from the utility pole to the service entrance conductors leading to the meter.

Service entrance box: box housing the electrical panel containing the main breaker and branch circuit breakers.

Shading coefficient: ratio of solar gain to the solar gain through a single layer of clear, double-strength glass.

Shake: wood shingle formed by splitting rather than sawing. Also a lumber defect in which the growth rings separate.

Shear: the effect of opposing forces acting in the same plane of a material.

Sheathing: layer of boards over the framing but under the finish.

Shellac: resinous secretion of the lac bug, dissolved in alcohol.

Shelter belt: band of trees and shrubs planted to reduce wind speed.

Shim: thin, tapered piece of wood used to level or plumb.

Shingle: small, thin piece of material, often tapered, for laying in overlapping rows as in roofing or siding.

Shiplap: rabbeted wood joint used in siding.

Siding: exterior finish for a wall.

Sill: lowest horizontal member in a frame. Also the bottom piece of the window rough opening.

Single-phase wiring: wiring in which the voltage exists only as a single sine wave. This is the type used in residences.

Single-strength glass: glass of thickness 0.085 to 0.100 inches.

Skylight: window set into a roof.

Slab on grade: concrete slab resting directly on the ground at near-grade level.

Sleeper: wood strip set into or on concrete as a fastener for flooring.

Slider: window that slides horizontally. Also called a *sliding window*.

Soffit: underside of a roof overhang, cornice, or stairway.

Soffit vent: inlet vent in the soffit. It may be individual or continuous.

Softwood: wood from coniferous, mostly evergreen, trees.

Soil line or pipe: pipe carrying human waste.

Solar radiation: total electromagnetic radiation from the sun.

Solar-tempered heating system: system deriving a significant fraction of the heating requirement from the sun.

Solder: metal alloy with a low melting point used in joining pipes, electrical wiring, and sheet metal.

Span: distance between supports.

Specific heat: ratio of the heat storage capacity of a material to that of an equal weight of water.

Square: 100 square feet of coverage. Also a carpentry tool for measuring and laying out.

Stack effect: buoyancy of warm gases within a chimney.

Standing-seam: metal roofing technique of folding the upturned edges of adjacent sheets to form a weatherproof seam.

Standing wave: sound wave in a space of a dimension equal to a multiple of the sound's wavelength.

Stile: vertical outside frame member in a door or window sash.

Stool: interior horizontal, flat molding at the bottom of a window.

Stop (molding): thin molding for stopping doors on closure or holding window sashes in place.

Storm door or window: removable, extra door or window for reducing winter heat loss.

Story: space between two floors. Also spelled *storey*.

Stringer: side member into which stair treads and risers are set.

Strip flooring: flooring of narrow strips with matched edges and ends.

Structural Insulated Panel: rigid foam sandwiched between two structural panels.

Stucco: plaster applied to the exterior.

Stud: vertical framing member to which wall sheathing and siding are attached.

Subfloor: first floor laid over the floor joists. The subfloor may also serve as the finish floor.

Supply plumbing: pipes supplying water to a building.

Suspended ceiling: modular ceiling panels supported in a hanging frame.

Tab: exposed portion of an asphalt shingle between the cutouts.

Taping: finishing gypsum drywall joints with paper tape and joint compound.

Tempered glass: glass that has been cooled rapidly to produce surface tension. The result is a stronger-than-normal glass that shatters into relatively harmless cubical fragments when broken.

Tenon: beam-end projection fitting into a mating tenon or hole in a second beam.

Tension: pulling apart; the opposite of compression.

Termiticide: chemical for poisoning termites.

Terne metal: sheet metal coated with a lead-and-tin alloy. Used in roofing.

Therm: 100,000 Btu.

Thermal mass: measure of the ability of a material to store heat (for later release).

Thimble: protective device installed in a combustible wall through which a stovepipe passes.

Threshold: beveled wood strip used as a door sill.

Tie beam: beam placed between mating rafters to form a triangle and prevent spreading. Also known as a *collar tie*.

Tilt angle: angle of a collector or window from the horizontal.

Timber: lumber that is 5 or more inches thick.

Toenailing: nailing a butt joint at an angle.

Tongue and groove: flooring and sheathing joint in which the tongue of one piece meets a groove in a mating piece.

Touch-sanding: sizing structural wood panels to a uniform thickness by means of light surface sanding.

Transit: surveying instrument, usually mounted on a tripod, for measuring horizontal and vertical angles.

Trap: section of plumbing pipe designed to retain water and block the flow of sewer gas into a building.

Tread: horizontal part of a step. The nosing is physically part of the tread but doesn't count from the design standpoint.

Trim: decorative building elements often used to conceal joints.

Truss: framing structure for spanning great distances, in which every member is purely in tension or in compression.

Tung oil: fast-drying oil from the seed of the Chinese tung tree. Used as a penetrating wood finish.

Ultraviolet radiation: radiation of wavelengths shorter than those of visible radiation.

Underlayment: sheet material or wood providing a smooth, sound base for a finish.

U-value: inverse of R-value.

Valley: intersection of two pitched roofs that form an internal angle.

Vapor barrier: material or surface designed to block diffusion of water vapor.

Varnish: mixture of drying oil and resin without pigment. With pigment added, it becomes enamel.

Veneer: thin sheet of wood formed by slicing a log around the growth rings.

Vent: pipe or duct allowing inlet or exhaust of air.

Vermiculite: mica that has been expanded to form an inert insulation.

Wall: a vertical structure whose height exceeds three times its thickness.

Wane: area of missing wood in lumber due to misjudgment of the log during sawing.

Water hammer: sound made by supply pipes when water is suddenly stopped by the quick closing of a valve.

Water softener: appliance that removes calcium ions from water.

Water table: level of water saturation in soil. Also a setback at foundation level in a masonry wall.

Watt: unit of electrical power. Watts equal volts across the circuit times amps flowing through it.

Weather strip: thin, linear material placed between a door or window and its jambs to prevent air leakage.

Weep hole: hole purposely built into a wall to allow drainage of trapped water.

Wind brace: T-section of metal strip let in and nailed diagonally to studs to provide racking resistance to a wall.

Wythe: single thickness of masonry in a wall.

Sources

Chapter 1: Design

"Human Dimensions" adapted from *Building Construction Illustrated* (New York, NY: Van Nostrand Reinhold, 1975).

"Kitchen Design Guidelines" adapted from *Kitchen Planning Guidelines* (Hackettstown, NJ: National Kitchen & Bath Association, 2005).

"Bath Design Guidelines" adapted from *Bathroom Planning Guidelines* (Hackettstown, NJ: National Kitchen & Bath Association, 2005).

"Stair Design" adapted from *Visual Interpretation of the IRC 2006 Stair Building Code* (Stafford, VA: Stairway Manufacturers' Association, 2006).

"Access" adapted from *28 CFR Part 36 Appendix A of the Code of Federal Regulations* (Washington, DC: Department of Justice, 1994).

"Meet the Code (IRC)" adapted from *International Residential Code for One- and Two- Family Dwellings* (Country Club Hills, IL: International Code Council, 2006).

Chapter 2: Site and Climate

"Unified Soil Classification System" adapted from *Classification of Soils for Engineering Purposes: Annual Book of ASTM Standards* (Conshohocken, PA: American Society for Testing and Materials, 2008).

"Magnetic Compass Variation" adapted from *Geodetic Survey, 1975* (Washington, DC: Department of the Interior, 1975).

"Safe Sight Distances for Passenger Cars Entering Two-Lane Highways" (Washington, DC: Institute of Traffic Engineers,1974).

"Shelterbelts" adapted from *Plants, People, and Environmental Quality* (Washington, DC: Department of the Interior, National Park Service, 1972).

"USDA Plant Hardiness Map" adapted from *American Horticultural Society USDA Plant Hardiness Zone Map* (Alexandria, VA: American Horticultural Society, 2003).

"Trees for Shade and Shelter" from *Landscaping Your Home* (Urbana-Champaign, IL: University of Illinois, 1975).

Chapter 3: Masonry

"Dimensions of Typical CMU" adapted from *Typical Sizes and Shapes of Concrete Masonry Units* (Herndon, VA: National Concrete Masonry Association, 2001).

"Concrete Pavers" adapted from *Passive Solar Construction Handbook* (Herndon, VA: National Concrete Masonry Association, 1984).

"Brick Sizes" adapted from *Dimensioning and Estimating Brick Masonry, Technical Note 10* (Reston, VA: Brick Institute of America, 2009).

"Brick Wall Positions and Patterns" from *Bonds and Patterns in Brickwork, Technical Note 30* (Reston, VA: Brick Institute of America, 1999).

"Brick Masonry Cavity Walls" adapted from *Brick Masonry Cavity Walls Detailing, Technical Note 21B* (Reston, VA: Brick Institute of America, 2002).

"Brick Veneer/Steel Stud Walls" adapted from *Brick Veneer/Steel Stud Walls, Technical Note 28B* (Reston, VA: Brick Institute of America, 1999).

"Brick Veneer/Wood Stud Walls" adapted from *Anchored Brick Veneer Wood Frame Construction, Technical Note 28* (Reston, VA: Brick Institute of America, 1991).

"Estimating Brick and Mortar" adapted from *Dimensioning and Estimating Brick Masonry, Technical Note 10* (Reston, VA: Brick Institute of America, 2009).

"Brick Pavement" adapted from *Unit Masonry: Brick Paving* (Redondo Beach, CA: Higgins Brick, 2001).

"Meet the Code (IRC)" adapted from *International Residential Code for One- and Two- Family Dwellings* (Country Club Hills, IL: International Code Council, 2006).

Chapter 4: Foundations

All materials except "Piers with Floor Insulation" and "Termite Control" adapted from *Builder's Foundation Handbook* (Oak Ridge, TN: Oak Ridge National Laboratory, 1991).

"Termite Control" from *Subterranean Termites, Their Prevention and Control in Buildings: Home and Garden* (Washington, DC: USDA Forest Service, 1972).

"Meet The Code (IRC)" adapted from *International Residential Code for One- and Two- Family Dwellings* (Country Club Hills, IL: International Code Council, 2006).

Chapter 5: Wood

"The Nature of Wood" adapted from *Wood Handbook* (Washington, DC: Department of Agriculture, 1987).

"Lumber Defects" adapted from *Wood Handbook* (Washington, DC: Department of Agriculture, 1987).

"Typical Lumber Grade Stamp" adapted from *Grade Stamps for West Coast Lumber* (Tigard, OR: West Coast Lumber Inspection Bureau, 2000).

"Properties of North American Species" condensed from *Wood Handbook* (Washington, DC: Department of Agriculture, 1987).

"Moisture Content and Shrinkage of Hardwoods and Softwoods" condensed from *Wood Handbook* (Washington, DC: Department of Agriculture, 1987).

"Typical Quality Stamp for Treated Lumber" adapted from *Grade & Quality Marks* at www.southernpine.com (Kenner, LA: Southern Pine Council, 2009).

Chapter 6: Framing

"Ground Snow Loads, PSF" adapted from *International Building Code* (Country Club Hills, IL: International Code Council, 2006).

"Stress Value Adjustment Factors" and "Span Tables for S4S Lumber" adapted from *The U.S. Span Book for Major Lumber Species* (Amherst, NY: Canadian Wood Council, 2004).

"I-Joists" adapted from *APA Performance Rated I-Joists* (Tacoma, WA: APA—The Engineered Wood Association, 2002).

"Wood Trusses" adapted from *Metal Plate Connected Wood Truss Handbook* (Madison, WI: Wood Truss Council of America, 1997).

"Glulam Beams" adapted from *Glulam Floor Beams* (Tacoma, WA: APA—The Engineered Wood Association, 2002).

"Plywood Box Beams" adapted from *APA Nailed Structural-Use Panel and Lumber Beams* (Tacoma, WA: APA—The Engineered Wood Association, 2009).

"Framing Details" adapted from *Manual for Wood Frame Construction* (Washington, DC: American Forest & Paper Association, 1988).

"Meet the Code" adapted from *International Residential Code for One- and Two- Family Dwellings* (Country Club Hills, IL: International Code Council, 2006).

Chapter 7: Sheathing

All material except "Wall Bracing" adapted from *Engineered Wood Construction Guide* (Tacoma, WA: APA—The Engineered Wood Association, 2005).

"Wall Bracing" adapted from *Whole House Wall Bracing* (Tacoma, WA: APA—The Engineered Wood Association, 2006).

Chapter 8: Siding

"Vinyl Siding" adapted from *Vinyl Siding Installation Manual* (Washington, DC: Vinyl Siding Institute, 2004).

"Fiber-Cement Lap Siding" adapted from *Hardiplank Lap Siding* (Mission Viejo, CA: James Hardie Building Products, 2005).

"Hardboard Lap Siding" adapted from *LP. ABT Siding, 7/16" Primed and Unprimed* (Roaring River, NC: Louisiana Pacific, 2005).

"Cedar Shingles" adapted from *Exterior and Interior Wall Manual* (Sumas, WA: Cedar Shake & Shingle Bureau, 2004).

"Vertical Wood Siding" adapted from *Redwood Siding Patterns and Application* (Mill Valley, CA: California Redwood Association).

"Plywood Siding" adapted from *Engineered Wood Construction Guide* (Tacoma, WA: APA—The Engineered Wood Association, 2005).

"Stucco" adapted from "Sticking with Stucco," *Professional Builder*, September, 1987.

"Meet the Code" adapted from *International Residential Code for One- and Two- Family Dwellings* (Country Club Hills, IL: International Code Council, 2006).

Chapter 9: Roofing

"Exposed-Nail Roll Roofing," "Concealed-Nail Roll Roofing," and "Double-Coverage Roll Roofing" adapted from *Residential Asphalt Roofing Manual* (Rockville, MD: Asphalt Roofing Manufacturers Association, 1984).

"Asphalt Shingles" adapted from *Certainteed Shingle Applicator's Manual* (Valley Forge, PA: CertainTeed Corporation, 2007).

"Cedar Shingles" and "Cedar Shakes" adapted from *New Roof Construction Manual* (Sumas, WA: Cedar Shake & Shingle Bureau, 2004).

"Slate" adapted from *Slate Roofing Manual* (Poultney, VT: Greenstone Slate Company, 2002).

"Metal Panel" adapted from *Residential Light Gauge Application Guide* (Lebanon, PA: Everlast Roofing, 2005).

"Meet the Code" adapted from *International Residential Code for One- and Two- Family Dwellings* (Country Club Hills, IL: International Code Council, 2006).

Chapter 10: Windows and Doors

"Dimensions of a Typical Double-Hung Window" adapted from *Andersen Narrowline Double-Hung Windows* (Bayport, MN: Andersen Corporation, 2005).

"Window Installation" adapted from *Installation Guide for Andersen 400-Series Tilt-Wash Double-Hung Windows* (Bayport, MN: Andersen Corporation, 2007).

"Window Energy Performance" data from Efficient Windows Collaborative (*www.efficientwindows.org*, 2008).

"Skylights" from *Residential Skylight Product Sizes* (Greenwood, SC: Velux America, 2009).

"Classic Wood Door Installation" adapted from *Wood Frame House Construction* (Washington, DC: Department of Agriculture, 1975).

"Modem Prehung Door Installation" from *Technical Data—Insulated Windows and Doors* (Norcross, GA: Peachtree Doors, 1987).

"Bulkhead Doors" adapted from *Planning or Adding an Areaway for a Bilco Basement Door* (New Haven, CT: The Bilco Company, 2008).

"Meet the Code" adapted from *International Residential Code for One- and Two- Family Dwellings* (Country Club Hills, IL: International Code Council, 2006)

Chapter 11: Plumbing

"Water Wells and Pumps" adapted from *How Your House Works* (Kingston, MA: R.S. Means, 2007).

"Allowed Supply Piping Materials" from *International Residential Code for One- and Two- Family Dwellings* (Country Club Hills, IL: International Code Council, 2006).

"Fixture Units for Plumbing Fixtures and Fixture Groups" from *International Residential Code for One- and Two-Family Dwellings* (Country Club Hills, IL: International Code Council, 2006).

"Sizing Drain and Waste Pipes," Rules for Running Drainpipe," "Traps," and "Venting" adapted from *International Residential Code for One- and Two-Family Dwellings* (Country Club Hills, IL: International Code Council, 2006).

"Water Treatment" adapted from *Choosing a Water Treatment Device* (Madison, WI: University of Wisconsin–Extension, 1993).

"Meet the Code" adapted from *International Residential Code for One- and Two- Family Dwellings* (Country Club Hills, IL: International Code Council, 2006).

Chapter 12: Wiring

"Electrical Circuit," and "Service Drops" from *How Your House Works* (Kingston, MA: R.S. Means, 2007).

"Electric Service Specifications" adapted from *Standard Requirements: Electric Service and Meter Installations* (Augusta, ME: Central Maine Power Company, 1981).

"Grounding" and "Panels and Subpanels" from *How Your House Works* (Kingston, MA: R.S. Means, 2007).

"Load Calculations," "Wire and Cable," and "Electrical Boxes" adapted from *International Residential Code for One- and Two- Family Dwellings* (Country Club Hills, IL: International Code Council, 2006).

"Typical Appliance Wattages" from *Appliance Operating Costs* (Madison, WI: Alliant Energy, 2005).

"Receptacles," "Switches," and "Wiring Switches, Receptacles and Lights" from *How Your House Works* (Kingston, MA: R.S. Means, 2007).

"Meet the Code" adapted from *International Residential Code for One- and Two- Family Dwellings* (Country Club Hills, IL: International Code Council, 2006).

Chapter 13: The Thermal Envelope

"The Thermal Envelope" from *How Your House Works* (Kingston, MA: R.S. Means, 2007).

"Building Material R-values" and "Insulation Materials" from *Maine Guide to Energy Efficient Residential Construction* (Augusta, ME: Maine Public Utilities Commission, 2006).

"Surface and Air Space R-Values" from *1989 ASHRAE Handbook Fundamentals* (Atlanta, GA: American Society of Heating, Refrigerating and Air Conditioning Engineers, 1989).

"Floor, Wall, and Roof Total R-Values" adapted from *Major Conservation Retrofits* (Washington, DC: Department of Energy, 1984).

"Moisture Control" and "Attic and Roof Ventilation" adapted from *Maine Guide to Energy Efficient Residential Construction* (Augusta, ME: Maine Public Utilities Commission, 2006).

"Envelope Air Leaks" adapted from *Cataloguing Air Leakage Components in Houses* (Washington, DC: American Council for an Energy Efficient Economy, 1982).

"Structural Insulated Panels (SIPs)" adapted from *Structural Insulated Panels* (Tacoma, WA: APA—The Engineered Wood Association, 2007).

"Sealing Envelope Air Leaks" adapted from *Air Sealing Homes for Energy Conservation* (Ottawa, Ont: Energy, Mines and Resources Canada, 1984).

Chapter 14:

Floors, Walls, and Ceilings

"Bases for Resilient Flooring" adapted from *Wood Underlayments for Resilient Flooring* (Amherst, MA: University of Massachusetts, 2002).

"Ceramic Tile" adapted from *American National Standard Specifications for Ceramic Tile* (Princeton, NJ: Tile Council of America, 1981).

"Tile Setting Materials" adapted from *Tiling 1-2-3* (Des Moines, IA: Meredith Books, 2001).

"Standard Tile Sizes" from *American National Standard Specifications for Ceramic Tile* (Princeton, NJ: Tile Council of America, 1981).

"Strip Flooring Installation" and "Plank Flooring Installation" adapted from *Installing Hardwood Flooring* (Memphis, TN: Oak Flooring Institute, 1997).

"Gypsum Wallboard" adapted from *National Gypsum Construction Guide, 10th Ed.* (Charlotte, NC: National Gypsum Corp., 2005).

"Wood Paneling" adapted from *Miracle Worker's Guide to Real Wood Interiors* (Portland, OR: Western Wood Products Association, 1986).

"Diagnosing Paint Failures" adapted from *www.paintquality.com/failures* (Philadelphia, PA: Paint Quality Institute, 2009).

"Wood Moldings" adapted from *WMI Series Wood Moulding Patterns* (Portland, OR: Wood Moulding and Millwork Association, 1986).

Chapter 15: Storage

"Typical Modular Bath Cabinetry" from www.kraftmaid.com.

Chapter 16: Heating

"Heating Climate Data" data from *Annual Degree Days to Selected Bases, 1971–2000* (Asheville, NC: National Climatic Data Center, 2002).

"Heating Degree Days, Base 65°F" from *International Residential Code for One- and Two- Family Dwellings* (Country Club Hills, IL: International Code Council, 2006).

"Heat Sources" from *How Your House Works* (Kingston, MA: R.S. Means, 2007).

"Fireplaces" adapted from *Residential Fireplaces, Design and Construction, Technical Note 19A* (Reston, VA: Brick Institute of America, 2000).

"Wood Stove Installation" adapted from *International Residential Code for One- and Two- Family Dwellings* (Country Club Hills, IL: International Code Council, 2006).

"Stove Pipe Installation" adapted from *Recommended Standards for the Installation of Woodburning Stoves* (Augusta, ME: Maine State Fire Marshal's Office, 1979).

"Metal Prefabricated Chimneys" adapted from *Premium Series Sure-Temp Catalog* (Nampa, ID: Selkirk Company, 2008).

"Meet the Code (IRC)" adapted from *International Residential Code for One- and Two- Family Dwellings* (Country Club Hills, IL: International Code Council, 2006).

Chapter 17: Cooling

"Human Comfort Zone" from *Design with Climate* (Princeton, NJ: Princeton University Press, 1963).

"Attic Radiant Barriers" adapted from *Designing and Installing Radiant Barrier Systems* (Cape Canavera, FL: Florida Solar Energy Center, 1984).

"Solar Radiation on Windows" from *Handbook of Air Conditioning, Heating, and Ventilating, 3rd Ed.* (New York, NY: Industrial Press, 1979).

"Window Shading Strategies" adapted from *Comparison of Window Shading Strategies for Heat Gain Prevention* (Cape Canaveral, FL: Florida Solar Energy Center, 1984).

"Evaporative Cooling" adapted from *How Your House Works* (Kingston, MA: R.S. Means, 2007).

"How a Window Air Conditioner Works" adapted from *How Your House Works* (Kingston, MA: R.S. Means, 2007).

"Work Sheet for Sizing Air Conditioners" adapted from *Air-Conditioning Guide* (Emmaus, PA: New Shelter Magazine, July 1984).

Chapter 18: Passive Solar Heating

"Glazing Orientation and Tilt" from *Handbook of Air Conditioning, Heating, and Ventilating* (New York, NY: Industrial Press, 1979).

"South Overhang Geometry" from *Passive Solar Construction Handbook* (Herndon, VA: National Concrete Masonry Association, 1984).

"Solar Absorptance" adapted from *Passive Solar Design Handbook, Vol. 3* (Washington, DC: Department of Energy, 1980).

"Heat Storage Capacity of Building Materials" from *Passive Solar Design Handbook, Vol. 3* (Washington, DC: Department of Energy, 1980).

"A Passive Solar Design Procedure" from *Adding Thermal Mass to Passive Designs: Rules of Thumb for Where and When* (Cambridge, MA: Northeast Solar Energy Center, 1981).

Chapter 19: Lighting

"Residential Lighting Guidelines" from *Residential Lighting Design Guide* (Davis, CA: California Lighting Technology Center, UC Davis, 2005).

"Meet the Code" adapted from *International Residential Code for One- and Two- Family Dwellings* (Country Club Hills, IL: International Code Council, 2006).

Chapter 20: Sound

"Sound Transmission" adapted from *Noise-Rated Systems* (Tacoma, WA: American Plywood Association, 1981).

"STCs of Walls" and "STCs and IICs of Floor-Ceilings" from *Gypsum Wallboard Construction* (Charlotte, NC: Gold Bond Products, 1982).

Chapter 21: Fasteners

"Nailing Schedule for Light Construction" from Table R602.3(1) in *International Residential Code for One- and Two- Family Dwellings* (Country Club Hills, IL: International Code Council, 2006).

"Estimating Nail Requirements" from *Keystone Steel & Wire Pocket Nail Guide* (Peoria, IL: Keystone Steel & Wire Company, 1989).

"Holding Power of Common Nails" and "Holding Power of Wood Screws" from *National Design Specification for Wood Construction* (Washington, DC: National Forest Products Association, 1986).

"Metal Framing Aids" adapted from *Wood Construction Connectors* (Pleasanton, CA: Simpson Strong-Tie Company, 2008).

Chapter 22: Decks

"Multilevel Deck Design" from *Multilevel Deck* (Pleasanton, CA: Simpson Strong-Tie Company, 2008).

Index

fastening schedule, 418
fire ratings, 417
floating corner techniques, 419
metal trim accessories, 418
perm rating, 383
R-values, 372
taping joints, 421
types/products, 416

H

Half-round moldings, 432
Hallways
    lighting, 537
    passageway dimensions, 3
Handrails, 17–19, 33, 434
Hangers, 566
Hardboard lap siding, 215, 228–29, 245
Hardiplank® siding. *See* Fiber-cement lap
    siding
Hardwood flooring, 413–15
Headers
    in exterior bearing walls, 135–37,
      146–47
    in interior bearing walls, 137, 147
    span tables, 135–37, 146–47
Heating, 455–85. *See also* Chimneys;
    Fireplaces; Wood stoves
    about: overview of, 455
    air-source heat pump, 465
    baseboard heater, 466, 470
    climate data, 460–61
    code requirements, 300, 484–85
    convection distribution, 469
    distribution systems, 468–71
    ducts in conditioned space, 595
    electric resistance, 595
    fuels and efficiencies, 472–73
    gas piping and shut-off valves, 485
    gas warm-air furnace, 463
    heat recovery ventilation system, 598
    hydronic distribution, 470
    life-cycle costing, 595
    load calculations, 350
    loads, calculating, 456–59
    minimizing load, 595
    oil-fired hydronic boiler, 462
    radiant distribution, 471
    sources, 462–67
    sustainable building and, 595
    typical wattages, 351
    warm-air distribution, 468
HEPA air cleaners, 598
Human dimensions, 2
Hydronic heating systems, 470

I

Ice dams, 384
I-joists, 148–55
    cantilevers for balconies, 152
    cantilevers for building offsets, 153
    characteristics, 148
    holes allowed in, 154

residential floor spans, 155
sustainable building and, 591
typical performance-rated floor framing,
    148–51
Impact insulation class (IIC) ratings, 545,
    548–49
Insulation. *See also* R-values; Thermal
    envelope
    foundation (basement, crawl space,
      slab), 81, 82–89, 90–95, 96–99,
      589
    structural insulated panels (SIPs),
      392–93, 591
    sustainable building and, 593
    weights of materials, 124
Interest on loans, 603
Ion-exchange water softeners, 331
Islands and peninsulas
    circuits, 346, 348
    fixture venting, 325
    kitchen cabinetry and, 443–45

K

Kitchens
    access design, 27
    cabinetry, 443–45
    circuits, 346, 348
    cleanup/prep sink placement, 7
    cooking surface design, 8
    countertop space, 9
    design guidelines, 4–9
    dishwasher placement, 7
    landing area/surface design, 8–9
    lighting, 9, 346, 348, 535
    receptacle requirements, 346, 348
    refrigerator landing area, 8
    seating clearances, 6, 27
    work aisle/walkway guidelines, 5–6, 27
    work center/work triangle guidelines, 4

L

Landings (stairway), 33
Landscaping
    about: overview of, 35
    grass seed zones/grasses, 52–53
    plant hardiness zones, 48–49
    shelterbelts, 46–47
    soil properties, 37
    tree specifications, 50–51
    for winter and summer, 47 *(see also*
      Climate)
    xeriscaping, 597
Laundry group
    circuits for, 346
    drain sizes and fixture units, 318
    drainage system. *See* Drain, waste, vent
      (DWV) system
    sources of water vapor, 382
    supply fixture units and, 308
    typical wattages, 351
Lawns, 52–53
Level changes, accessibility, 26

Life-cycle costing, 595, 596, 597
Light tubes, 594
Lighting, 527–39
    about: overview of, 527
    bath, 15, 32, 300, 346, 349, 534
    bedroom, 347
    caulking/sealing, 397
    circuits, 346 *(see also* Wiring)
    closet, 347, 539
    code requirements, 32, 300, 346–47,
      538–39
    color and, 529
    designing for daylighting, 596
    dining room, 536
    entry areas and foyers, 537
    fluorescent, 529, 530
    garage, 347
    glare and, 529
    hallways, 537
    high-intensity discharge (HID), 530,
      531
    incandescent, 529, 530, 531
    intelligent switches, 596
    kitchen, 9, 346, 348, 535
    lamp efficiencies, 530
    lamp shapes and bases, 532–33
    lamp types and characteristics, 529,
      530–31
    light-emitting diode (LED), 529, 530,
      531
    living room, 346–47, 536
    luminaire installation, 539
    outlets, 538 *(see also* Receptacles)
    recessed, 596
    residential guidelines, 534–37
    seeing and, 528–29
    spectral power curves of lamps, 529
    stairs and stairways, 32
    sustainable building and, 596
    switches, 361–65, 367, 596
    task, 596
    track, 539
    units and measurements, 528
    visual acuity/visual field and, 528
    wiring switches, receptacles and, 361–
      65, 367 *(see also* Wiring)
Live loads, 125
Living room lighting and receptacles,
    346–47, 536
Load calculations (cooling), 499–503, 595
Load calculations (electrical), 337, 350–51
Load calculations (heating), 456–59, 595
Loads. *See also* Spans
    about: overview of, 124
    APA roof sheathing, 207
    APA Sturd-I-Floor, 203
    dead, 124
    floor/roof load bearing for brick
      masonry walls, 66
    live, 125
    snow, 125
    weights of building materials and, 124
Loans. *See* Mortgages
Lumber. *See* Wood

PEX fittings, 315
pipe sizing, 308–09
pipe types/characteristics, 306–07
polyethylene fittings, 314
protection, 322, 332
PVC and CPVC fittings, 312–13
PVC pipe dimensions, 312
rough-in dimensions, 329
service pressures, 308, 309
sewer system and, 307
sustainable building and, 597
Water wells and pumps, 304–05
Watts, 336, 337, 350–51
Weather. See Climate
Weather strips, 398–99
Web joint layouts, 175
Wet venting, 324, 333
Whole-house fans, 494, 495
Whole-house filters, 331
Wind energy, 599
Wind speed and direction, 44–45. See also
    Shelterbelts
Window fans, 494, 495
Windows. See also Lighting
    about: overview of, 279
    air leakage, 284
    anatomy of, 281
    annual heating/cooling bills vs. window
        type, 287–89
    awnings for, 493
    climate-based design, 594
    code requirements, 32, 300–301
    dimensions, 3, 281
    Efficient Windows Collaborative
        (EWC), 287–89
    egress opening, 281, 301
    glass noise-reduction coefficients, 543
    installing, 282–83
    installing direct to framing, 292, 293
    installing in jambs, 292, 293
    insulated glazing units, 292–93, 594
    light tubes, 594
    light-to-solar gain, 284
    passive solar and. See Passive solar
    performance factors/labels, 284–89, 594
    rough opening, 281
    R-values, 373
    shading strategies, 492–93, 515
    site-built, 292–93
    skylights, 290–91, 594
    solar heat gain coefficient (SHGC), 284,
        285, 594
    solar/thermal properties of glazings, 286
    sustainable building and, 594
    types of, 280, 285, 287
    U-factor, 284, 285
    unit size, 281
    vinyl siding flashing/trim, 222–23
    visible transmittance (VT), 284, 285
    weather strips for retrofitting, 398
Wiring, 335–67. See also Receptacles
    about: overview of, 335
    ampacity, 353

amps, ohms, volts, watts and, 336–37
    (see also load calculations)
    bath, 15, 346, 349
    bedroom, 347
    branch circuits, 353, 367, 538
    circuit capacity and, 346
    circuit overview, 336–37, 346–47
    closet, 347
    code requirements, 346–47, 366–67
    color codes, 352
    conductors/connections, 366
    dining room/pantry, 346
    electrical boxes for, 354–55
    garage, 347
    GFCI circuits, 346, 347, 348, 349
    grounding, 342–43, 362, 366
    kitchen, 346, 348
    lighting requirements, 346–47, 367
    lights, switches, receptacles, 361–65
    living room, 346–47
    load calculations, 337, 350–51
    methods, 367
    panels and subpanels, 344–45, 366
    required circuits, 346–47
    running cable, 356–57
    running conduit, 358–59
    service drops, 338–41, 366
    stairway, 347
    switches, 361–65, 367
    wire and cable for, 352–53
Wood, 109–21
    about: overview of, 109
    cells, 111
    chemical composition, 111
    defects defined and illustrated, 112, 113
    density, paintability, cupping/checking
        resistance, R/inch, 114–15
    foundations, 88, 106, 107
    FSC-certified lumber, 591
    grade stamps, 112, 113, 120
    growth rings, earlywood, latewood, 111
    hardwood flooring, 413–15
    hardwoods, 114, 117
    horizontal siding, 215, 234–35, 244,
        245
    moisture and shrinkage, 116–17
    nature of, 110–11
    paneling, 422–23
    pressure-treated, 120–21
    properties of North American species,
        114–15
    R-values, 372
    shingles and shakes. See Roofing;
        Shingles and shakes
    softwoods, 115, 117
    standard lumber sizes, 118–19
    tree trunk components/functions, 110
    vertical siding, 215, 236–37
Wood stoves
    catalytic, 467
    clearances and specifications, 478–79
    heat distribution, 469
    installing, 478–79

metal prefabricated chimneys, 481–83
    non-catalytic, 467
    pros and cons, 467
    stovepipe installation, 480
Wood trusses, 156–68
    advanced (OVE) framing and, 190–91,
        591
    anatomy of, 156
    bearing and eave details, illustrated, 158
    code requirements, 192
    double fink, 162
    double Howe scissors, 167
    fink, 160
    floor, 168
    Howe scissors, 165
    modified queen post, 161
    mono, 163–64
    queen post, 159
    queen scissors, 166
    span tables, 159–68
    timber-frame, 178
    variety of types, illustrated, 157

X

Xeriscaping, 597